COMMON-LAW PLEADING:

ITS HISTORY AND PRINCIPLES.

INCLUDING

DICEY'S RULES CONCERNING PARTIES TO ACTIONS

AND

STEPHEN'S RULES OF PLEADING.

BY

R. ROSS PERRY,

OF THE BAR OF THE DISTRICT OF COLUMBIA.

LECTURER ON COMMON-LAW PLEADING IN THE GEORGETOWN (D.C.)
UNIVERSITY LAW SCHOOL.

THE LAWBOOK EXCHANGE, LTD.
Clark, New Jersey

ISBN 978-1-58477-105-0

Lawbook Exchange edition 2001, 2023

The quality of this reprint is equivalent to the quality of the original work.

THE LAWBOOK EXCHANGE, LTD.
33 Terminal Avenue
Clark, New Jersey 07066-1321

*Please see our website for a selection of our other publications
and fine facsimile reprints of classic works of legal history:*
www.lawbookexchange.com

Library of Congress Cataloging-in-Publication Data

Perry, R. Ross (Richard Ross), 1846-1915.
   Common-law pleading : its history and principles : including Dicey's
rules concerning parties to actions and Stephen's rules of pleading / by
R. Ross Perry.
      p. cm.
   Originally published: Boston : Little, Brown, 1897.
   Includes bibliographical references and index.
   ISBN 1-58477-105-4 (cloth : alk. paper)
   1. Pleading--Great Britain. I. Title.

KD7164 .P47 2000
347.42'072--dc21   00-036239

Printed in the United States of America on acid-free paper

COMMON-LAW PLEADING:

ITS HISTORY AND PRINCIPLES.

INCLUDING

DICEY'S RULES CONCERNING PARTIES TO ACTIONS

AND

STEPHEN'S RULES OF PLEADING.

BY

R. ROSS PERRY,

OF THE BAR OF THE DISTRICT OF COLUMBIA.

LECTURER ON COMMON-LAW PLEADING IN THE GEORGETOWN (D.C.)
UNIVERSITY LAW SCHOOL.

BOSTON:
LITTLE, BROWN, AND COMPANY.
1897.

University Press:
John Wilson and Son, Cambridge, U.S.A.

PREFACE.

———•———

IN my experience as a lecturer to students upon Common-Law Pleading, I have felt the need of a text-book containing the discoveries (for such they may properly be called) upon the subject made in the last twenty-five years by such men as Pollock and Maitland in the mother-country, and Bigelow, Holmes, Thayer, Ames, and others among ourselves. I have here endeavored to gratify that need. The fundamental principles of the common-law with respect to actions can never be better stated than they have been by Chitty. Stephen has performed a like task for the rules of pleading, while Dicey has embraced the law governing the selection of the parties to an action in an admirable series of rules. These three treatises have been, so far as was practicable, combined here, and the language of their authors has been used with the fewest possible modifications. Free use has been also made of the third book of Blackstone's Commentaries.

Therefore this work, if I may venture to give it that name, pretends to be only a re-statement in a condensed form of what has been said upon its subject by many authors in many books. Indeed, wherever the language of the particular author seemed to be the most appropriate it has been adopted. The only scope for original writing upon this subject is in the line of discovery followed by the distinguished men whom I have already named; this path is necessarily closed to the lawyer in active practice at the bar.

As this book is intended for the student and is designed to teach the principles of a science which was long since perfected, no effort has been made to digest recent decisions, or even to refer to them (save for some special purpose). The cases cited are almost exclusively the leading English authorities referred to by Chitty and by Stephen. Indeed, Saunders' Reports furnish the best collection of cases to be consulted by the student, who should supplement his studies by a close perusal of those Reports or of Ames' Cases on Pleading.

As the subject of this work is pleading as it existed at common-law, the present tense is frequently used in describing things which have long since ceased to exist.

It will perhaps be objected that in speaking (pp. 46, 47) of the modern conception of a contract, I have unduly magnified the element of consent at the expense of that of consideration. Sir Frederick Pollock is my authority for what I have said. In " The Principles of Contract " (p. 2), he states: " The first and most essential element of an agreement is the consent of the parties. There must be the meeting of two minds in one and the same intention." Again (p. 8), " Perhaps it (consideration) is to be regarded rather as a condition generally (though not always) imposed by a positive rule of English law as needful to the formation of a binding contract than as an elementary constituent of an agreement."

I am much indebted to Joseph J. Darlington, Leonard H. Poole, Henry W. Sohon, and E. Richard Shipp, of the District of Columbia bar, for assistance in the revision of proof, and also for suggestions as to the body of the work.

The index and the tables of cases and of contents have been carefully prepared by J. M. Gould of the Massachusetts bar, to whom I am under obligations for that part of the work.

R. ROSS PERRY.

Washington, D. C., *July* 26, 1897.

TABLE OF CONTENTS.

————————

	PAGE
INTRODUCTION	1

CHAPTER I.

Of Remedies	11
Self-help	12
by the mere act of the parties	15
by the joint act of all parties concerned	17
by sole operation of law	18

CHAPTER II.

Of Courts	20
Courts of record	21
not of record	21
in general	21
Ancient prominence of law of procedure	22
Anglo-Saxon courts	24
Anglo-Norman courts	28
The Curia Regis	28
Rise of the Court of Exchequer	29
Justices in Eyre	30
Birth of the Court of Common Pleas	31
Court of King's Bench	31
The judicial circuits	32
Jurisdiction of Court of King's Bench	34
of Court of Common Pleas	35
of Court of Exchequer	35
Court of Exchequer Chamber	36
House of Peers	36

CHAPTER III.

Of forms of Actions	38
Real actions	40
development of	42

	PAGE
Mixed actions	45, 93
Quare Impedit and Waste	45
Personal actions	46
division of, into	
(1) Formed actions ex contractu, which include : —	
debt	48
detinue	55
covenant	57
account	60
scire facias	60
(2) Formed actions ex delicto, or in tort, which include : —	
trespass	63
replevin	73
Inadequacy of formed actions	77
Actions on the case	77
assumpsit	82
trover	90
Ejectment	93
mesne profits	100
Consequences of a mistake in choosing the form of action	101
Extraordinary forms of actions	102
mandamus	102
procedendo	103
prohibition	103
quo warranto	104
informations	105
habeas corpus	105
certiorari	107
writs of error	108

CHAPTER IV.

OF THE JOINDER AND ELECTION OF ACTIONS	109
Joinder of actions	109
Election of actions	111

CHAPTER V.

PARTIES TO ACTIONS	116
Dicey's rules for the selection of parties	116
The persons who can sue and be sued	116
General rules applicable to all actions	117
Actions on Contract — Plaintiffs — General Rules	117
principal and agent	118
partners and unincorporated companies	119

	PAGE
corporations and incorporated bodies	120
husband and wife	121
bankrupt and trustee	121
executors, administrators, and heirs	122
Actions on Contract — Defendants — General Rules	124
principal and agent	125
partners and unincorporated companies	126
corporations and incorporated bodies	126
infants	127
husband and wife	127
bankrupt and trustee	128
executors, administrators, and heirs	129
Actions for Tort — Plaintiffs — General Rules	130
principal and agent	131
partners	131
husband and wife	131
bankrupt and trustee	132
executors and administrators	132
Actions for Tort — Defendants — General Rules	132
principal and agent	133
partners	133
corporations	133
infants	134
husband and wife	134
bankrupt and trustee	134
executors and administrators	134
Ejectment	134
Consequences of Non-Joinder and Mis-Joinder of Parties	135

CHAPTER VI.

OF THE ORIGINAL WRIT 137

CHAPTER VII.

OF THE PROCEEDINGS IN AN ACTION FROM ITS COMMENCEMENT
    TO ITS TERMINATION 148

The process	148
Bill of Middlesex, latitat and quo minus	153
The appearance of the defendant	158
The pleadings	159
Continuances	163
The declaration	164
Proceeding by bill	167

PAGE

Production of suit 168
The defence 169
Examination of the plaintiff's suit 1C9
Offer of proof 170
Origin of special pleading 171
The demurrer 174
Pleas 175
Dilatory pleas 175
Peremptory pleas 175, 178
The issue 179
Occasional pleas and incidents 182
Pleas puis darreign continuance 182
Demand of view 183
Voucher to warranty 184
Profert and oyer 185
Imparlances 187
Counter-pleas to oyer, &c. 188
Demurrer-book — paper-book 189
Amendments 189
Entering the issue on record 190
Modes of trial 191
Decision of issues in law 191
Trial of issues in fact 191
    old forms —
        (1) by witnesses 193
        (2) by oath 193
        (3) by ordeal 194
        (4) by battle 195
Miscellaneous proofs 196
The trial by the record 196
Trial by jury 197
    venire facias 201
    trials at nisi prius 201
    trial at bar 202
    conduct of jury trial 203
    variance 204
    the verdict 205
    incidents of jury trial 205
Bill of exceptions 206
Demurrer to evidence 206
Special verdict 207
General verdict subject to a special case 208
Proceedings subsequent to verdict 209
    motions, for a new trial 210
        in arrest of judgment 211
        for judgment non obstante veredicto 212
        for a repleader 213
        for a venire facias de novo 215

PAGE

The judgment 215
    for the plaintiff 216
    for the defendant 217
    by default, confession, &c. 218
Entering judgment on record 220
Execution 221
Writs of error 222

CHAPTER VIII.

OF THE RULES OF PLEADING 226

Abstract of proceedings in a supposed case 227

CHAPTER IX.

OF RULES WHICH TEND SIMPLY TO THE PRODUCTION OF AN ISSUE 231

RULE I. — AFTER THE DECLARATION THE PARTIES MUST AT EACH
STAGE DEMUR, OR PLEAD BY WAY OF TRAVERSE, OR BY WAY OF
CONFESSION AND AVOIDANCE 231
  I. Of demurrers 232
    1. Of the nature and properties of a demurrer 232
    2. Of the effect of passing a fault by without demurrer . 236
      of the aider of faults by pleading over 236
      of the aider of faults by verdict 237
      of the aider of faults by the statutes of jeofails and
      amendments 238
    3. Of the considerations which determine the pleader in
      his election to demur or plead 239
  II. Of pleadings 240
    1. Of the nature and properties of traverses 240
      of common traverses 240
      of general issues 241
      of the traverse de injuria 251
      of special traverses 255
        the inducement 263, 264, 266
        there must be no traverse upon a traverse . . . 264
      Of traverses in general 266
        (1) a traverse must deny " modo et forma " . . 266
        (2) a traverse must not be taken on matter of
        law 268
        (3) a traverse must not be taken upon matter not
        alleged 269
        (4) a party to a deed, who traverses it, must plead
        " non est factum " 270

PAGE

2. Of the nature and properties of pleadings in confession
and avoidance 272
of pleas in justification or excuse, and pleas in discharge 272
of color 273
3. Of the nature and properties of pleadings in general . 279
(1) every pleading must be an answer to the whole
of what is adversely alleged 279
(2) every pleading is taken to confess such traversable matters alleged on the other side as it does not
traverse 281
of protestation 281
Exceptions to the rule 283
In case of dilatory pleas 283
pleadings in estoppel 283
new assignments 283
extra viam 285
Inference from the rule — that it is sufficient to demur, traverse, or
confess and avoid 288
Exception, as to replication showing breach of award . . . 288
RULE II. — UPON A TRAVERSE ISSUE MUST BE TENDERED . . 289
Different forms of tendering issue 289
Another form of the rule, viz., that upon a negative and
affirmative the pleading shall conclude to the country,
but otherwise with a verification 290
Exception — that when new matter is introduced, the pleading
should always conclude with a verification 290
RULE III. — ISSUE, WHEN WELL TENDERED, MUST BE ACCEPTED 292
Of the similiter 292
Of the joinder in demurrer 293

CHAPTER X.

OF RULES WHICH TEND TO SECURE THE MATERIALITY OF THE
ISSUE 295

RULE. — ALL PLEADINGS MUST CONTAIN MATTER PERTINENT AND
MATERIAL 295
Rules subordinate and illustrative —
1. Traverse must not be taken on an immaterial point . 295
But where there are several material allegations, it is
in the option of the pleader to traverse which he
pleases 297
2. A traverse must not be too large nor too narrow . . . 297
But a party may, in general, traverse a material allegation of title or estate to the extent to which it is
alleged, though it needed not to be alleged to that
extent 299

CHAPTER XI.

PAGE

OF RULES WHICH TEND TO PRODUCE SINGLENESS OR UNITY IN
THE ISSUE 303

RULE I. — PLEADINGS MUST NOT BE DOUBLE 303
    Of the nature of duplicity in general 303
    Rules subordinate and illustrative —
        1. A pleading will be double that contains several answers,
           whatever be the class or quality of the answer . . . 307
        2. Matter may suffice to make a pleading double, though it
           be ill pleaded. 307
        3. But matter immaterial will not operate to make a plead-
           ing double. 308
        4. Nor matter that is pleaded only as necessary inducement
           to another allegation 309
        5. Nor matters, however multifarious, that together con-
           stitute but one connected proposition or entire point —
           cumulative traverses 310
        6. Nor a mere protestation 313
    Of several counts 313
    Of several pleas 317
        effect of the statute 4 Anne c. 16, § 4 . . . . . . 318, 320
RULE II. — IT IS NOT ALLOWABLE BOTH TO PLEAD AND TO
DEMUR TO THE SAME MATTER 322

CHAPTER XII.

OF RULES WHICH TEND TO PRODUCE CERTAINTY OR PARTICU-
LARITY IN THE ISSUE 323

RULE I. — THE PLEADINGS MUST HAVE CERTAINTY OF PLACE . 323
    Of venue —
        of the form in which the venue is to be laid 323
        of its effect upon the venire 328
        of the state of practice as to laying the venue truly . . 329
RULE II. — THE PLEADINGS MUST HAVE CERTAINTY OF TIME . 334
RULE III. — THE PLEADINGS MUST SPECIFY QUALITY, QUANTITY,
AND VALUE 336
RULE IV. — THE PLEADINGS MUST SPECIFY THE NAMES OF
PERSONS 339
RULE V. — THE PLEADINGS MUST SHOW TITLE 341
    I. Of the case where a party alleges title in himself, or in
        another whose authority he pleads 341
        1. Of alleging a title of possession 341

PAGE

2. Of alleging title in its full and precise extent . . . 342, 345

    of the allegation of the title itself 341–344

    of showing its derivation 345

        as to estates in fee simple 345

        as to particular estates 346

        where a party claims by descent 348

        where a party claims by conveyance 348

3. Of alleging a general freehold title 350

II. Of the case where a party alleges title in his adversary . 351

Exceptions to rule : No title need be shown where the opposite party is estopped from denying it 354

    No title need be shown in avowries or cognizances for rent, &c. 355

RULE VI. — THE PLEADINGS MUST SHOW AUTHORITY 355

RULE VII. — IN GENERAL, WHATEVER IS ALLEGED IN PLEADING MUST BE ALLEGED WITH CERTAINTY 358

SUBORDINATE RULES TENDING TO LIMIT OR RESTRAIN THE DEGREE OF CERTAINTY.

1. It is not necessary, in pleading, to state that which is merely matter of evidence 362

2. It is not necessary to state matter of which the court takes notice ex officio 364

3. It is not necessary to state matter which would come more properly from the other side 366

4. It is not necessary to allege circumstances necessarily implied 369

5. It is not necessary to allege what the law will presume . . 369

6. A general mode of pleading is allowed, where great prolixity is thereby avoided 370

7. A general mode of pleading is often sufficient, where the allegation on the other side must reduce the matter to certainty 372

8. No greater particularity is required than the nature of the thing pleaded will conveniently admit 377

9. Less particularity is required when the facts lie more in the knowledge of the opposite party than of the party pleading 378

10. Less particularity is necessary in the statement of matter of inducement or aggravation than in the main allegations 379

11. With respect to acts valid at common law, but regulated as to the mode of performance by statute, it is sufficient to use such certainty of allegation as was sufficient before the statute 380

CHAPTER XIII.

PAGE

OF RULES WHICH TEND TO PREVENT OBSCURITY AND CONFUSION
IN PLEADING 382

RULE I. — PLEADINGS MUST NOT BE INSENSIBLE OR REPUGNANT . 382
RULE II. — PLEADINGS MUST NOT BE AMBIGUOUS OR DOUBTFUL
IN MEANING; AND WHEN TWO DIFFERENT MEANINGS PRESENT
THEMSELVES, THAT CONSTRUCTION SHALL BE ADOPTED WHICH
IS MOST UNFAVORABLE TO THE PARTY PLEADING 383
  Of certainty to a common intent 383
  Of negatives pregnant 384
RULE III. — PLEADINGS MUST NOT BE ARGUMENTATIVE 386
RULE IV. — PLEADINGS MUST NOT BE HYPOTHETICAL, OR IN THE
ALTERNATIVE 388
  Two affirmatives or two negatives do not make a good issue 387, 388
RULE V. — PLEADINGS MUST NOT BE BY WAY OF RECITAL, BUT
MUST BE POSITIVE IN THEIR FORM 389
RULE VI. — THINGS ARE TO BE PLEADED ACCORDING TO THEIR
LEGAL EFFECT 390
RULE VII. — PLEADINGS SHOULD OBSERVE THE KNOWN FORMS OF
EXPRESSION, AS CONTAINED IN APPROVED PRECEDENTS . . . 391
RULE VIII. — PLEADINGS SHOULD HAVE THEIR PROPER FORMAL
COMMENCEMENTS AND CONCLUSIONS 392
RULE IX. — A PLEADING WHICH IS BAD IN PART, IS BAD ALTO-
GETHER 401

CHAPTER XIV.

OF RULES WHICH TEND TO PREVENT PROLIXITY AND DELAY IN
PLEADING 403

RULE I. — THERE MUST BE NO DEPARTURE IN PLEADING . . . 403
RULE II. — WHERE A PLEA AMOUNTS TO THE GENERAL ISSUE IT
SHOULD BE SO PLEADED 408
RULE III. — SURPLUSAGE IS TO BE AVOIDED 412

CHAPTER XV.

OF CERTAIN MISCELLANEOUS RULES 415

RULE I. — THE DECLARATION SHOULD COMMENCE WITH A RECITAL
OF THE ORIGINAL WRIT 415
RULE II. — THE DECLARATION MUST BE CONFORMABLE TO THE
ORIGINAL WRIT 417
RULE III. — THE DECLARATION SHOULD, IN CONCLUSION, LAY
DAMAGES, AND ALLEGE PRODUCTION OF SUIT 418
RULE IV. — PLEAS MUST BE PLEADED IN DUE ORDER 420

PAGE

RULE V. — PLEAS MUST BE PLEADED WITH DEFENCE 421

RULE VI. — PLEAS IN ABATEMENT MUST GIVE THE PLAINTIFF A BETTER WRIT OR BILL 424

RULE VII. — DILATORY PLEAS MUST BE PLEADED AT A PRELIMINARY STAGE OF THE SUIT 424

RULE VIII. — ALL AFFIRMATIVE PLEADINGS WHICH DO NOT CONCLUDE TO THE COUNTRY MUST CONCLUDE WITH A VERIFICATION 425

RULE IX. — IN ALL PLEADINGS, WHERE A DEED IS ALLEGED UNDER WHICH THE PARTY CLAIMS OR JUSTIFIES, PROFERT OF SUCH DEED MUST BE MADE 426

RULE X. — ALL PLEADINGS MUST BE PROPERLY ENTITLED OF THE COURT AND TERM 431

RULE XI. — ALL PLEADINGS OUGHT TO BE TRUE 432

APPENDIX 435

INDEX 453

ABBREVIATIONS,

In Addition to such as are in Current Use.

Anglo-Saxon Law . .	Essays in Anglo-Saxon Law. Little, Brown, & Co., Boston, 1876.
Bl. Com.	Blackstone's Commentaries, Hammond's edition, 1890.
Chit. Pl.	Chitty's Pleading, Volume I., 4th London edition, 1825.
Evans' Pl.	Evans' Pleading, Edward J. Coale, Baltimore, 1827.
Gould's Pl. . . .	Gould's Pleading, 4th edition, 1873.
Hist. Pr.	History of Procedure in England, by Melville M. Bigelow, 1880.
Ker. Eq. Ju. . . .	An Historical Sketch of the Equitable Jurisdiction of the Court of Chancery, by D. M. Kerly, 1890.
Holmes' C. L. . . .	The Common Law, by O. W. Holmes, Jr., 1881.
Min. Inst.	Institutes of Common and Statute Law, by John B. Minor, 1878.
P. & M. Hist. . . .	The History of English Law before the Time of Edward I., by Sir Frederick Pollock and Frederic William Maitland, 1895.
Reeves' Hist. . . .	Reeves' History of the English Law. Finlason's edition, London, 1869.
Steph. Pl.	Stephen's Pleading, Tyler's American, from 2d London (1827) edition.
Thay. Jury	Development of Trial by Jury, by James Bradley Thayer, 1896.

TABLE OF CASES CITED.

[THE REFERENCES ARE TO THE PAGES.]

ABBOT v. Chapman	248	Bayard v. Malcolm		434
Adams v. Cross	344, 347	Baylis v. Dinely		245
Aglionby v. Towerson	370	Beak v. Tyrrell		362
Alexander v. Mawman	423	Beal v. Simpson		268
Alsope v. Sytwell	379	Belasyse v. Hester		235
Amory v. Brodrick	324, 402	Belk v. Broadbent		356
Andrew v. Whitehead	336	Bell v. Alexander		433
Angle v. Chicago, &c. R. R. Co.	82	Bellamy's Case		427
Anon. (Kelw. 103 b)	278	Benbridge v. Day		402
—— (5 Mod. 18)	246	Bennet v. Filkins	259,	399
—— (12 Mod. 537)	410	Bertie v. Pickering		337
—— (2 Salk. 519)	236, 237, 330	Birch v. Bellamy		380
—— (2 Salk. 643)	343	—— v. Wilson	408, 410,	411
—— (3 Salk. 353)	263, 264	Bird v. Randall		250
—— (2 Vent. 196)	295	Bisse v. Harcourt	395,	399
—— (2 Wils. 150)	235	Blackborough v. Davis		348
Arlington (Lord) v. Merricke	375	Blackmore v. Tidderley		386
Arnfield v. Bate	332	Blake v. Foster	256,	352
Arundel (Corporation of) v. Bow-		Bleke v. Grove	307,	308
man	332	Blizard v. Kelly		391
Ashby v. White	11	Blockley v. Slater		347
Ashford v. Thornton	66	Bolton v. Carlisle (Bishop of)		233
Aslin v. Parkin	98	—— v. Cannon		322
Attorney-General v. Meller	351, 352,	Bond v. Dustin		212
	353, 378	Bonnel v. Fouke		86
Attwood v. Davis	400	Bonner v Wilkinson		271
Auberie v. James	385	Bonzi v. Stewart		311
Austin v. Jervoise	359	Bowdell v. Parsons		233
Aylesbury v. Harvey	427	Bowditch v. Mawley		340
		Bowyer's Case		327
		Bowyer v. Cook	392,	393
BAKER v. Blackman	297	Boyce v. Whitaker		365
—— v. Dewey	271	Braban v. Bacon	359,	370
Baldwin's Case	285	Bradburn v. Kennerdale		302
Ball v. Squarry	187	Braddish v Bishop		324
Banfill v. Leigh	427, 428	Bradley v. Fisher		69
Banks v. Pratt	370	Bray v. Freeman		332
Barker v. Braham	356	Bret v. Andar		374
—— v. Lade	390	Bridgewater v. Bythway		296
Barnes v. Hunt	287	Brindley v. Dennett	315,	413
Bartley v. Godslake	433	Bristow v. Wright	412,	413
Barton v. Webb	370	Britton v. Cole	296,	356
Bateman v. Allen	350	Broddeck v. Briggs		332
Bates v. Cort	235	Brooke v. Brooke		237
Batt v. Bradley	287	Brown's Case		347

Brown v. Cornish	399
—— v. Rands	359
Brudnell v. Roberts	256
Buckingham v. Francis	301
Buckley v. Kenyon	233
—— v. Rice Thomas	340, 377, 378, 391
Bultivant v. Holman	389
Burkley v. Wood	300
Burrell v. Dodd	347
Burton v. Webb	372
Butt's Case	382
CAIN v. C. & P. Telephone Co.	82
Calfe v. Nevil	308
Calvin's Case	324, 333
Cameron v. Reynolds	240
Campbell v. Lewis	237
—— v. St. John	293, 294
Careswell v. Vaughan	351
Carlisle v. Trears	335
Carmack v. Gundry	413
Carr v. Hinchliff	411
Carstairs v. Stein	210
Carver v. Pinckney	428
Carvick v. Blagrave	267, 297, 299
Case v. Barber	381
Casseres v. Bell	369
Chamberlain v. Greenfield,	337, 338, 379, 380
Chandler v. Roberts	387
Chapman v. Barney	101
—— v. Pickersgill	369, 370
Chasemore v. Richards	12
Chatland v. Thornly	393
Cheasley v Barnes	287, 357
Childes v. Westcot	350
Church v. Brownwick,	370, 371, 372, 373
Clarke v. Hougham	204
Clinton (Lord) v. Morton	319
Clue v. Baily	234
Cocker v. Crompton	285
Codner v. Dalby	359
Colborne v. Stockdale	298
Cole v. Hawkins	407
Collet v. Keith (Lord)	355, 357
—— v. Shrewsbury [Bailiffs of]	362
Collins v. Blantern	244, 245
Colt v. Coventry (Bishop of)	232
Colthirst v. Bejushin	383
Colton v. Goodridge	187, 245
Cook v. Cox	388, 391
—— v. Gerrard	207
Cooke v. Birt	334
Cooper v. Chitty	91
—— v. Monke	384
Cornwallis v. Savery,	290, 292, 304, 370, 371
Cotes v. Michill	356
Couling v. Coxe	213
Courtney v. Phelps	260, 387

Cowper v. Garbett	252
Craft v. Boite	326, 327
Crispin v. Williamson	332, 339
Crogate's Case	252, 254
Cromwell's (Lord) Case	240
Crosse v. Hunt	265, 269
Crosskeys Co. v. Rawlings	259
Croucher v. Oldfield	347
Cryps v. Baynton	370
Cudlip v. Rundle	354
Cuppledick v. Terwhit	307
Curwen v. Salkeld	324
Cutforthay v. Taylor	402
Cutter v. Powell	88, 89
—— v. Southern	405
DALE v. Phillipson	337
Dally v. King	391
Darby v. Boucher	245
Davies v. Aston	301
Davis v. Noake	391
Decker v. Pope	85
Denham v. Stephenson	348, 353, 378
Denison v. Richardson	334
Derisley v. Custance	351, 353, 378
De Wolf v. Bevan	311
Deybel's Case	364, 366
Digby v. Fitzharbert	264, 292
Dike v. Ricks	263
Dobbs v. Edmunds	389
Dodd v. Kyffin	247
Doe v. Ploughman	336
Doulson v. Matthews	330
Dovaston v. Payne	344, 368, 383, 384
Dowdale's Case	333
Dowland v. Slade	391
Dowman's Case	362
Draper v. Garratt	332
—— v. Glassop	246
Dudlow v. Watchorn	403, 407
Duffield v. Scott	401, 402
Dumsday v. Hughes	348
Dundass v. Weymouth (Lord)	412
Dunstall v. Dunstall	389
Dyster v. Battye	391, 392
EATON v. Southby	362, 363
Eden's Case	327
Edward v. Watkin	417
Ellison v. Isles	287
Elwis v. Lombe	285
Emerton v. Selby	257
Essington v. Boucher	307
Evans v. Prosser	397
—— v. Stevens	424
Evers (Lord) v. Buckton	359
Executors of Grenelefe, Case of the	308
FAIRCLAIM v. Shamtitle	98
Finlay v. Chirney	118

The references are to the pages.

Fisher v. Pimbley	403, 407
Fits v. Freestone	248
Fitzpatrick v. Robinson	359
Fletcher v. Pogson	237, 383
Foden v. Haines	266
Foster v. Jackson	235
Fowle v. Welsh	237
Francis Leke's (Sir) Case	299
Freeman v. Blewett	357
Fulmerston v. Steward	384, 406
GABELL v. Shaw	315
Gainsford v. Griffith	291, 375
Gale v. Read	378, 379
Gayle v. Betts	288
Georgia v. Brailsford	203
Gibbs v. Merrell	245
Gifford v. Perkins	274, 409
Gilbert v. Parker	270
Gladhill, ex parte	21
Gledstane v. Hewitt	56
Godfrey v. Saunders	60
Godson v. Good	400
Goodday v. Michell	383
Goodtitle v. Otway	336
Goram v. Sweeting	299
Gordon v. Ellis	214
Gourney v. Fletcher	389
Govett v. Radnidge	79, 112
Granger v. George	432
Green v. Cole	258
Greene v. Jones	257, 285
Greenhow v. Ilsley	342, 368
Griffith v. Crockford	293
Griffiths v. Eyles	388, 389
Grimstead v. Marlowe	342
Grimwood v. Barritt	335
Grocers' Co. v. Canterbury (Archbishop of)	268, 269
Groenvelt v. Burnell	362, 370
Guilford (Mayor of) v. Clarke	366
Gundry v. Feltham	234
HAITON v. Jeffreys	174, 322
Hallet v. Byrt	273, 274, 408
Hallowes v. Lucy	397
Halsey v. Carpenter	334, 359
Hammond v. Colls	301
Hamond v. Dod	384
Hampson v. Bill	421
Handford v. Palmer	369
Hard's Case	54
Harding v. Holmes	407
Hardy v. Cathcart	335
Harebottle v. Placock	45
Harlow v. Wright	384
Harmer v. Rowe	245
Harpur's Case	336
Harris v. Ferrand	267
—— v. Pett	374

Hart v. Longfield	304, 317
Hartley v. Herring	377
Hastrop v. Hastings	235
Hatton v. Morse	273, 274
Hawe v. Planner	336, 435
Hawke v. Bacon	285
Hawkins v. Eckles	344
Haworth v. Spraggs	424
Hayes v. Bryant	373
Hayman v. Gerrard	288, 292
Heard v. Baskerville	9
Hedges v. Chapman	401
Helier v. Whytier	264
Helliot v. Selby	416
Henderson v. Withy	290
Hendy v. Stephenson	346
Henry v. Earl	280
Henry Pigot's Case	244
Herlakenden's Case	279, 280
Herries v. Jamieson	318
Herring v. Blacklow	260, 387
Hickman v. Walker	404
Higgins v. Highfield	336
Hill v. Montagu	361, 370
—— v. Saunders	352
Hillier v. Plympton	373
Hinton v. Roffey	361
Hoe's Case	357
Holding v. Haling	333
Holland v. Shelley	427
Holler v. Bush	273, 408, 410, 411
Holmes v. Rhodes	374
Holt's Lessee v. Smith	98
Hore v. Chapman	389
Horne v. Lewin	261
Horsefall v. Testar	204
Hotham v. East India Co.	366, 368
Howel v. Richards	390
Huddart v. Rigby	287
Hudson v. Jones	281
Huggins v. Wiseman	370, 371
Hughes v. Phillips	264
Humphreys v. Bethily	236, 303, 304
—— v. Churchman	305
Huntingtower (Lord) v. Gardiner	237, 383
Hussey v. Jacob	411
—— v. More	420
Hutchinson v. Jackson	382
—— v. Piper	340
ILDERTON v. Ilderton	323
Isaac v. Farrer	252
JACKSON v. Pesked	237, 238
—— v. Wickes	293
Jacobs v. Nelson	384
J'Anson v. Stuart	361, 370
Jaques's Case	409
Jenkins v. Edwards	319

The references are to the pages.

Jermy v. Jenny	362, 370	Leyfield's Case	275, 426, 428
Jevons v. Harridge	187	Lightfoot v. Brightman	237
Johns v. Whitley	306, 846	Littleton v. Richardson	184
Johnson v. Picket	335	Lodge v. Frye	347
—— v. Warner	358	London (City of) v. Gorry	85
Johnstone v. Sutton	237	Long's Case	383
John Trollop's Case	393	Longueville v. Thistleworth	420
Jones v. Powell	295	Lumly v. Gye	82
Judin v. Samuel	402	Lynnet v. Wood	408, 409, 410
KEANE v. Boycott	245	MAGRUDER v. Belt	101
Keating v. Irish	370	Mainwaring v. Newman	427
Kempe v. Crews	214	Manser's Case	304, 373, 383
Kenicot v. Bogan	268	March v. Freeman	54
Kennedy v. Georgia State Bank	10	Market v. Johnson	280
Kent v. Hall	214	Marsh v. Bulteel	235, 369
Kerry (Earl of) v. Baxter	374, 375, 377	—— v. Newman	427
Kettle v. Bromsall	57	Marshall v. Riggs	389
Keyworth v. Hill	237	Martin v. Kesterton	285
King v. Frazer	391	—— v. Smith	388
—— v. Williams	194	Matthew v. Hassell	45
King, The, v. Brereton	888, 389	Matthews v. Carey	355, 358
—— v. Burdett	324, 333	McFaul v. Ramsey	8
—— v. Chester (Bishop of)	281, 334, 336	Medina v. Stoughton	395, 400
		Meeke v. Oxlade	315
—— v. Holland	324, 334	Mellor v. Spateman	440
—— v. Knollys	866	—— v. Walker	258
—— v. Lyme Regis	364, 365, 384	Merceron v. Dowson	232
—— v. Shakespeare	400	Meredith v. Alleyn	288, 289
—— v. Stevens	382	Merington v. Becket	433
—— v. Worcester (Bishop of)	264	Meriton v. Briggs	270
King qui tam v. Bolton	265	Middleton v. Price	357
Kingdon v. Nottle	123	Millner v. Crowdall	426
Kinlyside v. Thornton	78, 142	Mints v. Bethil	370, 371, 372, 373, 874
Kinnersley v. Cooper	297	Mole v. Wallis	405
Kirwan v. Raborg	101	Money v. Leach	206
Knight v. Farnaby	330	Moor v. Pudsey	297
—— v. Symms	336, 337	Moore v. Plymouth (Earl of)	390
Knights v. Quarles	123	—— v. Taylor	257
Knox v. Summers	159	Morant v. Sign	278
		Moravia v. Sloper	357
		Morewood v. Wood	302
LAKE v. Raw	367	Morgan v. Man	407
Lamb v. Mills	355, 356	Morley v. ——	280
Lambert v. Cook	264	Morrow v. Belcher	307
—— v. Prince	287	Mors v. Thacker	389
Lane v. Alexander	298	Morse v. James	356, 358
Langford v. Webber	342, 343	Moses v. Macferlan	86
Latham v. Rutley	204	—— v. United States	205
Lathbury v. Arnold	349	Mostyn v. Fabrigas	323
Lawley v. Gattacre	337	Mure v. Kaye	361
Layton v. Grindall	338	Murray v. East India Co.	386
Lea v. Luthell	386	—— v. Stair (Earl of)	244
Le Bret v. Papillon	235, 397, 399, 400	Myn v. Cole	384
Ledesham v. Lubram	386		
Lee v. Clarke	246		
—— v. Rogers	407	NASH v. Towne	205
Leech v. Widsley	206	Nelson v. Griffiths	315
Leneret v. Rivet	359, 374	Nerot v. Wallace	237, 238
Lethbridge v. Winter	285	Nevil and Cook's Case	267
Lewis v. Preston	362	Nevill v. Soper	882

Newcastle (Duke of) v. Wright 348, 353

Newhall v. Barnard 298

Newton v. Stubbs 391

Nichol v. Wilton 413

Nichols v. Pawlett 333

Nicholson v. Simpson 281, 288

Northumberland's (Countess of) Case 308

Nowlan v. Geddes 234, 399, 400

O'BRIEN v. Saxon 252, 253

Oglethorp v. Hyde 375, 376

Onslow v. Smith 393

Osborne v. Rogers 301

Osway v. Bristow 343

Outram v. Morewood 271

Owen v. Reynolds 406

PALMER v. Ekins 299

—— v. Lawson 367

Paramore v. Johnson 246, 249

Parkes v. Middleton 370

Parks v. Ross 207

Partridge v. Strange 365, 377, 378

Pasley v. Freeman 12

Peacock v. Bell and Kendal 446

Penn v. Ward 385

Phillips v. Fielding 412

—— v. Homfray 118

—— v. Howgate 287, 314

Piggot's Case 235

Pigot's (Henry) Case 244

Pillans v. Van Mierop 84

Pippet v. Hearn 237, 391

Pitt v. Knight 298

—— v. Russell 353

Plasket v. Beeby 393

Platt v. Hill 365

Playter's Case 337

Plomer v. Ross 360

Pope v. Skinner 267

—— v. Tillman 337

Porter v. Gray 349

Powdick v. Lyon 402

Powell v. Fullerton 399

Powers v. Cook 269, 270, 393

Poynter v. Poynter 384

Praed v. Cumberland (Duchess of) 407

Price v. Brown 205

—— v. Fletcher 412, 413

—— v. Seaman 237

Priddle and Napper's Case 268, 302

Pullin v. Nicholas 386

Purcell v. Bradley 383

Pyster v. Hemling 347

QUEEN (The) v. Dale 339

RABORG v. Peyton 54

Radford v. Harbyn 279

Ralph Bovy's (Sir) Case 296, 367

Rama Chitty v. Hume 320

Rann v. Hughes 84

Read's Case 297

Read v. Brookman 428

Renno v. Bennett 254

Rich v. Pilkington 235

Richards v. Hodges 291, 373, 403

Richardson v. Oxford (Mayor of) 265, 268

Richley v. Proone 433

Ricketts v. Loftus 296

Rider v. Smith 351, 378

Riggs v. Bullingham 379

Rivers v. Griffith 339

Robb v. Vos 115

Robert Bradshaw's Case 378, 379

Robert Pilford's Case 418

Roberts v. Mariett 404

Robinson v. Corbett 271, 272

—— v. Rayley 8, 253, 261, 310, 311

—— v. Smith 347

Roe v. Lord 348

—— v. Vernon 347

Rose v. Standen 383

Routh v. Weddell 235

Rowe v. Roach 340

—— v. Tutte 401

Rowland v. Veale 356, 357

SABINE v. Johnstone 395

St. Germains (Earl of) v. Willan 280, 401

St. John v. St. John 366, 367

St. Louis &c. Ry. v. McBride 159

Salisbury's (Bishop of) Case 379

Salter v. Purchell 254

Saunders's Case 408, 409, 410

Saunders v. Hussey 344, 345

Sayre v. Minns 290, 292, 360

Scavage v. Hawkins 345

Scilley v. Dally 346, 347

Scott v. Brest 324

Searl v. Bunnion 343, 346, 347

Selby v. Bardons 252

Shadwell v. Berthoud 433

Shaw v. Alvanley (Lord) 320

Sheers v. Brooks 369

Shepheard's Case 347

Sherland v. Heaton 389

Shum v. Farrington 370, 372

Sicard v. Davis 101

Skevill v. Avery 343, 347

Slade's Case 85

Slade v. Dowland 391

—— v. Drake 3, 385, 432

Smith v. Bellows 101

—— v. Dovers 262

—— v. Feverell 368

The references are to the pages.

Smith v. Yeomans   432
Spieres v. Parker   237
Stebbins v. Insurance Co.   101
Stephens v. Arthur   422
Stibbs v. Clough   187
Stone v. Bliss   359
Stowell v. Zouch (Lord)   366, 367
Street v. Hopkinson   399, 400
—— v. Rigby   18
Stroud v. Gerard (Lady)   390, 391
Swinnerton v. Stafford (Marquis
    of)   210
Symmons v. Knox   332

Talbot v. Hopewood   400
Tampian v. Newsam   421
Tatem v. Perient   299
Taylor v. Cole   287
—— v. Eastwood   278, 342
—— v. Needham   271, 272
—— v. Smith   287
Thomas v. Hanscombe   315
—— v. Heathorn   235, 280
—— v. Vandermoolen   433
Thornton v. Adams   383
Thrale v. London (Bishop of)   265
Tippet v. May   280
Tipping v. Johnson   293
Titley v. Foxall   358
Tolputt v. Wells   403
Tomlin v. Burlace   388
Took v. Glascock   398
Topping v. Fuge   431
Trevilian v. Seccomb   304
Trueman v. Hurst   401
Turner v. Felgate   356

Union Pacific R. R. Co. v. Wyler   405

Veale v. Warner   397, 398
Vere v. Smith   290, 291, 406
Vincent v. Beston   280
Vooght v. Winch   271
Vynior's Case   348, 369

Wade v. Baker   347
Wallis v. Savil   400
Walsingham's Case   366, 367
Walters v. Mace   340
Warbrook v. Griffin   85
Ward & Blunt's Case   411
Ware v. Boydell   324

Waring v. Griffiths   342
Warner v. Wainsford   408, 411
Washbourne v. Barrows   252
Washington, &c., S. P. Co. v. Sickles 229
Washington Gas Co. v. District of
    Columbia   184
Wats v. King   280
Webb v. Martin   401
Webber v. Tivill   401
Weeks v. Peach   398, 399
Weltale v. Glover   289
West v. Troles   317
Weston v. Charleston   20
—— v. Mason   237, 238
Wetherell v. Clerkson   379
—— v. Howard   267
Wettenhall v. Sherwin   389
Whelpdale's Case   245
White v. Cleaver   373, 374
Whitehead v. Buckland   290, 293
Whitwell v. Bennett   340
Wiat v. Essington   337
Wiggin's Ferry Co. v. O. & M. Ry.   9
Wilcox v. Skipwith (servant of)   281
Wilder v. Handy   389
Wilkes v. Williams   423
Williams v. Fowler   367
Wilson v. Kemp   292, 399
—— v. Hobday   369, 370
Wimbish v. Tailbois   377, 378
Wimbleton v. Holdrip   359
Winstone v. Linn   403
Wiscot's Case   350
Witham v. Lewis   215
Witherley v. Sarsfield   388
Witts v. Polehampton   214
Wood v. Budden   299, 300
—— v. Butts   386, 387
—— v. Hawkshead   407
Woodcock v. Cole   359
Woolaston v. Webb   379
Wright v. Clements   391
—— v. Ramscot   331
Wyat v. Aland   382

Yates v. Boen   244
—— v. Carlisle   412, 413
Young v. Gadderer   433
—— v. Rudd   297
—— v. Ruddle   297
—— v. Watson   417

Zouch v. Parsons   245
Zouch & Bamfield's Case   387

COMMON-LAW PLEADING.

INTRODUCTION.

In an address delivered in 1889, by Lord Chief Justice Coleridge, before the law students of Birmingham, he contrasted the law as it existed in England in 1847 with its condition at the time he spoke; incidentally, he referred to the late Baron Parke, of whom he said: "The ruling power in the courts in 1847 was Baron Parke, a man of great and wide legal learning, an admirable scholar, a kind hearted and amiable man, and of remarkable force of mind. These great qualities he devoted to heightening all the absurdities and contracting to the very utmost the narrowness of the system of special pleading. The client was unthought of. . . . The right was nothing, the mode of stating, everything." [1] After speaking further of Baron Parke's devotion to the technicalities of special pleading, Lord Coleridge resumed: "Peace be with him. He was a great lawyer, a man of high character and powerful intellect. No smaller man could have produced such results. If he ever were to revisit the glimpses of the moon, one shudders to think of his disquiet. No *absque-hoc*, no *et non*, no color, express or implied, given to trespass; no new assignment. Belief in the great doctrine of a negative pregnant no longer necessary to legal salvation, and the very nice question, as Baron Parke is reported to have thought, whether you could reply *de injuria* to a plea of deviation in an action on a marine policy not only still unsolved, but actually considered not worth solution." [2] Of other judges and advocates eminent in 1847, but since dead, Lord Coleridge said:

[1] The Contemporary Review, June, 1890, 799. [2] *Ibid.* 801.

1

"And with these men the system under which they flourished has gone to rest too; parties are examined, husband and wife are heard. Special pleading finds no refuge upon the habitable globe except, as I believe, in the State of New Jersey in America." [1] In confirmation of Lord Coleridge's statement, we find that the Common-Law Procedure Act of 1852, and the rules of court made pursuant thereto, abolished all common-law forms of actions, and substituted therefor the simplest possible statements of causes of demand. It may be accurately said that the tendency of English legislation is to the destruction of the science of special pleading at the hands of its creators. It is threatened with a like fate in this country. When, therefore, it is proposed to the student that he shall study special pleading as it was known at common-law, he may well ask why he should fit himself with an outworn and a cast-off garment. He may apparently well think that time and energy devoted to such a subject are wasted.

It is said by the most famous law-writer of this century, Savigny, that "The study of the law is of its very nature exposed to a double danger; that of soaring through theory into the empty abstractions of a fancied law of nature, and that of sinking through practice into a soulless, unsatisfying handicraft." [2] Only those students who have no higher ambition than to be mere craftsmen, and an inferior order even of these, can afford to refuse the study of special pleading because, in their opinion, it may not be of practical use to them to-day. I purpose to show briefly in this introduction how vitally this study is connected with the development of English law, and how indispensable a part of legal education it still is, and must ever be, wherever the common law of England is in force.

I. The remedial law of England developed with, and was stimulated and enlarged by, the development of special pleading. Littleton, writing in the reign of Edward IV., said: "And know ye this, my son, that it is one of the most honorable, laudable, and profitable things in our law to have the

---

[1] The Contemporary Review, June, 1890, 802.   [2] Howe's Studies in the Civil Law, 6.

science of well pleading in actions real and personal; and therefore I counsel thee especially to set all thy courage and care to learn that, &c."[1] That special pleading did not decline in importance between his time and that of Lord Coke is evident from what the latter has said of it in his judicial decisions and in his great Commentary. "Good pleading," says he, " is *Lapis Lydius*, the touchstone of the true sense and knowledge of the common law."[2] Again, in the Preface to his Commentary upon Littleton, he speaks of "The rules of good pleading (the *heart string* of the common law)." At page 115 b of the same Commentary, he has these words: "Note, one of the best arguments or proofes in law is drawn from the right entries or course of pleading; for the law itselfe speaketh by good pleading; and therefore Littleton here saith, 'it is proved by the pleading,' &c., as if pleading were *ipsius legis viva vox.*" It is said in Hobart's Reports that truth is the goodness and virtue of pleading, as certainty is the grace and beauty of it.[3]

It may be thought that these are extravagant expressions of men who were educated to see excellence in anything that was technical and abstruse. When Littleton says that the law is proved by the pleading, and when Coke adds, approvingly, "as if pleading were the living voice of the law itself," they are not using mere figures of rhetoric. Accordingly, we find in the recent work upon English law, by two men who have done more than all others to make its origin and growth plain (I refer to Pollock and Maitland's History of English Law), that the development of rights has depended upon the development of actions. In that work its authors show in great detail how closely advances in the conception of right have been associated with, and enforced by, corresponding advances in pleading. "Our forms of action are not mere rubrics nor dead categories; they are not the outcome of a classificatory process that has been applied to pre-existing materials; they are institutes of the law; they are, we say it without scruple, living things."[4]

---

[1] Tenures, sec. 534 (Tomlins).
[2] 10 Co. Rep. 29 b.
[3] Slade *v.* Drake, Hob. 295
[4] P. & M. Hist. II. 559.

"We shall do well to remember that the rule of law was the rule of writs." [1] Bracton, writing in the reign of Henry III., can still say, "There will be as many *formulæ* of writs as there are kinds of actions." A little later we shall have to take the tale of writs as the fixed quantity, and our maxim will be, "There will be as many kinds of actions as there are *formulæ* of writs." [2] Finally, at the conclusion of their work, speaking of English law prior to the time of Edward I., and resuming its influence upon the subsequent development of that law, these high authorities thus record their judgment: "Nor can we part with this age without thinking once more of the permanence of its work. Those few men who were gathered at Westminster, around Pateshull and Raleigh and Bracton, were penning writs that would run in the name of kingless commonwealths on the other shore of the Atlantic Ocean; *they were making right and wrong for us and for our children.*" [3]

Consonant with these opinions is what an eminent American jurist has written: "However much we may codify the law into a series of seemingly self-sufficient propositions, those propositions will be but a phase in a continuous growth. To understand their scope fully, to know how they will be dealt with by judges trained in the past which the law embodies, we must ourselves know something of that past. The history of what the law has been is necessary to the knowledge of what the law is." [4]

II. The study of special pleading is not only essential to a correct understanding of the historical development of the common law; it is most admirable and essential as an intellectual training. No man can be a strong reasoner who does not possess natural or acquired logic. No man can be a strong lawyer who has not, in addition to this logic, a clear knowledge of the logic of the law; and special pleading is the logic of the law.

The real function of education is not to charge the mind with facts; its object is, as the etymology of the word

[1] P. & M. Hist. II. 561.   [3] *Ibid.* 670.
[2] *Ibid.* 562.   [4] Holmes, C. L. 37.

expresses, to draw forth and develop all of the mental powers which the student has. This result cannot be accomplished by mere study. The mind may be a magazine charged with all sorts of knowledge, and yet not able to form a clear idea, or to express lucidly an idea when formed; still less able to reason upon, to develop and to defend it. For this purpose something more than study is necessary. It is related of John C. Calhoun, that, when a young man, he devoted an hour every morning to a solitary walk, during which he discussed, in every conceivable phase, some one proposition. He argued it on the one side and on the other. He held it up, as it were, to the sun, and endeavored to see through what thin places the light would pierce and betray weakness of structure. He pressed his mind against it as a farmer's boy holds the edge of an axe against a grindstone. Fatiguing as the process was, he persevered in it day after day and year after year until, as a result, he developed mental powers which, for clearness of conception, for lucidity and conciseness of expression, for rigid sequence of argument, and for strength of construction, were absolutely unrivalled. Such a process the student should aim to follow; it is the study of the science of special pleading, above all others, which will aid him in this pursuit. He should ever bear in mind the following advice of Lord Coke: " Mine advice to the student is, that before he read any part of our Commentaries upon any section, that first he read again and again our author himself in that section, and do his best endeavors, first of himself, and then by *conference with others* (*which is the life of study*), to understand it, and then to read our Commentary thereupon, and no more at any one time than he is able with a delight to bear away, and after to meditate thereon, which is the life of reading." [1] Clearly, Lord Coke knew the proper process for the development of the mind. The same thought is most admirably expressed by Sir William Hamilton in the introductory chapter to his Lectures upon Metaphysics, which chapter should be carefully read and pondered on by every teacher and student of law. " I must regard the main duty of a

---

[1] Co. Litt. Preface, xlii.

professor to consist not simply in communicating information, but in doing this in such a manner, and with such an
accompaniment of subsidiary means, that the information he
conveys may be the occasion of awakening his pupils to a
vigorous and varied exertion of their faculties. Self-activity
is the indispensable condition of improvement; and education
is only education, that is, accomplishes its purpose only, by
affording objects and supplying incitements to this spontaneous
exertion. Strictly speaking, every one must educate himself.
All profitable study is a silent disputation — an intellectual
gymnastic; and the most improving books are precisely those
which most excite the reader to understand the author, to
supply what he has omitted, and to canvass his facts and
reasonings. To read passively to learn is, in reality, not to
learn at all. In study, implicit faith, belief upon authority, is
worse even than, for a time, erroneous speculation. To read
profitably we should read the authors not most in unison with,
but most adverse to, our opinions; for whatever may be the case
in the cure of bodies, *enantiopathy*, and not *homœopathy*, is the
true medicine of minds. Accordingly, such sciences and such
authors as present only unquestionable truths, determining a
minimum of self-activity in the student, are, in a rational
education, subjectively naught. Those sciences and authors,
on the contrary, who constrain the student to independent
thought, are, whatever may be their objective certainty, subjectively, educationally best." [1] The science of special pleading cannot be mastered by one who merely studies. It must,
as Lord Coke says, be learned by conference with others, and
after meditation. How the truth of this was appreciated by
even a man of genius, who would popularly be supposed above
such aids as Lord Coke has indicated, is evident from what was
said before the Court of Common Pleas of Hampden, Massachusetts, on the occasion of Daniel Webster's death. "It was
a year or two since that he [Webster] spoke of having found
the Reports of Saunders when he was a student, accessible
only in their original Latin, and without the notes with which
Sergeant Williams has since enriched them, and he remarked:

---

[1] Hamilton's Metaphysics (Bowen), 11.

' I sat down and made a translation of them into English, and I have it now, and it was in that way that I made myself familiarly and greatly acquainted with the language of pleading.' " [1] On this fact Wallace, in his article upon Saunders' Reports, comments as follows: " Daniel Webster, it is said, once translated the Reports of Saunders into English. The book which trained Webster's mind to its ' *prodigious powers of legal logic*,' or in which *his* intellect found a dialectic harmony, may well receive the homage of the world." [2] As is well known, these volumes of Reports are the great repository of cases involving points of special pleading. It is related of one of the greatest lawyers whom this country has produced, the late Walter Jones of the Bar of the District of Columbia, that he wrote out, in all their detail, the pleadings of every case reported by Sir James Burrow. Surely the doing of such work by two such men is conclusive proof of its excellence as a discipline.

III. In addition to the general mental training given by this study, there is a particular advantage to be derived from it, notwithstanding the prevalent abolition of special pleading and the substitution therefor of what is called code pleading. No code can mar the beauty of pleading based upon the principles of the common-law science. Just as natural logic lies at the basis of all clear and effective discussion upon general topics, so special pleading is the foundation of all legal discussion. It is impossible that issues can be properly presented for decision, either by court or jury, unless, in the first place, the litigants, through their counsel, are capable of clearly conceiving the propositions of fact or of law upon which their claims rest. In the second place, there must be a lucid and concise expression of those propositions. Such expressions must, moreover, be relevant, and, as far as possible, single. After the propositions have been once stated, there must be no departure from them. A litigant must be compelled to pursue a definite and consistent course from the

---

[1] Remarks of Reuben A. Chapman upon the death of Daniel Webster. New York Daily Times, October 27, 1852.

[2] The Reporters, 338.

time he comes into court, until he obtains its judgment. He cannot do this unless he is thoroughly acquainted with the principles of special pleading.

In the sharp and hard competition of these modern days at the bar, the lawyer who is able to present his case in such manner as to enable the court or jury to at once possess itself of the salient points of the position which he occupies, is the lawyer who will, from the outset, secure the attention of court and bar, and who will speedily command success. Sir William Jones had such qualities in view when he wrote as follows: " The science of special pleading is an excellent logic ; it is admirably calculated for the purposes of analyzing a cause, of extracting, like the roots of an equation, the true points in dispute, and referring them with all imaginable distinctness to the court or jury. It is reducible to the strictest rules of pure dialectics, and tends to fix the attention, give a habit of reasoning clearly, quicken the apprehension and invigorate the understanding."[1]   To the same effect are the following observations of Lord Mansfield: " The substantial rules of pleading are founded in strong sense, and in the soundest and closest logic, and so appear when well understood and explained; though, by being misunderstood and misapplied, they are often made use of as instruments of chicane."[2]   More than one hundred years later, Mr. Justice Grier, speaking for the Supreme Court of the United States, in the case of McFaul v. Ramsey, thus said: " This system [of pleading], matured by the wisdom of ages, founded on principles of truth and sound reason, has been ruthlessly abolished in many of our States, who have rashly substituted in its place the suggestions of sciolists, who invent new codes and systems of pleading to order. But this attempt to abolish all species, and establish a single genus, is found to be beyond the power of legislative omnipotence. They cannot compel the human mind not to distinguish between things that differ. The distinction between the different forms of actions

[1] Sir William Jones' Works. Prefatory Discourse to the Speeches of Isæus, IV. 34. (f.) IX. 50, 51 (8 vo.).

[2] Robinson v. Rayley, 1 Burr. 319.

for different wrongs, requiring different remedies, *lies in the nature of things; it is absolutely inseparable from the correct administration of justice in common-law courts.* The result of these experiments, so far as they have come to our knowledge, has been to destroy the certainty and simplicity of all pleadings, and introduce on the record an endless wrangle in writing, perplexing to the court, delaying and impeding the administration of justice." [1] Undoubtedly, at the present moment, the swing of the pendulum is in the direction furthest from special pleading. Just as undoubtedly, if trial by jury be retained, it must again swing in the other direction.[2] It is essential for the proper administration of justice that the principles of special pleading should be observed in the statement of cases for decision by courts. There is an element of truth in the declaration of Baron Parke that, "Those who drew loose declarations brought scandal on the law." [3] Equally does the language of the court in the old case of Heard *v.* Baskerville express a truth. The court, in construing the statute of demurrers, 27 Eliz. c. 5, said: "Now the moderation of this statute is such that it doth not utterly reject form; for that were a dishonor to the law, and to make it in effect no art; but requires only that it be discovered, and not used as a secret snare to entrap." [4]

Perhaps the truth with respect to the proper use to-day of the rules of special pleading is nowhere better stated than by Mr. Justice Brown, delivering the opinion of the Supreme Court of the United States in the case of Wiggin's Ferry Co. *v.* O. & M. Railway: "Rules of pleading are made for the attainment of substantial justice, and are to be construed so as to harmonize with it if possible. A mistaken view of one's rights or remedies should not be permitted wholly to defeat a claim founded upon principles of equity and justice. And if the pleadings can be so amended as to admit proof of such claim, and such amendment does not introduce a new cause of action, though it

[1] 20 How. 525.
[2] Preface to Seventh Edition of Taylor on Evidence.
[3] Lord Coleridge. The Contemporary Review, June, 1890, 800.
[4] Hob. 232.

may set up a new measure of damages, or work a real hardship to the party defendant, it is within the discretion, even of the appellate court, to permit such amendment to be made." [1]   While this decision was made in an equity case, it nevertheless correctly indicates the trend of the law.[2]   Here, however, it must be again recollected that the lawyer who is so ignorant of these rules of pleading as to be compelled to apply frequently, and even in the appellate court, for leave to amend, in order that his clients may not suffer through his ignorance, is one who probably will do neither justice to these clients, nor credit to his profession.

[1] 142 U. S. 415.

[2] Encyclopædia of Pleading and Practice, I. 607.   Kennedy et al. v. Georgia State Bank et al., 8 How. 610.

CHAPTER I.

OF REMEDIES.

The vital principle of all systems of law is that a remedy must be given for the violation of every right. Our English law expresses this truth in the Latin words *ubi jus, ibi remedium* (wherever a right exists, there exists a corresponding remedy). This maxim has been freely translated by Lord Coke thus: "The law will, that in every case where a man is wronged and endammaged, that he shall have remedie."[1] Chief Justice Holt uses even terser and stronger language: "It is a vain thing to imagine there should be right without a remedy, for want of right and want of remedy are convertibles."[2]

So radical is this principle that the law expands by force of its inherent elasticity to admit new remedies. "It is not the novelty of the action that can be argued against it, if it can be supported by the old grounds and principles of the law. The ground of law is plain, certain, and indeed universal, that where any man is injured in his right by being either hindered in or defrauded of the enjoyment thereof, the law gives him an action to repair himself. . . . The law of England is not confined to precedents, but consists in the reason of them, which is much more extensive than the circumstances of this or that case. '*Ratio legis est anima legis,*' et '*ubi eadem ratio ibi idem jus*' ('the reason of the law is the soul of the law,' and 'where the same reason exists there is the same right'), are known maxims."[3]

[1] Co. Litt. 197 b.
[2] Ashby *v.* White, Ld. Raym. 938; s. c. 1 Smith's Leading Cases, 342; s. c. 1 English Ruling Cases, 521.

[3] Per Holt, C. J., Ashby *v.* White, English Ruling Cases, 525; s. c. (House of Lords) 1 Bro. P. C. 47.

But if an entirely new principle is attempted to be introduced, resort must be had to legislation, for in such case it is sought to create not only the remedy, but the right also.[1] For example, the Act of Parliament known as the Employer's Liability Act (43 & 44 Vict. c. 42) was required to create a right of action in favor of a servant, injured by the negligent act of a fellow-servant, against their common employer.

Again, the student must note that it is only the violation of a *right* for which a remedy is given. A man may suffer great *loss* and yet have no right violated. The law denominates such loss *Damnum absque injuria* (Loss without legal injury). For example: a proprietor digs a well on his own land and pumps up water to an extent exceeding what is required for his private use, with the result of absorbing water from the substrata and diminishing the supply enjoyed by neighboring proprietors, but without diverting water already collected in any definite channel; the loss thus suffered by those proprietors is *damnum absque injuria*, and affords no ground of action against the first proprietor.[2] The establishment of a rival school which draws away the pupils from a school previously established is another instance of such loss.[3]

Before considering the remedies given to injured persons through the instrumentality of the law, it is proper to advert to very ancient methods of redress by their own mere act, which were allowed to parties. Such redress could be effected in two manners : First, by the sole act of the party injured ; and second, by the joint act of all parties concerned.

SELF-HELP.

Such methods of redress were called self-help as distinguished from the help that the law gives.

In early societies the functions of the ruler, while large in power, were limited in application. The protection of private rights and the redress of private wrongs were relegated to

[1] Ashhurst, J., in Pasley v. Freeman, 3 T. R. 63.

[2] Chasemore v. Richards, 7 H. L. C. 349.

[3] Bacon, Abr., Actions in General, B.

the parties concerned. This was true among ancient peoples generally. We learn from Hunter's work on Roman Law that "at the time of the XII. Tables (B. C. 451, 450) the state did not as yet claim to decide civil disputes, although it sanctioned the use of force to bring an alleged wrong-doer before the tribunals. At an earlier period, as we may infer from the peculiarity of the oldest form of legal procedure, even this limited authority was denied. The earliest type of judicial proceedings is a mock combat followed by a reference to arbitration. The first judges were simply arbitrators. Civil jurisdiction sprang out of arbitration. The coercive authority of the state grew out of the voluntary submission of the subject." [1]

If we turn to what we to-day call crimes, we are confronted with the same private aspect. "The fact," says Mr. Justice Stephen, "that the private vengeance of the person wronged by a crime was the principal source to which men trusted for the administration of criminal justice in early times, is one of the most characteristic circumstances connected with English Criminal Law, and has had much to do with the development of what may, perhaps, be regarded as its principal distinctive peculiarity, namely, the degree to which a criminal trial resembles a private litigation." [2] This most interesting and instructive subject, so closely connected with the origin of all systems of positive law, cannot be dwelt on here, but the student is urged to pursue it in the works cited below.[3]

So complete was the revolution against this unrestrained self-help that we find in the Roman law the following radical provision existing in the fifth century of our era. "When a man shall have gone such lengths of frenzied arrogance as to have taken violent possession of things, . . . *if he be the owner*, he shall restore the possession abstracted by

[1] Roman Law, 967.

[2] Hist. of Criminal Law, I. 245.

[3] The Aryan Household (Hearn), c. xix.; Maine's Early Law and Custom, 170; Maine's Early History of Institutions, Lectures IX., X.; Stephen's History of Criminal Law, Vol. I.; Cherry's Growth of Criminal Law; Hunter's Roman Law, Book IV.; Muirhead's Roman Law, 51, 71, 105; Sohm's Institutes of Roman Law, 147, 148; Justinian's Institutes (ed. Moyle), I. 614.

him from the possessor and forfeit his ownership of such property." [1]

In England the change was no less fundamental. The law began early to stringently prohibit self-help, and to discourage a resort to force. In Bracton's time (Henry III.), "the man who has slain another in self-defence *deserves*, it is true, but he also *needs*, a royal pardon." [2] Without this pardon he was not guiltless. Probably in the reign of no other king was violence so universal and continuous in England as when Stephen sat in his usurped seat. "The earth bore no corn; you might as well have tilled the sea, for the land was all ruined by such deeds, and it was said openly that Christ and his saints slept." [3] Yet under the very next king (Henry II.) was invented that writ of *novel disseisin* (of which we shall say more hereafter) which protected a possession of real estate, acquired by violence and without a shadow of right. The owner of a stolen beast could only repossess himself of his property in a formal and prescribed way. Britton, writing in the reign of Edward I., supposes the following case: Peter has had his horse stolen and finds it in the possession of John, from whom he takes it by violence. Whereupon John appeals Peter of stealing the horse, and Peter says: "The horse was mine and as mine I took it." If Peter succeeds in proving this assertion he escapes the gallows, but as a punishment for his act of violence he loses the horse, "for," King Edward is supposed to say, "we will that every one shall have recourse to judgment rather than to force." [4]

It was inevitable that the law should recede from this extreme position, which it had been forced by the violence of half-civilized times to take against self-help. During the later middle ages a natural reaction in this respect took place. "In our own day our law allows an amount of quiet self-help that would have shocked Bracton. *It can safely allow this, for it has mastered* the sort of self-help that is lawless." [5]

---

[1] Imp. Valent. Cod. 8, 4, 7. Roman Private Law, Salkowski, 413.

[2] P. & M. Hist. II. 477, 572.

[3] The Anglo-Saxon Chronicle, *anno* 1137.

[4] P. & M. Hist. II. 167.

[5] *Ibid.* II. 572.

Self-Help by the Mere Act of the Parties.

There were five methods of self-help by his own mere act which the common law allowed to an injured person : —

(1) By Self-Defence.

(2) By Recaption of Persons or of Goods.

(3) By Entry upon Lands.

(4) By Abatement of Nuisances.

(5) By Distress.

These methods should be familiar to the student and require only brief mention here.

(1) *Self-defence:* In English law self-defence is recognized as the primary rule of nature; it is a right which society cannot take away. It includes not only the defence of one's self, but also the mutual and reciprocal defence of such as stand in the relation of husband and wife, parent and child, and master and servant. In these cases if the party himself, or any of these his relations, be forcibly attacked in person or property, it is lawful for him to repel force by force. Care must be taken, however, that the resistance does not exceed the bounds of mere defence and prevention, for then the defender would himself become an aggressor. Accordingly, it has been said that self-defence is only preventive and that therefore it should not be included among methods of redress.[1] But the law allows a blow to be repelled by a blow, and in this very act of prevention an element of redress seems to be present.

(2) *Recaption or reprisal:* This right exists when any one has deprived another unlawfully of his goods, or wrongfully detains his wife, child, or servant. In such case the injured party may lawfully claim and retake the property or person so detained wherever he happens to find the one or the other. But such recaption must not be in a riotous manner, nor attended with a breach of the peace.

(3) *Entry upon lands:* As recaption is a remedy given to the party himself, against one who unlawfully detains from him his personal property, so entry on lands and tenements, when another person without any right has taken possession

---

[1] Min. Inst. IV. 95.

thereof, is a remedy of the same kind for illegal deprivation of the possession of real estate.

(4) *Abatement of nuisances:* Whatever unlawfully annoys or does damage to another is a nuisance; and such nuisance may be abated, that is, taken away or removed, by the party aggrieved thereby, provided he commit no riot nor breach of the peace in doing it.

(5) *Distress:* A distress is the summary taking of a personal chattel out of the possession of the wrong-doer into the custody of the party injured, to procure a satisfaction of the wrong committed. It would seem originally to have been lawful only when authorized by a court. Its subsequent legalization as a mere private act is therefore an instance of modified feeling against all self-help as such. The student is referred to Bigelow's History of Procedure (Chapter V. Distraint) and to Pollock and Maitland's History (Vol. II. pp. 573–576) for a detailed account of its origin and incidents.[1] We have only space here to say that it was originally a means which the feudal lord could employ to compel his men to answer for default of services. Blackstone gives the following as its regular uses: a distress might be taken (1) for non-payment of rent in arrear; (2) for neglect to do suit to the lord's court or to perform other certain personal services; (3) for amercements in a court leet; (4) where a man finds beasts of a stranger wandering on his grounds, *damage feasant*, that is, doing him hurt or damage by treading down his grass or the like; (5) for several duties and penalties prescribed and inflicted by special acts of Parliament. All chattels upon the leased premises were liable for distress for rent. To this general rule there were, however, the following exceptions: things wherein no man can have an absolute and valuable property; whatever is at the time of distraint in the personal use or occupation of any man; valuable things in the way of trade, as a horse standing in a smith's shop to be shod; a man's tools and utensils of his trade, as the axe of a carpenter, the books of a scholar, beasts of the plough; things of a nature to be injured by keeping, and which can

---

[1] See also Maine's Early History of Institutions, Lectures IX., X.

not be rendered again in as good plight as when they were distrained, and things fixed to the freehold.

It must be noted that the right of distraint was not originally a right of self-satisfaction. The beast distrained could neither be sold nor used. It was in a sense in the custody of the law. The distrainer must always be ready to show it and to give it up if the tenant tenders payment of the amount due or resorts to his remedy of replevin. Subsequently, a sale of the thing distrained was allowed in certain cases by Act of Parliament. In making distraint it was a matter of the utmost importance to the distrainer to observe all of the formalities of the law. " He not only lost the goods seized in case he had made a false step, but he was also subjected to a fine in favor of the debtor." [1]

For an illegal distress the remedies allowed by common law to the tenant or owner of the thing distrained were the actions of replevin, of trespass and of trespass on the case, of all of which we shall speak hereafter. Trespass lay in all cases in which any irregularity of procedure rendered the distrainer a trespasser from the outset ; trespass on the case lay for excessive levy, for a wrongful seizure of property not liable to distress, and for irregularities which did not render the distrainer a trespasser from the outset.[2]

Blackstone mentions the seizing of heriots, when due on the death of a tenant, as another species of self-remedy. It is, however, not of sufficient historical importance to require more than mere mention in this connection.

Self-Help by the Joint Act of all Parties concerned.

We must next consider those remedies which arise from the joint act of all parties concerned. These are only two :

(1) Accord.
(2) Arbitration.

(1) *Accord*, or, as the term more commonly is, Accord and Satisfaction, occurs whenever parties who have a

---

[1] Hist. Pr. 211.

[2] In the United States the right of distraint has been generally abolished.

controversy mutually agree, the one to make or give, and the other to receive something (whether money, property, or a specific act performed), in satisfaction of the injury. The effect of this, when the satisfaction is actually given and accepted, is to entirely atone for the wrong. No right of action, by reason of the wrong, remains.

(2) *Arbitration* is where the parties, injuring and injured, submit all matters in dispute, concerning any personal chattel or personal wrong, to the judgment of two or more arbitrators, who are to decide the controversy; if they do not agree, it is usual to provide that another person be called in as umpire, to whose sole judgment the matter in dispute is then referred. The decision of the arbitrators or of the umpire is called an award. Thereby the question at issue is as fully determined, and the right transferred or settled, as it could have been by the agreement of the parties or the judgment of a competent court. The title to real estate cannot, however, pass by a mere award, although the award may require a conveyance, and it will be a breach of the arbitration bond to refuse compliance. This method of settling disputes is regarded by the law with much favor. Whatever its merits in theory, its practical benefit is open to serious doubts, which have been strongly stated by Lord Eldon (Street *v.* Rigby, 6 Ves. 818) and by Professor Minor (Institutes, Vol. IV. Pt. I. p. 138).

Remedies by Sole Operation of Law.

There are likewise only two instances of remedies given by the sole operation of the law.

(1) Retainer.
(2) Remitter.

(1) *Retainer:* If a person indebted to another make that creditor his executor, or if such creditor obtain letters of administration upon his debtor's estate, the law in each case gives the creditor a remedy for his debt, by allowing him to retain so much as will pay himself before any other creditors whose debts are of equal degree. The law gives him this remedy because he cannot, in his private, sue himself in

his representative capacity, and there is no one else whom he can sue. Hence, the law by its own act puts him in as good a position as if he had sued.[1]

(2) *Remitter*[2] applies only to real estate, and is where he who has the true property in lands, but is out of possession thereof, and has no right of entry thereon without recovering possession in an action, has the freehold cast upon him by some subsequent, and, of course, defective, title; in this case he is remitted, or sent back, by operation of law, to his ancient and more certain title. Again, where one is in wrongful possession of real estate as a disseisor, and then acquires by act of the law, as by a descent cast, the true property in the freehold of that real estate, there he is remitted to his true and better title. But the better title must always come to the party by act of the law, or at least without his participation. The same reason underlies this rule as in the case of retainer. Being himself in possession as disseisor, he cannot sue himself to establish his new and lawful title.[3]

We come now in due order to consider the redress of injuries effected by the concurring act of the parties and of the law; that is, by suit in court.

---

[1] In the United States this matter is generally regulated by statute.

[2] A case for the application of this doctrine could hardly arise to-day, for we have no proprietary as distinct from possessory actions for the recovery of real property.

[3] The student who may wish to study these methods of redress in greater detail is referred to Blackstone's Commentaries, Book III. chaps. 1 and 2, and Minor's Institutes, Book IV. Pt. I. 94–156.

CHAPTER II.

OF COURTS.

THE redress of injuries by suit in court requires the co-operation of the act of the parties and the act of the law. The term *suit* has been defined by Blackstone as " a lawful demand of one's right." [1] A better definition has been given by Chief Justice Marshall in these words : " The term [suit] is certainly a very comprehensive one, and is understood to apply to any proceeding in a court of justice, by which an individual pursues that remedy in a court of justice which the law affords him. The modes of proceeding may be various, but if a right is litigated between parties in a court of justice, the proceeding by which a decision of the court is sought is a suit." [2] The act of at least one of the parties is required to set the law in motion, and the process of the law is as a general thing the only instrument by which the parties are enabled to procure a certain and adequate redress. And it is to be noted that even where, as we have seen, the law allows an extra-judicial remedy, yet that does not exclude the ordinary course of justice. For example, I may defend myself, yet I am also entitled to an action of assault and battery against my assailant. Lord Coke says that, " *Curia*, court, is a place where justice is judicially ministered." [3] The definition is sounder than the etymology of the learned author, who derives the word from *cura, quia in curiis publicis curas gerebant* (care, because in public courts they transact business).[4] While this definition has

---

[1] Bl. Com. III. 116*.

[2] Weston *v.* Charleston, 2 Peters, 464.

[3] Co. Litt. 58 a.

[4] The verbal play is lost in translation.

been criticised in certain American cases,[1] it is sufficiently accurate. According to English law, the king was the fountain of all justice, and hence all courts of justice derived their jurisdiction and power from the crown.

COURTS OF RECORD.

Of courts, some are of record, others not of record. A court of record is a judicial, organized tribunal, having attributes and exercising functions independently of the person of the magistrate designated generally to hold it, and proceeding according to the course of the common-law.[2] The acts and judicial proceedings of these courts are recorded (originally they were enrolled in parchment) for a perpetual memorial and testimony. These records (or rolls) are called the records of the court, and they import absolute verity. Nothing can be averred against them, nor shall any plea or even proof be admitted to the contrary. If the existence of a record be denied, it shall be tried by itself, that is, by an inspection thereof by the court to ascertain whether or not it is a properly authenticated record. All English courts of record are the king's courts.

COURTS NOT OF RECORD.

A court not of record is a court of whose proceedings no solemn contemporaneous minute is made by a sworn officer. Such were the courts-baron incident to every manor. The proceedings of such courts are not enrolled or recorded, and are matters of fact to be tried and determined, if disputed, by a jury.

OF COURTS IN GENERAL.

Every court must be composed of at least three constituent elements: the *actor*, or plaintiff, who complains of an injury done; the *reus*, or defendant, who is called upon to make satisfaction for it; and the *judex*, or judicial power, who is to

---

[1] 45 Iowa, 503; 79 Ind. 375; 1 Gall. 499; 4 McCrary, 536; 5 Col. 381.

[2] Bouvier's Law Dict. *sub voc.* "Court of Record." *Ex parte* Gladhill, 8 Met. 170.

examine the accusation, to determine the law applicable in the premises, and, if any injury has been done, to ascertain and by proper officers to apply the remedy. We cannot here speak of attorneys-at-law or of counsel (who are officers of court) further than to say that originally every suitor was obliged to appear in person. In England, there was no definite legal profession till more than a century after the Norman Conquest.[1] Students who wish to follow the growth of this profession are referred to Minor's Institutes, Vol. IV. Pt. I. pp. 161–177.

The third and fourth chapters of Book III. of Blackstone's Commentaries are devoted to the consideration of courts in general and of the English public courts of common law and equity. This great system of courts existed continuously for about six hundred years, but has been recently entirely re-modelled by a series of statutes known as the Judicature Acts, beginning in 1873. Of these chapters of Blackstone his recent editor, Hammond, well says: "To the American student these chapters are now perhaps even more interesting and instructive than they are in England. They portray a system with which every American judge and lawyer of the first century was familiar, and which they regarded with a veneration hardly less than that paid the law itself. More remains of it may now be found in America than in the mother country; for no such sweeping change as that of the Judicature Acts is possible under our state and national organization. Moreover the English reports from the Year Books down are unintelligible to the student unless he understands the former organization of the courts." [2]

ANCIENT PROMINENCE OF LAW OF PROCEDURE.

But the study of the origin and organization of the great common-law courts has a more profound interest than a merely historical one. Upon an examination of ancient codes of law, we are surprised by the conspicuous and predominant place occupied by Courts of Justice and Rules of Procedure.[3] Sir

---

[1] P. & M. Hist. I. Introduction, xxvii.

[2] Bl. Com. III. 84.

[3] Hunter's Roman Law, 122.

Henry Sumner Maine, speaking of the ancient Indian code of laws, and especially of the compilation known as the Book of Narada, says: " The mechanism of a Court of Justice and its procedure are first elaborately described. . . . The principle and meaning of this ancient classification strike me as obvious. The compiler of Narada or his original makes the assumption that men do quarrel, and he sets forth the mode in which their quarrels may be adjudicated upon and settled without bloodshed or violence. The dominant notion present to his mind is not a Law, or a Right, or a Sanction, or the distinction between Positive and Natural Law, or between Persons and Things, *but a Court of Justice.* The great fact is that there now exists an alternative to private reprisals, a mode of stanching personal or hereditary blood-feuds other than slaughter or plunder. Hence, in front of everything he places the description of a Court, of its mechanism, of its procedure, of its tests of alleged facts. Having thus begun with an account of the great institution which settles quarrels, he is led *to distribute law* according to the subject-matter of quarrels, according to the relations between human beings which do, as a fact, give rise to civil disputes. Thus Debt, Partnership, the Marital Relation, Inheritance and Donation, are considered as matters about which men at a certain point of civilization do, as a fact, have differences, and the various rights and liabilities [as we should call them] to which they give rise, are set forth *simply as guides towards determining the judgment which a Court of Justice should give* when called upon to adjudicate on quarrels."[1] The same author says in another treatise: " It would not be untrue to assert that, in one stage of human affairs, rights and duties are rather the adjective of procedure than procedure a mere appendage to rights and duties. There have been times when the real difficulty lay, not in conceiving what a man was entitled to, but in obtaining it; so that the method, violent or legal, by which an end was obtained was of more consequence than the nature of the end itself. As a fact, it is only in the most recent times or in the most highly developed legal systems

---

[1] Early Law and Custom, 380, 381, 382.

that remedies have lost importance in comparison with rights, and have ceased to affect them deeply and variously." [1]

That this is true of the development of our English law is clearly stated by Pollock and Maitland. " That characteristic mark of ancient bodies of law, the prominent place given to what we sometimes speak of as ' adjective law,' the apparent subordination of rights to remedies, is particularly noticeable in our own case, and endures until modern times ; and naturally, *for our common law is the law of courts which gradually acquired their jurisdiction* by the development and interpretation of procedural formulas." [2] This is confirmed by our American jurist, Holmes, who says, speaking of the origin of the action of debt : " It seems strange that this crude product of the infancy of law should have any importance for us at the present time.   Yet whenever we trace a leading doctrine of substantive law far enough back, we are very likely to find some forgotten circumstance of procedure at its source." [3] To the same effect is what Hammond writes : " The old procedure had stood in all its substantial features at least since the reign of Edward I., and in that time had almost *created the English law of personal property, of contracts, and for the most part of torts.* In all these fields, if we try to trace the substantive law to its sources, we find most of its rules beginning as rules of practice in the appropriate action." [4]   These authorities should satisfy the student that he must understand the Law of Procedure, or, as Bentham and his school prefer to say, adjective law, before he can hope to master the substantive law of past centuries and of to-day.

ANGLO-SAXON COURTS.

Of the system of procedure and of the courts existing in England prior to the Norman Conquest, but little can be said here. The student who has leisure to pursue that subject can profitably read Bigelow's History of Procedure in England, and the first chapter of Pollock and Maitland's History of English Law. He is especially referred in

---

[1] Early History of Institutions, 252.   [3] Holmes, C. L. 253.
[2] P. & M. Hist. I. 208.   [4] Bl. Com. III. 187.

connection with the subject-matter of this entire chapter to "The King's Peace," a recent (1895) very instructive and accurate historical essay upon the English Law Courts by F. A. Inderwick, Q. C.

The natural tendency of a system whose main object was to repress self-help, was to localize the administration of justice. Self-help was prompt and ready to supply redress when and where the wrong was committed. The substitute for self-help must aim to be equally efficient. "To bring the view of justice to every man's door, to emulate the Cadi under the palm-tree, the justice-seat in the king's gate, the shout of the Wapentake, has ever been the ideal of law-reformers." [1] Accordingly, under the Anglo-Saxons the administration of justice was local. The several counties of England each did separately and completely its own judicial work. Appeals were discouraged and de-centralization was supreme. It is important to note this, for after the Norman Conquest the opposite course was pursued, and all the judicial work of the whole country was collected together and disposed of in one central court and by one supreme authority.[2]

The plan adopted by Alfred the Great and his successors was to divide the entire kingdom into sections, and to place each of these under the control of a chief officer. Each section was subdivided into smaller ones and these into still smaller, until finally a subdivision was reached at the head of which was a recognized officer, accountable directly to his superior officer, and through him and his superiors indirectly to the king. This ultimate subdivision was small enough to include a community of which each member was known to the other and to the common head, and was easily reached for purposes of legal process, of military service, and of taxation. The chief sections were called counties or shires, at the head of each of which was a judicial officer called the Shire-reeve, afterwards the Sheriff. Each county was then subdivided into hundreds, which were composed of either one hundred tithings or (it is uncertain which) one hundred hides of land, which would equal in extent about ten thousand acres, or a

---

[1] The King's Peace. Introduction, xvii.   [2] *Ibid.* Introduction, xiii.

little less than sixteen square miles. The tithing meant different things in different parts of the country. It is sufficient for our purpose to say that it meant a group of ten (or in some cases more) freemen subject to the law of frank-pledge, *i. e.*, the law which made each freeman of the group a pledge or surety for the good conduct or production, if need be, of any one or more of the same group. Each such group was presided over by one of the freemen thus associated, who was known as the chief-pledge, tithing-man, head-borough, or *bors*-holder (*i. e.* head or elder of the borh or pledge).[1] There were other subdivisions for various purposes, with which we are not here concerned.

The MANOR COURT or Court Baron was presided over by a Thane, a Baron, or the head of a tithing, as the case might be. One was ordinarily attached to each manor, and was held for the trial of cases arising within the manor, although, by consent of parties, its jurisdiction might extend to persons or things connected with the manor but not within it. But if the cause of action was between persons one of whom was not subject to the jurisdiction of the Manor Court, the suit, upon objection taken, could not proceed, but was removed to the Hundred or other proper court. Its most important business later was to determine, by writ of right, all controversies relating to the right of lands within the manor. The Court sat by custom once a fortnight, and was held in the Manor-House, which became the "local Temple of Justice."

The HUNDRED GEMOTE, otherwise called the Court of the Hundred or Wapentake,[2] was a court of higher and more extended jurisdiction than the Court Baron. King Edgar (A. D. 954–975) declared that it should meet always once in every four weeks, and that every man should do justice to another.[3] It tried civil, criminal, and ecclesiastical causes. It was presided over by a Sheriff or an Alderman who, with the freeholders acting also as judges, tried the cause. When the interests of the Church were concerned, a Bishop

---

[1] P. & M. Hist. *Passim sub voc. Frank-Pledge.*

[2] The court of assembled warriors bound to uphold by their arms the authority of their chief. Ancient Laws and Institutes, I. 455.

[3] *Ibid.* 259.

was usually associated with the presiding officer. The Court had jurisdiction only over persons or lands within its territorial limits. An appeal lay from this to the County Court, but not until the party seeking it had applied repeatedly and fruitlessly to the Hundred Court.[1]

The TRITHING, the LATHE COURT, and the COURT LEET were courts similar in character to the Hundred, but they tried cases over which the latter had no jurisdiction. They do not require any more extended notice in connection with our general purpose. The Hundred Court was "the judicial unit . . . for ordinary affairs." The County Court and the Hundred Court were the ordinary Anglo-Saxon Courts of Public Justice.[2]

The COUNTY COURT was the most ancient, the most active, and the most important in the kingdom. The student is especially referred to a just appreciation of its functions by the late John Richard Green, which will be found in Volume I. of his History of the English People, p. 353. This Court was held under the Presidency of the Sheriff once in each month. It was the Sheriff's Court. It had jurisdiction in civil, criminal, and ecclesiastical causes, the Sheriff generally associating with himself a Bishop and other ecclesiastical or learned persons to aid him in administering justice. The jurisdiction extended to the trial of title to land in the county, of the right to tithes, of bargains and sales of land, of services and customs, and of other causes of great moment. Appeals from the Hundred, Lathe, and Trithing Courts were also heard and determined here.[3]

The SHIREEVE'S TURN was a session of the County Court, and was held twice in the year in each Hundred by the Sheriff and Bishop. It inquired into frank-pledge, and had power to proceed both against those who broke the peace of the Church, and those who broke the peace of the king.[4]

The WITENAGEMOTE, or "assembly of the wise men," was both a legislative and a judicial body. But its legislative was

---

[1] P. & M. Hist. *Passim sub voc. Hundred Court.*

[2] P. & M. Hist. I. 18.

[3] The King's Peace, 12, 13, 14; P. & M. Hist. *Passim sub voc. County Court*

[4] The King's Peace, 15, 16, 17.

its main function. It adjudged incidentally upon the disputes of the king's thanes and great men, cleric and lay. It resembled, however, rather a great council than a court of justice, and can hardly be included among the judicial tribunals of the country.[1]

Such were the Anglo-Saxon courts. They were not "surrounded with such visible majesty of the law as in our times, nor were they furnished with any obvious means of compelling obedience."[2] They were frequently held in the open air. And yet archaic in form and weak in power as these courts were, they were nevertheless the source of our legal institutions. "From the Briton and the Roman of the fifth century we have received nothing. Our whole internal history testifies unmistakably to our inheritance of Teutonic institutions from the first immigrants after the cessation of Roman administration."[3]

The Anglo-Norman Courts.

When William the Conqueror had subdued armed opposition, he had to consider by what system of laws England should be governed. The system which he found was one of self-government, — one under which each local community tried its own cases with no right of appeal beyond the County Court, except to the clemency of the Crown. The system which he brought with him was a highly centralized one, in which the Grand Justiciar, or Chief of the Law, controlled absolutely the administration of justice. William chose a conservative course. He did not interfere with the existing Anglo-Saxon tribunals, save that he deprived them of any criminal jurisdiction over the offences of the clergy. On the other hand, he superseded the Witenagemote by one Supreme Court and one supreme officer of justice.

The Curia Regis.

The Court thus constituted was termed Curia Regis, or the King's Court; it was also called Aula Regia, or the Royal

---

[1] Hist. Pr. 20. The King's Peace, 18.
[2] P. & M. Hist. I. 14.
[3] Abdy's Feudalism (quoting Stubbs), 134.

Court. It was attached to the king's person, was held in his palace, followed him wherever he went, and was the embodiment of royal justice administered by the king himself. It was the only Royal Court, as distinguished from the English or Anglo-Saxon courts which continued in their old form. It had unlimited jurisdiction, and entertained appeals from inferior courts. Where the king had granted to certain of his subjects the privilege of suing and of being sued only in the Royal Court, it had exclusive jurisdiction. It was presided over by the Chief Justiciar, who was also a great officer of state, being the King's Lieutenant and, when necessary, the viceroy. It was composed of the Chief Justiciar, the Chancellor, and such of the Barons, ecclesiastics, and other learned persons as were from time to time summoned to assist in its deliberations. It took its inspiration from the king, and pronounced his judgments, which were binding upon the whole people. William's son built Westminster Hall for the more appropriate and frequent sittings of the Curia Regis, and at Whitsuntide, A. D. 1099, William Rufus wore his crown and sat for the first time in the royal justice seat in Westminster Hall.

Rise of the Court of Exchequer.

From this time we find the court and officers of the Exchequer existing as a part of the Curia Regis. Their duties were to receive the accounts of the Sheriffs and of all other accountants and collectors of the Crown, to give acquittance to those who paid, and to issue writs and orders to enforce payments by those in default.

We must pause here to observe the wisdom of the Conqueror's scheme. While he did not at the outset disturb the Anglo-Saxon local courts, he yet instituted a supreme royal court which contained within itself the possibility and the certainty of their ultimate overthrow. Bigelow says: "It was reserved for the Norman kings to make direct way for the great jurisdiction of the royal tribunals, by systematic encroachment upon the jurisdictions of the popular and franchise courts, a fact, however, not fully manifested before the twelfth century." [1] Again, he insists: "The ordinary King's Court, however, the full court sitting with the king, exercised a jurisdiction limited in fact only by the king's will. That is, there was nothing to prevent the king from drawing into his court all the causes of the people; and on one pretext or another he did seriously invade the jurisdictions of other courts, especially of the Manorial Courts." [2]

Of the consequences of these changes from the old order, the same author says: "The most salutary result accomplished in the history of English jurisprudence was the establishment of the [nearly] universal jurisdiction of the King's Court, including both of its branches, the central court about the king's person [with the exchequer and the council], and the eyre." [3]

The Curia Regis continued in this manner until the time of Henry II. (A. D. 1154–1189). Justice was dispensed in one department by the Justiciars, the Chancellors, and their assistants; questions of revenue were dealt with by the Barons in the other. In Henry's time, the King's Court had become overcrowded with suitors. The Conqueror's forethought was manifesting itself in results.[4] Men deserted, for many reasons, the local courts and flocked to the King's Court when life or property was in danger.

JUSTICES IN EYRE.[5]

To meet this difficulty, Henry, who had himself been Grand Justiciar, appointed (A. D. 1170) justices to go about the kingdom regularly and hear on the spot the complaints of his subjects. This was the origin of the judicial circuits which continued from that time on. Under this same king the Assizes (of which we shall speak hereafter) were instituted; their object was to enable litigants to escape the jurisdiction of the local court, with its ordeal of battle, and to refer themselves and their causes to the judgment of the king's justices. As litigation increased, and the suitors of the King's Court became more numerous, great dissatisfaction was caused by

[1] Hist. Pr. 75.   [4] P. & M. Hist. I. 181.
[2] *Ibid.* 76.   [5] Itinerant justices.
[3] *Ibid.* 199.

the fact that this Court followed the person of the king from place to place, and with it were forced to go its officers and its suitors.

BIRTH OF THE COURT OF COMMON PLEAS.

In the reign of King John a reform was effected, and in consequence the Court of Common Pleas was born. The language of the seventeenth clause of Magna Carta (A. D. 1215) was "*Communia placita non sequantur curiam nostram, sed teneantur in aliquo certo loco*" [1] (common pleas shall not follow our court, but shall be held in some certain place). From that time common pleas, or causes between party and party, as distinguished from Crown and revenue causes, were heard at Westminster, and this Court of Common Pleas retained its name and local habitation until 1875. In A. D. 1235, Thomas de Muleton was appointed Chief Justice of the Common Bench, being the first Chief Justice of either of the common-law courts. From this period personal actions gradually ceased to be heard in either the Curia Regis or the Exchequer, and under Edward I. such hearing was prohibited.

Dissatisfaction had been felt not only with the wandering character of the Curia Regis, but also with the composite functions of the Chief Justiciar, who was soldier and politician as well as administrator of law. This dissatisfaction culminated when two rival Chief Justiciars fought against each other, and one (Hugh le Despenser) fell on the field of Evesham (A. D. 1265). The other (Phillip Bassett) resigned. On March 8, 1268, Robert De Brus was appointed "*Capitalis Justiciarius ad placita coram Rege tenenda*" (Chief Justice for holding pleas before the king).[2] Without the passage of any formal statute the Curia Regis ceased to exist, and there was no longer a Grand Justiciar of England.

COURT OF KING'S BENCH.

The remnant of the great Royal Court became the Court of King's Bench, and at its head was the Lord Chief Justice newly created.

[1] 2 Inst. 21.

[2] Campbell's Lives of the Chief Justices, I. 59–65.

Thus we have seen the Curia Regis existing as the one great Royal Court of England for about two hundred years. Slowly it has broken up into three distinct tribunals: The Exchequer, Common Pleas, and, finally, the King's Bench. For six hundred years these three courts will continue to be the great common-law courts of England, and it is under their administration that the law will develop from its rudimentary beginnings into the system which to-day is so adequate to our needs, because the principles of growth and of adaptability which have made it what it is are still alive in it.

At the accession of Edward I. (A. D. 1272), we find the Courts of King's Bench, Common Bench (so Common Pleas was called), and Exchequer sitting in Westminster Hall. The King's Bench was presided over by the Lord Chief Justice with certain puisné or assistant judges, and had exclusive jurisdiction in all pleas of the Crown, and in all appeals from inferior courts. The Common Bench was presided over by its Chief Justice and other assistant judges, and had exclusive jurisdiction in all real actions and in actions between private persons to try private rights. The Exchequer was presided over by the Lord Treasurer, with the Chancellor of the Exchequer and other Barons, and its jurisdiction was limited to cases touching the king's revenue, with which it had exclusive power to deal. It however continued to sometimes hear cases between party and party, as it had done; but in A. D. 1300, it was directed by statute to cease such hearings.[1]

The Judicial Circuits.

We must pause here to inquire what provision was made for the trial of the numerous causes which were brought in or transferred to the King's Courts, now that suitors were forsaking the old tribunals for the stronger and completer Royal Justice. We have seen that Henry II. in A. D. 1170, appointed justices to regularly go around the kingdom and hear the complaints of his subjects, and that this was the origin of the judicial circuits. In 1176, the

[1] 28 Edw. I.

number of these Itinerant Justices was increased to eighteen, and they were sent into all the counties of England. In 1179, England was divided into four parts, and five justices were allotted to each part. These included in their number six justices of the Curia Regis. At about this time trial by inquest (the origin of our jury-trial) and also the Great Assize were introduced, and by these means, as we shall see more clearly when we come to consider the subject, " Modes of Trial," all issues of fact involved in causes pending in the Royal Courts at Westminster could be determined in the respective counties where these causes arose. The verdicts rendered in the several counties were certified back to the appropriate Westminster Courts. The Assizes and the Inquests also were held in the County Courts, which for many years were constituted as before. The Anglo-Saxon method of local trials was undisturbed. The county remained the unit for judicial administration. As the Shire-gemote (county-court) had been held twice each year for the trial of causes and criminals, so under the new system the Sheriff summoned the jurors and witnesses, and arranged the business, and twice in the year the king's justices came to each county and tried all causes and offences arising within its limits. After A. D. 1335, no more Itinerant Justices, or Justices in Eyre as they were also called, were appointed; circuits were thereafter perambulated by the Judges of Assize and *Nisi Prius*.[1] By virtue of the Statute Westminster 2 (13 Edw. I. c. 30) these judges were made up of the " king's sworn justices, associating to themselves one or two discreet knights of each county." Subsequent changes were made in the composition of the " commission" of assize ; but enough has been said to show the student the provision made for the ordinary trial of issues of fact.

It is not material to our purpose to trace the decadence of the old Anglo-Saxon courts, and the successive steps that were taken to relieve the Westminster courts by the creation of inferior jurisdictions. Nor will it aid us to dwell upon the

[1] This term will be explained in connection with the subject, "Modes of Trial."

equity side of the Exchequer Court or the law side of the
Court of Chancery. The study of the organization and jurisdiction of Ecclesiastical, Military, and Maritime Courts, and
of the great Court of Chancery itself exercising its extraordinary or equity jurisdiction, would be out of place here.
Nor can we stop to speak of courts of special jurisdiction,
interesting as some of them are, or of such petty courts as
the piepoudre and others. The student desirous of fuller information upon these points can find it in the authorities
cited at the end of this chapter.

JURISDICTION OF COURT OF KING'S BENCH.

It remains to consider somewhat more in detail the jurisdiction of the three great common-law courts as they existed
prior to the creation of the Supreme Court of Judicature.
The Court of King's Bench is the remnant of the Curia Regis.
Like that court, it purports to be presided over by the sovereign
in person, although for centuries he has had no voice in its
deliberations. It possesses the residuum of the ancient jurisdiction of the Curia Regis, which has not been parcelled out
to the other courts. Its judges are by their office the sovereign conservators of the peace. Its jurisdiction is very high
and transcendent. It controls all inferior jurisdictions. It
superintends all civil corporations, and commands magistrates
and others to do what their duty requires, in every case where
there is no other specific remedy. It protects the liberty of
the subject by speedy and summary interposition. It takes
cognizance both of criminal and of civil causes. On the plea
side, or civil branch, it has original jurisdiction of all actions
of trespass, or other injury alleged to be committed *vi et armis*
(by force and arms); of actions for forgery of deeds, for maintenance, conspiracy, and deceit, and of actions on the case
which allege any falsity or fraud, — all of which savor of a
criminal nature, although the action is brought for a civil
remedy, and make the defendant liable in strictness to pay a
fine to the king, as well as damages to the injured party. The
same doctrine is now extended to all actions on the case whatsoever; but no action of debt, or of detinue, or any other mere

civil action can, by the common law, be prosecuted by any subject in this court by original writ issuing out of chancery. And yet this court might always have held plea of any civil action (other than actions real), provided the defendant were an officer of the court, or in the custody of its marshal for a breach of the peace, or for any other offence. When we come to consider the subject, "process," we shall see how by a fiction this fact was so made use of as to give this court concurrent jurisdiction with the Court of Common Pleas in all personal actions whatsoever.

The Court of King's Bench is likewise a court of appeal, into which may be removed by writ of error all judgments of the Court of Common Pleas, and of all inferior courts of record in England.

Jurisdiction of Court of Common Pleas.

The Court of Common Pleas was originally the great common-law tribunal which acquired exclusive jurisdiction of pleas or causes between private or common persons. It retained always its exclusive jurisdiction of real actions. Sir Edward Coke named it, "the lock and key of the Common Law."[1] Another celebrated judge called it the "Common Shop for justice."[2] The early establishment and localization of this court at Westminster gave rise to the Inns of Court in its neighborhood, and collected there the whole body of the common-law lawyers, thus strengthening the law itself, promoting its development, and enabling it to resist the attacks of the canonists and the civilians who labored to substitute for it the system of the civil law.

Jurisdiction of Court of Exchequer.

The Court of Exchequer is inferior in rank to both of the others, although, as has been seen, it antedates them. Originally, it was charged only with those causes that concerned the king's revenue. It did, however, as we have said, hear other causes until forbidden by statute to do so, as was also

---

[1] 4 Inst. 79, 99.

[2] Sir Orlando Bridgman, State Trials, V. 993.

the case with the Curia Regis after the establishment of the Common Pleas. And when, after some hundreds of years had passed, increasing pressure upon the Common Pleas, or, possibly, emulation, induced the King's Bench to resort to a fictitious source of jurisdiction, and to resume its hearing of private suits generally, so, by a similar fiction which will be hereafter explained, the Exchequer usurped a like jurisdiction. The judges of the Court of Exchequer were for many centuries one Chief Baron and three puisné or junior Barons, although when it sat as a court of equity it was comprised, as at the outset, of the Lord Treasurer, the Chancellor of the Exchequer, the Chief Baron, and the junior Barons.

COURT OF EXCHEQUER CHAMBER.

The Court of Exchequer Chamber is exclusively an appellate court. It is composed of the judges of any two of the great Westminster courts to revise the judgments of the third. For example, the judgments of the King's Bench would be revised by the judges of the Common Pleas and the Barons of the Exchequer.

HOUSE OF PEERS.

The House of Peers or Lords is the supreme judicial tribunal of the kingdom in civil cases, succeeding in that respect the Curia Regis as originally constituted. It is the court of last resort in all causes, from whose judgment no further appeal is permitted. Theoretically, all peers sit as ultimate judges of the law. In fact, however, only those sit who are known as the " Law Lords ; " these are men who have filled high judicial stations, and most of whom have been advanced to the peerage (as chancellors or chief justices) by reason of their eminence in the profession. The peers can also, when they desire, call upon all the judges of England to advise them as to the law. For centuries the decisions of this august tribunal commanded, as it still commands, the respect of the profession both in England and in our own land.

We have briefly reviewed the organization, jurisdiction, and growth of that system of courts which has made English jurisprudence. This growth has been slow but healthy and strong. English law has not been a science, not " an ideal result of ethical or political analysis; it is the actual result of facts of human nature and history." [1] In our own new country we have accepted thankfully this result, and to-day the common law is at once the body of our own jurisprudence and the heart which nourishes that body and stimulates it to further development.

(NOTE. — In describing the origin and history of the common-law courts, we have condensed the account, and, wherever possible, used the words of Blackstone. For details, the student is referred to Book III. chap. 4, of his Commentaries. Also to Professor Minor's Commentaries, Vol. IV. Pt. I. pp. 177–190; Professor Bigelow's History of Procedure, chap. iii.; The King's Peace (Inderwick), chaps. ii. and iii., and finally to Pollock and Maitland's History, *passim*, under appropriate index references.)

[1] P. & M. Hist. I. Introduction, xxiii.

CHAPTER III.

OF FORMS OF ACTIONS.

" So great is the ascendency of the Law of Actions in the infancy of Courts of Justice, that substantive law has at first the look of being gradually secreted in the interstices of procedure; and the early lawyer can only see the law through the envelope of its technical forms." [1] What are these technical forms of actions? In all courts the party who seeks to set the court in motion has to make a statement which, by whatever name it may be called, is in fact an assertion that a wrong has been committed, including also generally in the civil courts a claim for redress.[2] Among our Anglo-Saxon ancestors these formal assertions grouped themselves into the following divisions: Actions for a Debt; Actions for Movables; Actions for Real Property, and Criminal Procedure.[3] These forms, sometimes complicated, were always stiff and unbending. With respect to all matters of procedure, there was an iron rigorism of form and a minute attention to external observances. As had happened among the Romans many centuries earlier, excessive subtlety brought things to such a pass, that a man who made even the most trifling mistake lost his suit.[4] And just as the Romans as they advanced in civilization replaced the solemn and unyielding *legis actiones* (actions of the law) by a more flexible formulary system, so English law passed under the dominion of a system of writs which issued from the royal chancery. This system grew up little by little. Its period of most rapid growth was from the

---

[1] Maine's Early Law and Custom, 389.
[2] Markby's Elements of Law, 251.
[3] Anglo-Saxon Law, 189.
[4] Hunter's Roman Law, 975.

accession to the throne of Henry II., in 1154, to the death of his grandson, Henry III., in 1272. It came into existence not in response to any theory, but to meet every-day needs.

It was through this system of royal writs that the jurisdiction of the old local courts was superseded. The King's Court had originally been established by the king's authority, and its jurisdiction in cases between subject and subject was in every case based upon the King's Writ. A suitor who wanted either to remove his case from a local into the royal court, or to sue at the outset in the latter, bought the King's Writ for that purpose. Thus the use of these writs was stimulated by motives both of royal policy and of royal finance. A limit was put to extortion through their sale by the memorable provision of Magna Carta: "*Nulli vendemus . . . justitiam vel rectum*"[1] (to no one will we sell justice or right).

It was originally "entirely foreign to any purpose of the writ to set forth the formal language of an action,"[2] and it had at the outset no connection whatever with the relief sought. But soon "a particular writ had come to be the only appropriate commencement of an action for a particular redress, and all writs to commence actions were issued from the Chancery, an office over which the Chancellor presided."[3] Of the Chancery in this connection Pollock and Maitland strikingly say: "The metaphor which likens the Chancery to a shop is trite; we will liken it to an armory. It contains every weapon of medieval warfare from the two-handed sword to the poniard. The man who has a quarrel with his neighbor comes thither to choose his weapon. The choice is large; but he must remember that he will not be able to change weapons in the middle of the combat and also that every weapon has its proper use and may be put to none other. If he selects a sword, he must observe the rules of sword play; he must not try to use his cross-bow as a mace. To drop metaphor, our plaintiff is *not merely choosing a writ; he is choosing an action*, and every action has its own rules."[4]

[1] 2 Inst. 45.
[2] Hist. Pr. 147.
[3] Ker. Eq. Ju. 9.
[4] P. & M. Hist. II. 559.

DIVISIONS OF ACTIONS.

The most ancient division of formed actions is into Real, Personal, and Mixed. By formed actions *(brevia formata)*[1] are signified such as were prescribed and provided by the common law, and which existed prior to the statute of Westminster 2d, authorizing actions on the case.

Real actions are brought for the specific recovery of lands, tenements, or hereditaments.

Mixed actions are brought for both the specific recovery of lands, tenements, or hereditaments, and damages for injury sustained in respect of such property.

Personal actions are brought for the specific recovery of goods and chattels, or for damages or other redress for breach of contract, or for other injuries of whatever description, the specific recovery of lands, tenements, and hereditaments only excepted.

REAL ACTIONS.

Of these divisions of actions English law was for centuries almost exclusively concerned with the first, and for manifest reasons. After the Norman conquest the warfare and fighting in England " were between the conquerors and the conquered. In spite of war, defections, and some scattered revolts, the Norman barons and their king work together, support one another, and march together with one common object. The cohesion of the feudal confederation and the vigor of the central power were matters of actual necessity for them. . . . The territory was divided into sixty thousand one hundred and fifteen knight's fees, whose owners swore, all of them, fealty to the king."[2]

The study of the growth and development of these real· actions is even at this day interesting and instructive. At the outset the student must recall the fact that no estate for less than life had the dignity of a freehold estate, or was of a feudal nature.[3] Consequently there was no real action which provided a remedy for injury to any estate less than for life. But this is not all. What a real action was originally concerned

---

[1] Chit. Pl. 82; Bracton, f. 413, b.   [3] Bl. Com. II. 143*.
[2] Abdy's Feudalism, 333, 334.

with was only the question of right or title to a freehold estate. The mere seisin or possession, as distinct from the right, was something which the law did not take under its protection, and for the deprivation of which it provided no remedy.

Just at this point it will be instructive to take an account of the remedies which the law originally offered for injuries to real estate. All real actions were at first included under the following divisions: Writs of Right, strictly so called, and Writs in the Nature of Writs of Right.

Writs of Right [1] dealt not merely with *seisina* (possession) but with *jus* (right). They did not apply to any save a fee-simple title. In such case the demandant (plaintiff) will appear and claim the land in dispute as his right and inheritance. "He will go on to assert that either he or some ancestor of his has been seised not merely ' as of fee ' but also ' as of right.' He will offer battle by the body of a champion who theoretically is also a witness, a witness who testifies this seisin either of his own knowledge or in obedience to the injunction of his dead father." [2] The person attacked in this action, who is called the tenant, always has it in his power to deny the demandant's case, and to put himself upon the battle. As the result of the trial a very solemn and absolutely conclusive judgment is pronounced; the land is adjudged to the successful party and his heirs and *abjudged* from the other party and his heirs forever. Because of the conclusiveness of the judgment, the law proceeds with great deliberation. Years may elapse before the termination of the action, and by collateral proceedings (vouchers to warranty)[3] the lifetime of the demandant may be consumed in vain.[4]

---

[1] "Note of writs of right (whereof the *praecipe in capite* is one), some be close, and some be patent.

"Writs of right returnable into the court of common pleas be patent, and writs directed into ancient demesne, are close ; and the reason wherefore in other courts of the lords, the writs shall be patent, is. because there is a clause in those writs, *et nisi feceris, vicecomes N. hoc faciat, ne amplius clamorem audiamus pro defectu recti* (and unless you will do this, let the sheriff of N. do it, that we may hear no more clamor thereupon for want of right): which clause is not in the other writs, and necessary it is that such writs should be patent, that the sheriffe might take notice thereof." — 2 Inst. 40.

But see Encyclopædia Britannica, *sub voc.* " Writs."

[2] P. & M. Hist. II. 62.

[3] See *post*, Voucher to Warranty.

[4] Booth on Real Actions, 58, 162.

Of these strict writs of right there were eight [1] forms, extending from the writ of right patent which was "in its nature
the highest writ in law," [2] lying only for the assertion of an
estate in fee simple of lands or tenements, down to the writ
of right close, which lay for lands in ancient demesne. The
following is the form of a writ of right patent: —

Henry by the grace of God, &c., to Henry Earl of Lancaster,
greeting: We command you, that without delay you do full right
to A. of B. of one messuage and twenty acres of land with the appurtenances in J. which he claims to hold of you by the free service of one penny *per annum* for all services; of which W. of T.
deforceth him; and unless you will do this, let the sheriff of
Nottingham do it, that we may hear no more clamour thereupon
for want of right. Witness, &c. [3]

Writs in the Nature of a Writ of Right included fourteen [4]
different forms, and they were so called because some of them
might be brought by tenant for life or in tail, and in others of
them battle did not lie, while in most of them relief was sought
for other things than injuries to the mere right to lands and
tenements. [5]

These forms covered a large remedial field, and, until the
time of Henry II., they were thought adequate for the needs
of the age with respect to injuries to real estate.

DEVELOPMENT OF REAL ACTIONS.

It appears that a distinctly possessory action is not native
in the law of the Anglo-Saxon race. [6] It required such a
king as Henry II. to transplant upon English soil the idea,
underlying the Roman interdict *unde vi*, [7] that a possession
acquired by force was wrongful. In the year 1166, we meet
first with the assize of novel disseisin, a new and possessory
action. This assize, in order to prevent further violence,
protects a possession which has been acquired without title

---

[1] Com. Dig. Action (D. 2).

[2] F. N. B. 1, A.

[3] F. N. B. 1, G.

[4] Com. Dig. Action (D. 2).

[5] Booth on Real Actions, Book II.
chap. IX.

[6] P. & M. Hist. II. 46.

[7] "Whence by force." The essential character of this interdict was that
it was available for a mere possessor,
whether he was owner or not. Hunter's Roman Law, 250, 332, 372.

and by force. A lawful tenant in fee or for life is ejected by one who has no right whatever to the land in dispute; the assize in such case puts a strict bound to the lawful owner's right of self-help; he must re-eject the disseisor promptly, or he must himself bring the assize of novel disseisin, and appeal to the law to restore to him that possession of which he has been wrongfully deprived. The law does evil that good may come of it, and "protects the land-grabber against his victim in order that land may not be grabbed." [1]

This assize of novel disseisin is quick in action and effective in remedy. No question of title is heard. Has there in fact been a novel (recent) disseisin? If so, the possession taken forcefully must be given up to the person from whom it was seized, though he himself may be a disseisor without right.

This, we see at once, is a long step forward. Yet it is soon apparent that the new remedy is incomplete. The action lies for the disseisee against the disseisor, but it does not lie for the heir of the disseisee, nor against the heir of the disseisor (to mention only two parties whom it fails to reach), because the heir of the disseisor is not himself guilty of any disseisin in the view of the law, and the heir of the disseisee has not been disseised.

Before, however, this defect is supplied, the law provides another speedy remedy for the recovery of possession in the case where, upon the death of an ancestor within a certain degree, a stranger enters and abates. This remedy is called the assize of mort d'ancestor. Where the ancestor is beyond this degree, then the writ is changed in name so as to express the relationship, for example, if the ancestor be a grandfather, it becomes *aiel*, great grandfather, *besaiel*, great-great-grand-father, *tresaiel*, and for collateral relations other than uncle and aunt (who come within the mort d'ancestor), it is called a writ of *cosinage*.

All of these assizes were much alike in that they turned upon the question of the demandant's possession; was he or his predecessor in right in peaceable possession at such or such a time?

1 P. & M. Hist. II. 52.

To provide a further remedy for cases in which these assizes had never applied, and also to extend their purpose to degrees which they failed to reach, a whole group of writs was invented which stood midway between the possessory assizes and the writ of right. We meet with the first of these writs in the year 1205.[1] All of these new writs assert the demandant's right by alleging a *recent* flaw in the tenant's title. They say that the tenant had no right of entry into the land in dispute save in a certain mode which they describe and attack. If there has been a disseisin, they say that the tenant had no entry unless through *(per)* the disseisor, or through B, to whom *(per* and *cui)* the disseisor had aliened or, when the degree is more remote still, after *(post)* the disseisin wrought by the original disseisor. So also, there were writs of entry upon intrusion after the death of the particular tenant, or after a certain term which had expired, or when land was given to a man by a woman whom he had promised to marry, which land he retained, although refusing to marry the woman. So these writs of entry lay upon alienation (1) by a person legally incapable of aliening [as an idiot or minor], (2) by a particular tenant, and (3) by the husband of the wife's estate.

There was one principle governing all of these actions: there was no going behind the entry charged. If that entry was unlawful, and if the tenant derived his possession through it, there could be no question of proprietary right.[2]

The advance which English real actions have made up to this point, has been thus graphically resumed by Pollock and Maitland: "A graduated hierarchy of actions has been established. 'Possessoriness' has become a matter of degree. At the bottom stands the novel disseisin, possessory in every sense, summary and punitive. Above it rises the mort d'ancestor, summary but not so summary, going back to the seisin of one who is already dead. Above this again are writs of entry, writs which have strong affinities with the writ of right, so strong that in Bracton's day an action begun by writ of entry may by the pleadings be turned into a final,

---

[1] P. & M. Hist. II. 64.　　　　　[2] *Ibid.* II. 67.

proprietary action. The writs of entry are not so summary as are the assizes, but they are rapid when compared with the writ of right; the most dilatory of the essoins (excuses) is precluded; there can be no battle or grand assize. Ultimately we ascend to the writ of right. Actions are higher or lower, some lie 'more in the right' than others. You may try one after another: begin with the novel disseisin, go on to the mort d'ancestor, then see whether a writ of entry will serve your turn, and, having failed, fall back upon the writ of right." [1]

It is true that this elaborate scheme of redress for injuries to the title or possession of real estate has been completely superseded. Real actions would be brought nowhere to-day. And yet it is necessary for the mastery of English law that their rise, development, and displacement should be studied and understood. The student is recommended to read Pollock and Maitland's History, Vol. II. chapters IV. and IX. Those desiring to pursue the subject further can consult Booth on Real Actions and Fitzherbert's Treatise on Writs (de Natura Brevium).

MIXED ACTIONS.

The only mixed actions which it is necessary to especially mention are Quare Impedit (wherefore he obstructed), by which, when the right of a party to a benefice was obstructed, he could recover the presentation; and Waste, to recover land wasted and treble damages for the waste committed thereon; but the equitable remedy to enjoin waste is so much more effective, that this action is obsolete. Ejectment cannot be called in strictness a mixed action; [2] we shall speak of it later in detail. It is enough to say here that it is to-day the general remedy for the trial of title to real estate, and has displaced all real actions. In the United States a forcible entry and detainer is punished by criminal proceedings, the English Statute of 5 Ric. 2, St. 1, or some substitute therefor

---

[1] P. & M. Hist. II. 74.

[2] Selw. N. P. II. 692, n. (1); Matthew v. Hassell, Cro. Eliz. 144: Harebottle v. Placock, Cro. Jac. 21. See also F. N. B. Ejectione firmæ, 220 H. n. (a); Steph. Pl. note 3.

applying to such cases. Very generally also in this country summary proceedings are provided by the law for the recovery of the possession of real estate, where the owner has been unlawfully deprived of such possession.

PERSONAL ACTIONS.

As we have seen, English procedure at its origin was almost entirely confined to remedies for injuries to real estate and to its possession. It is said by Mr. Buckler, in his recent monograph upon the origin and history of contract in Roman law, that "poverty of contract was, in fact, a striking feature of the early Roman law. . . . The origin of contract as a feature of social life was simultaneous with the birth of trade. . . . As Roman civilization progresses, we find commerce extending and contracts growing steadily to be more complex and more flexible."[1]

In striking similarity with the above statement, we learn from Pollock and Maitland's History of English Law that "the law of contract holds anything but a conspicuous place among the institutions of English law before the Norman conquest. In fact, it is rudimentary. Many centuries must pass away before it wins that dominance which we at the present day concede to it. Even in the schemes of Hale and Blackstone, it appears as a mere supplement to the law of property."[2]

Our ancestors did not at first conceive of what we to-day call a contract, that is, a transaction which depends for its validity upon the mere agreement of the parties thereto. They only knew what would be termed, in Roman law, formal and real contracts. A formal contract with the Romans was one which derived its binding force from the fact that it had been concluded through a certain ceremony (*per aes et libram*, with the copper and the scales), or that a certain prescribed question had been asked and answered in a manner also prescribed, or that an entry had been made in a certain book. A real contract on the other hand was one which

---

[1] Contract in Roman Law, Introduction, 1, 2.

[2] P. & M. Hist. II. 182.

required for its formation the delivery of some specific thing, as a deposit, a loan for use or a pledge.[1] Neither the formal nor the real contract was what we should to-day call a contract, for the consent of the parties involved was not the source of obligation. In the first case the question was, has a certain form been followed ? In the second case, has a certain thing been delivered by one party to the other ?

With our ancestors sale was a *real* and not a *consensual* proceeding. To them sale and exchange were known simply as completed transactions ; the money was paid when the object sold was delivered, and no such thing as a credit or an obligation to be discharged at some future time was thought of. Loans were made, but the borrower had to return the exact thing loaned. Pledges and gages were also given, but it was a long time before any idea of contractual obligation in connection with these arose. The recipient of the gage was bound to hand it back if, within due time, its giver came to redeem it. This was his duty rather than his contract obligation. If the gage was not restored, the owner would reclaim it thus : " You unjustly detain what is mine." We see clearly that such contracts were what were called *real*. They depended upon a fact and not upon an agreement. There is but one formal contract in English law, the deed or contract under seal; all others are simple contracts requiring, when executory, both consideration and consent.[2] The transition from the real to the formal contract in English law appears with what was called the pledge of faith. When men shook hands over a bargain, they went through a form which both made and bound that bargain, and gave it a certain legal status. Such a formal contract was never enforced among the English by the secular courts. It was, however, at once seized upon by the ecclesiastical courts as a source of jurisdiction. According to the Gregorian statute book, even the nude pact could be enforced, at any rate by penitential discipline. We find that early in the reign of Henry II., the

---

[1] Hunter's Roman Law, 451–490. Howe's Studies in the Civil Law, Lecture VI.

[2] Anson's Law of Contract, 56.

ecclesiastical courts, even the Roman Curia, were discussing agreements made by Englishmen with pledge of faith.[1] After the quarrel with Becket, and in consequence of that quarrel, the English justices in Glanvill's day had set their faces against what might otherwise have become the English formal contract, and had determined that the grasp of hands or the giving of the gage are not sufficient to constitute a formal contract. Blackstone has recorded how in his day men shook hands over a bargain.[2] The practice has come down to us, but all of the meaning went out of it when, in 1166, the fifteenth section of the Constitution of Clarendon provided thus: "Pleas of debt which are due by pledge of faith, or without pledge of faith, belong to the King's justiciar."[3] Thereafter the ecclesiastical courts could not, and the King's Court would not, enforce agreements made only with pledge of faith.

Division of Personal Actions.

We can now understand that when we divide personal actions into those arising *ex contractu*, or on contract, and *ex delicto*, or from tort, we are using a division which is younger than the actions included under it. The formed actions of debt, detinue, and covenant existed before the idea of contract, as we are familiar with it, was born.

Formed Actions ex Contractu.

Of these formed actions *ex contractu*, there are DEBT, DETINUE, COVENANT, ACCOUNT, and SCIRE FACIAS.[4]

Debt.

We must now turn to the action of debt which is probably the oldest of the formed actions upon contract. We do not meet with it more frequently in early days because a shrewd creditor then obtained as security a judgment or a recognizance against his would-be debtor before the loan

---

[1] P. & M. Hist. II. 196.
[2] Bl. Com. II. 448 *.
[3] Hist. Pr. 37.
[4] The action of *Annuity* was one in which the plaintiff demanded the arrears of an annual rent that was due to him. It has been for a long time obsolete, and merits no further notice here.

was made, and hence would not be compelled to sue on
non-payment of the loan. In Glanvill's time we find an
action of debt in the King's Court. From the form of the
original writ in debt the development of it from the original
writ in a real action is evident. The creditor is *being deforced
of money*, just as the demandant who brings a writ of right is
being deforced of land.[1] The modern action of debt is lineally
descended from the writ of right for money-debt, and *is therefore in its origin* what that always was, *a real action*.[2]

The very language of the writ is significant of the way in
which our ancestors thought of contract. A debtor was not
violating his agreement. He was deforcing his creditor of
his due. The action of debt was rare at first; but, as trade
developed, it became much more frequent. "First from the
Jew, then from the Lombard, Englishmen were learning to
lend money and to give credit for the price of goods."[3] We
may see the action of debt gradually losing some of the
features which it had in common with the actions in which
a man claimed his property. The idea of personal obligation
begins to manifest itself. The offer of battle as a mode of
proof of debt disappears so early that no record of a case of
it remains. Thus the writ of right for land, and "what we
might well call the writ of right for money," begin to
separate.

Very soon the action of detinue, in its turn, detaches itself
from the action of debt. In the writ for debt, it was said
"the *defendant debet* (owes) *et detinet* (and detains) the
sum claimed." But lawyers began to feel that in certain
cases the word "*debet*" should not be used. One ought not
to say *debet* when there has been a specific chattel loaned
(*commodatum*). Even when there is a money loan (*mutuum*)
the word "*debet*" should only be used so long as both parties
to the transaction are alive; if either dies, the money may be
unlawfully *detained* by the representative of the one from the
representative of the other; but there is no longer any *owing*
of money.

[1] Hist. Pr. 163.   [3] P. & M. Hist. II. 204.
[2] *Ibid.* 160.

4.

Debt is at first used to recover money loaned. Soon it is brought for the price of goods sold. Even in the time of Edward I. the action of debt was very rarely employed save for five purposes : it was used to obtain (1) money lent, (2) the price of goods sold, (3) arrears of rent due upon a lease for years, (4) money due from a surety, and (5) a fixed sum promised by a sealed document.[1] As this action is entirely independent of what we should call a contract, we soon find that it can be used whenever a fixed, a certain sum, is due from one man to another. Statutory penalties, forfeitures under by-laws, amercements inflicted by inferior courts, money adjudged by any court to be due, can each and all be recovered by it. There was as yet no thought of a *quid pro quo* (what for what), a consideration. The action began with an assertion of right to a sum of money unjustly withheld, and developed from that conception. That a promise is the ground of action is not imagined. The plaintiff in his declaration will also mention some *causam debendi* (cause of owing) and that cause will not be a promise. This is well expressed in a Norman maxim, " *Ex promisso autem nemo debitor constituitur, nisi causa precesserit legitima promittendi*," which translated is, " But no one is made a debtor by a promise, unless there has preceded a legitimate cause for the promise." [2] Thus if you sue in debt you must rely on a loan, a sale, or some other similar transaction, which is a legitimate support of a promise, and not on any one's promise distinct from such support.

In the action of debt, if the plaintiff had not something to show for his debt, for example, a sealed instrument, the defendant's denial of the debt by oath with oath-helpers turned the plaintiff out of court. This was called " wager of law," and will be more fully explained hereafter when we speak of modes of trial. It is enough to say here that it consisted in the defendant's swearing that he owed nothing, and then having eleven of his neighbors swear that they believed his assertion. The facility of escape which this privilege gave to the defendant in the case caused the partial disuse both of

[1] P. & M. Hist. II. 208. [2] *Ibid.* II. 210

this action and of detinue, its child. We have not space to
follow Mr. Justice Holmes in his inquiry into the development of this action, in connection with the vexed subject of
the birth and growth of the idea of " consideration " as necessary to sustain a simple contract; he maintains that this is
one of the instances in which " an accident of procedure "
became " a doctrine of substantive law." The student is referred for further information on this subject to Lectures VII.
and VIII. of " The Common Law." [1]

The action of debt, as ultimately developed, was an extensive
remedy. It lay to recover money in four classes of cases.[2]

I. On records, as upon the judgment of a superior or inferior court of record. At common law, debt was the only
remedy upon a judgment after a year and a day had elapsed
from the time of its recovery, for in such case execution could
not issue thereon, as it was presumed to be satisfied. Debt
was sometimes brought upon a recognizance against those
who were bound thereby. So it lay upon a statute merchant,
which was in the nature of a judgment. Debt also lay against
a sheriff who had collected money, and had not paid it over,
for his return of "*fieri feci* " (I have caused to be made) was
in the nature of a record.

II. On statutes. If a statute prohibit the doing of an act
under a penalty or forfeiture of a sum of money, to be paid to
the party aggrieved or to a common informer, and do not
prescribe any other mode of recovery, debt will lie at the suit
of those entitled to recover such sum.

It will be observed that in this and the preceding cases
there is no contract to support the action.

III. For money due on any specialty or contract under
seal to pay money, as on single bonds (bonds without condition), on charter parties, on policies of insurance under seal,
and on bonds conditioned for the payment of money (or for
the performance of any other act) it lay by or against the
parties to any such instrument, and their personal representatives. In all of these cases, the debt was created by the
act of the parties to be charged in executing the instrument

[1] See also Hist. Pr. 160–165.   [2] Chit. Pl. 97–102.

under seal which is sued on. In other words, we have here the formal contract of English law.

IV. On simple contracts and legal liabilities, debt lay to recover money lent, paid, had and received, or due on account stated; also for interest due on the loan or forbearance of money; for the reasonable worth *(quantum meruit)* of work and labor done, of goods sold, for fees, for use and occupation of a house, on a demise not under seal, and, generally, for the omission of any duty created by common law or custom; again it lay on an award to pay money, on by-laws for fines and on amercements, on judgments of domestic courts not of record, and of foreign courts. It lay generally wherever an act of the plaintiff had benefited the defendant in some certain sum of money which the defendant ought to pay; the duty creates the debt.

In none of these classes of cases was debt sustainable unless the demand was for a sum certain, or for a pecuniary demand which could readily be reduced by reference or computation to a certainty.

In some cases debt is the peculiarly appropriate remedy, as where a lessee has been ousted from a part of the demised premises by a third person, in which case he can be sued in debt for an apportionment of the rent, since privity of estate still exists between the lessor and lessee as to the part yet possessed by the latter, and debt is the peculiar remedy to recover rent where privity of estate exists, although privity of contract may never have existed. It is also the only remedy against a devisee of land for the breach by the devisor of a covenant relating to this land, since in such case the liability of the devisee depends upon his succession to the devised land, and his consequent legal duty to respond for any breach of such covenant by the person from whom he derived such succession.[1]

We will gain additional knowledge of the peculiar features of this action if we consider the instances in which it did not lie. Originally, debt for rent was confined to the recovery of arrears in cases where the estate in the rent was for

---

[1] Chit. Pl. 102.

years only. A remarkable doubt was long entertained in
England as to whether a personal action could be maintained
for the arrears of a freehold rent, the idea being that such
arrears, like a freehold estate in land, could be recovered only
by a real action, thus confounding the profits of the rent
(which are as much personalty as wheat or corn severed from
the land) with the rent itself.[1] In consequence of this doubt,
certain real actions *(cessavit* and others) were used to recover
the arrears of freehold rents wherever a distress would not
apply. It was not until the statutes of 8 Anne, c. 14, and
5 George III. c. 17, were passed that debt was used in such
cases. Debt could not be supported on a simple contract
against an executor, because in such case the testator could
have waged his law if sued when living. But as there was
no wager of law allowed in the Court of Exchequer, there
debt could be brought against an executor on a simple contract, as it could also be brought in the other courts in cases
in which the testator, if living, could not have waged his law.
Where the lessor has accepted rent from the assignee of the
lessee, he cannot sustain debt against the lessee or his personal representatives, but must proceed by action of covenant
on the express contract. The reason for this provision is
found in the fact above stated, that debt for rent was grounded
upon privity of estate (upon the duty of the occupier of land
to pay its owner the worth of such occupation) and not upon
privity of contract. Of course, the lessee remained liable
upon his express contract to pay rent; but this was absolutely
a contract liability, and covenant was the remedy for the
breach of that contract. It was doubtful at common law
whether debt would lie against the indorser of a negotiable
security, or the drawer of a bill of exchange, because in these
cases the liability depends not upon the writing only, but
upon collateral acts; *i. e.,* presentment and demand of payment and notice of dishonor. It was said debt would not lie
upon a bill of exchange against the acceptor; for, though the
acceptance binds by the custom of merchants, yet it does not
create a *duty* any more than a promise made by a stranger to

---

[1] Min. Inst. IV. 130; Com. Dig. Title "Debt," A. 7.

pay, etc., if the creditor will forbear his debt; the drawer of the bill is the debtor, and continues to be the debtor, notwithstanding the acceptance, for that is a collateral engagement only.[1] Debt was not sustainable where the simple contract was for the payment of the debt of a third person, or for other collateral act. Since debt lay only in cases where a legal duty arose from a fact, the mere *promise* of a man to pay the debt of another, or to do some collateral act, was not a fact which imposed a duty. It was, it is true, a promise, but a mere promise did not then create a duty; it could only be legally enforced when it was made in the form of a covenant. This primitive rule continued to apply after the law recognized promises made upon a consideration as creating a legal liability. This action does not lie for a debt payable by instalments, and not secured by penalty, until all are due, — a doctrine for which no satisfactory reason can be given, and which is in direct conflict with an early case,[2] but which is too well established by authority to be disregarded.[3] Formerly it was thought that in an action of debt on simple contract, the precise sum stated to be due in the declaration must be recovered, or the plaintiff would be non-suited; but this idea no longer prevails, and the plaintiff will recover if he prove any sum to be due to him.[4]

Actions of debt brought for money loaned, for money had and received, etc., differ from what are known as the "common counts," and which will be hereafter considered under the head of General Assumpsit; debt is brought upon a sale or loan as a fact in itself, and not on any promise connected therewith.

It is said that debt also lies in the *detinet* for goods, as

---

[1] Hard's case, Salk. 23. It will be perceived by the student that this reasoning is not harmonious. It is, however, characteristic. For a commentary upon it, reference should be made to the opinion of Story, J., in the case of Raborg *et al. v.* Peyton, 2 Wheaton, 388. The law upon the subject is stated in Byles on Bills, 333*, as follows: "Debt is of a limited application, and will only lie where there is a *privity of*

contract between the parties. It will, therefore, lie at the suit of the drawer against the acceptor; by the payee against the drawer of a bill or check, or maker of a note; by first indorsee against the drawer of a bill payable to his own order; and in all cases by indorsee against his immediate indorser."

[2] March *v.* Freeman, 3 Lev. 383.

[3] Min. Com. IV. 459.

[4] Chit. Pl. 103.

upon a contract to deliver a quantity of malt. This form of the action differs from detinue, in that the property in any specific goods need not be vested in the plaintiff at the time the action is brought, which is essential in detinue. But this form is probably a survival of the time when debt in the *debet* and debt in the *detinet* were the same action.

Since this action was brought for the recovery of a debt *eo nomine* and *in numero* (by that name and for a definite amount), only nominal damages were awarded for the detention of the debt, and they generally covered only interest thereon.

The declaration [1] in debt, if on simple contract, must show the fact from which the duty to pay arises, and should state either a legal liability or an express agreement, though not a promise, to pay the debt. But on specialties or on records, the action is supported by the specialty or the record itself.[2] Profert (proffer) of the specialty sued on should always be made, or its omission excused.[3]

The controlling feature of this action which the student should bear in mind is that it lies for the omission of a duty in not paying a definite sum of money, rather than for the violation of a contract to so pay. The characteristics of this and of the succeeding forms of actions can be studied at length in Selwyn's treatise on the law of " Nisi Prius."

DETINUE.

This action, originally identical with debt, slowly branched off from it. The first formula in debt alleges that the defendant owes the plaintiff so many marks " whereof he unjustly deforces him," as if the plaintiff were suing to recover certain specific coins. Shortly after Glanvill's time, the *deforces* is dropped and the formula becomes " which he owes *(debet)* and unjustly detains *(detinet)*." If, however, either creditor or debtor were dead, then the *owes* was omitted, and the defendant was charged as *detaining* only (debt in the *detinet*). Here detinue began to make its appearance. If

---

1 The formal statement of the plaintiff's demand, to be described hereafter.
2 Chit. Pl. 104.

3 Profert will be explained hereafter under the rule of pleading especially relating to it.

one claims a particular object, one must never say *debet*, but only *injuste detinet*. The idea of an obligation in connection with a contract is beginning to dawn, and debt in the *debet* is henceforth developed in that direction, while debt in the *detinet*, or detinue, remains a proprietary action.[1] It, however, never lost the marks of its origin. It could be joined with debt, although both the pleas and the judgments in the two actions became different. So also the defendant could always wage his law in detinue as in debt on simple contract. Originally detinue did not lie in a case of wrongful taking.[2] Indeed, it is said that it could only be maintained by a bailor against a bailee or his representatives, and that if the bailment were traversed it had to be proved.[3] Gradually the gist of the action becomes the wrongful detainer of the chattel against the demand of the true owner for its delivery, and the allegation of bailment is not allowed to be traversed.[4] Finally, it comes to be grouped by some writers among tort actions, notwithstanding the manifest traces of its origin.

Detinue[5] is the only remedy by suit at law for the recovery of a specific chattel *in specie*, unless in those cases where replevin lies. In trespass, trover, or *assumpsit* (forms of actions which will be presently explained), damages only can be recovered,[6] and in fact even in detinue an obstinate defendant can not be forced to give up the chattel itself, for the judgment is in the alternative, *i.e.*, for the return of the chattels claimed, or for their value, with damages for their detention, and costs.

This action could not be maintained for real property, and the goods or chattels for which it is brought must be distinguishable from others by some certain means. Thus it lies for a horse, a cow, or money in a bag; but for money or grain not in a bag or chest, or otherwise identified, it does not lie. Charters and title-deeds and any other specific chattel in which the plaintiff has the right of property may be recovered by it.[7]

---

[1] P. & M. Hist. II. 171, 172.
[2] Bl. Com. III. 151 *.
[3] P. & M. Hist. II. 174.
[4] Gledstane *v.* Hewitt, 1 Cromp. & J. 565.
[5] Chit. Pl. 110–114.
[6] *Ibid.* 110.
[7] *Ibid.* 111.

A person who has a right of property in the goods, and also the right of immediate possession, may support this action, although he has never had the actual possession. But if the plaintiff's interest be only in reversion, and he have not the right of immediate possession, he cannot sustain the action. One who has only a special property, as a bailee, may also support the action where he delivered the goods to the defendant or where they were taken out of his custody.

Detinue lies wherever a specific chattel is unlawfully withheld by the wrong-doer, whether it were originally taken lawfully or unlawfully. It cannot be supported against a person who never had possession of the goods, nor does it lie against a bailee if, before demand, he loses them. If the defendant claim that the goods were pledged to him as security for a loan still unpaid, or if he assert a lien of any kind on the goods, he must plead the same specially.

The declaration should contain a statement of the plaintiff's right to the goods in question, describing them with such certainty as to identify them, and should aver that they are in the defendant's possession; that the defendant acquired such possession by finding the said goods, or by their bailment to him; that he holds such possession subject to the plaintiff's right to have the same upon demand, and that such demand has been made and refused.[1] The value of the goods should be stated.

Covenant.

Glanvill does not mention the writ of covenant, but an instance of its use appears in the earliest extant plea roll (1194), and before the end of the reign of Henry III. it has become a popular writ. Commerce is increasing, and its wants have occasioned the practice of letting land for terms of years. The termor is protected by the writ of covenant, and for years this is his only protection.

Before the end of the reign of Edward I., it is established

---

[1] Kettle v. Bromsall. Willes' Rep. 120. Even in cases of unlawful taking, the form of the declaration in detinue seems to require a demand on the plaintiff's part to complete his right of action.

law that the only *conventio* (covenant) that can be enforced by
action is one that is expressed in a written document sealed
by the party to be charged therewith. Thenceforward the
term " covenant" denotes a sealed document. This is another instance of the moulding of substantive law by procedure. The man who relies upon a covenant must produce
in evidence a *deed*. Thenceforward the sealing and delivery
of a piece of parchment " has an operative force of its own
which intentions expressed, never so plainly, in other ways
have not. This sealing and delivering of the parchment is
the contractual act. Further, what is done by deed can only
be undone by deed." [1]

Covenant was first employed for the purpose of conveying
land by way of fine, and many such actions were brought
simply that they might be compromised. Family settlements
were also made with its aid, the settler taking a covenant for
re-feoffment from his feoffee. But, as has been said, its
principal use came to be the protection of a termor, who was
ousted from his term by an unscrupulous landlord. This will
be explained more fully when we come to speak of the action
of ejectment.

One limitation upon the functions of the action of covenant-
broken *(conventionem fractam)* soon becomes apparent;
it can not be employed for the recovery of a debt, even though
the existence of the debt is attested by a sealed instrument.
A debt can not have its origin in a *covenant*, but must arise
from some transaction, as a sale or a loan.

Covenant[2] is the only remedy for the recovery of unliquidated damages for the breach of a contract under seal.
It is the proper remedy where an entire sum is by deed
stipulated to be paid by instalments and the whole is not
due, nor the payment secured by a penalty. It is also the
proper remedy upon all collateral agreements under seal, in
order to recover damages to compensate for the breach of the
agreement.[3] Where an agreement has been sealed by only
one party thereto, covenant may be maintained against him

[1] P. & M. Hist. II. 218.   [3] Min. Inst. IV. 460.
[2] Chit. Pl. 105–110.

for its breach, although only *assumpsit* could be sustained against the other party for a breach by him. The action may be maintained on a covenant relating to some fact in the past, or the present, or for the performance of something in the future.

Covenant is the usual remedy on leases at the suit of the lessee against the lessor for the breach of a covenant for quiet enjoyment, etc., and by the lessor against the lessee for non-payment of rent, not repairing, etc.; and covenant appears to be generally a concurrent remedy with debt, for the recovery of any money demand, when there is an express or an implied contract contained in the deed. Where the demand is for rent, or any other liquidated sum, the lessor has an election to proceed in debt or covenant against the lessee.

At common law no person could support an action of covenant, or take advantage of any covenant or condition, unless he were a party or privy thereto, and of course no grantee or assignee of any reversion or rent could take such advantage. To remedy this defect the statute of 32 Hen. VIII. c. 34, gives the assignee of a reversion the same remedies against the lessee, or his representatives or assignees, upon covenants running with the land, as the lessor, or his heirs, had at common law; the assignee, on the other hand, is made liable for the breach of a covenant running with the land to the same extent that the lessor was at common law. As to the cases in which debt or covenant should be brought upon such covenants running with the land, and also as to the local or transitory nature of such actions, the student is referred to a careful review of the subject in Gould's Pleading, pp. 111–116.

The declaration in covenant must state that the contract was under seal, and should usually make profert thereof or excuse its omission. If performance of a condition precedent be required to establish the plaintiff's right of action, such performance must be averred. Only so much of the covenant as is essential to the cause of action should be set forth, and that not in full, but according to its legal effect; yet it is usual to declare, against this well-settled rule, in the very words of the deed. The breach may be alleged in the negative of the words of the covenant, or according to the legal effect. Several breaches may be assigned at common law. As damages are the main object of the suit, they should be laid in a sum sufficiently large to cover the real amount claimed.[1]

ACCOUNT.[2]

The action of account was closely modelled upon the proprietary writs. The defendant was called upon to *render* to the plaintiff justly and without delay a certain thing, to-wit: an account of his receipts and disbursements during the time he was the plaintiff's bailiff and, as such, receiver of his money. Even to-day we say that a man is under an obligation to render an account. This obligation does not rest upon contract, but upon a situation or a relation. An administrator, a trustee, a guardian owes an account to those who occupy a certain relation with respect to him as such officer. Accordingly the court first ascertained whether or not the duty to account existed, and if it found in the affirmative, it pronounced an interlocutory judgment, *quod computet* (let him account). Then auditors were appointed who stated the particulars of the account. This action would only lie where the amount sought to be recovered was uncertain and unliquidated.

It is perhaps worthy of note that this was the first action in which process of execution was given against the person of the defendant.

The action has been superseded, save in a very few of the United States, by the equitable remedy for an accounting. Its further details may be found in the record and proceedings in the case of Godfrey *v.* Saunders, 3 Wils. 73, and also in Selwyn's work before referred to.

SCIRE FACIAS.[3]

As the writ of *scire facias* is not an original but a judicial writ, it may seem irregular to class it among the formed actions. Of it Lord Coke says: "This is a judiciall writ,

[1] Chit. Pl. 110.
[2] Selw. N. P. I. 1–7.
[3] Foster on *Scire Facias, passim.*

and properly lyeth after the yeare and day after judgment. . . . So as by the writ it appeareth, that the defendant is to be warned to plead any matter in barre of execution ; and therefore albeit it be a judiciall writ, yet because the defendant may thereupon pleade this *scire facias* is accounted in law to bee in nature of an action."[1] It derived its name from the following necessary words in the writ : " *Quod scire facias præfat.* T. (the defendant) *quod sit coram*, etc., (that you the Sheriff *shall cause* the aforesaid T. to *know* that he must be before us, etc.)."

Scire Facias is an action which is always founded upon a record, and is the proper means of enforcing compliance with all obligations of record upon which an execution can not immediately issue, whether by reason of lapse of time, change of parties, or their own inherent nature. If the obligation imposed by the record be that of paying a liquidated sum of money, either debt or *scire facias* may be used. But if the obligation be of a different nature, *scire facias* is the only mode of proceeding. *Scire facias* and debt are the only actions which can be grounded upon a record.[2]

In real actions, and on a writ of annuity, the writ of *scire facias* lay at common law if the plaintiff did not take out an execution within a year and a day. In personal actions, before the Statute of Westminster 2d (13 Edw. I. St. 1, c. 45, A. D. 1285), if the plaintiff did not have execution within a year and a day, he was driven to a new action (debt) upon his judgment; by this statute the process upon *scire facias* was simplified and shortened, and its aid was extended to personal actions, and, while the plaintiff might still sue upon his judgment as before, yet he might have execution after *scire facias* upon his existing judgment.

In all cases where a new person, who was not a party to a judgment or recognizance, derives a benefit by, or becomes chargeable to, the execution, there must be a *scire facias* to make him a party to the judgment. Thus, where a judgment has been obtained by or against an unmarried woman who afterwards marries, and it is sought by the husband to have

---

[1] Co. Litt. 290 b.   [2] Evans' Pl. 84.

execution of the judgment, or by the wife's creditors to have execution *against him* for the judgment recovered against the wife whilst unmarried, a *scire facias* is necessary. So upon the death of a plaintiff pending a suit in a case where the cause of action survived, his personal representatives could through this writ be admitted to prosecute the action in his stead. And upon the death of a defendant in such a case, his personal and, when proper, his real representatives (including his *terre-tenants*, *i. e.*, those occupying his lands) could, by means of this writ, be substituted in his stead. The death of a sole plaintiff or defendant at any time before final judgment was, at common law, an abatement of the suit; but by the statute of 17 Car. II. c. 8, the benefit of the writ was extended to such cases. There were other uses to which this writ was applied, to-wit: in cases of bankruptcy or insolvency to enable the assignees to make themselves parties to suits by or against the bankrupt after judgment; and in case of judgment against an administrator or executor of assets *quando acciderint* (when they shall have come into possession), to reach subsequent assets on proof of their receipt by such officer. In England, when a bill of exceptions had been sealed, it lay to compel the judge who sealed it, or, in case of his death, his personal representatives, to acknowledge or deny his seal. If the judge died before sealing, there was no remedy on the bill. Formerly, the plaintiff in error in the Court of King's Bench had to give notice by *scire facias* to the defendant to appear and plead. There were other curious uses of this writ which we have not space to mention here; indeed, so many and important were the functions of *scire facias*, that extensive treatises [1] have been written upon them. It is proper to add that in certain cases this writ was the commencement of an original action, and therefore the writ itself was here called an original writ. Thus in England it was used to repeal letters-patent; to repeal the grant of a franchise, where such grant is injurious to another, as also in the case of the abuse of a franchise by negligence; and to repeal a patent granting an office, where the officer

---

[1] Foster on *Scire Facias.* Kelly on *Scire Facias.*

neglects his duties. As in the nature of an original action, it lies to have execution of a forfeited recognizance; upon recognizance of bail in error; against pledges in replevin, and against the sheriff for taking insufficient pledges; on bond to the Crown for the payment of excise or other duties, or for the faithful discharge of an office; and on inquest of office (inquisitions) to recover simple contract debts found due to the Crown, since the Crown, although it may sue a private subject in debt in the common-law courts, can nevertheless proceed by inquest-of-office in a manner more consistent with its dignity and with the royal prerogative.

Having described as briefly as was possible, in view of the importance of the subject, the formed actions on contract, we come now to consider the

FORMED ACTIONS EX DELICTO, OR IN TORT.

Tort actions are for the redress of wrongs unconnected with contract. They are for the violation of natural, as contrasted with acquired, rights. Natural rights are those which we all possess to security of person, reputation, and estate. "The purpose of the law of torts is to secure a man indemnity against certain forms of harm to person, reputation, or estate at the hands of his neighbors."[1] No more striking contrast exists in the history of the Anglo-Saxon people than that afforded by a comparison of the law of torts of to-day with that which existed only one hundred years ago. Of the formed actions in tort there were only two, — TRESPASS and REPLEVIN.

TRESPASS.

The action of trespass cannot be understood unless we revert to the primitive times when self-help was at once the measure of responsibility and the means of redress. In the most archaic German society, before the organization of courts and of a civil government, each individual was, to the extent of his power, the protector of his own rights and the avenger of his wrongs. With respect to both the civil remedy of distress and private vengeance for injuries, this

[1] Holmes' C. L. 144.

was a period of summary action by the individual. German society was organized on the basis of the *peace, i. e.*, a particular protection or security under which certain persons and places stood; this particular and, as it were, *local* peace, since it was protected by some local lord, afterwards became co-extensive with the realm under the name of the king's peace. Every violation of this primitive peace was a wrong. Upon the gradual growth of society, and the development of courts for the protection of the individual from wrongs, this private vengeance was at first retained; but it was not allowed unless clearly used by the individual as an instrument of law. It became a fundamental rule of German law that vengeance must be authorized by previous permission of the court; or, if it preceded that permission, it must afterwards be justified to the court.

As a survival of the primitive right of private and unrestrained vengeance, there lingered the *feud*, or, as it was commonly called, the blood feud, which obliged the kindred of a dead man to avenge his blood. This was outside of the law, and in bold opposition to it; but it rested upon a foundation so strong in human nature that it held its position, even in England, long after the Conquest, although many attempts were made to control it.

The great step towards the limitation of vengeance and of these blood feuds was the extension of the system of compositions. Vengeance and feud could be bought off. The wrath of the dead man's kindred could be extinguished with a money-payment.[1] Under Anglo-Saxon law, a money value was placed on the life of every free man, according to his rank, and a corresponding sum on every wound that could be inflicted on his person, and for nearly every injury that could be done to his civil rights, honor, or peace, — the same being aggravated according to adventitious circumstances.[2] If neither the lord nor the kinsman of the offender could pay this compensation, then only might vengeance be taken.

When an offender broke the peace he became by that very

---

[1] Anglo-Saxon Law, 262–305.   [2] Kemble's Anglo-Saxons, I. 197, 276, 277.

act "peaceless;" he was outside the pale of law and protection; vengeance against him was not regarded as a crime, and his life was forfeit. By bringing the charge before the court, the permission of the community enlarged the right of vengeance by binding all members of that community to assume a state of warfare against the peace-breaker; he became an outlaw on whose head a price was set, a "*lupinum caput*," a wolf, glad to escape the country, and spend his life as a wretch; and when excommunication from the Church was added, his cup was full.

Although the payment of composition, or "blood-money," was at first the result of private agreement, yet later the state asserted the right to avert vengeance from him who had paid or offered to pay the fixed sum. Of this sum a part went to the state as "peace money" (*wite*), and another to the individual injured as damages (*bot*). We must not, however, omit to note carefully that certain very grave crimes did not come within this system of composition. They were *unemendable*, and could not be bought off. Such were house-breaking, arson, open theft, certain forms of aggravated homicide, and treason against one's lord. These were punished with death, sometimes preceded by mutilation and other torture.

We cannot stop here to discuss the development of the true idea of criminal law, — of the offence against the state and the infliction of punishment as such for the offence. " The difference between an offence against the state and an offence merely against the individual that suffers, although very clear and important, is not apprehended at an early stage in the history of law. Even after it is recognized a long period generally elapses before a proper distribution of offences is made. Thus theft in the early Roman law was treated purely as a civil wrong. . . . The true distinction between crime and civil wrong is to be found in the remedy that is applicable. The aim of the Civil Law is to give redress to a sufferer in the form either of restitution or of compensation. The aim of the Criminal Law is punishment." [1]

[1] Hunter's Roman Law, 1053, 1064.

In England, by the time we meet with our first judicial records (*temp*. Ric. I.) this differentiation of criminal law has begun. There are a few crimes defined in broad terms which place the life and limb of the offender at the king's mercy. The other crimes are punished chiefly by discretionary money penalties which have taken the place of the old pre-appointed *wites*, while the old pre-appointed *bot* has given way to " damages " assessed by a tribunal. Outlawry is no longer a punishment; it is mere *process* compelling the attendance of the accused.[1] At about the same time we meet with a communal accusation (what we should to-day call an indictment or a presentment) against an alleged criminal. Prior to this, even the gravely punishable offences have been looked at from the point of view of the person who has been wronged, and the wrong-doer has been prosecuted on his complaint. A felony, according to the old law, is a crime which can be prosecuted by an *appeal*, *i. e.*, by an accusation in which the accuser must, as a general rule, offer battle. The king himself cannot protect the man-slayer from the suit of the dead man's kin. He cannot pardon a man appealed of a felony, for "appeals of all kinds are the suit not of the king but of the party injured;"[2] this right of private prosecution remained until it was abolished by act of Parliament in 1819.

The woundings and house-burnings of an earlier day became the appeals of mayhem and of arson. The appeals *de pace et plagis* (of peace broken and of blows given) became, or rather were in substance, the action of trespass which is still familiar to lawyers.[3]

The writs of trespass are closely connected with these appeals for felony. The action of trespass is, it is said, an *attenuated appeal*. The charge of felony is omitted; no battle is offered; but the basis of the action is a *wrong* done to the plaintiff in his body, his goods, or his lands, by force and arms and against the king's peace. We can now understand the quasi-criminal character of this action and the jurisdic-

[1] P. & M. Hist. II. 457.

[2] Bl. Com. IV. 312–317*, 398*. See also Ashford *v.* Thornton, 1 B. & Ald. 405.

[3] Holmes' C. L. 2, 3.

tion asserted over it by the King's Bench, which court alone held Pleas of the Crown, *i. e.*, criminal causes.

The early English appeals for personal violence seem to have been confined to intentional wrongs. It was only at a late day, and after argument, that trespass was extended so as to embrace harms which were foreseen, but which were not the intended consequence of the defendant's act. Thence again it extended to unforeseen injuries.[1]

This action of trespass became common near the end of the reign of Henry III. It was a flexible action; the defendant was called upon to say why with force and arms and against the king's peace he did some wrongful act; he was threatened with a semi-criminal action; the plaintiff was using a weapon which had in the past been reserved for felons, and was urging against the defendant the terrible process of outlawry.

In the course of time the cases of trespass grouped themselves into three great divisions. Violence was done to the goods of the plaintiff; they were taken and carried away; this form became trespass *de bonis asportatis* (for goods carried away). Violence was done to the plaintiff's land; it was forcibly entered upon and trees were destroyed or other damage done; this form became trespass *de clauso fracto*, or *quare clausum fregit* (for a close broken, or wherefore he broke the close). Finally violence was done to the plaintiff's person; he was assaulted and beaten; this form became trespass for assault and battery (the old appeal *de pace et plagis*).

As has been said, the process against a contumacious defendant aimed at his outlawry. If convicted, he was imprisoned until he made fine with the king; in addition he was compelled to pay damages to the plaintiff.

In course of time the criminal element becomes weakened. There will be a trespass with force and arms if a man's body, goods, or lands have been even so much as unlawfully touched. The fine due the king will become obsolete, and only the civil and private aspect of the action will remain.

One other historical incident of the action must, however,

---

[1] Holmes' C. L. 3, 4.

be mentioned, for it is the origin of the anomalous practice still in force to-day of giving punitive damages in what is theoretically a merely compensatory suit. It seems that the old law did not place much reliance in public instrumentalities for the punishment of wrong-doers. It was not thought that royal officials or people in general would be active in bringing malefactors to justice. " More was to be hoped from the man who had suffered. He would move if they made it worth his while. And so in a characteristically English fashion punishment was to be inflicted in the course of civil actions ; it took the form of manyfold reparation, of penal and exemplary damages." [1]

Coming now to consider the fully developed action of trespass,[2] we have to remark that its most general characteristic is that it lies only for injuries committed with actual or implied force, or, as the Latin phrase is, *vi et armis* [3] (with force and arms).

It is not easy to define that force which the law implies ; but it is sufficient to say that the law will imply violence, though none was actually used, when the injury is of a direct and immediate kind, and committed against the person, or tangible and corporeal property of the plaintiff, which is in his possession.[4] The old words *contra pacem* (against the peace) remain, and in some cases are material to the foundation of the action, for an action of trespass to land not within the king's dominion could not be sustained. In this action the intention of the wrong-doer, be it never so innocent, is immaterial.

The action can not be maintained where the wrong complained of was a mere *non-feasance ;* or where the matter affected was not tangible, as reputation or health, and consequently not capable of immediate injury by force ; or where the right invaded is incorporeal, as an incorporeal hereditament of any sort ; or where the plaintiff's interest is in reversion and not in possession ; or where the injury was not immediate but consequential ; or where the act com-

---

[1] P. & M. Hist. II. 521.
[2] Chit. Pl. 151–172.
[3] Co. Litt. 161 b.
[4] Steph Pl. 47.

plained of was not the direct act of the defendant, but of his servant in the course of his employment; or generally where such act was not unlawful in its inception. In such cases force does not actually exist and can not be implied.[1]

Trespass may be divided into two large classes: injuries committed under color of legal proceedings,[2] and injuries not so committed.

In general no action whatever can be supported for any act, however erroneous or even malicious, of a judicial officer acting within the scope of his jurisdiction.[3] But when the court has no jurisdiction over the subject-matter, trespass is the proper form of action against all the parties for any act which comes properly within its scope. When a court has jurisdiction, but the proceeding is defective because it is irregular or void, trespass against the attorney and the plaintiff is generally the proper form of action; and where a judgment has been set aside for irregularity, this is the appropriate remedy for any act done under it. When the process has been misapplied, as where A or his goods are taken upon process against B, trespass is generally the only remedy. When the process of a court has been abused, trespass against the sheriff and his officer committing the abuse is the proper action, if the act of such officers was in the first instance illegal and an immediate injury to the body or to personal or real property. So also where the conduct of the officer was in the first instance lawful, but he abused his authority, and thereby became a trespasser *ab initio* (from the outset). When a ministerial officer proceeds without warrant, on the information of another, trespass is the proper form of action against the informer if the information prove to be false. But no person who acts upon a regular writ or warrant can be liable in trespass, however malicious his conduct.

When we consider injuries not committed under color of legal proceedings,[4] and where consequently the mere act of injury is to be dealt with, we find that one may himself injure another in person or with respect to personal or real property.

1 Chit. Pl. 150.
2 *Ibid.* 167–171.
3 Bradley *v.* Fisher, 13 Wall. 335.
4 Chit. Pl. 151–167.

He may also injure through persons or things for whom he is responsible.

Trespass is the only remedy for a menace to the plaintiff, attended with consequent damages, and for an illegal assault, battery, or imprisonment, when not under color of process. So it lies for an injury occasioned by force to the relative rights, as by menacing tenants or servants, or by beating or imprisoning a wife, child, or servant, whereby the landlord, husband, father, or master has sustained a loss ; it lies for the seduction or debauching of a wife, or servant, and in the case of a daughter debauched the most liberal meaning is given to the term *service* in this connection in order to allow the benefit of the action to the father.

Trespass lies for taking or injuring all inanimate personal property, and all domiciled and tame animals, including all animals usually marketable, as parrots, monkeys, etc. The person who has the absolute or general property in the thing injured may support this action, although he has never had the actual possession, or although he has parted with his mere possession to a carrier or servant, it being a rule of law that the general property in personal chattels *prima facie* as to all civil purposes draws to itself the possession. But if the general owner part with his possession, and the bailee at the time of injury have an exclusive right to use the chattel, there the inference of possession is rebutted, and the general owner, having only an interest in reversion, cannot maintain trespass. A bailee who has an authority coupled with an interest, as a factor or consignee of goods in which he has an interest to the extent of his commission, may support trespass for any injury done to the goods during the continuation of his interest, though he never had actual possession of the goods. So a bailee with a mere naked authority coupled only with an interest as to remuneration, as a carrier, pawnee, etc., may maintain this action for any injury done while he was in actual possession of the thing, but a mere servant cannot maintain it. The finder of any article, and even a person having an illegal possession of a chattel, may support trespass against any person but the real owner.

The injury may be inflicted either by the unlawful taking of the chattel, or by damaging it while in the possession of another. Trespass is a concurrent remedy with trover for most illegal takings, even in the case of an illegal distress for rent. It also lies though there has been no wrongful intent, as if a sheriff take the goods of a wrong person. It may be supported against a bailee who has only a bare authority, as if a servant take goods of his master out of his shop and convert them. But trespass is not sustainable against a bailee who has the possession coupled with an interest, unless he destroy the chattel; nor against a joint-tenant or tenant-in-common for merely taking away and holding the property exclusively from his co-owner, for each has an interest in the whole; but if the thing be destroyed, then trespass lies against the co-owner guilty of the destructive act. When the taking is unlawful, either the general owner, or the bailee, if answerable over, may support trespass; but if the taking were lawful, trespass will not lie for a refusal to deliver. Trespass can be maintained for any immediate injury to personal property occasioned by actual or implied force, as for shooting or beating a dog or other live animal, chasing sheep, mixing water with wine, etc., although in none of these cases is there any taking away or disposing of the chattel by the wrong-doer. It may also be supported for an injury done to personal property whilst in the lawful adverse possession of the wrong-doer, if he has been guilty of an abuse which renders him a trespasser *ab initio*, as where a horse which had been distrained was worked by the distrainer.

Trespass is the proper remedy to recover damages for an illegal entry upon, or an immediate injury to, real property corporeal in the possession of the plaintiff. The real property must be something tangible and fixed, as a house, an out-building or land, or anything which is covered by the technical word *close*, which signifies an interest in the soil, and not merely an inclosure. Trespass lies no matter how temporary the plaintiff's interest, and although this interest be merely in the profits of the soil, if such interest be to the exclusion of others. In England, the parson might support trespass against a person preaching in his church without his leave. It lies for an injury to land covered by water, but the close must be described as so covered; so it lies for breaking and entering the several fishery of the plaintiff.

The *gist* of the action is the injury to the possession of real estate, and unless at the time the injury was committed the plaintiff was actually in possession, he cannot maintain the action. The possession of a servant is the possession of his master for this purpose. Any possession is sufficient against a wrong-doer or a person who can not make out a title *prima facie* conferring the right to the possession. But there must be actual possession, for even the owner of the freehold can not maintain trespass until he has actually entered upon his land. If the plaintiff was in possession of the close at the time when the injury was committed, it is no objection to his suit that he gave up this possession before bringing his action.

Trespass for injury to real property can only be supported when the injury is immediate and was committed with force actual or implied. It lies, no matter how unintentional the trespass, and although the *locus in quo* (place in which) were not inclosed, or although the door of the house were open, if the entry was not for a justifiable purpose. Even shooting at or killing or wounding game or any animal on another's land, without an actual entry, is an entry in law, and in such case trespass will lie. If one tenant in common forcibly prevent his co-tenant from entering or occupying the land, trespass may be maintained. Though the original entry of a party be lawful, yet by a subsequent abuse of an authority in *law* to enter, as to distrain, etc., such party may become a trespasser *ab initio*.

A person will be liable for a trespass committed by his command or procurement, or by subsequently assenting to such act committed for his benefit. In the case of animals, if they are of such kind as to have a natural propensity to do the act complained of (as is the case with horses and cattle with respect to trespasses on land, and with notoriously ferocious or wild animals, which have not been properly confined, as to other injuries), trespass may be supported for injuries inflicted by such animals.

The declaration in trespass should contain a concise statement of the injury complained of, whether to the person or to personal or real property, and should allege that such injury was committed *vi et armis* and *contra pacem*.

REPLEVIN.

Where goods had been illegally distrained, their owner could *at once regain their possession* by an original writ of replevin. The student will note at the outset the peculiar characteristic of this action in that, at the inception of the suit, it put the plaintiff in possession of the property claimed. Distress was a very severe kind of self-help, as we have seen, and the king's courts were much concerned when it was abused. The offence that the distraining lord committed, when he retained the beasts distrained after the tenant had offered gage and pledge for their return to him, was known as *vetitum namii* (refusal of the *nam* or distress), and stood next door to robbery. [1] If the distrainer will not deliver the beasts after gage and pledge have been offered, then it is the sheriff's duty to deliver them. To deter the person distraining from refusing or neglecting to deliver a distress which had been driven into a stronghold, the Statute of Westminster I. c. 17, directed that such stronghold or castle *should be razed* and thrown down by the sheriff, aided, if necessary, by the *posse comitatus* (power of the county). Under this name of replevin, in the time of Henry II., an action was developed which proved to be convenient for the settlement of disputes between landlord and tenant, and which owed its vigor and its rapidity to the supposition that a serious offence had been committed against the king. Replevin gave back at once to the husbandman his chattels, so that his labors might not be interfered with, and ultimately, if he prevailed in the suit, gave him damages for their wrongful distraint.

It is said in Comyn's Digest (*Title Pleader*, 3 K. 1),[2] " If a man tortiously takes the person or goods or chattels of

[1] P. & M. Hist. II. 575.   [2] See also Selw. N. P. II. 1184.

another, and detains them, a replevin lies, upon which the sheriff shall be commanded upon pledges to make deliverance of the same person or goods." By the common law the person of a man was replevied by a writ *de homine replegiando* (for the replevying of a man). Of this last writ we shall speak again when considering the writ of *Habeas Corpus.*

Originally in this action the plaintiff procured from the Chancery the writ of replevin commanding the sheriff to seize and restore to him his chattels. He could not get this writ until he had given security to prosecute an action against the tortious taker to determine the right to the chattels, and to return them, if the right should be determined against him, to that taker who was of course the defendant in the action. If the sheriff made return to this writ that the defendant had *eloigned* (removed afar off) the chattels, or that they were dead, etc., then the plaintiff could have a *capias in withernam* (you shall take as a further distress) authorizing the sheriff to seize so many of the defendant's cattle as were equivalent in value to those distrained.[1]

Under the original writ the plaintiff, whether or not he got back his chattels or their equivalent in value, was compelled, in accordance with the terms of his engagement and security given, to prosecute his action against the tortious taker. In his declaration, the plaintiff alleged, if he had recovered his chattels, that the defendant had detained (*detinuit*) them ; and he only got damages for their detention ; but if he had not recovered the chattels, then he declared that the defendant detains (*detinet*) them, and he got damages not only for the detention but also for the value of the goods. These forms were called respectively replevin in the *detinuit* and in the *detinet ;* if only a part of the goods had been recovered the action was in the *detinuit* as to those that were restored and in the *detinet* as to the rest.[2]

From the necessity of an application to Chancery, when the distress was taken in a distant part of the kingdom, delay and expense resulted. To remedy this, the Statute of Marlebridge

[1] Com. Dig. *ubi supra.*

[2] McKelvey on Pleading, 49 ; Com Dig. Title Pleader (3 K. 10).

(52 H. III.) provided that "if the beasts of any person are taken and unjustly detained, the sheriff, after complaint made to him, may deliver them without the hindrance or refusal of the person who shall have taken the beasts."[1] After this statute was enacted, the tenant made his complaint to the sheriff, gave his security as before to prosecute his suit and at the same time filed his declaration, which was always in the *detinuit* and assumed that the goods or their equivalent would be taken by the sheriff upon the writ and delivered to the plaintiff. But the damages recovered included the value of the chattels in case they were not restored to the plaintiff, and for this purpose it was customary to allege their value.[2]

Upon these points there is some confusion. It is said by Gilbert: "When the sheriff does not replevy the beasts, there you must recite the writ in the *detinet* and count in the *detinet* also because the beasts are not delivered; and there you recover as well the value of the beasts in damages, as damages for the detention and this is a shorter way than to sue a *withernam*, etc."[3]

A more recent writer confirms him thus: the plaintiff may, if the cattle be withheld, proceed in the cause, and recover damages to the full amount of the goods, as well as for the detention.[4] But in fact the goods were almost universally delivered to the plaintiff in the replevin.[5] Hence, we find Chitty saying that replevin in the *detinet* has become obsolete; that only replevin in the *detinuit* remains in force, in which the plaintiff can not recover the value of the goods themselves.[6] And this is fortified by a note of Sergeant Williams to the effect that it was not usual to insert the price of the chattels in the declaration in replevin, as their value could not be recovered.[7]

Replevin[8] can only be supported for taking a personal chattel, and not for an injury to things affixed to the freehold. The plaintiff must at the time of the tortious taking

---

[1] Selw. N. P. II. 1186.

[2] McKelvey on Pleading, 50; F. N. B. 69 L. note (c).

[3] Gilbert on Replevin, 167.

[4] Wilkinson on Replevin, 20, 43.

[5] *Ibid.* 43.

[6] Chit. Pl. 146.

[7] 2 Saund. 320, n. (I). See also Selw. N. P. II. 1215.

[8] Chit. Pl. 145–149.

have had either the general property in the goods taken, or a special property in them as bailee, pawnee, etc. Replevin can not be supported if the plaintiff have not the immediate right of possession. At common law, it lay only for an unlawful taking. An excessive distress was not therefore remediable by this action, and consequently if any rent, however small, were due, replevin would not lie.

In this action both the plaintiff and the defendant are considered as actors. The defendant, having distrained, is called on to justify his action; this he does in his plea which, if he justify in the right of himself or of his wife is called an avowry, or a cognizance, if he justify in the right of another by whose command he acted. This plea, as it contains the defendant's justification and presents the real question to be tried, *i. e.*, the legality of the distress, is in its functions a declaration, and the plaintiff's replication, a plea; and so in this case the pleadings are all postponed one step.

The defendant might not justify, but might deny the taking. He might also claim property in the chattels, in which case the sheriff's power to replevy them was suspended until the question of property was settled.[1] Again, he might deny taking the chattels in the place alleged. None of these incidents is of importance to us here.

The declaration in this action, which is local, requires certainty in the description of the place where the distress was taken, and the description, number, and value of the goods taken must be given with certainty. The judgment, when for the plaintiff, is that he recover his damages and costs; when for the defendant, it was at common law *pro retorno habendo* (to have a return) to him of the goods replevied.

The action of replevin has in many of the United States displaced detinue and trover, and is the common remedy to recover possession of a chattel and damages for its wrongful detention, or, in case it can not be specifically recovered, damages for its value as well as for its detention. Space is

---

[1] The student may consult Wilkinson on Replevin, 46, and *passim*, as to the details of this action.

wanting here to consider this development of the action, but the student who understands the common-law action will have little difficulty in mastering its present form and functions.[1]

INADEQUACY OF FORMED ACTIONS.

Pausing now to reckon and estimate the means of redress offered to us by the old common law, we find that we are provided with remedies more or less adequate with respect to injuries to land and to its possession. Injuries to incorporeal hereditaments are, however, not remediable by a personal action. When we consider personal rights, there are many serious defects in the legal machinery. No remedy is provided for the enforcement of an agreement not itself under seal or protected by a sealed instrument. The remedy which is given for the recovery of a debt not evidenced by a judgment, statute, or sealed instrument is miserably inefficient, for the defendant can defeat it by wager of law. The remedy for the recovery of specific articles of personal property is liable to this same disaster, and moreover requires a definiteness of description of the article pursued, which often cannot be given. When we consider the protection afforded against acts of personal wrong, we find that only direct, forceful, immediate injuries are recognized. No remedy exists for injuries to reputation, or to health; none for acts of omission, of negligence, or of deceit; and none for the violation of personal rights which are not in possession.

ACTIONS ON THE CASE.

It is thus apparent that the formed actions had ceased to be adequate. There were many cases which did not fall exactly within the definition of a trespass, but which required a remedy. But in order to have a new remedy a new form of writ must first be provided. Accordingly the famous Statute of Westminster 2d (13 Edward I. c. 24) authorized the Chancery to frame new writs in cases similar in principle to those in which the old formed writs had applied. Thus writs of trespass on the case

[1] See Cobbey, Morris, or Wells on Replevin.

began to make their appearance. These writs stated a ground of complaint analogous to, but not quite amounting to, a trespass as sued for in the old writs. Thus a smith might lame a horse, left with him to be shod, by negligently driving a nail in his hoof. The owner could not bring trespass, if he had left the horse in the smith's possession. But laming the horse was equally a wrong whether the owner held the horse by the bridle or left it in the possession of the smith, and as, in the latter case, the wrong was closely connected with a trespass, although not one, the new law gave the owner a writ of trespass on the case.[1]

In his commentary on this statute Lord Coke asserts that it is merely declaratory of the common law, and Mr. Bigelow has shown that in earlier times the framing of writs had been to some extent in the discretion of the Chancery.[2]

" The words of the statute give no power to make a completely new departure ; writs are to be framed to fit cases similar to, but not identical with, cases falling within existing writs, and the examples given in the statute itself are cases of extension of remedies against a successor in title of the raiser of a nuisance, and for the successor in title of a person who had been disseised of his common. . . . In the course of centuries, by taking certain writs as starting points, and accumulating successive variations upon them, the judges added great areas to our common law, and many of its most famous branches, *assumpsit* and *trover and conversion* for instance, were developed in this way ; but the expansion of the common law was the work of the 15th and subsequent centuries, when, under the stress of eager rivalry with the growing equitable jurisdiction of the Chancery, the judges strove, not only by admitting and developing actions on the case, but also by the use of fictitious actions, following the example of the Roman Praetor, to supply the deficiencies of their system." [3]

The student will note that only the deficiencies of the formed

---

[1] Holmes, C. L. 274, 275. Chit. Pl. 83 ; Kinlyside *v.* Thornton
[2] Ker. Eq. Ju. 10; Hist. Pr. 198; *et al.,* 2 Bla. Rep. 1113.
[3] Ker. Eq. Ju. 10, 11.

actions with respect to remedies for wrongs were provided for at the outset. The defects on the side of contract had to wait. As he will presently see, more than two hundred years elapsed before the action of special *assumpsit* was sustained, and the writ of general *assumpsit* was later still.

After *assumpsit* and trover had split off from the general action on the case, the latter remained, as it had been from its origin, distinctly a tort action. Nevertheless, as will be seen when we speak of the election of actions, case is a concurrent remedy with *assumpsit* for many breaches of contract, the plaintiff being allowed to state the *gravamen* of his action as a neglect of duty, instead of as a breach of contract.[1]

Actions on the case[2] lie generally to recover damages for torts not committed with force actual or implied, or for acts committed by force when the thing injured is not tangible; or when the injury is not immediate but only consequential; or where the interest in the property affected is only in reversion; or where the wrongful act is not done directly by the person to be charged, but by his servant, without his authority yet in the course of his business. Torts of this nature are to the absolute or relative rights of persons, or to personal property in possession or reversion, or to real property, corporeal or incorporeal, in possession or reversion. These injuries may be either by non-feasance (the omission of some act which the defendant ought to perform), or by mis-feasance (the improper performance of some lawful act), or by mal-feasance (the doing of an act which the defendant ought not to do). These respective torts are commonly the performance or omission of some act contrary to the general obligation of the law, or to the particular rights or duties of the parties, or to the obligation of some express or implied contract between them.[3]

Case is the proper remedy for any injury to the absolute rights of persons where the injury is not immediate but mediate or consequential. Thus for hurt done by mischievous animals which their owner, having notice of their propensities,

---

[1] Govett *v.* Radnidge, 3 East, 70.   [3] *Ibid.* 123.
[2] Chit. Pl. 122–135.

has kept; for special damage resulting from a public nuisance; for injury received by falling over a log which the defendant has negligently thrown in the public highway; in all these instances *case* and not trespass is the remedy. But if the injury were immediate, as if the defendant incited the dog to bite, or let loose a dangerous animal which did injury, or threw the log and hit the plaintiff therewith, the remedy would be trespass.

Again if the injury be inflicted through the regular process of a court of competent jurisdiction, though this process be maliciously set in motion, case for malicious prosecution is the proper remedy.

Case is the appropriate action for injuries to health (nuisance) or to reputation (libel and slander). It is the remedy against sheriffs and other officers acting *ministerially* (where they have no discretion as to the performance of a duty) and not judicially, for refusing bail, etc.; it also lies against surgeons, attorneys, and others, for want of skill or care in the discharge of their duties, in which cases, however, *assumpsit* may be brought.

Actions for injuries to the relative rights of persons, as for seducing or harboring wives, and enticing away or harboring servants or apprentices, are properly in case, although, as we have seen, trespass also will lie for the seduction or debauching of a wife, daughter, or servant.

Where there has been any fraud, misrepresentation, or deceit independent of written contract, case is the proper remedy.

For the negligent driving of a servant, the master can only be sued in case, and it is clearly the proper remedy for an injury occasioned by negligence in navigating ships.

For injury to personal property not committed with force, or not immediate (injuries resulting from negligence or omission), or where the plaintiff's right thereto is in reversion, case should be brought.

This action lies against a sheriff for making a false return of "*nulla bona*" (no goods) to a writ of *fi. fa.*, or for not levying under it when he should have done so.

With respect to injuries to real property corporeal, case lies where the injury is not immediate but consequential, as for so placing a spout near the plaintiff's land as to discharge water thereon; it also lies where the plaintiff's interest is only in reversion, for injuries affecting the reversion, as for cutting down trees on land of the plaintiff's leased to a tenant, or for any other waste committed by the tenant or by a stranger during the lease. Case is the proper remedy for all injuries to incorporeal hereditaments.

It is impossible to name here all of the instances in which an action on the case can be maintained. In fact, the law has never put a limit to this action. As has been seen, it was the instrument which the judges used in building up the law of England as we know it to-day. "It is often alleged that by a liberal construction of this statute (Westminster 2d), the need for the Chancellor's extraordinary jurisdiction would have been avoided. Austin with characteristic vigor of language says that 'Equity arose from the sulkiness and obstinacy of the common-law courts, which refused to suit themselves to the changes which took place in opinion and in the circumstances of society.'[1] Blackstone writes to the same effect: this 'provision (with a little accuracy in the clerks of the Chancery, and a little liberality in the judges, by extending rather than narrowing the remedial effects of the writ) might have effectually answered all the purposes of a court of equity, except that of obtaining discovery by the oath of the defendant;'[2] and the idea is not confined to modern writers, for a judge of the reign of Edward VI. said that, 'the subpœna (the equity process) would not be so often used as it is, if we paid heed to actions upon the case.' . . . The suggestion is however an unfounded one. . . . It is not true that without wholly revolutionizing their procedure, as well as extending their jurisdiction, the courts could have afforded the kinds of relief that Equity ultimately gave."[3] It is, however, true, so potent is this action on the case, that to-day courts admit its adaptability

---

[1] Austin's Jurisprudence, 615.
[2] Bl. Com. III. 51 *.
[3] Ker. Eq. Ju. 11, 12.

to circumstances which only the growth of our civilization has made possible. If our law can respond to this growth, it must do so mainly through the capabilities of this action.[1]

The declaration in an action on the case ought not to state the injury to have been committed *vi et armis*, nor should it conclude *contra pacem*. In other points the form of the declaration depends upon the particular circumstances on which the action is founded, and consequently there is greater variety in this than in any other form of action.[2]

ASSUMPSIT.[3]

The Statute of Westminster 2d authorizing these new writs was enacted in the year 1285. It was not until 1520 that it was decided that one who sold goods to a third person, on the faith of the defendant's promise that the price should be paid, might have an action on the case upon the promise. This decision introduced the whole law of parol guaranty. Cases in which the plaintiff gave his time or his labor were as much within the principle of the new action as those in which he parted with property. And this fact was speedily recognized. In Saint-Germain's book (Doctor and Student), published in 1531, the student of law thus defines the liability of a promisor: " ' If he to whom the promise is made have a charge by reason of the promise, . . . he shall have an action for that thing that was promised, though he that made the promise have no worldly profit by it.' From that day to this a detriment has always been deemed a valid consideration for a promise if incurred at the promisor's request." [4]

How was an action of tort transformed into an action of contract, "becoming afterwards a remedy where there was neither tort nor contract?"

Nothing, save perhaps the history of the action of eject-

---

[1] Cain *v.* C. & P. Telephone Co , 3 App. D. C. 546; Lumly *v.* Gye, 3 E. & Bl. 114; Angle *v.* Chicago, &c. R. R. Co., 151 U. S. 1.

[2] Chit. Pl. 135.

[3] See "The History of Assumpsit," by J. B. Ames, Harvard Law Review, II. 1-19, 53-69.

[4] Ames' History of Assumpsit. Harvard Law Review, II. 14.

ment, more strongly and characteristically indicates the development of English law than this very transformation. Its history can only be given here in outline; but students are especially urged to study it closely as detailed by Professor Ames in the articles cited.[1]

The actions of debt, detinue, covenant, and account were, as we have already said, soon found to be inadequate as general remedies for breach of contract. But, as these were the only contractual remedies, resort was necessarily had to the tort action of trespass on the case. This action lay originally for a mal-feasance, or the doing an act which was wrongful *ab initio*. Its next development was in the way of remedying cases of mis-feasance; for example, where a person promised to do a certain thing, and did it negligently, or in part only, and then abandoned it. Lastly, and with difficulty, the final step was taken, and this action was allowed in a case of pure non-feasance, *i. e.*, a case where one refused or neglected to do what he was bound to do. In this form it was applied to executory contracts not under seal, and became firmly established as the action of special *assumpsit*. Every such contract required a consideration to render it enforceable. What is *consideration?* Mr. Justice Markby characterizes it as a " shifting and almost unintelligible term." [2] Professor Ames speaks of " the mystery of consideration," and advances a theory of his own with respect to its origin, dissenting from each of the three distinct hypotheses of Mr. Justice Holmes,[3] Mr. Salmond,[4] and Judge Hare.[5] The wisest course to pursue here will be to quote for the student the words of Mr. Anson in his treatise on Contracts: " It is a hard matter to say how consideration came to form the basis upon which the validity of informal *(i. e.*, not under seal) contracts might rest. Probably the *quid pro quo* (the *causa debendi)*, which furnished the ground of the

---

[1] See also The Law of Contract in Salmond's Essays in Jurisprudence; Hare on Contract, chaps. VII., VIII.; Holmes, C. L. 274–288.

[2] Elements of Law, Appendix C, 271.

[3] Holmes, C. L. 285.

[4] History of Contract, 219.

[5] Contracts, chaps. VII. and VIII. See also Jenk's Doctrine of Consideration and Pollock's Principles of Contract, App. note E.

action of debt, and the *detriment to the promisee* on which was based the delictual action of *assumpsit*, were both merged in the more general conception of consideration as it was developed in the chancery. . . . 'Was the party making the promise to gain anything from the promisee, or was the promisee to sustain any detriment in return for the promise?' If so, there was a *quid pro quo* for the promise, and an action might be maintained for the breach of it. So silent was the development of the doctrine as to the universal need of consideration for contracts not under seal, and so marked was the absence of any express authority for the rule in its broad and simple application, that Lord Mansfield in 1765 raised the question whether, in the case of commercial contracts made in writing, there was any necessity for consideration to support the promise. In the case of Pillans *v.* Van Mierop,[1] he held that consideration was only required as evidence of intention, and that where such evidence was effectually supplied in any other way, the want of consideration would not affect the validity of a parol promise. This doctrine was emphatically disclaimed in the opinion of the judges delivered not long afterwards in the House of Lords, in Rann *v.* Hughes.[2] The logical completeness of our law of contracts, as it stands at present, is apt to make us think that its rules are inevitable and must have existed from all time. To such an impression the views set forth by Lord Mansfield in 1765 are a useful corrective."[3]

Up to this point we have been dealing with cases in which there has been a definite bargain or agreement. But there were many other cases in which this element did not exist. Services would be rendered by a tailor, or other workman, without any agreement as to compensation. Here, formerly, debt could not be maintained, because there was no liquidated sum to sue for,[4] and *assumpsit* would not lie for want of an express

[1] 3 Burr. 1663.
[2] 7 T. R. 350, n. (a).
[3] Law of Contract, 54, 55.
[4] While, as has been stated, debt could be maintained on a *quantum meruit* count, yet there was strong authority against such use of the action. (Bl. Com. III. 154*; Warren's Law Studies, 479; Chit. Pl. ed. of 1844, I. 121, n. q; and Ames, Harvard Law Review, VIII. 260). Moreover the notion, prevalent until after Blackstone wrote, that in

promise to pay; to imply a promise to pay so much as the work or goods were reasonably worth was to take a long and a strong step forward. It was not until 1609 that this step was taken,[1] and thenceforth a *quantum meruit* (so much as he deserved) was a common count. A further innovation was made in 1757, when Lord Mansfield ruled, in the case of Decker *v.* Pope, that "When a debtor desires another person to be bound with him or for him, and the surety is afterwards obliged to pay the debt, this is a sufficient consideration to raise a promise in law."[2]

The origin of general *assumpsit (indebitatus assumpsit,* being indebted, he undertook) is generally attributed to Slade's case,[3] decided in 1603. But in 1542 mention is made of this form upon an express promise, and in 1573 the Court of Queen's Bench held that it would be supported by proof of a simple contract debt, without an express promise, and Slade's case confirmed and established this position.[4]

This form of *indebitatus assumpsit* came also to be used as a remedy upon *quasi*-contracts; these are, in truth, no contracts at all. The judgment debtor has not contracted to pay the judgment rendered against him. But when he does not pay he cannot be said to be guilty of any tort. Hence, as the division of actions was arbitrarily limited to contract and tort actions, these cases were ranged as *quasi*-contracts under the contractual head. In all such cases, which are neither truly contract nor tort actions, a fictitious promise will be implied. The first instance of such an action is the city of London *v.* Gorry,[5] decided in 1673, which was *assumpsit* for money due by custom for scavage. The action was sustained. although the jury found specially that no promise to pay was expressly made. "*Assumpsit* was allowed upon a foreign judgment in 1705, and 'the metaphysical notion' of a promise implied in law became fixed in our law."[6] This fictitious promise enabled *indebitatus assumpsit* to compete with debt

debt only the exact amount sued for could be recovered, must have prevented the frequent use of this count.

[1] Warbrook *v.* Griffin, 2 Brownl. 254
[2] Selw. N. P. I. 77, n.
[3] 4 Co. Rep. 92 a.
[4] Ames, *ubi supra*, 16, 17.
[5] 2 Lev. 174.
[6] Ames, *ubi supra*, 66.

on simple contract; for example, a sale of goods as a fact would support debt, for it was a *causa debendi;* but it would also enable the law to imply a promise on the part of the vendee to pay their value to the vendor. Thus was established, in 1657, the equitable and most beneficial action of *assumpsit* for money had and received to recover money paid to the defendant by mistake.[1]   Lord Mansfield so encouraged this action that it became almost the universal remedy where a defendant had received money which he was obliged by the ties of natural justice and equity to refund.[2]

Actions of *assumpsit* upon parol contracts came to be regarded as actions on contract.   But they had the marks of their origin *ex delicto* strongly impressed upon them.   Every remediable breach of a parol promise was at the outset regarded as a deceit.   Accordingly the language of the declaration is: "*Yet the said defendant, not regarding his said promise, but contriving and fraudulently intending, craftily and subtly, to deceive and defraud the plaintiff,*" etc.   The plea of "not guilty" instead of "*non-assumpsit*" was good after verdict, because there is a deceit alleged.

It must be remembered by the student that, during these centuries of development, equity was also growing, and was from time to time even aggressively intervening to help those suitors for whom the common law had no remedy.   It was mainly owing to her rivalry with the common-law courts, that the action on the case was both expanded beyond its delictual limits, and also pushed to such extreme lengths within those limits.[3]

As developed, the action of *assumpsit*[4] became the characteristic remedy for the recovery of unliquidated damages for the violation of an express contract not under seal, or of a promise implied by law from an executed consideration or from a legal duty.   It derived its name from the Latin word *assumpsit* (he undertook), which was originally always inserted in the declaration as descriptive of the defendant's under-

---

[1] Bonnel *v.* Fouke, 2 Sid. 4.

[2] Moses *v.* Macferlan, 2 Burr. 1012; Ames, *ubi supra*, 68.

[3] Ker. Eq. Ju. 11, 37, 86.

[4] Chit. Pl. 85-97

taking. As has been seen, there were two forms of this action, the one *special*, brought upon an express contract, and the other *general*, brought upon an implied or a fictitious promise.

We shall the better understand its functions if we consider, first, the cases in which neither of these forms could be used.[1]

When a party has a security of a higher nature than a simple contract, as an instrument under seal or a record, then he must proceed in debt, covenant, or *scire facias* as the case may require. But if a deed be only executed by the plaintiff and not by the defendant, there only *assumpsit* can be brought for a breach by the defendant,[2] and so *assumpsit* can be brought upon an invalid deed if there be a consideration from which a promise can be implied, or on a new contract upon a new consideration to pay or perform a contract under seal, or where such a contract has been varied by a simple contract. The taking of a *collateral* security of a higher nature does not prevent a suit in *assumpsit* upon the original contract. *Assumpsit* cannot be supported for the use and occupation of real estate where the possession is adverse, for of course that circumstance excludes the idea of any contract; nor is *assumpsit* the proper remedy in a case of deceit not apparent on the face of a written contract, because there the matter of the alleged deceit would be a variance of the writing, and an action on the case for the fraudulent representation is the proper remedy.

As this action of *assumpsit* was invented to remove the inconveniences and to make up the deficiencies of the action of debt, we find that it was generally the only remedy against an executor or administrator for the breach of a contract not under seal; and for the recovery of money payable by instalments where the whole debt is not due; also in all cases where the simple contract is for the payment of the debt of a third person or the performance of some collateral thing, and upon an award to perform any act except the payment of money. It not only entirely escaped the wager of law, but general

---

[1] Chit. Pl. 91–94. [2] *Ibid*, 92.

assumpsit avoided the great particularity with which the plaintiff was required to set forth his cause of action in debt.[1]

SPECIAL ASSUMPSIT lay for the breach of all simple contracts, whether oral or in writing, made in express terms.[2]

GENERAL ASSUMPSIT, equally with special *assumpsit*, lay to recover damages for breach of a promise; but in this case the promise was an implied or fictitious one, the consideration of which was found in the existence of circumstances creating a duty.[3] In debt on simple contract the obligation arose directly from these circumstances. In general *assumpsit*, it arose from the fictitious promise which the law implied from those same circumstances and in consideration of their existence, and the law implied this promise for the express purpose of providing a substitute for the action of debt.

It will be evident to the student, from what has been said, that wherever a valid simple contract can be made or implied from the acts of the parties, there *assumpsit* can be brought for its violation. Hence a catalogue of the cases in which special *assumpsit* can be brought would require to be co-extensive with the sphere of simple contract.

General *assumpsit*, or the Common Counts, as they are popularly called, cannot be supported by proof of a special executory contract. The law will not imply a promise where an express promise exists. Hence, so long as the special contract remains executory, it must be declared upon in special *assumpsit*. But where it has been performed, there it may be given in evidence under the common counts, as showing the receipt by the defendant of work, or goods, etc., from which fact a promise will be implied to pay the stipulated price for them; if there be no such stipulation, their value can be recovered under these counts. In cases where the special contract is void, or has been abandoned, or where an innocent

---

[1] Ames, *ubi supra*, 57.

[2] It is not thought advisable to complicate the subject by treating of contracts which, though implied as to fact, *i. e.*, contents, are nevertheless express contracts, and therefore to be sued for in special *assumpsit*. See Bishop on Contracts, §§ 257-263.

[3] For the clearest statement of the difference between special and general *assumpsit*, see Cutter *v.* Powell, 2 Smith's Leading Cases (8th ed.), 48, notes.

party thereto is justified in abandoning it, there a remedy can be had under these common counts for the fair value (*quantum meruit*, or *quantum valebant*) of the labor done or goods furnished.[1]

The COMMON COUNTS[2] included what were called the money counts, and they were so called because they set forth certain money transactions as a debt, and from the existence of this debt the consideration for the feigned promise to pay the money arose. They were as follows: money paid to the defendant's use, or money had and received by the defendant under such circumstances as to impose upon him the obligation of returning it, or money lent to the defendant, or interest due by the defendant on a loan, or forbearance of money, or on an account stated showing a balance due from the defendant. These common counts also included claims for the use and occupation of land, for board and lodging, for goods sold and delivered, for goods bargained and sold, for work, labor, and services, and for work, labor, and materials. In these also circumstances were alleged which created the duty or obligation to pay, and the promise to pay was implied upon this consideration.

In the *quantum meruit* (so much as he deserved to have) and the *quantum valebant* (so much as they were worth) counts, the first of which related to services performed, and the second to goods, etc., sold, the facts of services performed or of goods sold were directly alleged as the consideration of the fictitious promise to pay, in the one case what the plaintiff deserved, and in the other what the goods were worth.

It must be noted that nothing but money could be recovered under the common counts.

The declaration in *assumpsit* must invariably disclose the consideration upon which the contract was founded, the contract itself, whether express or implied, and its breach. The claim of damages should be large enough to cover the real amount of money.[3]

---

[1] Cutter *v.* Powell, 2 Smith's Leading Cases (8th ed.), 48, notes.

[2] Chit. Pl. 297–309.

[3] *Ibid.* 96.

TROVER.

It was as desirable to devise some action in the room of *detinue* as it had been to substitute one for debt, since the wager of law was a legal method of defence in both, and in detinue even greater exactness and definiteness of description were required than in debt. According to Reeves' History of English Law this action was split off from the action on the case in the 33d and 34th years of the reign of Henry VIII. (1542–3).[1] But it appears that it did not receive its precise form until the fourth year of Edward VI. (1551). At this time " a writ had been framed which surmised, that the plaintiff being possessed of the thing in question, lost it; and that the defendant found it, and converted it to his own use, upon which the action accrued. This, from the suggestion which gave the cue to the demand, was called an action *sur trover et conversion*, or an action of trover; that is, grounded upon a supposed *trover* (finding) by the defendant of the thing demanded, and *converting* it to his own use." [2] By a fiction of law, actions of trover were at length permitted to be brought against any person who had in his possession, no matter how that possession was acquired, the personal property of another, and who sold or used that property without the consent of the owner, or who refused to deliver it upon demand to such owner. The injury lies in the conversion of the plaintiff's property and the depriving him of its use, which is the gist of the action; the allegation of the finding or trover is immaterial and not traversable; the fact of conversion does not necessarily import an acquisition of property by the defendant; the action is brought for the recovery of damages to the value of the thing converted, and not for the thing itself, which can only be recovered, if at all, in detinue or replevin. Lord Mansfield thus described this action: " In *form* it is a fiction; in *substance* it is a remedy to recover the value of personal chattels wrongfully converted by another to his own use; the form supposes that the defendant might have come

[1] Reeves' Hist. IV. 385, 386 (2d London ed).   [2] *Ibid*. 526.

lawfully by it, and if he did not, yet by bringing this action the plaintiff waives the trespass ; no damages are recoverable for the act of taking ; all must be for the act of converting. This is the tort or *maleficium* (misdeed), and to entitle the plaintiff to recover, two things are necessary : 1st, property in the plaintiff ; 2d, a wrongful conversion by the defendant." [1]

Trover [2] lies only for the conversion of some personal chattel, and not for injuries to real property. It is sustainable only for specific articles, but these articles need not be described with certainty, because only damages for the conversion, and not the thing itself, are recovered in the action. Hence, unlike detinue, it lies for money, though it be not in a bag or distinguishable from other coin.

In order to support this action the plaintiff must, at the time of the conversion, have had a general or special property in the chattel converted, and also the actual possession, or the right to immediate possession thereof. The person who has the absolute or general, and not the mere special, property in a personal chattel may sustain this action, although he has never had the actual possession. So a person having a special property in the goods, may support trover against a stranger who takes them out of his actual possession, and a party entitled to the temporary possession may bring trover against the general owner. Generally, a special property must have been accompanied by possession in order to sustain the action, but there is an exception to this rule in the case of one who has also an interest in the goods converted. Without such absolute or special property the action can not be maintained ; but it may in most cases be brought by either such general or special owner, and a recovery by one bars an action by the other.[3]

The acts of conversion are manifold. They may consist of a wrongful taking of a personal chattel, or an illegal assumption of its ownership, or an illegal use or misuse or a wrongful detention thereof. The wrongful taking of the goods of another, who has the right of immediate possession, is of it-

---

[1] Cooper *et al. v.* Chitty *et al.*, 1 Burr. 31.

[2] Chit. Pl. 135–145.

[3] *Ibid.* 138.

self a conversion, and so are the wrongful assumption of ownership with respect thereto, and the illegal use or misuse thereof. But unless there be an illegal assumption of property, trover can not generally be supported for a mere omission or non-feasance; therefore trover will not lie against a carrier or other bailee who by negligence loses goods intrusted to his care.[1]

In the preceding instances, proof of the wrongful taking, etc., is sufficient, without evidence of a demand by the plaintiff upon the defendant for the delivery of the goods in question, and a refusal of such demand; for such acts are in themselves a conversion. But where the plaintiff is not prepared to prove some such act, he should make an actual demand upon the defendant for the possession of the chattels in question before instituting his suit; for in such case trover can not be supported without proof of a demand and refusal, or at least of such neglect to comply with the demand as will be equivalent in law to a refusal. Such a demand and non-compliance therewith are *prima facie* evidence of a conversion. But the defendant may rebut this presumption by showing that he was a carrier, and lost the goods in his possession as such by negligence, or that he had reasonable ground to doubt the plaintiff's right to the goods, and that he offered to deliver them to the true owner, etc. Such refusal will not amount to a conversion.

In such cases, where it is doubtful whether the evidence will establish a conversion so as to support a count in trover, a count in case for negligence, etc., should be added, if there be any proof to sustain it. If there has been a conversion, trover lies, although the goods converted be afterwards restored to the owner, for the restoration only goes in mitigation of damages.[2]

One joint-tenant, or tenant in common, or co-parcener can not support trover against his co-tenant, unless the latter has destroyed or sold the chattel in question.

For a wrongful taking, trover may be brought concurrently with trespass; but trover may often be brought where tres-

[1] Chit. Pl. 142.   [2] *Ibid.* 144.

pass will not lie, for trespass can not be brought where the taking was lawful or excusable; yet in such cases trover can be maintained for the unlawful conversion.[1]

The declaration in this action should state that the plaintiff was possessed of the goods in question as of his own property, and that they came to the defendant's possession by finding; but the omission of the formal words is not material after verdict, and these words are not traversable. As the conversion is the gist of the action, it must necessarily be stated in the declaration. The judgment is for damages and full costs, and the damages should be laid large enough to cover the value of the goods and the loss through their detention.[2]

MIXED ACTIONS. — EJECTMENT.

The history of the growth of the action of ejectment is, perhaps, even more characteristic of English law than the development of the action on the case which we have just considered. We know that no estate for a less period than life was acknowledged by the feudal law as a freehold. No less estate was considered worthy of a freeman's acceptance. But, as we have seen, with advancing civilization Englishmen were learning, " first from the Jew, then from the Lombard, . . . to lend money and to give credit for the price of goods." [3] With the development of trade, and the consequent increase of town population, the practice grew of letting lands for terms of years. These terms, however long they might run, were nothing more than chattels real; i. e., mere personal property, related, it is true, to the realty, but sharing nothing of its sacred quality. They gave the termor no rights in, no possession or seisin of, the land itself, but merely the benefit of an agreement with his lessor. He has a right in personam against the lessor and his heirs. His action is, as we have seen, an action of covenant, " an action which seems to have been invented for the enforcement of what we should call leases." [4] In this action (in which in all other cases only damages are recoverable) he

---

[1] Chit. Pl. 144.
[2] Ibid. 145.
[3] P. & M. Hist. II. 204.
[4] Ibid. II. 106.

can recover seisin of the land, and thus get a specific per-, formance of his covenant, as against his lessor, as well as damages. But the lessor's assignees were not bound by the lessor's covenant; hence, the lessor's feoffee could oust the termor, and leave him to his personal remedy for damages for covenant broken against the lessor or the lessor's heir. As against strangers, the termor was entirely unprotected. If he was ejected by some third person, not in privity with his lessor, such ejectment would be a disseisin of the lessor, who thereupon would bring his assize of novel disseisin, and thus regain possession; but his recovery would not enure to the benefit of the termor. So slight was the estimation in which these terms for years were held, that it was not until the time of Henry III. that any remedy was found for this deficiency. About the year 1235 a new action — the *quare ejecit infra terminum* (wherefore he ejected him during his term) — was given to the termor. This action required the defendant to show why he deforced the plaintiff of certain lands which A had demised to him (plaintiff) for a term then unexpired, within which term the said A sold the lands to the defendant, whereupon the defendant ejected the plaintiff therefrom. But, strange to say, the complete remedy is missed. This action cannot be used against ejectors in general; it will only lie against one who has purchased from the lessor. By this writ the termor recovered, as by the old writ of covenant, both his term and damages, if the term were unexpired, or his damages only in case of its expiration before judgment. Yet the lessee was still without remedy when dispossessed by a mere stranger not claiming under his lessor.

As the importance of these terms for years increased, the termors began to demand a more adequate remedy. We find in the forty-fourth year of Edward III. (1371), the first recorded instance of the new writ of *ejectione firmæ* (ejectment from the farm).[1]

This writ was in its nature one of trespass. It gave the termor a remedy against all persons whomsoever who ousted

---

[1] Adams on Ejectment, 7, note (a) (1st American edition, 1846).

him from his term, except the lessor's feoffee, who, coming into possession by means of a title, could not be said to be a trespasser, and who, consequently, had to be proceeded against by the former remedy of *quare ejecit*. As, however, the plaintiff had not a freehold interest, he could only recover damages for the injury he had sustained, and did not have restored to him the possession of his term. But this possession was the thing of main value. Hence disappointed suitors, dissatisfied with the common-law remedy, applied to courts of equity for redress. There they found an ear open to their complaints, and a strong hand eager to redress their grievances. These courts granted, as against the lessor and his privies, a specific performance of the covenant, and against third persons a perpetual injunction to quiet the possession; they also required restitution of the land itself

The courts of common law, unwilling to yield their jurisdiction to their civil-law rival, soon responded to this move of the equity courts, by themselves granting in this action of trespass a relief not warranted by the original writ, nor demanded by the declaration, viz., a judgment to recover the term and a writ of possession thereupon. This step was made at some time between the years 1455 and 1499.

We have now reached the point at which the modern action of ejectment was conceived of as a possibility. Here we have an action which will restore a termor, ejected by a stranger or even by his lessor, to the possession of his term, in addition to giving him damages for his ejectment; we have moreover an action in which the title of the plaintiff or termor to the possession of the land in question was incidentally determined. If his lessor had no such title, then the term was void. This question of title could always be raised by the defendant's plea of not guilty. Hence, so often as real ejectment occurred, the question of title could be settled in this action of *ejectione firmæ* without a resort to the long, intricate, and costly process of a real action.

The first step in the adaptation of this action to its larger use was what we may call a *factitious* as contrasted with the second *fictitious* process. As a term was recovered in the action, necessarily a term must be created; and as the action must be brought by an ejected termor, this *artificial* termor, if we may use the expression, must go upon the land in dispute and be ejected therefrom. Accordingly the party out of possession claiming title to the disputed land, whom we shall call the adverse claimant, entered upon the land accompanied by a friend to whom, whilst actually on the land (to avoid the offence of maintenance) he sealed and delivered a lease for years. The claimant so entering must have a present right to the possession, for otherwise his entry will be illegal and will not authorize him to convey a title to his lessee. The lessee, having acquired a right to the possession by means of the lease spoken of, remained upon the land until the claimant in possession, whom we shall call the occupant, came upon the freehold, *i. e.*, spied him and came his way, when he departed, and was esteemed to have been ejected, and to have had his possession trespassed upon by the occupant. He was even permitted to consider the mere presumed presence of the occupant upon the land in dispute as an ouster. It will be seen that by this process an artificial ejectment has been contrived; in the actual *ejectione firmæ* we had a real lease, an entry by the lessor, and an ouster by the occupant of the lessee or termor. Here we have, and are able to establish by proof, the same three things, but we have made them to order.

This however did not detract from their efficacy, and accordingly the lessee served a writ of *ejectione firmæ* on the occupant treating him as an ejector. Upon the trial the plaintiff (the lessee) had to establish his right to the possession of the land in dispute; but he derived this title through his lessor, the adverse claimant, and thus the latter's title was brought into question and determined. If the lessee succeeded, he recovered possession, but immediately gave it up to the adverse claimant.

This process worked no injustice so long as the occupant was made the defendant, or actually knew of this collusive action. But after a while a trick was practised. The adverse claimant proceeded as before, entering, sealing, and delivering the lease and departing, leaving his friend in possession; but he immediately procured a second friend to enter upon the land and eject the first friend, who thereupon made this second friend, instead of the occupant, the defendant to the action. This second friend was called the casual ejector. The lessee would thereupon get judgment against the casual ejector, who made default, and in this knavish way the occupant might be ousted of his lands, without any opportunity of defending his title. But very soon the courts by rule refused to permit the plaintiff in ejectment to proceed against the casual ejector without giving the occupant notice, and affording him an opportunity to come in and defend his title, as he was always allowed to do.

The action of ejectment continued in this condition until the time of the Commonwealth (1649–1660). There were many inconveniences connected with it. These actual entries could not always be peacefully or conveniently made. Again, if several persons were in possession of the disputed lands, it was necessary to execute separate leases upon the premises of the different tenants, and to commence separate actions upon the several leases. Lord Chief Justice Rolle discovered a remedy for all of these inconveniences, and by one stroke converted the factitious into a fictitious process. No lease is sealed and no entry or ouster is really made; the plaintiff lessee and the defendant casual ejector are men of straw.

A, the adverse claimant, delivers to B, the occupant, a declaration in ejectment, in which John Doe and Richard Roe, fictitious persons, are made respectively plaintiff and defendant; John Doe states in his declaration a fictitious demise of the lands in question from the adverse claimant to himself for a term of years, and complains of an ouster from them by Richard Roe during its continuance. To this declaration is annexed a notice by Richard Roe to the occupant, informing him of the proceedings, and advising him to apply to the court for permission to defend the action as he, Richard Roe, has no title and will make no defence. If the occupant does not make this application within a reasonable time, the court will, on proper proof of the service on him of the declaration and notice, give judgment against the casual ejector and execution for the possession of the lands to the plaintiff lessee. But if the occupant apply, as he surely will, for leave to defend, then he is required to enter into what is called the consent-rule. In the original form of the action, the lease, entry, and ouster were real and could readily be proved, as was required to be done; under the factitious process, the same facts, although collusively created, were yet facts, and could therefore be proved as readily as before. But the last step had made them mere fictions; they could not be proved. Therefore the consent-rule was a matter of necessity. The occupant was compelled to admit a series of fictions, to-wit: the lease, the entry, and the ouster.[1] Then, and not until then, he was permitted to come in and defend. The declaration was changed by making him, instead of the casual ejector, the defendant, and then the cause regularly proceeded to trial.[2]

We have no space here to consider the question of morality involved in this and other fictions of the law. They seem to be essential to all systems of jurisprudence. In English law they are a mark of the intense conservatism of the race, and of its strong adherence to precedent and customary law. They made pretence of doing as had always been done, and yet by means of the pretence they advanced through broader procedure to higher ideas.[3]

In this last form the action of ejectment persisted until the present generation. It was not changed in the District of Columbia until the year 1870. To-day it probably exists nowhere upon the globe in that form. Yet its history can never cease to be a characteristic story of the growth of English law.

Ejectment lies for the recovery of the possession of real property, in which the lessor of the plaintiff has the legal

---

[1] The entry admitted by the consent-rule is the entry of the adverse claimant for the purpose of making the lease, and not, as stated by Blackstone, the entry of the lessee, for his entry was admitted by the confession of his ouster. Evans' Pl. 264; Min. Inst. IV. 362; Holt's Lessee v. Smith, 1 Harr. & McH. 273, and authorities there cited; Bl. Com. III. 202*, 203*.

[2] See Lord Mansfield's description of this action in Fairclaim v. Shamtitle, 3 Burr. 1294, and in Aslin v. Parkin, 2 Burr. 668.

[3] The student should carefully read on this subject Chap. II. of Sir H. S. Maine's Ancient Law, and an essay by Oliver R. Mitchell, Harvard Law Review, VII. 249.

interest, and a possessory right not barred by the statute of limitations. It is only sustainable for the recovery of possession of property upon which an entry may in point of fact be made, and of which the sheriff can deliver actual possession; hence it does not lie for the recovery of an incorporeal hereditament. Any party having a right of entry may support an ejectment, but the right of possession must be exclusive and more than a mere license. The plaintiff must recover on the strength of his lessor's title, and not on the weakness of his adversary's, for possession gives the defendant a title against every person who cannot show a *sufficient* title. The plaintiff must also show in his lessor a strict legal title, for no recovery can be had in this action upon a mere equitable interest. The lessor of the plaintiff must have had the right of possession both at the time of the sealing and delivery of the lease mentioned in the declaration, and at the commencement of the action; but if the lease expire during the trial, the plaintiff, if he succeed, shall have judgment with a perpetual stay of execution as to possession, so that he can recover mesne profits and costs.

This action is only sustainable for what in fact, or in point of law, amounts to an ouster or dispossession of the lessor of the plaintiff; and it is necessary that the possession of the defendant should be adverse or illegal at the time of the execution and delivery of the lease mentioned in the declaration. If there be no ouster, or if the defendant be not in possession at the time of suit brought, the action will fail. A wrongful detention, even after a lawful entry made, will amount to an ouster in law. Hence ejectment is not brought where there has been no actual ouster, until after a demand made for possession and a refusal thereof.[1]

Ejectment has been very generally changed by the abolition of the fictions, and the action is brought in the name of the adverse claimant against the occupant. These statutory ejectments vary in form, and do not require a detailed review here.

[1] For the general subject of "Ejectment," see Adams on Ejectment, 1st American edition, 1846.

Mesne Profits.

Until the invention of fictions in ejectment, the successful plaintiff recovered not only the unexpired portion of his term, but also his costs and damages for the deprivation of his possession. But after the introduction of these fictions the courts could not permit the recovery of substantial damages for an imaginary ouster. Hence, the judgment in ejectment was only for possession and nominal damages. To recover the real damages sustained, the plaintiff, after a judgment in his favor in ejectment, brought another action of trespass, called an action for mesne profits.[1] In this action the plaintiff complains of his ejection and loss of possession, states the time during which the defendant held the lands and took the profits, and prays judgment for the damages which he has thereby sustained.

Upon the trial of the ejectment suit, the plaintiff's lessor has had to prove title in himself at the time of the sealing and delivery of the lease mentioned in the declaration in that suit. Consequently the judgment in ejectment is conclusive evidence, upon the trial of the action for *mesne profits*, of the plaintiff's title from that time. But it is not evidence of the defendant's possession, for the consent-rule establishes such possession only from the time of the service on him of the declaration. Hence, the plaintiff must prove the length of time that the defendant has been in possession of the disputed premises, and also the amount of his damages.

But if the plaintiff seeks to recover the mesne profits accruing antecedent to the day of the demise in the declaration, he must produce the regular proof of his title to the premises, for the judgment in ejectment is only proof of title subsequent to the date of the demise. He must also in such case prove an entry upon the lands.

Mesne profits are now usually recoverable in a count joined with the count in ejectment.

---

[1] Adams on Ejectment, 1st American edition, 1846, chap. XIV.

CONSEQUENCE OF A MISTAKE IN CHOOSING THE FORM OF ACTION.

At common law a mistake in the Form of Action brought was very serious, for the courts considered it of great importance to preserve the boundaries between the different actions,[1] and hence they would not allow the parties, even by agreement, to try a question, or to recover, in the wrong action. When the objection to the form of the action is substantial, and appears upon the face of the declaration, it may be taken by demurrer, by motion in arrest of judgment, or by writ of error. Thus, where the plaintiff in an action on the case stated that the defendant *wilfully* drove his horses against the plaintiff's carriage, the court arrested the judgment because it appeared from such allegation that the action should have been trespass and not case. When the objection to the form of action does not appear on the face of the pleadings, it can only be taken as a ground of non-suit. If for such mistake the plaintiff fail in his action, and judgment be given against him for that reason, and not upon the merits, this judgment is no bar to a fresh action.[2]

But such mistake will not now, so liberal is the law in permitting amendments, be productive of more serious consequences than delay, expense, and mortification. A suitor may amend a defective statement of his cause of action by changing from one form of contract or tort action to another of the same class;[3] some authorities have even permitted the change of a contract to a tort form, and *vice versa* of a tort form to one in contract.[4] But if he introduce *a new cause of action* by his amendment, as he may do, the statute of limitations will, in a proper case, apply to the new cause of action stated for the first time by the amendment.[5]

[1] Chit. Pl. 84 n. (e).
[2] *Ibid*. 179.
[3] Kirwan *v*. Raborg, 1 Harr. & J. 296; Stebbins *v*. Insurance Co., 59 N. H. 143;
Chapman *v*. Barney, 129 U. S. 677; Magruder *v*. Belt, 7 App. D. C. 303.
[4] Smith *v*. Bellows, 77 Penn. St. 441; Chapman *v*. Barney, *ubi supra*.
[5] Sicard *v*. Davis, 6 Peters, 124.

Extraordinary Forms of Actions.

It seems proper to indicate to the student those extraordinary actions which are not ordinarily needed for the vindication of a right, but which upon occasion are the only remedies adapted to the administration of justice. No more can be done than to name them in order, and to briefly describe their functions. They are generally in force in this country, and are obtainable from the local courts of record of original jurisdiction at common law. Nearly all of them are the subjects of special treatises, and to these the student must be referred for detailed information. These actions are MANDAMUS, PROCEDENDO, PROHIBITION, QUO WARRANTO, INFORMATION, HABEAS CORPUS, CERTIORARI, and WRITS OF ERROR.[4]

Mandamus.

A writ of *mandamus* (we command) is a mandate issuing in England in the king's name from the Court of King's Bench, and directed to any person, corporation, or inferior court of judicature within the king's dominions, requiring to be done some particular *ministerial* act therein specified, which appertains to their duty, and which the Court of King's Bench has previously determined to be consonant to right and justice. It is a high prerogative writ of an extensively remedial nature, and may be employed in all cases where the applicant has a right to have anything done of a ministerial character, and has no other adequate specific means of compelling its performance. The student must especially note that it lies only to compel the doing of a specific ministerial act, and therefore it can not be used to control in any way the judgment or discretion of a judicial or other officer charged with a public duty. A *mandamus* lies to compel the admis-

---

[4] The writ of *audita querela* (the complaint having been heard) is an antiquated proceeding, whereby a defendant, against whom judgment is recovered, and who is in danger of execution, or perhaps actually in execution, may be relieved upon good matter of discharge which has happened *since the judgment,* as, *e. g.,* a general release executed and delivered to him by the plaintiff after the rendition of the judgment. Such relief is now generally given upon motion. Min. Inst. IV, 846, 847.

sion or restoration of the applicant to any office or franchise
of a public nature; for the production, inspection, or delivery
of public books and papers; to compel bodies corporate to
affix their common seal; and for an infinite number of other
purposes.[1]

Writ of Procedendo.

A writ of *procedendo ad judicium* (for proceeding to judgment) issues in England out of the *Court of Chancery*, commanding an inferior court, which improperly delays judgment,
to proceed to give it, but, of course, without specifying the
judgment to be given; for that, if erroneous, must be corrected by means of a writ of error or appeal. Disobedience
of this order may be punished as a contempt. This writ is
sometimes confused with the preceding; but a *mandamus*
commands the doing of a specific ministerial thing, while a
procedendo requires a judicial officer to go on with the discharge of a judicial function.[2] Professor Minor calls attention to this confusion in several cases in the Supreme Court
of the United States.[3] For the details of this writ, see Fitzherbert (*de Natura Brevium*), 153 B. 240 D.

Writ of Prohibition.

When a subordinate tribunal is solicited, or manifests a
disposition, to encroach upon the jurisdiction of the higher
courts, and to exercise a cognizance not belonging to it, it is
a grievance for which the common law has provided a remedy
by the writ of prohibition. This, in England, is the king's
prerogative writ, issuing properly out of the King's Bench
(but sometimes out of the Court of Chancery, Common Pleas,
or Exchequer), directed to the judge and parties to a suit in
any inferior court, commanding them to cease from the prosecution thereof. It issues upon a suggestion that either the
case originally, or some collateral matter arising therein, did
not belong to the jurisdiction entertaining the suit in question, but to some other court. It was directed in proper cases

---

[1] Min. Inst. IV. 311.
[2] *Ibid.* 310.

[3] 8 Peters, 291; 13 Peters, 290; 14 How. 25.

to a great variety of inferior courts, to wit: the ecclesiastical, the university, and the admiralty courts, the court of chivalry, military and naval courts-martial, and, of course, to inferior courts of common law. If either judge or parties proceeded after such prohibition, they were punished for contempt. Where the jurisdiction which is impeached is defended by the inferior court, or where the question whether or not this jurisdiction exists in that court is a difficult or doubtful one, there the superior court will try the matter upon a feigned contempt by the lower court in disobeying the prohibition, and, if satisfied that the lower court rightfully has jurisdiction, it will grant a writ of *consultation*, returning thereby the cause to the lower court to be there proceeded with.[1]

QUO WARRANTO.

A writ of *quo warranto* (by what warrant or authority) is *in the nature of a writ of right for the king* against him who claims or usurps any office, franchise, or liberty, to inquire by what authority he supports his claim, in order to determine the right. It lies also in case of non-user, or long neglect of a franchise, as well as for mis-user or abuse of it. It commands the defendant to show by what warrant he exercises such a franchise, having never had any grant of it, or having forfeited it by neglect or abuse. If, upon hearing, judgment were given for the defendant, it was final and conclusive, even against the Crown; in case of judgment for the king, the franchise was either seised into the king's hands, or, if that were not proper, there was merely a judgment of ouster of the defendant.

By virtue of the statute of 9 Ann. c. 20, an information in the nature of a *quo warranto*, without a resort to the prerogative writ of which we have just spoken, may be brought by leave of the court, at the relation of any person desiring to prosecute the same (who is called the relator) against any person usurping, intruding into, or unlawfully holding any franchise or office in any city, borough, or town corporate. And now, generally, when any individual or body politic has

---

[1] Min. Inst. IV. 312–315; F. N. B. 39 H.

intruded into, usurped, or assumed to act on any franchise, liberty, office, or privilege, not being legally entitled to it, and is supposed to have thereby injured either another party really entitled to the office or franchise, or the public, — in such case, by this information, the party whose conduct is challenged is called upon to show by what authority he has so acted. If the defendant be convicted, judgment of ouster may be given against him, and he may also be fined, for the information in the nature of a *quo warranto* is a *quasi*-criminal proceeding.[1]

INFORMATIONS.

In England an information on behalf of the Crown, filed in the Exchequer by the king's attorney-general, is a method of suit for recovering money or other chattels due the king, or for obtaining satisfaction in damages for any personal wrong committed to the land or other possessions of the Crown. It is grounded on no writ under seal, but merely on the intimation of the attorney-general who " gives the court to understand and to be informed of " the matter in question, upon which the party informed against is put to his answer, and trial is had as in suits between private subjects. The most usual informations were those of intrusion and debt: intrusion, for any trespass upon the Crown-lands, and debt, upon any contract for money due the king or for any forfeiture to the Crown.[2] With criminal informations we have no concern here.

HABEAS CORPUS.

No more grievous injury can be inflicted upon a person than the deprivation of his personal liberty. To redress this wrong the ancient law provided several nominal remedies. By the writ *of mainprize*, which issued out of the Chancery, the sheriff was directed to take sureties (called mainpernors) for the appearance of a man who was imprisoned, and to set him at large, where he had committed a bailable offence and bail had been refused by the committing officer, or where such

---

[1] Bl. Com. III. 262 *; Warren's Law Studies, 600.   [2] Bl. Com. III. 261 *.

officer had no authority to admit to bail. The writ *de homine replegiando* (for replevying a man) lay to replevy a man out of prison, or out of the custody of any private person, upon giving security to the sheriff that the man should be forthcoming to answer any charge against him. And if the man were *eloigned, a capias in withernam*, exactly as in the case of replevin of a chattel, would issue to imprison the defendant himself till he produced the party. But for many offences a man could not be replevied, as for homicide, or the breach of the forest laws ; this writ was especially ineffectual in cases of imprisonment where the Crown was concerned and where consequently the subject most needed protection. The writ *de odio et atia* (for hatred and ill-will) issued out of Chancery, and commanded the sheriff to inquire whether a prisoner charged with murder was committed upon just ground of suspicion, or merely *propter odium et atiam ;* and if, upon inquisition, due cause of suspicion do not appear, then there issues another writ commanding the sheriff to admit him to bail. We shall have to return to this writ in another connection.

As we have said these writs were nominal remedies, but they were miserably inefficient to protect the subject against the Crown.

The great and efficacious writ in all manner of illegal confinement is that of *habeas corpus ad subjiciendum* (you shall have the body for submission). This most potent and famous writ of the law is the citizen's writ of right, and is the means whereby any imprisonment, or restraint of liberty, alleged to be illegal, may be formally inquired into, and, if found to be illegal, the party may be finally discharged. The person having in his custody the party restrained of his liberty must forthwith produce him before the court or judge issuing the writ. If upon inquiry the imprisonment or restraint is found to be lawful and under sufficient authority, as, for instance, in pursuance of the commitment of a magistrate acting within his jurisdiction, there no further inquiry can be made as to the guilt or innocence of the accused, and he must be remanded to custody. But if he be held without lawful authority, he must be released. The benefits of this writ extend to the domain of private as well as of public life. A wife or a child may be released from every unjust restraint upon personal freedom, though imposed by a husband or a father.

We have only space to add that this writ existed at common law. By Statute 16 Car. I. c. 10, the right to its use and protection was solemnly acknowledged and affirmed, and safeguards were added to prevent its denial. These proving insufficient, in 1680 the famous *habeas corpus* act of 31 Car. II. c. 2, was enacted. This is the original of all American statutes upon the subject, and its provisions are so complete that it has for more than two centuries accomplished its purpose with wonderful success. It is provided by Article I., Section 9, Paragraph 2, of the Constitution of the United States, that " The Privilege of the Writ of Habeas Corpus shall not be suspended, unless when in case of Rebellion or invasion the public Safety may require it." [1]

CERTIORARI.

A writ of *certiorari* is a writ issued from a superior court to one of inferior jurisdiction, commanding the latter to certify to the former the record or proceedings in a particular case. Upon reception of the record the superior court may proceed with the cause as if it had originated there; or the superior court may simply inspect the record, where the proceeding is a summary one, and not according to the common law, and determine whether there has been any material irregularity therein. Sometimes the writ is used for the purpose of obtaining a fuller and more complete transcript of a record of a lower court where the first copy is imperfect.[2] This writ is used in connection with *habeas corpus* where it is desired to test the sufficiency of a commitment, in order that the superior court may have before it, on the hearing, the record of the proceedings by virtue of which the commitment was issued.

---

[1] The student is referred for a most concise, and yet complete, account of the history and functions of this great writ to Professor Minor's Institutes, IV. 402–429, and also to Hurd's Treatise on Habeas Corpus.

[2] Min. Inst. IV. 300; F. N. B. 242 B

WRITS OF ERROR.

These will be described in connection with the review of the proceedings in an action.

The student has thus considered, necessarily briefly, the principal remedies afforded by the common law. He can profitably study elsewhere that remedial scheme more in detail than space has here permitted. He will find most interesting and abundant information in three articles by Professor Maitland, upon the history of the register of original writs, published in the Harvard Law Review, Vol. III. pp. 97, 167, 212. Especially let him go carefully over the writs described in Fitzherbert's book, and arrange them under appropriate heads of relief. He will then appreciate these words of Pollock and Maitland: "*The more we read of thirteenth century law, the fewer will seem to us the really new ideas that were introduced by the chancellors of the later middle ages.*" [1]

----

[1] P. & M. Hist. II. 594.

CHAPTER IV.

OF THE JOINDER AND ELECTION OF ACTIONS.

JOINDER OF ACTIONS.

IT is a maxim of the law that no one should be twice pursued for the same cause of action. It is also said that the law abhors a multiplicity of actions. That a plaintiff who has two or more causes of action, which may be joined in one action, should be compelled to so join them, is another illustration of the same general principle. If under such circumstances he bring several actions, he may be forced to consolidate them and to pay the costs of the application for such consolidation.

The subject of joinder may be considered as it affects different *forms* and different *rights* of actions.[1]

With respect to the joinder of different forms of actions, the rule originally was that counts in the same form of action might be joined, but that those in different forms of actions might not. And this resulted from the fact that every proceeding was begun by an original writ of a particular form, which also determined the particular form of the action. No action could be grounded on two original writs, nor could one writ be in two forms. Consequently only such counts could be joined as could properly be grouped under one and the same original writ. The most forcible illustration and relic of this rule is the fact that counts in debt and detinue can be joined, because at the outset they were the same action and were covered by the original writ in debt. This continued to be the case, although they ultimately separated so widely that the pleas differed in the respective actions as did also

[1] Chit. Pl. 179–188.

the judgments entered in them. But when the origin of the rule was forgotten, in consequence of the many cases in which original writs were not sued out, artificial reasons were invented to account for its continuance. It is said that wherever two counts admit of the same plea and the same judgment, they may be joined. But this is a very imperfect expression of the rule, for in an action of debt counts may be joined upon records, upon contracts under seal, and upon simple contracts; yet these counts require three different pleas. The old rule is the simplest in statement and the most universal; all counts or forms of actions may be joined which could originally have been included under one original writ. But it must be restrained in the following particular. After the action on the case so developed as to include *assumpsit* which sounded in contract, and trover or case generally, which sounded in tort, the courts, applying the reason of the rule, held that counts which sounded in contract could not be joined with counts which sounded in tort.

Thus in *assumpsit* the plaintiff may join as many counts as he has causes of action upon an express or an implied simple contract or upon a *quasi*-contract. And this principle is true generally of each form of action. So debt on bond, on judgment, on a statute, and on a simple contract may all be joined in one action. So several distinct trespasses may be joined in the same declaration. And several causes of action in case may be joined with trover.

But actions in form *ex contractu* can not be joined with those in form *ex delicto*. Thus debt can not be joined with trespass, nor covenant with trover. Nor can different forms of actions, whether the same be on contract or for tort, be joined; thus debt can not be joined with covenant, trespass with case, *assumpsit* with trover.

Coming now to consider the joinder of different rights of action, we find the rule to be this: where the same form of action may be adopted for several distinct injuries, the plaintiff may generally proceed for all in one action, though the several rights affected were derived from different titles.

Thus, in the case of a surviving partner, a demand by or against him as partner may be joined with a demand due in his own right. So an executor or administrator may declare as such for money paid by him in that character, and may join such count with counts on promises to the testator or intestate.

But a person can not in the same action join a demand in his own right and a demand *in autre droit* (in another right); thus an executor or administrator can not join claims made in his representative with claims made in his personal character. So, in an action against an executor or administrator, a count can not be introduced which would charge him personally, for the judgment in the one case would be *de bonis testatoris* (from the testator's goods), and in the other *de bonis propriis* (from his own goods).

The consequences of a misjoinder of forms of actions are serious. However perfect in form each count may be, yet if they be improperly joined the declaration will be bad on a general demurrer, or in arrest of judgment, or upon writ of error. A demurrer for misjoinder must be to the whole declaration.

Under the modern latitude as to amendments, a misjoinder could, before verdict, be cured by entering a *nolle prosequi* (unwilling to pursue) upon one or more counts. But after a general verdict for damages, and judgment entered thereon, the judgment would even now have to be arrested, for the court could not say on what count or counts the jury assessed the damages.

ELECTION OF ACTIONS.

In certain cases the party injured has the right to elect one of several remedies for the same injury.[1] The proper exercise of this right may be a matter of great importance to his interests. What are the considerations which should govern him in making his election?

(1) In some actions the plaintiff may recover upon a mere naked possession of the thing affected, while in others a strict

[1] Chit. Pl. 188–194.

legal title is essential. Therefore where the title of the plaintiff is doubtful, he should choose the remedy requiring only proof of possession; *e. g.* trespass, and not ejectment. So where a person's property has been taken away or withheld from him, he may generally waive the tort and sue in *assumpsit* for the value; but it will not be advisable to do this if he can not clearly establish his title to the property, as he must do in *assumpsit*, whereas bare possession is generally sufficient to sustain an action of trover or trespass.

(2) In an action on contract, if a person who ought to be made co-plaintiff be omitted, it is a ground of non-suit (except in the case of persons suing *in autre droit)*, whereas in tort-actions such non-joinder can only be pleaded in abatement. Again, in contract-actions the joinder of too many defendants is a ground of non-suit, and the omission of a necessary defendant may be pleaded in abatement; whereas in tort-actions, where the offence may in the eye of the law have been committed by several, the joinder of too many defendants will be no ground of objection, and the omission of a party jointly concerned in committing the injury can not generally be pleaded in abatement. Therefore, in many cases of uncertainty as to how many persons should be made plaintiffs or defendants, it may be advisable to declare in case rather than in *assumpsit*. The following judgment[1] of Lord Ellenborough explains the advantages arising in many instances from the adoption of the action on the case, in preference to the action of *assumpsit:* " There is no inconvenience in suffering the party to allege his gravamen as a breach of duty, arising out of an employment for hire, and to consider that breach of duty as tortious negligence, instead of considering the same circumstances as forming a breach of promise implied from the same consideration of hire; by allowing it to be considered in either way, according as the neglect of duty or the breach of promise is relied upon as the injury, a multiplicity of actions is avoided; and the plaintiff, according as the convenience of his case requires, frames his

[1] Govett *v.* Radnidge, 3 East, 70.

principal count in such a manner as either to join a count in trover therewith, if he have another cause of action other than the action of *assumpsit*, or to join with the *assumpsit* the common counts, if he have another cause of action to which they are applicable; and other advantages ensue from the adoption of case instead of . *assumpsit*, viz. that in the former action, the defendant can not plead in abatement the non-joinder of other parties as defendants; and the plaintiff will recover, if he prove one of several defendants to be liable."

(3) Where the plaintiff has several demands, recoverable in different forms of actions, he may and frequently ought to declare for all in one action. Thus, in case of neglect by a bailee, the bailor may proceed against him either in *assumpsit* for violating his implied contract to keep safely, or in tort for negligence. But if he have also at the same time a money demand against the bailee, he should, to prevent multiplicity of suits, declare for both causes of action in *assumpsit ;* if, on the other hand, the second cause of action be, for example, trover, then the declaration should, for the same reason, be in case.

(4) By an astute and somewhat questionable election of remedy, advantage may be gained in depriving an adversary of a defence which he might otherwise avail himself of. Thus, a bankrupt may plead his discharge in bar of an action in *assumpsit* against him for money had and received, however wrongfully, by him before his bankruptcy; but by declaring in case or trover, he is prevented from using this defence. So a set-off can be pleaded in *assumpsit*, but not in case. In cases of fraud the statute of limitations may not begin to run until the fraud is discovered, and therefore in such instances the *assumpsit* should be waived and suit brought in tort for the fraud. By a judicious election the defendant may be compelled, either to take issue upon some particular allegation in the declaration (instead of putting the plaintiff to prove his whole case), or to plead his ground of defence specially. Thus, in covenant for rent, the defendant must plead to some particular allegation, for there

is no general issue in covenant;[1] but in debt on a lease the defendant can plead the general issue of *nil debet*, and thus compel the plaintiff to prove the whole of his declaration. So, trespass is generally preferable to case, for under the general issue of *not guilty* in the latter the defendant may not only dispute the averments of the declaration, but may give in evidence matters of defence, which in trespass he would be compelled to plead specially.

(5) In some cases the party injured may have his choice between a local action (one which can only be brought in the county where it arose), and a transitory action (which may be brought in any jurisdiction where the defendant is found). Thus debt for rent by the assignee or devisee of the lessor against the lessee is local; but, upon an express covenant to pay rent, the action of covenant may be maintained between the same parties, and, as this action is transitory, it should be chosen where it is desired to try the cause out of the county where the land is situated.

(6) It was a rule of the common law that when a *tort-feasor* (wrong-doer) died, the cause of action against him died with him. Hence trover could not be maintained against the personal representative of one who had wrongfully seized and converted goods. But the owner of the goods could waive the wrong, and sue the personal representatives of the wrong-doer for the value of the goods, as for money had and received by him in his lifetime for the use of the plaintiff.

(7) An infant is liable for his tort; but where it is too closely connected with his contract, as for instance when he obtains credit through his false statement as to his majority, he is not liable; a husband and wife are liable for the wife's tort, subject to the same limitation. A lunatic is liable for his tort. Hence, where it can be done, such persons may be sued in tort, the contract being waived.

(8) The nature and amount of damages recoverable in different actions is an important consideration in this connection. It is generally held in the United States that a

---

[1] Stephen contradicts this statement; see *post*, 242, text and note 2.

passenger injured by a common carrier can sue in *assumpsit* upon the breach of the contract to carry safely, or in case for negligence in not carrying safely. By suing in tort, the plaintiff may obtain the benefit of a different rule of damages, for he may recover more remote and consequential damages than in *assumpsit*, and, in a proper case, even punitive or exemplary damages. Again, it may be more profitable to replevy an article wrongfully taken, whose value has been increased by labor done upon it since its taking, than to sue in trespass for its unlawful caption and asportation, or in trover for its value. So the owner of land, whose trees have been cut down, and carried off after a prolonged severance, by a trespasser, may sue the wrong-doer in trespass *quare clausum fregit* or *de bonis asportatis*, or he may waive the tort and sue for the value of the trees in *assumpsit*, and in each case a different measure of damages would be applied. It must be borne in mind by the student that not every tort can be waived, and yet support an *assumpsit*. Thus a mere trespasser cannot be sued for use and occupation of land, nor can one in adverse possession of land be so sued.

(9) In some jurisdictions stringent process exists against defendants in tort-actions. The plaintiff may avail himself of this by waiving his contract and suing in tort, where he may properly do so.

(10) In debt the judgment by *nil dicit*, or, generally, on default, is final, and execution may be taken out at once without the expense and delay of an inquisition to assess damages, as is required in *assumpsit* or covenant.

Where a party has elected one form of action, he may nevertheless abandon it, and after duly discontinuing it, he may resort to another. But, where there are two inconsistent remedies, he is bound by his election, and cannot afterwards change his form of action.[1]

[1] Robb *v.* Vos, 155 U. S. 13.   Encyclopædia of Pleading and Practice, VII. 364.

CHAPTER V.

PARTIES TO ACTIONS.

It is observed by Chitty that there are no rules connected with the science of pleading so important as those which relate to the persons who are to be the parties to the action; for, if there be any mistake in this respect, the plaintiff is, generally, compellable to abandon his suit, and to proceed *de novo*, after having incurred great expense.[1]

While the modern license of amendment has interfered to prevent the sacrifice of the particular suit through an error in this respect, yet it still remains true that this subject is of prime importance. Certainly the litigating parties should be the proper parties and only those.

It is thought that the doctrine of the law upon this subject has been best stated in the following rules, formulated by Dicey in his excellent "Treatise on the Rules for the Selection of the Parties to an Action." It has been found that this clear, formal, and concise treatment of the matter impresses itself upon the attention and memory of the student, and enables him to more thoroughly understand the radical principles underlying the rules themselves.

DICEY'S RULES FOR THE SELECTION OF THE PARTIES TO AN ACTION.

THE PERSONS WHO CAN SUE AND BE SUED.

Rule 1. All persons can sue and are liable to be sued in an action at law.

> *Exception* 1. Felons, outlaws, and alien enemies cannot sue.
>
> *Exception* 2. The sovereign, foreign sovereigns and ambassadors can not be sued.

[1] Chit. Pl. 1.

GENERAL RULES APPLICABLE TO ALL ACTIONS.

Rule 2. No action can be brought except for the infringement of a right.

Rule 3. No action can be brought except for the infringement of a common-law right.

Subordinate rule. Where one person has a legal and another an equitable interest in the same property, any action in respect of such property must be brought by the person who has the legal interest.

Rule 4. An action may be brought for every infringement of a "legal" right.

Exception 1. Where an injurious act amounts to a public nuisance, unless the plaintiff has suffered from it particular damage.

Exception 2. Where the wrong done amounts to a felony, until the felon has been prosecuted.

Rule 5. The same person can not be both plaintiff and defendant.

Rule 6. The right to bring an action cannot be transferred or assigned.

Rule 7. No person can be sued who has not infringed upon the right in respect of which the action is brought.

Rule 8. Every person can be sued who infringes upon the right of another.

Rule 9. The liability to be sued cannot be transferred or assigned.

ACTIONS ON CONTRACT — PLAINTIFFS — GENERAL RULES.

Rule 10. No one can sue for the breach of a contract who is not a party to the contract.

Rule 11. The person to sue for the breach of a *simple* contract must be the person from whom the consideration for the promise moves.

Exception 1. Actions by a person appointed by statute to sue on behalf of others.

Exception 2. Actions which can be brought either by a principal or an agent.

Exception 3. Some actions for money had and received.

Rule 12. The person to sue for the breach of a contract *by deed* is the person with whom the contract is expressed by the deed to be made; *i. e.*, the covenantee.

Subordinate rule. No one can sue on a covenant in an indenture who is not mentioned among the parties to the indenture.

Rule 13. All the persons with whom a contract is made must join in an action for the breach of it.

Rule 14. One and the same contract, whether it be a *simple* contract or a contract *by deed,* can not be so framed as to give the promisees or covenantees the right to sue upon it both jointly and separately.

Rule 15. The right to bring an action on contract can not be transferred or assigned.

> *Exception 1.* Contracts made assignable by statute.
>
> *Exception 2.* Contracts or choses in action assignable by custom.
>
> *Exception 3.* Assignment of a debt by agreement of all the parties.
>
> *Exception 4.* Covenants annexed to or running with estates in land.
>
> *Exception 5.* Assignment by marriage, bankruptcy, and death.[1]

Rule 16. The right of action on a contract made with several persons jointly passes on the death of each to the survivors, and on the death of the last to his representatives.

> *Exception.* Covenants with tenants in common.

PRINCIPAL AND AGENT.

Rule 17. A contract entered into with a principal through an agent is in law made with the principal, and the principal, not the agent, is the proper person to sue for the breach of it.

> *[Only agent can sue.]*
>
> *Exception 1.* Where an agent is contracted with by deed in his own name.
>
> *Exception 2.* Where the agent is named as a party to a bill of exchange or other commercial paper.
>
> *Exception 3.* Where the right to sue on a contract is, by the terms or circumstances of it, expressly restricted to the agent.

---

[1] In the older English law the maxim: *actio personalis moritur cum persona* (a personal action dies with the person), was of general application; it extended both to actions based upon an obligation and to all actions based on tort. Its application has been from time to time restricted by statute. Phillips *v.* Homfray, 1883, 24 Ch. D. 439; Finlay *v.* Chirney, 1888, 20 Q. B. D. 494; Encyclopædia of the Laws of England, I. 105.

Exception 4. Where the contract is made with the agent himself; *i. e.*, where the agent is treated as the actual party with whom the contract is made.

Exception 5. Where the agent is the only known or ostensible principal, or where the agent has made a contract not under seal in his own name for an undisclosed principal.

Exception 6. Where an agent has made a contract, in the subject-matter of which he has a special interest or property.

Exception 7. Where the agent has paid away money of the principal's under circumstances which gave a right to recover it back.

(Left margin bracket: Either principal or agent may sue.)

Rule 18. A person who enters into a contract in reality for himself, but apparently as agent for another person, whom he does not name, can sue on the contract as principal.

Rule 19. A person who contracts, in reality for himself, but, apparently, as agent for another person, whose name he gives, can not sue on the contract as principal.

PARTNERS AND UNINCORPORATED COMPANIES.

Rule 20. A firm or an unincorporated company can not sue in its name as a firm or as a company, but must sue in the names of the individual members of the firm or of the company.

Exception 1. Where an unincorporated company is empowered by statute to sue, etc., in the name of its public officer.

Exception 2. Where an unincorporated company is being wound up.

Rule 21. All persons who are partners in a firm, or members of an unincorporated company, at the time when a contract is made with the firm or the company, should join in an action for the breach of it.

Exception. One partner must or may sue alone, on contracts made with him on behalf of the firm, in the same cases in which an agent must or may sue on contracts made with him on behalf of his principal.

Rule 22. One partner or member of an unincorporated company can not sue another upon any matter involving the accounts of the partnership or company.

> *Exception* 1. Where there is an agreement which, though relating to partnership business, can be treated as separate and distinct from other matters in question between the partners.
>
> *Exception* 2. Where the matters, in respect of which an action is brought, are connected with the partnership business only through the wrongful act of the partner sued.

Rule 23. Actions for breaches of contracts made with a firm must be brought:

1. On the bankruptcy of the firm, by the trustee or trustees of the bankrupts.

2. On the bankruptcy of one or more partners, by the solvent partners together with the trustee or trustees of the bankrupt partner or partners.

Rule 24. On the death of a partner, the surviving partners and ultimately the last survivor, or his representative, must sue on contracts made with the firm.

CORPORATIONS AND INCORPORATED BODIES.

Rule 25. A corporation or incorporated body must sue in its corporate name.

Rule 26. A corporation or incorporated body can not sue on a contract not under seal.

> *Exception* 1. Where a corporation enters into a contract concerning matters necessarily incidental to the purposes of the business of the corporation.
>
> *Exception* 2. Where the contract relates to acts of trivial importance or of constant recurrence.
>
> *Exception* 3. Where the consideration for the contract is executed on the part of the corporation.
>
> *Exception* 4. Where there is a contract implied by law.
>
> *Exception* 5. Where a corporation is authorized by statute to contract otherwise than under seal.

Rule 27. A corporation or incorporated body can not sue on contracts *ultra vires* (beyond its powers).

Rule 28. When an incorporated company is in the course of winding up, actions on behalf of such company are brought and continued in its corporate name by the official liquidator.

HUSBAND AND WIFE.

Rule 29.   A wife can not during coverture sue without her husband.[1]

Exception 1. Where the husband is civilly dead.

Exception 2. Where the husband is legally presumed to be dead.

Exception 3. Where a wife has a "judicial separation" or "protection order" under statute.

Exception 4. Where by statute a wife is empowered to sue as a *feme sole*.

Subordinate rule. A husband can not bring an action against his wife, or a wife against her husband.

Rule 30.   A husband and wife must sue jointly in two cases:

1. On contracts made by the wife before marriage.

2. On contracts in which the wife claims as executrix, or administratrix.

Rule 31.   A husband may sue either alone or jointly with his wife in three cases:

1. On negotiable instruments (*e. g.*, bills of exchange) given to his wife before marriage.

2. On contracts made after marriage with his wife alone.

3. On contracts made after marriage with himself and his wife.

Rule 32.   The following are the results of errors as to joinder of parties in actions by husband or wife:

1. If a husband sues alone where the wife must be joined, the error is fatal.

2. If a wife sues alone where she either must or may be joined, the only result is to expose her to a plea in abatement.

3. If a husband sues with his wife where she neither must nor may be joined, the error is fatal.

Rule 33.   Where a husband is bankrupt and the trustee in bankruptcy sues in the right of the wife, he must join the wife with him in suing.

BANKRUPT AND TRUSTEE.

Rule 34.   The trustee of the property of a bankrupt must sue for the breach of any contract, made with the bank-

---

[1] For the law upon this subject, the legislation of the particular jurisdiction must be consulted.

rupt before bankruptcy, in which the bankrupt has both a legal and a beneficial interest.

> *Exception* 1. Contracts, the breach of which involves injury to the person or to the feelings of the bankrupt.
>
> *Exception* 2. Contracts uncompleted at the time of bankruptcy in which the personal service of the bankrupt is of the essence of the contract.

Rule 35.   For the breach of any contract made with the bankrupt during the continuance of the bankruptcy (in which the bankrupt has both a legal and a beneficial interest), either the trustee may sue, or the bankrupt may sue, if the trustee does not interfere.

> *Exception* 1. Contracts, the breach of which involves injury to the person or the feelings of the bankrupt.
>
> *Exception* 2. Contracts to pay for the personal labor of the bankrupt performed after his bankruptcy.

Rule 36.   Actions on contracts made with the bankrupt after the "close of the bankruptcy"[1] must be brought by the bankrupt.

Rule 37.   All the trustees must join in suing.

Rule 38.   On the removal, retirement, death, etc., of a trustee his rights pass to and vest in his successor.

Rule 39.   The bankruptcy of a plaintiff does not cause the action to abate.

Rule 40.   If an action be brought by the bankrupt in cases in which the trustee must sue, or by the trustee in cases in which the bankrupt must sue, the error is fatal.

EXECUTORS, ADMINISTRATORS, AND HEIRS.

Rule 41.   The personal representatives of a deceased person (*i. e.*, his executors or administrators) can sue on all contracts of whatever description made with him, whether broken before or after his death.

> *Exception* 1. Contracts, the breach of which occasioned merely personal suffering to the deceased.

---

[1] When the whole property of the bankrupt has been realized for the benefit of his creditors, the court may make an order that the bankruptcy *has closed*, and such order *closes the bankruptcy.*

Exception 2. Contracts limited to the lifetime of the deceased.

Exception 3. Covenants real broken during the lifetime of the deceased.[1]

Exception 4. Contracts on which the deceased must have sued jointly with other persons.

Subordinate rule 1. An executor can commence an action before probate; but an administrator can not commence an action before letters of administration granted to him.

Subordinate rule 2. On the death of a plaintiff the action can be carried on by his executor or administrator.

Rule 42. An executor or administrator:

1. Must sue in his representative character on all contracts made with the deceased.

2. May sue either in his representative or in his personal character on contracts made with him as executor after the death of the deceased.

Subordinate rule. An executor or administrator can not join claims made in his representative with claims made in his personal character.

Rule 43. Co-executors or co-administrators must all join as plaintiffs in an action.

Exception 1. Where a contract is made with some of several co-executors only.

Exception 2. Where an executor renounces the executorship.

Subordinate rule. One co-executor or co-administrator can not bring an action against another concerning matters connected with the executorship.

Rule 44. On the death of a co-executor or co-administrator, his rights of action pass to the survivors, and ultimately to the last survivor.

Rule 45. The executor of a sole, or of a sole surviving, executor represents the original testator; but the administrator of an executor does not represent the testator,

---

[1] *Covenants real*, as the term is here used, mean *covenants which both run with the land and descend to the heir or devisee,* i. e., covenants which affect the freehold. But where there has been a substantial breach of such covenants during the ancestor's lifetime, his personal representatives may sue for such breach in respect of any damage caused thereby to the personal estate. Kingdon v. Nottle, 1 M. & S. 355, 364; Knights v Quarles, 2 B. & B. 102, 105.

nor does the administrator of an administrator, or the executor of an administrator represent the original intestate.

ACTIONS ON CONTRACT — DEFENDANTS — GENERAL RULES.

Rule 46. No person can be sued for a breach of contract who is not a party to the contract.

Rule 47. The person to be sued for the breach of a *simple* contract is the person who promises or who allows credit to be given to him.

> *Exception* 1. Actions against a person appointed by statute to be sued on behalf of others.
>
> *Exception* 2. Actions on some contracts implied by law or actions *quasi ex contractu.*

Rule 48. The person to be sued for the breach of a contract *by deed* is the person by whom the contract is expressed by the deed to be made, *i. e.*, the covenantor.

Rule 49. Where several persons are jointly liable on a contract, they must all be sued in an action for the breach thereof, *i. e.*, joint contractors must be sued jointly.

> *Exception* 1. Where a co-contractor has become bankrupt.
>
> *Exception* 2. Where a claim is barred against one or more joint debtors, and not against others.
>
> *Exception* 3. Where a co-contractor is resident out of the jurisdiction.
>
> *Exception* 4. Where an action is brought against common carriers.
>
> *Exception* 5. Where an action is brought against a firm, some of the members of which are nominal or dormant partners.
>
> *Exception* 6. Where a co-contractor is an infant or a married woman.

Rule 50. Covenantors and other contractors may be at once jointly and severally liable upon the same covenant or contract, in which case they may be sued either jointly or separately.

Rule 51. The liability to an action on contract can not be transferred or assigned.

> *Exception* 1. Where there is a change of credit by an agreement between all the parties.
>
> *Exception* 2. Where there are covenants between lessor and lessee which run with the land.

Rule 52.

The liability to an action on a contract made by several persons jointly, passes at the death of each to the survivors, and on the death of the last to his representatives.

PRINCIPAL AND AGENT.

Rule 53.

A contract entered into by a principal, through an agent, is in law made by the principal, and the principal, not the agent, is the person to be sued for the breach of it.

Only agent can be sued.

Exception 1. Where an agent contracts by deed in his own name.

Exception 2. Where an agent draws, indorses, or accepts a bill of exchange or promissory note, in his own name.

Exception 3. Where credit is given exclusively to the agent.

Exception 4. Where an agent contracts for persons incapable of contracting.

Either principal or agent can be sued.

Exception 5. Where the contract is made by the agent himself, *i. e.*, where the agent is treated as the actual party by whom the contract is made, or in other words, where the agent, though acting as such, incurs a personal responsibility.

Exception 6. Where the agent is the only known or ostensible principal, or where a contract (not under seal) has been made by an agent in his own name for an undisclosed principal.

Exception 7. Where money received by an agent for his principal has been paid under a mistake of fact, or obtained by means of a tort.

Exception 8. Where an agent has signed certain contracts on behalf of a limited company without using the word "limited," in which case probably only the agent can be sued.

Rule 54.

An agent who, without having authority, enters into a contract on behalf of a principal, can not himself be sued on the contract, but is otherwise liable.

Exception. Where the authority of an agent has without his knowledge expired at the time of his making the contract.

PARTNERS AND UNINCORPORATED COMPANIES.

Rule 55.　　A firm or unincorporated company can not be sued in its name as a firm or as a company, but must be sued in the names of the individual partners or members composing the firm or company.

Rule 56.　　All persons who are partners in a firm, or members of an unincorporated company, at the time when a contract is made by or on behalf of the firm or company, should be joined in an action for the breach of it.

> *Exception.* One partner must or may be sued alone, on contracts made by him on behalf of the firm, in the same cases in which an agent must or may be sued on contracts made by him on behalf of his principal.

Rule 57.　　Actions on contracts made by a firm:

1. Can not, on the bankruptcy of the firm, be brought either against the trustee or (as a general rule) against the individual partners.[1]

2. Must, on the bankruptcy of one or more partners, be brought against the solvent partner or partners.

Rule 58.　　On the death of a partner, the surviving partners, and ultimately the last survivor or his representative, must be sued on contracts made with the firm.

CORPORATIONS AND INCORPORATED BODIES.

Rule 59.　　A corporation or incorporated body must be sued in its corporate name.

Rule 60.　　A corporation or incorporated body can not be sued on a contract not under seal.

> *Exception* 1. Where a corporation contracts concerning matters necessarily incidental to the purposes or business of the corporation.
>
> *Exception* 2. Where the contract relates to matters of trivial importance or of constant recurrence.
>
> *Exception* 3. In some cases of an implied contract.
>
> *Exception* 4. Where a corporation is authorized by statute to contract otherwise than under seal.

---

[1] The remedy is by proof against the bankrupt's estate, or by action against him if his order of discharge is no bar to the claim.

Rule 61.   A corporation or incorporated body can not be sued on contracts *ultra vires*.

Rule 62.   When a company is in course of winding up, actions against the company can either be stayed, or can not be brought without leave of the court.

INFANTS.

Rule 63.   An infant can not be sued on any contract made by him.

> *Exception* 1. Contracts for necessaries.
>
> *Exception* 2. Contracts in respect of permanent property occupied or possessed by an infant.

Rule 64.   An adult (*i. e.*, a person of or over twenty-one years of age) can not be sued on contracts made by him during infancy.

> *Exception* 1. Contracts on which an infant might be sued.
>
> *Exception* 2. Contracts ratified in writing [1] after full age.
>
> *Exception* 3. Contracts connected with the possession of permanent property and not repudiated after full age.

Rule 65.   If one of several co-contractors is an infant and the others are adults, the adults alone must be sued.

HUSBAND AND WIFE.

Rule 66.   A wife can not during coverture be sued alone.

> *Exception* 1. Where the husband is civilly dead.
>
> *Exception* 2. Where the husband is legally presumed to be dead.
>
> *Exception* 3. Where a wife has a judicial separation or protection order.
>
> *Exception* 4. Where the husband is an alien enemy.
>
> *Exception* 5. Where the wife is permitted by statute to be sued alone.
>
> *Subordinate rule.* A wife can not be sued by her husband.

---

[1] Written ratification is required in England by 9 Geo. IV. c. 14, s. 5, which is not in force in the United States; here a ratification in writing is not required.

Rule 67.   A husband and wife must be sued jointly in two cases, *sc.:*

    1. On contracts made by the wife before marriage.

    2. On contracts on which a claim is made against the wife as executrix or administratrix.

Rule 68.   In all actions brought to charge a husband on contracts made by his wife during coverture, the husband must be sued alone.

Rule 69.   The following are the results of errors in joinder of parties in actions against husband or wife:

    1. If a husband is sued alone where his wife must be joined, the error is fatal.

    2. If a wife is sued alone, where she must be joined, the only result is to expose the plaintiff to a plea in abatement.

    3. If a husband is sued jointly with his wife, where he ought to be sued alone, the error is fatal unless amended.

BANKRUPT AND TRUSTEE.

Rule 70.   A bankrupt can not, after his discharge, be sued on contracts made before bankruptcy.

    Exception 1. Debts or liabilities held not to be provable by the court of bankruptcy.

    Exception 2. Debts or liabilities contracted after notice to the creditor of an act of bankruptcy.

    Exception 3. Debts or liabilities incurred by means of fraud or breach of trust.

    Exception 4. Debts or liabilities whereof the bankrupt has obtained forbearance by fraud.

    Exception 5. Debts due to the Crown.

    Exception 6. Debts with which the bankrupt stands charged for an offence against a statute relating to any branch of the public revenue, or at the suit of the sheriff or other public officer on a bail bond, entered into for the appearance of any person prosecuted for any such offence.

Rule 71.   An undischarged bankrupt remains liable on contracts made by him before bankruptcy.

Rule 72.   The trustee can be sued as a trustee on contracts entered into by him in his character as a trustee.

EXECUTORS, ADMINISTRATORS, AND HEIRS.

Rule 73. The personal representatives of a deceased person (*i. e.*, his executors or administrators) can be sued on all contracts made with him, whether broken before or after his death.

> *Exception* 1. Contracts limited to the lifetime of the deceased.
>
> *Exception* 2. Covenants in law [1] not broken during the lifetime of the deceased.
>
> *Exception* 3. Contracts on which the deceased must have been sued jointly with other persons.
>
> *Subordinate rule* 1. An action can be commenced against an executor before probate, but an action can not be commenced against an administrator before letters of administration granted to him.
>
> *Subordinate rule* 2. On the death of a defendant the action may be carried on against his executor or administrator.

Rule 74. An executor or administrator must be sued in his representative character; *i. e.*, as executor or administrator, on all contracts made by the deceased.

Rule 75. An executor or administrator must be sued in his personal character on contracts made by himself.

> *Exception.* Contracts made by executor distinctly as executor.
>
> *Subordinate rule.* In an action against an executor or administrator, claims made against him in his representative character cannot be joined with claims made against him in his personal character.

Rule 76. All co-executors or co-administrators who have administered, should be joined as defendants in an action.

---

[1] Certain covenants are annexed by the law to the use of certain expressions. Whenever, for example, certain terms are used in a lease, it is inferred, as a matter of law, that the person using them enters into certain covenants. Thus under a lease by deed, the word demise or let, or any equivalent words sufficient to constitute a lease, import a covenant for title and for quiet enjoyment, unless there be an express cove- nant on either point, in which case no implication can be raised from such words. Such implied contracts are limited to the duration of the lessor's estate, and cease upon its determination. No action lies against an executor or administrator upon such a covenant at law which is not broken until after the death of the testator. 2 Williams on Executors (6th ed.), 1752.*

Rule 77.   The heir may be sued on contracts of the deceased in three cases, *sc. :*

1. On contracts *by deed* in which the ancestor expressly binds himself and his heirs.

2. On contracts of record.

3. On covenants real.

> *Subordinate rule* 1. A devisee is liable under the same circumstances under which the heir would be liable.

> *Subordinate rule* 2. In no case can an executor or administrator be sued together with an heir or devisee.

ACTIONS FOR TORT — PLAINTIFFS — GENERAL RULES.

Rule 78.   No one can bring an action for any injury which is not an injury to himself.

Rule 79.   The person who sustains an injury is the person to bring an action for the injury against the wrong-doer.

> *Subordinate rule* 1. The person to sue for any interference with the immediate enjoyment or possession of land or other real property is the person who has possession of it, and no one can sue merely for such an interference who has not possession.

> *Subordinate rule* 2. For any permanent injury to the value of land, or other real property, *i. e.*, for any act which interferes with the future enjoyment of, or title to, the land, an action may be brought by the person entitled to a future estate in it, *i. e.*, by the reversioner.

> *Subordinate rule* 3. Any person may sue for an interference with the possession of goods, who, as against the defendant, has a right to the immediate possession of such goods ; and no person can sue for what is merely an interference who has not a right to the immediate possession of the goods.

> *Subordinate rule* 4. Any person entitled to the reversionary interest in goods (*i. e.*, the reversioner) may bring an action for any damage to such interest, or, in other words, to his right of ultimate possession.

Rule 80.   1. Persons who have a separate interest and sustain a separate damage must sue separately.

2. Persons who have a separate interest, but sustain a joint damage, may sue either jointly or separately in respect thereof.

3. Persons who have a joint interest must sue jointly for an injury to it.

Rule 81. The right of action for a tort cannot be transferred or assigned.

Rule 82. Where several persons have a joint right of action for a tort it passes on the death of each to the survivors, and on the death of the last (if the right of action be one that survives) to his representatives.

PRINCIPAL AND AGENT.

Rule 83. A principal (or employer) can never sue for what is merely an injury to his agent (or servant), nor an agent (or servant) for what is merely an injury to his principal (or employer).

PARTNERS.

Rule 84. All the partners in a firm, or members of an unincorporated company, should join in an action for a wrong done to the firm or company. ·

Rule 85. An action for an injury to the property of a firm must be brought:

1. On the bankruptcy of the firm, by the trustee or trustees of the bankrupts.

2. On the bankruptcy of one or more partners, by the solvent partners, together with the trustee or trustees of the bankrupt partner or partners.

HUSBAND AND WIFE.

Rule 86. A husband and wife must sue jointly in three cases :

1 For injuries to the person, character, or property of the wife, committed before marriage.

2. For injuries to the person or character of the wife committed during coverture; and

3. For injuries for which the wife must sue as executrix or administratrix.

Rule 87. A husband may sue either alone or jointly with his wife for all injuries done during coverture to real property, of which the husband and wife are seised, or to which they are entitled in right of the wife.

Exception. Where a permanent injury is done to the wife's freehold.

Rule 88.   The husband must sue alone in respect of any injuries to personal property committed during coverture.

BANKRUPT AND TRUSTEE.

Rule 89.   The trustee and not the bankrupt must sue for injuries to the real or personal property of the bankrupt committed before the bankruptcy.

    Exception. Trespass to land before bankruptcy.

Rule 90.   For injuries to property acquired by the bankrupt after bankruptcy, either the trustee may sue or the bankrupt may sue if the trustee does not interfere.

Rule 91.   The bankrupt alone can sue for injuries to his person, feelings, or reputation.

EXECUTORS AND ADMINISTRATORS.

Rule 92.   The personal representatives of the deceased (*i. e.,* his executors or administrators) can sue for injuries to the property of the deceased done during his lifetime.

Rule 93.   The personal representatives of the deceased can not sue for injuries to the person, feelings, or reputation of the deceased.

    Exception. Where deceased has been killed by wrongful act or by negligence.

Rule 94.   The personal representatives of the deceased can sue for injuries to his personal property committed after his death.

Rule 95.   The real representative of the deceased (*i. e.,* his heir or devisee) can not sue for any wrong done to him.

ACTIONS FOR TORT — DEFENDANTS — GENERAL RULES.

Rule 96.   No person is liable to be sued for any injury of which he is not the cause.

Rule 97.   Any person who causes an injury to another is liable to be sued by the person injured.

    Exception. Where persons are protected from actions for torts by their positions, *e. g.,* a judge.

Rule 98.   One, or any, or all of several joint wrong-doers may be sued.

    Exception. Persons sued as joint owners of land.

Rule 99.
The liability to be sued for a tort can not be transferred or assigned.

Exception. Assignment by death.

Rule 100.
Each wrong-doer's separate liability to be sued for a tort passes on his death (if it survives at all) to his personal representatives. The joint liability of several wrong-doers passes on the death of each to the survivors.

PRINCIPAL AND AGENT.

Rule 101
A principal is liable to be sued for the torts of an agent either committed by the command of the principal, or subsequently assented to or ratified by him.

Rule 102.
An employer or master is liable to be sued for the torts of his servant if committed in the course of the servant's employment, and for his master's benefit, or in other words, in the service of his master.

Exception 1. Where the servant is injured by a fellow-servant.

Exception 2. Where the master is compelled by statute to employ a particular person.

Exception 3. Where the employer is a public officer under government.

Rule 103.
A servant or other agent is liable to the person wronged for acts of misfeasance, or positive wrong, in the course of his employment, but not for acts of non-feasance, or mere omission.

Subordinate rule. An action for tort may be brought either against the principal or against the immediate actor in the wrong, but can not be brought against an intermediate agent.

PARTNERS.

Rule 104.
One, or any, or all of the partners in a firm, or members of an unincorporated company, may be sued jointly for a wrong committed by the firm or company.

Exception. Where partners are sued as co-owners of land.

CORPORATIONS.

Rule 105.
A corporation or incorporated body can be sued for torts.

INFANTS.

Rule 106.
An infant may be sued for torts committed by him.

Exception. Where his fraud is closely connected with a contract.

HUSBAND AND WIFE.

Rule 107.
A husband and wife must be sued jointly for all torts committed by the wife either before marriage or during coverture.

Exception. Where her fraud is closely connected with a contract.

BANKRUPT AND TRUSTEE.

Rule 108.
A bankrupt can be sued both before and after obtaining an order of discharge for all torts committed by him.

EXECUTORS AND ADMINISTRATORS.

Rule 109.
The personal representatives of the deceased (*i. e.*, his executors or administrators) can not be sued for torts committed by him.

Exception 1. Injuries to property within 3 and 4 Will. IV. c. 42.[1]

Exception 2. Actions for dilapidations.[2]

Exception 3. Actions for tort brought in the form of actions on contract.

EJECTMENT — PLAINTIFFS.

Rule 110.
The claimant, or plaintiff, in ejectment must be a person who has the legal right to enter and take possession of the land, etc., in respect of which action is brought, as incident to some estate or interest therein.

Rule 111.
All the claimants, or plaintiffs, in whom the title is alleged to be, should join in bringing an action of ejectment.

EJECTMENT — DEFENDANTS.

Rule 112.
The persons to be made defendants in an action of ejectment (*i. e.*, to be named in the writ) are all the tenants in possession of the land, etc., sought to be recovered.

Rule 113.
The persons who have a right to defend in an action of ejectment are any persons named in the writ, and any person who is in possession by himself or his tenant.

[1] Not in force in the United States.

[2] The destruction or waste of buildings or other property belonging to a benefice in England.

CONSEQUENCES AT COMMON LAW OF NON-JOINDER AND OF
MIS-JOINDER OF PARTIES.

Ex-Contractu — Plaintiffs.

Non-joinder: If it *appears upon the face of the
pleadings* that there are other obligees, covenantees, or parties to the contract, who ought
to be, but are not, joined in the action, it
is fatal on *demurrer*, or *on motion in arrest
of judgment*, or *on error;* and though the
objection *may not appear on the face of the
pleadings*, the defendant may avail himself
of it either by *plea in abatement*, or as a
ground of non-suit on the trial upon the plea
of general issue.[1]

Mis-joinder: If it appears upon the face of the
pleadings that *too many* persons have been
made plaintiffs, the error will be fatal upon
demurrer, motion in arrest of judgment, or
on error; if the objection *does not appear
upon the face of the pleadings* the defendant
may avail himself of it as a *ground of non-
suit* on the trial.[2]

Defendants.

Non-joinder: If it appears upon the face of the
pleadings that one who should be a defendant is omitted, and that such person so
omitted is *still living*, the error will be fatal
on *demurrer*, on *motion in arrest of judgment*, or *on error;* but if the objection does
not so appear, it can only be taken by *plea
in abatement*, verified by affidavit.[3]

Mis-joinder: If *too many* persons be made defendants, and the objection appear on the
pleadings, any of the defendants may *demur,
move in arrest* of judgment or support a
writ of error; and if the objection do not
appear upon the pleadings the plaintiff may
be *non-suited* upon the trial, if he fail in
proving a joint contract.[4]

[1] Chit. Pl. 7, 8.
[2] *Ibid.* 8.
[3] *Ibid.* 32.
[4] *Ibid.* 34.

Ex-Delicto — Plaintiffs.

Non-joinder: In actions in form *ex-delicto*, if a party who ought to join be omitted, the objection can only be taken by *plea in abatement*, or by way of *apportionment of damages* on the trial.[1]

Mis-joinder: If, however, *too many* persons be made co-plaintiffs, the objection, if it appear on the record, may be taken advantage of by *demurrer*, by motion in *arrest of judgment*, or by *writ of error*, or, if the objection do not appear on the face of the pleadings, it will be a *ground of non-suit* on the trial.[2]

Defendants.

Non-joinder: If several persons jointly commit a tort, the plaintiff generally has his election to sue all or any of the parties, and non-joinder is not error.[3]

Mis-joinder: If several persons be made defendants jointly, *where the tort could not in point of law be joint*, they may *demur, move in arrest of judgment*, or have a *writ of error*, but the objection may be aided by the plaintiff's taking a verdict against one only. Where the tort may be joint, the joinder of more persons than were liable constitutes no objection, and one or more of them may be acquitted and a verdict taken against the others.[4]

---

[1] Chit. Pl. 55.
[2] *Ibid.* 56.

[3] *Ibid.* 75.
[4] *Ibid.* 74.

CHAPTER VI.

OF THE ORIGINAL WRIT.

Up to this point we have considered the necessary preliminaries to the bringing of an action. We must now learn how the action was in fact instituted at common law.

At the outset we must understand that, according to the rule of the Conqueror and of his successors, the Crown was "the fountain of all justice."[1] This conception was the opposite of that obtaining before the Conquest. "Neither at the beginning nor at the end of the Anglo-Saxon time, was the king considered in law as the fountain of justice. The law was administered in the popular courts, theoretically as the act of the freemen. It was strict law; the decision, when reached, was final in the eye of the law; and not even the Witan itself wielded any process by which the letter of the common law could be escaped."[2] There was a complete absence of equitable powers.

We have seen how William superseded the Witenagemote of the Saxon kings and instituted in its stead the one Supreme King's Court, the Aula Regis, a court of unlimited jurisdiction.[3]

This court very soon became a disturbing and an uncertain influence in the regular administration of justice. It was furnished with new processes of law in aid of its large and undefined jurisdiction, and very early in its history it clearly showed that it would not be confined by the limits of its predecessor, and that the object of its founder was to substitute *its* administration of justice for that of the prior local

---

[1] Bl. Com. III. 273 *.
[2] Anglo-Saxon Law, 26.

[3] The King's Peace, 46, 47.

tribunals.   We are now to inquire concerning the instrumentality which successfully transferred jurisdiction from
the old popular and local to the new royal centralized court.

"Under special commissions, the jurisdiction of the court
was limited to the trial of such causes as had been delegated
to the special members of the court.   The ordinary King's
Court, however, the full court sitting with the king, exercised a jurisdiction limited in fact only by the king's will.
That is, there was nothing to prevent the king from drawing
into his court all the causes of the people."[1]   This, in fact,
he did, and the means by which he accomplished this great
result was the original writ.

"Prior to the Conquest, writs were almost unknown in
England as judicial process.   No use for them had been
found, except for authorizing the trial of a cause before
some special delegate not possessed of the requisite jurisdiction.   It (the original writ) served this purpose afterwards
usefully, upon a more extensive scale; but it was now the
embodiment of the principle that the king personally was
the fountain of justice.   It was, indeed, the symbol and
expression of arbitrary power.   It expressed the king's sole
right over the dispensation of justice, a right which he exercised on his own terms until Magna Carta was extorted
from John."[2]

We learn from Glanvill that when any one complained to
the king, or to his justiciars, concerning his fee or his freehold, if the complaint was such as was proper for the determination of the King's Court, *or if the king was pleased to
have it decided there*, a writ called a writ of *præcipe* (command) was granted.[3]   This writ directed the sheriff to
command the defendant to surrender, without delay, to
the plaintiff the land in question; and if the defendant
failed to do so, to summon him before the king or his
justiciars at a certain time, to show why he had so failed.
There was another writ of *præcipe* of a similar character,
designed to give the King's Court jurisdiction over the

---

[1] Hist. Pr. 76.   [3] Glanv. Lib. 1, c. 5.
[2] *Ibid.* 199.

debts of the laity.[1] Again, in all writs addressed to the manorial courts issued by the king or his justiciar, it was provided that if the lord to whom the writ was addressed failed to do justice, in his manorial court, in favor of the party who sought it, then the king's officers (the sheriff or justiciar usually) should do it, and through this *nisi feceris* (unless you shall do it) clause many causes were drawn into the King's Court.[2]

Finally, by a fictitious averment that a tortious act had been committed within the *king's peace* (as contrasted with the *peace* of some local lord), the King's Court entertained jurisdiction of trespass to the person or to the property of an individual.

"Thus, by the writ process generally, partly by virtue of an insidious clause in the manorial writs of right, partly by open usurpation under the writs of *præcipe*, and partly by the use of a fiction in a plaintiff's appeal of trespass or theft, was finally obtained the jurisdiction which has supplied the superior courts of England and their new successor with business until the present day."[3] All of this jurisdiction thus acquired was in derogation of the rights of the popular courts and of manorial franchises, and rested upon the sole authority of the king.

We are now in a position to understand the full extent of Blackstone's meaning when he speaks of the original writ as "the foundation of the jurisdiction of that court (Common Pleas) *being the king's warrant for the judges to proceed to the determination* of the cause."[4] Again he says: "The original writ out of Chancery being the foundation and warrant of the whole proceedings in the Common Pleas, if the declaration does not pursue the nature of the writ, *the court's authority totally fails.*"[5] This is the reason why "the judges could not allow amendments, or pardon mistakes; they could not permit a party to change his cause of action, or to recover more than his writ called for; because any

---

[1] Hist. Pr. 77.
[2] *Ibid.* 79.
[3] *Ibid.* 85.

[4] Bl. Com. III. 273 *.
[5] *Ibid.* 393.

such departure from the original would have been a trans-
gression of their own instructions. The judges were not
commissioned simply to judge between the parties on such
evidence as might be produced, and to render an equitable
decision thereon; they were authorized to render only a
certain judgment if they found the party entitled to it. . . .
Viewed in this light, the technical strictness of the early
common-law judges is reasonable, and not the motiveless
quibbling about trifles that it is often represented to be." [1]

So purely personal to the king issuing it was this original
writ conceived to be that "antiently (until 1 Edw. VI.) by
the demise of the king, all suits depending in his courts
were at once discontinued, and the plaintiff was obliged to
renew the process by suing out a fresh writ from the successor; the virtue of the former writ being totally gone, and
the defendant no longer bound to attend in consequence
thereof." [2]

The first step, therefore, which an intending suitor took at
common law was to sue out an original writ suited to his
particular case. Blackstone speaks of suing it "from the
Court of Chancery, which is the *officina justitiæ* (the shop
or mint of justice) wherein all the king's writs are
framed." [3] The student must not be misled by this sentence; original writs were sued out centuries before the
equitable jurisdiction of the Court of Chancery was established.[4] The office of Chancellor had existed, according
to Lord Coke, from extreme antiquity,[5] and a charter of
Edward the Confessor is sealed by "Rembald, the King's
Chancellor." [6]

The Chancellor was the "King's Secretary, the Chaplain
of his Chapel, and the Keeper of his Seal. . . . By reason
of his position as custodian of the Great Seal he was the
head of the office in which the King's Charters were enrolled,
and whence the Original Writs were issued." [7] In Glan-

---

[1] Hammond's note to Bl. Com. III.
372.

[2] Bl. Com. III. 296 *.

[3] Bl. Com. III. 273 *.

[4] The Court of Chancery was regu-

larly established towards the end of the
reign of Edward III. Ker. Eq. Ju. 4, 30.

[5] 4 Inst. 78.

[6] The King's Peace, 31.

[7] Ker. Eq. Ju. 23.

vill's time, as we have seen, when any one was injured concerning his freehold, he complained to the king or to his justiciars, and petitioned that right should be done to him. These petitions passed through the Chancellor's Office, which was in its functions "a great secretarial bureau, a home office, a foreign office, and a ministry of justice."[1] Very little was done by the king that was not done by a document bearing the Great Seal, which was the *key of the kingdom.* Almost every message or mandate that came from the king, whether addressed to an emperor or to an escheator, to all of the king's liege subjects, or to one man only, was a document settled in the Chancery and sealed with the Great Seal.[2]

Originally, as has been shown, writs were granted in response to these petitions if the complaint was such as was proper for the determination of the King's Court, or if the king was pleased to have it decided there. While these writs specified with some particularity the subject-matter of the complaint, yet at the outset they had no connection whatever with the form of action or with the subsequent count or declaration, but were only general directions to do right to the plaintiff. Their office was simply to set on foot a suit under supreme authority.[3] "As the king's interference becomes more frequent and more normal, the work of penning such writs will naturally fall into the hands of subordinate officials, who will follow precedents and keep blank forms. A classification of writs will be the outcome; some will be granted more or less as a matter of course, will be *brevia de cursu,* writs of course; those which are directed to a feudal lord will be distinguished from those which are directed to a sheriff; those which bid the sheriff do justice, from those which bid him to summon the defendant to the king's own court; those which relate to the ownership of land from those which relate to debts."[4] Ultimately a particular form of writ became the only appropriate commencement of an action for a particular redress. But even

---

[1] P. & M. Hist. I. 172.
[2] *Ibid.* I. 173.

[3] Hist. Pr. 196. See also Min. Inst IV. 517, 518.
[4] P. & M. Hist. I. 129.

after the writ had thus come to be so closely connected with the remedy sought for, and until about the time of Glanvill, a writ to suit each case was framed and issued, until in 1258 the Provisions of Oxford[1] expressly forbade the Chancellor to frame new writs without the consent of the king and his council. "This, with the growing independence of the judiciary on the one hand, and the settlement of legal process on the other, terminated the right to issue special writs, and at last fixed the common writs in unchangeable form; most of which had by this time become developed into the final form in which for six centuries they were treated as precedents of declaration."[2]

These fixed forms were inadequate to meet the needs of a developing society. As we have seen a partial remedy was furnished by the 24th Chapter of the Statute of Westminster II., which, after providing for a few special cases to which no existing writ applied, enacts further that

" And whensoever from henceforth it shall fortune in the Chancery, that in one case a writ is found, and in like case falling under like law, and requiring like remedy, is found none, the clerks of the Chancery shall agree in making the writ; or the plaintiffs may adjourn it until the next Parliament; and let the cases be written in which they can not agree, and let them refer themselves until the next Parliament; and by consent of men learned in the law, a writ shall be made, lest it might happen after that the court should long time fail to minister justice unto complainants."[3]

As has been already noticed, Lord Coke asserts that this statute is merely declaratory of the Common Law, and Mr. Bigelow contends that it "was only an attempt to return to what had existed throughout English history until writs of course, supplemented by the restrictions contained in the Provisions of Oxford, had tied the hands of the courts."[4]

While it is true that the words of the statute gave no power

---

[1] So called because Parliament then sat at Oxford.

[2] Hist. Pr. 198.

[3] 2 Inst. 405.

[4] Hist. Pr. 198. See also Chit. Pl. 84; Kinlyside *v.* Thornton *et al.*, 2 Bl. Rep. 1113.

to make a completely new departure, for writs were only to be framed to fit cases similar to, but not identical with, cases falling within the existing writs *de cursu*, yet, as we have already said, the growth of English law has been accomplished through these actions on the case provided by this Statute of Westminster II.

In petty actions, wherein less than the value of forty shillings was involved, and which were brought in the court-baron or in the county court, no original writ was necessary; the foundation of such suits continued to be (as in the times of the Saxons) by *plaint*, that is, by a personal petition presented in open court to the judge, wherein the party injured sets forth his cause of action.[1]

It is proper here to refer again to a great grievance which was only remedied by the strong words of Magna Carta. Our ancestors had to purchase justice. These original writs were bought at a great price. "We may find creditors promising the king a quarter or a third of the debts they hope to recover by means of his writs."[2] "The idea that litigants were to be taxed as such, and that too without uniformity, for purposes of general revenue, and not merely to the extent of the cost of the clerical and ministerial work required in the course of an action, was never abandoned or relaxed in the twelfth century, even if the justice of it was questioned. . . . '*Nulli vendemus, nulli negabimus aut differemus rectum aut justiciam*'[3] — the most familiar passage of Magna Carta — has an unmistakable meaning. The practice, introduced by the Conqueror, of setting a price upon the dispensation of justice in the new forms, continued without intermission until a power had arisen strong enough to assert its right to stamp it out."[4]

An authoritative book called "The Register of Writs" was from most ancient times kept in the Chancery, wherein were entered all forms of writs once issued. This Register was not regarded as complete and final, but a common form

---

[1] Bl. Com. III. 273*.
[2] P. & M. Hist. I. 174.

[3] Lord Coke has *justitiam vel rectum* 2 Inst. 45.
[4] Hist. Pr. 190.

once settled was not to be lightly departed from, and any variations had to be supported by sufficient authority.[1]

The original writ was a mandatory letter issuing out of the Chancery, under the Great Seal and in the king's name, directed to the sheriff of the county where the injury was alleged to have been committed, containing a summary statement of the cause of complaint, and was in form either optional or peremptory; it was termed, according to the introductory words of the writ, either a *præcipe* (command) or a *si te fecerit securum* (if he shall make you secure). Whenever the plaintiff demanded something certain, which the defendant might himself perform, as the restoration of the possession of land, the payment of a liquidated debt, the rendition of an account, and the like, he might properly have a *præcipe*, an example of which is the following: —

ORIGINAL WRIT OF DEBT.

George the Fourth, &c., to the Sheriff of   , greeting :

  Command C. D., late of   , gentleman, that justly and without delay he render to A. B. the sum of   pounds, of good and lawful money of Great Britain, which he owes to and unjustly detains from him, as it is said.   And unless he shall do so, and if the said A. B. shall make you secure of prosecuting his claim, then summon, by good summoners, the said C. D., that he be before us, in eight days of St. Hilary, wheresoever we shall then be in England, to show wherefore he hath not done it; and have you there the names of the summoners and this writ.

  Witness ourself at Westminster, the   day of   , in the year of our reign.

Where nothing specific was demanded, but only unliquidated damages, to obtain which the intervention of a court was required, as in writs of trespass or case, there a *si te fecerit securum* was issued; an example of this is the following: —

ORIGINAL WRIT OF TRESPASS (FOR AN ASSAULT AND BATTERY).

George the Fourth, &c., to the Sheriff of   , greeting:

  If A. B. shall make you secure of prosecuting his claim, then put by gages and safe pledges C. D., late of   yeoman,

---

[1] P. & M. Hist. I. 174 ; Reeves' Hist. III. 437.

that he be before us on the morrow of All Souls, wheresoever we shall then be in England, to show wherefore, with force and arms, at   aforesaid, he made an assault upon the said A. B., and beat, wounded, and ill-treated him, so that his life was despaired of, and other wrongs to him there did to the damage of the said A. B. and against our peace; and have you there the names of the pledges and this writ.

 Witness ourself at Westminster, the ·   day of   , in the year of our reign.

It will be observed that the optional form, the *præcipe*, commands the defendant either himself to pay the debt to the plaintiff, or to show at a given time, and in the King's Court, why he has not paid it. In the peremptory form, however, the defendant is immediately called upon to appear in court, provided the plaintiff give good security to prosecute his claim. Both species of writs are *tested* (witnessed) in the king's own name, and are under the Great Seal of the realm. Originally, the plaintiff actually gave security in each case to prosecute his claim; if he brought his action without cause, or failed in the prosecution of it when brought, he was liable to an amercement from the Crown for making a false accusation; and the judgment against him still is "that he be in mercy." This giving of security became later a mere matter of form, and two men of straw,[1] John Doe and Richard Roe, were always returned as the standing pledges for this purpose.

The day on which the defendant is ordered to appear in court, and on which the sheriff is ordered to bring in the writ, and to report what he has done in pursuance of its commands, is called the *return* of the writ; it is then returned by him to the king's justices at Westminster. The writ was made returnable always upon some day in one of the four terms in which the court sat for the despatch of business, and at least fifteen days were allowed from its date, in order that the defendant might have time to come up to Westminster, even from the most remote part of the kingdom. These four annual terms of court were very ancient, and

---

[1] See Black's Law Dictionary, 767.

originated by reason of the exemption by the Church of certain holy seasons of the year from what was thought to be the profanation of legal strife. Thus Advent and Christmas were sacred seasons, and after them came the Hilary term, in January; Lent and Easter-tide were followed by the Easter term; Pentecost preceded Trinity term; and finally the long vacation, between midsummer and Michaelmas, which was allowed for the haytime and harvest, preceded Michaelmas term, in October. In every term there were stated days called days in bank, which were days of appearance in the Court of Common Pleas. These were generally a week apart, and had reference to some festival of the Church. On some one of these days in bank, all original writs were necessarily made returnable, and these were called the returns of that term. Although many of these return days were fixed on Sunday, yet the court never sat to receive them until the following Monday. On the first day in each term the court sat to take *essoins* (excuses) for such as did not appear in obedience to the writ, wherefore this is usually called the *essoin* day of the term. But, according to a very ancient practice, the person summoned had three days of grace, beyond the return of the writ, in which to make his appearance; for if he appeared on the fourth day inclusive (*quarto die post*) it was sufficient.[1]

In the United States original writs, properly so-called, never existed. The constitutions and the laws of the United States, and of the several States, confer and fix jurisdiction upon the courts. While these writs have been abolished in England, their original functions and their history are yet vital and instructive. For this reason they have been considered more in detail than their practical importance demands. In theory, some conduit pipe is still requisite to transfer jurisdiction from the sovereign, whether monarch or people, to the delegated tribunal. Such conduit was the original writ.

It is stated by Stephen that, "One object of the original writ, therefore, is to compel the appearance of the defendant

[1] Bl. Com. III. 278*.

in court."[1]   As has been pointed out by Hammond, it is a mistake to identify the original writ with our modern summons, or with other original process to bring the defendant into court.[2]   A defendant cannot be damaged by the mere suing out against him of the original, so that no action lies for the issuing of that original.[3]   But if the original were process upon which the defendant could be compelled to come into court, an action would manifestly lie.   As we shall presently see, the first step to compel the defendant's appearance was *judicial*, as contrasted with *original*, process.

In the King's Bench the plaintiff's attorney commences the suit by preparing a draft (called a *præcipe*) of the original writ, appropriate to the proposed action, in such form as is thought conformable to precedent, and the subsequent steps are taken by the proper officers of the court.   In this country, the *præcipe* signifies the written direction given by the plaintiff's attorney to the clerk of the court to issue process in a particular case.

[1] Steph. Pl 41.
[2] Bl. Com. III. 372.

[3] F. N. B. 95, note a.

CHAPTER VII.

OF THE PROCEEDINGS IN AN ACTION, FROM ITS COMMENCEMENT TO ITS TERMINATION.

AFTER an action at law has been commenced, the regular steps in succession are, The Process, The Appearance of the Defendant, The Pleadings, The Trial, The Judgment, and The Execution. Finally there may be Proceedings in Error.

THE PROCESS.

After suing out the original writ, the next step in the prosecution of the suit is called the *process*, and is the means of compelling the defendant to appear in court.

All process having this object in view was called *original*, as distinguished from *mesne* process, issuing pending the suit for interlocutory matters, and from *final* process which was always in execution of the court's judgment. Only the *original writ* issued from the Chancery, and was under the Great Seal of the Kingdom. All subsequent *process*, whether *original, mesne, or final*, was *judicial process*, and issued out of the court of common law, into which the original writ was made returnable, under the private seal of that court; it bore *teste* in the name of the chief justice of that court.

Process at common law varied "in stringency from the polite summons to the decree of outlawry."[1] The initial process, the *summons*, was a warning to appear in court at the return of the original writ, given to the defendant in person, or left on his farm or land by two of the sheriff's messengers, called *summoners*. In real actions the warning on the land was given by erecting a white stick or wand on the defendant's ground, and, later, notice had also to be

[1] P. & M. Hist. II. 576.

proclaimed on some Sunday before the door of the parish church. If the defendant disobeyed this verbal summons, the next compulsory step was a writ of *Attachment* or *pone*, so-called from the words of the writ "*pone per vadium et salvos plegios*" (put by gage and safe pledges). This writ commanded the sheriff to attach the defendant by taking *gage*, *i. e.*, certain of his goods, which he forfeited if he did not appear, or by making him find *safe pledges*, *i. e.*, sureties, who should be fined in case of his non-appearance. In cases of trespass *vi et armis*, or for other injuries which though not forcible are yet trespasses against the peace, as *deceit*, and *conspiracy*, where the violence of the wrong requires a more speedy remedy, this was the first and immediate process. If the defendant still proved obdurate, then he was further compelled by a writ of *distringas* (you shall distrain), or *distress infinite*, under which he was gradually stripped of all his goods by repeated distresses, until he rendered obedience to the king's writ by appearing in court. Here process ended in the case of injuries without force; for the law regarded a man who had no property as incapable of making satisfaction, and therefore looked upon all further process as useless. Besides, it did not permit the feudal lord to be deprived of *his man's* services by process against his person for injuries merely civil. But, in cases of injuries accompanied with force, the law punished the breach of the peace, and endeavored to prevent its recurrence by allowing process against the *defendant's person* in case he neglected to appear upon the former process of attachment, or if he had no property whereby to be attached. This process was a *capias ad respondendum* (you shall take for answering), under which the defendant's body could be subjected to imprisonment. Subsequently, in order to reach indigent wrong-doers, this process was also allowed by statute in actions of account, of debt, of detinue, in all actions on the case, and finally in almost every species of complaint. As an instance of the indirect way in which English law has surmounted obstacles for the removal of which the times were not yet ripe, it should be noted, that, before this amendatory legislation was had, a practice had been introduced of bringing an original writ of trespass *quare clausum fregit*, for breaking the defendant's close *vi et armis*, which, by the old common law, subjected the defendant's person to be arrested by writ of *capias;* and then, by connivance of the court, the plaintiff might proceed to prosecute the defendant, who was under arrest for an imaginary trespass, for any other less forcible injury. This writ of *capias* commanded the sheriff to take the body of the defendant, if he were found in the sheriff's bailiwick or county, and him safely to keep, so that he might be produced in court on the return day to answer to the complaint against him. If the sheriff of Oxfordshire (in which county the injury may be supposed to be committed and the action to be laid) cannot find the defendant in his jurisdiction, he returns that the defendant is not found (*non est inventus*) in his bailiwick; whereupon another writ issues, called a *testatum capias*, directed to the sheriff of the county where the defendant is supposed to reside, for example, Berkshire; this second recites the first writ, and adds that *it is testified* (*testatum est*) that the defendant *latitat et discurrit* (lurks and wanders about) in his bailiwick, wherefore he (the sheriff of Berkshire) is commanded to take the defendant, as in the first *capias*. But where a defendant absconds, and the plaintiff desires to proceed to outlawry against him, if the sheriff cannot find him upon the first writ of *capias*, and returns a *non est inventus*, there issues out an *alias* (formerly) writ of *capias*, and after that a *pluries* (often), to the same general effect as the former. And, if a *non est inventus* is returned upon all of them, then a writ of *exigent* or *exigi facias* (you shall cause to be exacted) may be sued out, which requires the sheriff to cause the defendant to be proclaimed or exacted in five county courts, successively, to surrender himself; if he does, then the sheriff shall take him, as in a *capias;* but if he does not appear, and is returned *quinto exactus* (for the fifth time exacted), he shall then be outlawed by the coroners of the county. For greater publicity, it was subsequently required that a *writ of procla-*

mation should issue at the same time with the *exigent*, commanding the sheriff of the county, wherein the defendant dwells, to make three proclamations of the impending process in places the most public, and where the fact would most likely come to the defendant's knowledge, a month before the outlawry shall take place. This judgment of outlawry put a man out of the protection of the law, made him incapable of bringing a legal action, and forfeited all his goods and chattels to the king. If, after outlawry, the defendant appeared publicly, he could be arrested by a writ of *capias utlagatum* (you shall take the outlaw), and committed to prison until the outlawry should be reversed, which reversal was made, in civil cases, upon almost any pretext. "Outlawry was usually a last resort. It was seldom proclaimed except as punishment for contumacy; that is, for unyielding disobedience of the requirements of the law when once set in motion, or of the commands of the king or of the courts. . . . The contumacy of an alleged criminal, or of a recusant defendant, if not already known to the king, was reported to him, on judgment of court, for the final sentence of the law. And now, unless the influence of others or the king's own disposition towards him availed, the hopeful outlaw, who had preferred the uncertainty of concealment and flight to the doubtful event of the ordeal or the duel, or to the certainty of imprisonment, was turned over to the tender mercies of that disproportionate part of the population who, strangers to pity, knew no shrinking at the sight of blood."[1]

Two things are especially to be noted by the student in connection with this procedure enforced through so many centuries. The first is the tedious forbearance of the law. "Very slowly it turns the screw which brings the pressure to bear upon the defendant. . . . If we would understand its patience, we must transport ourselves into an age when steam and electricity had not become ministers of the law, when roads were bad and when no litigant could appoint an attorney until he had appeared in court. Law must be slow

[1] Hist. Pr. 348, 349.

in order that it may be fair."[1] Secondly, we must especially
observe that no judgment can be given against the absent in
a personal action. There is no *judgment by default*. "One
thing our law would not do, the obvious thing. It would
exhaust its terrors in the endeavor to make the defendant
appear, but it would not give judgment against him until he
had appeared, and, if he was obstinate enough to endure imprisonment or outlawry, *he could deprive the plaintiff of his
remedy*. . . . Instead of saying to the defaulter, 'I don't
care whether you appear or no,' it sets its will against his
will: 'But you shall appear.' To this we may add, that the
emergence and dominance of the semi-criminal action of
trespass prevents men from thinking of our personal actions
as mere contests between two private persons. The contumacious defendant has broken the peace, is defying justice
and must be crushed. *Whether the plaintiff's claim will
be satisfied is a secondary question*."[2] It required nearly six
centuries to correct this primitive misconception.[3]

As the king, at first actually and later in contemplation of
law, always sat in person in the Court of King's Bench, it
might be supposed that no original writ was required for the
institution of a case in that court, yet, as a matter of fact,
suits were frequently there begun by original, particularly
in actions of ejectment and of trespass. An explanation of
this is furnished by the following sentence of Blackstone:
"As the justices of this court have, by its fundamental
constitution, power to determine all offences and trespasses,
by the common law and custom of the realm, *it needed no
original writ from the Crown to give it cognizance of any
misdemeanor in the county wherein it resides*."[4] In other
cases, therefore, it would need an original writ to entertain
jurisdiction of civil causes. In this court all writs were
returnable, not at Westminster, where the Court of
Common Pleas was fixed by Magna Carta, but, "*ubicunque
fuerimus in Anglia*" (wheresoever we (the king) shall
be in England), the Court of King's Bench having been

---

[1] P. & M. Hist. II. 589.
[2] P. & M. Hist. II. 592, 593.
[3] Stat. 2 Will. IV. c. 39, sec. 16 (1832).
[4] Bl. Com. III. 285 *.

removable into any part of England at the pleasure of the Crown.

BILL OF MIDDLESEX, LATITAT AND QUO MINUS.

This brings us to the consideration of the fictions, whereby the King's Bench and the Exchequer intruded upon the civil jurisdiction exclusively belonging to the Common Pleas.

As has been said, the King's Bench needed no original writ to give it cognizance of any misdemeanor committed in the county wherein it happened to sit. But, as by the very fact of its coming into any county it superseded the ordinary administration of justice therein by the usual authorities thereof, it had to invent a process of its own to bring in such persons as were accused of committing any forcible injury therein. Such process was called a bill of Middlesex, when the court was sitting in Middlesex, of Kent, when sitting there, and, in a word, always took the name of the particular county where the King's Bench was at the time sitting. This bill of Middlesex (for the court ordinarily sat in that county) was formerly always issued in consequence of a *plaint* of trespass *quare clausum fregit*, entered in the records of the court, and was in form a *capias* directed to the sheriff of that county, commanding him to take the defendant and have him before the king at Westminster, on a day named, to answer to the plaintiff of a plea of trespass. If the sheriff does not find the defendant in Middlesex, he returns "*non est inventus,*" whereupon, as we have before seen, there issues out a writ of "*latitat*" (called *testatum capias* in the Common Pleas) to the sheriff of the county where the defendant actually is, upon which he can be arrested and compelled to give bail to appear at Westminster to answer the supposed trespass. Of course, if the defendant be actually arrested in Middlesex upon the bill of Middlesex, no "*latitat*" is required. It is by means of this proceeding that the King's Bench acquired its usurped jurisdiction, and in this way: the accusation of trespass in Middlesex gives this court jurisdiction of the alleged trespass without any original writ. But when once the defendant is in the custody of the court he is its prisoner. "By practice of very ancient date in all personal suits, where an officer or *prisoner* of the King's Bench, or an officer of the Common Pleas, is defendant, the course has been to proceed against such defendant in the court in which he is officer or prisoner by exhibiting (*i. e.*, filing) a *bill* against him, among the records of the court, *without suing out any original writ*. For when the defendant is in either of the privileged characters above mentioned the two great purposes of the original writ are superseded. As he is actually present in court, or considered as being so, no original, of course, is requisite to enforce his appearance;[1] and, as he is already within the jurisdiction of the court as its officer or prisoner, an instrument of that kind is not deemed necessary to give authority for the institution of the suit. This practice, however, is confined to personal actions, and it does not appear that actions real or mixed have ever been allowed to be thus commenced."[2]

In order to found this jurisdiction, it is not necessary that the defendant be actually in the custody of the marshal of the court or in its prison (the marshalsea); for, as soon as he appears, or puts in bail, to the process, he is deemed by so doing to be in such custody of the marshal as will give the court jurisdiction to proceed. Hence, in the bill of process, a complaint of trespass is always suggested, whatever else may be the real cause of action. Thus we have the artifice completely successful. Upon an imaginary trespass, a constructive prisoner has been brought within the jurisdiction of the court; once there, he can be proceeded against upon any personal cause of action whatsoever, although independently of the fictitious trespass and arrest the court would have no jurisdiction in the premises.

The Court of Exchequer was not to be outdone by the King's Bench.[3] In this court there was no proceeding by original writ, because in it the king was always plaintiff,

---

[1] It will be recollected that the original writ did not enforce the defendant's appearance. *Ante*, 147.

[2] Steph. Pl. 76.

[3] It is said by Kerly (Eq. Ju. 12) that the fictitious use of the writ of *quo minus* by the Exchequer ante dated the similar use of the bill of Middlesex by

and was there calling upon his debtors to account to him for their debts, "as the withholding and non-payment thereof is an injury to his *jura fiscalia* [revenue rights]."[1] As all the officers of this court have, like those of the other superior courts, the privilege of suing and of being sued only in their own court, so also the king's debtors and farmers, and all accountants of the Exchequer, are privileged to sue and implead one another, or any stranger, in all common-law actions where only the personalty is concerned. This gave a foundation for a fictitious complaint that the intended defendant, in a proposed case, owes money to the intending plaintiff, who avers himself to be a debtor of the king, and the less able to pay that debt because the defendant has failed to pay him. The writ upon which all proceedings are based in this court is called a *quo minus* (by which the less). The plaintiff suggests that he is the king's farmer or debtor, and that the defendant has done him the injury or damage complained of, *quo minus sufficiens existit*, "by which he is the less able," to pay the king his debt or rent. Upon this writ the defendant may be arrested as upon a *capias*, and, when he is thus brought within the jurisdiction of the court, he may be proceeded against for any personal cause of action. By this suggestion of privilege, as the king's debtor, which was permitted to all as a mere fiction, any person, as well as the king's accountant, might be admitted to sue in the Exchequer, and so the Court of Exchequer successfully rivalled the King's Bench in the enlargement of its jurisdiction.[2] The *quo minus* was an instance of the process called an *attachment of privilege*, which was in nature a *capias*, and which issued at the suit of any officer of the King's Bench, Common Pleas, or Exchequer, against any person liable to him in a personal cause of action. In such cases, by a very ancient privilege, the officer was allowed to

the King's Bench. But he cites no authority for his statement. Blackstone, Reeves, and Stephen write as if the King's Bench led the way in this assumption of jurisdiction. It is stated in Hargrave's Law Tracts (422), that

the date of innovation in either court is not certainly known.

[1] Bl Com. III. 45 *.

[2] For observations on these fictions, see Harg. Law Tracts, 422.

file a declaration in his own court against the defendant with-out having obtained an original writ, and the defendant's appearance was enforced by this attachment of privilege.[1]

The ancient rules connected with the arrest of the defend-ant, the giving of *common* and of *special bail*, and the reason for adding the clause *ac etiam* (and also) to the usual complaint of trespass and later to the writ of *capias*, have now no sufficient interest to require their consideration here. A reference to Tidd's Practice will fully inform the student upon these points.

In England, as has been said, original writs have been abolished, and the rules of the Supreme Court of Judicature, promulgated in 1883, authorize and require the simplest form of process. Order II., Paragraph I., provides as follows: —

"Every action in the High Court shall be commenced by a writ of summons, which shall be indorsed with a statement of the nature of the claim made, or of the relief or remedy required in the action, and which shall specify the Division of the High Court to which it is intended that the action should be assigned."

The general form of this writ of summons is the follow-ing: —

In the High Court of Justice.   Between A. B., Plaintiff,
          Division.   and
                                   C. D. and E. F., Defendants.

Victoria, by the Grace of God, &c.

To C. D., of   , in the county of

We command you, That within eight days after the service of this writ on you, inclusive of the day of such service, you do cause an appearance to be entered for you in an action at the suit of A. B.; and take notice that in default of your so doing the plaintiff may proceed therein, and judgment may be given in your absence.

Witness: ROUNDELL, EARL OF SELBORNE, Lord High Chan-cellor of Great Britain, the   day of   , in the year of Our Lord one thousand eight hundred and

[1] Steph. Pl. 77.

Memorandum to be subscribed on the writ.

N. B. — This writ is to be served within twelve calendar months
from the date thereof, or, if renewed, within six calendar months from the date of the last renewal, including
the day of such date, and not afterwards.

The defendant (or defendants) may appear hereto by entering
an appearance (or appearances), either personally or by solicitor,
at the Central Office, Royal Courts of Justice, London.

Indorsements to be made on the writ before issue thereof.

The plaintiff's claim is for, &c.
This writ was issued by the said plaintiff, who resides at
, or, this writ was issued by E. F., of , whose
address for service is , solicitor for the said plaintiff,
who resides at (mention the city, town, or parish, and
also the name of the street and number of the house of the plaintiff's residence, if any).

Indorsement to be made on the writ after service thereof.

This writ was served by me at on the defendant
on the day of
Indorsed the day of 18
(Signed)
(Address)

In this country generally a *summons* is the form of process
used to institute a suit, and to require the defendant to
appear in court. The form now in force in the Supreme
Court of the District of Columbia is the following (Rule
11): —

SUMMONS.

In the Supreme Court of the District of Columbia.

A. B., Plaintiff,
  vs. } At Law, No.
C. D., Defendant.

The President of the United States to the defendant,
  greeting:
You are hereby commanded to appear in this court on or before the twentieth day, exclusive of Sundays and legal holidays,
after the day of the service of this writ on you, to answer the

plaintiff's suit and show why he should not have judgment against you for the cause of action stated in his declaration.

Witness the honorable   , chief justice of said court, the   day of   A. D. 18 .

By   , Clerk.
          , Assistant Clerk.

Rule 10.

A notice to plead shall be subscribed to every declaration in the following form:

The defendant is to plead hereto on or before the twentieth day, exclusive of Sundays and legal holidays, occurring after the day of the service hereof; otherwise, judgment.

Except this notice to plead, subscribed to the declaration, no rule to plead or demand of plea shall be necessary.

A *capias ad respondendum*, authorizing the arrest of the defendant's person, is of very limited use in this country as original process. It is allowed in some jurisdictions by express statutory authority in cases of fraud, breach of trust, or other gross wrong-doing.

An *attachment* is similarly authorized against the property of absconding debtors, non-residents, and other classes of persons specifically designated in the statutes providing for this summary process.

Reference must be had to local legislation upon these subjects, and to books of practice for information as to the proper service of process and kindred topics.

The Appearance of the Defendant.

The main object of all process was to compel the appearance of the defendant, for until that was effected there could, in a *personal* action, be no pleading, and of course no judgment given, nor could any other act be done in court beyond the issuing of the process, which, as we have seen, had its final resource in outlawry. When the defendant appeared the following entry was made upon the records of the court: "*And the said C. D.* [the defendant] *by E. F., his attorney, comes*" (*venit*), &c. This word, *venit*, is the statement on record of the defendant's appearance in court, and was at one time erroneously said to be necessary to make

him a party to the suit.[1] The appearance may be stated to
be in person or by attorney, according to the fact, but in
pleas to the jurisdiction it must be in person. Actual and
personal appearance in open court, either by the defendant
or by his attorney, was originally necessary.[2] This, however, is no longer required, and the defendant's appearance
is effected by making a formal entry of the fact in the proper
office, or, if he has been arrested, by his giving bail.[3] An
entry of a general appearance will waive objection to the
jurisdiction of the court over the person of the defendant, to
a misnomer, to want of service of process, and to formal
defects. If, therefore, the defendant desire to urge these
objections, he should appear *specially*, and, where a plea to
the jurisdiction is interposed, in person.[4] As the appearance was at first *actually* and afterwards *constructively* in
open court, it, of course, always purported to be in term
time, when only pleading and all proceedings whatever in
open court can take place.

As the plaintiff has, by the institution of the suit, himself
appeared, no formal entry of his appearance is made, and,
upon appearance of the defendant, both parties are considered as in court, and the *pleadings* begin.[5]

THE PLEADINGS.

"Pleadings are the mutual altercations of the parties to
a suit, expressed in legal form, and in civil actions reduced
to writing. In a more limited sense, however, ' the pleadings' [in the plural] comprehend only those allegations, or
altercations, which are subsequent to the count or declaration. In England these altercations were anciently *oral*,
having been offered *viva voce* by the respective parties or
their counsel, in open court; as is still generally done in
the pleadings on the part of the defendant, or prisoner, in
criminal prosecutions. And hence it is in the Norman

---

[1] Chit. Pl. 367.
[2] Stéph. Pl. 58.
[3] *Ibid.* 61.
[4] Knox *v.* Summers, 3 Cranch, 496;

St. Louis, &c. Railway *v.* McBride, 141
U. S. 127.

[5] The learning on the Subject of
Appearance will be found in Com. Dig.
Title Pleader, B.

language, in which most of the ancient books of the English law are written, the pleadings are frequently denominated the *parol;* though for centuries past all pleadings in civil actions have been required to be written. In some instances, however, the term *parol* is still used to denote the entire pleadings in a cause, as when in an action brought against an infant heir, on an obligation of his ancestor's, he prays that the *parol may demur, i. e.,* that the pleadings may be stayed, till he shall attain full age. The mutual altercations, which constitute the pleadings in civil actions, consist of those formal allegations and denials, which are offered on one side for the purpose of maintaining the suit, and on the other for the purpose of defeating it; and which, generally speaking, are predicated only of matters of *fact.* For pleading is practically nothing more than affirming or denying, in a formal and orderly manner, those *facts* which constitute the ground of the plaintiff's demand and of the defendant's defence. Pleading therefore consists in merely alleging matters of fact, or in denying what is alleged as such by the adverse party." [1]

But we have very imperfectly described Pleading when we have said that it consists in merely affirming or denying facts. Every pleading involves a syllogism "of which the body of judicial rules is the major, and the declaration of facts the minor premise." [2] Even the final judgment of a court "may be described as a conclusion from a legal syllogism. The question, Are such cases as that alleged entitled to redress? involves the major premise; Is this case such? the minor; and if both inquiries are answered affirmatively, the judgment follows as a necessary inference." [3]

In pleading, therefore, every averment of fact *implies* some principle of law by virtue of which the statement of fact becomes a claim of right. If it does not, then it is *demurrable, i. e.,* the opposite party can reply: " *Whether your averment of fact be true or not, it can not be made the foundation of any legal claim against me.*" An illustration

[1] Gould's Pl. 1, 2.   [3] Hare on Contracts, 43, 44.
[2] Anglo-Saxon Law, 183.

will make this clear. In an action brought for a trespass committed upon land, we may suppose the plaintiff to say: "*Against him who has forcibly entered upon my land, I have a right by law to recover damages: The defendant has forcibly entered upon my land: Therefore, against him I have a right by law to recover damages.*" We may suppose the defendant to answer: "*If he upon whose land I have forcibly entered, releases to me his right of action for such entry, he has thenceforth no right by law to recover damages for such entry against me: But the plaintiff has released to me his right of action for my entry upon his land: Therefore he has, by law, no right to recover damages for that cause against me.*" To this the plaintiff may have his reply ready as follows: "*A release extorted from me by duress does not in law destroy any pre-existing right of mine to recover damages: But the release pleaded by the defendant was extorted from me by duress: Therefore that release does not destroy my right to recover damages against him.*" [1]

In this process, which might be prolonged, the major premise, containing the affirmation of the rule of law relied upon by the plaintiff or by the defendant in their respective pleadings, has been expressed; the pleadings are, in fact, made substantially as follows: *The defendant has forcibly entered upon my land.* To which the defendant answers: *The plaintiff has released to me his right of action.* Whereto the plaintiff replies: *That release was extorted from me by duress.* It is thus seen that the pleadings in the case supposed have consisted only of the several minor premises, each asserting matter of fact, and that the major premise, involving the rule of law relied upon to give legal vitality to its minor, is in each case only implied.

Let us now suppose a case in which the minor premise is this: "*For ten years I conducted a profitable school in London, when the defendant established a new school near mine, and my pupils deserted me and resorted to his school to my great loss.*" Here it is at once perceived that there is no valid

---

[1] Gould's Pl. chap. I.

major premise implied, and hence the plaintiff's averment of fact is impotent, and therefore demurrable.

The facts are alleged because they are supposed to be unknown to the judges. But, as these judges are presumed to know judicially what the law applicable to any state of facts is, it is not necessary to allege the general rules of the law.

As has been said, these pleadings were originally spoken by the parties themselves or by their counsel in open court.[1] They were then minuted down by the chief clerk or prothonotary, and, together with the entries from time to time made touching the cause, they constituted the *record* in the cause.

This record, when complete, was preserved as a *perpetual, intrinsic,* and *exclusively admissible* testimony of all the judicial transactions which it comprised. From the beginning of the reign of Richard I. (1189) commences a still extant series of records down to the present day; and such, as far back as can be traced, has always been the stable and authentic quality of these documents in contemplation of law.[2]

As this record was originally the contemporaneous minute made by the prothonotary, it was entered as a narrative in the third person, and hence the pleadings follow the same form of expression, *e. g.,* " *C. D comes and defends the wrong and injury, &c., and says, &c.*"

It was the office of the judges to direct and control this oral contention conducted before them. This they so managed as to compel the disputants to come finally to some specific fact, affirmed by one and denied by the other, or to some disputed point of law. Then the parties were said to be *at issue (ad exitum, i. e., at the end* of their pleading). The question so determined upon was specifically called *The Issue,* and was, from its nature, either an issue *in fact,* or an issue in *law.* The latter the judges themselves decided; the former was referred to such one of the various methods'

---

[1] Interesting examples of this early *viva voce* pleading are given by Reeves in his History of the English Law, II. 219–223 ; also by Warren in his Law Studies, 722, 723, note.

[2] Steph. Pl. 61.

of trials then practised as the court thought applicable, or was, when proper, by mutual agreement of the parties, referred to a trial by jury.[1]

CONTINUANCES.

These proceedings of course required time, and yet in contemplation of law the parties were supposed to be always in court ready to urge their respective contentions. To meet this difficulty, the law allowed the proceedings to be adjourned over from one term to another, or from one day to another in the same term. When this happened, an entry of an adjournment to a given day, and of its cause, was made on the parchment roll (the record), and by that entry the parties were also appointed to re-appear on the given day in court.

Such adjournment was called a continuance. If any interval took place without such an adjournment, duly obtained and entered, the break or chasm thus occasioned was called a *discontinuance,* and the cause was considered as *out of court* by the interruption, and was not allowed afterward to proceed.[2]

It was probably in the middle of the reign of Edward III. (1327–1377) that pleadings ceased to be had orally or in open court. Gradually the pleader discontinued the oral delivery, and in lieu of it entered his statement, in the first instance, upon the parchment roll on which the record used to be drawn up. The pleader of the other party had access to this roll in order that he might prepare his answer, which he afterwards entered in the same manner, and the roll thus became both the pleadings themselves and also their record. Later, as more convenient, the pleadings were first put on paper, then delivered in that shape to the adverse party, or filed in the proper court office, and not entered of record until a subsequent stage of the cause.[3] These pleadings so written are framed upon the same principles as those which governed the oral allegations. The

[1] Steph. Pl. 59.   [2] *Ibid.* 60.   [3] *Ibid.* 63.

parties are made to come to *issue* exactly in the same manner as when really opposed to each other in verbal altercation at the bar of the court; and all the rules which the judges of former times prescribed to the actual disputants before them are, as far as possible, still enforced with respect to these paper pleadings.[1]

The oral pleadings could formerly be delivered by none but regular advocates, and so it is now necessary that these paper pleadings should be signed by a *barrister;* in fact, however, they are frequently prepared by persons of learning, not barristers, who are known by the name of *special pleaders.*[2]

Having learned generally what the pleadings in a cause are, we must next consider their respective titles, functions, and order. We have reached the point when the parties are in court. As they stand opposite to each other, it next becomes necessary for the plaintiff to state his case by his own mouth or by that of his pleader. His statement is called in Latin *narratio* (story or narrative), in French *conte;* in English it was probably first called *tale,*[3] but later *count* in real, and *declaration* in personal and mixed actions; ultimately the term " declaration " was applied commonly in all actions.

THE DECLARATION.

Originally the declaration was "a formal statement bristling with sacramental words, an omission of which would be fatal. . . . In a civil action begun by writ the plaintiff's count must not depart by a hair's breadth from the writ, or there will be a variance of which the defendant will take advantage."[4] In Anglo-Saxon times, when, according to the old procedure, a defendant had to repeat the claim of the plaintiff and to deny it word for word, *he lost his suit if he stammered* in the repetition.[5]

The brief statement of the original writ must be expanded, and also made more detailed, by the declaration. "Thus a

[1] Steph. Pl. 64.
[2] *Ibid.* 64.
[3] P. & M. Hist. II. 602.

[4] *Ibid.* II. 603.
[5] Anglo-Saxon Law, 183.

writ of Debt will merely tell William that he must say why he has not paid fifty marks which he owes to Alan and unjustly detains; but the count [declaration] will set forth how on a certain day came this William to this Alan and asked for a loan of fifty marks, how the loan was made and was to have been repaid on a certain day, and how, despite frequent requests, William has refused and still refuses to pay it. The count on a Writ of Right will often be an elaborate history. A seisin as of fee and of right with a taking of *esplees* [profits or produce of the land] will be attributed to some ancestor of the demandant [plaintiff], and then the descent of this right will be traced down a pedigree from which no step may be omitted."[1]

The pleading is said to begin with the declaration or count, which is a statement on the part of the plaintiff of his cause of action. In the declaration, the plaintiff, as we have seen, states the nature and quality of his case more fully than in the original writ, but still in strict conformity with the tenor of that instrument.[2]

This will be more readily understood by a consideration of two forms of declarations, corresponding with the specimens of original writs already given.

DECLARATION IN DEBT.

On a Bond.

In the King's Bench,   Term,   in the   year of
    the reign of King George the Fourth:

Middlesex, to wit, C. D. was summoned to answer A. B. of a plea, that he render to the said A. B. the sum of   pounds, of good and lawful money of Great Britain, which he owes to and unjustly detains from him. And thereupon the said A. B. by   , his attorney, complains: For That Whereas the said C. D. heretofore, to wit, on the   day of   , in the year of our Lord   , at   , in the County of   , by his certain writing obligatory, sealed with his seal, and now shown to the court here (the date whereof is the day and year aforesaid) acknowledged himself to be held and firmly bound to the said A. B. in the sum of   pounds, above demanded, to be paid to the said A. B. Yet the said C. D. (although often requested)

---

[1] P. & M. Hist. II. 603.   [2] Steph. Pl. 65.

hath not as yet paid the said sum of   pounds above demanded, or any part thereof, to the said A. B.; but so to do hath
hitherto wholly refused and still refuses, to the damage of
the said A. B. of   pounds; and therefore he brings his
suit, &c.

DECLARATION IN TRESPASS (FOR AN ASSAULT AND BATTERY).

In the King's Bench,   Term, in the   year of the reign
     of King George the Fourth:

Middlesex, to wit, C. D. was attached to answer A. B. of a
plea, wherefore he, the said C. D., with force and arms at   ,
in the county of   , made an assault upon the said A. B., and
beat, wounded, and ill-treated him, so that his life was despaired
of, and other wrongs to him there did, to the damage of the said
A. B. and against the peace of our Lord the now King. And
thereupon the said A. B., by   , his attorney, complains:
For that the said C. D. heretofore, to wit, on the   day of
    , in the year of our Lord   , with force and arms, at
     aforesaid, in the county aforesaid, made an assault upon
the said A. B. and then and there beat, wounded, and ill-treated
him, so that his life was despaired of, and other wrongs to the
said A. B. then and there did, against the peace of our said Lord
the King, and to the damage of the said A. B. of   pounds;
and therefore he brings his suit, &c.

Similar declarations to the two preceding would to-day in
the English Supreme Court of Judicature be in the following
form: —

ACTION ON AN ANNUITY BOND.

1. The plaintiff's claim is for principal and interest due upon
the defendant's bond to the plaintiff, dated the first day of January, 1883, and conditioned for payment to the plaintiff of £150
half-yearly, on the 1st of July and the 1st of January in every
year during the life of the plaintiff.

2. Two instalments, of £150 each, due on the 1st of July,
1883, and the 1st of January, 1884, are due and unpaid.

Particulars: —

Principal £300 0 0
Interest 5 0 0
                         £305 0 0

The plaintiff claims £305.

ACTION FOR ASSAULT AND BATTERY.

1. The plaintiff has suffered damage from personal injuries to the plaintiff, caused by the defendant assaulting him on the 1st of May, 1882, and beating him about the head and shoulders.

Particulars of expenses: —

Mr. Jones, Surgeon £20 0 0

The plaintiff claims £100.[1]

It does not consist with the purpose of this work to consider in detail the forms of declarations proper to the various forms of actions. For these, reference must be had to books of Practice and of Forms. It is sufficient here to say generally that "the declaration must allege all the circumstances necessary for the support of the action, and contain a full, regular, and methodical statement of the injury which the plaintiff has sustained, and the time and place, and other circumstances, with such precision, certainty, and clearness, that the defendant, knowing what he is called upon to answer, may be able to plead a direct and unequivocal plea, and that the jury may be able to give a complete verdict upon the issue, and that the court, consistently with the rules of law, may give a certain and distinct judgment upon the premises."[2] The formal parts of the declaration will be considered hereafter, in connection with certain definite rules of pleading, and others of these rules will prescribe the manner of making those substantial averments upon which the cause of action must rest. The facts set forth by these averments of course vary in each particular case. Their legal virtue is matter of substantive rather than of adjective law, and consequently not the subject of our study here.

PROCEEDING BY BILL.

Proceeding by bill, instead of by declaration, without the suing out of an original writ, requires only a brief explanation. We have seen how the King's Bench, by its process of *bill of Middlesex* and *latitat*, and the Exchequer by its

---

[1] Cunningham & Mattinson's Precedents (2d ed.), 134, 193.

[2] Chit. Pl. 229.

attachment of privilege (quo minus), extended their respective civil jurisdictions in personal actions, and brought defendants within their control by process founded upon fictions. We have further learned that such defendants could, when once within the jurisdiction of these courts, be proceeded against by bill instead of by declaration. The *bill*, as it is called, filed in such cases is exactly equivalent to a declaration, differing from it only in some formal words at the commencement and conclusion; this bill is, therefore, considered as belonging to one of the regular forms of actions as strictly as if an original writ had issued to determine the form.[1] It was used of necessity because a declaration was regularly preceded by an original writ, and in these cases there was no original.

PRODUCTION OF SUIT.

We must not leave this subject without calling attention to the concluding words of the declaration: *And therefore he brings suit and good proof.*[2]

"It is not enough that the plaintiff should tell his tale: he must offer to prove its truth. In an Appeal of Felony he offers 'proof by his body;' in a Writ of Right he offers proof by the body of a certain free man of his, A. B. by name, who, or whose father, witnessed the seisin that has been alleged; in other cases he produces a suit *(secta)* of witnesses. No one is entitled to an answer if he offers nothing but his bare assertion, his *nude parole*. . . . What the plaintiff relies on as a support for his word is *suit*. This suggests that the suitors *(sectatores)* whom the plaintiff produces in a civil action have been, at least in theory, men who along with him have *pursued* the defendant. . . . When we first obtain records from the King's Court, the production of suit is beginning to lose its importance, and we know little as to what the suitors did or said when they had thus been introduced to the court. But we may gather from the Norman books that each of them in turn ought to have stepped forward and said, ' This I saw and heard, and

---

[1] Steph. Pl. 76. [2] Evans' Pl. 29.

(by way of proof) I am ready to do what the court shall award.' At this stage the suitors make no oath and are not questioned. They are not yet making proof; *the proof will not be made until the court has spoken after hearing what the defendant has to say."* [1] As to the number of these suitors requisite when no battle was offered, they could not be less than two; the rule was *testis unus, testis nullus* (one witness, no witness), and was thought to be deduced from the Bible. There might be as many as thirteen suitors. [2]

THE DEFENCE.

"The time has now come when the defendant must speak, and as a general rule the only plea that is open to him is a flat denial of all that the plaintiff has said. He must ' *defend* ' all of it, and in this context to defend means *to deny*. In the past he has been bound to ' defend ' the charge word by word, with painful accuracy. By the end of the thirteenth century he is allowed to employ a more general form of negation." Gradually this defence becomes a mere form, but it remains to tell us of a time, *before the science of special pleading was conceived*, when a downright No! (a *thwertutnay*, as it was called) was the one possible answer to the plaintiff's *tale;* until our own day it remained the *indispensable preliminary to every possible answer.* [3]

EXAMINATION OF THE PLAINTIFF'S SUIT.

If the defendant wished to rely upon this original common traverse, this *thereto-nay*, or defence, he might demand an examination of the plaintiff's *suit*. He may object that no suit at all has been produced. In such cases he insists that he is not bound to answer the *nude parole* (naked word) of the plaintiff. If suit has been produced, the defendant can demand that it be examined, but in so doing he abandons every other defence. This demand would have led to a purely formal and indisputable oath on the part of the suitors, and if they duly pronounced the necessary formal

1 P. & M. Hist. II. 603, 604 ; Thay. Jury, 10–13.

2 P. & M. Hist. II. 605.
3 *Ibid.* II. 605, 606.

words of this oath, the defendant lost his case. But later these suitors could, on the demand of the defendant, be examined one by one by the court to discover whether they really knew anything about the facts of the plaintiff's claim. If they break down under examination, and disclose their ignorance of the alleged facts, or disagree, the *suit is null* and the plaintiff fails. If they agree, then the defendant's cause is lost by the examination which he has himself demanded.[1] This examination of the plaintiff's suit begins to be questioned as early as 1314, and finally in 1343 it was denied as antiquated; yet the allegation of the production of suit was continued on as a form to our own day.[2]

Offer of Proof.

When the defendant did not wish to stake his case upon the examination of the plaintiff's suit, he had to offer to make good his downright No! When battle has been offered, he must accept the offer. Having verbally *defended* the charge, he professes his willingness to again *defend* it, in some cases by his own body, in others by the body of his freeman, "When and where the court shall consider that defend he ought." Where the plaintiff has not offered battle, the defendant will follow up his defence by the words: "And this he is ready and willing to defend when and where he ought as the court shall consider." In the former case the court will award a wager of battle. In the latter it will award the defendant some other *law*, to wit: an oath with helpers; the defendant must at once *wage this law*, that is, find gage and pledges that he will, on a later day, *make* this law by producing compurgators or *oath-helpers* to sustain by their oaths his denial of the plaintiff's claim.[3]

"Such have been the modes whereby a man made good his *thwertutnay*. In Bracton's day (*temp.* Hen. III.), they are being concealed from view by an overgrowth of special pleading and the verdicts of jurors. But the background of the

---

[1] P. & M. Hist. II. 607; Thay. Jury, 12, 15.

[2] Thay. Jury, 15.

[3] P. & M. Hist. II. 608.

law of pleading and trial still is this, that the defendant must take his stand upon a downright No, whereupon there will be a wager of battle or of some other law."[1]

ORIGIN OF SPECIAL PLEADING.

Although it was not until a century after Bracton that English lawyers had grasped the first principles of that system of pleading which, in the future was to become the most exact, if the most occult, of the sciences,[2] yet already the idea of the *exceptio* of the Roman law was developing in England.

According to Roman law the prætor in some cases denied to a person having a perfect legal right his proper remedy. The plaintiff's claim might be valid by the civil law, and yet to give effect to it might work injustice. In order to prevent this result, the prætor recognized a merely equitable defence, which was called an *exceptio* (exception).[3] The English medieval lawyer was familiar with the well-known language of Justinian: "*It often happens that although the action which the plaintiff prosecutes is lawful, nevertheless it is unjust to prosecute it against the particular defendant.*"[4]

He, however, knew little or nothing of any system of equity as contrasted with a system of law, and therefore could not mark off any proper sphere for these exceptional cases in which it was unjust to pursue a legal right. Hence, he was led to believe that every kind of answer to an action was an *exceptio*, and that Roman law allowed an almost unlimited license to the pleader of *exceptions*. "This new idea set up a ferment in England and elsewhere. When the old rigid rules had once been infringed, our records became turbid with exceptions."[5] The right of exception first obtained a firm footing in the then new procedure of the Petty Assizes, of which we shall speak later. In certain cases, from the very nature of the procedure, it was evident

---

1 P. & M. Hist. II. 608.

2 *Ibid*. II. 609.

3 Hunter's Roman Law, 40.

4 Inst. 4, 13 pr.

5 P. & M. Hist. II. 609.

from the outset that gross injustice would be done the defendant.[1]   Hence he was allowed to assert that for a given reason the assize ought not to proceed, and that assertion was an *exceptio*, and was also a special plea.   "From the province of the Petty Assizes the *exceptio* spread with great rapidity throughout the domain of the other actions.   For one thing, the old reasons for refusing to answer were brought under the new rubric.   From of old a defendant must have had some power of urging such reasons; of saying, for example, *I will not answer, for this court is not competent to decide this cause,* or *I will not answer you, for you are an outlaw.* Under the influence of the Romano-canonical procedure these preliminary objections were now called exceptions; they were ' temporary ' or ' dilatory ' exceptions.   A classification of exceptions and a theory about the order in which they should be propounded were borrowed.   First you must except to the jurisdiction of the court, then to the person of the judge, then to the writ, then to the person of the plaintiff, then to the person of the defendant, and so on. . . .   In a very short time we find the defendant propounding, by way of exception, pleas that we cannot regard as mere preliminary objections, for they are directed to the heart of the plaintiff's case; these are ' peremptory ' or ' perpetual ' exceptions, the ' special pleas in bar ' of later law.   For a while the utmost laxity prevails.   Of this the best examples are to be found among the Appeals.   By way of exception to an appeal of homicide, the appellee is suffered to plead that the appeal is not a ' true ' [that is, not a *bona fide*] appeal but is the outcome of spite and hatred [*odium et atia*].   A climax seems to be reached when an appellee pleads an *alibi* by way of *exceptio;* a climax, we say, for the plea of *alibi* can be nothing but an argumentative traverse of the charge that has been made against him, a charge that he will already have traversed in large and explicit words by his ' defence.'

---

[1] A son and heir might enter upon the father's land at his death, and then enfeoff a third person. It would be scandalous if this son could then re- cover the land from his feoffee, yet he could do it if in such case a *mort d' ancestor* were allowed to proceed. P. & M. Hist. I. 610.

And here we may see how exotic the *exceptio* once was, though it is now flourishing but too luxuriantly in our soil: it is always, or almost always, preceded by a *thwertutnay*, that is, by a flat denial of the plaintiff's assertions. The exception may be met by a replication, the replication by a triplication, and so on *ad infinitum*. We may occasionally find long debates between the parties. Not only are they long, but, if judged by the standard of a later time, they are loose and irregular. The pleaders must be charged with many faults which would have shocked their successors; they habitually ' plead evidence,' they are guilty of argumentativeness and duplicity. The curious rule that in later days will confine a man to a single ' plea in bar' appears already in Bracton, justified by the remark that a litigant must not use two staves to defend himself withal. But this rule had not always been observed; defendants were allowed a second staff, at all events if when using the first they expressly reserved the right of picking up another. These men are drunk with the new wine of Romanism: such may be the comment which a modern reader will make when for the first time he watches the exploits of our ancient pleaders. But we ought to see that there is an under-current of good sense running beneath their vagaries. The extension of the *exceptio* is the extension of *a new mode of proof;* it is the extension of a mode of proof which will become famous under the name of *trial by jury,*" [1] as we shall see more fully hereafter.

Here, plainly, we have the birth of special pleading, and the history of its earliest years. The *defence*, instead of being "one of those verbal subtleties, by which the science of special pleading was, in many instances, anciently disgraced," [2] was, as has been discovered since Stephen wrote, the original denial by the defendant of the plaintiff's claim. It existed before special pleading came into being, and for centuries after the birth of the latter the special plea had to be almost invariably preceded by the unequivocal and direct *defence* of the earlier law.

[1] P. & M. Hist. II. 611–614.   [2] Steph. Pl. 377.

THE DEMURRER.

The plaintiff having made or filed his declaration, and the defendant having duly *defended* the same, the latter had next to consider the specific nature of his response to the attack of the former. We have seen that every averment of fact implies a rule of law on which it relies for its potency. The first care, therefore, of the defendant, or of his pleader, was to examine the declaration narrowly, and to determine whether the facts averred in it, supposing them to be true as averred, state a legal cause of action. If the matter of the plaintiff's declaration be insufficient in law, then the defendant *demurs* to the declaration.

"A demurrer cometh of the Latin word *demorari*, to abide; and therefore he which demurreth in law, is said, he that abideth in law; *moratur* or *demoratur in lege*." [1] To demur, therefore, is to *rest* or *pause;* and the party who demurs in law upon his adversary's pleading *rests* or *pauses* upon it as requiring no answer by reason of its supposed legal insufficiency. A demurrer, therefore, is no plea, but is, on the contrary, an excuse for not pleading.[2]

The defect apparent upon the face of the plaintiff's declaration may be one of substance, in that no legal cause of action is stated, or one of form, in that the declaration is not framed according to the rules of pleading. Under the common law, either defect was a ground of demurrer; the objection for defect of substance was called a *general*, and that for want of form a *special* demurrer. The following is an instance of the former : —

GENERAL DEMURRER TO THE DECLARATION (IN DEBT).

In the King's Bench,   Term, in the   year of the reign of King George the Fourth :

C. D. ⎱   And the said C. D., by   , his attorney, comes and
ats. ⎰   defends the wrong and injury, when, &c. ; and says that
A. B. ⎰   the said declaration and the matters therein contained, in

---

[1] Co. Litt. 71, b.   [2] Haiton *et al. v.* Jeffreys, 10 Mod. R. 280.

OF THE PROCEEDINGS IN AN ACTION.

manner and form as the same are above stated and set forth, are not sufficient in law for the said A. B. to have or maintain his aforesaid action against him, the said C. D.; and that he, the said C. D., is not bound by the law of the land to answer the same. And this he is ready to verify. Wherefore, for want of a sufficient declaration in this behalf, the said C. D. prays judgment, and that the said A. B. may be barred from having or maintaining his aforesaid action against him, &c." [1]

Here the defendant says plainly that he is not bound to answer the declaration, and prays the judgment of the court, which judgment he will await. The subject of *the demurrer* will be more fully discussed hereafter. It is proper to add here that special demurrers have been quite universally abolished.

PLEAS.

If the defendant does not demur, he must *answer* the declaration by counter-averments of fact, and in doing this he is said to *plead*, as distinguished from *demurring*, and his answer of fact so made is called the *plea*.

Pleas are divided into pleas *Dilatory* and *Peremptory*, this is their most general division. Dilatory Pleas are again subdivided into the following:—

(1) PLEAS TO THE JURISDICTION OF THE COURT;

(2) PLEAS IN SUSPENSION OF THE ACTION; AND

(3) PLEAS IN ABATEMENT OF THE WRIT.

Peremptory Pleas are always in bar of the action.[2]

DILATORY PLEAS.

(1) *A Plea to the Jurisdiction* is one by which the defendant excepts to the jurisdiction of the court, in which he is sued, to entertain the action against him. As we have seen, he must appear and plead in proper person, and not by attorney; in the conclusion of his plea *he prays judgment, if the court of our lord the king here will or ought to have further cognizance of the plea (action) aforesaid.*[3]

(2) *A Plea in Suspension of the Action* is one which alleges

[1] Steph. Pl 82, 83.   [2] *Ibid.* 83.   [3] *Ibid.* 84.

some fact constituting an objection to the proceeding in the suit at that time by the court, and prays that the pleading may be suspended until that objection be removed.   The number of these pleas is small.   Among them is that which alleges the non-age of an infant heir who is sued on an obligation of his ancestor, and which is called a *parol demurrer* (a suit-stayer); it concludes with the infant's averment (through his guardian) that *he does not conceive that during his minority he ought to answer the said A. B. in his said plea.   And he prays that the parol may demur until the full age of him, the said C. D.*[1]

(3) *A Plea in Abatement of the Writ* is one which shows some ground for *abating or quashing* the original writ, and it concludes with a prayer that this may be done.

The grounds for thus abating the writ are any matters of fact which assail its correctness, without denying the right of action itself.   If the original writ vary from the declaration, or if it has been sued out pending another action already brought for the same cause, or if it name only one person as defendant, when it should have named several, or if it appear to have been defaced in a material part, — all or any of these facts are grounds for its abatement.

Pleas in abatement are addressed —

(1) To the Person of the Plaintiff,
(2) To the Person of the Defendant,
(3) To the Count or Declaration, and
(4) To the Original Writ.

A plea in abatement addressed to the person (1) of the plaintiff, or (2) of the defendant, avers some fact of personal disability in the plaintiff to sue or in the defendant to be sued.   It may allege that the plaintiff is an alien enemy or an outlaw, or that the defendant is a married woman or a bankrupt.   These pleas to the person are not strictly in abatement, for they do not pray *that the writ be quashed;* they pray judgment *if the plaintiff ought to be answered.* As, however, they do not deny the right of action itself, but

[1] Steph. Pl. 84.

urge an objection of form and not of substance, they are considered as, and classed with, pleas in abatement.

(3) A plea in abatement to the count or declaration is founded on some objection applying immediately to the declaration, and only indirectly affecting the writ. All cases of variance between the declaration and the original are instances of such objections. But this sort of plea was generally founded on facts that could only be ascertained by an examination of the writ itself, and hence the pleader was compelled to demand the reading (oyer) of the original before pleading in abatement on such grounds. To discourage such pleas, the courts refused to grant oyer of the original in these cases, and hence pleas in abatement based on such facts were no longer possible. But there are pleas in abatement of the declaration which do not require any examination of the writ itself, *e. g.*, the non-joinder as defendant of one of two joint-contractors, the suing out of a writ pending another action, pleas to the person of the plaintiff or defendant, — these and many others do not require oyer of the original, for the defendant has the right to assume that the original and the declaration agree with each other, and he may plead such matters in abatement without the production and reading of the original.[1]

(4) A plea in abatement to the writ is based on some objection to the writ itself, as, for example, where in an action on a joint contract it omits to name as defendants all of the joint-contractors. These pleas are subdivided into such as are addressed to the *form* of the writ, and such as relate to its *action*. The former are again subdivided into such as are founded on objections *apparent on the writ itself*, and such as are founded on *extraneous matter*.[2] Of these subdivisions Mr. Stephen says that they are " more subtle than useful." [3] Objections to the action of the writ are that the wrong form of action has been brought, as, *e. g.*, case instead of trespass, or that the action is prematurely brought. Objections to the form of the writ apparent on its face are

---

[1] Steph. Pl. 86, 88.
[2] *Ibid.* 86.
[3] *Ibid.* 86, n.

repugnancy, variance from the record or specialty sued on, and the like. Objections not apparent on its face, and founded on extraneous matter, are misnomer of the plaintiff or defendant, non-coverture of persons suing or sued as husband and wife, and generally the want of proper parties.[1]

Pleas in abatement applied as well to proceedings by bill as to those by original writ, only the necessary verbal changes being made in the wording of the plea.[2]

The effect of all pleas in abatement, if successful, is to defeat the particular action. The right of action itself, however, is not destroyed, and the plaintiff, on obtaining a better form of writ, may maintain a new action if the objection were founded on matter of abatement; or, if the objection were only to the disability of the person, and in mere suspension of the action, he may bring a new action when that disability is removed.[3]

By Statute 4 Ann. c. 16, s. 11, all dilatory pleas must be verified by affidavit, or, at least, some probable matter must be shown to the court to induce it to believe that the fact of the plea is true.

PEREMPTORY PLEAS.

A Peremptory Plea, or a Plea in Bar of the Action, may be defined as one which shows some ground for barring or defeating the action, and its prayer is to that effect.

A plea in bar is, therefore, distinguished from all pleas of the dilatory class in that it denies the right of action altogether, instead of seeking to divert the proceedings to another jurisdiction, to suspend them, or to abate the particular writ. It aims to be a substantial and conclusive answer to the action. Obviously, then, it must deny all, or some essential part, of the averments of fact in the declaration; or, admitting these allegations to be true, it must allege new facts which either qualify or destroy the legal effect of the former. In the first case, the defendant is said, in the language of pleading, to *traverse* (deny) the matter of the declaration; in the latter, to *confess and avoid* it.

---

[1] Chit. Pl. 391, 392.　　　　　[3] *Ibid.* 87.
[2] Steph. Pl. 89.

Pleas in bar are consequently divided into pleas *by way of traverse*, and pleas by way of *confession and avoidance*.[1]

' THE ISSUE.

If we suppose the defendant to plead in bar to the declaration by way of *traverse*, it is evident that a question is at once raised between the parties; this question is one of *fact*, viz., whether the averments in the declaration which the defendant denies are true. Here is a specific matter, affirmed on one side and denied on the other. According to the ancient practice the defendant, who is the party traversing, is generally obliged to offer to refer this disputed matter to some mode of trial, and he does this by closing his traverse with an appropriate formula, proposing either a trial by the country, *i. e.*, by a jury, or some other proper method of decision. We shall explain this more fully when we speak of the modes of trial. If this offer of the defendant's be accepted by the plaintiff, the parties are then, conformably to the language of the ancient pleading, said to be *At Issue*, and the question itself is called the *Issue*. Hence, a party who thus traverses, annexing such formula, is said to *tender issue*, and the issue so tendered is called an issue in fact.[2]

If, however, the defendant, instead of traversing the declaration, demurs, it is obvious that in this case also a question is raised between the parties, only here it is a question of *law*, and involves the legal sufficiency of the facts, alleged in the declaration, to maintain the action. Here, again, the defendant is the denying party, and he accordingly uses a formula referring the question of law involved to the judgment of the court, which is the only proper mode of trial of such question. As upon a traverse he tenders an issue in fact, so upon a demurrer he tenders an issue in law. A party may sometimes, as will be hereafter seen, traverse or deny without offering any mode of trial; but, upon a demurrer, he always necessarily tenders an issue in law, for the only known form of a demurrer contains an appeal to the judgment of the court. This tender of an issue in law is necessarily accepted

---

[1] Steph. Pl. 89.   [2] *Ibid.* 91.

by the plaintiff, for he can not object either to the question itself (since he prepared his own declaration, and must maintain its sufficiency or abandon it), or to the proposed mode of decision, for only the court can decide issues in law. He is therefore obliged to accept or join in the issue in law, and this he does by a formula called a *joinder in demurrer*.[1]

But, when an issue in fact is tendered, the plaintiff is not obliged to accept it, for manifest reasons. The traverse, as we have seen, may only involve a part of the declaration, and the defendant may, in the case supposed, have so framed his traverse as to involve only an *immaterial* part of the declaration, or a part *insufficient to decide the action*. Again, the plaintiff may consider the traverse *defective in point of form*, and he may object to its sufficiency in law on that ground. Or, the *mode of trial proposed* may be legally inapplicable to the particular kind of issue. For any of these grounds he may demur to the traverse as insufficient in law. This, however, would only postpone the acceptance of issue one step; for, by the demurrer, he himself tenders an issue of law which must be accepted at once.

If the tender of issue in fact be not demurred to, it must be accepted along with the mode of trial which it proposes, and this acceptance is expressed by a formula called a *joinder in issue*, or a *similiter* (likewise).

The issue in law or fact being thus tendered and accepted by the other side, the parties are *at issue*, and the pleading is at an end.

But this end may not come so soon as we have hitherto supposed. Instead of demurring, or pleading in bar by way of traverse to the declaration, the defendant may plead some one of the *dilatory pleas*, which we have described, or a *plea in bar by way of confession and avoidance*. In either case the plaintiff has the option of *demurring* to the plea, as insufficient in law to answer the declaration by reason of a defect in form or substance, or of pleading to it by way of *traverse*, or by way of *confession and avoidance* of its allegations. Such pleading on the part of the plaintiff is called the *replication*. If this *rep-*

---

[1] Steph. Pl. 92.

lication be by way of traverse, it should generally tender issue. So, if the plaintiff demur, an issue in law is tendered, and in either case a joinder in issue results. But, if the replication be in *confession and avoidance*, the defendant has in his turn the opportunity to demur to, traverse, or confess and avoid its allegations. If he so plead, his pleading is called *the rejoinder*.

In the same manner, and subject to the same law of proceeding, viz., that of demurring, traversing, or pleading in confession and avoidance, is conducted all the subsequent altercation to which the nature of the case may lead. These alternate allegations of fact, or *pleadings*, are in order and name as follows : DECLARATION, PLEA, REPLICATION, REJOINDER, SUR-REJOINDER, REBUTTER, and SUR-REBUTTER, after which last the pleadings seldom extend, and have no distinctive name.[1]

However the altercation be prolonged, it is obvious that this process must sooner or later end in a demurrer or a traverse. *The parties can not go on indefinitely alleging relevant new matter* by way of confession and avoidance. So they arrive at *issue* after a long series of pleadings, precisely in the same manner as when the process ends with the plea.

After thus discussing the respective functions of the demurrer and of the pleading, the student will hardly need to have his attention called to the fact that a demurrer is never based upon matter extraneous to the pleading which it opposes, but must be supported by the face of that pleading ; a pleading, on the other hand, is always founded on extraneous matter. A demurrer admits facts, alleged in proper form ; a pleading brings into the case new facts, *e. g.*, if the declaration in a given case fail to name the plaintiff, this defect is apparent on its face, and should be taken advantage of by demurrer ; but if the defendant be improperly named in the declaration as William instead of John, the fact that his name is John is an extraneous fact, not disclosed by the declaration itself, and must be brought into the case, therefore, by way of a plea in abatement.[2]

---

[1] Steph. Pl. 93, 94.   [2] *Ibid.* 96, 97.

Occasional Pleas and Incidents.

The pleading has been hitherto supposed to take its direct and simple course. There are, however, *some pleas and incidents* of occasional occurrence by which its progress is sometimes interrupted, and such pleas are called

Pleas Puis Darreign Continuance.

It will be remembered that under the ancient law there were continuances, *i. e.*, adjournments of the proceedings, for certain purposes, from one day or one term to another; and that, in such cases, there was an entry made on the record, expressing the ground of the adjournment, and appointing the parties to re-appear at the given day. In the intervals, between such continuances and the day appointed, the parties were of course *out of court*, and consequently not in a situation to plead. But it sometimes happened that, after a plea had been pleaded, and while the parties were out of court in consequence of such a continuance, a new matter of defence arose which did not exist, and which the defendant had consequently no opportunity to plead, *before* the last continuance. This new defence he was therefore entitled, at the day given for his re-appearance, to plead as a matter that had happened *after the last continuance (puis darreign continuance — post ultimam continuationem)*. In the same cases that occasioned a continuance in the ancient law, but in no other, a continuance still takes place. At the time, indeed, when the pleadings are filed and delivered, no record actually exists, and there is therefore no entry at that time made on record of the award of a continuance; but the parties are, from the day when, by the ancient practice, a continuance would have been entered, supposed to be out of court, and the pleading is suspended till the day arrives to which, by the ancient practice, the continuance would extend. At that day the defendant is entitled, if any new matter of defence has arisen in the interval, to plead it according to the ancient plan, *puis darreign continuance.*

A plea *puis darreign continuance* is always pleaded by way of substitution for the former plea, on which no proceeding is afterwards had.   It may be either in bar or abatement, and is followed like other pleas, by a replication and other pleadings, till issue is attained upon it.[1]

DEMAND OF VIEW.

One of the *incidents* of occasional occurrence, by which the progress of the pleading was sometimes varied, was the demand of view.

In most real and mixed actions, in order to ascertain the identity of the land claimed with that in the tenant's possession, the tenant is allowed, after the demandant has counted (*i.e.*, filed his count or declaration), to *demand a view* of the land in question ; or, if the subject of claim be a rent, a right of advowson, a right of common, or the like, a view of the land out of which it issues.   This, however, is confined to real or mixed actions.   For in actions personal, the view does not lie.

The view being granted, the course of proceeding is to issue a writ, commanding the sheriff to cause the tenant to have view of the land.   It being the interest of the demandant to expedite the proceedings, the duty of suing out the writ lies upon *him*, and not upon the tenant ; and when, in obedience to its exigency, the sheriff causes view to be made, the demandant is to show to the tenant, in all ways possible, the thing in demand with its metes and bounds.

On the return of the writ into the court, the demandant must count *de novo*, that is, declare again, and the pleading proceeds to issue.[2]

Under modern practice, and, generally, in pursuance of statutory authority, what is called a view is now, in the discretion of the court, granted to the jury in civil and criminal cases, in order that, by an examination of the premises involved in the evidence, they may be the better able to apply that evidence.   But this practice has no connection with this incident of pleading which we are considering, and pertains properly to the law of evidence.[3]

[1] Steph. Pl. 98.
[2] *Ibid.* 99.   Booth on Real Actions, 37.
[3] Min. Com. IV. 607.

VOUCHER TO WARRANTY.

A warranty is a covenant real, annexed to lands and tenements, whereby a man is bound to defend such lands and tenements for another person, and, in case of eviction by title paramount, to give him lands of equal value.[1] Voucher to warranty *(vocatio ad warrantizandum)* is the calling of such warrantor into court by the party warranted (when tenant in a real action, brought for recovery of such lands) to defend the suit for him; and the time of such voucher is after the demandant has counted. It lies in most real and mixed actions, but not in personal.

Where the voucher has been made and allowed by the court, the vouchee either voluntarily appears, or there issues a judicial writ, called a *summons ad warrantizandum*, commanding the sheriff to summon him.

When he, either voluntarily or in obedience to this writ, appears, and offers to warrant the land to the tenant, it is called *entering into the warranty;* after which he is considered as tenant in the action, in the place of the original tenant. The demandant then counts against him *de novo*, the vouchee pleads to the new count, and the cause proceeds to issue.[2]

Voucher to warranty does not exist in modern practice, as real actions have been abolished; but the rule seems to be established that when a person is responsible over to another, either by operation of law or by express contract, and notice has been given him of the pendency of the suit, and he has been requested to take upon himself the defence of it, he is no longer regarded as a stranger to the judgment that may be recovered, because he has the right to appear and defend the action equally as if he were a party to the record. When notice is thus given, the judgment, if obtained without fraud or collusion, will be conclusive against him whether he has appeared or not.[3]

---

[1] Co. Litt. 365.
[2] Steph. Pl. 100.
[3] Littleton *v.* Richardson, 34 N. H 179, 187; Washington Gas Co. *v.* District of Columbia, 161 U. S. 327, 328, 330.

PROFERT AND OYER.[1]

Where either party alleges any deed, he is generally obliged, by a rule of pleading that will afterwards be considered in its proper place, to make *profert* (proffer) of such deed, that is, to produce it in court simultaneously with the pleading in which it is alleged. This, in the days of oral pleading, was of course an actual production in court. Since then, it consists of a formal allegation that he shows the deed in court, it being in fact retained in his own custody.

Where a profert is thus made by one of the parties, the other, before he pleads in answer, is entitled to *demand oyer*, that is, *to hear the deed read.* For it is to be observed that the forms of pleading do not in general require that the whole of any instrument which there is occasion to allege should be set forth. So much only is stated as is material to the purpose. The other party, however, may reasonably desire to hear the whole, and this, either for the purpose of enabling him to ascertain the genuineness of the alleged deed, or of founding on some part of its contents, not set forth by the adverse pleader, some matter of answer. He is therefore allowed this privilege of hearing the deed read *verbatim*.

When the *profert* was actually made in *open court* the demand of oyer, and the oyer given upon it, took place in the same manner, and the course was that, on demand by one of the pleaders, the deed was read aloud by the pleader on the other side. By the present practice, the attorney for the party by whom it is demanded, before he answers the pleading in which the profert is made, sends a note to the attorney on the other side, containing a demand of oyer, on which the latter is bound to carry to him the deed, and deliver to him a copy of it, if required, at the expense of the party demanding; and this is considered as oyer, or an actual reading of the deed in court.

Oyer is demandable in all actions, real, personal, and mixed.

It is said to have been formerly demandable not only of *deeds*, but of *records* alleged in pleading, and (as has been

[1] Steph. Pl. 100-104.

before stated) of the *original writ* also ; but, by the present practice, it is not now granted either of a record or of an original writ, and can be had only in the cases of deeds, probates, and letters of administration, etc., of which profert is made on the other side; of private writings not under seal, oyer has never been demandable.[1]

Oyer can be demanded only where profert is made.[2] In all cases where profert is necessary, and where it is also, in fact, made, the opposite party has a right, if he pleases, to demand oyer ; but if it be unnecessarily made, this does not entitle to oyer ; and so, if profert be omitted when it ought to have been made, the adversary cannot have oyer, but must demur.

When a deed is pleaded with profert, it is supposed to *remain in court* during all the term in which it is pleaded, but no longer, unless the opposite party, during that term, plead in denial of the deed, in which case it is supposed to remain in court till the action is determined. Hence, it is a rule, that oyer can not be demanded *in a subsequent term to that in which profert is made.*

A party having a right to demand oyer is yet not obliged, in all cases, to exercise that right; nor is he obliged, in all cases, after demanding it, to notice it in the pleading that he afterwards files or delivers.[3] Sometimes, however, he is obliged to do both, viz., where he has occasion to found his answer upon any matter contained in the deed of which profert is made, and not set forth by his adversary. In these cases the only admis-

---

[1] But where an action is founded on a written instrument not under seal, though the defendant cannot pray oyer, yet the court will in some cases make an order for delivery of a copy of it to the defendant or his attorney, and that all proceedings in the meantime be stayed (1 Tidd, 639, 8th ed.; 1 Saund. 9 d, n. g.). It seems that oyer is not demandable of an act of Parliament (1 Tidd, 637); nor of letters patent (1 Arch. 169); nor of a recognizance (*Ibid.*). But it is demandable of a deed enrolled, or of the exemplification of the enrolment, according to the terms of the profert (*Ibid.*).

[2] Therefore, in an action on a bond conditioned for performance of the covenant in another deed, the defendant cannot crave oyer of such deed, but must himself plead it with a profert (Chit. Pl. 370).

[3] 1 Tidd, 638, 8th ed., where it is said that if the defendant omits to set forth the oyer in his plea, the plaintiff in Common Pleas may insert it for him at the head of his plea in making up the issue; but in King's Bench can only avail himself of the deed by praying that it be enrolled at the head of his own replication. And see Com. Dig. Pleader, P. 1.

sible method of making such matter appear to the court is to demand oyer, and from the copy given to set forth the whole deed *verbatim* in his pleading.[1]

When oyer is demanded and the deed thus set forth, the effect is as if it had been set forth in the first instance by the opposite party; and the tenor of the deed, as it appears upon oyer, is consequently considered as forming a part of the preceding pleading. Therefore, if the deed, when so set forth by the plea, be found to contain in itself matter of objection or answer to the plaintiff's case, as stated in the declaration, the defendant's course is to demur, as for matter apparent on the face of the declaration; and it would be improper to make the objection the subject of plea.

IMPARLANCES.[2]

By the ancient practice, if a party found himself unprepared to answer the last pleading of his adversary immediately, his course was to pray the court to allow him a further day for that purpose; which was accordingly granted by the court to any day that, in their discretion, they might award, either in the same or the next succeeding term. The party was, in this case, said to pray, and the court to grant, an imparlance *(interlocutio*, or *interloquela)*, a term derived from the supposition that in this interval the parties might *talk together* and amicably settle their controversy.

An imparlance, when granted, was one of the cases of *continuance*, of which doctrine some general explanation has already been given. It was grantable in almost all actions, real, personal, and mixed.

The prayer of imparlance, when made by the defendant prior to his plea, was either *general* or *special*. The first was simply a prayer for leave to imparl. Of such general imparlance it was a consequence that the defendant was afterwards

---

[1] Com. Dig. Pleader, 2 V. 4; 2 Saund. 410, n. 2; 1 Saund. 9 b, n. 1; Stibbs *v.* Clough, 1 Stra. 227; Ball *v.* Squarry, Fort. 354; Colton *v.* Goodridge, 2 Bl. R. 1108. If he does not set forth the whole deed, or misrecites it, the plaintiff may either sign judgment for want of plea, or by his replication may pray that the deed be enrolled (Jevons *v.* Harridge, 1 Saund. 9 b; and see Com. Dig. P. 1).

[2] Steph. Pl. 104; Chit. Pl. 375-378.

precluded from certain proceedings of a dilatory tendency, which might before have been competent to him. Thus he could not, after a general imparlance, demand oyer, nor (according to some authorities) a view, nor could he plead a plea *to the jurisdiction* or *in abatement*. Accordingly, if he wished to preserve his right to these advantages, he varied the form of his prayer, and made it with a reservation of such right. If his object was to preserve the right of pleading in abatement, he prayed what is called a *special* imparlance; but, if he desired to plead to the jurisdiction, he had to resort to a *general-special* imparlance, which reserved all *advantages* and *exceptions whatsoever*.

This subject is now of no practical importance, and any further notice of it is unnecessary. In modern practice the rules of court allow a fixed time to the parties wherein to plead, which allowance may be enlarged upon cause shown.

COUNTER-PLEAS TO OYER, ETC.

These, and other incidents of a similar kind, may occur in pleading. If they take their course without opposition, they do not, as we have seen, long interrupt the main series of the allegations. But, with respect to most of them, the opposite party has a right, if he pleases, to oppose the prayer made on the other side; and for this purpose he was entitled, in the ancient practice of pleading, to demur or plead to it, as if it were a statement of fact made in the direct course of the pleading. Thus, if a party demanded oyer in a case where, upon the face of the pleading, his adversary conceived it to be not demandable, the latter might demur, or if he had any matter of fact to allege as a ground why the oyer could not be demanded, he might plead such matter. If he pleaded, the allegation was called a counter-plea to the oyer. So the demandant might have occasion, in the same manner, to counterplead the voucher or counterplead the view; all pleadings of this incidental kind, diverging from the main series of the allegations, were termed counterpleas. And in the latter instances, as well as upon oyer, it would seem there might be demurrer instead of counterplea, if the objection appeared on the face of the proceedings. Again, on the counterplea, in all these cases, there might be a replication and other subsequent pleadings; and so the parties might come to issue in law or in fact on this collateral subject, in the same manner as upon the principal matters in controversy.[1]

DEMURRER-BOOK. — PAPER-BOOK.

Supposing the cause to be at issue, the next proceeding is to make a transcript upon paper of the whole pleadings that have been filed or delivered between the parties. This transcript, when the issue joined is an issue in law, is called the *demurrer-book;* when an issue in fact, it is called, in the King's Bench, in some cases, *the issue,* in others, *the paper-book*, and in the Common Pleas, *the issue*. It contains not only the pleadings, but also entries, according to the ancient forms used in recording, of the appearance of the parties, the continuances, and other acts supposed to be done in court up to the period of issue joined, even though such entries have not formed part of the pleadings as filed or delivered; and it concludes with an entry of an award by the court of the mode of decision tendered and accepted by the pleadings. The making of this transcript upon an issue in law, is called making up the demurrer-book; upon an issue in fact, making up the issue or paper-book. The demurrer-book, issue, or paper-book, when made up, is delivered to the defendant's attorney, who, if it contains what he admits to be a correct transcript, returns it unaltered; but, if it varies from the pleadings that were filed or delivered, he makes application to the court to have it set right.[2]

AMENDMENTS.

During the course of the pleading, if either party perceives any mistake to have been committed in the manner of his allegation, or if, after issue joined on demurrer for matter of form, he should think the issue likely to be decided against him, he ought to apply, without delay, for leave to *amend*.

[1] Steph. Pl.*107.   [2] *Ibid*. 108.

Under the ancient system, the parties were allowed to correct and adjust their pleadings during the oral altercation, and were not held to the form of statement that they might first advance. So, at the present day, until the judgment is signed, in the manner to be afterwards mentioned, either party is generally at liberty to amend his pleading as at common law ; the leave to do which is granted, as of course, upon proper and reasonable terms, including the payment of the costs of the application, and sometimes the whole costs of the cause up to that time. And, even after the judgment is signed, and up to the latest period of the action, amendment is, in most cases, allowable at the discretion of the court, under certain statutes passed for allowing amendments of the record ; and in late times the judges have been much more liberal than formerly in the exercise of this discretion. Amendments are, however, always limited by a due consideration of the rights of the opposite party ; and where, by the amendment, he would be prejudiced or exposed to unreasonable delay, it is not allowed.[1]

ENTERING THE ISSUE ON RECORD.

The pleadings and issue being adjusted by the making up, delivery, and return of the demurrer-book, issue, or paper-book, the next step is to enter the issue on record. It will be remembered that the pleadings are framed as if they were copied from a roll of the oral pleadings. Such a roll, as has been shown, did, in the time of oral pleading, exist, and still exists in contemplation of law ; but no roll is now actually prepared or record made till after issue joined and made up, in the manner above described. At that period, however, a record is drawn up on a parchment roll. This proceeding is called entering the issue ; and the roll on which the entry is made is called the issue roll. The issue roll contains an entry of the term, of which the demurrer-book, issue, or paper-book is entitled ; and (in the King's Bench) the warrants of attorney supposed to have been given by the parties at the commencement of the cause, authorizing their attorneys to appear for

[1] Steph. Pl. 110.

them respectively; and then proceeds with a transcript of the declaration and subsequent pleadings, continuances, and award of the mode of decision, as contained in the demurrer-book, issue, or paper-book. When drawn up, it is filed in the proper office of the court.[1]

MODES OF TRIAL.

The action being now brought to that stage at which the issue is recorded, the next subject for consideration is the manner in which that issue is decided.

DECISION OF ISSUES IN LAW.

The decision of issues *in law* is vested, as it always has been, exclusively in the judges of the court. Therefore, when, upon a demurrer, the issue in law has been entered on record in the manner above described, the next step is to *move for a concilium;* that is, to move to have a day appointed on which the court will hear the counsel of the parties argue the demurrer. And such day being appointed, the cause is then *entered for argument* accordingly. On that day, or as soon afterwards as the business of the court will permit, it is accordingly argued *viva voce* in court by the respective counsel for the parties; and the judges, in the same manner and place, pronounce their decision according to the majority of voices.[2]

TRIAL OF ISSUES IN FACT.

The manner of deciding issues *in fact* will require explanation at greater length. The decision of the issue in fact is called the *trial*.

Before we can understand the immense function assigned to the trial by jury to-day, and for centuries past, in all English speaking countries,[3] we must go back to a time when such a mode of trial did not exist; to a time, in fact, when there was no such thing as a trial at all, as we understand that word. " We must once for all discard from our thoughts that familiar

---

[1] Steph. Pl. 111.

[2] *Ibid.* 114.

[3] " All we see about us, Kings, Lords, and Commons, the whole machinery of the state, all the apparatus of the system, and its varied workings, end in simply bringing twelve good men into a box." — Lord Brougham, *Present State of the Law,* Feb. 7, 1829.

picture of a trial in which judges and jurymen listen to the
evidence that is produced on both sides, weigh testimony
against testimony, and by degrees make up their minds about
the truth. The language of the law, even in Bracton's day,
has no word equivalent to our *trial*. We have not to speak of
trial; we have to speak of proof." [1] " That thing [trial], so
obvious and so necessary, as we are apt to think it, *was only
worked out after centuries.*" [2]

Among the Germanic races popular courts and popular
justice were ancient and abiding institutions. These courts
were originally an assembly of the people, in which all were
judges. Of law so administered, Maine says : " I will say no
more of its general characteristics than that it is intensely
technical, and that it supplies in itself sufficient proof that
legal technicality is a disease, not of the old age, but of
the infancy of societies." [3] These courts assembled, not to
hear witnesses and to balance doubtful testimony, but to see
that certain forms were strictly observed. The conception
of a trial was that of a public proceeding between the parties,
carried on in a certain prescribed way. As we have seen,
it was once true that if a man stammered in repeating a
formula, or if, while holding the Bible in the act of swearing, every finger was not placed in a certain prescribed
position, the suit was irretrievably gone.[4] *Proof* meant, not
what we call evidence, but *the due observance of prescribed rules
of procedure.* And hence some room for choice existed.

There were many modes of such trial, but the proof was
largely *one-sided, i. e.*, to be performed by one of the parties
only. In some cases the right to supply this proof was a
privilege, in others a danger ; hence an important question to
be decided was this : who has the right to go to the proof in
this case ? For determining this question there were tradi-
tional rules, and the judgment upon it (called the MEDIAL
JUDGMENT) came before the trial, for the actual trial was
simply the following out of a certain form which the judgment itself prescribed.[5]

[1] P. & M. Hist. II. 596.   [4] Thay. Jury, 25.
[2] Thay. Jury, 10.   [5] *Ibid.* 9.
[3] Early Law and Custom, 170.

We must recall here what has already been said as to the *secta* or suit. No complaint made on the *naked word* of the plaintiff could put a defendant to his proof; there must be something to support the complaint, the *secta*, or the defendant's own writings, or his tally, etc.[1]

The old forms of trial were, in cases not conclusively determined by the production of the defendant's own deeds, the following: (1) Witnesses; (2) The Party's Oath, with or without fellow-swearers (compurgators); (3) The Ordeal; (4) Battle.

(1) THE TRIAL BY WITNESSES.

This appears to be one of the oldest, as it is also one of the most formal, kinds of " one-sided proof." Under Anglo-Saxon law certain transactions, such as sales, had to take place before official witnesses;[2] a woman was endowed at the church-door, and a charter was executed, both before witnesses. In case of controversy as to any of these facts, the formal oath of these witnesses, who could not be cross-examined, ended the matter. So too if the question were of the non-age of a party, or, originally, of the ownership of chattels, or of the death of the husband in an action of dower, in all of these cases trial by witnesses was had. But when these witnesses came it was merely in order to swear to a set formula. *They made no promissory oath to tell the truth in answer to questions, but an assertory oath.*[3] This mode of trial is obsolete, and requires no further notice.

(2) THE TRIAL BY OATH.

The most common and popular medieval form of trial by oath was where the party swore with oath-helpers, and was called *compurgation*. It consisted in the producing, by the party adjudged to make the proof, of a specific number of persons to make oath in his favor; the requisite number varied with the rank of the parties and of the compurgators, the value of the property in dispute, and the nature of the suit. These persons were not witnesses, and they swore,

---

1 Thay. Jury, 10, 11.
2 Anglo-Saxon Law, 187, 216.
3 P. & M. Hist. II. 599.

not as to facts, but as to the truthfulness of the party who produced them in his behalf.[1] In small matters the oath taken was an informal one, but in serious criminal cases it was made so intricate that its words could only with great difficulty be repeated, and if a wrong word was used the oath *burst* and the adversary won. " In the twelfth century such elaborate forms of asseveration had been devised that, rather than attempt them, men would take their chance at the ' hot iron ' [the ordeal]." [2]

" From being a favored mode of trial, this ' *law* ' or, as it is commonly called, *wager of law* [from its preliminary stage of giving pledges to perform it] steadily tended to become a thing exceptional ; not going beyond the line of the precedents, and within that line being a mere privilege along side of the growing . . . trial by jury. In the newer forms of action it was not allowed, and finally it survived mainly in detinue and debt." [3] It did survive in these actions, however, and so late as 1824 it was demanded as a right.[4] In 1833 it was abolished by act of Parliament.

(3) THE TRIAL BY ORDEAL.

Primitive man lived very closely in contact with what we call the supernatural. In doubt or in perplexity he turned to the miraculous as the *natural* source of help. Men have at all times and everywhere required God to denounce guilt or to protect innocence by some action manifestive of His power ; by making the flowing water uphold the guilty body cast into it, or the hot iron spare the innocent hand that grasped it. This trial by ordeal was at first adopted and consecrated by the church ; later (1215) she repudiated it, and in consequence of that repudiation it ceased to be practised generally, and especially in England. No case of trial by ordeal later than 1214 is found recorded in English books, but in the year 1679 a defendant is reported to have seriously demanded this form of trial.[5]

---

[1] Hist. Pr. 301.

[2] P. & M. Hist. II. 599.

[3] Thay. Jury, 28, 29.

[4] King *v.* Williams, 2 Barn. & Cress. 538 ; s. c. 4 Dow. & Ry. 3.

[5] Thay. Jury, 38.

It was only when the party had no charters, and could furnish neither witnesses nor compurgators, that he resorted to the ordeal, except in cases provided for by special legislation. It was the typical mode of trial among the English, as contrasted with the Norman trial by battle. It was used frequently in civil, as well as in criminal, cases before and for a considerable time after the Conquest.[1]

When the accused was unable, through age, sex, or bodily infirmity, to fight in the duel, then this trial by ordeal was found to be a convenient last resort. The three varieties of ordeal in Anglo-Saxon law were those of fire, water, and the morsel or *corsned*.[2]

(4) THE TRIAL BY BATTLE.

The judicial combat or duel is a two-sided ordeal. The combatant who was vanquished was looked upon as a convicted perjurer, and it was truth that was thought to triumph, not the mere superior strength or skill of the conqueror.

This mode of trial was introduced into England by William the Norman, but was, according to Blackstone, only used in three cases, one military, one criminal, and the third civil. The first was in the court of chivalry or honor; the second in appeals of felony, and the third upon issue joined in a writ of right.[3] But Glanvill writes of it as of one of the chief modes of trial in the king's courts, and even in the courts-baron.[4]

It was a new thing in England, and was hated by the natives as the Frenchman's mode of trial. In form, it was a fight between two champions, one appearing for each of the contending parties, armed with staves, and he who was conquered was forced to cry "*craven*," and became an infamous man. The combatants were bound to fight until the stars appeared in the evening; if the champion of the tenant can defend

[1] Hist. Pr. 322.
[2] For a particular description of the ordeal, the student is referred to "Essays on Anglo-Saxon Law," 300–303, and to the fourth book of Blackstone's Commentaries, 342–346 *.
[3] Bl. Com. III. 337 *, 338 *.
[4] Lib. 10, c. 17; Lib. 9, c. 1; Thay. Jury, 39, 40.

himself so long he shall prevail, for he has maintained his ground and the battle is a drawn one.[1]

It was not until 1819, that this barbarous relic of a long past age was formally abolished in England by act of Parliament.[2]

MISCELLANEOUS PROOFS.

There were, in addition to the foregoing regular modes of trial, a few miscellaneous methods of proving particular facts. Certain questions were decided by the certificate of the bishop, such as the questions whether a certain church had a properly constituted parson; whether two people were lawfully married; whether a child was legitimate.

Again, there was a trial by *inspection*. If it was asserted that a litigant was a minor, the justices would sometimes decide the fact upon an inspection of him with their own eyes.[3]

THE TRIAL BY THE RECORD.

Before proceeding to consider the next mode of trial and its immediate forerunner, we must notice the proof required in cases where the contents of a record are drawn in question.

The trial by the record applies to cases where an issue of *nul tiel record (no such record)* is joined in any action. If a record be asserted on one side to exist, and the opposite party deny its existence, under the form of traverse that *there is no such record* remaining in court as alleged, and issue be joined thereon, this is called an issue of *nul tiel record ;* and the court awards, in such case, a trial by *inspection and examination of the record.* Upon this, the party affirming its existence is bound to produce it in court, on a day given for the purpose; and, if he fail to do so, judgment is given for his adversary. The trial by record is not only in use when an issue of this kind happens to arise for decision, but it is the only legitimate mode of trying such issue, and the parties can not put themselves *upon the country.*[4]

---

[1] For a very detailed and interesting account of this mode of trial the student is referred to the third book of Blackstone's Commentaries, 337–341*.

[2] Stat. 59 Geo. III. c. 46.
[3] P. & M. Hist. II. 637.
[4] Steph. Pl. 130.

If we pause now to reckon our available modes of proof, we find that for the most important and numerous class of actions, the writs of right, we have the proof by battle; for actions of debt and detinue, the proof by wager of law; for actions of covenant, the papers or charters of the defendant himself; for sales, the proof by witnesses; for records, the proof by inspection of the record; for exceptional cases, the proof by ordeal. But as yet we have not heard even mention of the proof by jury.

TRIAL BY JURY.

It is impossible to do more than to present the barest outline of the introduction and growth of this remarkable institution of our own race. Fortunately, in the recently published work by Professor Thayer upon this topic, the student has a masterly and thorough exposition of the subject.

It seems to be conceded to-day that Henry II. was a " great and sagacious king;"[1] under him " England takes for a short while the lead among the States of Europe in the production of law and of a national legal literature."[2] He was Duke of Normandy before he was Chief Justiciary, and later King, of England. As Duke of Normandy, he had there developed and organized the *Norman Inquisition*, which was simply *the practice of ascertaining facts by summoning together, by public authority, a number of people most likely and most competent, as being neighbors, to know and tell the truth about a given matter, and calling for their answer under oath.*[3] This was the origin of our jury of to-day. In Normandy, this process of inquisition was applied both in legal controversy and in political administration. When the King of the Franks wanted a point determined which involved the royal revenue, he ordered that inquiry should be made, not by witnesses brought forward by the party interested, but " *through those who in that county are known to be of the best character and most truthful; let inquiry be made through their testimony, and according to what they shall testify in the premises, let*

---

[1] Thay. Jury, 53.
[2] P. & M. Hist. II. 145, 146.

[3] Thay. Jury, 7.

them (taxes) be withheld or rendered." This reformed process for the ascertainment of facts connected with the revenue naturally extended to the administration of justice. And yet only a strong central power could compel parties to abandon the old familiar formal procedure in favor of this new and strange trial. Only royal authority could put a man to an oath as a juryman, and this fact made and kept trial by jury the special possession of the royal courts.[1]

This strong kingly power the Normans brought with them to England. With them came also the inquisition. It appears to have been occasionally resorted to in judicature prior to the reign of Henry II.; of its administrative use the compilation of Domesday Book in 1085-6 is an example. But with this great king the *inquisition* began to assume the place which its inherent potency fitted it for. He established the use of this mode of trial as a right, and compelled suitors to accept it in lieu of the old established *proofs*. Before his time, it had been granted merely as a royal favor to particular suitors; under him in certain cases any suitor had *a right* to the king's writ ordering it. It now began to be called a *recognition* instead of an *inquisition*, but the new name only signified the *answer* of the jurors, while the old one denoted the *inquiry* which they made.[2]

" These recognitions were so many new modes of trial on particular questions, established by a dead lift of royal power." By the old law men had *tried* their own cases. " To put upon a man, who had the right to go to the proof, instead of the proof (the defence, the purgation of the older law, where he produced the persons or things that cleared him), the necessity of submitting himself to the test of what a set of strangers, witnesses selected by a public officer, might say — this was a wonderful thing." [3] It was only by continued effort that the change was accomplished. The writer of the *Mirror* (1291–2) says : "*It is an abuse that the justices drive a lawful man to put himself on the country when he offers to defend himself against the approver by his body.*" [4]

---

[1] Thay. Jury, 49.
[2] *Ibid.* 55.
[3] *Ibid.* 55, 56.
[4] *Ibid.* 57.

We now understand why a man in pleading has to offer to put himself upon the country, and why in criminal procedure the terrible torture of *la peine forte et dure* (the strong and hard punishment) was used to open the mouth of a prisoner who stood mute. The trial by jury was not originally a lawful trial, and could not be forced on a man without at least the form of his assent.

It was probably at the council of Clarendon (1166) that Henry II. authorized the proceeding known as the assize of *novel disseisin.*[1] We have already seen that this new remedy was devised to protect the mere possession of land. "The ownership of land may be a matter for the feudal courts; the king himself will protect by royal writ and inquest of neighbors every seisin of a free tenement."[2] Later, the same king took a fresh step in advance, and decreed that no man need answer for his tenement without a royal writ. He decreed further that a *tenant* (defendant), pursued in the local feudal court (court-baron) in a proprietary action for land, might, if he so desired, have the action removed into the King's Court, and there have the whole question of right determined by a verdict of neighbors. In this case the inquest was called *the grand assize,* and was made more solemn in form than the assize of *novel disseisin* and other similar ones subsequently instituted, which were called, by way of distinction, the *petty assizes.* To constitute the grand assize the sheriff chose four knights "girt with swords," who, in the presence of the court, then chose twelve other knights, likewise "*gladiis cinctos;*" this jury of twelve (but some authorities say, of sixteen) constitute the jury for the trial of all writs of right,[3] and for that purpose only.

To form a petty assize or an ordinary jury, twelve free and lawful men of the neighborhood were summoned directly by the sheriff.[4]

We must now recur to the development of the *exception* and of special pleading in connection with the spread of the new method of trial by jury.

[1] P. & M. Hist. I. 124.
[2] *Ibid.* 125.
[3] P. & M. Hist. II. 618 (*cf.* Steph. Pl. 129).
[4] *Ibid.* II. 619.

In the case of these petty assizes, which were all of recent institution, when the litigants came into court they found there these twelve *recognitors* or jurymen, who formed a convenient body to try the truth of any exception which might be pleaded in the case. In fact, these jurymen were used for that purpose, either by the consent of parties or by the order of the court. It soon became common that the court would compel the plaintiff to submit the question of the truth of an *exception* pleaded by the defendant to the verdict of a jury, under penalty of having his cause decided against him if he refused.[1] This procedure spread rapidly beyond the domain of the petty assizes. In civil causes generally the defendants became desirous of referring not only the new exceptions, but also the old absolute denials, to a form of trial which enabled them to escape the dangerous and costly modes of proof under the old law. " By its intrinsic fairness as contrasted with the older modes, and by the favor of the Crown and the judges, it grew fast to be regarded as the one regular common-law mode of trial, always to be had when no other was fixed." [2] Then, too, all new writs and forms of action in civil cases required by their terms a jury trial, and as these were demandable as of right they gave a great impetus to the new mode of proof.

It will be interesting to turn for a moment to the instrumentality of introducing the inquisition into the domain of the criminal law. On an appeal of felony it was open to the party so appealed of crime to plead that the appeal was not made *bona fide*, but that it was brought maliciously to disinherit or otherwise injure him (the innocent appellee). This was called the *exceptio de odio et atia (exception of spite and hatred)*. This plea often involved practically a decision of the real guilt or innocence of the appellee. By Magna Carta this writ of spite and hatred issued *gratis* and without any denial, and the sheriff must under its terms *take an inquest* to determine the truth of the appellee's exception. In this way the accused could ask for and obtain the benefit of a trial by jury.[3] But if he did not demand it, if, on the

---

[1] P. & M. Hist. II. 615. [3] *Ibid.* 68; P. & M. Hist. II. 585, 586
[2] Thay. Jury, 60.

contrary, he remained mute and refused to " put himself on the country," then came, as we have seen, the torture, which brought either death or consent to the jury-trial.

As showing emphatically, however, the intrusion of this method of trial, and the persistence of the old regular customary modes of proof, we must recur to the fact that the trial by battle was not dead in 1819, and that wager of law lingered on until 1833 ; in each case, as has been said, an act of Parliament was required to terminate an outworn but a long and a once vigorous life.

The student must pursue elsewhere the study of that course of development which converted the ancient witnesses as to facts, for such the inquisition was, into the modern triers of facts, for such the jury came to be. It belongs properly to the law of evidence.[1]

Venire Facias.

Recurring now to the general subject of trial by jury, it will be remembered that, when the parties have mutually referred the issue to decision by jury, or (as it is technically termed) have *put themselves upon the country*, there is entered upon the roll (as in all other cases) the award of the mode of decision so adopted. In the case of the trial by jury, that award directs the issuing of the writ of *venire facias* (you shall cause to come) commanding the sheriff of the county, where the facts are alleged by the pleading to have occurred, to summon a jury to try the issue ; and such writ is accordingly sued out.

Trials at Nisi Prius.

The *venire facias* directs the jury to be summoned to appear in *the superior court*. This is because the trial was, in fact, anciently had there. But, except in some few cases, to be presently noticed, the trial by jury no longer takes place before the superior court. It is now usually conducted in the county where the facts are alleged, in pleading, to have occurred, and into which the *venire facias* issues, and before

[1] Thay. Jury, *passim ;* P. & M. Hist. *sub voc.* " Jury."

certain judges called the *justices of assize and nisi prius*. The trial is, in such cases, said to be had at *nisi prius*. The term is derived from the Latin words at one time used in the writ of *venire facias*, by which the sheriff was commanded to summon the jurors to be, by a given day, at Westminster, to try the issues, *unless before (nisi prius)* that time, the justices came into the sheriff's own county, on their semi-annual circuit, as they were sure to do; when the jurors, instead of going to Westminster, were summoned to the assize town of their own county.[1] When the trial is to be so had, the course of proceeding is, after an issue to be tried by jury has been entered on record on the issue roll, to sue out the *venire facias*, together with another writ, for compelling the attendance of the jury, called the *distringas* in the King's Bench; in the Common Pleas the *habeas corpora*. The next step is to make up and pass, at the proper offices, another record, on a parchment roll, called *the record of nisi prius*, which is a transcription from the issue roll, and contains a copy of the pleadings and issue. This *nisi prius* record is then delivered to the judges of assize and *nisi prius*, and serves for their guidance as to the nature of the issue to be tried. The trials at *nisi prius* now take place, in London and Middlesex, several times in the course of each term, and also during a considerable part of each vacation; in every other county they are held twice a year, and always in time of vacation. The justices of assize and *nisi prius*, for trials in London and Middlesex, consist of the chief justices of the three courts respectively, each trying only the issues from his own court. For trials in the other counties, they consist of such persons as are appointed for the purpose by temporary commission from the Crown, among whom are usually, for each circuit, two of the judges of the superior courts, the whole kingdom being divided into six circuits for the purpose.[2]

TRIAL AT BAR.

Though the trial by jury is thus, in general, had at *nisi prius*, this is not universally the case; for, in causes of great

---

[1] Min. Inst. IV. 189.   [2] Steph. Pl. 116.

difficulty and consequence, these inquests are allowed to be taken before the four judges in the superior court in which the pleading took place, as in the ancient practice. The proceeding is then technically said to be a trial at *bar*,[1] by way of distinction from the trial at *nisi prius*.

After these explanations as to the time and place of trial by jury, the next subject for consideration is the course of the proceeding itself.

CONDUCT OF JURY TRIAL.

The whole proceeding of trial by jury takes place under the superintendence of the presiding judge or judges, who usually decide all points as to the admissibility of evidence, and direct the jury on all such points of law arising on the evidence as is necessary for their guidance in appreciating its legal effect, and drawing the correct conclusion in their verdict.

After hearing the evidence of the witnesses, the addresses of counsel, and the charge of the judge, the jury pronounce their *verdict*, which the law requires to be unanimously given. The verdict is usually in general terms, " for the plaintiff," or " for the defendant," finding at the same time (in case of verdict for the plaintiff, and where damages are claimed by the action) the amount of *damages* to which they think him entitled.[2]

The principles upon which the law requires the jury to form their decision, are these : —

1. They are to take no matter into consideration but the question *in issue ;* for it is to try the issue, and that only, that they are summoned.

Example : Where to an action of assumpsit the defendant pleaded that he did not promise within six years, to which there was a replication that he did promise within six years, on which issue was joined, it was held not to be competent to the plaintiff to offer evidence that the action was grounded on a fraudulent receipt of money by the defendant, and that the fraud was not

---

[1] For an instance of a trial at bar in the Supreme Court of the United States, see State of Georgia *v.* Brailsford, 3 Dallas, 1.

[2] Steph. Pl. 117.

discovered till within six years of the action, for the issue was merely upon the promise within six years.[1]

2. They are bound to give their verdict for the party who, upon the proof, appears to them to have succeeded in establishing his side of the issue.

3. The burden of proof, generally, is upon that party who, in pleading, maintained the *affirmative* of the issue ; for a *negative* is, usually, incapable of proof. Consequently, unless he succeed in proving that affirmative, the jury are to consider the opposite proposition, or negative of the issue, as established.[2]

VARIANCE.

The proof offered may, in some cases, *wholly* fail to support the affirmative of the issue ; but in others, it may fail by a *disagreement in some particular point or points only* between the allegations and the evidence. Such disagreement, when upon a material point, is called a *variance* and is as fatal to the party on whom the proof lies as a total failure of evidence, the jury being bound, upon *variance*, to find the *issue against him*.

Examples : (1) The plaintiff declared in covenant for not repairing, pursuant to the covenant in the lease, and stated the covenant as a covenant to " repair when and as need should require ; " and issue was joined on a traverse of the deed alleged. The plaintiff, at the trial, produced the deed in proof, and it appeared that the covenant was thus : to repair " when and as need should require, *and at farthest after notice,*" the latter words having been omitted in the declaration. This was held to be a variance, because the additional words were material, and qualified the legal effect of the contract.[3]

(2) So where the plaintiff declared in *assumpsit* that for certain hire and reward the defendants undertook to carry goods from London and deliver them safely at Dover, and the contract was proved to have been to carry and deliver safely, *fire and robbery excepted*, this was held to be a variance.[4]

---

[1] Clarke *v.* Hougham, 2 Barn. & Cress. 149.

[2] Steph. Pl. 118.

[3] Horsefall *v.* Testar, 7 Taunt. 385.

[4] Latham *v.* Rutley, 2 Barn. & Cress. 20.

On the other hand, however, the principle is not so rigorously observed as to oblige the party on whom the proof lies to make good his allegation to the *letter*. It is enough if the *substance* of the issue is exactly proved,[1] and a variance in *mere form*, or in *matter quite immaterial*, will not be regarded.

Example : In debt on bond conditioned for payment of money, where the defendant pleaded payment of principal and interest, and the plaintiff replied that he had not paid all the principal and interest, and issue was joined thereon, and the proof was that the whole interest was not, in fact, paid, but that the defendant paid a sum in gross, which was accepted in full satisfaction of the whole claim, the issue was considered as sufficiently proved on the part of the defendant.[2]

THE VERDICT.

The verdict, when given, is afterwards drawn up *in form*, and entered on the back of the record of *nisi prius*. This is done upon trials in King's Bench, in London and Middlesex, by the attorney for the successful party ; in other cases, by an officer of the court. Such entry is called the *postea* (afterward) from the word with which, at a former period (when the proceedings were in Latin), it commenced. The *postea* is drawn up *in the negative or affirmative of* the issue, according as it may be for the plaintiff or for the defendant.[3]

Such is the course of trial at *nisi prius*, in its direct and simple form ; and the practice of a trial *at bar* is generally the same. Trials by jury, however, whether *at bar* or *nisi prius*, are subject to certain varieties of proceeding, some of which require to be here noticed.

INCIDENTS OF JURY TRIAL.

If, at a trial, a point of law arises, either as to the *legal effect* or the *admissibility* of the *evidence*, the usual course (as already stated) is for the judge to decide these matters. But it may happen that one of the parties is dissatisfied with the

[1] Com. Dig. Pleader, S. 26.

[2] Price *v.* Brown, Str. 690. The old rule as to variance has been greatly relaxed in this country. See Nash *v.* Towne, 5 Wall. 689, 698, and Moses *v* United States, 166 U. S. 579.

[3] Steph. Pl. 120.

decision, and may wish to have it revised by a superior jurisdiction. If he is content to refer it to the superior court in
which the issue was joined, and out of which it is sent (called,
by way of distinction from the court at *nisi prius*, the court
in banc), his course is to move in that court for a *new trial*, —
a subsequent proceeding which will be considered hereafter
in its proper place. But, as the *nisi prius* judge himself frequently belongs to that court, a party is often desirous, under
such circumstances, to obtain the revision of some court of
error, *i. e.*, some court of appellate jurisdiction, having authority
to correct the decision.

For this purpose, it becomes necessary to put the question
of law on *record* for the information of such court of error ;
and this is to be done pending the trial, in a form marked out
by an old statute (Westminster 2, 13 Edward I. c. 31).

Bill of Exceptions.

The party excepting to the opinion of the judge *tenders*
him a *bill of exceptions ;* that is, a statement, in writing, of the
objection made by the party to his decision, to which statement, if truly made, the judge is bound to set his seal in confirmation of its accuracy. The cause then proceeds to verdict
as usual, and the opposite party, for whom the verdict is given,
is entitled, as in the common course, to judgment upon such
verdict in the court *in banc*, for that court takes no notice of
the bill of exceptions. But, the whole record being afterwards
removed to the appellate court by *writ of error* (a proceeding
to be hereafter explained), the bill of exceptions is then taken
into consideration in the latter court, and there decided.[1]

Demurrer to Evidence.

Though the judge usually gives his opinion on such points
of law as above supposed, yet it may happen that, for various
reasons, he is not required by the parties, or does not wish to
do so. In such case several different courses may be pursued
for determining the question of law.

---

[1] Steph. Pl. 121, and see especially Money *v.* Leach, 3 Burr. 1692.

First, a party disputing the legal effect of any evidence offered may *demur to the evidence*. A *demurrer* to *evidence* is analogous to a demurrer in pleading; the party from whom it comes declaring that he will not proceed, because the evidence offered on the other side is not sufficient to maintain the issue. Upon joinder in demurrer by the opposite party, the jury are generally discharged from giving any verdict; and the demurrer, being entered on record, is afterwards argued and decided in the court *in banc*, and the judgment there given upon it may ultimately be brought before a court of error.[1]

SPECIAL VERDICT.

A more common, because more convenient, course than this to determine the legal effect of the evidence is, to obtain from the jury a *special verdict*, in lieu of that *general* one of which the form has been already described; for the jury have an option, instead of finding the *negative or affirmative of the issue*, as in a general verdict, to find *all the facts of the case as disclosed upon the evidence before them*, and, after so setting them forth, to conclude to the following effect : " *That they are ignorant, in point of law, on which side they ought, upon these facts, to find the issue ; that if, upon the whole matter, the court shall be of opinion that the issue is proved for the plaintiff, they find for the plaintiff accordingly, and assess the damages at such a sum, etc. ; but if the court are of an opposite opinion, then vice versa.*" This form of finding is called a *special verdict*.[2] However, as on a general verdict the jury do not themselves actually frame the *postea*, so they have, in fact, nothing to do with the formal preparation of the special verdict. When it is agreed that a verdict of that kind is to be given, the jury merely declare their opinion as to any fact remaining in doubt, and then the verdict is adjusted without their further interference. It is settled, under the correction of the judge, by the counsel and

---

[1] Steph. Pl. 122. In this country, generally, a demurrer to evidence was heard by the trial-justice. But here it has fallen into disuse; in lieu of it, the practice prevails of requesting the trial court to give an absolute instruction to the jury that, admitting the evidence to be true, the party offering it is not entitled to recover. Parks *v.* Ross, 11 How. 362.

[2] The form of this will be found in Cook *v.* Gerrard, 1 Saund. 171 a.

attorneys on either side, according to the state of facts as found by the jury, with respect to all particulars on which they have delivered an opinion, and, with respect to other particulars, according to the state of facts which it is agreed that they *ought* to find upon the evidence before them. The special verdict, when its form is thus settled, is, together with the whole proceedings on the trial, then entered *on record;* and the question of law arising on the facts found is argued before the court *in banc,* and decided by that court as in case of demurrer. If the party be dissatisfied with their decision, he may afterwards resort to a court of error.

It is to be observed that it is a matter entirely in the *option of the jury* whether their verdict shall be general or special. The party objecting in point of law cannot therefore *insist* on having a special verdict, and may consequently be driven to *demur to the evidence,* at least if he wishes to put the objection *on record,* without which no writ of error can be brought nor the decision of a *court of error* obtained.[1]

A *special verdict* differs from a *demurrer to evidence* in two marked particulars : (1) the former ascertains the facts proved, the latter recites the whole evidence adduced ; (2) in favor of the former no inferences as to matter of fact are allowable, whilst it is the court's duty in deciding a demurrer to the evidence to draw, from the evidence demurred to, all inferences that a jury must or might reasonably draw.

GENERAL VERDICT SUBJECT TO A SPECIAL CASE.

But if the object be merely to obtain the decision of the court *in banc,* and it is not wished to put the legal question *on record,* with a view to a writ of error, then the more common, because the cheaper and shorter course, is neither to take a special verdict nor to demur to the evidence, but to take a general verdict, subject (as the phrase is) to a special case ; that is, to a written statement of all the facts of the case drawn up for the opinion of the court *in banc,* by the counsel and attorneys on either side, under correction of

[1] Steph. Pl. 123.

the judge at *nisi prius*, according to the principle of a special verdict, as above explained. The party for whom the general verdict is so given is of course not entitled to judgment till the court *in banc* has decided on the special case ; and, according to the result of that decision, the verdict is ultimately entered either for him or his adversary. A special case is not (like a special verdict) entered on record, and consequently a writ of error cannot be brought on this decision.[1]

A special verdict differs from a *general verdict subject to a special case* or a *case agreed*, as it is sometimes called, in this respect also : the case agreed may occur at any time after the suit is instituted, but a special verdict only after issue joined. Like the special verdict, the case agreed admits of no inferences of fact, but is rigorously construed.[2]

The object of all of these three proceedings is by their operation to withdraw facts, pregnant with disputed law, from the jury, and to bring them before the court for its decision of the law.[3]

PROCEEDINGS SUBSEQUENT TO VERDICT.

We must now return to the course of proceeding, after trial by jury in what has been here called its direct or simple form.

The proceedings on trial by jury, at *nisi prius* or at bar, terminate with the verdict.

In case of trial at *nisi prius*, the return day of the last jury process (the *distringas* or *habeas corpora*, which, like all other judicial writs, is made returnable into the court from which it issues) always falls on a day in term subsequent to the trial, and forms the next continuance of the cause. On the day given by this continuance, therefore (which is called the day *in banc)*, the parties are supposed again to appear in the court *in banc*, and are in a condition to receive judgment. On the other hand, in case of trial at bar, the trial takes place on or after the return day of the last jury process ; and, therefore, immediately after the trial, the parties are in court, so that

---

[1] Steph. Pl. 124.   [3] Warren's Law Studies, 738.
[2] Min. Inst. IV. 752, 753.

judgment may be given. In either case, however, a period of four days elapses before, by the practice of the court, judgment can be actually obtained. And during this period certain proceedings may be taken by the unsuccessful party to avoid the effect of the verdict. He may move the court to grant a new trial, or to arrest the judgment, or (if he be the plaintiff) to give judgment *non obstante veredicto* (despite the verdict), or to award a repleader, or to award a *venire facias de novo*. Of these briefly in their order.[1]

MOTIONS FOR A NEW TRIAL.

With respect to a new trial. It may happen that one of the parties may be dissatisfied with the opinion of the *nisi prius* judge, expressed on the trial, whether relating to the effect or the admissibility of evidence; or he may think the evidence against him insufficient in law, where no adverse opinion has been expressed by the judge, and yet may not have obtained a special verdict, or demurred to the evidence, or tendered a bill of exceptions. He is at liberty, therefore, after the trial, and during the period above mentioned, to move the court *in banc* to grant a new trial, on the ground of the judge's having misdirected the jury, or having admitted or refused evidence contrary to law, or (where there was no adverse direction of the judge) on the ground that the jury gave their verdict contrary to the evidence, or on evidence insufficient in law. And resort may be had to the same remedy in other cases, where justice appears not to have been done on the first trial, as where the verdict, though not wholly contrary to evidence, or on insufficient evidence in point of law, is manifestly wrong in point of discretion, as contrary to the weight of the evidence and on that ground disapproved by the *nisi prius* judge.[2] So,

---

[1] Steph. Pl. 124.

[2] But not unless the finding is manifestly wrong; for where there is a contrariety of evidence, which brought the question fairly within the discretion of the jury, the court will not disturb the verdict, though disapproved by the judge who tried the cause. And "the court, in granting new trials, does not interfere, unless to remedy some manifest abuse or to correct some manifest error in law or fact." Carstairs *v.* Stein, 4 M. & S. 192; and see Swinnerton *v.* Marquis of Stafford, 3 Taunt. 91, 232.

too, a new trial may be moved for, where a new and material fact has come to light since the trial, which the party did not know, and had not the means of proving before the jury, or where the damages given by the verdict are *excessive*, or where the jury have misconducted themselves, as by casting lots to determine their verdict, etc. In these and the like instances the court will, on motion, and in the exercise of their discretion, under all the circumstances of the case, grant a new trial, that opportunity may be given for a more satisfactory decision of the issue. A new jury process consequently issues, and the cause comes on to be tried *de novo*. But except on such grounds as these, tending manifestly to show that the discretion of the jury has not been legally or properly exercised, a new trial can never be obtained; for it is a great principle of law, that the decision of a jury, upon an issue in fact, is in general irreversible and conclusive.[1]

Motions in Arrest of Judgment.

Again, the unsuccessful party may move in arrest of judgment; that is, that the judgment for the plaintiff be arrested or withheld, on the ground that there is some error appearing on the face of the record, which vitiates the proceedings. In consequence of such error, on whatever part of the record it may arise, from the commencement of the suit to this period, the court are bound to arrest the judgment. It is, however, only with respect to objections apparent on the record that such motion can be made. Nor can it be made, generally speaking, in respect of formal objections. This was formerly otherwise, and judgments were constantly arrested for errors of mere form; but this abuse has been long remedied by certain statutes, passed at different periods, to correct inconveniences of this kind, and commonly called the statutes of amendments and *jeofails*,[2] by the effect of which, judgment, at the present day, can not generally be arrested for any objection of form.[3]

[1] Steph. Pl. 126.
[2] Old form of *J'ai failli (I have failed)*.
[3] Steph. Pl 126.

Perhaps the student will best understand the nature of a motion in arrest of judgment if he consider it as a *postponed demurrer, i. e.*, a demurrer interposed after verdict, instead of during the pleadings, and applying to all substantial errors appearing on the face of the record from the institution of the suit down to the making of the motion itself.[1]

MOTION FOR JUDGMENT NON OBSTANTE VEREDICTO.

If the verdict be for the defendant, the plaintiff, in some cases, moves for judgment *non obstante veredicto :* that is, that judgment be given in his own favor, *without regard to the verdict* obtained by the defendant. This motion is made in cases where, after a pleading by the defendant in confession and avoidance, as, for example, a plea in bar and issue joined thereon and verdict found for the defendant, the plaintiff, on retrospective examination of the record, conceives that such plea was bad in substance, and might have been made the subject of demurrer on that ground. *If the plea was itself substantially bad in law, of course the verdict, which merely shows it to be true in point of fact, can not avail to entitle the defendant to judgment ; while, on the other hand, the plea, being in confession and avoidance, involves a confession of the plaintiff's declaration, and shows that he was entitled to maintain his action.* In such case, therefore, the court will give judgment for the plaintiff without regard to the verdict ; and this, for the reason above explained, is also called a judgment as upon confession. Sometimes it may be expedient for the plaintiff to move for judgment *non obstante*, etc., even though the verdict be in his own favor ; for if, in such a case as above described, he takes judgment as upon the verdict, it seems that such judgment would be erroneous, and that the only safe course is to take it as upon confession.[2]

Before the Statute of Anne (allowing several pleas), the question whether there should be a *repleader* or judgment *non obstante veredicto,* depended on whether the plea, on

---

[1] A motion in arrest of judgment can only be maintained for a defect apparent upon the record, and *the evidence is no part of the record* for this purpose. Bond *v.* Dustin, 112 U. S. 604, 608.

[2] Steph. Pl. 127.

which the immaterial issue arises, admits a cause of action by
way of confession and avoidance. But since that statute it
has been held that, although the plea (on which the immaterial issue was found for the defendant) did not confess the
cause of action, yet *if it was confessed or proved on the other
pleas which were found for the plaintiff*, there should be no
repleader, but judgment for the plaintiff. And even *although
the pleas on which the good issues have been taken and found
for the plaintiff were not pleas in confession and avoidance*,
but traverses of material allegations in the declaration, and
although some of the material allegations were neither traversed nor proved, nor admitted by way of confession and
avoidance, nevertheless, it has been held that, *when the other
material pleas enabled the court to give judgment* — without
requiring the parties to replead in order to show on which
side the right was — there should be no repleader, but judgment *non obstante veredicto*.[1]

MOTION FOR A REPLEADER.

The motion for a repleader is made where the unsuccessful
party, on examination of the pleadings, conceives that the
issue joined was an immaterial issue, that is, not taken on a
point proper to decide the action. It has been shown that
the issue joined is always some question raised between the
parties, and mutually referred by them to judicial decision;
but that point may nevertheless, on examination, be found
not proper to decide the action. For either of the parties
may, from misapprehension of the law, or oversight, have
passed over without demurrer a statement on the other
side insufficient and immaterial in law; and an issue in
fact may have been ultimately joined on such immaterial
statement; and so the issue will be immaterial, though the
parties have made it the point in controversy between
them.

It was said that a repleader was never granted to the party
who had made the first fault in the pleading, but to that suggestion Tindal, C. J., once answered: " A repleader is rather

[1] Couling *v.* Coxe, 6 Dow. & L. 399.

the act of the court, where it sees that justice can not be done without adopting that course." [1]

The difference between a *repleader* and a judgment *non obstante veredicto* is best expressed by the following language of Chief Justice Holt: —

" Where the plea of the defendant confesses the duty for which the plaintiff declared, but doth not sufficiently avoid it, and thereupon issue is joined on an immaterial thing, if it is found for (or against) the plaintiff, he shall have judgment, though the issue was immaterial ; but where the defendant's plea avoids the plaintiff's duty, who replies and traverses a matter not material, and issue is taken upon such immaterial traverse, and it is found for (or against) him, the statute of jeofails will not help in such case ; but there must be a repleader.[2]

If the issue might in any aspect of the case have been material, a repleader will not be awarded.[3] According to the English practice the motion for a judgment *non obstante veredicto* could be made by the plaintiff only, the defendant availing himself of the same ground by a motion in arrest of judgment ; the motion for a repleader could be made by either party.   Again, it must be noted that a judgment *non obstante veredicto* is always *upon the merits*, as shown in the pleadings, while a repleader is upon a formal defect in the pleadings.[4]

Example : If in an action of debt on bond, conditioned for the payment of ten pounds ten shillings at a certain day, the defendant pleads payment of *ten pounds*, according to the form of the condition, and the plaintiff, instead of demurring, tenders issue upon such payment, it is plain that, whether this issue be found for the plaintiff or the defendant, it will remain equally uncertain whether the plaintiff is entitled or not to maintain his action ; for in an action for the penalty of a bond, conditioned to pay a certain sum, the only material question is, whether the exact sum were paid or not, and a payment in part is a question quite beside the legal merits.[5]

---

[1] Gordon *v.* Ellis, 7 M. & G. 607.

[2] Witts *v.* Polehampton, 3 Salk. 305.

[3] Kempe *v.* Crews, 1 Ld. Raym. 167.

[4] Min. Inst. IV. 774, 775.

[5] Kent *v.* Hall, Hob. 113.

In such cases, therefore, the court, not knowing for whom to give judgment, will award a repleader, that is, will order the parties to plead *de novo* (anew), for the purpose of obtaining a better issue.[1]

VENIRE FACIAS DE NOVO.

A *venire facias de novo*, that is, a new writ of *venire facias*, will be awarded when, by reason of some irregularity or defect in the proceedings on the first *venire*, or the trial, the proper effect of that writ has been frustrated, or the verdict become void in law ; as, for example, where the jury has been improperly chosen, or given an uncertain, or ambiguous, or defective verdict. The consequence and object of a new *venire* are, of course, to obtain a new trial ; and accordingly this proceeding is, in substance, the same with a motion for a new trial. Where, however, the unsuccessful party objects to the verdict, in respect of some irregularity or error in the practical course of proceeding, rather than on the merits, the form of the application is a motion for a *venire de novo*, and not for a new trial.[2]

THE JUDGMENT.

It has now been shown in what manner the issue, whether in law or fact, is decided. It has been explained, too, by what means the unsuccessful party may, upon an issue in fact, avoid in some cases by motion in court the effect of the decision. Supposing, however, that such means are not adopted, or do not succeed, or that the issue be an issue in law, the next step is the judgment.[3]

As the issue is the question which the parties themselves have, by their pleading, mutually selected for decision, they are generally considered as having each put the fate of the cause upon that question ; and as soon, therefore, as the issue is decided in favor of one of them, that party generally becomes victor in the suit ; and nothing remains but to award the judicial consequence which the law attaches to such

---

[1] Steph. Pl. 128 ; 2 Saund. 319 b, n. 6.

[2] Witham *v.* Lewis, 1 Wils. 48.

[3] Steph. Pl. 132.

success : The award of this judicial consequence is called the judgment, and is the province of the judges of the court.

The nature of the judgment varies with that of the action, the plea, the issue, and the manner and result of the decision.

Judgment for the Plaintiff.

It shall be first supposed that the issue is decided for the plaintiff.

In this case, if it be an issue in law, arising on a dilatory plea, the judgment is only that the defendant *answer over*, which is called a judgment of *respondeat ouster*. The pleading is accordingly resumed, and the action proceeds. This judgment, therefore, does not fall within the definition of the term just given, but is of an anomalous kind. Upon all other issues in law, and, generally, upon all issues in fact, the judgment is that the plaintiff *do recover*, which is called a judgment *quod recuperet*. The nature of such judgment, more particularly considered, is as follows : It is of two kinds, *interlocutory* and *final*. If the action sound in damages (according to the technical phrase), that is, be brought not for specific recovery of lands, goods, or sums of money (as is the case in real and mixed actions, or the personal actions of debt and detinue), but for damages only, as in covenant, trespass, etc. ; and if the issue be an issue in law, or any issue in fact not tried by jury, then the judgment is only that the plaintiff ought to recover his damages, without specifying their amount ; for, as there has been no trial by jury in the case, the amount of damages is not yet ascertained. The judgment is then said to be interlocutory. On such interlocutory judgment the court does not, generally, itself undertake the office of assessing damages, but issues a *writ of inquiry* directed to the sheriff of the county where the facts are alleged by the pleading to have occurred, commanding him to inquire into the amount of the damage sustained, "by the oath of twelve good and lawful men of his county," and to return such inquisition, when made, to the court. Upon the return of the inquisition, the plaintiff is entitled to another judgment, viz.: that he recover the amount of the damages so assessed; and this is called final judgment. But if the issue be in fact, and was tried by a jury, then the jury, at the same time that they tried the issue, assessed the damages. In this case, therefore, no writ of inquiry is necessary; and the judgment is final in the first instance, and to the same effect as just mentioned, viz.: that the plaintiff do recover the damages assessed. Again, if the action do not sound in damages, the judgment is in this case also generally final in the first instance; and to this effect, that the plaintiff recover seisin of the land, etc., or recover the debt, etc. But there is, beside this, in mixed actions, a judgment for damages also; and this is either given at the same time with that for recovery of seisin, if the damages have been assessed by a jury, or, if not so assessed, a writ of inquiry issues, and a second judgment is given for the amount found by the inquisition.[1]

JUDGMENT FOR THE DEFENDANT.

The issue shall next be supposed to be decided for the defendant.

In this case, if the issue, whether of fact or law, arise on a dilatory plea, the judgment is, that *the writ (or bill) be quashed (quod breve* (or *billa) cassetur)* upon such pleas as are in abatement of the writ or bill, and that the pleading *remain without day*, until, etc., upon such pleas as are in suspension only; the effect, in the first case, of course being that the suit is defeated, but with liberty to the plaintiff to prosecute a better writ or bill; in the second, that the suit is suspended until the objection be removed. If the issue arise upon a declaration or peremptory plea, the judgment generally is that the plaintiff *take nothing by his writ* (or bill), and that the defendant go thereof without day, etc., which is called a judgment of *nil capiat per breve*, or, *per billam.*

What has been said as to the different forms of judgment relates to those on direct issues. Upon an issue of the collat-

---

[1] 2 Saund. 44 n. 4.

eral or incidental kind (which is a case that does not occur in modern practice), the judgment is sometimes *respondeat ouster ;* in other cases, *quod recuperet ;* but the law, with respect to the judgment on issues of this kind, does not seem to be, in every instance, clearly settled.[1]

JUDGMENTS BY DEFAULT, CONFESSION, ETC.

Judgment has hitherto been supposed to be awarded only upon the decision of an issue. There are several cases, however, in which judgment may be given though no issue have arisen, and these cases will now require notice. In the description given in this chapter of the manner of suit, it will be observed that the action has been uniformly supposed to proceed to issue, and this has been done to prevent digression and complexity. But an action may be cut off in its progress and come to premature termination by the fault of one of the parties in failing to pursue his litigation ; and this may happen either with the intention of abandoning the claim or defence, or from failing to follow them up within the periods which the practice of the court in each particular case prescribes. In such cases the opposite party becomes victor in the suit, as well as where an issue has been joined and is decided in his favor, and is at once entitled to judgment. Thus, in a real *(though not in a personal)* action, if the defendant holds out against the process, judgment may be given against him for default of appearance. So, in actions real, mixed, or personal, if after appearance he neither pleads nor demurs, or if after plea he fails to maintain his pleading till issue joined, by rejoinder, rebutter, etc., judgment will be given against him for want of plea, which is called judgment by *nil dicit* (he nothing says). So if, instead of a plea, his attorney says he is not informed of any answer to be given to the action, judgment will be given against him ; and it is in that case called a judgment by *non sum informatus* (I am not informed). Again, instead of a plea, he may choose to confess the action ; or, after pleading, he may at any time before trial both confess the action and withdraw his plea or other allegations ;

[1] Steph. Pl. 135.

and the judgment against him in these two cases is called a judgment by confession or by confession *relicta verificatione* (proof being waived). On the other hand, judgment may be given against the plaintiff, in any class of actions, for not declaring or replying, or surrejoining, etc., or for not entering the issue; and these are called judgments of *non pros.* (from *non prosequitur*, he does not pursue). So, if he chooses, at any stage of the action after appearance and before judgment, to say that he " will not further prosecute his suit," or that " he withdraws his suit," or (in case of plea in abatement) prays that his " writ " or " bill may be quashed, that he may sue or exhibit a better one," there is judgment against him of *nolle prosequi*, *retraxit*, or *cassetur breve*, or *billa*, in these cases respectively. Again, judgment of nonsuit may pass against the plaintiff, which happens when, on trial by jury, the plaintiff, on being called or demanded, at the instance of the defendant, to be present in court while the jury give their verdict, fails to make his appearance. In this case no verdict is given, but judgment of nonsuit passes against the plaintiff. So if, after issue is joined, the plaintiff neglects to bring such issue on to be tried in due time, as limited by the course and practice of the court in the particular case, judgment will also be given against him for this default; and it is called judgment as in case of nonsuit.

These judgments by default, confession, etc., when given for the plaintiff, are generally *quod recuperet*, and may be either *interlocutory* or *final*, according to a distinction already explained. For the defendant, the form generally is *nil capiat* (let him take nothing).[1]

Upon judgment in most personal and mixed actions, whether upon issue, or by default, confession, etc., it will be observed that it forms part of the adjudication that the plaintiff or defendant recover his costs of suit or defence, which costs are taxed by an officer of the court at the time when the judgment is given.

There is generally an addition, too, when the judgment is for the plaintiff, that the defendant " be in mercy " *(in miseri-*

[1] Steph. Pl. 135, 136, 137.

cordia), that is, be amerced or fined for his delay of justice ; when for the defendant, that the plaintiff be in mercy, for his false claim. The practice, however, of imposing an actual amercement has been long quite obsolete.

Judgments, like the pleadings, were formerly pronounced in open court, and are still always supposed to be so ; and they are consequently always considered as taking place in term time. But, by a relaxation of practice, there is now, generally, except in the case of an issue in law, no actual delivery of judgment, either in court or elsewhere. The plaintiff or defendant, when the cause is in such a state that by the course of practice he is entitled to judgment, obtains the signature or allowance of the proper officer of the court, expressing generally that judgment is given in his favor, and this is called signing judgment, and stands in the place of its actual delivery by the judges themselves.[1] Though supposed to be pronounced during term, judgments are frequently signed in time of vacation.

ENTERING JUDGMENT ON RECORD.

Regularly, the next proceeding is to enter the judgment on record. Where it has been signed after trial or demurrer, it will be remembered that the proceedings up to the time of issue and the award of *venire*, or the continuance by *curia advisare vult* (the court wishes to consider), have already been recorded. It will remain, however, to enter the subsequent proceedings to the judgment inclusive, which is called entering the judgment. This is done by drawing them up with continuances, etc., on the same roll on which the issue was entered, by way of continuation, or further narrative, of the proceedings there already recorded ; and the judgment is entered in such form as the attorney for the successful party conceives to be legally appropriate to the particular case, supposing that it were actually pronounced by the court. The roll, when complete by the entry of final judgment, is no longer called the *issue roll*, but has the name of the *judgment roll*, and is deposited and filed of record in the treasury of the

[1] Steph. Pl. 137.

court. This whole proceeding of entering the judgment on record is, in practice, usually neglected. Yet there are several cases in which, by the practice of the court, it becomes essential, after final judgment, to do so, and in which it is, therefore, actually done.

When judgment is signed, not after trial or demurrer, but as by default, confession, etc., there having been no issue roll yet made up, the whole proceedings, to the judgment inclusive, are to be entered for the first time on record. This is accordingly done by the attorney upon a parchment roll, and upon the same principles as to the form of entry that have been already stated with respect to recording the issues and judgment thereon.[1]

EXECUTION.

The course of the action, till the entry on record of the final judgment, has now been described, but the student will not have a complete view of the history of a suit without taking some notice of two other subsequent proceedings. These are the writ of execution and the writ of error.[2]

Upon judgment, the successful party is, generally, entitled to execution, to put in force the sentence that the law has given. For this purpose he sues out a writ, addressed to the sheriff, commanding him, according to the nature of the case, either to give the plaintiff possession of the lands, or to enforce the delivery of the chattel which was the subject of the action, or to levy for the plaintiff the debt or damages and costs recovered, or to levy for the defendant his costs; and that either upon the body of the opposite party,[3] his lands, or goods, or, in some cases, upon his body, lands, and goods; the extent and manner of the execution directed always depending upon the nature of the judgment. Like the judgment, writs of execution are supposed to be actually awarded by the judges in court, but no such award is generally made. The attorney, after signing final judgment, sues out of the proper office a writ of

[1] Steph. Pl. 138.
[2] *Ibid.* 141.
[3] The abolition of imprisonment for debt has taken away this method of execution.

execution in the form to which he conceives he would be entitled upon such judgment as he has entered, if such entry has been actually made, and, if not made, then upon such as he thinks he is entitled to enter; and he does this, of course, upon peril that if he takes a wrong execution, the proceeding will be illegal and void, and the opposite party entitled to redress.[1]

Writs of Error.

After final judgment is signed, the unsuccessful party may bring a writ of error; and this, if obtained and allowed before execution, suspends (generally speaking) the latter proceeding till the former is determined. A writ of error is an original writ, and therefore is sued out of Chancery, directed to the judges of the court in which judgment was given, and commanding them, in some cases, themselves to examine the record; in others, to send it to another court of appellate jurisdiction to be examined, in order that some alleged error in the proceedings may be corrected. The first form of writ, called a *writ of error coram nobis (or vobis)* before us (or you) is where the alleged error consists of matter of fact; the second, called a *writ of error* generally, where it consists of matter of law.

The words *coram nobis* (before us, the king) were used when reference was made to the King's Bench, where the king was supposed in contemplation of law to actually sit; the Common Pleas was designated by the other formula, *coram vobis* (before you, the judges).

When a writ of error is obtained, the whole proceedings, to final judgment inclusive, are then always actually entered (if this has not before been done) on record; and the object of the writ of error is to reverse the judgment for some error of fact or law that is supposed to exist in the proceedings as so recorded. It will be proper here to explain in what such error may consist.

Where an issue in fact has been decided, there is (as formerly observed) no appeal in the English law from its decision, except by way of motion for a new trial; and its

[1] Steph. Pl. 142.

being wrongly decided is not error in that technical sense to which a writ of error refers. So, if a matter of fact should exist, which was not brought into issue, but which, if brought into issue, would have led to a different judgment, the existence of such fact does not, after judgment, amount to error in the proceedings. For example, if the defendant has a release, but does not plead it in bar, its existence can not, after judgment, on the ground of error or otherwise, in any manner be brought forward. But there are certain facts which affect the validity and regularity of the legal decision itself; such as the defendant having, while under age, appeared in suit by attorney, and not by guardian, or, the plaintiff or defendant having been a married woman when the suit was commenced. Such facts as these, however late discovered and alleged, are errors in fact, and sufficient to traverse the judgment upon writ of error. To such cases the writ of error *coram nobis* applies, because the error in fact is not the error of the judges, and reversing it is not reversing their own judgment.[1]

But the most frequent case of error is when, upon the face of the record, the judges appear to have committed a mistake in law. This may be by having wrongly decided an issue in law brought before them by demurrer, but it may also happen in other ways. As formerly stated, the judgment will generally follow success in the issue. It is, however, a principle necessary to be understood, in order to have a right apprehension of the nature of writs of error, that the judges are, in contemplation of law, bound, before in any case they give judgment, to examine the whole record, and then to adjudge either for the plaintiff or defendant, according to the legal right as it may on the whole appear, notwithstanding, or without regard to, the issue in law or fact that may have been raised and decided between the parties; and this, because the pleader may, from misapprehension, have passed by a material question of law without taking issue upon it. Therefore, whenever, upon examination of the whole record, right appears on the whole not to have been done, and judg-

[1] Steph. Pl. 143.

ment appears to have been given for one of the parties, when it should have been given for the other, this will be error in law. And it will be equally error, whether the question was raised on demurrer, or the issue was an issue in fact, or there was no issue, judgment having been taken by default, confession, etc. In all these cases, indeed, except the first, the judges have really committed no error; for it may be collected from preceding explanations, that no record, or even copy of the proceedings, is actually brought before them, except upon demurrer; but, with respect to a writ of error, the effect is the same as if the proceedings had all actually taken place and been recorded in open court, according to the fiction and supposition in law. So, on the same principle, there will be error in law if judgment has been entered in a wrong form, inappropriate to the case; although, as we have seen, the judges have in practice nothing to do with the entry on the roll. But, on the other hand, nothing will be error in law that does not appear on the face of the record; for matters not so appearing are not supposed to have entered into the consideration of the judges. Upon error in law, the remedy is not by writ of error *coram nobis* (for that would be merely to make the same judges reconsider their own judgment), but by a writ of error requiring the record to be sent into some other court of appellate jurisdiction (that the error may be there corrected), and called a writ of error generally.[1]

With respect to the writ of error of this latter description, it is further to be observed, that it cannot be supported unless the error in law be of a substantial kind. For as, by the effect of the statutes of amendments and *jeofails*, errors of mere form are no ground for arresting the judgment, so, by the effect of the same statutes, such objections are now insufficient to support a writ of error, though at common law the case was otherwise.

When, on the ground of some error in law, the record is removed by writ of error, the following is the course of appeal among the different courts: From the Common Pleas the record may be removed into the Court of King's Bench,

---

[1] Steph. Pl. 144.

and from thence, by a new writ of error, into the House of Lords; from the Exchequer into the Court of Exchequer Chamber, held before the Lord Chancellor, Lord Treasurer, and the judges of the Courts of King's Bench and Common Pleas, and from thence into the House of Lords; from the King's Bench, in proceedings by bill, in most of the usual actions, into the Court of Exchequer Chamber, held before the judges of the Common Pleas, and the Barons of the Exchequer, and from thence into the House of Lords; in proceedings by original writ, into the House of Lords in the first instance.[1]

By what course of proceeding the error in the record is discussed and corrected in the appellate court, and the judgment reversed or affirmed, it is not material to the purpose of the present treatise to explain. The student is referred for information on that subject to the many valuable books of practice.

[1] Steph. Pl. 145. This whole process has been changed by the Supreme Court of Judicature Acts.

CHAPTER VIII.

OF THE RULES OF PLEADING.

It is evident that, in the administration of justice, there must be an orderly method of ascertaining the exact point or points to be decided in each particular case. The contending parties naturally state their respective claims. By the rules of the Roman law, which are substantially followed in the modern civil law and in our equity jurisprudence, the respective parties were allowed to state their case *at large, i. e.*, in a narrative form and upon all points involved. This process requires a review by the court of the opposing statements of the litigants, and a winnowing by it of the substantial questions controverted from what is often a mass of irrelevant and immaterial (therefore improper and unnecessary) matter.

The common law of England pursued from the outset a different course. It obliged the parties themselves to so state their cases, or, as it was called, to *plead*, as to develop a single issue by means of their opposing statements; it further compelled them to agree upon this issue as the sole point for decision in the cause. The student will the better comprehend this by a study of the following practical example from Minor's Institutes.[1] He will especially note how, in the supposed case, the proceedings are so conducted as at each stage to put aside matters which are not in dispute, until finally the real question controverted is alone presented for decision. Thus, the execution and delivery of the bond sued on, and of the release pleaded, are only mentioned to be conceded and passed over, until at last the real matter to be decided (the alleged offer to deliver the horse) is affirmed on one side and denied on the other, and thus becomes the sole issue for trial.

[1] Min. Inst. IV. 554, 555.

Abstract of Proceedings in a Supposed Cause.

A. holds a bond of Z.'s for $1,000, on which he proposes to institute suit by causing Z. to be summoned to answer his complaint, which purports to be a *plea of debt*. At the return day of the summons (supposing it to be returned "*executed*"), and from time to time afterwards, the following altercations and proceedings might occur: —

Declaration.	A. — This man Z. owes me $1,000, as appears by his bond here, which I now *produce to the court*, yet he has not paid me.
Oyer.	Z. — Let me *hear it read!*
Pleas.	I say it does not bind me:
	1, Because I was an *infant* when I executed it;
	2, Because it was founded on an *usurious consideration;*
	3, Because it is *not my deed;* and
	4, Because the plaintiff afterwards *released* the bond to me by this writing here, *under his seal*, which I now *produce to the court*.
Demurrer to Pleas.	A. — Stop! I say you cannot make more than *one distinct answer* to my demand; and I submit it to the court.
Joinder in Demurrer.	Z. — Let the court say!
Judgmt. on Demurrer.	COURT. — Defendant *by the common law* (it is otherwise by statute) can make *only one answer*.
Deft. relies on 4th plea.	Z. — Then I rely *on the fourth*, — the release.
Replication.	A. — I say that the so-called release does not bar my demand:
	1, Because it was obtained from me by *duress of violent threats;*
	2, Because I delivered it to W. *as an escrow*, to take effect only on condition that Z. should deliver me a horse the next day, which he did not do.
Demurrer to Replic'n.	Z. — Stop! I say you cannot make more than one distinct answer to my plea; and I submit it to the court.
Joinder in Demurrer.	A. — Let the court say!

Judgmt. on Demurrer.

COURT. — Plaintiff is not permitted by the law to make *more than one answer*.

Plaintiff relies on Second Replication.

A. — Then I rely *on the second*, — that the so-called release was delivered by me as an *escrow*.

Rejoinder.

Z. — I offered to deliver the horse and you refused to receive it.

Demurrer to rejoinder.

A. — Stop ! I admit that you offered to deliver the horse, and that I refused to receive it ; but I say that that is not a sufficient answer to my replication, for you do not say that you have *ever since been ready* to deliver it ; I submit it to the court, if that is not necessary.

Joinder in Demurrer.

Z. — Let the court say !

Judgment (*quasi*) on Demurrer.

COURT. — I am inclined to think *it is not necessary ;* but I will take time to consider.

Demurrer withdrawn with leave.

A. — I will not trouble the court to consider it ; but with its permission I will withdraw my objection to the rejoinder, and answer *to the fact.*

Leave given.

COURT. — Leave is given *of course.*

Sur-Rejoinder and Issue tendered.

A. — I say that the defendant did not offer to deliver me the horse as he has said ; and I *submit it to the country.*

Similiter and Issue.

Z. — And I *do the like.*

Jury Impanelled.

And thereupon comes a jury, to wit Wouter Van Twiller, and eleven others, who being duly elected, tried, and sworn the truth to speak upon the issue joined, upon their oath

Verdict.

do say that the said Z. did not offer to deliver the horse to the said A. as the said Z. hath in pleading alleged, and, therefore, they find for the plaintiff the debt in the declaration mentioned, with lawful interest from the 1st day

Judgment.

of January, 18 —, until paid. Wherefore it is considered by the court that the plaintiff recover against the defendant, the sum of one thousand dollars, with interest thereon, after the rate of *six per centum per annum*, from the 1st day of January, in the year of our Lord eighteen hundred and —— until paid, and his costs by him about his suit in this behalf expended ; and the said defendant in mercy, etc.

Mr. Stephen is of the opinion that this characteristic of the English law is to be attributed to the original practice of *oral* pleading, and that it was adopted to avoid charging the memory with too many and too complicated points of dispute. Another reason assigned for its development is that the different modes of trial formerly existing required the preliminary settlement of the exact question to be tried, in order that the particular mode of trial, appropriate to that question, might be determined.

Whatever is its origin, it is certain that this method has been followed in the English courts from the time of Henry II.[1]

The introduction of an issue was not the only object of this system. An issue might be reached and yet be of such nature as not to involve the merits of the question to be decided. This would, of course, render the trial useless, and would, as we have seen, be occasion for the awarding of a repleader. Therefore, to avoid this mishap, the issue must in all cases be *material* to the question to be tried.

Again, it was important to the judges, when the contention was conducted orally, that the process should be as brief and as simple as possible. Therefore, it was originally established as a rule that the pleaders should be confined to a single issue in respect of each single claim.

It was hardly less essential that the issue should be specific or, as it was called, certain.[2] This was required in order that the mode of decision might be marked out by the issue itself. But especially was it demanded by the nature of the trial by jury as originally practised. As the jurors were then witnesses, the sheriff was directed to summon them from the immediate neighborhood where the facts occurred, and from among those

---

[1] These rules of pleading do not seem to have been originally of legislative enactment, or to have had any authority, except usage or judicial regulation. They grew gradually into an entire and a connected system of pleading. Steph. Pl. 147.

[2] Certainty, in the broad sense of that word, was required in the pleadings and issue in order that the matter tried might become *res judicata* (an adjudicated thing), and might always thereafter be identified as such, and therefore not subject to be tried again. Washington, &c., S. P. Co. *v.* Sickles, 24 How. 341-346. Certainty in the issue was also necessary in connection with the evidence to be adduced on the trial. A definite law of evidence is an offshoot from the system of special pleading. Tyler's Pleading, 48.

persons who best knew the truth of the matter. Hence the issue must specify the *place* where the alleged matter was said to have occurred, and also the *time* and other particulars of the transaction in question in order to guide the sheriff in summoning proper persons as jurors.

It is apparent, from the foregoing considerations, that the chief objects of pleading are these: That the parties be brought to an issue, and that the issue so produced be material, single, and certain in its quality. Moreover, this result should be reached without obscurity in the process, and further, without prolixity and delay. The whole body of the established rules of pleading has been accordingly distributed by Mr. Stephen under the following heads: —

I. RULES WHICH TEND SIMPLY TO THE PRODUCTION of AN ISSUE.

II. RULES WHICH TEND TO SECURE THE MATERIALITY OF THE ISSUE.

III. RULES WHICH TEND TO PRODUCE SINGLENESS OR UNITY IN THE ISSUE.

IV. RULES WHICH TEND TO PRODUCE CERTAINTY OR PARTICULARITY IN THE ISSUE.

V. RULES WHICH TEND TO PREVENT OBSCURITY AND CONFUSION IN PLEADING.

VI. RULES WHICH TEND TO PREVENT PROLIXITY AND DELAY IN PLEADING.

VII. CERTAIN MISCELLANEOUS RULES.

These rules and their discussion will lay before the student a general but complete view of the whole system of pleading. The following pages will consist in the main of the text of Mr. Stephen's work (2d London edition), with such departures therefrom, principally by way of illustration and detail, as experience has suggested.

CHAPTER IX.

OF RULES WHICH TEND SIMPLY TO THE PRODUCTION OF AN ISSUE.

Upon examination of the system of allegation by which the parties are brought to issue, as that process has been described, it will be found to resolve itself into the following fundamental rules or principles : —

I. After the Declaration the Parties must at each stage Demur, or plead by Way of Traverse, or by Way of Confession and Avoidance.

II. Upon a Traverse, Issue must be tendered.

III. The Issue, when well tendered, must be accepted.

Either by virtue of the first rule, a demurrer takes place (which is a tender of an issue in law), or, by the joint operation of the first two, the tender of an issue in fact; and then, by the last of these rules, the issue so tendered, whether in fact or in law, is accepted, and becomes finally complete. It is by these rules, therefore, that the production of an issue is effected ; and they will consequently form the subject of the present chapter.

Rule I. After the Declaration, the Parties must at each stage Demur, or plead by Way of Traverse, or by Way of Confession and Avoidance.

Exceptions : (1) *Where a Dilatory Plea is interposed.*

(2) *Pleadings in Estoppel.*

(3) *Where a New Assignment is necessary.*

This rule has two branches —

1. The party must *demur* or *plead*. One or other of these courses he is bound to take (while he means to maintain his

action or defence) until issue be tendered. If he does neither, but confesses the right of the adverse party, or says nothing, the court immediately gives judgment for his adversary; in the former case, as by confession; in the latter, by *non pros.* or *nil dicit.*

2. If the party *pleads*, it must either be by way of *traverse* or of *confession* and *avoidance.* If his pleading amount to neither of these modes of answer, it is open to demurrer on that ground.[1]

Such is the effect of this rule generally and briefly considered. But, for its complete illustration, it will be necessary to enter much more deeply into the subject, and to consider at large the doctrines that relate both to *demurrers* and to *pleadings.*

I. Of Demurrers.

Under this head it is intended to treat, (1) of the nature and properties of a demurrer; (2) of the effect of passing a fault by without demurrer, and pleading over; (3) of the considerations which determine the pleader in his election to demur or plead.

(1) Of the Nature and Properties of a Demurrer.

A demurrer may be for insufficiency either in *substance* or in *form ;* that is, it may be either on the ground that the case shown by the opposite party is *essentially insufficient*, or on the ground that it is stated in an *inartificial manner ;* for " the law requires in every plea " (and the observation equally applies to all other pleadings) " two things : the one that it be in matter sufficient, the other that it be deduced and expressed according to the forms of law; and if either the one or the other of these be wanting, it is cause of demurrer." [2] A violation of any of the rules of pleading that will be hereafter stated is, in general, *ground for demurrer ;* and such fault occasionally amounts to matter of *substance*, but usually to matter of *form* only.

---

[1] Reg. Plac. 59; 21 Hen. VI. 12; 5 Hen. VII. 13 a, 14 a, b; 1 Tidd, 665, 8th ed.; Merceron *v.* Dowson, 5 Barn. & Cress. 479.

[2] Per Lord Hobart, Colt *v.* Bishop of Coventry, Hob. 164.

A demurrer, as in its *nature*, so also in its *form*, is of two kinds : it is either *general* or *special*. A general demurrer excepts to the sufficiency in general terms, without showing specifically the nature of the objection ; a special demurrer adds to this a specification of the particular ground of exception.[1] A general demurrer is sufficient where the objection is on a matter of *substance*. A special demurrer is necessary where it turns on matter of *form* only ; that is, where, notwithstanding such objection, enough appears to entitle the opposite party to judgment, as far as relates to the merits of the cause. For, by two statutes, 27 Elizabeth, c. 5, and 4 Anne, c. 16, passed with a view to the discouragement of merely formal objections, it is provided, in nearly the same terms, that the judges " shall give judgment according as the very right of the cause and matter in law shall appear unto them, without regarding any imperfection, omission, defect, or want of form, except those only which the party demurring shall specially and particularly set down and express, together with his demurrer, as causes of the same ; " the latter statute adding this proviso : " So as sufficient matter appear in the said pleadings, upon which the court may give judgment according to the very right of the cause." Since these statutes, therefore, no mere matter of form can be objected on a general demurrer ; but the demurrer must be in the special form, and the objection specifically stated.[2] But, on the other hand, it is to be observed that, under a special demurrer, the party may, on the argument, not only take advantage of the particular faults which his demurrer specifies, but also of all such objections in substance, or regarding " the very right of the cause " (as the statutes express it) as do not require, under those statutes, to be particularly set down.[3] It follows, therefore, that unless the objection be clearly of this substantial kind, it is the safer course, in all cases, to demur

[1] Co. Litt. 72 a; Reg. Plac. 125, 126; Bac. Ab. Pleas, &c. n. 5.

[2] For examples of cases where a special demurrer is considered as necessary, and where, on the other hand, a general one is sufficient, see Buckley *v.* Kenyon, 10 East 139 ; Bowdell *v.* Parsons, *ibid.* 359 ; Bolton *v.* Bishop of Carlisle, 2 H. Bl. 259. A demurrer to a plea in *abatement* need not be special. (2 Saund. 2 b, n. *k.*)

[3] Chit. Pl. 576.

specially.[1]   Yet, where a general demurrer is plainly sufficient,
it is more usually adopted in practice ; because, the effect of
the special form being to apprise the opposite party more distinctly of the nature of the objection, it is attended with the
inconvenience of enabling him to prepare to maintain his
pleading in argument, or of leading him to apply the earlier
to amend.   With respect to the *degree* of particularity with
which, under these statutes, the special demurrer must assign
the ground of objection, it may be observed, that it is not sufficient to object, in general terms, that the pleading is " uncertain, defective, informal," or the like ; but it is necessary
to show *in what respect* uncertain, defective, or informal.[2]

EFFECT OF A DEMURRER.   With respect to the *effect* of a
demurrer, it is, first, a rule that *a demurrer admits all such
matters of fact as are sufficiently pleaded.*[3]   The meaning of
this rule is, that the party, having had his option whether to
plead or *demur*, shall be taken, in adopting the latter alternative, to admit that he has no ground for denial or traverse.
A demurrer is consequently an admission that the facts alleged
are true ; and therefore the only question for the court is,
whether, assuming such facts to be true, they sustain the case
of the party by whom they are alleged.   It will be observed,
however, that the rule is laid down with this qualification,
that the matter of fact be *sufficiently pleaded*.   For, if it be
not pleaded in a formal and sufficient manner, it is said that
a demurrer, in this case, is no admission of the fact.[4]   But
this is to be understood as subject to the alterations that have
been introduced into the law of demurrer by the statutes
already mentioned ; and therefore, if the demurrer be *general*,
instead of *special*, it amounts, as it is said, to a confession,
though the matter be informally pleaded.[5]

Again, it is a rule that *on demurrer the court will consider
the whole record, and give judgment for the party who, on the*

---

[1] 1 Arch. 313 ; Clue *v.* Baily, 1 Vent.   1 East. 634 ; Gundry *v.* Feltham, 1
240.   T. R. 334.

[2] 1 Saund. 160, n. 1 ; 337 b, n. 3.   [4] Com. Dig. Pleader, Q. 6.

[3] Bac. Ab. Pleas, &c. n. 3 ; Com.   [5] 1 Saund. 337 b, n. 3 ; 1 Arch. 318.
Dig. Pleader, Q. 5 ; Nowlan *v.* Geddes,

whole, appears to be entitled to it.[1] Thus, on demurrer to the replication, if the court think the replication bad, but perceive a substantial fault in the *plea*, they will give judgment, not for the defendant, but the plaintiff,[2] provided the *declaration* be good ; but if the declaration also be bad in substance, then, upon the same principle, judgment would be given for the defendant.[3] This rule belongs to the general principle already stated, that when judgment is to be given, whether the issue be in law or fact, and whether the cause have proceeded to issue or not, the court is always bound to examine the whole record, and adjudge for the plaintiff or defendant, according to the legal right, as it may on the whole appear. It is, however, subject to the following

Exceptions : First, if the plaintiff demur to a *plea in abatement*, and the court decide against the plea, they will give judgment of *respondeat ouster*, without regard to any defect in the declaration.[4]

Secondly, though on the whole record the right may appear to be with the plaintiff, the court will not adjudge in favor of such right, unless the plaintiff have himself put his action upon that ground.

Example : Where, on a covenant to perform an award, and not to prevent the arbitrators from making an award, the plaintiff declared in covenant, and assigned as a breach that the defendant would not pay the sum awarded, and the defendant pleaded that, before the award made, he revoked, by deed, the authority of the arbitrators, to which the plaintiff demurred, the court held the plea good, as being a sufficient answer *to the breach alleged,* and therefore gave judgment for the defendant, although they also were of opinion that the matter stated in the plea would have entitled the plaintiff to maintain his action, if he had alleged, by way of breach, that the defendant prevented the arbitrators from making their award.[5]

---

[1] Com. Dig. Pleader, M. 1, M. 2 ; Bac. Ab. Pleas, &c. A. n. 3 ; 5 Co. Rep. 29 a ; 1 Saund. 285, n. 5 ; Foster *v.* Jackson, Hob. 56 ; Anon. 2 Wils. 150 ; Le Bret *v.* Papillon, 4 East. 502.

[2] Anon. 2 Wils. 150 ; Thomas *v* Heathorn, 2 Barn. & Cress. 477.

[3] Piggot's Case, 5 Co. Rep. 29 a ; Bates *v.* Cort, 2 Barn. & Cress. 474.

[4] Belasyse *v.* Hester, Lutw. 1592 ; Ronth *r.* Weddell, *Ibid.* 1667 ; Hastrop *r.* Hastings, 1 Salk. 212 ; Rich *v.* Pilkington, Carth. 172.

[5] Marsh *r.* Bulteel, 5 B. & Ald. 507.

Lastly, the court, in examining the whole record, to adjudge according to the apparent right, will consider only the right in *matter of substance*, and not in respect of mere *form*, such as should have been the subject of special demurrer.

Example: Where the declaration was open to an objection of form, such as should have been brought forward by special demurrer — the plea bad in substance — and the defendant demurred to the replication, the court gave judgment for the plaintiff, in respect of the insufficiency of the plea, without regard to the formal defect in the declaration.[1]

(2) Effect of Pleading over without Demurrer.

It has been shown that it is the effect of a demurrer to admit the truth of all matters of fact sufficiently pleaded on the other side; but it cannot be said, *e converso*, that it is the effect of a pleading to admit the sufficiency in law of the facts adversely alleged. On the contrary, as has been seen upon a demurrer arising at a subsequent stage of the pleading, the court will take into consideration, retrospectively, the sufficiency in law of matters to which an answer in fact has been given. And, as has been shown, even after an issue in fact and verdict thereon, the court are bound to give judgment on the whole record, and therefore to examine the sufficiency in law of all allegations through the whole series of the pleadings; and, accordingly, advantage may often be taken by either party of a legal insufficiency in the pleading on the other side, by motion in arrest of judgment or motion for judgment *non obstante veredicto*[2] or writ of error, according to the circumstances of the case.

It thus appears that in many cases a party, though he has pleaded over without demurring, may nevertheless afterwards avail himself of an insufficiency in the pleading of his adversary. But this is not universally true. For, first, it is to be observed, *that faults in the pleading are, in some cases, aided by pleading over.*[3]

---

[1] Humphreys *v.* Bethily, 2 Vent. 222.

[2] According to English practice, as has been noted, the defendant moved in arrest of judgment in cases similar to those in which the plaintiff moved for judgment *non obstante veredicto.*

[3] Com. Dig. Pleader, C. 85, E. 37; Co. Litt. 303 b.; Pract. Reg. 351; Anon.

Example : In an action of trespass, for taking a hook, where the plaintiff omitted to allege in the declaration that it was *his* hook, or even that it was in his possession, and the defendant pleaded a matter in confession and avoidance, justifying his taking the hook *out of the plaintiff's hand*, the court, on motion in arrest of judgment, held, that as the plea itself showed that the hook was in the possession of the plaintiff, the objection, which would otherwise have been fatal, was cured.[1]

And with respect to all *objections of form*, it is laid down as a general proposition, " that if a man pleads over he shall never take advantage of any slip committed in the pleading of the other side, which he could not take advantage of upon a general demurrer." [2]

Again, it is to be observed *that faults in the pleading are, in some cases, aided by a verdict.*[3] Thus, if the grant of a reversion, a rent charge, an advowson, or any other hereditament which lies *in grant*, and can only be conveyed by deed, be pleaded, such grant ought to be alleged to have been made *by deed*, and, if not so alleged, it will be ground of demurrer; but if the opposite party, instead of demurring, pleads over, and issue be taken upon the grant, and the jury find that the grant was made, the verdict aids or cures the imperfection in the pleading, and it can not be objected in arrest of judgment or by writ of error.[4] The extent and principle of this rule of *aider by verdict* is thus explained in a modern decision of the Court of King's Bench : " Where a matter is so essentially necessary to be proved that, had it not been given in evidence, the jury could not have given such a verdict, there the want of stating that matter in express terms in a declaration, provided it contains terms sufficiently general to comprehend it in fair and reasonable intendment, will be

---

2 Salk. 519; Fowle *v.* Welsh, 1 Barn. & Cress. 29 ; Fletcher *v.* Pogson, 3 Barn. & Cress. 192.

1 Brooke *v.* Brooke, Sid. 184, cited Bac. Ab. Trespass, 603.

2 Per Holt, C. J.; Anon. 2 Salk. 519 ; Bac. Ab. Pleas, &c. 322.

3 Com. Dig. Pleader, C. 87 ; 1 Saund. 228, n. 1; Weston *v.* Mason, 3 Burr. 1725 ; Spieres *v.* Parker, 1 T. R. 141;

Johnstone *v.* Sutton, *ibid.* 545 ; Nerot *v.* Wallace, 3 T. R. 25 ; Jackson *v.* Pesked, 1 M. & S. 234; Campbell *v.* Lewis, 3 Barn. & Ald. 392; Keyworth *r.* Hill, *ibid.* 685; Pippet *v.* Hearn, 5 Barn. & Ald. 634 ; Lord Huntingtower *v.* Gardiner, 1 Barn. & Cress. 297 ; Price *v.* Seaman, 4 Barn. & Cress. 525.

4 1 Saund. 228 a, n. 1 ; Lightfoot *v* Brightman, Hutt. 54.

cured by a verdict; and where a general allegation must, in fair construction, so far require to be restricted that no judge and no jury could have properly treated it in an unrestrained sense, it may reasonably be presumed, after verdict, that it was so restrained at the trial."[1] In entire accordance with this are the observations of Mr. Sergeant Williams: " Where there is any defect, imperfection, or omission in any pleading, whether in substance or form, which would have been a fatal objection upon demurrer, yet if the issue joined be such as necessarily required, on the trial, proof of the facts so defectively or imperfectly stated or omitted, and without which it is not to be presumed that either the judge would direct the jury to give or the jury would have given the verdict, such defect, imperfection, or omission is cured by the verdict."[2] It is, however, only where such " fair and reasonable intendment " can be applied that a verdict will cure the objection ; and, therefore, if a necessary allegation be altogether omitted in the pleading, or if the pleading contain matter adverse to the right of the party by whom it is alleged, and so clearly expressed that no reasonable construction can alter its meaning, a verdict will not aid.[3]

Example: Where the plaintiff brought an action of trespass on the case, as being entitled to the reversion of a certain yard and wall, to which the declaration stated a certain injury to have been committed, but omitted to allege that the *reversion* was, in fact, prejudiced, or to show any grievance which, in its nature, would necessarily prejudice the reversion, the court arrested the judgment, after a verdict had been given in favor of plaintiff, and held the fault to be one which the verdict could not cure.[4]

Lastly, it is to be observed, *that at certain stages of the cause all objections of form are cured by the different statutes of jeofails and amendments*, the cumulative effect of which is to provide that neither after verdict or judgment by confession, *nil dicit*, or *non sum informatus*, can the judgment be arrested or reversed by any objection of that kind.

[1] Jackson v. Pesked, 1 M. & S. 234.
[2] 1 Saund. 228, n. 1.
[3] Jackson v. Pesked, *ubi supra;* Nerot
v. Wallace, 3 T. R. 25 ; Weston v. Mason, 3 Burr. 1725.
[4] Jackson v. Pesked, *ubi supra.*

Example: In an action of trespass, where the plaintiff omits to allege in his declaration on what certain day the trespass was committed (which is a ground of demurrer), and the defendant, instead of demurring, pleads over to issue, and there is a verdict against him, the fault is cured by the statutes of jeofails,[1] if not also by the mere effect of pleading over.

(3) Considerations by which the Pleader ought to be governed, in making his Election to Demur or to Plead.[2]

He is first to consider whether the declaration, or other pleading opposed to him, is sufficient in substance and in form to put him to his answer. If sufficient in both, he has no course but to plead. On the other hand, if insufficient in either, he has ground for demurrer; but whether he should demur or not is a question of expediency, to be determined by the following considerations: If the pleading be insufficient in *form*, he is to consider whether it is worth while to take the objection, recollecting the indulgence which the law allows in the way of *amendment;* but also bearing in mind that the objection, if not taken, will be aided by pleading over, or, after pleading over, by the verdict, or by the statutes of amendments and jeofails. And, if he chooses to demur, he must take care to demur specially, lest, upon general demurrer, he should be held excluded from the objection. On the other hand, supposing an insufficiency in substance, he is to consider whether that insufficiency be in the case itself, or in the manner of statement; for, on the latter supposition, it might be removed by an amendment, and it may, therefore, not be worth while to demur. And, whether it be such as an amendment would remove or not, a further question will arise, whether it be not expedient to pass by the objection for the present, and plead over; for a party, by this means, often obtains the advantage of contesting with his adversary, in the first instance, by an issue in fact, and of afterwards urging

---

[1] Bl. Com. III. 394 *; 1 Saund. 228 c, n. 1, where Mr. Sergeant Williams corrects a mistake in the passage in Blackstone's Commentaries.

[2] As, according to modern practice, the judgment against a demurrer is generally not final, but permits the demurrant to plead over, the pleader now has more freedom in making his election.

the objection in law by motion in arrest of judgment or writ of error.[1] This double aim, however, is not always advisable; for, though none but *formal* objections are cured by the statutes of jeofails and amendments, there are some defects, of *substance* as well as *form*, which are aided by pleading over or by a verdict; and therefore, unless the fault be clearly of a kind not to be so aided, a demurrer is the only mode of objection that can be relied upon. The additional delay and expense of a trial is also sometimes a material reason for proceeding in the regular way by demurrer, and not waiting to move in arrest of judgment or to bring a writ of error. And a concurrent motive for adopting that course is, that costs are not allowed when the judgment is arrested,[2] nor where it is reversed upon writ of error[3] (each party in these cases paying his own); but on demurrer the party succeeding obtains his costs.

II. Of Pleadings.

Under this head it is proposed to examine, (A) the nature and properties of *traverses;* (B) the nature and properties of pleadings in *confession and avoidance;* (C) the nature and properties of *pleadings in general*, without reference to their quality, as being by way of traverse or confession and avoidance.

(A) Of the Nature and Properties of Traverses.

Of *traverses*, there are various kinds. The most ordinary kind is that which may be called a *common* traverse.

The Common Traverse.

The common traverse consists of a *tender of issue;* that is, of a denial, accompanied by a formal offer of the point denied for decision; and the denial that it makes is by way of *express contradiction, in terms of the allegation traversed.*

---

[1] "When the matter in fact will clearly serve for your client, although your opinion is that the plaintiff hath no cause of action, yet take heed that you do not hazard the matter upon a demurrer, in which, upon the pleading and otherwise, more will perhaps arise than you thought of; but first take advantage of the matters of fact, and leave matters in law, which always arise upon the matters in fact, *ad ultimum*, and never at first demur in law when, after trial of the matters in fact, the matters in law will be saved to you." (Lord Cromwell's Case, 4 Co. Rep. 14 a.)

[2] 1 Sel. Pract. 497; Cameron *v.* Reynolds, Cowp. 407.

[3] 2 Tidd, 1243, 8th ed.

These are generally expressed in the *negative*. That, however, is not invariably the case with a common traverse; for, if opposed to a precedent negative allegation, it will, of course, be in the *affirmative*.

THE GENERAL ISSUES.

Besides this, the common kind, there is a class of traverses which, from its great frequency and importance in practice, requires particular notice. It is that of the *general issues*. In most of the usual actions there is an appropriate plea, fixed by ancient usage, as the proper method of traversing the declaration, in cases where the defendant means to deny the whole or the principal part of its allegations.[1] This form of plea or traverse is called the *general issue* in that action; and it appears to be so called, because the issue that it tenders, involving the whole declaration or the principal part of it, is of a more general and comprehensive kind than that usually tendered by a common traverse. From the examples of it that will be presently given, it will be found that, not only in extent or comprehensiveness, but in point of form also, it differs somewhat from a common traverse; for though, like that, it *tenders issue*, yet, in several instances, it does not contradict *in terms of the allegation traversed*, but in a more general form of expression.

In *debt* on *bond* or *other specialty* the general issue is called the plea of *non est factum;* and is as follows: —

And the said C. D., by ———, his attorney, comes and defends the wrong and injury, when, &c., and says that the said supposed writing obligatory (*or* "*indenture*," *or* "*articles of agreement*," *according to the subject of the action*) is *not his deed;* and of this he puts himself upon the country.

In *debt* on *simple contract* the general issue is called the plea of *nil debet;* and is thus: —

And the said C. D., by ———, his attorney, comes and defends the wrong and injury, when, &c., and says that he *does not owe* the said sum of money above demanded, or any part thereof,

---

[1] Reg. Plac. 57; Doct. & Stud. 272.

16

in manner and form as the said A. B. hath above complained; and of this the said C. D. puts himself upon the country.[1]

In *covenant* [2] the general issue is *non est factum*, and its form is similar to that in debt on specialty.

In *detinue* the general issue is called the plea of *non detinet;* and is as follows: —

And the said C. D., by ———, his attorney, comes and defends the wrong and injury, when, &c., and says that he *does not detain* the said goods and chattels *(or "deeds and writings," according to the subject of the action)* in the said declaration specified, or any part thereof, in manner and form as the said A. B. hath above complained; and of this the said C. D. puts himself upon the country.

In *trespass* the general issue is called the plea of *not guilty;* and is as follows: —

---

[1] *Nil debet* is the proper form of the general issue, not only in debt on simple contract, but in all other actions of debt not founded on a deed or specialty. And an action is not considered as founded on a deed or specialty, so as to require a plea of *non est factum*, if the deed be mentioned in the declaration only as introductory to some other main cause of action. Therefore *nil debet* is a good plea in debt for rent upon an indenture, or in debt for an escape, or in debt upon a *devastavit* (he has wasted). (1 Tidd, 701, 8th ed.)

[2] " According to respectable authorities (Tidd, 593. Lawes' Pl 113. 1 Chit. Pl. 482), there is, to a declaration in *covenant broken, no* general issue: Since the plea of *non est factum*, which denies the *deed* only, and not *the breach*, does not put the *whole* declaration in issue. And therefore, it is said, that this plea, when used in this particular action, is to be called '*the common issue.*' It must indeed be admitted. that there is a difference between the effect of the plea of *non est factum*, in covenant broken, and in *debt* on specialty. A valid bond, or single bill, necessarily creates a *present debt;* and the plea in question, by denying the deed, necessarily and *directly* denies the alleged *debt:* Whereas a *covenant* does not necessarily create, in the covenantee, a right to damages; because a breach may never occur. And though, if there be no covenant, there can be no *breach;* yet a denial of the covenant denies the breach, only by *consequence*, and not *directly.* As, however, *non est factum* is confessedly a *good* plea, in covenant broken, and also the most general form of denial, of which the action admits, there appears to be little use in distinguishing it, by the anomalous appellation of a 'common issue.' Indeed, the only peculiarity which distinguishes it in this action, from other general issues, — viz., that it does not put the *whole* declaration directly in issue, — would seem rather to bring it within the description of a *special* issue. At any rate, if it is necessary or proper to give this plea, in the action of *covenant broken*, the peculiar denomination of a *common issue*, it would seem equally so, to distinguish the same plea by the same name when pleaded to a *special* declaration, in debt *on a penal bond.* For the same reason, which authorizes its peculiar designation in the former action, exists, to the same extent, in the latter." Gould's Pl. 284, n. 2.

And the said C. D., by ———, his attorney, comes and defends the force and injury, when, &c., and says that he is not guilty of the said trespasses above laid to his charge, or any part thereof, in manner and form as the said A. B. hath above complained; and of this the said C. D. puts himself upon the country.

In *trespass on the case* (in the species of *assumpsit)* the general issue is called the plea of *non-assumpsit;* and is as follows : —

And the said C. D., by ———, his attorney, comes and defends the wrong and injury, when, &c., and says that he *did not undertake* or promise, in manner and form as the said A. B. hath above complained: and of this the said C. D. puts himself upon the country.

In *trespass on the case, in general*, the general issue is *not guilty;* and is thus : —

And the said C. D., by ———, his attorney, comes and defends the wrong and injury, when, &c., and says that he is not guilty of the premises above laid to his charge, in manner and form as the said A. B. hath above complained ; and of this the said C. D. puts himself upon the country.

In *replevin* the general issue is called the plea of *non cepit;* and is as follows : —

And the said C. D., by ———, his attorney, comes and defends the wrong and injury, when, &c., and says that he *did not take* the said cattle *(or " goods and chattels," according to the subject of the action)* in the said declaration mentioned, or any of them, in manner and form as the said A. B. hath above complained ; and of this the said C. D. puts himself upon the country.

A very important effect attends the adoption of the general issue, viz., that by tendering the issue on the declaration, and thus closing the process of the pleading at so early a stage, it throws out of use, wherever it occurs, a great many rules of pleading, applying exclusively to the remoter allegations. For it is evident that, when the issue is thus tendered in the plea, the whole doctrine relating to pleadings in confession and avoidance, replications, rejoinders, etc., is superseded.

At the same time, the general issue is of very frequent occurrence in pleading; and it has, therefore, on the whole, the
effect of narrowing, very considerably, the application of
the greater and more subtle part of the science.

The important character of this plea makes it material to
explain distinctly in what cases it may and ought to be used;
and this is the more necessary, because an allowed relaxation
in the modern practice has, in some actions, given it an
application more extensive than belongs to it in principle.
To obtain a clear view of this subject, we must examine the
language of the different general issues, in reference to
the declarations which they respectively traverse.

In *debt* on *specialty* and in *covenant*, the general issue, *non
est factum*, denies that the deed mentioned in the declaration
is the deed of the defendant. Under this, the defendant at
the trial may contend, either that he never executed such
deed as alleged, or that it is absolutely void in law.

Examples : He may so contend on the ground that the alleged
obligor or covenantor was, at the time of execution, a married
woman or a lunatic;[1] or that since its execution, and before the
commencement of the suit, it has been erased or altered by the
obligee or covenantee himself, or (if in a material point) by a
stranger.[2]

But if the defendant's case consist of anything but a denial
of the execution of such deed as alleged, or some fact showing
its absolute invalidity, the plea of *non est factum* will be improper.[3] And it is to be observed that, in point of pleading,

[1] Com. Dig. Pleader, 2 W 18; Yates
v. Boen, 2 Str. 1104; Collins v. Blantern,
2 Wils. 347.

[2] Henry Pigot's Case, 11 Co. Rep.
26 b   But, according to modern
authority, an alteration, although
material. can not invalidate a written
instrument, when made by a stranger
to the contract. See Parsons on Contracts (7th ed.), II. 716*, n. 1, where
the authorities are collected and discussed.

[3] If the statement of the deed in the
declaration materially varies from the
tenor of the deed itself, the plea of *non
est factum* will of course be as applicable
as where no deed has been executed by
the defendant; for in either case the
deed, as *alleged*, is not his. So, if the
instrument was delivered as an *escrow.*
this is evidence under *non est factum* (1
Tidd, 701, 8th ed.), because it shows
the invalidity of the instrument as a
deed. But it seems that its delivery as
an escrow may be also specially pleaded.
(Murray v. Earl of Stair, 2 Barn. &
Cress. 82.)

a deed is on some grounds absolutely *void* in law, on others *voidable* only.   Thus, though it is void for the lunacy of the party who executes, his infancy makes it only voidable.[1] And its execution under duress is also an objection of the latter kind.[2] Now, the rule is, that while matters which make a deed absolutely void may be given in evidence under *non est factum*, those which make it voidable only must be specially pleaded.[3] And it seems that, generally, objections to the legality of the consideration on which a deed was founded are referable to the latter class ; for it has been decided, that where the condition of a bond is in restraint of matrimony, that ground of defence is not evidence under *non est factum ;* [4] and that where a bond is given to compound a felony, that is matter which must be specially pleaded.[5] And it is a general rule that any illegality arising from the prohibition of *an act of Parliament*, as in the case of usury, or gaming, is matter for special plea, and is not evidence under *non est factum ;* [6] a rule apparently founded on the same principle ; for its reason seems to be, that the statute is always so construed as to make the instrument not absolutely void, but voidable by special plea.[7]

If the general issue in *debt on simple contract* be now examined, its effect and application will be found to be much more extensive. The declaration alleges that the defendant was indebted to the plaintiff on some consideration, *e. g.*, for goods sold and delivered. The general issue alleges " that he does not owe the sum of money," etc. Were the allegation merely that "the goods were not sold and delivered," it would of course be applicable to no case but that where the defendant means to deny the sale and delivery ; but, as the allegation

[1] Whelpdale's Case, 5 Co. Rep. 119 a ; 2 Inst. 483 ; Darby *v.* Boucher, 1 Salk. 279 ; Zouch *v.* Parsons, 3 Burr. 1805 ; Gibbs *v.* Merrell, 3 Taunt. 307 ; Baylis *v.* Dinely, 3 M. & S. 477 ; Keane *v.* Boycott, 2 H. Bl. 515.

[2] 2 Inst. 482, Com. Dig. Pleader, 2 W. 19.

[3] Com. Dig. Pleader, 2 W. 18.

[4] Colton *v.* Goodridge, 2 Bl. Rep. 1108.

[5] Harmer *v.* Rowe, 2 Chit. Rep. 334 ; s. c. 2 Stark. 36 ; and see Collins *v.* Blantern, 2 Wils. 347.

[6] Whelpdale's Case, *ubi supra.* With respect to *usury*, it is said that, even if the condition of a bond, as set forth in the pleadings, appears on the face of it to be usurious, yet the defendant cannot *demur*, but must plead the usury. (1 Saund. 295 a, n. 1.)

[7] See Whelpdale's Case, *ubi supra.*

is that he *does not owe*, it is evident that the plea is adapted to any kind of defence that tends to deny *an existing debt ;* and, therefore, not only to a defence consisting in a denial of the sale and delivery, but to those of *release, satisfaction, arbitrament*,[1] and a multitude of others, to which a general issue of a narrower kind (for example, that of *non est factum*) would, in its appropriate actions, be inapplicable. In short, there is hardly any matter of defence to an action of debt to which the plea of *nil debet* may not be applied, because almost all defences resolve themselves into a denial *of the debt*.[2]

In *detinue*, the declaration states that the defendant detains certain goods of the plaintiff; the general issue alleges that he " does not detain the said goods in the said declaration specified," etc. This will apply either to a case where the defendant means to deny that he detains the goods mentioned, or to a case where he means to deny that the goods so detained are the *property of the plaintiff;* for, if they are not the plaintiff's property, then it is true that the defendant does not detain the goods specified in the declaration ; the only goods there specified being described as the goods *of the plaintiff*.[3]

In *trespass*, the general issue, *not guilty*, evidently amounts to a denial of the trespasses alleged, and no more. Therefore, if in trespass for assault and battery the case be, that the defendant has *not* assaulted or beat the plaintiff, it will be proper that he should plead the general issue ; but if his case be of any other description, the plea will be inapplicable. So, in trespass *quare clausum fregit*, or for taking the plaintiff's goods, if the defendant did not, in fact, break and enter the

---

[1] Anon. 5 Mod. 18 ; Paramore *v.* Johnson, 1 Ld. Raym. 566 ; s. c. 12 Mod. 376.

[2] It was even holden, per Holt, C. J., that as the plea is in the present tense, the defendant may give in evidence the *statute of limitations*. (Draper *v.* Glassop, 1 Ld. Raym. 153 ; Lee *v.* Clarke, 2 East, 336. Per Lawrence, J. *Qu. tamen* (questioning). See 1 Saund. 283, n. 2, 2 Saund. 62 c, n. 6.) But under this plea, defendant cannot give in evidence a *tender*, nor (without notice) a *set-off;* nor (in an action for rent on indenture) that the plaintiff *had nothing in the tenements ;* nor (in debt, *qui tam*) *a former recovery* against him for the same cause by another person. (1 Tidd, 700, 8th ed.)

[3] Therefore he may give in evidence, under *non detinet*, a *gift* from the plaintiff ; for that proves that he does not detain the plaintiff's goods ; but he can not give in evidence that they were *pawned* to him. (Co. Litt. 283.)

close in question or take the goods, the general issue, " not guilty," will be proper. It will also be applicable if he *did* break and enter the close, but it was not *in the possession of the plaintiff*, or not *lawfully in his possession, as against the better title of the defendant*.[1] So it will be applicable if he did take the goods, but they did not *belong to the plaintiff;* for, as the declaration alleges the trespass to have been committed on the close or goods *of the plaintiff*, the plea of *not guilty* involves a denial that the defendant broke and entered the close or took the goods *of the plaintiff ;* and is, therefore, a fit plea, if the defendant means to contend that the plaintiff had no possession of the close, or property in the goods, sufficient to entitle him to call them his own. But if the defence be of any other kind, the general issue will not apply.

So far, all is consistent with the form and principle of these several pleas ; but, with respect to the two general issues that next follow, the case is somewhat different.

First, with respect to that in *assumpsit*. The declaration in this action states that the defendant, upon a certain consideration therein set forth, made a certain promise to the plaintiff. The general issue, in this action, states that the defendant " did not promise and undertake in manner and form," etc. This, at first sight, would appear to put in issue merely the fact of his having made a promise such as is alleged. A much wider effect, however, belongs in practice to this plea, and was originally allowed (as it would appear), with reference to the following distinction. It has been already stated that the law will always *imply* a promise, in consideration of an existing debt or liability ; and that the action of *assumpsit* may be consequently founded on a promise either *express* or *implied*. When the promise relied upon was of the *latter kind*, and the defendant pleaded the general issue, the ·plaintiff's mode of maintaining the affirmative of this issue, on the trial, was, of course, by proving that debt or liability on which the implied promise would arise ; and in such case it was evidently reasonable that the defendant also should, under his plea denying the promise, be at liberty to show any circumstance

[1] Dodd *v.* Kyffin, 7 T. R. 254.

by which the debt or liability was disproved; such, for example, as performance or a release. Accordingly, in actions on *implied assumpsits*, this effect was, on the principle here mentioned, allowed to the general issue. But it was at first allowed in the case of *implied assumpsits only;* and, where an *express* promise was proved, the defendant, in conformity with the language and strict principle of his plea, was permitted, under the general issue, only to contest the fact of the promise, or at most to show that, on the ground of some illegality, it was a promise void in law.[1] This practice, however, was by relaxation gradually applied to *actions* on *express* promises also; and at length, in *all* actions of *assumpsit* without distinction, the defendant was, under the general issue, permitted not only to contend that no promise was made, or to show facts impeaching the validity of the promise, but (with some few exceptions)[2] to prove any matter of defence whatever which tends to deny his debt or liability; for example, a release or performance.

This is a great deviation from principle; for it is to be observed that many of these matters of defence are such (in the case of express promise) as ought regularly to be pleaded in *confession and avoidance.* Thus, if the defendant be charged with an express promise, and his case be, that, after making such promise, it was *released* or *performed*, this plainly *confesses and avoids* the declaration. To allow the defendant, therefore, to give this in evidence under the general issue, which is a plea by way of *traverse*, is to lose sight of the distinction between the two kinds of pleading. And even where the matters of defence thus admitted in evidence are *not* such as would have been pleadable by way of confession and avoidance, but are in the nature of a traverse of the declaration, yet they are almost always inconsistent with the form and language of the general issue in this action; which (as has been seen) consists of a denial of the *promise* only, and pur-

---

[1] Fits *v.* Freestone, 1 Mod. 310; Abbot *v.* Chapman, 2 Lev. 81; Vin. Ab. Evidence, Z, a.

[2] He can not give in evidence a *tender, bankruptcy of defendant*, the *statute of limitations, a discharge under the insol-* vent *act*, nor (in some cases) a defence under the *court of conscience acts*. Nor is a *set-off* evidence under *non-assumpsit*, unless notice of set-off be given with the plea. (Chit. Pl. 420; 1 Tidd, 700, 8th ed.)

ports to traverse no other part of the declaration. Thus, in an action which has become, of all others, the most frequent and general in its application, the science of pleading has been, in a great measure, superseded by an innovation of practice, which enables the parties to come to issue upon the plea (the second step in the series of allegations) in a great variety of cases, which would formerly have led to much remoter or more specific issues. This important inroad on the ancient dominion of pleading has been effected for more than a century past,[1] and was probably first encouraged by the judges in consequence of a prevalent opinion that the rules of this science were somewhat more strict and subtle than is consistent with the objects of justice ; and that, as the general issue tended to abbreviate its process, and proportionably to emancipate the suitors from its restrictions, it was desirable to extend, as much as possible, the use and application of that plea.

Next in order is the general issue which belongs to the action of *trespass on the case in general.* The declaration in this action sets forth specifically the circumstances which form the subject of complaint. The general issue, *not guilty*, is a mere traverse or denial of the facts so alleged ; and, therefore, on principle, should be applied only to cases in which the defence rests on such denial. But here a relaxation has taken place similar to that which prevails in *assumpsit ,* for, under the plea now in question, a defendant is permitted not only to contest the truth of the declaration, but, with certain exceptions,[2] to prove any matter of defence that tends to show that the plaintiff has no right of action, though such matters be in confession and avoidance of the declaration ; as, for example, a release given or satisfaction made. This latitude was, no doubt, originally allowed for the same reasons that prompted

---

[1] See Paramore *v.* Johnson, 12 Mod. 377, where Holt, C. J., says : " It is indulgence to give *accord with satisfaction* in evidence upon *non-assumpsit* pleaded, but that has crept in, and now is settled."

[2] In an action of libel or words of slander he cannot give in evidence the *truth* of the charges, but must plead it specially ; nor *retaking on fresh pursuit*, in an action for escape ; nor in any action on the case, the *statute of limitations.* (1 Tidd, 702, 8th ed. ; Chit Pl. 436)

the encouragement of the general issue in *assumpsit*. It is not, however, easy to conceive by what artifice of reasoning the relaxation was, in this case, held to be reconcilable with the principles of pleading, to which it stands in apparent variance ; and perhaps the truth is, that the practice in question was first applied to the general issue in trespass on the case *in general*, without regard to any principle beyond that of a forced analogy to the similar practice in trespass on the case in *assumpsit*.[1]

Thus, in *assumpsit* and trespass on the case in general, the defendant is allowed, under the general issue, to give in evidence matters which do not fall within the strict principles of that plea ; and, among these, matters in confession and avoidance. It is to be observed, however, with respect to matters of this latter description, that, though allowed, he is in no case obliged to take that course, but may still bring forward, by way of special plea in confession and avoidance, all such allegations as properly fall within the principle of such pleadings ; that is, all which confess what is adversely alleged, but repel or obviate its legal effect. Thus the defendant may, in *assumpsit* and other actions of trespass on the case, plead a release, though it is also competent to him to rely upon it in evidence under the general issue.[2] As this course is allowable, so there are reasons of convenience which sometimes dictate its adoption ;[3] but the general issue, where capable of being applied, is much the more usual form of plea, and that which, from its generality, is commonly the most advantageous to the defendant.

---

[1] See, however, Lord Mansfield's explanation of the reason for allowing this practice in trespass on the case. (Bird v. Randall, 3 Burr. 1353.)

[2] Upon this principle the defendant may plead specially, not only a *release, performance, payment, accord and satisfaction*, or other matter in *discharge*, but any matter also which tends to show the contract *void* or *voidable in point of law*, while it admits it to have been made in fact, such as *infancy, lunacy, coverture,*

duress, usury, gaming, or the *statute of frauds*. All these, however, are evidence under the general issue.

[3] The chief advantage of pleading specially is, that it obliges the plaintiff to *reply ;* in doing which, he is confined (as will be shown hereafter) to a single answer. This often puts him to great disadvantage, for he may have several answers to the defendant's case ; and, if the general issue be pleaded, may avail himself of all.

Lastly, the general issue, *non cepit*, in *replevin*, applies to the case where the defendant has not in fact taken the cattle or goods, or where he did not take them, or have them, in the *place* mentioned in the declaration.[1] For the declaration alleges that the defendant "took certain cattle or goods of the plaintiff, in a certain place called," etc., and the general issue states that he did not take the said cattle or goods " in manner and form as alleged;" which involves a denial both of the taking and of the place in which the taking was alleged to have been ; the *place* being a material point in this action.

On the subject of general issues, it remains only to remark, that other pleas are ordinarily distinguished from them by the appellation of *special pleas ;* and, when resort is had to the latter kind, the party is said to plead *specially*, in opposition to pleading the *general issue*.[2] So the *issues* produced upon special pleas, as being usually more specific and particular than those of *not guilty, nil debet*, etc., are sometimes described in the books as *special issues*, by way of distinction from the others, which were called *general issues*,[3] the latter term having been afterwards applied not only to the issues themselves, but to the pleas which tendered and produced them.[4]

THE TRAVERSE DE INJURIA.

There is another species of traverse, which varies from the common form, and which, though confined to particular actions, and to a particular stage of the pleading, is of frequent occurrence. It is the traverse *de injuria sua propria, absque tali causa* (of his own wrong without such excuse), or (as it is briefly called) the traverse *de injuria*. It always *tenders issue ;* but, on the other hand, differs, like many of the gen-

---

[1] Chit. Pl. 436.

[2] These terms, it may be remarked, have given rise to the popular denomination of the whole science to which this work relates, which, though properly described as that of *pleading*, is generally known by the name of *special pleading*.

[3] Co. Litt. 126 a ; Heath's Maxims, 53 ; Com. Dig. Pleader, R. 2.

[4] By the Rules of Court of Hilary Term, 1834, 3 and 4 Wm. IV, the general issues were materially restricted. The student is referred to the Report of the Common Law Commissioners, and to those rules which he will find in full in 5 Barn. & Adolph. i.–xx. As these rules were never in force in this country, they are only of scientific interest to the American student.

eral issues, from the common form of a traverse, by denying in general and summary terms, and *not in the words of the allegation traversed.*

This species of traverse occurs in the *replication* in actions of trespass,[1] trespass on the case,[2] replevin,[3] *assumpsit*,[4] debt,[5] and covenant,[6] but is not used at any other stage of the pleading. In these actions it is the *proper* form, when the plea consists merely of matter of *excuse.* But when it consists of or comprises matter of *title* or *interest* in land, etc., or the *commandment* of another, or *authority of law,* or *authority in fact,* derived from the opposite party, or matter of *record,* — in any of these cases, the replication *de injuria* is generally improper,[7] and the traverse of any of these matters should be in the common form ; that is, in the words of the allegation traversed.

As the general issue allowed the defendant to deny by a brief formula the material averments of the plaintiff's declaration, so this species of traverse, which occurs only as a replication, gave the plaintiff a similar privilege in · certain cases with respect to the defendant's plea. These cases are when, in any of the above-named actions, the defendant undertakes in his plea to excuse by a plea of confession and avoidance the act alleged against him in the declaration. An illustration will make this plain :

Example : A. sues B. in trespass *vi et armis* for an assault and battery.   B. pleads what is technically called a plea of *son assault demesne* (his own assault) ; ˙by this plea he confesses that he did assault as charged in the declaration ; but he *excuses* his apparently wrongful act by averring that A. has not told the whole truth in his declaration, for, as B. now alleges, A. made the first assault upon him, and he only *molliter manus imposuit* (gently hands laid) upon A. to defend himself from A.'s assault *prout bene ei licuit* (as well he might), using no more force than was necessary to repel A.'s assault.

---

[1] Crogate's Case, 8 Co. Rep. 67 a.

[2] O'Brien *v.* Saxon, 2 Barn. & Cress. 908.

[3] Selby *v.* Bardons, 3 Barn. & Adolph. 2.

[4] Isaac *v.* Farrer, 1 M. & W. 65.

[5] Cowper *v.* Garbett, 13 *ibid.* 33

[6] Washbourne *v* Barrows, 1 Ex. 107.

[7] Crogate's Case, *ubi supra ;* Doct. Pl. 113, 115.   See the law on this subject more fully explained, and the exceptions noticed, Chit. Pl. 512–518 ; 1 Arch. 238 ; 2 Saund. 295, n. 1 ; 1 Saund. 244 c, n. 7.

Now, the student will observe that by this plea B. has offered an excuse which is made up of several elements, to wit : the prior assault by A. upon him, and his battery of A. in self-defence.   Instead of being compelled to traverse specif-ically the material allegations of this plea, A. is permitted to reply generally that B. assaulted him as charged in the decla-ration *of his (B.'s) own wrong and without the excuse* set out in the plea.

Let us take another more complicated illustration : —

Example: The plaintiff sued the defendant for maliciously, and without any reasonable or probable cause, suing out a com-mission of bankruptcy against him, the plaintiff.   The defendant pleaded confessing the suing out of the commission of bankruptcy, but excusing his act by averring that the plaintiff was a trader, and as such became indebted to him and then became a bankrupt, wherefore he (defendant) sued out the said commission.   To this the plaintiff replied that the defendant *of his own wrong and without the excuses* in his plea alleged committed the grievance charged in the declaration.[1]

Here the student will notice that the defendant's plea con-tains three several material averments, to wit : the plaintiff's trading, his bankruptcy, and the petitioning creditor's debt. Yet by this form of replication the plaintiff is permitted to put them all in issue.

This privilege of the plaintiff is however restrained within reasonable bounds.   It may be that the defendant's plea contains matter which can not properly be put in issue in this general way.   The defendant, sued for an assault, may plead that he was an officer of the law charged with the execution of a warrant for the arrest of the plaintiff, and that he com-mitted the assault in question only to enforce his arrest over the plaintiff's resistance thereto.   To permit the replication *de injuria sua propria absque tali causa* in this case, would be to send to the jury for trial a question of record (the warrant) combined with a question of fact (the resistance of the plain-tiff to the arrest), and this the law will not do.

Again, questions of title to or interest in land were con-

[1] O'Brien *v.* Saxon, 2 Barn. & Cress 908   See also Robinson *v.* Rayley, 1 Burr. 316.

sidered too important to be tried in this general way, and a specific traverse was required to put them in issue.[1] So if the defendant claimed authority for the act alleged from the plaintiff, he was entitled to know by a specific traverse whether the plaintiff denied that authority.[2]

In these cases another form of this replication was, however, open to the plaintiff, and this was called *de injuria sua propria absque residuo causæ* (of his own wrong without the remainder of the excuse).

Example: The plaintiff sues the defendant for assault and battery. The defendant confesses that he did commit the alleged assault, but only under the following circumstances: On the day in question he was an officer of the law, and as such was charged to arrest the plaintiff upon the warrant of a competent court; he attempted to arrest the plaintiff upon this warrant, when the plaintiff assaulted him, and he was compelled to beat the plaintiff to enforce his arrest.

Now it may be that, in the case supposed, the defendant really was acting under a warrant, and yet did assault and beat the plaintiff without justification. In such case the plaintiff would usually *protest*[3] the warrant, and reply *de injuria . . . absque residuo causæ* as to the remainder of the plea, thus putting in issue the defendant's averment that he was compelled to beat the plaintiff to enforce his arrest.

Thus in each case the plaintiff can waive or admit the forbidden subject, and reply *de injuria . . . absque residuo causæ* as to the remainder of the excuse.[4] In any case he can contest the question of *authority, title,* etc., *but not under this replication;* it must be *by an appropriate traverse.*

This replication *de injuria* in any form could not be used where the plea was the general issue, a specific traverse, or a plea by way of confession and avoidance in discharge. Nor could it be resorted to in reply to a plea of set-off, for that is a cross-demand of the defendant and is not matter in excuse.[5]

---

[1] Crogate's Case, 8 Co. Rep. 66.

[2] Com. Dig. Pleader, F. 22.

[3] The subject of *protestation* will be hereafter considered.

[4] For an example of the use of the traverse *de injuria . . . absque residuo causæ,* see Renno *v.* Bennett, 3 Gal. & Dav. 54; s. c. 3 Ad. & E. (N. S.) 768.

[5] Salter *v.* Purchell, 1 Q. B. 197.

THE SPECIAL TRAVERSE.

There is still another species of traverse, which differs from the common form, and which will require distinct notice. It is called the *special traverse*, and is a form of pleading governed by rules which are considered intricate. Its tendency to illustrate the general spirit and character of the science justifies its consideration at length, although it has fallen into disuse and has finally been abolished in the land of its birth.

A special traverse is a pleading which sets out with a detail of circumstances, inconsistent with those stated in the preceding pleading to which it purports to be an answer; it then directly denies some fact stated in that preceding pleading, and concludes with a verification.[1] The detail of inconsistent circumstances, with which it commences, is termed the *inducement* to the traverse; the denial is called, from its introductory words, the *absque hoc* (without this).

Why should this *special traverse* be necessary in any case?

In many instances, occurring in ordinary discussion, a proposition may be so stated as to require contradiction, and yet not to admit of a point-blank or, as it is called, a categorical, denial. In juridical disputation the same situation is sometimes presented, and the special traverse is the form of qualified denial which the science of pleading supplies for use in that emergency. The student must recollect that the Nay! of the common traverse was nay indeed. If the pleader used that, he had to deny in the very words of his antagonist's pleading. When it was inconvenient or impossible for him to do this, he, of necessity, resorted to the indirect or qualified denial of the special traverse.

Now there were four classes of circumstances which made it desirable for the pleader to adopt this indirect form of denial:

(1) The case might be one in which some principle or rule of law was opposed to a direct denial;

(2) Some fact, ordinarily immaterial but material in the particular case, might be falsely pleaded by the adversary, and

[1] Evans' Pl. 31.

the purposes or the defence would require the materiality of that fact to be made apparent on the face of the pleading;

(3) It might be desirable in the particular case to separate questions of law from those of fact;

(4) The defendant (or the party pleading the special traverse) might wish to open and conclude the cause.

These several instances may be made plain by examples. ·

(1) Employment of a special traverse because an unqualified and unexplained denial is opposed to some principle or rule of law.

Example : If in an action of covenant by the *heir of a lessor*, against the lessee of land for *non-payment of rent*, the fact be that the lessor had no more than an estate *for his life* in the premises, so that the heir has no interest therein, and the lessee should traverse in the common form, by averring " that after the making of the said lease, the reversion of the said demised premises did not belong to the said lessor *and his heirs*," etc., it would expose him to the objection of violating the well-known rule of law, whereby a tenant is precluded (or in technical phrase, estopped), to say that his lessor *had no title* in the premises demised. Instead, therefore, of the general assertion that the reversion did not belong to the lessor and his heirs, which would fall within this prohibition, the lessee, by means of a special traverse, says what he is permitted by law to say, to wit: that his lessor had only a particular estate, which has since expired.[1]

In a case, therefore, in which the declaration alleged a seisin in fee in the lessor, and the nature of the defence was, that he had a particular estate only (*e. g.*, an estate for life), since expired, the pleader would resort to a special traverse, setting forth the lessor's limited title, by way of inducement, and traversing his seisin of the reversion in fee under the *absque hoc.* He thus would avoid the objection that might otherwise arise on the ground of estoppel.

(2) It may be necessary to show that in the particular case certain averments of fact are material and should be truly pleaded.

Example : The plaintiff in an action for false imprisonment declares that the defendant, in Montgomery County, in the

---

[1] Blake *v.* Foster, 8 T. R. 487; Brudnell *v.* Roberts, 2 Wills, 143; Min. Inst. IV. 648.

State of Maryland, on the 1st day of May, 1896, unlawfully arrested and detained him for two days. Now ordinarily averments of time and place are immaterial, it being manifest that what is an injury at one time or place is equally so at another. But in the case supposed these averments may both be very material,[1] for the truth may be that the arrest sued for was made not in Montgomery, but in Prince George's County, Maryland, by the defendant, who was at the time in question sheriff of the latter county; it may be further true that the arrest was made not on the first but on the tenth day of May, 1896, by virtue of a competent warrant of that date which the sheriff had on that day, but which he did not have on the first day of May as charged. Here it is evident that the defendant must rely for his defence on the warrant and on the fact that he executed it within his jurisdiction. In other words, the averments of time and place are, in the particular case, both material for the justification of the arrest so made by him. Now he can not deny the truth of the plaintiff's declaration, for it is true save as to the averments of time and place, which the plaintiff need not prove as alleged. He can not defend himself by pleading the warrant as a justification, because it had no existence on the first day of May, 1896, and in any event it would not protect him beyond the limits of his own county. His only remedy, therefore, is a special traverse. In the inducement of this traverse he will state that on the tenth day of May, 1896, he was the sheriff of Prince George's County aforesaid; that a writ had on that day been legally issued, and placed in his hands, by virtue of which he afterwards, upon that day, and in the same county, arrested the plaintiff, and that this is the same arrest complained of in the declaration.

Here is a statement of facts inconsistent with that of the plaintiff, yet not directly denying any matter stated in the declaration. This statement of inconsistent matter shows that the place and time of the arrest, although generally immaterial, are, in this special case, material, and that it is necessary for the defendant's justification that they be averred with exactness.[2]

But subsequently it was permitted in such cases to plead in confession and avoidance, justifying the arrest by a statement

[1] "In these transitory actions not only the place but the time may be made material by the plea." Greene v. Jones, 1 Saund. 300 f, n. (6), Emerton v. Selby, 2 Ld. Raym 1015.

[2] Evans' Pl. 33, 34.

17

of the true particulars thereof, and adding an averment that the circumstances so stated are the same as those complained of in the declaration.[1] This, however, was a departure from the accuracy of special pleading, for a tort can not be confessed and then justified.

(3) Employment of a special traverse in order to separate questions of law from those of fact.

Example: In an action on the case *for waste*, if the defendant plead the general traverse (or issue) *not guilty*, the whole case upon that issue must be determined by a jury. Now suppose that the destruction or waste in question has been committed, not by *public enemies*, but by *rebels in arms*. It might be very desirable to the defendant not to submit to the jury the question of law, whether destruction so occasioned is technical waste or not, but to have it determined by the court. If that be his object, he might effect it by pleading by way of *special traverse*, setting forth by way of *inducement* that the destruction was occasioned by the overpowering violence of rebels, marshalled in arms and in warlike array, against the existing government, which violence it was impossible for him to resist; and then under the *absque hoc*, denying the waste charged: "*without this* that the said defendant was guilty of the said waste and destruction in the declaration mentioned." [2]

To such a special traverse the plaintiff must either demur, upon the ground that destruction wrought by rebels, however irresistible, is no less *waste in law* than when occasioned by a mob, or he must join issue *upon the fact* alleged, and insist that the waste was not brought about by rebels in arms, as stated in the plea. In the latter case, all question as to the law is waived, and the jury are charged with a mere matter of fact; in the former, the question is one exclusively of law, which the court decides.[3]

(4) Employment of a *special traverse* in order to obtain for the party pleading the privilege of opening and concluding the cause.

The defendant is allowed upon such a plea to open and conclude the cause, because the *affirmative of the issue, and, therefore, the burden of proof, is upon him.*

[1] Mellor *v.* Walker, 2 Saund. 4, 5 a, n. (3).   [3] Min. Inst. IV. 648, 649.
[2] Green *v.* Cole, 3 Saund. 252.

Example: The plaintiffs sued the defendant in trespass for breaking their drawbridge, by carelessly "bringing a vessel, under the command of the defendant, in violent collision with it. The defendant, instead of pleading the general issue and denying that he was guilty of the wrong, undertook to do so with an *inducement,* by way of explanation, alleging that the plaintiffs had so obstructed the water-way between the piers of their draw, that a constant and very strong current was created just at that point, whereby vessels passing through the draw were liable, notwithstanding the utmost pains and care which those who navigated them could take, to be carried violently against one or the other of the piers, and that defendant had used due care in the management of his vessel; *without this,* that he was guilty of any negligence," etc.[1]

It will be seen at once that this last example is not a legitimate special traverse; no occasion exists for its use. A plea of the general issue would answer every proper purpose of the pleader. But this abuse of the special traverse was formerly allowed, and by means of it the pleader obtained his object and had the affirmative of the issue.

A similar abuse of this traverse was practised by the plaintiff, but it requires no detailed notice.

A special traverse must always consist of three parts:

(1) The affirmative part, or inducement, which generally introduces new matter and constitutes the indirect or argumentative denial.

(2) The negative part, which contains the direct denial, and, as has been seen, is called the *absque hoc* (without this) from the Latin words with which this part formerly began, although similar words as *et non*[2] (and not) might also be used.

(3) The verification and prayer for judgment, with which this form of traverse originally concluded.

The regular method of pleading in *answer* to a special traverse is to tender issue upon it, with a repetition of the allegation traversed.

It will be perceived, therefore, that the *effect* of a special

---

[1] Crosskeys Co. *v.* Rawlings, 3 Bingh. N. C. 71.

[2] Bennet *v.* Filkins, 1 Saund. 21.

traverse is to postpone the issue to one stage of the pleading later than it would be attained by a traverse in the common form.

The ancient pleader appears to have been mainly influenced by the preceding considerations in his frequent adoption of an inducement of new affirmative matter, tending to explain or qualify the denial. But, though these considerations show the purpose of the *inducement*, they do not account for the two other distinctive features of the special traverse, viz.: the *absque hoc* and the *conclusion with a verification*. For, it will naturally suggest itself, the affirmative matter might, in each of the above cases, have been pleaded *per se*, without the addition of the *absque hoc*. So, whether the *absque hoc* were added or not, the pleading might, consistently with any of the above reasons, have *tendered issue*, like a common traverse, instead of concluding with a verification. These latter forms were dictated by *other* principles. The direct denial under the *absque hoc* was rendered necessary by this consideration : that the affirmative matter, taken *alone*, would be only an *indirect* (or, as it is called in pleading, *argumentative)* denial of the preceding statement ; and, by a rule which will be considered in its proper place hereafter, all *argumentative* pleading is prohibited. In order, therefore, to avoid this fault of *argumentativeness*, the course adopted was, to follow up the explanatory matter of the inducement with a *direct* denial.[1] Thus, to allege, as in the first example, that the lessor was seised for life, would be to deny by implication, but by implication *only*, that the reversion belonged to him in fee ; and therefore, to avoid argumentativeness, a direct denial that the reversion belonged to him in fee is added, under the formula of *absque hoc*. With respect to the *verification*, this conclusion was adopted in a special traverse, in obedience to another rule, of which there will also be occasion to speak hereafter, viz.: *that wherever new matter is introduced in a pleading it is improper to tender issue, and the conclusion must consequently be*

[1] Reeves' Hist. II. 625 ; Bac. Ab. 301 ; Herring *v.* Blacklow, Cro. Eliz. 30; Pleas, &c. H. ; Courtney *v.* Phelps, 1 Sid. 10 Hen. VI. 7 Pl. 21.

with a verification. The inducement setting forth new matter makes a verification necessary, in conformity with that rule.

Having now explained the form, the effect, and the use and object of a special traverse, it remains to show in what cases this method of pleading is or ought to be applied at the present day. First, it is to be observed that this form was at *no* period applicable to *every case* of denial, at the pleasure of the pleader. There are many cases of denial to which the scheme of special traverse has never been applied, and which have always been and still are the subjects of traverse in the common form exclusively.[1] These it is not easy to enumerate or define; they are determined by the course of precedent, and in that way become known to the practitioner. On the other hand, in many cases where the special traverse anciently occurred, it is now no longer used, especially that species of it which is illustrated by the last example. Even when the formula was most in repute, the use of that species does not appear to have been regarded as matter of *necessity ;* and, in cases which admit or require no allegation of new matter, we find the special and the common traverse to have been indifferently used by the pleaders of those days.[2] But in modern times the special traverse, without an inducement of new matter, has been considered, not only as *unnecessary,* but as frequently *improper.* As the taste in pleading gradually simplified and improved, the prolix and dilatory effect of a special traverse brought it into disfavor with the courts ; and they began, not only to enforce the doctrine that the common form might be substituted in cases where there was no inducement of new matter, but often intimated their preference of that form to the other.[3] Afterwards they appear to have gone further, and to have established in favor of the common plan of traverse, in cases where there is no allegation of new matter, the following rule of distinction : *That where the whole substance of the last pleading is denied, the conclusion must be to the country,* or, in other words, the

---

[1] Horne *r.* Lewin, 1 Ld. Raym. 641.

[2] Rast. Ent. 622 ; and see Horne *v.* Lewin, *ubi supra.*

[3] Robinson *v.* Rayley, 1 Burr. 320.

traverse must be in the common form; *but where one of several facts only is the subject of denial, the conclusion may be either to the country or with a verification ;* that is, the traverse may be either common or special, *at the option of the pleader.*[1] It is not easy to trace either the original authority, or even a very satisfactory reason, for this distinction. It does not appear to coincide with the practice at a former period, which certainly allowed special traverses, though without an inducement of new matter, in many cases where the whole substance of the pleading was denied; and its true origin is perhaps to be referred to the inclination of the courts to discourage this formula. From the time that the special traverse thus fell into disrepute, it has been much neglected, even in cases where permissible; and it now rarely occurs in any instance where there is no inducement of new matter, although the denial relate to one out of several facts only. With respect to the *other* kind of special traverse, viz., that which is attended with an inducement of new matter, the case is very different. This was originally devised, as has been shown, for certain reasons of convenience or necessity; and those reasons still occasionally apply. However, in the general decline of the method of special traverse there is felt in practice a great disinclination to adopt in any case whatever, without a clear reason for doing so, this discredited form; and this more particularly because of the disadvantages with which it is attended. These disadvantages consist not only in prolixity and delay, but in the additional inconvenience that the inducement tends to disclose the real nature of the party's case, by giving notice to his adversary of the precise grounds on which the denial proceeds, and thus facilitates to the latter the preparation of his proofs, or otherwise guides him in his further proceedings. For these reasons the special traverse is perhaps daily becoming more rare. And even though the case be such as would admit of an inducement of new matter explanatory of the denial, the usual course is to omit any such inducement, and to make the denial in

[1] See 1 Saund. 103 a, b, n. 3; Bac. Ab. Pleas, &c. 381, notes; Smith *v.* Dovers, 2 Doug. 430.

an absolute form, with a tender of issue; thus substituting the common for the special formula. The latter, however, appears to be still always allowable when the case is such as admits of an inducement of new matter, except in certain instances before noticed, to which, by the course of precedent, the common form of traverse has always been exclusively applied. And, where allowable, it should still be occasionally adopted, by reason of the various grounds of necessity or convenience by which it was originally suggested. Accordingly, it is apprehended that in the first three examples a special traverse would be as proper at the present day as it was at the period when the precedents first occurred.

It will be necessary now to advert to certain principles laid down in the books relative to this form.

The Inducement should be such as in itself Amounts to a Sufficient Answer in Substance to the Last Pleading.[1]

For, as has been shown, it is the use and object of the inducement to give an explained or qualified denial; that is, to state such circumstances as tend to show that the last pleading is not true; the *absque hoc* being added merely to put that denial in a positive form, which had previously been made in an indirect one. Now, an indirect denial amounts, in substance, to an answer; and it follows, therefore, that an inducement, if properly framed, must always in itself contain, without the aid of the *absque hoc*, an answer in substance to the last pleading. Thus, in the first example, the allegation that the lessor was seised for life, and that his estate is since determined, is in itself, in substance, a sufficient answer, as denying, by implication, that the fee descended from the lessor to the plaintiff.

The Inducement must not consist of a Direct Denial.

It follows, from the same consideration as to the object and use of a special traverse, that the answer given by the inducement can properly be of *no other* nature than that of an

---

[1] Bac. Ab. H. 1; Com. Dig. Pleader, G. 20; Anon. 3 Salk. 353; Dike *v.* Ricks, Cro. Car. 336.

indirect denial. Accordingly, we find it decided, in the first place, *that it must not consist of a direct denial.*

Example: The plaintiff in an *audita querela*, being bound by recognizance to pay J. Bush £300 in six years, by £50 per annum, at a certain place, alleged that he was ready every day, at that place, to have paid to Bush the said £50, but that Bush was not there to receive it. To this the defendant pleaded, that J. Bush was ready at the place to receive the £50, *absque hoc*, that the plaintiff was there ready to have paid it. The plaintiff demurred, on the ground that the inducement, alleging Bush to have been at the place ready to receive, contained a direct denial of the plaintiff's precedent allegation that Bush was *not* there, and should therefore have concluded to the country, without the *absque hoc;* and judgment was given accordingly for the plaintiff.[1]

The Inducement must not be in the Nature of a Confession and Avoidance.[2]

Example: If the defendant makes title as assignee of a term of years of A., and the plaintiff, in answer to this, claims under a prior assignment to himself from A. of the same term, this is a confession and avoidance; for it admits the assignment to the defendant, but avoids its effect, by showing the prior assignment. Therefore, if the plaintiff pleads such assignment to himself by way of inducement, adding under an *absque hoc*, a denial that A. assigned to the defendant, this special traverse is bad.[3] The plaintiff should have pleaded the assignment to himself as in confession and avoidance, without the traverse.

There must be no Traverse upon a Traverse.

Again, it is a rule with respect to special traverses, that the opposite party has no right to traverse the inducement,[4] or (as the rule is more commonly expressed) *that there must be no traverse upon a traverse.*[5] Thus, in the first example, if the plaintiff, instead of taking issue on the traverse, should traverse the inducement, either in the common or the special

[1] Hughes *v.* Phillips, Yelv. 38; and see 36 Hen. VI. 15.

[2] Com. Dig. Pleader, G. 3; Lambert *v.* Cook, 1 Ld. Raym. 238; Helier *v.* Whytier, Cro. Eliz. 650.

[3] Com. Dig. *ubi supra;* Helier *v.* Whytier, *ubi supra.*

[4] Anon. 3 Salk. 353.

[5] Com. Dig. Pleader, G. 17; Bac. Ab. Pleas, &c. H. 4; The King *v.* Bishop of Worcester, Vaughan, 62; Digby *v.* Fitzharbert, Hob. 104.

form, denying that the lessor, at the time of making the indenture, was seised in his demesne as of freehold for the term of his
natural life, etc., such replication would be bad, as containing
a traverse upon a traverse. The reason of this rule is clear
and satisfactory. By the first traverse a matter is denied by
one of the parties which had been alleged by the other, and
which, having once alleged it, the latter is bound to maintain
instead of prolonging the series of the pleading and retarding
the issue by resorting to a new traverse.

*Exception : There may be a traverse upon a traverse when the
first is a bad one.*[1]

In other words, if the denial under the *absque hoc* of the
first traverse be insufficient in law, it may be passed by, and
a new traverse taken on the inducement.

Example : In an action of prohibition, the plaintiff declared
that he was elected and admitted one of the common council of
the city of London, but that the defendants delivered a petition
to the court of common council, complaining of an undue election,
and suggesting that they themselves were chosen ; whereas
(the plaintiff alleged) the common council had no jurisdiction to
examine the validity of such an election, but the same belonged to
the court of the mayor and aldermen. The defendants pleaded
that the common council, time out of mind, had authority to
determine the election of common councilmen ; and that the
defendants, being duly elected, the plaintiff intruded himself into
the office ; whereupon the defendants delivered their petition to
the common council, complaining of an undue election ; *without
this, that* the jurisdiction to examine the validity of such election
belonged to the court of the mayor and aldermen. The plaintiff
replied [2] by traversing the inducement ; that is, he pleaded that
the common council had not authority to determine the election
of common councilmen, concluding to the country. To this the
defendant demurred, and the court adjudged that the first traverse
was bad, because the question in this prohibition was not whether
the court of aldermen had jurisdiction, but whether the common
council had ; and that, the first traverse being immaterial, the
second was well taken.

---

[1] Com. Dig. Pleader, G. 18, 19 ;
Thrale *v.* Bishop of London, 1 H. Bl.
376 ; Richardson *v.* Mayor of Oxford, 2
H. Bl. 186 ; King *qui tam v.* Bolton, Str.
117 ; Crosse *v.* Hunt, Carth. 99.

[2] "Though the plaintiff might have
demurred, yet he was at liberty to go
on to try the right." (Pratt, C. J.,
King *qui tam v.* Bolton, Str. 117, 119.)
[3] *Ibid.*

The Inducement can not be Confessed and Avoided.

As the inducement can not, when the denial, under the *absque hoc,* is sufficient in law, be traversed, so, for the same reasons, it can not be answered by *a pleading in confession and avoidance.* But, on the other hand, if the denial be insufficient in law, the opposite party has then a right to plead in confession and avoidance of the inducement, or (according to the nature of the case) to traverse it; or he may demur to the whole traverse for the insufficiency of the denial.

As the inducement of a special traverse, when the denial under the *absque hoc* is sufficient, can neither be traversed nor confessed and avoided, it follows that there is, in that case, no manner of *pleading* to the inducement. The only way, therefore, of answering a good special traverse is to plead to the *absque hoc,* which is done by tendering issue on such denial.

But, though there can be no *pleading* to an inducement, when the denial under the *absque hoc* is sufficient, yet the inducement may be open, in that case, to exception in point of *law.* If it be faulty in any respect, as, for example, in not containing a sufficient answer in substance, or in giving an answer by way of direct denial, or by way of confession and avoidance, the opposite party may demur to the whole traverse, though the *absque hoc* be good, for this insufficiency in the inducement.[1]

Rules pertaining to Traverses in General.

The *different kinds, or forms of* traverse, having been now explained, it will be proper next to advert to certain principles which belong to *traverses in general.*

(1) A Traverse must Deny "Modo et Forma."

The first of these that may be mentioned is, that it is the nature of a traverse to deny the allegation in the *manner and form* in which it is made, and therefore to put the opposite party to prove it to be true in manner and form, as well as in

[1] Com. Dig. Pleader, G. 22; Foden *v.* Haines, Comb. 245.

general effect. Accordingly, he is often exposed at the trial to the danger of a *variance*, for a slight deviation in his evidence from his allegation.

This doctrine of *variance* we now perceive to be founded on the strict quality of the traverse here stated. It has been explained, however, that this strictness is so far modified that it is, in general, sufficient to prove *accurately* the *substance* of the allegation; and that a deviation in point of *mere form, or in matter quite immaterial*, will be disregarded.

On this subject of variance, or the degree of strictness with which, in different instances, the traverse puts the fact in issue, there are a great number of adjudged cases, involving much nicety of distinction; but it does not belong to this work to enter into it more fully. The general principle is that which is here stated, that the traverse brings the fact into question, according to the *manner and form in which it is alleged;* and that the opposite party must consequently prove that, in substance, at least, the allegation is *accurately true.* The existence of this principle is indicated by the *wording* of a traverse, which, when in the negative, generally denies the last pleading *modo et forma,* "in manner and form as alleged." [1] This will be found to be the case generally, except in the general issue *non est factum* and the replication *de injuria,* which are almost the only negative traverses that are not pleaded *modo et forma.* These words, however, though usual, are said to be in no case strictly essential, so as to render their omission cause of demurrer.[2]

It is naturally a consequence of the principle here mentioned, that great accuracy and precision, in adapting the allegation to the true state of the fact, are observed in all well-drawn pleadings; the vigilance of the pleader being always directed to these qualities, in order to prevent any risk of variance or failure of proof at the trial, in the event of a traverse by the opposite party.

---

[1] But, notwithstanding the words *modo et forma*, it is enough to prove the substance of the allegation. (See Litt. sect. 483; Doct. Pl. 344; Harris v. Ferrand, Hardr. 39; Pope v. Skinner, Hob. 72; Carvick v. Blagrave, 1 Brod. & Bing. 536) As to the effect of these words, as covering the whole matter of the allegation traversed, see Weathrell v. Howard, 3 Bing. 135.

[2] Com. Dig Pleader, G. 1; Nevil and Cook's Case, 2 Leo. 5.

(2) A Traverse must not be taken on Matter of Law.

Again, with respect to all traverses, it is laid down as a rule, that a *traverse must not be taken upon matter of law*.[1] For a denial of the law involved in the preceding pleading is, in other words, an exception to the sufficiency of that pleading in point of law, and is therefore within the scope and proper province of a *demurrer* and not of a *traverse*.

Example: Where, to an action of trespass for fishing in the plaintiff's fishery, the defendant pleaded that the *locus in quo* was an arm of the sea, in which every subject of the realm had the liberty and privilege of free fishing, and the plaintiff, in his replication, traversed that in the said arm of the sea every subject of the realm had the liberty and privilege of free fishing, this was held to be a traverse of a mere inference of law, and therefore bad.[2]

Upon the same principle, if a matter be alleged in pleading, " by reason whereof " (*virtute cujus*) a certain legal inference is drawn, as that the plaintiff " became seised," etc., or the defendant " became liable," etc., this *virtute cujus* is not traversable;[3] because, if it be intended to question the facts from which the seisin or liability is deduced, the traverse should be applied to the facts, and to those only ; and, if the legal inference be doubted, the course is to demur. But, on the other hand, where an allegation is *mixed of law and fact*, it may be traversed.[4]

Examples: (1) In answer to an allegation that a man was "taken out of prison by virtue of a certain writ of *habeas corpus*," it may be traversed that he was " taken out of prison by virtue of that writ." [5]

(2) Where it was alleged in a plea that, in consequence of certain circumstances therein set forth, it belonged to the wardens

---

[1] 1 Saund. 23, n. 5 ; Doct. Pl. 351 ; Kenicot *v.* Bogan, Yelv. 200 ; Priddle and Napper's Case, 11 Co. Rep. 10 b ; Richardson *v.* Mayor of Orford, 2 H. Bl. 182.

[2] Richardson *v.* Mayor of Orford, *ubi supra.* (A most interesting case, which the student should carefully examine.)

[3] Doct. Pl. 351 ; Priddle and Napper's Case, *ubi supra.*

[4] 1 Saund. 23, n. 5, and see the instances cited ; Bac. Ab. Pleas, &c. 380, note *b*, 5th ed. ; Beal *v.* Simpson, 1 Ld. Raym 412 ; Grocers' Company *v.* Archbishop of Canterbury, 3 Wils. 234.

[5] Beal *v.* Simpson, *ubi supra ;* Treby, Ch. J., *cont.*

and commonalty of a certain body corporate to present to a certain church, being vacant, in their turn, being the second turn, and this was answered by a special traverse, *without this, that* it belonged to the said wardens and commonalty to present to the said church, at the second turn, when the same became vacant, etc., in manner and form as alleged, the court held the traverse good, as not applying to a *mere* matter of law, "but to a matter of law, or rather of right resulting from facts." [1]

(3) So it is held, upon the same principle, that traverse may be taken upon an allegation that a certain person obtained a church by simony. [2]

(3) A Traverse must not be taken upon Matter not Alleged.

It is also a rule, *that a traverse must not be taken upon matter not alleged.* [3] The meaning of this rule will be sufficiently explained by the following cases : —

Examples : (1) A woman brought an action of debt on a deed, by which the defendant obliged himself to pay her £200 on demand, if he did not take her to wife, and alleged in her declaration that, though she had tendered herself to marry the defendant, he refused, and married another woman. The defendant pleaded that, after making the deed, he offered himself to marry the plaintiff, and she refused ; *absque hoc,* "that he refused to take her for his wife before she had refused to take him for her husband." The court was of opinion that this traverse was bad ; because there had been no allegation in the declaration "that the defendant had refused before the plaintiff had refused ;" and therefore the traverse went to deny what the plaintiff had not affirmed. [4] The plea in this case ought to have been in *confession and avoidance ;* stating merely the affirmative matter, that before the plaintiff offered the defendant offered, and that the plaintiff had refused him ; and omitting the *absque hoc.*

(2) Again, in an action of debt on bond against the defendant, as *executrix* of J. S., she pleaded in abatement that J. S. died *intestate,* and that *administration* was granted to her. On demurrer, it was objected, that she should have gone on to traverse "that she meddled as executrix before the administration granted ;" because, if she so meddled, she was properly charged

---

[1] Grocers' Company *v.* Archbishop of Canterbury, 3 Wils. 234.

[2] *Ibid.;* Rast. Ent. 532 a.

[3] 1 Saund. 312 d, n. 4 ; Doct. Pl. 358 ;

Crosse *v.* Hunt, Carth. 99 ; Powers *v.* Cook, 1 Ld. Raym. 63 ; s. c. 1 Salk. 298

[4] Crosse *v.* Hunt, *ubi supra.*

as executrix, notwithstanding the subsequent grant of letters of administration. But the court held the plea good in that respect; and Holt, C. J., said, "that, if the defendant had taken such traverse, it had made her plea vicious; for it is enough for her to show that the plaintiff's writ ought to abate, which she has done, in showing that she is chargeable only by another name. Then, as to the traverse, that she did not administer as executrix before the letters of administration were granted, it would be to traverse what is not alleged in the plaintiff's declaration; which would be against a rule of law, that a man shall never traverse that which the plaintiff has not alleged in his declaration." [1]

Exception: A traverse may be taken upon matter which, though not expressly alleged, is necessarily implied. [2]

Example: In replevin for taking cattle, the defendant made cognizance that A. was seised of the close in question, and, by his command, the defendant took the cattle damage feasant. The plaintiff pleaded in bar, that he himself was seised of one third part, and put in his cattle, *absque hoc,* "that the said A. was *sole seised.*" On demurrer, it was objected that this traverse was taken on matter not alleged, the allegation being that A. was *seised,* not that A. was *sole* seised. But the court held, that in the allegation of seisin that of sole seisin was necessarily implied, and that whatever is necessarily implied is traversable, as much as if it were expressed. Judgment for plaintiff. [3]

The court, however, observed that, in this case, the plaintiff was not *obliged* to traverse the sole seisin; and that the effect of merely traversing the *seisin modo et forma,* as alleged, would have been the same on the trial as that of traversing the *sole* seisin.

(4) A PARTY TO A DEED, WHO TRAVERSES IT, MUST PLEAD "NON EST FACTUM."

Another rule that may be referred to this head, though of a more special and limited application than the former, is the following: *that a party to a deed, who traverses it, must plead "non est factum," and should not plead that he did not grant,*

---

[1] Powers *v.* Cook, 1 Ld. Raym. 63; s. c. 1 Salk. 298.
Parker, 2 Salk. 629; s. c. 6 Mod. 158; Meriton *v.* Briggs, 1 Ld. Raym. 39.

[2] 1 Saund. 312 d, n. 4; Gilbert *v.*

[3] Gilbert *v.* Parker, *ubi supra.*

did not demise, etc.[1] This rule seems to depend on the doctrine of *estoppel*.

A man is sometimes precluded, in law, from alleging or denying a fact in consequence of his own previous act, allegation, or denial to the contrary, and this preclusion is called an *estoppel*.[2] It may arise (1) from matter of *record*, (2) from the *deed* of the party, or (3) from matter in *pais*, that is, matter of *fact*.[3]

(1) Thus, any confession or admission made in pleading in a court of record, whether it be express or implied from pleading over without a traverse, will forever preclude the party from afterwards contesting the same fact, in any subsequent suit, with the same adversary.[4] This is an estoppel by matter of record.

(2) As an instance of an estoppel by *deed*, may be mentioned the case of a bond reciting a certain fact. The party executing that bond will be precluded from afterwards denying, in an action brought upon that instrument, the fact so recited.[5]

(3) An example of an estoppel by matter in *pais* occurs when one man has accepted rent of another. He will be estopped from afterwards denying, in any action, with that person, that he was, at the time of such acceptance, his tenant.[6]

It is from this doctrine of estoppel, apparently, that the rule now under consideration as to the mode of traversing deeds has resulted.[7] For though a party against whom a deed is alleged may be allowed, consistently with the doctrine of estoppel, to say *non est factum*, viz., that the deed is not his, he is, on the other hand, precluded by that doctrine from denying its effect or operation ; because, if allowed to say *non concessit* or *non demisit*, when the instrument purports to *grant*

---

[1] Doct. Pl. 261 ; Robinson *v.* Corbett, Lutw. 662 ; Taylor *v.* Needham, 2 Taunt. 278.

[2] An estoppel is, "when a man's own act or acceptance stoppeth or closeth up his mouth to allege or plead the truth." (Co. Litt. 352 a.)

[3] Co. Litt. 352 a.

[4] Bract. 421 a ; Com. Dig. Estoppel, A. 1 ; and see Outram *v.* Morewood, 3 East. 346 ; Vooght *v.* Winch, 2 Barn. & Ald. 662.

[5] Bonner *v.* Wilkinson, 5 Barn. & Ald. 682 ; and see Baker *v.* Dewey, 1 Barn. & Cress. 704.

[6] Com. Dig. Estoppel, A. 3 ; Co. Litt. *ubi supra.*

[7] See 39 Ed. III. 3 ; Taylor *v.* Needham, *ubi supra.*

or to *demise*, he would be permitted to contradict his own deed. Accordingly, it will be found that in the case of a person not a party, but a *stranger* to the deed, the rule is reversed, and the form of traverse in that case is *non concessit*, etc.,[1] the reason of which seems to be, that estoppels do not hold with respect to strangers.[2]

The doctrine of traverse being now discussed, the next subject for consideration is —

(B) Pleadings in Confession and Avoidance.

The Nature and Properties of Pleadings in Confession and Avoidance.

Pleas in confession and avoidance are divided, with respect to their subject-matter, into two classes : —

(1) Pleas in justification or excuse.

(2) Pleas in discharge.[3]

(1) Pleas in Justification or Excuse.

These set forth some justification or excuse of the matter charged in the declaration ; their effect, therefore, is to show that the plaintiff never had any right of action, because the act charged was lawful. An example of this class is the plea of *son assault demesne.*

(2) Pleas in Discharge.

These show some discharge or release of the matter charged in the declaration ; their effect is to show that, though the plaintiff once had a right of action, it is discharged or released by some subsequent matter. An example of this latter class is a release.

This division applies to *pleas* only ; for *replications and other subsequent pleadings* in confession and avoidance are not subject to any such classification.

As to the *form* of pleadings in confession and avoidance, it

---

[1] Taylor *v.* Needham, 2 Taunt. 278. N. B. The court there lay it down that the plea of *non concessit*, etc., brings into issue the title of the grantor, as well as the operation of the deed.

[2] In accordance with the same doctrine of estoppel, it is held, with respect to *real* or *personal representatives*, that they are in the same situation with *parties*, and must plead *non est factum*. (Robinson *v.* Corbett, Lutw. 662. As to *privies in estate*, see 2 Hen. IV. 20; Taylor *v.* Needham, *ubi supra*.)

[3] Com. Dig. Pleader, 3 M. 12.

will be sufficient to observe that, in common with all pleadings whatever which do not tender issue, they always conclude *with a verification and prayer of judgment.*

COLOR.

With respect to the *quality* of these pleadings, it is a rule, *that every pleading by way of confession and avoidance must give color.*[1] This is a rule which it is very essential to understand, in order to have a correct apprehension of the nature of these pleadings ; yet it appears to have been not hitherto adequately explained or developed in the books of the science.

Color is a term of the ancient rhetoricians, and was adopted at an early period into the language of pleading.[2] As a term of pleading, it signifies an apparent or *prima facie* right ; and the meaning of the rule, that every pleading in confession and avoidance must give color, is, that *it must admit an apparent right in the opposite party, and rely, therefore, on some new matter by which that apparent right is defeated.*

Example : In the case of a plea of release to an action for breach of covenant, the tendency of the plea is to admit an apparent right in the plaintiff, viz., that the defendant did, as alleged in the declaration, execute the deed and break the covenant therein contained, and would, therefore, *prima facie*, be chargeable with damages on that ground ; but shows new matter, not before disclosed, by which that apparent right is done away with, viz., that the plaintiff executed to him a release. Again, if the plaintiff claims that the release was obtained from him by duress, he, in his replication, impliedly admits that the defendant has, *prima facie*, a good defence, viz., that such release was executed as alleged in the plea, and that the defendant, therefore, would be apparently discharged ; but he relies on new matter, by which the effect of the plea is avoided, viz., that the release was obtained by duress.

The plea in this case, therefore, *gives color* to the declaration, and the replication to the plea.

But let it be supposed that the plaintiff had replied that the release was executed by him, but *to another person*, and *not to*

---

[1] See Reg. Plac. 304 ; Hatton *v.* Morse, 3 Salk. 273 ; Hallet *v.* Byrt, 5 Mod. 252 ; Holler *v.* Bush, 1 Salk. 394. [2] It occurs at least as early as the reign of Ed. III. (See Year-Book, 40 Ed. III. 23.)

the defendant ; this would be an informal replication, as *want-ing color*, because, if the release were not to the defendant, there would not exist even an apparent defence, requiring the allegation of new matter to avoid it, and the plea might be sufficiently answered by a *traverse*, denying that the deed stated in the plea is the deed of the plaintiff.[1]

IMPLIED COLOR.

The kind of color to which these observations relate, being a latent quality naturally inherent in the structure of all reg-ular pleadings in confession and avoidance, has been called *implied color*, to distinguish it from another kind, which is, in some instances, formally inserted in the pleading, and is there-fore known by the name of *express* color.[2]

EXPRESS COLOR.

It is the latter kind to which the technical term most usually applies ; and to this the books refer when color is mentioned *per se*, without the distinction between express and implied.

Color, in this sense, is defined to be " *a feigned matter, pleaded by the defendant in an action of trespass, from which the plaintiff seems to have a good cause of action, whereas he has, in truth, only an appearance or color of cause.*"[3]

This is one of the most curious subtleties that belong to the science of pleading ; and, though now rather of rare occur-rence, yet, as it is still sometimes practised, and is, besides, illustrative of the important doctrine of *implied* color, deserves attention. Its nature and use may be thus explained.

The necessity of an implied color has evidently the effect of obliging the pleader to traverse in many instances in which his case, when fully stated, does not turn on a mere denial of fact, but involves some considerations of law. In the example first above given, of want of color, this would not be so ; for, if the

---

[1] See Gifford *v.* Perkins, 1 Sid. 450, where a *plea* of this kind was held to be bad. The objection, indeed, in that case, took a somewhat different shape, viz., that the plea *amounted to the general issue.* But this objection, as will be explained in a subsequent part of the work, is in substance the same with the *want of color.*

[2] Hallet *v.* Byrt, 5 Mod. 252 ; Hatton *v.* Morse, 3 Salk. 273 ; Reg. Plac. 304.

[3] Bac. Ab. Trespass, T. 4.

deed of release were executed not to the defendant, but to a different person, this, of course, amounts to no more than a mere denial that the deed, as alleged in the plea, is the deed of the plaintiff; and no question of *law* can be said to arise under this traverse.

But a case may easily be supposed in which a point of law is involved in some part of the defendant's title, which point it is desirable to so introduce in the pleading as to enable a demurrer to be interposed to it, and thus segregate it from the remaining matters of fact.

If the defendant is compelled to traverse the plaintiff's declaration, then, upon the general issue so made up, he must prove his whole title, deducing it through all its steps, and the jury must determine *the law as well as the facts* involved therein.

The question, therefore, for the defendant to solve is this: Can he by an expedient plead what is really an argumentative traverse, as a confession and avoidance? He can, by resorting to this device of *express color.*

Example: In an action of *trespass quare clausum fregit*, for breaking the plaintiff's close, the defendant would confess that the plaintiff, at the time of the act complained of, was *in possession* of the close in question, by virtue of a *parol demise* for life from one Z.; but that afterwards (nothing passing by the parol demise for life),[1] Z.'s title became legally vested in the defendant, who thereupon entered upon the close so in possession of the plaintiff; which is the same trespass complained of by the plaintiff..

In alleging his title in the foregoing plea, the defendant would trace it truly and minutely from Z., in whom the plea admits the title to have been vested at the time of the *parol demise* to the plaintiff. Thus, he might aver, according as the fact was, that he derived his title by *last will* from X., who got it *by deed* from Y., on whom it *descended* from Z. In a word, he would set out every link, including of course the one involving the doubtful point of law, constituting his claim of title.

---

[1] The defect in the title, given by this color, is, that the parol demise, or charter for life, is not pleaded as a *feoffment*, and does not appear to have been accompanied by *livery of seisin*. It is therefore void. (Doct. Pl. 73, Leyfield's Case, 10 Co. Rep. 89 b.)

Now the plaintiff must meet this plea. If he mean to contest the point of law involved, he must demur to the plea, when the legal question thus segregated will be argued to the court. If, on the other hand, he mean to controvert the facts of the title, he must *reply ;* and, in replying, he must select for attack some one of the links of title in the defendant's chain, and must admit the validity of all the rest, thus separating the facts from the law, and obliging the defendant to prove *one only* of the facts of title instead of all of them.[1]

The student will be aided by contrasting a common traverse with a traverse converted, by this expedient, into a plea by confession and avoidance with express color.

By Way of Traverse.

Pltff. Defendant broke my close, to my damage of $1,000.

Dfdt. Not guilty, and issue tendered.

Pltff. Issue joined.

By Confession and Avoidance with Express Color.

Pltff. Defendant broke my close, to my damage of $1,000.

Dfdt. One Z. was seised of the close in question, and before the alleged trespass, by conveyance duly executed, transferred the land to Y. in fee, from whom it lawfully descended to the defendant as his son and heir. And the plaintiff claiming the said close by color of a *parol demise* for his life, by the said Z. made to him long before the conveyance aforesaid by Z. to Y., entered on the premises, and was possessed of the same; and the defendant afterwards entered upon the plaintiff's possession as lawfully he might, and that is the trespass complained of.

Pltff. Defendant is not *son and heir* to Y., and issue tendered.

Dfdt. Issue accepted.

---

[1] Min. Inst. IV. 650, 651.

By pleading thus by way of confession and avoidance, the defendant gains these several advantages: (1) He *spreads his title on the record*, and obliges the plaintiff, if he regards it as not a lawful title as thus exhibited, to *demur* and present the question to the court, instead of its going mixed with all the facts to the jury, as it might have done upon the plea by way of traverse.

(2) He obliges the plaintiff to traverse or attack but one of the links in the defendant's chain of title; and thus, by the rules of pleading, to admit all the other links as good.

(3) He gains, according to the English practice, the affirmative of the issue, and, hence, the opening and conclusion of the cause.[1]

The most abstruse points of law might be presented in this way by the pleadings, so that a demurrer could segregate them from the surrounding facts. Thus, the example given by Stephen, upon this head, presents the legal question whether or not continued claim of title by a disseisee will preserve in him the right of entry upon the premises in dispute, notwithstanding a descent cast on the heir of the disseisor.[2]

It is to be understood that, when color was thus given, the plaintiff was not allowed, in his replication, to traverse the fictitious matter suggested by way of color;[3] for, its only object being to prevent a difficulty of *form*, such traverse would be wholly foreign to the merits of the cause, and would only serve to frustrate the fiction which the law in such case allows. The plaintiff would, therefore, pass over the color without notice, and either traverse the title of the defendants, if he meant to contest its truth in point of fact, or demur to it, if he meant to except to its sufficiency in point of law; and thus the defendants would obtain their object, of bringing any legal question raised upon their title under consideration of the court, and withdrawing it from the jury.

The practice of giving express color obtained in the mixed actions called an *assize*, and the *writ of entry in nature of an*

---

[1] Min. Inst. IV. 910, 911.   [3] Chit. Pl. 445.

[2] Co. Litt. 250, a, b; Bl. Com. III. 175 *.

assize, and the personal action of *trespass.*[1] The two former kinds of proceeding being now out of use, it occurs at present in the action of trespass only, nor is it, even in trespass, often found to be expedient. As the practice of giving express color seems to be confined to these actions, so also it is restrained to pleas, and does not extend to replications or other subsequent pleadings.[2] It is also to be understood, with respect to giving express color, that though, originally, *various* suggestions of apparent right might be adopted, according to the fancy of the pleader,[3] and though the same latitude is, perhaps, still allowable, yet, in practice, it is unusual to resort to any except certain known fictions which long usage has applied to the particular case. Thus, in trespass to land, the color universally given is that of a defective *charter of demise,* as in the above example.

There are some rules, with respect to express color, immediately resulting from the nature of the fiction and the object for which it is adopted. Thus, it is laid down that, *it must consist of such matters as, if it were effectual, would maintain the nature of the action.*[4]

Example: In an action of assize, where the demandant complains of a disseisin of his *freehold,* the tenant should not, by way of giving color, suggest a demise to the demandant for *years,* because this would not give him even a colorable ground to maintain an assize.[5]

On the other hand, it is to be observed that the right suggested must be *colorable* only, and that it must not amount to a *real* or *actual* right. For, if it does, then the plaintiff would, of course, upon the defendant's own showing, be entitled to recover, and the plea would be an insufficient answer.

Example: In trespass for taking away one hundred loads of wood, if the defendant pleads that I. S. was possessed of them *ut de bonis propriis* (as of his own goods), and the plaintiff, claim-

---

[1] Doct. & Stud. 271. But see an example of express color in trover, Morant *v.* Sign, 2 M. & W. 94; S. C. 5 Dowl. 319. The color here is a delivery by the defendant to John Doe and a wrongful delivery by him to the plaintiff.

[2] Chit. Pl. 541. And see Taylor *v.* Eastwood, 1 East. 212.

[3] Reeves' Hist. III. 629.

[4] Bac. Ab. Pleas, &c. I. 8; Com. Dig. Pleader, 3 M. 41.

[5] Anon. Keilw. 103 b.

ing them *by color of a deed of gift by the said I. S. afterwards made*, took them, and then the defendant retook them, the plea is bad; for if the plaintiff took possession of the goods under a deed of gift from the lawful owner, he has a good title to them, and ought to recover.[1]

So, in the example of color before given, it would be bad pleading, if, instead of alleging that the plaintiff claimed by color of a certain *charter of demise* for the term of his life, etc., it were alleged that he claimed by color of a certain *feoffment* for the term of his life; for in the word *feoffment* the law intends not only the charter of demise, but the delivery of seisin also; and the title allowed to the plaintiff would, therefore, not be defective or colorable, but valid.[2]

There are other rules relating to express color,[3] but as they seem, on examination, to be either resolvable into the same principles that have been already considered, or, where this is not the case, to be obscure and unimportant, they need not be here discussed.

The pleadings by way of *traverse*, and those by way of *confession and avoidance*, having been now separately considered, there are yet to be noticed :

(C) THE NATURE AND PROPERTIES OF PLEADINGS IN GENERAL.

We shall now consider the nature and properties of *pleadings in general*, without reference to their quality, as being by way of traverse or confession and avoidance. The rules on this subject are the following : —

(1) EVERY PLEADING MUST BE AN ANSWER TO THE WHOLE OF WHAT IS ADVERSELY ALLEGED.[4]

Example : In an action of trespass for breaking a close and cutting down three hundred trees, if the defendant pleads, as to cutting down all but two hundred trees, some matter of justification or title, and as to the two hundred trees says nothing, the

---

[1] Radford v. Harbyn, Cro. Jac. 122.
[2] Doct. Pl. 73.
[3] See Com. Dig. Pleader, 3 M. 40, 3 M. 41.
[4] Com. Dig. Pleader, E. 1, F. 4; 1 Saund. 28, n. 3; Herlakenden's Case, 4 Co. Rep. 62 a.

plaintiff is entitled to sign judgment, as by *nil dicit*, against him in respect of the two hundred trees, and to demur or reply to the plea as to the remainder of the trespasses.[1]

In such cases the plaintiff should take care to avail himself of his advantage by this (which is the only proper) course; for if he demurs or replies to the plea, without signing judgment for the part not answered, the whole action is said to be *discontinued*.[2] The principle of this is, that the plaintiff, by not taking judgment, as he was entitled to do for the part unanswered, does not follow up his entire demand, and there is consequently that sort of chasm or interruption in the proceedings which is called in the technical phrase a *discontinuance*;[3] and such discontinuance will amount to error on the record.[4]

It is to be observed, however, that as to the plaintiff's course of proceeding, there is a distinction between a case like this, where the defendant does not profess to answer the whole, and a case where, by the commencement of his plea, he professes to do so, but in fact gives a defective and partial answer, applying to part only. The latter case amounts merely to insufficient pleading; and the plaintiff's course therefore is not to sign judgment for the part defectively answered, but to *demur* to the whole plea.[5]

It is also to be observed, that where the part of the pleading to which no answer is given is immaterial, or such as requires no separate or specific answer — for example, if it be mere matter of *aggravation* — the rule does not in that case apply.[6]

---

[1] Henry *v.* Earl, 8 M. & W. 228.

[2] Com. Dig. Pleader, E. 1, F. 4; 1 Saund. 28, n. 3; Herlakenden's Case, 4 Co. Rep. 62 a; Morley *v.* ——, 12 Mod. 421; Vincent *v.* Beston, 1 Ld. Raym. 716; Market *v.* Johnson, 1 Salk. 180.

[3] The proper and original meaning of a *discontinuance* has been explained. By analogy to this, whenever a suit is not regularly carried on from its commencement to its conclusion, but a chasm of any kind, either in the process or pleading, occurs, there is also a discontinuance. Besides the example in the text, see another in Tippet *v.* May, 1 Bos & Pul. 411.

[4] Wats *v.* King, Cro. Jac. 353. *A discontinuance is cured, however, after verdict,* by the statute of jeofails, 32 H. VIII. c. 30; *and after judgment* by *nil dicit,* confession, or *non sum informatus,* by 4 Ann. c. 16.

[5] 1 Saund. 28, n. 3; Thomas *v.* Heathorn, 2 Barn. & Cress. 477; Earl of St. Germains *v.* Willan, *ibid.* 216.

[6] 1 Saund. 28, n. 3.

(2) Every Pleading is taken to Confess such Traversable Matters alleged on the Other Side as it does not Traverse.[1]

Thus, in the example given of an action on an indenture of covenant, the plea of release, as it does not traverse the indenture, is taken to admit its execution; and the replication of duress, on the same principle, is an admission of the execution of the release. The effect of such admission is extremely strong, for, first, it concludes the party, even though the jury should improperly go out of the issue and find the contrary of what is thus confessed on the record,[2] and, in the next place, the confession operates not only to prevent the fact from being afterward brought into question in the same suit, but is equally conclusive as to the truth of that fact in any *subsequent action* between the same parties. The rule, however (it will be observed), extends only to such matters as are *traversable;* for matters of *law*, or any other matters which are not fit subjects of traverse, are not taken to be admitted by pleading over.[3]

PROTESTATION.

It is this rule which has given rise to the practice of *protestation* in pleading.[4] When the pleader passes over, without traverse, any traversable fact alleged, and, at the same time, wishes to preserve the power of denying it *in another action,* he makes, collaterally or incidentally to his main pleading, a declaration, importing that this fact is untrue; and this is called a *protestation,* and it has the effect of enabling the party to dispute, in another action, the fact so passed over.[5] It is wholly without avail *in the action in which it occurs;* and, under the rule already laid down, every traversable fact not traversed

[1] Com. Dig. Pleader, G. 2; Bac. Ab. Pleas, &c. 322, 386, 5th ed.; Hudson v. Jones, 1 Salk. 91; Nicholson v. Simpson, Fort. 556.

[2] Bac. Ab. Pleas, &c. 322, 5th ed.; Wilcox v. Servant of Skipwith, 2 Mod. 4.

[3] 10 Ed. IV. 12; The King v. The Bishop of Chester, 2 Salk. 561.

[4] Bac. Ab. Pleas, &c. 386, n. a, 5th ed.

[5] Com. Dig. Pleader, N.; Co. Litt. 124 b; 2 Saund. 103 a, n. 1; 17 Ed. II. 534; 43 Ed. III. 17; 40 Ed. III. 17, 46; 48 Ed. III. 11.

is, notwithstanding the protestation, to be taken as admitted *in the existing suit.*

It is also a rule, that if upon the traverse the issue be found *against* the party protesting, the protestation does not avail; and that it is of no use except in the event of the issue being determined *in his favor;* with this exception, however, that if the matter taken by protestation be such as the pleader could not have taken issue upon, the protestation in that case shall avail, even though the issue taken were decided against him.[1]

A protestation ought not to be *repugnant to the pleading which it accompanies,*[2] nor ought it to be *taken on such matter as the pleading itself traverses.*[3]

The rules, however, with respect to the *form* of a protestation, become the less material, because it has been decided that neither a superfluous nor repugnant protestation is sufficient ground for *demurrer;*[4] the protestation itself having in view *another suit* only, and its faults of form being, therefore, immaterial in the present action.

It has been already observed, that the necessity of the protestation arises from the rule, " that every traversable fact not traversed is confessed." But it has been seen that an answer in fact is no admission of the sufficiency in point of *law* of the matter answered. It follows, therefore, that it is not necessary, in passing over an insufficient pleading without demurrer, and answering in point of fact, to make any protestation of the insufficiency in law of such pleading; for, even without the protestation, no implied admission of its sufficiency arises. In practice, however, it is not unusual, in such case, to make a protestation of *insufficiency in law,* the form having apparently been adopted by analogy to the proper kind of protestation, viz., that against the truth of a *fact.*

Such are the doctrines involved in the general rule, *that the party must demur, or plead either by way of traverse, or by way of confession and avoidance.*

---

[1] See 2 Saund. 103 a, n. 1, for further explanation on this subject.

[2] Com. Dig. Pleader, N; 2 Saund. *ubi supra.*

[3] Com. Dig. Pleader, N.

[4] Com. Dig. and Saund. *ubi supra.*

Exceptions to Rule I.

We must recur now to the exceptions already noted to the main rule, which requires a party to plead either by way of *traverse* or by way of *confession and avoidance.*

(1) Where a Dilatory Plea is interposed.

There is an exception in the case of *dilatory pleas,* for a plea of this kind merely opposes a matter of form to the declaration, and does not tend either to deny or to confess its allegations.

But *replications* and *subsequent pleadings,* following on dilatory pleas, *are not within this exception.*

(2) Pleadings in Estoppel.

These are pleadings which, without confessing or denying the matter of fact adversely alleged, rely merely on some matter of estoppel, as a ground for excluding the opposite party from the allegation of the fact, and, after stating the previous act, allegation, or denial, on which the estoppel is supposed to arise, pray judgment if he *shall be received or admitted to aver* contrary to what he before did or said.

(3) Where a New Assignment is Necessary.

Another exception to that branch of the general rule, which requires the pleader either to traverse, or confess and avoid, arises in the case of what is called a *new assignment.*

It has been seen that the declarations are conceived in very general terms; a quality which they derive from their adherence to the tenor of those simple and abstract *formulæ,* the original writs. The effect of this is, that, in some cases, the defendant is not sufficiently guided by the declaration to the real cause of complaint, and is, therefore, led to apply his plea to a different matter from that which the plaintiff has in view. A new assignment is a method of pleading to which the plaintiff in such cases is obliged to resort in his replication, for the purpose of setting the defendant right.

Example: In an action for assault and battery, a case may occur in which the plaintiff has been *twice assaulted* by the defendant; and one of these assaults may have been justifiable, being committed in self-defence, while the other may have been committed without legal excuse.   Supposing the plaintiff to bring his action for the *latter*, it will be found, by referring to the example formerly given, of declaration for assault and battery, that the statement is so general as not to indicate to which of the two assaults the plaintiff means to refer.[1]   The defendant may, therefore, suppose, or affect to suppose, that the *first* is the assault intended, and will plead *son assault demesne*.   This plea the plaintiff can not safely *traverse;* because, as an assault was in fact committed by the defendant under the circumstances of excuse here alleged, the defendant would have a right, under the issue joined upon such traverse, to prove those circumstances, and to presume that such assault, and no other, is the cause of action.   And it is evidently *reasonable* that he should have this right; for if the plaintiff were, at the trial of the issue, to be allowed to set up a different assault, the defendant might suffer, by a mistake into which he had been led by the generality of the plaintiff's declaration.   The plaintiff, therefore, in the case supposed, not being able safely to traverse, and having no ground either for demurrer or for pleading in confession and avoidance, has no course but, by a new pleading, to correct the mistake occasioned by the generality of the declaration, and to declare that he brought his action, not for the *first*, but for the *second* assault; and this is called a *new assignment*.[2]

The mistake being thus set right by the new assignment, it remains for the defendant to plead such matter as he may have in answer to the assault last mentioned, the first being now out of the question.

By way of further example, may be mentioned a case that arises in trespass *quare clausum fregit*, and was formerly of very

---

[1] As for the *day* and *place* alleged in the declaration (which may be supposed sufficient, in general, to identify the assault referred to), it will be shown hereafter that they are not considered as generally material to be proved in such a case, and are consequently alleged without much regard to the true state of fact.

[2] He may guard himself, by anticipation, against this necessity, in the particular case supposed, by charging the defendant in the declaration with *both* the assaults, which (in the form of different counts) is allowable. If both assaults are thus charged, the defendant of course must answer both in his plea, and the reason for the new assignment fails.

frequent and ordinary occurrence. In this action, if the plaintiff declares for breaking his close in a certain parish, without naming or otherwise describing the close (a course which in point of pleading is allowable),[1] if the defendant happen to have any freehold land in the same parish, he may be supposed to mistake the close in question for his own, and may therefore plead what is called *the common bar*,[2] viz., that the close in which the trespass was committed is his own freehold.[3] And then, upon the principle already explained, it will be necessary for the plaintiff to new-assign, alleging that he brought his action in respect of a different close from that claimed by the defendant as his freehold.[4]

New Assignment Extra Viam.

The examples that have been given consist of cases where the defendant in his plea *wholly* mistakes the subject of complaint. But it may also happen that the plea correctly applies to *part* of the injuries, while, owing to a misapprehension occasioned by the generality of the statement in the declaration, it fails to cover the whole.

[1] Martin *v*. Kesterton, 2 W. Bla. 1089.

[2] "It was anciently the most usual practice in trespass *quare clausum fregit*, to declare generally of breaking the plaintiff's close at A. This general mode of declaring put the defendant under a difficulty of knowing in what part of the *vill* of A. the trespass which the plaintiff meant by his declaration was committed. The defendant was therefore permitted to plead that the close was his freehold, which he might do without giving it a name, because as the plaintiff was *general* in his count, the defendant might be *as general* in his plea. And if the plaintiff traversed it — as he unquestionably might (6 Mod. 119) — he ran a great risk; for if the defendant had any part of his land in that *vill*, the verdict would be for him on that issue. This turned the difficulty upon the plaintiff, and therefore he was almost always driven to a new assignment, in which he ascertained the place with proper exactness. . . . This general plea of freehold is usually called the *common bar*, and sometimes the general issue." Greene *v*. Jones, 1 Saund. 299 b, 297 c, n. 6.

[3] In the common bar, it seems that the defendant is not bound to name his close. (1 Saund 299 b, n. 5; Elwis *v*. Lombe, 6 Mod. 117; s. c. Salk. 453, *sed. qu.?* (but it is doubtful). See Cocker *v*. Crompton, 1 Barn. & Cress. 489; and Martin *v*. Kesterton, *ubi supra*.

[4] See examples, Baldwin's Case, 2 Co. Rep. 18. But if the plaintiff has named his close in the declaration, the plea of freehold does not drive him to new-assign, though the defendant may have another close of the same name in the same parish; unless, at least, the defendant, in his plea, describes his close by its abuttals. (Cocker *v*. Crompton, *ubi supra*; and see Lethbridge *v*. Winter, 2 Bing. 49.) And on the subject of the common bar generally, see 1 Saund. 299 b, n. 5; Martin *v*. Kesterton, *ubi supra*; Hawke *v*. Bacon, 2 Taunt. 156.

N. B. — In order to avoid the prolixity of the common bar and new assignment, it is now usual to name the close in the declaration.

Example : In trespass *quare clausum fregit,* for repeated tres-passes, the declaration usually states, that the defendant, on divers days and times before the commencement of the suit, broke and entered the plaintiff's close, and trod down the soil, &c., without setting forth, more specifically, in what parts of the close or on what occasions the defendant trespassed.[1] Now, the case may be, that the defendant claims a right of way over a certain part of the close, and, in exercise of that right, has repeatedly entered and walked over it; but has also entered and trod down the soil, &c., on other occasions, and in parts out of the supposed line of way ; and the plaintiff, not admitting the right claimed, may have intended to point his action both to the one set of trespasses and to the other. But, from the generality of the declaration, the defendant is entitled to suppose that it refers only to his entering and walking in the line of way. He may, therefore, in his plea allege, as a complete answer to the whole complaint, that he has a right of way by grant, &c., over the said close ; and if he does this, and the plaintiff confines himself in his replication to a traverse of that plea, and the defendant at the trial proves a right of way as alleged, the plaintiff would be precluded (upon the principle already explained) from giving evidence of any trespasses committed out of the line or track in which the defendant should thus appear entitled to pass.

The plaintiff's course of pleading in such a case, there-fore, is, *both to traverse the plea* and *also to new-assign,* by alleging that he brought his action not only for those tres-passes supposed by the defendant, but for others, committed on other occasions and in other parts of the close, out of the supposed way, which is usually called a new assignment *extra viam* (out of the way) ; or, if he means to admit the right of way, he may new-assign simply, without the traverse.[2]

As the object of a new assignment is to correct a mistake occasioned by the generality of the *declaration,* it always occurs in answer to a *plea,* and is therefore in the nature of a *repli-cation.* It is not used in any other part of the pleading because the statements subsequent to the declaration are not, in their nature, such, when properly framed, as to give rise to the kind of mistake which requires to be corrected by a new assignment.

---

[1] See an example, 9 Went. 97.   [2] See examples of a new assignment *extra viam,* 9 Went. 323, 396.

A new assignment chiefly occurs in an action of *trespass*, but it seems to be generally allowed in all actions in which the form of declaration makes the reason of the practice equally applicable.[1]

Several new assignments may occur in the course of the same series of pleading. Thus, in the first of the above examples, if it be supposed that *three* different assaults had been committed, two of which were justifiable, the defendant might plead, as above, to the declaration, and then, by way of plea to the new assignment, he might again justify, in the same manner, another assault; upon which it would become necessary for the plaintiff to new-assign a third, and this upon the same principle by which the first new assignment was required.[2]

A new assignment is said to be *in the nature of a new declaration*.[3] It seems, however, to be more properly considered as a repetition of the declaration, differing only in this, that it distinguishes the true ground of complaint as being different from that which is covered by the plea. Being in the nature of a new or repeated declaration, it is consequently to be framed with as much *certainty* or specification of circumstances as the declaration itself. In some cases, indeed, it should be even *more* particular, so as to avoid the necessity of *another* new assignment. Thus, if the plaintiff declares in trespass *quare clausum fregit* without naming the close, and the defendant pleads the common bar, which, as we have seen, obliges the plaintiff to new-assign, he must, in his new assignment, either give his close its name or otherwise sufficiently describe it,[4] though such name or description was not required in the declaration.[5]

---

[1] Chit. Pl. 543; Vin. Ab. Novel Assignment, 4, 5; 3 Went. 151; Batt v. Bradley, Cro. Jac. 141.

[2] Chit. Pl. 544; 1 Saund. 299 c.

[3] Bac. Ab. Trespass (1), 4, 2; 1 Saund. 299 c.

[4] *Semb.* (it seems) Dy. 264 a; Com. Dig. Pleader, 3 M. 34. (See an example, 9 Went. 187.)

[5] On the subject of new assignment, see 1 Saund. 299 a, n. 6; Barnes v. Hunt, 11 East. 451; Cheasley v. Barnes, 10 East 73; Taylor v. Smith, 7 Taunt. 156; Taylor v. Cole, 3 T. R. 292; Lambert v. Prince, 1 Bing. 317; Phillips v. Howgate, 5 Barn. & Ald. 220. Some of these cases will be found to involve nice distinctions as to the necessity, in particular instances, of a new assignment. See specially, Huddart v. Rigby, 5 L. R. Q. B. 139, and Ellison v. Isles, 11 Ad. & E. 665.

The rule under consideration and its exceptions[1] being now discussed, the last point of remark relates to an inference or deduction to which it gives rise.

It is implied in this rule, that *as the proceeding must be by demurrer, traverse, or confession and avoidance,* SO ANY OF THESE FORMS OF OPPOSITION TO THE LAST PLEADING IS IN ITSELF SUFFICIENT.

There is, however, *an exception* to this in a case which the books consider as *anomalous* and *solitary.* It is as follows :

If in debt on a bond, conditioned for the performance of an award, the defendant pleads that no award was made, and the plaintiff, in reply, alleges that an award was made, setting it forth, it is held that he must also proceed to state a *breach* of the award, and that without stating such breach the replication is insufficient.[2]

" The reason was, because an award may be good in one part, and void in another; and therefore it is incumbent upon the plaintiff to show a breach thereof, that the court may judge whether he has well conceived his action or not; for perhaps he has brought his action for a breach of that part of the award which is void in itself, and consequently has not any cause of action." [3]

This, as has been observed, is an anomaly; for, as by alleging and setting forth the award he fully *traverses* the plea which denied the existence of an award, the replication

[1] There are also certain specific pleas which present the anomaly of being neither by way of traverse nor of confession and avoidance, and which therefore deserve notice in this place. These are the pleas of *Tender* and of *Payment into Court.* By the first of these, the defendant alleges that he has been always ready to pay the debt demanded, and before the commencement of the action tendered it to the plaintiff, and now brings it into Court ready to be paid to him. By the second of these pleas, the defendant alleges simply that he brings a sum of money into Court ready to be paid to the plaintiff, and that the latter has no claim to any larger amount. They are both in the nature of pleas in bar, as they give an answer in point of fact, and upon the merits; but they are in the nature of confession only, without avoidance, for they admit the right of action to exist. (Stephen, 5th English ed. 331.)

[2] 1 Saund. 103, n. 1; Meredith *v.* Alleyn, 1 Salk. 138; s. c. Carth. 116; Nicholson *v.* Simpson, Str. 299. Though this is considered as a solitary case, it may be observed that another analogous one is to be found (Gayle *v.* Betts, 1 Mod 227).

[3] Hayman *v.* Gerrard, 1 Saund. 103; Jones, *arguendo* (in argument), quoting Holt, C. J., in Meredith *v.* Alleyn, *ubi supra.* This reason is not satisfactory to Mr. Stephen.

would seem, according to the general rule under consideration, to be sufficient without the specification of any breach. And in accordance with that rule it is expressly laid down, that in all other cases, "*if the defendant pleads a special matter that admits and excuses a non-performance, the plaintiff need only answer and falsify the special matter alleged;* for he that excuses a non-performance supposes it, and the plaintiff need not show that which the defendant hath supposed and admitted." [1]

RULE II. UPON A TRAVERSE, ISSUE MUST BE TENDERED.

In the account already given of traverses, it was shown that, with the exception of a *special* traverse, the different forms all involve a *tender of issue*. The rule under consideration prescribes this as a necessary incident to them; and establishes it as a general principle, that wherever a traverse takes place, or, in other words, wherever a denial or contradiction of fact occurs in pleading, issue ought, at the same time, to be tendered on the fact denied. The reason is, that as by the contradiction it sufficiently appears what is the issue or matter in dispute between the parties, *it is time that the pleading should now close*, and that the method of deciding this issue should be adjusted.

The *formulæ* of tendering the issue in fact vary, of course, according to the mode of trial proposed.

The tender of an issue to be tried by *jury* is by a formula called the *conclusion to the country*. This conclusion is in the following words, when the issue is tendered by the *defendant* : " And of this the said *C. D. puts himself* upon the country." When it is tendered by the *plaintiff*, the formula is as follows : " And this the said *A. B.* prays *may be inquired of* by the country." [2] It is held, however, that there is no material difference between these two modes of expression, and that if *ponit se* be substituted for *petit quod inquiratur*, or *vice versa*, the mistake is unimportant. [3]

---

[1] Per Holt, C. J., Meredith *v.* Alleyn, 1 Salk. 138.

Glover, 10 Mod. 166; Bract. 57; Ry Plac. Parl. 146.

[2] Heath's Maxims, 68; Weltale *v.*

[3] Weltale *v.* Glover, *ubi supra.*

19

With respect to the *extraordinary* methods of trial, their occurrence is too rare to have given rise to any illustration of the rule in question. It refers chiefly to traverses of such matters of fact as are triable by the *country ;* and, therefore, we find it propounded in the books most frequently in the following form : *That upon a negative and affirmative the pleading shall conclude to the country, but otherwise with a verification.*[1]

EXCEPTION.

To the rule, in whatever form expressed, there is the following exception : *That when new matter is introduced, the pleading should always conclude with a verification.*[2]

To this exception belongs the case, formerly noticed, of *special traverses.* These, as already explained, never tender issue, but always conclude with a verification ; and the reason seems to be, that in such of them as contain new matter in the inducement, the introduction of that new matter will give the opposite party a right to be heard in answer to it if the *absque hoc* be immaterial, and consequently makes a tender of issue premature. And, on the other hand, with respect to such special traverses as contain no new matter in the inducement, they seem in this respect to follow the analogy of those first mentioned, though they are not within the same reason.

Not only in the case of special traverses, but in other instances also, to which that form does not apply, a traverse may sometimes involve the allegation of new matter ; and in all such instances, as well as upon a special traverse, and for a similar reason, the conclusion must be with a verification, and not to the country.

Examples : (1) Where the action is in debt on a bond conditioned for performance of covenants, if the defendant pleads generally performance of the covenants, and the plaintiff, in his replication, relies on a breach of them, he must show specially in what that breach consists ; for to reply generally that the defendant

---

[1] Com. Dig. Pleader, E. 32 ; 1 Saund. 103, n. 1.
[2] 1 Saund. 103, n. 1, and the authorities there cited ; Whitehead *v.* Buckland, Stile, 401 ; Cornwallis *v.* Savery, 2 Burr. 772 ; Vere *v.* Smith, 2 Lev. 5 ; s. c. Vent. 121 ; Sayre *v.* Minns, Cowp. 575 ; Henderson *v.* Withy, 2 T. R. 576

did not perform them would be too vague and uncertain.[1] His replication, therefore, setting forth, as it necessarily does, the circumstances of the breach, discloses new matter; and consequently, though it is a direct denial or traverse of the plea, it must not tender issue, but must conclude with a verification.[2]

(2) In an action of debt on bond conditioned to indemnify the plaintiff against the consequences of a certain act, if the defendant pleads *non damnificatus* (not damaged), and the plaintiff replies, alleging a damnification, he must, on the principle just explained, set forth the circumstances, and the new matter thus introduced will make a verification necessary.[3]

(3) The plaintiff declared in debt, on a bond conditioned for the performance of certain covenants by the defendant in his capacity of clerk to the plaintiff, one of which covenants was to account for all the money that he should receive. The defendant pleaded performance. The plaintiff replied, that on such a day such a sum came to his hands, which he had not accounted for. The defendant rejoined that he *did* account, and in the following manner: that thieves broke into the counting-house and stole the money, and that he acquainted the plaintiff with the fact; and he concluded with a verification. The court held, that though there was an express affirmative that he did account, in contradiction to the statement in the replication that he did not account, yet that the conclusion with a verification was right; for that, *new matter* being alleged in the rejoinder, the plaintiff ought to have liberty to come in with a surrejoinder, and answer it by traversing the robbery.[4]

The application, however, to particular cases, of this exception, as to the introduction of *new matter*, is occasionally nice and doubtful; and it becomes difficult sometimes to say whether there is any such introduction of new matter as to make the tender of issue improper.

Example: In debt on a bond conditioned to render a full account to the plaintiff of all such sums of money and goods as were belonging to W. N. at the time of his death, the defendant pleaded that *no goods or sums of money came to his hands*. The plaintiff replied, *that a silver bowl*, which belonged to the said W. N. at the time of his death, *came to the hands* of the defendant,

---

[1] This results from a rule which will be discussed hereafter.

[2] See an example in Gainsford *v.* Griffith, 1 Saund. 54.

[3] See an example in Richards *v.* Hodges, 2 Saund. 82.

[4] Vere *v.* Smith, 2 Lev. 5; s. c. Vent. 121.

viz., on such a day and year; "and this he is ready to verify," &c. On demurrer, it was contended that the replication ought to have concluded to the country, there being a complete negative and affirmative; but the court thought it well concluded, as *new matter was introduced*. However, the learned judge who reports the case thinks it clear that the replication was *bad;* and Mr. Serjeant Williams expresses the same opinion, holding that there was *no* introduction of new matter, such as to render a verification proper.[1]

RULE III.   ISSUE, WHEN WELL TENDERED, MUST BE ACCEPTED.[2]

If issue be well tendered, both in point of substance and in point of form, nothing remains for the opposite party but to accept or join in it, and he can neither demur, traverse, nor plead in confession and avoidance; *but he may plead in estoppel.*

The acceptance of the issue, in case of a conclusion to the *country*, *i. e.*, of trial by *jury*, may, as already explained, either be added in making up the issue or paper-book, or may be filed or delivered before that transcript is made up. It is in both cases called the *similiter*, and in the latter case a *special similiter*. The form of a *special similiter* is thus: "And the said *A. B.*" (or "*C. D.*"), "as to the plea" (*or* "replication," etc.), "of the said *C. D.*" (or "*A. B.*"), "whereof he hath put himself upon the country" (*or* whereof he hath prayed it may be "inquired by the country"), "doth the like." The *similiter*, when added in making up the issue or paper-book, is simply this: "And the said *A. B.*" (*or* "*C. D.*"), "doth the like."

As the party has no option in accepting the issue, when well tendered, and as the *similiter* may in that case be added for him, the acceptance of the issue, when well tendered, may be considered as a mere matter of *form*. It is a form, however, which should be invariably observed; and its omission

---

[1] Hayman *v.* Gerrard, 1 Saund. 101. But see Cornwallis *v.* Savery, Burr. 772; Sayre *v.* Minns, Cowp. 575.

[2] Bac. Ab. Pleas, &c. 363; 5th ed.; Digby *v.* Fitzharbert, Hob. 104;

Wilson *v.* Kemp, 2 M. & S. 549. "*In all pleadings, wherever a traverse was first properly taken, the issue closed.*" (Gilb., C. P. 66.)

has sometimes proved a ground of successful objection, even after verdict.[1]

The rule expresses that the issue must be accepted only when it is *well* tendered. For if the opposite party thinks the *traverse* bad, in substance or in form, or objects to the *mode of trial* proposed, in either case he is not obliged to add the *similiter*, but may *demur*,[2] and, if it has been added for him, may strike it out and demur.

The *similiter*, therefore, serves to mark the acceptance both of the question itself and the mode of trial proposed. It seems originally, however, to have been introduced with a view to the *latter* point only. As has been already explained, the resort to a jury, in ancient times, could generally be had only by the mutual *consent* of each party. It appears to have been with the object of expressing such consent that the *similiter* was in those times added in drawing up the record; and from the record it afterward found its way into the written pleadings. Accordingly, no *similiter* or other acceptance of issue is necessary when recourse is had to any of the *other modes* of trial; and the rule in question does not extend to these. Thus, when issue is tendered to be tried by the *record*, the plaintiff is entitled to consider the issue as complete upon such tender,[3] and no acceptance of it, on the other side, is essential.

The rule in question extends to an issue in *law*, as well as an issue in *fact;* for, by analogy (as it would seem) to the *similiter*, the party whose pleading is opposed by a demurrer is required formally to accept the issue in law which it tenders by the formula called a *joinder in demurrer*. However, it

---

[1] Griffith *v.* Crockford, 3 Brod. & Bing. 1. But see Saund. 319, n. 6 ; and Tidd. 955, 8th ed.

[2] But he can not *plead over*, as we have seen he may do in case of an immaterial traverse with an *absque hoc.* Whitehead *v.* Buckland, Stile, 402; where Roll, C. J., says the plaintiff "must either demur or join issue with you; and I have not heard of *passing over* in this case, as may be done in the case of a traverse" (meaning a traverse with an *absque hoc).* So it is said, per Holt, C. J., that pleading over, when issue is offered, is a *discontinuance.* (Campbell *v.* St. John, 1 Salk. 219.)

[3] And the replication may, therefore, conclude with an entry that a day is given to inspect the record. (Tipping *v.* Johnson, 2 Bos & Pul. 302; Jackson *v.* Wickes, 2 Marsh. 354 ; s. c. 7 Taunt. 30; Pitt *v.* Knight, 1 Saund. 96 a, Tidd, 800, 801, 8th ed.)

differs in this respect from the *similiter*, that, whether the issue in law be well or ill tendered — that is, whether the demurrer be in proper form or not — the opposite party is equally bound to join in demurrer.   For it is a rule, *that there can be no demurrer upon a demurrer*,[1] because the first is sufficient, notwithstanding any inaccuracy in its form, to bring the record before the court for their adjudication ; and as for *traverse* or *pleading in confession and avoidance*, there is of course no ground for them while the last pleading still remains unanswered, and there is nothing to oppose but an exception in point of law.

[1] Bac. Ab. Pleas, &c. N. 2.   *Demurrer upon demurrer* is *a discontinuance.* Campbell *v.* St. John, 1 Salk. 219.

CHAPTER X.

OF RULES WHICH TEND TO SECURE THE MATERIALITY OF THE ISSUE.

In order to secure the materiality of the issue, it is of course necessary that at each step of the series of pleadings, by which it is to be produced, there should be some pertinent and material allegation or denial of fact. On this subject, therefore, a general rule may be propounded in the following form : —

RULE. ALL PLEADINGS MUST CONTAIN MATTER PERTINENT AND MATERIAL.

Examples : (1) If to an action of *assumpsit* against an administratrix, laying promises by the intestate, she pleads that she, the *defendant* (instead of the intestate), did not promise, the plea is obviously immaterial and bad.[1]

(2) So where, in replevin for taking cattle, the defendant avowed taking them in the close in which, etc., for rent in arrear, and the plaintiff pleaded in bar to the avowry that the cattle were not *levant* (rising) and *couchant* (lying down) on the close in which, etc., the plea was holden bad on demurrer; for it is a general rule, that all things upon the premises are distrainable for rent in arrear, and the *levancy* and *couchancy* of the cattle is immaterial, unless under special circumstances, such as did not appear by the plea in bar to have existed in this case.[2]

With respect to *traverses* in particular, this general doctrine is illustrated in the books by *subordinate rules* of a more special kind. Thus it is laid down : —

(1) *That traverse must not be taken on an immaterial point.*[3]

---

[1] Anon., 2 Vent. 196.
[2] Jones *v.* Powell, 5 Barn. & Cress. 647.
[3] Com. Dig. Pleader, R. 8, G. 10; Bac. Ab. Pleas, &c. H. 5.

This rule prohibits, first, the taking of a traverse on a point *wholly immaterial*.

Example: Where, to an action of trespass for assault and battery, the defendant pleaded that a judgment was recovered, and execution issued thereupon against a third person, and that the plaintiff, to rescue that person's goods from the execution, assaulted the bailiffs, and that in aid of the bailiffs, *and by their command*, the defendant *molliter manus imposuit* upon the plaintiff, to prevent his rescue of the goods, it was holden that a traverse of the *command of the bailiffs* was bad; for even without their command the defendant might lawfully interfere to prevent a rescue, which is a breach of the peace.[1]

So, by this rule, *a traverse is not good when taken on matter the allegation of which was premature*, though in itself not immaterial to the case.

Example: If in debt on bond the plaintiff should declare that, at the time of sealing and delivery, the defendant was of full age, the defendant should not traverse this, because it was not necessary to allege it in the declaration; though if in fact he was a minor, this would be a good subject for a plea of infancy, to which the plaintiff might then well reply the same matter, viz., that he was of age.[2]

Again, *this rule prohibits the taking of a traverse on matter of aggravation;* that is, matter which only tends to increase the amount of damages, and does not concern the right of action itself.

Example: In trespass for chasing sheep, *per quod* (through which) the sheep died, the dying of the sheep, being aggravation only, is not traversable.[3]

So it is laid down that, in general, *traverse is not to be taken on matter of inducement;* that is, matter brought forward only by way of explanatory introduction to the main allegations.

---

[1] Bridgewater *v.* Bythway, 3 Lev. 113. *Aliter* (otherwise), if not done to prevent a rescue; for in a case where defendant justifies merely as assistant to, and by command of, a person executing legal process, the command is traversable. (Britton *v.* Cole, 3 Salk. 409.)

[2] Sir Ralph Bovy's Case, 1 Vent. 217; Ricketts *r.* Loftus, 14 Q. B. 482.

[3] Leech *v.* Widsley, 1 Vent. 54; s. c. Lev. 283.

But this is open to many exceptions, for it often happens that introductory matter is in itself essential, and of the substance of the case, and in such instances, though in the nature of inducement, it may nevertheless be traversed.[1]

While it is thus the rule, that traverse must not be taken on an immaterial point, it is, on the other hand, to be observed *that, where there are several material allegations, it is in the option of the pleader to traverse which he pleases.*[2]

Examples: (1) If, in trespass, the defendant pleads that A. was seised and demised to him, the plaintiff may traverse either the seisin or the demise.[3]

(2) Again, in trespass, the defendant pleads that A. was seised, and enfeoffed B., who enfeoffed C., who enfeoffed D., whose estate the defendant hath : in this case the plaintiff may traverse which of the feoffments he pleases.[4]

The principle of this rule is sufficiently clear; for it is evident that where the case of any party is built upon several allegations, each of which is essential to its support, it is as effectually destroyed by the demolition of any one of these parts as of another.

It is also laid down —

(2) *That a traverse must not be too large, nor, on the other hand, too narrow.*[5]

As a traverse must not be taken on an immaterial allegation, so, when applied to an allegation that is material, it ought, generally, to take in *no more and no less of that allegation than is material.* If it involves *more,* the traverse is said to be too *large;* if less, too *narrow.*

Traverses too Large.

A traverse may be too large, by involving in the issue quantity, time, place, or other circumstances, which, though

---

[1] Com. Dig. Pleader, G. 14; Kinnersley *v.* Cooper, Cro. Eliz. 168; Carvick *v.* Blagrave, 1 Brod. & Bing. 531.

[2] Com. Dig. Pleader, G. 10; Read's Case, 6 Co. Rep. 24; Doct. Pl. 354, 365; Baker *v.* Blackman, Cro. Jac. 682; Young *v.* Rudd, Carth. 347; Young *v.*

Ruddle, Salk. 627; Bac. Ab. Pleas, &c. H. 5, 392, 5th ed.

[3] Com. Dig. Pleader, G. 10; Moor *v.* Pudsey, Hardr. 317.

[4] Doct. Pl. 365.

[5] 1 Saund. 268, n. 1, 269, n. 2; Com. Dig. Pleader, G. 15, G. 16.

forming part of the allegation traversed, are immaterial to the merits of the cause.

Examples: (1) In an action of debt on bond conditioned for the payment of £1,550, the defendant pleaded that part of the sum mentioned in the condition, to wit, £1,500, was won by gaming, contrary to the statute in such case made and provided, and that the bond was consequently void. The plaintiff replied that the bond was given for a just debt, and traversed that the £1,500 was won by gaming, in manner and form as alleged. On demurrer, it was objected that the replication was ill, because it made the precise sum parcel of the issue, and tended to oblige the defendant to prove that the whole sum of £1,500 was won by gaming; whereas the statute avoids the bond if *any part* of the consideration be on that account. The court was of opinion that there was no color to maintain the replication, for that the material part of the plea was that *part* of the money for which the bond was given was won by gaming; and that the words "to wit, £1,500," were only form, of which the replication ought not to have taken any notice.[1]

(2) Where the condition of a bond was that the obligor should serve the obligee half a year, and, in an action of debt on the bond, the defendant pleaded that he had served him half a year at D., in the county of K., and the plaintiff replied that he had not served him half a year *at D., in the county of K.*, this was adjudged to be a bad traverse, as involving the *place*, which was immaterial.[2]

(3) Where the plaintiff pleaded that the queen, at a manor court, held on such a day, by I. S., her steward, and by copy of court-roll, etc., granted certain land to the plaintiff's lessor, and the defendant rejoined, traversing that the queen, at a manor court, held such a day, by I. S., her steward, granted the land to the lessor, the court held that the traverse was ill, "for the jury are thereby bound to find a copy on such a day, and by such a steward, which ought not to be." The traverse, it seems, ought to have been, that the queen did not grant, *in manner and form as alleged,*[3] words which, as already observed, bring into issue only the *substance* of the allegation.

(4) Where, in an action on the case for stopping *three lights* (windows), the defendant traversed that *he stopped* the *said three lights,* it was held bad, for if he stopped any of them, the action lay.[4]

---

[1] Colborne *v.* Stockdale, Str. 493; s. c. 8 Mod. 58.

[2] Doct. Pl. 360.

[3] Lane *v.* Alexander, Yelv. 122.

[4] Com. Dig. Pleader, G. 15; Newhall *v.* Barnard, Yelv. 225.

Again, a traverse may be too large, by being taken in the *conjunctive*, instead of the *disjunctive*, where it is not material that the allegation traversed should be proved conjunctively.

Example: In an action of *assumpsit*, the plaintiff declared on a policy of insurance, and averred " that the ship insured did not arrive in safety; but that the said ship, tackle, apparel, ordnance, munition, artillery, boat, and other furniture, were sunk and destroyed in the said voyage." The defendant pleaded with a traverse, " Without this, that the said ship, tackle, apparel, ordnance, munition, artillery, boat, and other furniture, were sunk and destroyed in the voyage, in manner and form as alleged." Upon demurrer, this traverse was adjudged to be bad; and it was held that the defendant ought to have denied, disjunctively, that the ship *or* tackle, etc., was sunk or destroyed, because, in this action for damages, the plaintiff would be entitled to recover compensation for any part of that which was the subject of insurance, and had been lost; whereas (it was said), if issue had been taken in the conjunctive form, in which the plea was pleaded, " and the defendant should prove that only a cable or anchor arrived in safety, he would be acquitted of the whole." [1]

On the other hand, however, *a party may, generally, traverse a material allegation of title or estate, to the extent to which it is alleged, though it need not have been alleged to that extent;* and such traverse will not be considered as too large. [2]

Examples: (1) In an action of replevin, the defendant avowed the taking of the cattle, as *damage feasant,* in the place in which, etc.; the same being the freehold of Sir F. L. To this the plaintiff pleaded that he was seised in his demesne as of fee of B. close, adjoining to the place in which, etc.; that Sir F. L. was bound to repair the fence between B. close and the place in which, etc.; and that the cattle escaped through a defect of that fence. The defendant traversed, that the plaintiff *was seised in his demesne as of fee* of B. close; and on demurrer the court was of opinion that it was a good traverse, for though a less estate than a seisin in fee would have been sufficient to sustain the plaintiff's case, yet, as the plaintiff, who should best know

---

[1] Goram *v.* Sweeting, 2 Saund. 205. Blagrave, 1 Brod. & Bing. 531. Palmer *v.* Ekins, 2 Str. 818, is apparently *contra,*
[2] Com. Dig. Pleader, G. 16; Sir Francis Leke's Case, Dy. 365 ; 2 Saund. but, from the report of the same case 207, n. 24; Wood *v.* Budden, Hob. 119; (2 Ld. Raym. 1550), it may be reconciled Tatem *v.* Perient, Yelv. 195; Carvick *v.* with the other authorities.

what estate he had, had pleaded a seisin in fee, his adversary was entitled to traverse the title so laid.[1]

(2) Again, in an action of trespass, for trespasses committed in a close of pasture, containing eight acres, in the town of Tollard Royal, the defendant pleaded that W., Earl of Salisbury, was seised in fee and of right of an ancient chase of deer, called Cranborn, and that the said chase did extend itself, as well in and through the said eight acres of pasture as in and through the said town of Tollard Royal; and justified the trespasses as committed in using the said chase. The plaintiff traversed, *that the said chase extended itself as well to the eight acres as to the whole town ;* and, issue being taken thereon, it was tried and found for the plaintiff. It was then moved, in arrest of judgment, "that this issue and verdict were faulty, because, if the chase did extend to the eight acres only, it was enough for the defendant ; and therefore the finding of the jury, that it did not extend as well to the whole town as to the eight acres, did not conclude against the defendant's right in the eight acres, which was only in question. But it was answered by the court, that there was no fault in the issue, much less in the verdict (which was according to the issue), but the fault was in the defendant's plea; for he puts in his plea more than he needed, viz., the whole town, which, being to his own disadvantage and to the advantage of the plaintiff, there was no reason for him to demur upon it, but rather to admit it, as he did, and so to put it in issue. And so judgment was given for the plaintiff." [2]

Traverses too Narrow.

A traverse is too narrow when it fails to answer fully the whole of the adversary's allegation, which it proposes to answer.[3]

Examples : (1) If to an action on the case for slander, charging the words to have been spoken at S., on a day named, the defendant plead that he spoke the words imputed to him at W., as counsel in a judicial proceeding, *absque hoc* " that he spoke the words at S. *before or after* the day mentioned in the declaration," by which he excluded the day itself, and answered not to it, the traverse is *too narrow,* and for that reason is bad.[4]

(2) In an action of *assumpsit,* to recover a recompense for service from March 21, 1647, to November 1, 1664, the defendant

---

[1] Sir Francis Leke's Case, Dy. 365 ;
[2] Saund. 206 a, n. 22.
[2] Wood *v.* Budden, Hob. 119.

[3] Min. Inst. IV. 930.
[4] Com. Dig. Pleader, G. 16 ; Burkley *v.* Wood, 4 Co. Rep. 14 b.

pleaded that the plaintiff left the service on December 31, 1658; *without this* that the plaintiff served until November 1, 1664; it was held to be too narrow a traverse, because the plaintiff was entitled to recover in proportion to the time he served. In another aspect it was also *too large*, because it put in issue the whole time of service, thus calling upon the plaintiff to prove more than he was obliged to in order to recover.[1]

(3) In an action of trespass for *breaking open the outer doors of the plaintiff's dwelling-house*, the defendants pleaded that they were sheriff's officers, and that an execution of *fieri facias* upon the plaintiff's goods came to their hands as such officers, by virtue of which they entered the house. The court held the plea bad, because it did not answer *the breaking*, and therefore tended to raise an *immaterial* issue.[2] This case illustrates the principle under consideration, although, being a plea by way of confession and avoidance, it is not an example of too narrow a traverse. Many similar cases can be found in the books.

(4) In an action of *trover* for the value of cattle and goods of the plaintiff, to wit, beasts of the plough, implements of husbandry, *books*, *bedsteads*, etc., the defendant by his plea justified the seizure as for distress, for *rent in arrear*. The plaintiff replied that he was an husbandman, and that the goods mentioned in the count were beasts of the plough and implements of husbandry, there being then on the premises other available distress. This replication was held bad as being *too narrow*, not traversing the legality of the distress as to the *books and bedsteads*, although it professed to answer the whole plea.[3]

(5) In an action of trespass *quare clausum fregit* for breaking plaintiff's close, the plea of the defendant stated that the plaintiff was his lessee of the *locus in quo* (place in which), and that in the lease was, amongst others, a condition that the lessee should not assign in any way, notwithstanding which the lessee had assigned *in a particular* manner *which was specified*. The plaintiff replied that he had not assigned *in that manner*. This replication was held to be bad, because *it limited* the denial to the specific mode of assignment stated in the plea.[4]

So, a traverse may be too narrow by being applied to part only of an allegation, which the law considers as in its

---

[1] Com. Dig. Pleader, G. 16; Osborne v. Rogers, 1 Saund. 268, n. 1, 269 a, b, and n. 2.

[2] Buckingham v. Francis, 11 Moore, 40.

[3] Davies v. Aston, 1 Man. Gr. & Scott, 746.

[4] Hammond v. Colls, *ibid*. 916.

nature *indivisible and entire,* such as that of a prescription or grant.

Example : In an action of trespass for breaking and entering the plaintiff's close, called S. C., and digging stones therein, the defendant pleaded that there are certain wastes lying open to one another, one, the close called S. C., and the other called S. G., and so proceeded to prescribe for the liberty of digging stones in both closes, and justified the trespasses under that prescription. The replication traversed the prescriptive right in S. C. *only,* dropping S. G.; but the court held that the traverse could not be so confined, and must be taken on the whole prescription as laid.[1]

The principle, which forbids too narrow a traverse, is the same as that which requires that *every pleading shall really answer so much of the adversary's pleading as it professes and undertakes to answer.*

[1] Morewood *v.* Wood, 4 T. R. 157; and see Doct. Pl. 351, 352, 370; Priddle and Napper's Case, 11 Co. Rep. 10 b; Bradburn *v.* Kennerdale, Carth. 164; 1 Saund. 268, n. 1.

CHAPTER XI.

OF RULES WHICH TEND TO PRODUCE SINGLENESS OR UNITY IN THE ISSUE.

THE following rules enforce singleness in the method of pleading or allegation, and, by consequence, tend to produce a single issue.

RULE I. PLEADINGS MUST NOT BE DOUBLE.[1]

This rule applies both to the declaration and to subsequent pleadings. Its meaning, with respect to the former, is that *the declaration must not*, in support of a single demand, *allege several distinct matters, by any one of which that demand is sufficiently supported.* With respect to the subsequent pleadings, the meaning is that *none of them is to contain several distinct answers to that which preceded it,* and the reason of the rule in each case is, that such pleading tends to several issues concerning a single claim.

The rule in its terms points to *doubleness* only, as if it prohibited only the use of *two* allegations or answers of this description; but its meaning, of course, equally extends to the case of more than two, the term *doubleness,* or *duplicity,* being applied, though with some inaccuracy, to either case.

Of this rule, as applied to the *declaration,* the following are

Examples: (1) The plaintiff declared in debt on a penal bill,[2] by which the defendant was to pay ten shillings on the 11th of June, and ten shillings upon the 10th of July next following, and ten shillings every three weeks after, till a certain total sum were

---

[1] Com. Dig. Pleader, C. 33, E. 2, F. 16; Bac. Ab. Pleas, *x* K.; Humphreys *v.* Bethily, 2 Vent. 198, 222; Doct. Pl. 135.

[2] *Bills penal* are instruments not now in use, having been superseded by *bonds with conditions.* The example in the text would, therefore, not occur in modern practice, but serves equally well the purpose of illustration.

satisfied by such several payments, and by the said bill the defendant bound himself for the true payment of the said several sums in the penal sum of seven pounds, and the plaintiff alleged that the defendant did not pay the said *total sum, or any part thereof, upon the several days aforesaid ;* whereby an action had accrued to him to demand the said penalty of seven pounds. This was held bad for duplicity. For, if the defendant had failed in payment of *any one* of the sums, such failure would alone be a breach of the condition, and sufficient to entitle the plaintiff to the penalty he claimed; and the plaintiff ought, therefore, to have confined himself to the allegation of the non-payment of one of those sums only.[1]

(2) Where the plaintiff declared in *assumpsit,* that the defendant was indebted to him in such a sum, for nourishing one E. L., at the request of the defendant, which the latter promised to pay, and also that the defendant promised to pay him so much as he reasonably deserved to have for nourishing the said E. L. during the same time ; this was bad for duplicity, and, indeed, also for repugnancy (another fault in pleading that will be hereafter considered), as the two promises — to pay a sum certain, and to pay *quantum meruit* — were inconsistent, and could not stand together.[2]

Of duplicity in *pleadings, subsequent to the declaration,* the following instance occurs in a *plea in abatement :*

Example : The defendant pleaded, in disability of the person of the plaintiff, ten different outlawries adjudged against him, and it was held that the plea was ill for duplicity; because the plaintiff was disabled as well by one outlawry as by the whole ten.[3]

The following is an instance of duplicity in a *plea in bar :*

Example : In trespass for breaking a close and depasturing the herbage with cattle, if the defendant pleads that A. had a right of common, and B. also a right of common, in the close, and that the defendant, as their servant and by their command, entered and turned in the cattle, in exercise of their rights of common, the plea is bad for duplicity; [4] because the title of either one or other

---

[1] Humphreys *v.* Bethily, 2 Vent. 198, 222.

[2] Hart *v.* Longfield, 7 Mod. 148. As to duplicity in the *declaration,* see also

Cornwallis *v.* Savery, 2 Burr. 773 ; Manser's Case, 2 Co. Rep. 4.

[3] Trevilian *v.* Seccomb, Carth. 8.

[4] Vin. Ab. tit. Double Pleas, A. 114, cites 15 Henry VII. 10.

of the commoners, and the authority derived as his servant, would have alone constituted a sufficient answer to the declaration.

An instance of duplicity in the *replication* is the following

Example: The plaintiff declared in trespass for breaking and entering his stable, cutting asunder a beam, and throwing down the tiles of the roof. The defendant justified, as servant to Sir H. G., and pleaded that Sir H. G. was seised of a wall in his demesne as of fee, and because the beam was placed in the wall of the said Sir H. G. without his consent, the defendant, as his servant, in order to remove this nuisance, did enter the stable and cut the beam as near to the wall as he could, doing as little damage as possible, and thereby the tiles were thrown down. The plaintiff replied, traversing that the wall was Sir H. G.'s; and then, with a protestation that the wall was not his, further pleaded that the defendant, of his own wrong, did throw down the tiles, for the cutting the beam as aforesaid. The court held that, the first traverse being a complete answer to the whole, the second made the replication double.[1]

The object of this rule is to enforce a single issue upon a *single subject of claim* or defence; the rule is, accordingly, carried no further than is necessary to secure this object.

The declaration, therefore, may, in support of several demands, allege as many distinct matters as are respectively applicable to each.

Example: Let one of the examples above given, with respect to the declaration, be so far varied as to substitute, for the case of an action in debt on a penal bill for the penalty accrued in consequence of non-payment of a sum by several instalments, the case of an action of covenant, on a covenant to pay that sum by similar instalments. In this latter case the plaintiff might, without duplicity, declare that the defendant " did not pay the said total sum, or any part thereof, upon the several days aforesaid." For he does not, as in the action upon the penal bill, found upon such non-payments a single claim, viz., the claim to the penalty of seven pounds; there being no penalty in question, his claims are multiplied in proportion to the number of non-payments; that is, he is entitled to ten shillings in respect of the first default, and ten shillings more upon each of the rest; the allegation of several

---

[1] Humphreys *v.* Churchman, Rep. *temp.* Hard. 289.

20

defaults is, therefore, in this case, the allegation of so many distinct demands, and consequently allowable.[1]

So the *plea*, though it must not contain several answers to the whole of the declaration, may nevertheless make distinct answers to such parts of it as relate to different matters of claim or complaint.[2]

Example : Thus, in the preceding example of duplicity in a plea in bar, if the case were a little varied, and the defendant, being charged with putting five beasts on the common, had pleaded that A. and B. had respectively rights of common there, and that he, as the servant of A., put in two of the beasts in respect of *his* common right, and, as the servant of B., put in three in respect of *his* common right, there would no longer be duplicity ; for he pleads the several titles, not as several answers to the same subject of claim or complaint, but as distinct answers to different matters of complaint, arising in respect of different cattle.[3]

So, in the *replication* and other subsequent parts of the series, a severance of pleading may take place in respect of several subjects of claim or complaint.

Example : If an action be brought for trespasses in closes A. and B., and the defendant pleads a single matter of defence applying to both closes, the plaintiff is still at liberty, in his replication, to give one answer as to so much of the plea as applies to close A., and another answer as to so much of the plea as applies to close B.[4]

The power, however, of alleging in a plea distinct matters, in answer to such parts of the declaration as relate to different claims, seems to be subject to this restriction : that neither of the matters so alleged be such as would alone be a sufficient answer to the whole.

Example : If an action be brought on two bonds, though the defendant may plead, as to one, payment, and as to the other, duress ; yet if he pleads as to one a release *of all actions*, and as to the other duress, it will be double ; for the release is alone a sufficient answer to both bonds.[5]

---

[1] See Bac. Ab. Pleas, &c. 446, 5th ed.

[2] Com. Dig. Pleader, E. 2 ; Co. Litt. 132.
304 a.

[3] Vin. Ab. tit. Double Pleas, A. 115.

[4] See Johns *v.* Whitley, 3 Wils.

[5] Doct. Pl. 136 ; Vin. Ab. tit. Double Pleas, D. In Viner, however, some

Again, if there be several defendants, the rule against duplicity is not carried so far as to compel each of them to make the same answer to the declaration.

Each defendant is at liberty to use such plea as he may think proper for his own defence, and they may either join in the same plea or sever, at their discretion.[1] But *if the defendants have once united* in the plea, *they can not afterward sever* at the rejoinder or other later stage of the pleading.[2]

Where, as to several subjects or several defendants, a severance has thus taken place in the pleading, this may, of course, lead to a corresponding severance in the whole subsequent series, and, as the ultimate effect, to the production of *several issues.* And where there are several issues, they may, respectively, be decided in favor of different parties, and the judgment will follow the same division.

Such being the nature of duplicity, the following rules will tend to its further illustration.

(1) *A pleading will be double that contains several answers, whatever be the class or quality of the answer.*

Example : It will be double by containing several matters in abatement or several matters in bar,[3] or by containing one matter in abatement and another in bar.[4] So a pleading will be double by containing several matters in confession and avoidance, or several answers by way of traverse, or by combining a traverse with a matter in confession and avoidance.[5]

(2) *Matter may suffice to make a pleading double, though it be ill pleaded.*

Example : In trespass for assault and battery, the defendant pleaded that he committed the trespasses in the moderate correc-

cases are cited which show that this restriction has not been uniformly observed, or is at least open to several exceptions.

[1] Co. Litt. 303 a ; Essington *v.* Boucher, Hob. 245. It is said, however, *arguendo,* in the case cited, that they cannot sever in *dilatory* pleas. *Sed qu.?* (See Cuppledick *v.* Terwhit, Hob. 250.)

[2] And see a case where, upon a replication to a plea by one defendant, a rejoinder by all the defendants was adjudged to be bad. (Morrow *v.* Belcher, 4 Barn. & Cress. 704.)

[3] Com. Dig. Pleader, E. 2 ; and see the cases already cited on the subject of duplicity.

[4] *Semb.* Com. Dig. Pleader, E. 2 ; Bleke *v.* Grove, 1 Sid. 176.

[5] Com. Dig. Pleader, E. 2 ; Bac. Ab. Pleas, &c. K. ; and see the cases already cited.

tion of the plaintiff as his servant, and further pleaded, that since that time the plaintiff had discharged and released to him the said trespasses, without alleging, as he ought to have done, a release *under seal*. The court held that this plea was double, the moderate correction and the release being each a matter of defence; and, though the release was insufficiently pleaded, yet, as it was a matter that a material issue might have been taken upon, it sufficed to make the plea double.[1]

On the other hand, it seems that

(3) *Matter immaterial can not operate to make a pleading double*.[2]

Example: In an action by the executors of J. G. on a bond conditioned that the defendant should warrant to J. G. a certain meadow, the defendant pleaded that the said meadow was copyhold of a certain manor, and that there is a custom within the manor, that if the customary tenants fail in payment of their rents and services, or commit waste, then the lord for the time being may enter for forfeiture; and that the said J. G., during his life, peaceably enjoyed the meadow; which descended after his death to one B., his son and heir; who, of his own wrong, entered without the admission of the lord, against the custom of the manor; and because three shillings of rent were in arrear on such a day, the lord entered into the meadow, as into lands forfeited. On demurrer, it was objected (among other things) that the plea was double; because, in showing the forfeiture to have accrued by the heir's own wrongful act, two several matters are alleged: first, that he entered without admission, against the custom; secondly, that three shillings of rent were in arrear. But the judges held, that the only sufficient cause of forfeiture was the non-payment of rent; that, there being no custom alleged for forfeiture in respect of entry without admission, the averment of such entry was mere surplusage, and could not, therefore, avail to make the plea double.[3]

It is, however, to be observed, that the plea in this last case seems to *rely* on the non-payment of the rent as the only

---

[1] Bac. Ab. Pleas, &c. K. 2; Bleke *v.* Grove, 1 Sid. 175.

[2] Bac. Ab. *ubi supra;* 1 Hen. VII. 16; Countess of Northumberland's Case, 5 Co. Rep. 98 a; Case of the Executors of Grenelefe, Dy. 42 b; Doct. Pl. 138. There is, however, a *dictum* of Doddridge, J., that a plea may be double, though only one of the matters be material. (Calfe *v.* Nevil, Poph. 186.) But the weight of the authorities, and the reason of the thing, are opposed to this opinion.

[3] Case of the Executors of Grenelefe, *ubi supra*.

ground of forfeiture ; for it alleges that, "because three shillings of the rent were in arrear, the lord entered ;" and the court noticed this circumstance. The case, therefore, does not explicitly decide, that where two several matters are not only pleaded, but *relied upon,* the immateriality of one of them shall prevent duplicity ; but the manner in which the judges express themselves seems to show that the doctrine goes to that extent ; and there are other authorities the same way.[1]

This doctrine, that a plea may be rendered double by matter *ill pleaded,* but not by *immaterial* matter, quite accords with the *object* of the rule against duplicity, as formerly explained. That object is the avoidance of several issues. Now, whether a matter be well or ill pleaded, yet if it be sufficient in substance, so that the opposite party may go to issue upon it, if he chooses to plead over, without taking the formal objection, such matter tends to the production of a separate issue, and is on that ground held to make the pleading double. On the other hand, if the matter be immaterial, no issue can properly be taken upon it; it does not tend, therefore, to a separate issue, nor, consequently, fall within the rule against duplicity.

(4) *No matter will operate to make a pleading double that is pleaded only as necessary inducement to another allegation.*

Example : It may be pleaded without duplicity that, after the cause of action accrued, the plaintiff (a woman) took husband, and that the husband afterwards released the defendant; for, though the coverture is itself a defence, as well as the release, yet the averment of the coverture is a necessary introduction to that of the release.[2]

This exception to the general rule is prescribed by an evident principle of justice ; for the party has a right to rely on any single matter that he pleases in preference to another ; as in this instance, on the release, in preference to the coverture ; but if a necessary inducement to the matter on which he relies, when itself amounting to a defence, were held to make his pleading double, the effect would be to exclude him from this right, and compel him to rely on the inducement only.

[1] Bac. Ab. Pleas, &c. K. 2.   [2] Bac. Ab. Pleas, &c. K. 2 ; Com. Dig. Pleader, E. 2 ; 24 E. III. 75 b.

(5) *No matters, however multifarious, will operate to make a
pleading double that together constitute but one connected proposition or entire point.*

Example: To an action for assault and imprisonment, if the
defendant plead that he arrested the plaintiff on suspicion of
felony, he may set forth any number of circumstances of suspicion, though each circumstance alone may be sufficient to justify
the arrest; for all of them taken together do but amount to one
connected cause of suspicion.[1]

CUMULATIVE TRAVERSES.

This qualification of the rule against duplicity applies not
only to pleadings in confession and avoidance, but to traverses
also; so that *a man may deny as well as affirm, in pleading,
any number of circumstances that together form but a single
point or proposition.*

Example: In an action of trespass for breaking the plaintiff's
close and depasturing it with cattle, the defendant pleaded a right
of common in the close for the said cattle, being his own commonable cattle, *levant* and *couchant*, upon the premises. The
plaintiff, in the replication, traversed, " that the cattle were the
defendant's own cattle, and that they were *levant* and *couchant*
upon the premises, and commonable cattle." On demurrer for
duplicity, it was objected that there were three distinct facts put
in issue by this replication, any one of which would be sufficient
by itself; but the court held that the point of the defence was,
that the cattle in question were entitled to common; that this
point was single, though it involved the *three several facts*, that
the cattle were the defendant's own, that they were *levant* and
couchant, and that they were commonable cattle; that the replication traversing these facts, in effect, therefore, only traversed
the single point, whether the cattle were entitled to common;
and was, consequently, not open to the objection of duplicity.[2]

---

[1] Vin. Ab. Double Pleas, A. 7, cites
2 Ed. IV. 8.

[2] Robinson *v.* Rayley, 1 Burr. 316.
Upon this case Mr. Williston, in a note
to the fifth edition of Stephen on Pleading, comments as follows: "It should
be observed that the allowance of cumulative traverses (other than *de injuria*,
for the use of which special boundaries

were fixed) is destructive of the fundamental aim of common-law pleading,
that of bringing the parties to issue on
a single narrow point. Robinson *v.*
Rayley is the leading case for the allowance of such traverses, and the distinction there laid down by Lord Mansfield is
'that you must take issue upon a single
point; but it is not necessary that this

The most frequent instance of this cumulative traverse, as it may be called, occurs in the case of the replication, *de injuria absque tali causa.* This replication (it will be recollected) alleges that the defendant did the act (the subject of complaint) of his own wrong, and " *without the cause alleged ;* " and this *cause* frequently consists of several connected circumstances. It is, however (as was formerly stated), a restriction in the use of this replication, that it can not be applied so as to include in the traverse any matter alleged on the other side in the nature of *title, interest, commandment, authority,* or *matter of record.* If, therefore, any such matter be contained in the plea, and the plaintiff wishes to deny it, such matter must be traversed separately ; or, if he chooses not to point the denial to this, but to other matters in the plea, these other matters must separately form the subject of traverse. In the former case, the denial is in the words of the allegation; in the latter, the usual form is to plead with a protestation, and a traverse *de injuria absque residuo causæ,* thus : —

" Protesting that the said C. D. is not seised, etc. For replication, nevertheless, in this behalf, the said A. B. says that the said C. D., of his own wrong, and *without the residue of the cause* in his said plea alleged, broke and entered the said close, etc." [1]

This restriction, by which matter of *title, interest, commandment, authority,* or *record* is required to be separately traversed, is not to be taken as applicable merely to the use of the replication *de injuria,* but extends (it is conceived) in its principle to *all* cases of cumulative traverse, so that it may be said to be generally true, that where any such matter is alleged in connection with other circumstances, it is not a case in which it is competent to the other party

single point should consist only of a single fact. Here the point is, the cattle being entitled to common ; this is the single point of the defence.' But any good affirmative plea contains but a single point of defence. If it contains more, it is double, and the only logical consequence of Robinson *v.* Rayley is that all the material facts of a preceding pleading may always be traversed together. This consequence was never admitted, nor was Robinson *v.* Rayley overruled, but, though followed in some recent cases, it was not followed in others, and, though distinctions were attempted, the cases in fact seem indistinguishable. DeWolf *v.* Bevan, 13 M. & W. 160 ; Bonzi *v.* Stewart, 7 M. & G. 746."

[1] See the precedent, 9 Went. 327.

to traverse cumulatively ;[1] and that, if he include all these circumstances in the same traverse, his pleading will be double.

In some cases the *general issues* appear to partake of the nature of these cumulative traverses. For some of them are so framed as to convey a denial, not of any particular fact, but generally of the whole matter alleged, as *not guilty* in trespass or trespass on the case, and *nil debet* in debt. And in *assumpsit* the case is the same in effect, according to a relaxation of practice formerly explained, by which the defendant is permitted, under the general issue, in that action, to avail himself, with some few exceptions, of any matter tending to disprove his liability. The consequence is, that under these general issues the defendant has the advantage of disputing, and therefore of putting the plaintiff to the proof of every averment in the declaration. Thus, by pleading *not guilty*, in trespass *quare clausum fregit*, he is enabled to deny, at the trial, both that the land was the plaintiff's and that he committed upon it the trespasses in question, and the plaintiff must establish both these points in evidence. Indeed, besides this advantage of double *denial*, the defendant obtains, under the general issue, in *assumpsit* and other actions of trespass on the case, the advantage of double *pleading in confession and avoidance*. For, upon the principles formerly explained, he is allowed, in these actions, to bring forward, upon the general issue, almost any matters (though in the nature of confession and avoidance), which tend to disprove his debt or liability ; so he is not limited (as he would be in special pleading), to a reliance on any single matter of this description, but may set up any number of these defences. While such is the effect of many of the general issues in mitigating or evading the rule against duplicity, the remark does not apply to all. Thus, the general issue of *non est factum* raises only a single question, namely, whether the defendant executed a valid and genuine deed, such as is alleged in the declaration. The defendant may, under this plea, insist that the deed was not executed by him, or that it was executed under circumstances

---

[1] See Bull. N. P. 93.

which absolutely annul its effect as a deed, but can set up no other kind of defence.

(6) *A protestation will not make the pleading double.*[1]

A protestation (as already explained) does not tend to issue in the action, but is made merely to reserve to the party the right of denying or alleging the same matter in a future suit. It consequently can not fall within the object of the rule against duplicity, which is, to avoid a plurality of issues.

THE USE OF SEVERAL COUNTS.

Having explained the rule against duplicity in pleading, it is necessary, in the next place, to advert to certain *modes of practice* by which the effect of that rule is materially qualified and evaded. These are, the use of *several counts* and the allowance of *several pleas*, the former being grounded on ancient practice, the latter on the statute 4 Ann. c. 16.

First shall be considered the subject of *several counts*.

Where a plaintiff has several distinct causes of action, he is allowed to pursue them cumulatively in the same original writ, subject to certain rules which the law prescribes, as to joining such demands only as are of similar quality or character.[2]

Examples : He may join a claim of debt on bond with a claim of debt on simple contract, and pursue his remedy for both by the same original writ in debt. So, if several distinct trespasses have been committed, these may all form the subject of one original writ in trespass ; but, on the other hand, a plaintiff can not join in the same suit a claim of debt on bond and a complaint of trespass, these being dissimilar in kind.

Where a plaintiff thus makes several demands by the same writ, his course of proceeding in debt, covenant, and detinue, and the real and mixed actions, where the writs are in a simple and general form, is merely to enlarge his claim in point of sums and quantities; but in trespass, and trespass on the case, where the form is more special, the original writ separately specifies each subject of claim or complaint.

[1] Bl. Com. III. 311 *.   [2] Upon this subject, see Bac. Ab Actions. C.

Examples : If the action be brought in trespass for two assaults and batteries, the original writ, after setting forth one, proceeds to detail the other. And, when the time for the *declaration* arrives, the plaintiff, in *all* forms of action, sets forth in the declaration, separately, each different subject of claim or complaint thus put together in the same writ. So, in the case of proceeding by *bill*, the different claims or complaints are separately brought forward in the bill or declaration, care, however, being taken to join only such as might have been jointly claimed by the same original.

Such different claims or complaints constitute different parts or sections of the declaration, and are known in pleading by the description of *several counts.*

When several counts are thus used, the defendant may, according to the nature of his defence, demur to the whole ; or plead a single plea applying to the whole ; or may demur to one count and plead to another ; or plead a several plea to each count; and in the two latter cases the result may be a corresponding severance in the subsequent pleadings, and the production of *several issues.* But, whether one or more issues be produced, if the decision, whether in law or fact, be in the plaintiff's favor, as to any one or more counts, he is entitled to judgment *pro tanto* (for so much), though he fail as to the remainder.[1]

The use of several counts, when applied to *distinct causes of action,* is quite consistent with the rule against duplicity ; for the object of that rule, as formerly explained, is to prevent several issues in respect to the same demand only ; there being no objection to several issues where the demands are several.

But it happens more frequently than otherwise that, when various counts are introduced, they do *not* really relate to distinct claims, but are adopted merely *as so many different forms of propounding the same cause of action,* and are therefore a mere evasion of the rule against duplicity. This is a relaxation of very ancient date, and has long since passed, by continual sufferance, into allowable and regular practice. It

---

[1] See Phillips *v.* Howgate, 5 Barn. & Ald. 220.

takes place when the pleader, in drawing the declaration or bill in any action, or in preparing the *præcipe* for an original writ in trespass, or trespass on the case, after having set forth his case in one aspect, feels doubtful whether, as so stated, it may not be insufficient in point of law, or incapable of proof in point of fact; and at the same time perceives another mode of statement, by which the apprehended difficulty may probably be avoided.   Not choosing to rely on either view of the case exclusively, he takes the course of adopting both; and accordingly inserts the second form of statement in the shape of a second count, in the same manner as if he were proceeding for a separate cause of action.   If, upon the same principle, he wishes to vary still further the method of allegation, he may find it necessary to add many other succeeding counts besides the second; and thus, in practice, a great variety of counts often occurs in respect to the same cause of action; the law not having set any limits to the discretion of the pleader, in this respect, if fairly and rationally exercised.[1]

The Object of using Several Counts.

It may be desirable, however, to explain more particularly in what case, and with what objects, resort is had to several counts for the same cause of action.   This may happen either

(1) Where the state of facts to which each count refers is really different, or

(2) Where the same state of facts is differently represented.

(1) An instance of the first case is the following

Example : In an action of debt on a penal bill, whereby the defendant engaged to pay £7, as penalty, in the event of non-payment of 10s. on the 11th of June, and 10s. more on the 10th of July, and 10s. every three weeks after, till a certain sum was satisfied, let it be supposed that the plaintiff complains of a failure in payment both on the 11th June and 10th July.   Either failure entitles him to the penal sum for which he brings the

---

[1] See Meeke *v.* Oxlade, 1 N. R. 289;   Brindley *v.* Dennet, 2 Bing. 184 ; Nelson Gabell *v.* Shaw, 2 Chit. Rep. 299;   *v.* Griffiths, *ibid.* 412; 1 Tidd, 667, Thomas *v.* Hanscombe, 1 Bing. 281;   8th ed.

action; but, if he states them both in the same count, the declaration, as we have seen, will be double. The case, however, may be such as to make it convenient to rely on both defaults; for there may be a doubt whether one or other of the payments were not made, though it may be certain that there was at least one default; and if, under these circumstances, the plaintiff should set forth one of the defaults, and the defendant should take issue upon it, he might defeat the action by proving payment on the day alleged, though he would have been unable to prove the other payment. To meet this difficulty, the pleader might resort to two counts. The first of these would set forth the penal bill, alleging a default of payment on the 11th of June; the second would again set forth the same bill, describing it as "a certain *other* bill," etc., and would allege a default on the 10th of July. The effect of this would be, that the plaintiff, at the trial, might rely on either default, as he might then find convenient.

In this instance, the several counts are each founded on a *different state of facts* (viz., a different default in payment), though in support of the same demand.

(2) But it more frequently happens that it is the *same state of facts differently represented* which forms the subject of different counts.

Example: Where a man has ordered goods of another, and an action is brought against him for the price, the circumstances may be conceived to be such as to raise a doubt whether the transaction ought to be described as one of *goods sold and delivered,* or of *work and labor done;* and, in this case, there would be two counts, setting forth the claim both ways, in order to secure a verdict, at all events, upon one of them.

Common Money-Counts.

It may be useful to observe here that, upon this principle, the counts for *money lent and advanced, money paid, money had and received,* and *money due on account stated* (commonly called the *money counts),* are, some or all of them, generally inserted, as a matter of course, in every *præcipe,* declaration, or bill in *assumpsit,* though the cause of action be also stated in a more special form in other counts. This is done because it often happens that, when the special counts are found incapable of proof at the trial, the cause of action will resolve itself into one of these general pecuniary forms of demand, and thus the plaintiff may obtain a verdict on one of these money counts, though he fail as to all the rest. Again, the same state of facts may be varied, by omitting, in one count, some matter stated in another. In such a case the more special count is used, lest the omission of this matter should render the other insufficient in point of law. The more general count is adopted, because, if good in point of law, it will relieve the plaintiff from the necessity of proving such omitted matter in point of fact. If the defendant demur to the latter count as insufficient, and take issue in fact on the former, the plaintiff has the chance of proving the matter alleged, and also the chance of succeeding on the demurrer. If, on the other hand, the defendant do not think proper to demur, but take issue in fact on both, the plaintiff will have no occasion at the trial to rely at all upon the former count, but will succeed by merely proving the latter.

Whether the subjects of several counts be *really* distinct or identical, they must always *purport* to be founded on distinct causes of action, and not to refer to the same matter; and this is effected by the insertion of such words as "*other*," "*the further sum*," etc. This is evidently rendered necessary by the rule against duplicity, which, though *evaded*, as to the declaration, by the use of several counts, in the manner here described, is not to be directly *violated*.[1]

THE USE OF SEVERAL PLEAS.

It has been already stated that the rule against duplicity does not prevent a defendant from giving distinct answers to different claims or complaints on the part of the plaintiff. To several counts, or to distinct parts of the same count, he may, therefore, plead several pleas, viz., one to each.[2]

Example: In an action of trespass for two assaults and batteries, he may plead, as to the first count, *not guilty;* and as to

---

[1] Hart *v.* Longfield, 7 Mod. 148; West *v.* Troles, 1 Salk. 213; Bac Ab. Pleas, &c. B.

[2] Or he may plead to one count, and demur to another. And it seems that in pleading different pleas to different

the second, the statute of limitations, viz., that he was *not guilty within four years.*

But it may also happen that a defendant may have several distinct answers to give to the *same* claim or complaint.

Example : To an action of trespass for two assaults and batteries, he may have ground to deny both the trespasses, and also to allege that they were neither of them committed within four years.

Anterior, however, to the regulation which will be presently mentioned, it was not competent to him to plead these several answers to both trespasses, as that would have been an infringement of the rule against duplicity. The defendant was, therefore, obliged to elect between his different defences, where more than one thus happened to present themselves, and to rely on that which, in point of law and fact, he might deem strongest. But as a mistake in that selection might occasion the loss of the cause, contrary to the real merits of the case, this restriction against the use of several pleas to the same matter, after being for ages observed in its original severity, was at length considered contrary to the true principles of justice, and was accordingly relaxed by legislative enactment.

The statute 4 Ann. c. 16, s. 4, provides that " it shall be lawful for any defendant or tenant, in any action or suit, or for any plaintiff in replevin, in any court of record, with leave of the court, to plead as many several matters thereto as he shall think necessary for his defence." Since this act the course has been for the defendant, if he wishes to plead several matters to the same subject of demand or complaint, to apply previously for a rule of court permitting him to do so ; and, upon this, a rule is accordingly drawn up for that purpose.[1]

When several pleas are pleaded, either to different matters, or (by virtue of the statute of Anne) to the same matter, the

parts of the declaration, the defendant is not confined to pleas of the *same kind*. Thus, it is laid down that he may plead in abatement to part, and demur or plead in bar to the residue. (2 Saund. 209 e, n. 1) And see Herries v. Jamieson, 5 T. R. 553.

[1] But the court have a discretion, either to permit or refuse, according to the nature of the matters proposed

plaintiff may, according to the nature of his case, either demur to the whole, or demur to one plea and reply to the other, or make a several replication to each plea ; and, in the two latter cases, the result may be a corresponding severance in the subsequent pleadings, and the production of *several issues*.   But, whether one or more issues be produced, if the decision, whether in law or fact, be in the defendant's favor, as to any one or more pleas, he is entitled to judgment, though he fail as to the remainder, — *i. e.*, he is entitled to judgment in respect of that subject of demand or complaint to which the successful plea relates ; and, if it were pleaded to the whole declaration, to judgment generally, though the plaintiff should succeed as to all the other pleas.

USE OF SEVERAL PLEAS SIMILAR TO THAT OF SEVERAL COUNTS.

By a relaxation similar to that which has obtained with respect to *several counts*, the use of *several pleas* (though presumably intended by the statute to be allowed only in a case where there are really several grounds of defence) [1] is, in practice, carried much further.   For it was soon found that, when there was a matter of defence by way of special plea, it was generally expedient to plead that matter in company with the general issue, whether there were any real ground for denying the declaration or not ; because the effect of this is to put the plaintiff to the proof of his declaration before it can become necessary for the defendant to establish his special plea ; and thus the defendant has the chance of succeeding, not only on the strength of his own case, but by the failure of the plaintiff's proof.   Again, as the plaintiff, in the case of several counts, finds it convenient to vary the mode of stating the same subject of claim, so, for similar reasons, defendants were led, under color of pleading distinct matters of defence, to state variously, in various pleas, the same defence, and this, either by presenting it in an entirely new aspect, or by omitting in one plea some circumstances alleged in another.   To this

to be pleaded.   (Jenkins *v.* Edwards, 5 T. R. 97.)

[1] See Lord Clinton *v.* Morton, 2 Str. 1000.

extent, therefore, is the use of several pleas now carried. Some efforts, however, were at one time made to restrain this apparent abuse of the indulgence given by the statute. For that *leave of the court* which the statute requires was formerly often refused where the proposed subjects of plea appeared to be *inconsistent;* and on this ground leave has been refused to ·plead to the same trespass *not guilty* and *accord* and *satisfaction,* or *non est factum* and *payment* to the same demand.[1] In modern practice, however, such pleas, notwithstanding the apparent repugnancy between them, are permitted;[2] and the only pleas, perhaps, which have been uniformly disallowed, on the mere ground of inconsistency, are those of the general issue and a *tender*.[3]

Statute 4 Ann. c. 16, s. 4, does not extend to Replications or Subsequent Pleadings.

On the subject of several pleas it is to be further observed, that the statute extends to the case of pleas *only*, and not to *replications* or *subsequent pleadings*. These remain subject to the full operation of the common law against duplicity, so that, though to each plea there may, as already stated, be a separate replication, yet there can not be offered to the same plea more than a single replication, nor to the same replication more than one rejoinder; and so to the end of the series.

The legislative provision allowing several matters of *plea* was confined to that case, under the impression, probably, that it was in that part of the pleading that the hardship of the rule against duplicity was most seriously and frequently felt, and that the multiplicity of issues (which would be occasioned by a further extension of the enactment) would have been attended with expense and inconvenience more than equivalent to the advantage. The effect, however, of this state of law is somewhat remarkable.

---

[1] Com. Dig. Pleader, E. 2.

[2] *Vide* 1 Sell. Pract. 299. See Rama Chitty *v.* Hume, 13 East, 255.

[3] But the Court of Common Pleas refused to allow the defendant in *scire facias,* on a judgment, to plead, (1) payment; (2) that the judgment was obtained by fraud; (3) that the warrant of attorney on which judgment was entered was obtained by fraud. (Shaw *v.* Lord Alvanley, 2 Bing. 325.)

Examples: It empowers a defendant to plead to a declaration in *assumpsit*, for goods sold and delivered, (1) the general issue ; (2) that the cause of action did not accrue within six years ; (3) that he was an infant at the time of the contract. On the first plea the plaintiff has only to join issue, but with respect to each of the two last he may have several answers to give. The case may be such as to afford either of these replications to the statute of limitations, viz., that the cause of action *did* accrue within six years, or that at the time the cause of action accrued he was *beyond sea*, and that he commenced his suit within six years after his return. So, to the plea of infancy, he may have ground for replying, either that the defendant was *not* an infant, or that the goods for which the action is brought were *necessaries* suitable to the defendant's condition in life. Yet, though the defendant had the advantage of his three pleas cumulatively, the plaintiff is obliged to make his election between these several answers, and can reply but one of them to each plea.

STATUTE DOES NOT APPLY TO DILATORY PLEAS.

It is also to be observed, that the power of pleading several matters extends to pleas in *bar* only, and not to those of a *dilatory* class, with respect to which the leave of the court will not be granted.[1]

Again, it is to be remarked, that the statute does not operate as a total abrogation, even with respect to pleas in bar, of the rule against duplicity. For, first, it is necessary (as we have seen) to obtain *the leave of the court* to make use of several matters of defence ; and then the several matters are pleaded formally, with the words "by leave of the court for this purpose first had and obtained." The several defences must also each be pleaded as a *new* or *further* plea, with a formal commencement and conclusion as such ; so that, notwithstanding the statute, and the leave of the court obtained in pursuance of it to plead several matters, it would still be improper to incorporate several matters in *one plea* in any case in which the plea would be thereby rendered double at common law.

EFFECT OF PLEADING OVER.

Such are the nature and extent of the rule against double pleading, and of the modifications to which, in practice, it is

[1] See 1 Sell. Pract. 275.

subject. Under this rule, it remains only to observe that, if, *instead of demurring for duplicity*, the opposite party passes the fault by, and *pleads over*, he is, in that case, *bound to answer each matter alleged ;* and has no right, on the ground of the duplicity, to confine himself to any single part of the adverse statement.[1]

RULE II.   IT IS NOT ALLOWABLE BOTH TO PLEAD AND TO DEMUR TO THE SAME MATTER.[2]

This rule depends on exactly the same principles as the last.   As it is not allowable to *plead* double, lest several issues in fact in respect of the same matter should arise, so it is not permitted both to *plead and demur* to the same matter, lest an issue in fact and an issue in law, in respect of a single subject, should be produced.   The party must, therefore, make his election.

The rule, however, it will be observed, only prohibits the pleading and demurring *to the same matter*.   It does not forbid this course as applicable to *distinct statements*.   Thus, a man may plead to one count, or one plea, and demur to another.   The reason of this distinction is sufficiently explained by the remarks already made on the subject of duplicity in pleading.

Lastly, it is to be remarked, that the statute of Anne, which authorizes the pleading of *several pleas*, gives no authority for *demurring and pleading* to the same matter.   The rule now in question, therefore, is not affected by that provision, but remains as it was at common law.[3]

---

[1] Bolton *v.* Cannon, 1 Vent. 272.   [3] Haiton *v.* Jeffreys, 10 Mod. 280.
[2] Bac. Ab. Pleas, &c. K. 1.

CHAPTER XII.

OF RULES WHICH TEND TO PRODUCE CERTAINTY OR PARTICULARITY IN THE ISSUE.

THE rules tending to certainty in the pleadings, and, by consequence, certainty in the issue, are very numerous, and in their nature do not easily admit of methodical arrangement; but an enumeration shall here be attempted of such of them as appear to be of principal importance.

RULE I. THE PLEADINGS MUST HAVE CERTAINTY OF PLACE.[1]

VENUE.

It has been explained that the nature of the trial by jury, while conducted in the form which first belonged to that institution, was such as to render particularity of *place* absolutely essential in all issues which a jury was to decide. Consisting, as the jurors formerly did, of witnesses, or persons in some measure cognizant of their own knowledge of the matter in dispute, they were of course, as a rule, to be summoned from the particular place or neighborhood where the fact happened,[2] and, in order to know into what county the *venire facias* for summoning them should issue, as well as to enable the sheriff to execute that writ, it was necessary that the issue, and therefore the pleadings out of which it arose, should show particularly what that place or neighborhood was.[3] Such place or

---

[1] Com. Dig. Pleader, C. 20; *Ibid.* Abatement, H. 13; Co. Litt. 125 a.

[2] Co. Litt. by Harg. 125 a, n. 1. "The *venire* was to bring up the *pares* (*equals, peers*) of the place where the fact was laid, in order to try the issue; and originally every fact was laid in the place where it was really done; and

therefore the written contracts bore date at a certain place." (Gilb. Hist. C. P. 84.)

[3] Ilderton *v.* Ilderton, 2 H. Bl. 161; per Lord Mansfield, Mostyn *v.* Fabrigas, Cowp. 176; Co. Litt. 125 a, b. See 2 Hen. VII. 4.

neighborhood was called *the venue*, or *visne* (from *vicinetum*),[1] and the statement of 'it in the pleadings obtained the same name; to allege the place being, in the language of pleading, to *lay the venue*.

THE VENUE OF THE ACTION.

The present law of *venue* may be stated as follows: —

The *original writ* must be directed to the sheriff of some county; and in that county the *action* is said to be *brought* or *laid*. Each affirmative traversable allegation in the writ is to be laid with a *venue* or place, comprising not only the *county* in which the fact occurred, but the *parish, town,*[2] or *hamlet* within the county;[3] but in a mere denial, of course, no *venue* is to be used, nor is any required in respect of facts not traversable; for example, matter of inducement or aggravation.[4] The pleader has his election to lay either the parish, the town, or the hamlet; but a more extensive division than a parish (for example, a hundred) is not a sufficient *venue;* that having apparently been considered, in ancient times, as too large an allegation of place to instruct the sheriff properly as to the summoning of the jurors.[5] Of the different facts alleged in the writ, it is necessary that some principal one, at least, should be laid in some parish, town, or hamlet, within the county in which the *action is brought,* in order to justify the bringing of the action in that county,[6] and

---

[1] Bac. Ab. *Visne* or *Venue*, A.; Bl. Com. III. 294 *.

[2] A *town* is, in pleading, otherwise called *vill.* (Bl. Com. I. 114 *.) See Curwen *v.* Salkeld, 3 East, 538.

[3] Co. Litt. 125 a; Com. Dig. Abatement. H. 13; *ibid.* Pleader, C. 20; Braddish *v.* Bishop, Cro. Eliz. 260; The King *v.* Holland, per Buller, J., 5 T. R. 620; Amory *v.* Brodrick, 5 Barn. & Ald. 712. But in Ware *v.* Boydell, 3 M. & S. 148 (which was an action on a promissory note), the court held it sufficient to allege a county for *venue,* in the declaration, without a parish, because the jury now come *de corpore* comitatus (from the body of the county).

[4] Com. Dig. Pleader, C. 20, cites Pl. Com. 190 b.

[5] Co. Litt. by Harg. 125, n. 1. If the fact happened out of any parish, town, or hamlet, but in some other *known place,* such as a forest, or the like, such *known place* may be laid for *venue.* (Co. Litt. 125 a, b; Bac. Ab. Visne, E in marg.) And if it happened out of any parish, town, hamlet, or *known place,* the *venue* may be laid in the county generally. (Bac. Ab. *ibid.*)

[6] See The King *v.* Burdett, 4 Barn. & Ald. 175, 176. Calvin's Case, 7 Co. Rep. 1; Scott *v.* Brest, 2 T. R. 238.

such county, and the particular place so laid within it, are called the *venue in the action* or the *venue where the action is laid*.

VENUE OF THE TRAVERSABLE ALLEGATIONS.

As the *declaration* conforms to the writ in other particulars, so it adheres of necessity to the same *venue*. The county where the action is laid is placed at the commencement, in the margin of the declaration; and all the different affirmative traversable allegations are to be laid with a *venue* of parish, town, or hamlet, as well as county, in the same manner as above explained with regard to the writ, and in accordance with that instrument.

In proceedings by *bill*, the law of *venue* is exactly the same as that already described, subject only to the difference necessarily introduced by the absence of the original writ, the only effect of which is, that the declaration, instead of the original, first determines where the *action is laid*, and, as in proceedings by original the *action* is said to be *brought or laid* in the county into which the writ issues, so, in proceedings by bill, it is said to be *brought or laid* in the county named in the margin of the declaration. Again, as in proceedings by original, the county into which the writ issues, and the place within that county at which the principal fact is laid, are called the *venue in the action*, so, in proceedings by bill, the same term applies to the county in the margin of the declaration, and the place within that county laid to the principal fact.

Whether the action be by original or by bill, the *plea, replication, and subsequent pleadings* lay a *venue* to each affirmative traversable allegation, according to the principles already stated, until issue joined.

It having been stated that the original object of thus laying a *venue* was to determine the place from which the *venire facias* should direct the jurors to be summoned, in case the parties should put themselves upon the country, it will be proper now to consider how far the same use is made of the *venue* in modern practice. And, in order to explain clearly the existing law on this subject, it will be convenient to take a short retrospect of its former state and progress.

ANCIENT USE OF THE VENUE.

The most ancient practice, as established at the period when juries were composed of persons cognizant of their own knowledge of the fact in dispute, was, of course, to summon the jury from that *venue* which had been laid to the particular fact *in issue*, and from the *venue* of *parish, town, or hamlet*, as well as county.[1]

Examples: (1) In an action of debt on bond, if the declaration alleged the contract to have been made at Westminster, in the County of Middlesex, and the defendant, in his plea, denied the bond, issue being joined on this plea, it would be tried by a jury from Westminster.

(2) If he pleaded an affirmative matter, as, for example, a release, he would lay this new traversable allegation with a *venue ;* and, if this *venue* happened to differ from that in the declaration, being laid, for example, at Oxford, in the County of Oxford, and issue were taken on the plea, such issue would be tried by a jury from Oxford, and not from Westminster.[2]

And it may here be incidentally observed, that as the place or neighborhood in which the fact arose and also the allegation of that place in the pleadings were called the *venue,* so the term was often applied to the jury summoned from thence. Thus, it would be said in the case last supposed that *the venue was to come from Oxford.* With respect to the *form* of the *venire* at this period, it was as follows : *venire facias duodecim liberos et legales homines, de vicineto de W. (or O.), (i. e.,* the parish, town, or hamlet), *per quos rei veritas melius sciri poterit,* etc. (you shall cause to come twelve free and legal men, from the neighborhood of W., through whom the truth of the matter may be the better known).[3]

---

[1] Co. Litt. 125 a ; Bac. Ab. *Visne* or *Venue,* E. ; and see an illustrative case, 43 Ed. III. 1.

[2] Craft *v.* Boite, 1 Saund. 246 b ; Com. Dig. Action, N. 12 ; 8 Ed. III. 8 pl. 20 ; 45 Ed. III. 16.

[3] *De vicineto tali* (is the expression of Bracton) *per quos rei veritas melius sciri poterit,* &c. Bract. 309 b, 310 a, 396 b, 397 a. In the statute 27 Eliz. c. 6, sec. 1, the form is, 12 *liberos et legales homines de vicineto de B., per quos rei veritas,* &c. ; and see Litt. sec. 234.

CHANGES IN PRACTICE AS TO VENUE.

While such appears to have been the most ancient state of practice, it soon sustained very considerable changes. When the jury began to be summoned no longer as witnesses, but as judges, and, instead of being cognizant of the fact on their own knowledge, learned the fact from the testimony of others judicially examined before them, the reason for summoning them from the immediate neighborhood ceased to apply, and it was considered as sufficient if, by way of partial conformity with the original principle, a *certain number of the jury* came from the same *hundred* in which the place laid for *venue* was situate, though their companions should be of the county only, and neither of the *venue* nor even of the *hundred*. This change in the manner of executing the *venire* did not, however, occasion any alteration in its *form*, which still directed the sheriff, as in former times, to summon the whole jury from the particular *venue*.[1] The number of hundredors which it was necessary to summon was different at different periods; in later times no more than *two* hundredors were required in a personal action.[2]

CHANGES IN LAW OF VENUE.

In this state of the law was passed the statute 16 and 17 Car. II. c. 8. By this act (which is one of the statutes of *jeofails)* it is provided, " that after verdict judgment shall not be stayed or reversed, for that there is no right *venue*, so as the cause were tried by a jury of the proper county or place *where the action is laid*." This provision was held to apply to the case (among others) where issue had been taken on a fact laid with a different *venue* from that *in the action*, but where the *venire* had improperly directed a jury to be summoned from the *venue in the action*, instead of the *venue laid to the fact in issue*.[3] This had formerly been matter of *error*, and, therefore, ground for arresting or reversing the judgment;[4]

---

[1] 27 Eliz. c. 6, s. 1 ; Litt. sec. 234.
[2] 27 Eliz. c. 6, s. 5.
[3] Craft *v.* Boite, 1 Saund. 247.
[4] 1 Saund. 247, n. 1 ; 2 Saund. 5,

n. 3 ; Bowyer's Case, Cro. Eliz. 468 ; Eden's Case, 6 Co. Rep. 15 b ; Co. Litt. by Harg. 125 a, n. 1.

but by this act (passed with a view of removing what had become a merely formal objection) the error was cured, and the staying or reversal of the judgment disallowed.

While such was its direct operation, it has had a further effect, not contemplated, perhaps, by those who devised the enactment. For what the statute only purported to cure as an error, it has virtually established as regular and uniform practice ; and issues taken on facts laid with a different *venue* from that *in the action* have, for a long time past, been constantly tried, not by a jury of the *venue* laid to the *fact in issue*, but by a jury of the *venue in the action*.[1]

Another change was introduced by the statute 4 Ann. c. 16, sec. 6. This act provides that " every *venire facias* for the trial of any issue shall be awarded of the *body* of the proper county where such issue is triable," instead of being (as in the ancient form) awarded from the particular *venue* of parish, town, or hamlet. From this time, therefore, the form of the *venire* has been changed, and directs the sheriff to summon twelve good and lawful men, etc., "*from the body of his county;*" and they are accordingly, in fact, all summoned from the body of the county only, and no part of them necessarily from the hundred in which the particular place laid for venue is situate.[2]

Modern Rule as to Venue.

On the whole, then, by the joint effect of these two statutes, the *venire*, instead of directing the jury to be summoned from that *venue* which had been laid to the fact *in issue*, and from the *venue* of *parish, town, or hamlet*, as well as county, now directs them, in all cases, to be summoned from the *body of the county in which the action is laid*, whether that be the county laid to the fact in issue or not, and without regard to the parish, town, or hamlet.

[1] 2 Saund. 5, n. 3.

[2] And even in criminal proceedings it is now expressly enacted, that no jurors shall be required to be returned from any hundred or hundreds, or from any particular *venue*, within the county, and that the want of hundredors shall be no cause of challenge. (6 Geo. IV. c. 50, sec. 13.)

When Venue must be truly laid.

What has been hitherto said on the subject of *venue* relates only to the form in which the *venue* is laid and its effect as to the *venire*. There is, however, another very important point still remaining to be considered, viz., how far it is necessary to lay the *venue truly*.

Before the change in the constitution of juries above mentioned, the *venue* was of course always to be laid in the true place where the fact arose, for so the reason of the law of *venue* evidently required. But when, in consequence of that change, this reason ceased to operate, the law began to distinguish between cases in which the truth of the *venue* was material, or of the substance of the issue, and cases in which it was not so. A difference began now to be recognized between *local* and *transitory* matters. The former consisted of such facts as carried with them the idea of some certain place, comprising all matters relating to the *realty*, and hardly any others; the latter consisted of such facts as might be supposed to have happened anywhere; and, therefore, comprised debts, contracts, and generally all matters relating to the person or personal property. With respect to the former, it was held, that if any local fact were laid in pleading at a certain place, and issue were taken on that fact, the place formed part of the substance of the issue, and must, therefore, be proved as laid, or the party would fail as for want of proof. But as to transitory facts, the rule was, that they might be laid as having happened at one place, and might be proved on the trial to have occurred at another.[1]

The present state of the law, with respect to the necessity of laying the true *venue*, is accordingly as follows : —

Local and Transitory Actions.

Actions are either LOCAL or TRANSITORY.

An action is LOCAL, if all the principal facts on which it is founded be local.

An action is TRANSITORY, if any principal fact be of the transitory kind.

[1] Vin. Ab. Trial, M. f; Co. Litt. 282 a.

In a local action, the plaintiff must lay the *venue in the action truly*. In a transitory one, he may lay it in any county, and any parish, town, or hamlet within the county, that he pleases.

FACTS ARISING OUT OF THE REALM.

From this state of the law, it follows, first, that if an action be local, and the facts arose *out of the realm*, such action can not be maintained in the English courts ; [1] for, as the *venue in the action* is to be laid truly, there is no county into which, consistently with that rule, the original writ can be directed. But, on the other hand, if the action be transitory, then, though all the facts arose abroad, the action may be maintained in England ; because the *venue in the action* may be laid in any English county, at the option of the plaintiff.

CHANGE OF VENUE.

The same state of law also leads to the following inference : that, in a transitory action, the plaintiff may have the action tried in any county that he pleases ; for (as we have seen) he may lay the *venue in the action* in any county, and upon issue joined the *venire* issues into the county where the *venue in the action* is laid. And such, accordingly, is the rule, subject only to a check interposed by another regulation, viz , that which relates to the *changing of the venue*. The courts established, about the reign (as it is said) of James I.,[2] a practice, by which defendants were enabled to protect themselves from any inconvenience they might apprehend from the *venue* being laid contrary to the fact, and to enforce, if they pleased, a compliance with the stricter and more ancient system. By this practice, when the plaintiff in a transitory action lays a *false venue*, the defendant is entitled to *move the court to have the venue changed*, i. e., altered to the right place ; and the court, upon *affidavit* that the cause of action arose wholly in the county to which it is proposed to change the *venue*, will in most cases grant the application, and oblige the plaintiff to amend his declaration in this particular, unless he, on the other hand,

---

[1] Per Buller, J., Doulson *v.* Matthews, 4 T. R. 503.   [2] Knight *v.* Farnaby, 2 Salk. 670.

will undertake to give, at the trial, some material evidence arising in the county where the *venue* was laid.

VENUE OF LOCAL FACTS MUST BE TRULY LAID.

Whether the action be local or transitory, every *local fact* alleged in the *writ and declaration* must still be laid with its true *venue*, on peril of a variance, if the fact should be brought in issue ; but transitory facts may be laid with any *venue*, at the choice of the plaintiff ; though it is the usual and most proper course to lay all these with the *venue in the action*. As in the writ and declaration, so in the *plea* and *subsequent pleadings*, every *local* fact must be laid with its true *venue*, under peril of variance.

TRANSITORY FACTS MUST BE LAID WITH THE VENUE OF THE ACTION.

With respect to *transitory* facts, the rule is, that they must be laid with the *venue in the action;* [1] and even to lay the true place is, in this case, not allowable, if it differ from that *venue*.

Example : In the case of an action on a bond, where the action is laid in Middlesex, if the defendant should plead a release at Oxford, this departure from the *venue in the action*, would be bad,[2] though the release should really have been executed there. For as the plaintiff may, for a transitory matter, choose any *venue* that he likes, in his writ and declaration, so, upon the same principle, it would have followed, that the defendant might also, for a transitory matter, have chosen any *venue* in his plea ; and thus, who ever happened to make the last affirmative allegation, and, therefore, to lay the last *venue*, would have been able (prior to the alteration of practice introduced by the statute of Charles II.), to draw the *venire facias* and the trial to any place that he pleased. But it was thought more reasonable and convenient that this option should rest with the plaintiff, who, having in the first instance chosen a *venue*, ought not to be removed from it without cause.

The defendant, therefore, is obliged to follow the *venue* that the plaintiff has laid ; and, in consequence of the estab-

---

1 Wright *v.* Ramscot, 1 Saund. 85 ;   2 Co. Litt. 282 b.
2 Saund, 5, n. 3.

lishment of this rule, it seems now to be held that, to transitory
matters, *no venue* need now be laid in pleadings subsequent to
the declaration, because, with respect to every matter of this
description, the original *venue* will be taken to be *implied*.[1]
In practice, however, it is usual to lay a *venue* in these as well
as in the declaration ; and, perhaps, in point of strict form, it
is the better course.

ALLEGATIONS UNDER A VIDELICET.

Another point to be noticed on this subject of the true allegation of *venue*, is, that when transitory matters are alleged
out of their true place, it seems to be necessary that they
should be laid, as the phrase is, *under a videlicet, i. e.,* with
the prior intervention of the words " *to wit,*" or " *that is to
say.*" The effect and object of the *videlicet* are to mark that
the party does not undertake to prove the precise place. And,
accordingly, there is some doubt whether the omission of a
videlicet does not occasion a necessity, in the event of a traverse
even of a transitory matter, of proving the place alleged.[2] On
the other hand, however, it is clear, that where the place is
material, or, in other words, where the matter is local, the
use of a *videlicet* will not prevent the necessity of proving the
venue laid. This doctrine as to a *videlicet*, it will be observed,
is not peculiar to *venue*, but applies (as will afterward appear)
to many other of the points on which certainty is required in
pleading.

HOW TO ALLEGE LOCAL MATTER OCCURRING OUT OF THE REALM.

The last point of remark that occurs on this subject, relates
to the case where a *local* matter, occurring *out of the realm*, is
alleged in the course of the pleading. This was formerly
considered as a case of difficulty : for, on the one hand, all
local facts are to be alleged (as has been shown) in the true

---

[1] Chit. Pl. 248.

[2] Mr. Chitty inclines to consider the
omission as immaterial. (See Chit. Pl.
276, n. *q*) Opposed, however, to the
authorities on which the learned author
relies, are Symmons *v.* Knox, 3 T. R.
68 ; Arnfield *v.* Bate, 3 M. & S. 173 ;
2 Saund. 291 c, n. 1 ; Bray *v.* Freemen,
2 J. B. Moore, 114 ; Corporation of
Arundel *v.* Bowman, *ibid.* 93 ; Crispin
v. Williamson, 8 Taunt. 107 ; Draper *v.*
Garratt, 2 Barn. & Cress. 2.

place, and, on the other hand, if a place out of the realm be laid for *venue*, and issue be joined on the fact, it was, at one time, supposed that the issue could not be tried, because no jury could be summoned from the place; and prior to the statute of Charles, it was, by the general rule, essential (as already stated) that the jury should be summoned from the *venue* laid to the fact in issue.[1] It was, however, early decided, that notwithstanding that general rule, such matter might be tried by a jury from the *venue in the action*.[2] And, by way of more effectually preventing the objection, a form has long been in use, which satisfies the double object of conforming to the true place, and, at the same time, laying a *venue* within the realm; the *venue* of a fact arising abroad being often alleged with a *videlicet*, under the following form of expression: "*In parts beyond the seas, at Fort St. George, in the East Indies*" (the real place), "*to wit, at Westminster, in the County of Middlesex*" (the *venue in the action*).[3] With respect to this method, indeed, of laying the true place, with the addition of the *venue* in the action, under a *videlicet*, we may take occasion to observe, that it is usually applied, not only to local facts arising out of the realm, but to those arising *in England* also, if they happened at a different *venue* from that *in the action*.

DESCRIPTIVE ALLEGATIONS OF PLACE.

Where place is alleged as matter of *description*, and not as *venue*, it must, in all cases, be stated truly and according to the fact, under peril of variance, if the matter should be brought into issue.[4]

DEFECTS IN LAYING VENUE.

If no *venue* be laid in the declaration, the defendant may demur or plead the defect in abatement. Even in local and

---

[1] See a curious instance of the difficulty formerly found in such cases, cited per Abbott, C. J., The King *v.* Burdett, 4 Barn. & Ald. 172; and another instance, cited in Dowdale's Case, 6 Co. Rep. 47 b; and see Broddeck *v.* Briggs, Carth. 265; Nichols *v.* Pawlett, *ibid.* 302; Holding *v.* Haling, 3 Keb. 150.

[2] Dowdale's Case, *ubi supra;* Calvin's Case, 7 Co. Rep. 27 a.

[3] Com. Dig. Action, n. 7.

[4] Steph. Pl. (5th ed.) 292.

penal actions the only modes of objecting to the *venue* are by *demurrer*, or at the trial as a *ground of nonsuit*.[1]

Rule II. The Pleadings must have Certainty of Time.[2]

In personal actions, the pleadings must allege the *time ;* that is, *the day, month, and year* when each traversable fact occurred; and, when there is occasion to mention *a continuous act, the period of its duration* ought to be shown.[3]

The necessity of laying a time, like that of laying a *venue,* extends to *traversable* facts only, and therefore no time need be alleged *to matter of inducement or aggravation.* The courts, indeed, are in the habit of considering the allegations of place and time as connected together; and have laid down this general principle, that wherever it is necessary to lay a *venue,* it is also necessary to mention time.[4]

As the place, in transitory matters, is considered as forming no material part of the issue, so that one place may be alleged and another proved, the same law has obtained with respect to time, in all matters generally.[5] The pleader, therefore, as a rule, assigns any time that he pleases to a given fact. This option, however, is subject to certain restrictions :

(1) He should lay the time under a *videlicet,* if he does not wish to be held to prove it strictly.

(2) He should not lay a time that is *intrinsically impossible,* or *inconsistent with the fact to which it relates.*

A time so laid would, generally, be sufficient ground for demurrer. But, on the other hand, there is no ground for demurrer, where such time is laid to a fact not traversable, or where, for any other reason, the allegation of time was unnecessarily made; for an unnecessary statement of time, though impossible or inconsistent, will do no harm, upon the principle that *utile, per inutile, non vitiatur* (the useful is not hurt by the useless).[6]

---

[1] Chit. Pl. 253, 254.

[2] Com. Dig. Pleader, C. 19; Halsey v. Carpenter, Cro. Jac. 359; Denison v. Richardson, 14 East, 291.

[3] *Ibid.*

[4] Per Buller, J., The King v. Holland, 5 T. R. 620.

[5] Co. Litt. 283 a; The King v. Bishop of Chester, 2 Salk. 561; Cooke v. Birt, 5 Taunt. 765.

[6] This appears to be a correct general statement of the law with respect to demurrer for an impossible or inconsistent date; but the current of authorities is not quite clear and uniform on this subject. (See Com. Dig. Pleader, C.

When Averments of Time are Material.

Again, there are some instances in which time happens to form *a material point in the merits of the case;* and, in these instances, if a traverse be taken, the time laid is of the substance of the issue, and must be strictly proved; just as in local matters it is necessary to prove the alleged *venue.* The pleader, therefore, with respect to all facts of this description, must state the time truly, at the peril of failure, as for a variance. And here, as in the case of a local fact, the insertion of a *videlicet* will give no help.

Examples: (1) Where the declaration stated a usurious contract, made on the 21st day of December, 1774, for giving day of payment of a certain sum to the 23d day of December, 1776, and the proof was that the contract was on the 23d December, 1774, giving day of payment for two years, it was held that the verdict must be for the defendant; the principle of this decision being, that the time given for payment being of the substance of a usurious contract, such time must be proved as laid.[1]

(2) Where the declaration stated a usurious agreement on the 14th of the month, to forbear and give day of payment for a certain period, but it was proved that the money was not advanced till the 16th, the plaintiff was nonsuited;[2] it being held by Lord Mansfield at the trial, and afterwards by the court *in banc,* that the day from whence the forbearance took place was material, though laid under a *videlicet.*[3]

When not Material.

Where the time needs not to be truly stated (as is generally the case), it is subject to a rule of the same nature with one

---

19; 2 Saund. 291 c, n. 1; *ibid.* 171 a, n. 1.) N. B. The objection is often aided, after verdict, or cured by the statutes of jeofails.

[1] Carlisle *v.* Trears, Cowp. 671.

[2] The nature of judgment of *nonsuit* has been stated. It will be proper to explain here, however, that when, on account of a variance, or any other matter of form, the plaintiff understands that the judge is going to direct the jury to find a verdict against him, he usually takes the course of avoiding a verdict, by voluntarily submitting to judgment of nonsuit; and for that purpose he is supposed to absent himself from the court. The reason is, that such judgment does not prevent his bringing another action, but by a verdict he is barred forever. (See Bl. Com. III. 377 *.)

[3] Johnson *v.* Picket, cited Grimwood *v.* Barritt, 6 T. R. 483; see also Hardy *v.* Cathcart, 5 Taunt. 2.

that applies to *venue* in transitory matters, viz., that the plea
and subsequent pleadings should follow the day alleged in the
writ and declaration,[1] and if, in these cases, *no time at all* be
laid, the omission is aided, after verdict, or judgment by confession or default, by the operation of the statute of *jeofails*.[2]
But where, in the plea or subsequent pleadings, the time
happens to be material, it must be alleged; and there (as in
the case of a *venue* to a local fact) the pleader may be obliged
to depart from the day in the writ and declaration.

EXCEPTION TO RULE.

Certainty of time is said to be required in *personal* actions
only; it being held that in *real* and *mixed* actions it is generally not necessary to allege the day, month, and year, and
that it is sufficient to show in what king's reign the matter
arose.[3]

RULE III. THE PLEADINGS MUST SPECIFY QUALITY, QUANTITY, AND VALUE.[4]

AVERMENTS OF QUALITY, QUANTITY, AND VALUE.

It is, generally, necessary, where the declaration alleges
any injury to *goods and chattels*, or any contract relating to
them, that their *quality*, *quantity*, and *value* or *price*, should
be stated. In any action brought for the *recovery of real
property*, its *quality* should be shown, as, whether it consists
of houses, lands, or other hereditaments, and, as a rule, it
should be stated whether the lands are meadow, pasture, or
arable, etc. And the *quantity* of the lands or other real estate
must also be specified. So, in an action brought for *injuries*
to real property, the *quality* should be shown, as, whether it
consists of houses, lands, or other hereditaments.

---

[1] 2 Saund. 5, n. 3; Hawe *v.* Planner, 1 Saund. 14.

[2] Higgins *v.* Highfield, 13 East, 407.

[3] Com. Dig. Pleader, C. ;9; The King *v.* Bishop of Chester, 2 Salk. 561; Skin. 660; 9 Henry VI. 115, 116.

[4] *Oportet quod petens rem designet, quam petit, videlicet, qualitatem,* &c., *item quantitatem,* &c. (the plaintiff must designate the thing that he seeks, to wit: its quality, &c., and also the quantity, &c.). Bract. 431 a; Harpur's Case, 11 Co. Rep. 25 b; Doct. Pl. 85, 86; Knight *v.* Symms, Carth. 204; Doe *v.* Ploughman, 1 East, 441; Goodtitle *v.* Otway, 8 East, 357; Andrew *v.* Whitehead, 13 East, 102; 1 Saund. 333, n. 7; 2 Saund. 74, n. 1.

Examples: (1) In an action of trespass, for breaking the plaintiff's close and taking away his fish, without showing the number or nature of the fish, it was, after verdict, objected, in arrest of judgment, first, "that it did not appear by the declaration of what nature the fish were: pikes, tenches, breams, etc.; " and, secondly, that "the certain number of them did not appear." And the objection was allowed by the whole court.[1]

(2) Where, in an action of trespass, the declaration charged the taking of cattle, the declaration was held to be bad, because it did not show of what species the cattle were.[2]

(3) In an action of trespass, where the plaintiff declared for taking goods generally, without specifying the particulars, a verdict being found for the plaintiff, the court arrested the judgment for the uncertainty of the declaration.[3]

(4) In a modern case, where, in an action of replevin, the plaintiff declared that the defendant, "in a certain dwelling-house, took divers goods and chattels of the plaintiff," without stating what the goods were, the court arrested the judgment for the uncertainty of the declaration, after judgment by default and a writ of inquiry executed.[4]

(5) In an action of dower, where blanks were left in the count for the number of acres claimed, the judgment was reversed after verdict.[5]

(6) In ejectment, the plaintiff declared for five closes of land, arable and pasture, called Long Furlongs, containing ten acres; upon not guilty pleaded the plaintiff had a verdict, and it was moved in arrest of judgment, that the declaration was ill, because the quantity and quality of the lands were not distinguished and ascertained, so as to show how many acres of arable there were and how many of pasture. And for this reason the declaration was held ill, and the judgment arrested.[6]

With respect to *value*, it is to be observed, that it should be specified with reference to the *current coin of the realm*, thus : " divers, to wit, three tables of great value, to wit, the value

---

[1] Playter's Case, 5 Co. Rep. 34 b. N. B. — Sergeant Williams observes, that in this case the omission would, perhaps, *now* be held to be aided, after verdict. or cured, by the statutes of jeofails; and as the action was not merely for taking fish, but also for breaking the close, he doubts if the declaration would now be held bad, even on special demurrer. (2 Saund. 74, n. 1.)   And see Chamberlain *v.* Greenfield, 3 Wils. 292.

[2] Dale *v.* Phillipson, 2 Lutw. 1374.

[3] Bertie *v.* Pickering, 4 Burr. 2455; Wiat *v.* Essington, 2 Ld. Raym. 1410, S. P.

[4] Pope *v.* Tillman, 7 Taunt. 642.

[5] Lawley *v.* Gattacre, Cro. Jac. 498.

[6] Knight *v.* Symms, Carth. 204.

of twenty pounds, of lawful money of Great Britain." With
respect to *quantity*, it should be specified by the ordinary
measures of extent, weight, or capacity, thus : " divers, to
wit, fifty acres of arable land," " divers, to wit, three bushels
of wheat."

EXCEPTIONS TO RULE.

The rule in question, however, is not so strictly construed,
but that it sometimes admits the specification of *quality* and
quantity in a *loose and general way*.

Examples : (1) A declaration in trover, for two *packs* of flax and
two *packs* of hemp, without setting out the weight or quantity of
a pack, is good after verdict, and, as it seems, even upon special
demurrer.[1]

(2) A declaration in trover, for a *library* of books, has been
allowed, without expressing what they were.

(3) Where the plaintiff declared in trespass for entering his
house, and taking *several keys* for the opening of the doors of
his said house, it was objected, after verdict, that the kind and
number ought to be ascertained. But it was answered and resolved, that the keys are sufficiently ascertained by reference to
the house.[2]

(4) It was held, upon special demurrer, that it was sufficient to declare, in trespass for breaking and entering a house,
damaging the goods and chattels, and wrenching and forcing open
the doors, without specifying the goods and chattels, or the
number of doors forced open ; because the essential matter of the
action was the breaking and entering of the house, and the rest
merely aggravation.[3]

There are also some *kinds of actions*, to which the rule
requiring specification of quality, quantity, and value, does
not apply in modern practice. Thus, in actions of *debt* and
indebitatus assumpsit (where a more general form of declaration obtains than in most other actions), if the debt is claimed
in respect of goods sold, etc., the quality, quantity, or value of
the goods sold is never specified. The amount of the debt, or
sum of money due upon such sale, must, however, be shown.

[1] 2 Saund. 74 b, n. 1.

[2] Layton *v.* Grindall, 2 Salk. 643 ;
and see many other instances, 2 Saund.
74 b, n. 1.

[3] Chamberlain *v.* Greenfield, 3 Wils.
292.

AVERMENTS OF QUANTITY AND VALUE GENERALLY IMMATERIAL.

As with respect to *place* and *time,* so, with respect to *quantity* and *value,* it is not necessary, when these matters are brought into issue, that the proof should correspond with the averment. The pleader may, generally, allege any quantity and value that he pleases (at least if it be laid under a *videlicet*), without risk from the variance, in the event of a different amount being proved.[1] But it is to be observed, that *a verdict can not generally be obtained for a larger quantity or value than is alleged.* The pleader, therefore, takes care to lay them to an extent large enough to cover the utmost case that can be proved.

It is also to be observed, that, as with respect to place or time, so with respect to quantity or value, there may be instances in which they form part of the substance of the issue ; and there they must be strictly proved as laid.

Example : To a declaration in assumpsit for £10 4s., and other sums, the defendant pleaded, as to all but £4 7s. 6d., the general issue ; and, as to the £4 7s. 6d., a tender. The plaintiff replied that, after the cause of action accrued, and before the tender, the plaintiff demanded the said sum of £4 7s. 6d., which the defendant refused to pay ; and on issue joined, it was proved that the plaintiff had demanded not £4 7s. 6d., but the whole £10 4s. This proof was held not to support the issue.[2]

AVERMENTS OF QUALITY MATERIAL.

With respect to the allegation of *quality, this generally requires to be strictly proved as laid.*

RULE IV. THE PLEADINGS MUST SPECIFY THE NAMES OF PERSONS.[3]

(1) *This rule applies to the parties to the suit.*

The original writ and the declaration must both set forth accurately the names of both parties.[4] The plaintiff must be

---

[1] Crispin *v.* Williamson, 8 Taunt. 19, F. 17, F. 18 ; *Ibid,* Pleader, C. 18 ; 107.

[2] Rivers *v.* Griffith, 5 Barn. & Ald. 630.

[3] Com. Dig. Abatement, E. 18, E.

[4] Com. Dig. *ubi supra* ; Bract. *ubi supra.* But in Queen *v.* Dale, 17 Q. B. 64 (proceedings in *scire facias* on

described by his Christian name and surname ; and, if either be mistaken or omitted, it is ground for plea in abatement. The case is the same with respect to the defendant. If either party have a name of *dignity*, such as *earl*, etc., he must be described accordingly ; and an omission or mistake in such description has the same effect as in the Christian name and surname of an ordinary person.[1]

(2) *The rule also relates to persons not parties to the suit, of whom mention is made in the pleading.*

The names of such persons, viz., the Christian name and surname, or name of dignity, must generally be given ; but, if not within the knowledge of the party pleading, an allegation to that effect should be made, and such allegation will excuse the omission of name.[2]

CONSEQUENCES OF A MISTAKE.

A mistake in the name of a *party to the suit* is ground for plea in abatement only, and can not be objected as a variance at the trial ; but the name of a person not a party, is a point on which the proof must correspond with the averment, under peril of a fatal variance, for it is matter of description.

Examples: (1) Where a bill of exchange drawn by John *Couch* was declared upon as drawn by John *Crouch*, and the defendant pleaded the general issue, the plaintiff was nonsuited.[3]

(2) Where the declaration stated that the defendant went before Richard Cavendish, Baron Waterpark, of *Waterfork*, one of the justices, etc., for the County of Stafford, and falsely charged the plaintiff with felony, etc., and, upon the general issue, it appeared in evidence that the charge was made before Richard Cavendish, Baron Waterpark, of *Waterpark* — this was held a fatal variance in the name of dignity.[4]

---

a recognizance), the declaration stated that the recognizance had been acknowledged before " J. H. Harper." A demurrer was overruled, the court saying that " J " may have been the full Christian name of the person, and adding, " There is no doubt that a vowel may be a good Christian name, why not a consonant ? "

[1] Com Dig. Abatement, E. 20, F. 19.

[2] Buckley *v.* Rice Thomas, Plowd. 128 a ; Rowe *v.* Roach, 1 M. & S. 304.

[3] Whitwell *v.* Bennett, 3 Bos. & Pull. 559. See also Bowditch *v.* Mawley, 1 Camp. 195 ; Hutchinson *v.* Piper, 4 Taunt. 810

[4] Walters *v.* Mace, 2 Barn & Ald. 756.

RULE V. THE PLEADINGS MUST SHOW TITLE.[1]

When, in pleading, any right or authority is set up in respect of property, personal or real, some *title* to that property must of course be alleged in the party, or in some other person from whom he derives his authority.

So, if a party be charged with any *liability*, in respect of property, personal or real, his title to that property must be alleged.

It is proposed to consider : —

I. The case of a party's alleging title *in himself*, or *in another whose authority he pleads ;*

II. That of his alleging it *in his adversary.*

I. OF THE CASE WHERE A PARTY ALLEGES A TITLE IN HIMSELF, OR IN ANOTHER WHOSE AUTHORITY HE PLEADS.

(A) IT IS OFTEN SUFFICIENT TO ALLEGE A TITLE OF POSSESSION ONLY.

The form of laying a title of possession, in respect of *goods and chattels*, is either to allege that they were the "*goods and chattels of the plaintiff*," or that he was "*lawfully possessed of them as of his own property*."

With respect to *corporeal hereditaments*, the form is, either to allege that the close, etc., was the "*close of*" the plaintiff, or that he was "*lawfully possessed of a certain close*," etc.

With respect to *incorporeal hereditaments*, a title of possession is generally laid by alleging that the plaintiff was possessed of the corporeal thing, in respect of which the right is claimed, and by reason thereof was entitled to the right at the time in question; for example, that he "*was possessed of a certain messuage, etc., and by reason thereof, during all the time aforesaid, of right ought to have had common of pasture*," etc.

A title of possession is *applicable*, that is, will be sufficiently sustained by the proof, in all cases where the interest is of a present and immediate kind. Thus, when a title of possession is alleged with respect to *goods and chattels*, the statement will be supported by proof of any kind of *present interest* in

---

[1] Com. Dig. Pleader, 3 M. 9; Bract. 372 b, 373 b.

them, whether that interest be temporary and special, or absolute in its nature; as, for example, whether it be that of a
carrier or finder only, or that of an owner and proprietor.[1]
So, where a title in possession is alleged in respect of *corporeal*
or *incorporeal hereditaments*, it will be sufficiently maintained
by proving any kind of *estate in possession*, whether fee simple,
fee tail, for life, for term of years, or otherwise.   On the other
hand, with respect to any kind of property, a title of possession would not be sustained in evidence by proof of an interest
in *remainder* or *reversion* only; and, therefore, when the interest is of that description, the preceding forms are inapplicable,
and title must be laid in remainder or reversion, according to
the fact, and upon the principles that will be afterwards
stated on the subject of alleging title in its *full and precise
extent.*

Where a title of possession is *applicable*, the allegation of it
is, in many cases, *sufficient*, in pleading, without showing title
of a superior kind.   The rule on this subject is as follows:

It is sufficient to allege possession as against a wrong-doer.[2]

In other words, it is enough to lay a title of possession
against a person who is stated to have committed an injury
to such possession, having, as far as it appears, no title
himself.

Examples : (1) If the plaintiff declares in trespass, for breaking
and entering his close, or in trespass on the case, for obstructing
his right of way, it is enough to allege in the declaration, in the
first case, that it is the " *close of the plaintiff,*" in the second
case, that " *he was possessed of a certain messuage, etc., and, by
reason of such possession, of right ought to have had a certain way,*"
etc.   For, if the case was that the plaintiff being possessed of
the close, the defendant, having himself no title, broke and entered
it, or, that the plaintiff being possessed of a messuage and right
of way, the defendant, being without title, obstructed it, then,
whatever was the nature and extent of the plaintiff's title, in
either case, the law will give him damages for the injury to his

---

[1] 2 Saund. 47 a, n. 1.

[2] Com. Dig. Pleader, C. 39, C. 41;
Taylor *v.* Eastwood, 1 East, 212; Grim-
stead *v.* Marlowe, 4 T. R. 717; Green-

how *v.* Ilsley, Willes, 619; Waring *v.*
Griffiths, 1 Burr. 440; Langford *v.*
Webber, 3 Mod. 132.

possession; and it is the possession, therefore, only that needs to be stated.   It is true that it does not yet appear that the defendant had no title, and, by his plea, he may possibly set up one superior to that of the plaintiff; but as, on the other hand, it does not yet appear that he *had* title, the effect is the same, and till he pleads he must be considered as a mere *wrong-doer*, that is, he must be taken to have committed an injury to the plaintiff's possession, without having any right himself.

(2) In an action of trespass for assault and battery, if the defendant justifies, on the ground that the plaintiff wrongfully entered his house and was making a disturbance there, and that the defendant gently removed him, the form of the plea is, that *"the defendant was lawfully possessed of a certain dwelling-house, etc., and, being so possessed, the said plaintiff was unlawfully in the said dwelling-house,"* etc.; and it is not necessary for the defendant to show any title to the house beyond this of mere possession.[1]   For the *plaintiff* has, at present, set up no title at all to the house; and, on the face of the plea, he has committed an injury to the defendant's possession, without having any right himself.

(3) In an action of trespass for seizing cattle, if the defendant justifies, on the ground that the cattle were *damage-feasant* on his close, it is not necessary for him to show any title to his close, except that of mere possession.[2]

Exceptions: It is to be observed, however, with respect to this rule, as to alleging possession against a wrong-doer, that it seems not to hold in *replevin*.   For, in that action, it is held not to be sufficient to state a title of possession, even in a case where it would be allowable in trespass, by virtue of the rule above mentioned.

Example: In replevin, if the defendant, by way of avowry, pleads that he was possessed of a messuage, and entitled to common of pasture, as appurtenant thereto, and that he took the cattle *damage-feasant*, it seems that this pleading is bad, and that

[1] Skevill *v.* Avery, Cro. Car. 138.
[2] 1 Saund. 221, n. 1, 346 e, n. 2; 2 Saund. 285, n. 3; Anon. 2 Salk. 643; Searl *v.* Bunnion, 2 Mod. 70; Osway *v.* Bristow, 10 Mod. 37; 2 Bos. & Pull. 361, n. *a*; Langford *v.* Webber, 3 Mod. 132; but see s. c. Carth. 9; 3 Salk. 356.

N. B. — It is sometimes said, that the reason why it is sufficient to lay a possessory title in such cases is, that the title is matter of *inducement* only to the main subject of the plea.   But this doctrine, if well examined, resolves itself into the broader and more satisfactory rule given in the text.

it is not sufficient to lay such mere title of possession in this action.[1]

It is to be observed, too, that this rule has little or no application in *real* or *mixed* actions; for, in these, an injury to the possession is seldom alleged; the question in dispute being, for the most part, on the *right of possession,* or the *right of property.*

(B) Where Superior Title must be shown.

Where this rule as to alleging possession against a wrong-doer *does not apply,* there, though the interest be present or possessory, *it is,* generally, *not sufficient* to state a title of possession, but *some superior title must be shown.*

Examples : (1) In trespass for breaking the plaintiff's close, if the defendant's justification is that the close was his own copyhold estate of inheritance, his plea, as it does not make the plaintiff a wrong-doer, but, on the contrary, admits his possessory title in the close, and pleads in confession and avoidance of it, must allege not merely a possession, but a seisin in fee of the copyhold.

(2) In a similar action, if the defendant relies on a right of way over the plaintiff's close, it will not be sufficient to plead that he, the defendant, was lawfully *possessed* of another close, and, by reason of such possession, was entitled to a right of way over the plaintiff's, but he must set forth some superior title to his close and right of way; as, for example, that of seisin in fee of the close, and a prescription in a *que estate*[2] to the right of way.

The manner of stating a superior title to that of possession will be shown under the following head, relative to the allegation of title in its *full and precise extent.*

---

[1] Hawkins v. Eckles, 2 Bos. & Pull. 359, 361, n. a; per Buller, J. Dovaston v. Payne, 1 H. Bl. 530; 1 Saund. 346 e, n. 2; 2 Saund. 295, n. 3; Saunders v. Hussey, 2 Lutw. 1231; s. c. Carth. 9; 1 Ld. Raym. 333; but see Adams v. Cross, 1 Vent. 181.

[2] Where a prescriptive right is claimed to an easement, or to any profit or benefit taken or arising out of land, such as a prescriptive right of way or of common, it is required to allege a seisin in fee of the close or other corporeal hereditament *in respect of which the right is claimed,* and then *to prescribe for that right,* in a *que estate; i. e.,* to allege that the person so seised, and all those *whose estate* he has in the premises, have, from time immemorial, exercised the right in question. Min. Inst. IV. 968; Bl. Com. II. 264*; 1 Saund. 346, n. 3.

(C) WHERE A TITLE OF POSSESSION IS EITHER NOT APPLICABLE, OR NOT SUFFICIENT, THE TITLE SHOULD, GENFRALLY, BE STATED IN ITS FULL AND PRECISE EXTENT.[1]

Upon this head, two subjects of remark present themselves :

(a) THE ALLEGATION OF THE TITLE ITSELF,
(b) THE STATEMENT OF ITS DERIVATION.

(a) THE ALLEGATION OF THE TITLE ITSELF.

With respect to the *allegation of the title itself*, there are certain forms used in pleading, appropriate to each different kind of title, according to all the different distinctions as to *tenure, quantity of estate, time of enjoyment,* and *number of owners*. These forms are too various to be here stated, and it will be sufficient to refer the student to the copious stores in the printed precedents.[2]

(b) THE DERIVATION OF THE TITLE.

With respect to the *derivation of the title*, there are certain rules of which it will be necessary to give some account.

There is a leading distinction, on this subject, between *estates in fee simple* and *particular estates*.

(1) *Generally, it is sufficient to state a seisin in fee simple per se.*

In this case it is enough simply to state (according to the usual form of alleging that title), that the party was " *seised in his demesne as of fee of and in a certain messuage,*" etc., without showing the *derivation*, or (as it is expressed in pleading), the *commencement* of the estate.[3] For, if it were requisite to show from whom the present tenant derived his title, it might be required, on the same principle, to show from whom that person derived *his*, and so *ad infinitum*. Besides, as mere seisin will be sufficient to give an estate in fee simple, the estate may, for anything that appears, have had no other com-

---

[1] Therefore, to allege mere *seisin*, without showing whether in fee, in tail, or for life, is, generally, not sufficient. (Saunders *v* Hussey, Carth. 9; s. c. 2 Lutw. 1231 ; 1 Ld. Raym. 333.)

[2] The best books of precedents are Wentworth's Pleading, and the 2d and 3d volumes of any edition prior to 1834 of Chitty's Pleading.

[3] Co. Litt. 303 b; Scavage *v*. Hawkins, Cro. Car. 571.

mencement than the seisin itself which is alleged. So, though the fee be *conditional* or *determinable* on a certain event, yet a seisin in fee may be alleged, without showing the commencement of the estate.[1]

(2) *However, it is sometimes necessary to show the derivation of the fee; viz., where, in the pleading, the seisin has already been alleged in another person, from whom the present party claims.*

In such case it must, of course, be shown how it passed from one of these persons to the other.

Examples : (1) In debt or covenant brought on an indenture of lease by the heir of the lessor, the plaintiff, having alleged that his ancestor was seised in fee and made the lease, must proceed to show how the fee passed to himself, viz., by descent.

(2) If, in trespass, the defendant plead that E. F., being seised in fee, demised to G. H., under whose command the defendant justifies the trespass on the land (giving color), and the plaintiff, in his replication, admits E. F.'s seisin, but sets up a subsequent title in himself to the same land, in fee simple, prior to the alleged demise, he must show the derivation of the fee from E. F. to himself, by conveyance antecedent to the lease under which G. H. claims.[2]

(3) *With respect to particular estates, the general rule is, that the commencement of particular estates must be shown.*[3]

If, therefore, a party sets up in his own favor an estate tail, an estate for life, a term of years, or a tenancy at will, he must show the derivation of that title from its commencement, that is, from the last seisin in fee simple; and, if derived by alienation or conveyance, the substance and effect of such conveyances should be precisely set forth. For examples of the manner of thus showing the commencement of particular estates, under all the different kinds of conveyances, and other *media* of title, the student must again have recourse to the books of precedents.

---

[1] Doct. Pl. 287.

[2] See Upper Bench Precedents, 196, cited 9 Went., Index, xl, xli.

[3] Co. Litt. 303 b ; Scilly *v.* Dally, 2 Salk. 562 ; s. c. Carth. 444 ; Searl *v.* Bunnion, 2 Mod. 70 ; Johns *v.* Whitley, 3 Wils. 72 ; Hendy *v.* Stephenson, 10 East, 60 ; Rast. Ent. 656 ; and the case of title derived from the king is no exception. (1 Saund. 186 d, n. 1.)

Under this rule, *that the commencement of particular estates must be shown*, it is necessary to show the commencement of a *copyhold*, even though it be copyhold of *inheritance*.[1] This is on the ground that a copyhold, even in fee, is in the nature of a particular estate, in respect of the freehold inheritance in the lord. And the difficulty that would arise, if the title were to be deduced from the earliest or original grantee, is obviated by the practice of going back to the admittance of the last heir or surrenderee only; which admittance is considered as in the nature of a grant from the lord, and is so pleaded.[2] It is in this manner that the commencement of a copyhold estate is, generally, alleged, namely, by stating it as a grant from the lord.[3] But, where an estate has been already laid in another copyholder, from whom the present party claims, and it becomes necessary, therefore, to show how the estate passed from one to the other, the conveyances between the copyhold tenants, by surrender, and the admittance by the lord, etc., must then be set forth according to the fact.

Exception : To the rule *that the commencement of particular estates must be shown*, there is this exception, that it need not be shown where the title is alleged by way of *inducement* only.[4]

Example : If an action of debt or covenant be brought on an indenture of lease by the executor or assignee of a lessor, who had been entitled for a term of years, it is necessary, in the declaration, to state the title of the lessor, in order to show that the plaintiff is entitled to maintain the action, as his representative or assignee. But as the title is, in that case, alleged by way of inducement only (the action being mainly founded on the lease itself), and therefore it is probable that the title may not come

[1] Pyster *v.* Hemling, Cro. Jac. 103; Shepheard's Case, Cro. Car. 190; Robinson *v.* Smith, 4 Mod. 346.

[2] See same cases, and Brown's Case, 4 Co. Rep. 22 b; Bac. Ab. Pleas, &c. 422, 5th ed.

[3] As to *customary freeholds*, see Croucher *v.* Oldfield, Salk. 365; Roe *v.* Vernon, 5 East, 51 ; Burrell *v.* Dodd, 3 Bos. & Pull. 378.

[4] Com. Dig. Pleader, E. 19, C. 43; Blockley *v.* Slater, Lutw. 120; Searl *v.* Bunnion, 2 Mod. 70; Scilly *v.* Dally, Carth 444; Skevill *v.* Avery, Cro. Car. 138; Lodge *v.* Frye, Cro. Jac. 52; Adams *v.* Cross, 2 Vent. 181; Wade *v.* Baker, 1 Ld. Raym. 130.

into question, the particular estate for years may be alleged in the lessor, without showing its commencement.

(4) *Where a party claims by inheritance, he must, generally, show how he is heir,*[1] *and if he claims by mediate, not immediate, descent, he must show the pedigree.*

If he claims by inheritance, he must show how he is heir, whether as son or otherwise; if he claims as nephew, he must show how he is nephew.[2]

(5) *Where a party claims by conveyance or alienation, the nature of the conveyance or alienation must, generally, be stated.*

It must be shown whether it is by devise, feoffment, etc.[3]

(6) *The nature of the conveyance or alienation should be stated according to its legal effect, rather than its form of words.*

This depends on a more general rule, which we shall have occasion to consider in another place, viz., " that things are to be pleaded according to their legal effect or operation." For the present, the doctrine, as applicable to conveyances, may be thus illustrated. In pleading a conveyance for *life*, with livery of seisin, the proper form is to allege it as a " demise " for life,[4] for such is its effect in proper legal description. So, a conveyance in *tail*, with livery, is always pleaded, on the same principle, as a " gift " in tail,[5] and a conveyance of the fee, with livery, is described by the term " enfeoffed."[6] And such would be the form of pleading, whatever might be the *words* of donation used in the instrument itself; which, in all the three cases, are often the same,

---

[1] Denham *v.* Stephenson, 1 Salk. 355; The Duke of Newcastle *v.* Wright, 1 Lev. 190; 1 Ld. Raym. 202.

[2] Dumsday *v.* Hughes, 3 Bos. & Pull. 453; Blackborough *v.* Davis, 12 Mod. 619; and see Roe *v.* Lord, 2 Bl. Rep. 1099, and the cases there cited.

[3] See Com. Dig. Pleader, E. 23, E. 24.

[4] Rast. Ent. 647 a, 11 d.

[5] See Co. Ent. tit. Formedon, &c., &c.

[6] " Feoffment properly betokeneth a conveyance in fee; and yet, sometimes improperly, it is called a feoffment, when an estate of freehold only doth passe." (Co. Litt. 9 a.) *Feoffare dicitur, qui feodum simplex feoffatorio confert; donare, qui feodum talliatum. (He is said to enfeoff, who confers a fee simple on a feoffee; to donate, who confers a fee tail.)* (Spelm. Gloss. verbo *feoffare.*) And Lord Coke, in another place, makes the distinction laid down in the text between *feoffment, gift,* and *demise.* (Vynior's Case, 8 Co. Rep. 82 b.)

viz., those of "give" and "grant."[1] So, in a conveyance by lease and release, though the words of the deed of release be "grant, bargain, sell, alien, release, and confirm," yet it should be pleaded as a *release* only, for that is the legal effect.[2] So, a *surrender* (whatever words are used in the instrument) should be pleaded with *sursum reddidit* (again he rendered), which alone, in pleading, describe the operation of a conveyance as a surrender.[3]

(7) *Where the nature of the conveyance is such that it would, at common law, be valid without deed or writing, there no deed or writing need be alleged in the pleading, though such document may in fact exist; but where the nature of the conveyance requires, at common law, a deed, or other written instrument, such instrument must be alleged.*[4]

Therefore, a conveyance, with livery of seisin, either in fee, tail, or for life, is pleaded without alleging any charter, or other writing of feoffment, gift, or demise, whether such instrument, in fact, accompanied the conveyance or not. For such conveyance might, at common law, be made by parol only,[5] and though, by the statute of frauds, 29 Car. II. c. 3, s. 1, it will not now be valid unless made in writing, yet the form of *pleading* remains the same as before the act of Parliament.[6] On the other hand, a *devise* of lands (which, at common law, was not valid, and authorized only by the statutes 32 Hen. VIII. c. 1, and 34 Hen. VIII. c. 5), must be alleged to have been made in writing,[7] which is the only form in which the statutes authorize it to be made. So, if a conveyance by way of *grant* be pleaded, a deed must be alleged,[8] for matters that "lie in grant" (according to the legal phrase) can pass by deed only.[9]

---

[1] "*Do* (I give) or *dedi* (I have given) is the aptest word of feoffment." (Co. Litt. 9 a.)

[2] 1 Arch. 127 ; 3 Went. 483, 515.

[3] 1 Saund. 235 b, n. 9.

[4] Vin. Ab. *Faits* or Deeds, M. a, 11.

[5] Vin. Ab. Feoffment, Y.; Co. Litt. 121 b.

[6] This depends upon a more general rule, viz., that regulations introduced by statute do not alter the form of pleading at common law. This rule will be noticed hereafter, in its proper place.

[7] 1 Saund. 276 a, n. 2.

[8] Porter *v.* Gray, Cro. Eliz. 245 ; 1 Saund. 234, n. 3 ; Lathbury *v.* Arnold, 1 Bing. 217.

[9] Vin. Ab. tit. Grants, G a.

Exception: There is one case, however, in which a deed is usually alleged in pleading, though not necessary, at common law, to the conveyance, and which, therefore, in practice at least, forms an exception to the above rule. For, in making title under a lease for years, by indenture, it is usual to plead the indenture, though the lease was good at common law by parol, and needs to be in writing only where the term is of more than three years' duration, and then only by the statute of frauds.

On the other hand, in the case where a demise by husband and wife is pleaded, it seems that it is not necessary to show that it was by deed; and yet the lease, if without deed, is at common law void as to the wife, after the death of the husband, and is not within the statute 32 Hen. VIII. c. 28, s. 1, which gives efficacy to leases by persons having an estate in right of their wives, etc., only where such leases are " by writing indented, under seal." The reason seems to be that a lease by husband and wife, though without deed, is good during the life of the husband.[1]

Thus far with respect to the allegation of title, in its *full and precise extent*. Another mode, however, of laying title, still remains to be considered.

ALLEGATION OF GENERAL FREEHOLD TITLE.

Where a *title of possession* is inapplicable or insufficient, it is not always necessary to allege the title in its *full and precise extent;* for in lieu of this, it is occasionally sufficient to allege what may be called a *general freehold title.* In a plea in trespass *quare clausum fregit*, or an avowry in replevin,[2] if the defendant claim an estate of freehold in the *locus in quo*, he is allowed to plead generally that the place is his " *close, soil, and freehold.*" This is called the plea or avowry of *liberum tenementum* (free-holding).

This allegation of a *general freehold title* will be sustained by proof of *any* estate of *freehold*, whether in fee, in tail, or

[1] 2 Saund. 180 a, n. 9; Wiscot's Case, 2 Co. Rep. 61 b; Bateman *v.* cot, *ibid.* 482; Dy. 91 b.   Allen, Cro. Eliz. 438; Childes *v.* West-

[2] 1 Saund. 347 d, n. 6.

for life only, and whether in possession or expectant on the determination of a term of years.[1]   But it does not apply to the case of a freehold estate in remainder or reversion, expectant on a particular estate of freehold, nor to copyhold tenure.

The plea or avowry of *liberum tenementum* is the only case of usual occurrence in modern practice in which the allegation of a *general freehold title*, in lieu of a *precise* allegation of title, is sufficient.[2]

In alleging a general freehold title, it is not necessary (as appears by the above example) to *show its commencement*.

II. WHERE A PARTY ALLEGES TITLE IN HIS ADVERSARY.

The rule generally applicable upon this subject is the following : —

IT IS NOT NECESSARY TO ALLEGE TITLE MORE PRECISELY THAN IS SUFFICIENT TO SHOW A LIABILITY IN THE PARTY CHARGED OR TO DEFEAT HIS PRESENT CLAIM.

Except as far as these objects may require, a party is not compellable to show the precise estate which his adversary holds, even in a case where, if the same person were pleading his own title, such precise allegation would be necessary. The reason of this difference is, that a party must be presumed to be ignorant of the particulars of his adversary's title, though he is bound to know his own.[3]

WHEN SUFFICIENT TO ALLEGE A TITLE OF POSSESSION.

To answer the purpose of showing a liability in the party charged, according to the rule here given, it is, in most cases, sufficient to allege a *title of possession*, the forms of which are

---

[1] See 5 Henry VII. 10 a, pl. 2, which shows, that where there is a lease for years it must be replied in confession and avoidance, and is no ground for traversing the plea of *liberum tenementum*.

[2] See 1 Saund. 347 d, n. 6. This form of allegation occurred, however, in the now disused actions of assize, the count or plaint in which lays only a general freehold title. (Doct. Pl. 289.) It occurs also in the count on a writ of entry *sur disseizin* (on a disseisin) brought by tenant for life or in tail. (Booth, 177 ; 33 Hen. VI. 14 b ; Careswell v. Vaughan, 2 Saund. 30.)

[3] Rider v. Smith, 3 T. R. 766 ; Derisley v. Custance, 4 T. R. 77 ; The Attorney-General v. Meller, Hardr. 459.

similar to those in which the same kind of title is alleged in favor of the party pleading.

A title of possession, however, can not be sustained in evidence, except by proving some *present interest* in chattels, or *actual possession* of land. If, therefore, the interest be by way of reversion or remainder, it must be laid accordingly, and the title of possession is *inapplicable*. So, there are cases in which to charge a party with mere possession would not be *sufficient* to show his liability.

Example: In declaring against a party in debt for rent, as assignee of a term of years, it would not be sufficient to show that he was possessed, but it must be shown that he was possessed as assignee of the term.

Where Superior Title must be shown.

Where a title of possession is thus inapplicable or insufficient, and some other or superior title must be shown, it is yet not necessary to allege the title of an adversary with as much precision as in the case where a party is stating his own;[1] and it seems sufficient that it be laid fully enough to show the liability charged. Therefore, though it is the rule, with respect to a man's own title, *that the commencement of particular estates should be shown*, unless alleged by way of *inducement*, yet, in pleading the title of an adversary, it seems that this is, generally, not necessary.[2] So, in cases where it happens to be requisite to show whence the adversary derived his title, this may be done with less precision than where a man alleges his own. And, generally, it is sufficient to plead such title by a *que estate;* that is, to allege that the opposite party has the same estate, or that the same estate is vested in him, as has been precedently laid in some other person, without showing in what manner the estate passed from the one to the other.[3]

Example: In debt, where the defendant is charged for rent, as assignee of the term, after several *mesne* assignments, it is

[1] Com. Dig. Pleader, C. 42; Hill *v.* Saunders, 4 Barn. & Cress. 536.

[2] Blake *v.* Foster, 8 T. R. 487.

[3] As to making title by a *que estate,* see the Attorney-General *v.* Meller, Hardr. 459; Doct. Pl. 302; Com. Dig. Pleader, E. 23, E. 24; Co. Litt. 121 a.

sufficient, after stating the original demise, to allege that, "*after making the said indenture, and during the term thereby granted, to wit, on the —— day of ——, in the year ——, at ——, all the estate and interest of the said E. F.*" (the original lessee) "*of and in the said demised premises, by assignment, came to and vested in the said C. D. ;*" without further showing the nature of the *mesne* assignments.[1]

But, if the case be reversed, that is, if the plaintiff, claiming as assignee of the reversion, sue the lessee for rent, he must precisely show the conveyances, or other *media* of title, by which he became entitled to the reversion; and to say, generally, that it came by assignment, will not, in this case, be sufficient, without circumstantially alleging all the *mesne* assignments.[2] Upon the same principle, if title be laid in an adversary by descent, as, for example, where an action of debt is brought against an heir on the bond of his ancestor, it is sufficient to charge him as *heir*, without showing *how* he is heir, viz., as son, or otherwise ;[3] but if a party entitle himself by inheritance, we have seen that the mode of descent must be alleged.

AVERMENTS OF TITLE MUST BE STRICTLY PROVED.

The manner of showing title, both where it is laid in the party himself, or the person whose authority he pleads, and where it is laid in his adversary, having been now considered, it may next be observed, that the title so shown must generally, when issue is taken upon it, be strictly *proved*. With respect to the allegations of *place, time, quantity*, and *value*, it has been seen, that when issue is taken upon them, they, in most cases, do not require to be proved as laid — at least, if laid under a *videlicet*. But with respect to *title*, it is, ordinarily, of the substance of the issue; and, therefore, under the doctrine of *variance* requires to be maintained accurately by the proof.

---

[1] 1 Saund. 112, n. 1 ; The Attorney-General *v.* Meller, Hardr. 459 ; The Duke of Newcastle *v.* Wright, 1 Lev. 190 ; Derisley *v.* Custance, 4 T. R. 77.

[2] 1 Saund. *ubi supra ;* Pitt *v.* Russell, 3 Lev. 19.

[3] Denham *v.* Stephenson, 1 Salk. 355.

23

Example : In an action on the case, the plaintiff alleged, in his declaration, that he demised a house to the defendant for seven years, and that, during the term, the defendant so negligently kept his fire, that the house was burned down ; and the defendant having pleaded *non demisit modo et forma* (he did not demise in manner and form), it appeared in evidence, that the plaintiff had demised to the defendant several tenements, of which the house in question was one ; but that, with respect to this house, it was, by an exception in the lease, demised at will only. The court held, that, though the plaintiff might have declared against the defendant as tenant at will only, and the action would have lain, yet, having stated a demise for seven years, the proof of a lease at will was a variance, and *that* in substance, not in form only ; and, on the ground of such variance, judgment was given for the defendant.[1]

Exceptions to Rule V.

The rule which requires that title should be shown having been now explained, it will be proper to notice certain exceptions to which it is subject.

(1) Estoppel.

No title need be shown where the opposite party is *estopped* from denying the title.

Examples : (1) In an action for goods sold and delivered, it is unnecessary, in addition to the allegation that the plaintiff sold and delivered them to the defendant, to state that they were the goods *of the plaintiff ;*[2] for a buyer who has accepted and enjoyed the goods cannot dispute the title of the seller.

(2) In debt or covenant, brought by the lessor against the lessee, on the covenants of the lease, the plaintiff need allege no title to the premises demised; because a tenant is estopped from denying his landlord's title.

On the other hand, however, a tenant is not bound to admit title to any extent greater than might authorize the lease ; and, therefore, if the action be brought not by the lessor himself, but by his heir, executor, or other representative or assignee, the title of the former must be alleged, in order to show that the reversion is now legally vested in the plaintiff, in the character in which he sues. Thus, if he sue as heir,

---

[1] Cudlip *v.* Rundle, Carth. 202. [2] Bull. N. P. 139.

he must allege that the lessor was seised in fee; for the tenant is not bound to admit that he was seised in fee; and, unless he was so, the plaintiff can not claim as heir.

(2) Avowries and Cognizances.

Another exception to the general rule, requiring title to be shown, has been introduced by statute, and is as follows :

In making avowry or cognizance in replevin. upon distresses for rent, quit-rents, reliefs, heriots, or other services, the defendant is enabled, by the provision of the act 11 Geo. II. c. 19, s. 22,

"to avow or make cognizance generally that the plaintiff in replevin, or other tenant of the lands and tenements whereon such distress was made, enjoyed the same, under a grant or demise, at such a certain rent, during the time wherein the rent distrained for accrued, which rent was then and still remains due, or that the place where the distress was taken was parcel of such certain tenements held of such honor, lordship, or manor, for which tenements the rent, relief, heriot, or other service distrained for, was, at the time of such distress, and still remains, due, without further setting forth the grant, tenure, demise, or title of such landlord or landlords, lessor or lessors, owner or owners of such manor, any law or usage to the contrary notwithstanding." [1]

RULE VI. THE PLEADINGS MUST SHOW AUTHORITY.[2]

When a party has occasion to justify under a writ, warrant, precept, or any other authority whatever, he must, as a rule, *set it forth particularly* in his pleading. And he ought also to show *that he has substantially pursued* such authority.

Example : In trespass for taking a mare, the defendant pleaded that Sir J. S. was seised in fee of the manor of B., *and that he, and all those whose estate he had in the said manor,*[3] had always held a lawful court twice a year, to which the tenants of the manor used to resort; that such as had right of common were appointed by the steward to be of the jury; that by-laws were

---

[1] See remarks on this enactment and on the previous state of the law, 2 Saund. 284 c, n. 3.

[2] "Regularly, whensoever a man doth anything by force of a warrant or authority, he must plead it." (Co. Litt.

283 a; *ibid.* 303 b; Com. Dig. Pleader, E. 17; 1 Saund. 298, n. 1; Lamb *v.* Mills, 4 Mod. 377; Matthews *v.* Cary, 3 Mod. 137; s. c. Carth. 73; Collet *v.* Lord Keith, 2 East, 260; Selw. N. P. 826.)

[3] Instance of pleading a *que estate.*

accustomed to be made there, and that such as had right of common obeyed those laws or paid a forfeiture of a reasonable sum to be imposed on them ; that at one of these courts a jury was sworn and a law made, that every person who had common should pay forty shillings for depasturing his cattle on any place where corn was standing; that the plaintiff had right of common, and permitted his sheep to depasture on certain ground on which corn was standing ; that such offence was presented at the next court ; and that the defendant, *being bailiff of the lord of the said manor*, did take the mare for the forfeiture, etc. Upon demurrer, the court held the plea bad ; "for the bailiff can not take a forfeiture *ex officio*. There must be a precept directed to him for that purpose, which he must show in pleading," etc. And judgment was given for the plaintiff.[1]

So, in all cases where the defendant justifies under judicial process, he must *set it forth particularly* in his plea, and *it is not sufficient to allege generally* that he committed the act in question by virtue of a certain writ or warrant directed to him.[2] But on this subject there are some important distinctions as to the degree of particularity which the rules of pleading in different cases require : —

(1) It is not necessary that any person, justifying under judicial process, should set forth *the cause of action* in the original suit in which that process issued.[3]

(2) If the justification be by the officer executing the writ, he is required to plead such *writ* only, and not the *judgment* on which it was founded, for his duty obliged him to execute the former, without inquiring about the validity or existence of the latter. But, if the justification be by a party to the suit, or by any stranger, except an officer, the judgment, as well as the writ, must be set forth.[4]

(3) Where it is an officer who justifies, he must show that the writ was *returned*, if it was such as it was his duty to

---

[1] Lamb v. Mills, 4 Mod. 377.

[2] 1 Saund. 298, n. 1 ; Co. Litt. 303 b.

[3] Rowland v. Veale, Cowp. 18; Belk v. Broadbent, 3 T. R. 183 ; 1 Saund. 92, n. 2.

[4] Per Holt, C. J., Britton v. Cole, Carth. 443 ; s. c. 1 Salk. 408 ; Turner v. Felgate, 1 Lev. 95 ; Cotes v Michill,

3 Lev. 20 ; per De Grey, C. J., Barker v. Braham, 3 Wils. 368. But in Britton v. Cole, 1 Salk. 408, it is said that the court "seemed to hold that, if one comes in aid of the officer at his request, he may justify as the officer may do." (See Morse v. James, Willes, 122)

return, and all *mesne* process is of that description. But, as
a rule, a writ of execution need not be returned, and therefore no return of it need generally be alleged.[1] However, it
is said that, "if any ulterior process in execution is to be
resorted to to complete the justification, there it may be necessary to show to the court the return of the prior writ, in order
to warrant the issuing of the other."[2] Again, there is a distinction as to this point between a principal and a subordinate
officer : "The former shall not justify under the process,
unless he has obeyed the order of the court in returning it ;
otherwise it is of one who has not the power to procure a
return to be made."[3]

(4) Where it is necessary to plead the judgment, that may
be done (if it was a judgment of a superior court) without
setting forth any of the previous proceedings in the suit.[4]

(5) Where the justification is founded on process issuing
out of an inferior English court, or (as it seems) a court of
foreign jurisdiction, the nature and extent of the jurisdiction
of such court ought to be set forth, and it ought to be shown
that the cause of action arose within that jurisdiction, though
a justification founded on process of any of the superior courts
need not contain such allegations.[5] And, in pleading a
judgment of inferior courts, the previous proceedings are, in
some measure, stated. But it is allowable to set them forth
with a *taliter processum est* (such proceedings were had) ;
thus, that A. B., at a certain court, etc., held at, etc., levied
his plaint against C. D., in a certain plea of trespass on the
case, or debt, etc. (as the case may be), for a cause of action
arising within the jurisdiction, and *thereupon such proceedings were had*, that afterwards, etc., it was considered by the
said court that the said A. B. should recover against the said
C. D., etc.[6]

---

[1] Middleton *v.* Price, Str. 1184 ; s. c. 1 Ld. Raym. 633 ; s. c. 1 Salk. 409 ; 1 Wils. 17 ; Cheasley *v.* Barnes, 10 East, 73 ; Rowland *v.* Veale, Cowp. 18 ; Hoe's Case, 5 Co. Rep. 90 ; 1 Saund. 92, n. 2.

[2] Cheasley *v.* Barnes, *ubi supra.*

[3] Per Holt, C. J., Freemen *v.* Blewett, Moore *v.* Taylor, 5 Taunt. 69.

[4] See the precedents, 9 Went. 22, 53, 120, 351.

[5] Collet *v.* Lord Keith, 2 East, 274 ; Moravia *v.* Sloper, Willes, 30.

[6] 1 Saund. 92, n. 2 ; Rowland *u*

EXCEPTION TO RULE.

Notwithstanding the general rule under consideration, *it is allowable, where an authority may be constituted verbally and generally, to plead it in general terms.*

Example : In replevin, where the defendant makes cognizance, confessing the taking of the goods or cattle, as bailiff of another person, for rent in arrear, or as *damage-feasant*, it is sufficient to say that, " *as bailiff of the said E. T., he well acknowledges the taking, etc., as for and in the name of a distress*," etc., without showing any warrant for that purpose.[1]

AVERMENTS OF AUTHORITY MUST BE STRICTLY PROVED.

The allegation of *authority*, like that of *title*, must, generally, be strictly proved as laid.

The above-mentioned particulars of *place, time, quality, quantity*, and *value, names of persons, title*, and *authority*, though, in this work, made the subject of distinct rules, with a view to convenient classification and arrangement, are to be considered but as examples of that infinite variety of circumstances, which it may become necessary, in different cases and forms of action, to particularize, for the sake of producing a certain issue; for it may be laid down as a comprehensive rule, that —

RULE VII. In GENERAL, WHATEVER IS ALLEGED IN PLEADING, MUST BE ALLEGED WITH CERTAINTY.[2]

This rule, being very wide in its terms, it will be proper to illustrate it by a variety of examples.

In pleading *the performance of a condition or covenant*, it is a rule, though open to exceptions that will be presently noticed, that the party must not plead generally that he performed the covenant or condition, but must show specially the time, place, and manner of performance; and even though the subject to

---

Veale, Cowp. 18; Morse *v.* James, Willes, 122; Johnson *v.* Warner, *ibid.* 528; Titley *v.* Foxall, *ibid.* 688.

[1] Matthews *v.* Cary, 3 Mod. 138.
[2] Com. Dig. Pleader, C. 17, C. 22, E. 5, F. 17.

be performed should consist of several different acts, yet he must show in this special way the performance of each.[1]

Examples : (1) In debt on bond, conditioned for the payment of £30 to H. S., I. S., and A. S., *tam cito* (so soon) as they should come to the age of twenty-one years, the defendant pleaded that he paid those sums *tam cito* as they came of age, and the plaintiff demurred, because it was not shown when they came of age, and the certain times of the payment. "And for this cause all the court held the plea to be ill; for although it be a good plea, regularly, to the condition of a bond, to pursue the words of the condition, and to show the performance, yet Coke said there was another rule, that he ought to plead in certainty the time and place and manner of the performance of the condition, so as a certain issue may be taken; otherwise it is not good. Wherefore, because he did not plead here in certainty, it was adjudged for the plaintiff.

(2) "And between the same parties, in another action of debt upon an obligation, the condition being for performance of legacies in such a will, he pleaded performance generally, and, not showing the will, nor what the legacies were, it was adjudged for the plaintiff." [2]

(3) In debt on a bond, conditioned for the performance of several specific things, "the defendant pleaded *performavit omnia* (he performed all), etc. Upon demurrer it was adjudged an ill plea; for, the particulars being expressed in the condition, he ought to plead to each particularly, by itself." [3]

EXCEPTIONS TO RULE.

This rule, requiring performance to be specially shown, *admits of relaxation where the subject comprehends such multiplicity of matter as would lead to great prolixity;* and a more general mode of allegation is in such cases allowable. It is open also to the following exceptions: Where the condition is for the performance of matters set forth in another instru-

---

[1] Com. Dig. Pleader, E. 25, E. 26, 2 W. 33; Halsey *v.* Carpenter, Cro. Jac. 359; Wimbleton *v.* Holdrip, 1 Lev. 303; Woodcock *v.* Cole, 1 Sid. 215; Stone *v.* Bliss, 1 Bulst. 43; Fitzpatrick *v.* Robinson, 1 Show. 1; Austin *v.* Jervoise, Hob. 69, 77; Brown *v.* Rands, 2 Vent. 156; Lord Evers *v.* Buckton, Benl. 65; Braban *v.* Bacon, Cro. Eliz. 916; Codner *v.* Dalby, Cro. Jac. 363; Leneret *v.* Rivet, *ibid.* 503; 1 Saund. 116, n. 1.

[2] Halsey *v.* Carpenter, *ubi supra.*

[3] Wimbleton *v.* Holdrip, *ubi supra*

ment, and these matters are in an affirmative and absolute form, and neither in the negative nor the disjunctive, a general plea of performance is sufficient. And where a bond is conditioned for indemnifying the plaintiff from the consequences of a certain act, a general plea of *non damnificatus*, viz., that *he has not been damnified*, is proper, without showing how the defendant has indemnified him. These variations from the ordinary rule, and the principles on which they are founded, will be explained hereafter.

When, in any of these excepted cases, however, *a general plea of performance* is pleaded, the rule under discussion still requires the *plaintiff to show particularly* in his replication *in what way the covenant or condition has been broken;* for, otherwise, no sufficiently certain issue would be attained.

Example: In an action of debt on a bond, conditioned for performance of affirmative and absolute covenants contained in a certain indenture, if the defendant pleads generally (as in that case he may) that he performed the covenants according to the condition, the plaintiff can not in his replication tender issue with a mere traverse of the words of the plea, viz., that the defendant did not perform any of the covenants, etc. ; for this issue would be too wide and uncertain; but he must assign a breach, showing specifically in what particular, and in what manner, the covenants have been broken.[1]

Not only on the subject of *performance*, but in a variety of other cases, the books afford illustration of this general rule.

Examples: (1) In debt on bond, the defendant pleaded that the instrument was executed in pursuance of a certain corrupt contract, made at a time and place specified, between the plaintiff and defendant, whereupon there was reserved above the rate of £5 for the forbearing of £100 for a year, contrary to the statute in such case made and provided. To this plea there was a demurrer, assigning for cause, that the particulars of the contract were not specified, nor the time of forbearance, nor the sum to be forborne, nor the sum to be paid for such forbearance. And the court held that the plea was bad, for not setting forth particularly the corrupt contract and the usurious interest; and Bayley, J.,

---

[1] Plomer *v.* Ross, 5 Taunt. 386; per Lord Mansfield, Sayre *v.* Minns, Cowp 578; Com. Dig. Pleader, F. 14.

observed, that he "had always understood that the party who pleads a contract must set it out, if he be a party to the contract."[1]

(2) To an action on the case for a libel, imputing that the plaintiff was connected with swindlers and common informers, and had also been guilty of deceiving and defrauding divers persons, the defendant pleaded that the plaintiff had been illegally, fraudulently, and dishonestly concerned with, and was one of, a gang of swindlers and common informers, and had also been guilty of deceiving and defrauding divers persons with whom he had had dealings and transactions. To this plea there was a special demurrer, assigning for cause, *inter alia* (among other things), that the plea did not state the *particular instances of fraud ;* and though the Court of Common Pleas gave judgment for the defendant, this judgment was afterwards reversed upon writ of error, and the plea adjudged to be insufficient, on the ground above mentioned.[2]

(3) In an action of trespass for false imprisonment, the defendants pleaded, that before the said time, when, etc., certain persons unknown had forged receipts on certain forged dividend warrants, and received the money purporting to be due thereon, in Bank of England notes, amongst which was a note for £100, which was afterwards exchanged at the bank for other notes, amongst which was one for £10, the date and number of which were afterwards altered; that afterwards, and a little before the said time, when, etc., the plaintiff was *suspiciously* possessed of the altered note, and did in a *suspicious* manner dispose of the same to one A. B., and afterwards, in a *suspicious* manner, left England and went to Scotland; whereupon the defendants had *reasonable cause to suspect,* and did suspect, that the plaintiff had forged the said receipts, and so proceeded to justify the taking and detaining his person, to be dealt with according to law. Upon general demurrer, this plea was considered as clearly bad, because it did not show the *grounds* of suspicion with sufficient certainty to enable the court to judge of their sufficiency; and it was held that the use of the word *suspiciously* would not compensate that omission.[3]

(4) In an action of trover, for taking a ship, the defendant pleaded that he was captain of a certain man-of-war, and that he seized the ship mentioned in the declaration as prize; that he carried her to a certain port in the East Indies; and that the

---

[1] Hill *v.* Montagu, 2 M. & S. 377; Hinton *v.* Roffey, 3 Mod. 35, S. P.

[2] J'Anson *v.* Stuart, 1 T. R. 748.

[3] Mure *v.* Kaye, 4 Taunt. 34.

admiralty court there gave sentence against the said ship as prize. Upon demurrer, it was resolved that it was necessary for the plea to show some special cause for which the ship became a prize, and that the defendant ought to show who was the judge that gave sentence and to whom that court of admiralty did belong. And for the omission of these matters the plea was adjudged insufficient.[1]

(5) In an action of debt on bond, conditioned to pay so much money yearly, while certain letters patent were in force, the defendant pleaded, that from such a time to such a time he did pay, and that then the letters patent became void and of no force. The plaintiff having replied, it was adjudged, on demurrer to the replication, that the plea was bad, because it did not show *how* the letters patent became void.[2]

(6) Where the defendant justified an imprisonment of the plaintiff, on the ground of a contempt committed *tam factis quam verbis* (as well by acts as by words), the plea was held bad upon demurrer, because it set forth the contempt in this general way, without showing its nature more particularly.[3]

With respect to all points on which certainty of allegation is required, it may be remarked that the allegation, when brought into issue, must commonly be proved, in substance, as laid; and that the relaxation from the ordinary rule on this subject, which is allowed with respect to *place, time, quantity, and value*, does not, generally speaking, extend to other particulars.

SUBORDINATE RULES.

Such are the principal rules which tend to certainty; but it is to be observed, that these receive considerable *limitation* and *restriction* from some other rules of a subordinate kind, to the examination of which it will now be proper to proceed.

(1) *It is not necessary in pleading to state that which is merely matter of evidence.*[4]

[1] Beak *v.* Tyrrell, Carth. 31.

[2] Lewis *v.* Preston, 1 Show. 290; s. c. Skin. 303.

[3] Collet *v.* The Bailiffs of Shrewsbury, 2 Leo. 34.

[4] "Evidence shall never be pleaded, because it tends to prove matter in fact; and therefore the matter in fact shall be pleaded." (Dowman's Case, 9 Co. Rep. 9 b; and see 9 Ed. III. 5 b, 6 a, there cited; Eaton *v.* Southby, Willes, 131; Jermy *v.* Jenny, 1 Ld. Raym. 8; Groenvelt *v.* Burnell, Carth. 491.)

In other words, it is not necessary, in alleging a fact, to state such circumstances as merely tend to prove the truth of the fact.

Example: In an action of replevin, for seventy cocks of wheat, the defendant avowed under a distress for rent arrear. The plaintiff pleaded in bar, that before the said time, when, etc., one H. L. had recovered judgment against G. S., and sued out execution; that G. S. was tenant at will to the defendant, and had sown seven acres of the premises with wheat, and died possessed thereof as tenant at will; that, after his death, the sheriff took the said wheat in execution, and sold it to the plaintiff; that the plaintiff suffered the wheat to grow on the *locus in quo* till it was ripe and fit to be cut; that he afterwards cut it, and made it into cocks, whereof the said seventy cocks were parcel; that, the said cocks being so cut, the plaintiff suffered the same to lie on the said seven acres until the same, in the course of husbandry, were fit to be carried away; and that, while they were so lying, the defendant, of his own wrong, took and distrained the same, under pretence of a distress, the said wheat not then being fit to be carried away, according to the course of husbandry, etc. The defendant demurred, and, among other objections, urged that it ought to have been particularly shown how long the wheat remained on the land after the cutting, that the court might judge whether it were a reasonable time or not. But the court decided against the objection. "For though it is said (in Co. Litt. 56 b) that, in some cases, the court must judge whether a thing be reasonable or not, as in case of a reasonable fine, a reasonable notice, or the like, it is absurd to say that, in the present case, the court must judge of the reasonableness; for, if so, it ought to have been set forth in the plea, not only how long the corn lay on the ground, but likewise what sort of weather there was during that time, and many other incidents, which would be ridiculous to be inserted in a plea. We are of opinion, therefore, that this matter is sufficiently averred, and that the defendant might have traversed it, if he had pleased, and then it would have come before a jury, who, upon hearing the evidence, would have been the proper judges of it." [1]

The reason of this rule is evident, if we revert to the general object which all the rules, tending to certainty, contemplate, viz., the attainment of a certain issue. This implies (as has been shown) a development of the question in contro-

---

[1] Eaton *v.* Southby, Willes, 131.

versy in a specific shape; and it has been elsewhere attempted to define, in a general way, the degree of specification with which this should be developed. But, if that object be attained, there is, generally, no necessity for further minuteness in the pleading; and, therefore, those subordinate facts, which go to make up the evidence by which the affirmative or negative of the issue is to be established, do not require to be alleged, and may be brought forward, for the first time, at the trial, when the issue comes to be decided. Thus, in the above example, if we suppose issue joined, whether the wheat cut was afterwards suffered to lie on the ground a reasonable time or not, there would have been sufficient certainty, without showing on the pleadings any of those circumstances (such as the number of days, the state of the weather, etc.) which ought to enter into the consideration of that question. These circumstances, being matter of evidence only, ought to be proved before the jury, but need not appear on the record.

This is a rule so elementary in its kind, and so well observed in practice, as not to have become frequently the subject of illustration by decided cases; and (for that reason, probably) is little, if at all, noticed in the digests and treatises. It is, however, a rule of great importance, from the influence which it has on the general character of English pleading; and it is this, perhaps, more than any other principle of the science, which tends to prevent that minuteness and prolixity of detail, in which the allegations, under other systems of judicature, are involved.

Another rule, that much conduces to the same effect, is that —

(2) *It is not necessary to state matter of which the court takes notice ex officio.*[1]

Therefore it is unnecessary to state matter of law,[2] for this the judges are bound to know, and can apply for themselves to the facts alleged.

---

[1] Co. Litt. 303 b; Com. Dig. Pleader, C. 78; Deybel's Case, 4 Barn. & Ald. 243.

[2] Doct. Pl. 102. Per Buller, J., The King v. Lyme Regis, Doug. 159.

Example: If it be stated in pleading, that an officer of a corporate body was removed for misconduct, by the corporate body at large, it is unnecessary to aver that the power of removal was vested in such corporate body ; because that is a power by law incidental to them, unless given by some charter, by-law, or other authority, to a select part only.[1]

Nor is it the principles of the *common law* alone, which it is unnecessary to state in pleading. The *public statute law* falls within the same reason and the same rule ; as the judges are bound, officially, to notice the tenor of every public act of Parliament.[2] It is, therefore, never necessary to set forth a public statute.[3] The case, however, of *private* acts of Parliament is different; for these the court does not officially notice,[4] and therefore, where a party has occasion to rely on an act of this description, he must set forth such parts of it as are material.[5]

It may be observed, however, that though it is generally unnecessary to allege matter of law, yet there is sometimes occasion to make mention of it, for the convenience or intelligibility of the statement of fact.

Examples : (1) In an action of *assumpsit* on a bill of exchange, the form of the declaration is to state that the bill was drawn or accepted by the defendant, etc. (according to the nature of the case), and that the defendant, as drawer or acceptor, etc., *became liable* to pay ; and, being so liable, in consideration thereof promised to pay.

(2) It is sometimes necessary to refer to a public statute in general terms, to show that the case is intended to be brought within the statute ; as, for example, to allege that the defendant committed a certain act against the *form of the statute in such case made and provided ;* but the reference is made in this general way only, and there is no need to set the statute forth.

This rule, by which matter of law is omitted in the pleadings, by no means prevents (it will be observed) the attainment of the requisite certainty of issue. For even though

---

[1] The King *v.* Lyme Regis, Doug. 148.

[2] Bl. Com. I. 86 *.

[3] Boyce *v.* Whitaker, Doug. 97; Partridge *v.* Strange, Plow. 84.

[4] Bl. Com. *ibid. ;* Platt *v.* Hill, 1 Ld. Raym. 331.

[5] Boyce *v.* Whitaker, *ubi supra.*

the dispute between the parties should turn upon matter of law, yet they may evidently obtain a sufficiently specific issue of that description without any *allegation* of law : for *ex facto jus oritur* (from fact the law arises) ; that is, *every question of law necessarily arises out of some given state of facts;* and therefore nothing more is necessary than for each party to state, alternately, his case in point of fact ; and, upon demurrer to the sufficiency of some one of these pleadings, the issue in law must at length (as formerly demonstrated) arise.

As it is unnecessary to allege matter of law, so, if it *be* alleged, it is improper (as it has been elsewhere stated) to make it the subject of traverse.

Besides points of *law,* there are many other matters of a public kind, of which the court takes official notice, and with respect to which, it is, for the same reason, unnecessary to make allegation in pleading, such as matters antecedently alleged in the same record,[1] the time of the king's accession, his proclamations, his privileges, the time and place of holding Parliament, the time of its sessions and prorogations, and its usual course of proceeding; the ecclesiastical, civil, and maritime laws; the customary course of descent in gavelkind, and borough-English tenure; the course of the almanac;[2] the division of England into counties,[3] provinces, and dioceses; the meaning of English words, and terms of art (even when only local in their use); legal weights and measures, and the ordinary measurement of time; the existence and course of proceeding of the superior courts at Westminster, and the other courts of general jurisdiction ; and the privileges of the officers of the courts at Westminster.[4]

(3) *It is not necessary to state matter which would come more properly from the other side.*[5]

---

[1] Co. Litt. 303 b; The King v. Knollys, 1 Ld. Raym. 13.

[2] But see Mayor of Guilford v. Clarke, 2 Vent. 247.

[3] But not the local situation and distances of the different places in a county from each other. (Deybel's Case, 4 Barn. & Ald. 243.)

[4] This enumeration is principally taken from Chit. Pl. 196–204, where further information on the subject will be found.

[5] Com. Dig. Pleader, C. 81; Stowell v. Ld. Zouch, Plow. 376; Walsingham's Case, *ibid.* 564; St. John v. St. John, Hob. 78; Hotham v. East India Company,

This, which is the ordinary form of the rule, does not fully express its meaning. The meaning is, that *it is not necessary to anticipate the answer of the adversary*, which, according to Hale, C. J., is "like leaping before one comes to the stile."[1] It is sufficient that each pleading should, in itself, contain a good *prima facie* case, without reference to possible objections not yet urged.

Examples : (1) In pleading a devise of land by force of the statute of wills (32 Hen. VIII. c. 1), it is sufficient to allege that such an one was seised of the land in fee, and devised it by his last will, in writing, without alleging that such devisor was of full age. For, though the statute provides that wills made by *femes covert*, or persons within age, etc., shall not be taken to be effectual, yet, if the devisor were within age, it is for the other party to show this in his answer,[2] and it need not be denied by anticipation.

(2) In a declaration of debt upon a bond, it is unnecessary to allege that the defendant was of full age when he executed it.[3]

(3) Where an action of debt was brought upon the statute 21 Henry VI., against the bailiff of a town, for not returning the plaintiff, a burgess of that town, for the last Parliament (the words of the statute being that the sheriff shall send his precept to the mayor, and, if there be no mayor, then to the bailiff), the plaintiff declared that the sheriff had made his precept unto the bailiff, without averring that there was no mayor. And, after verdict for the plaintiff, this was moved in arrest of judgment. But the court was of opinion, clearly, that the declaration was good, "for we shall not intend that there was a mayor, except it be showed ; and if there were one, it should come more properly on the other side."[4]

(4) Where there was a covenant in a charter-party, "that no claim should be admitted, or allowance made for short tonnage, unless such short tonnage were found and made to appear on the ship's arrival, on a survey to be taken by four shipwrights, to be indifferently chosen by both parties ; " and, in an action of covenant, brought to recover for short tonnage, the plaintiff had a verdict, the defendant moved, in arrest of judgment, that it had

<hr/>

1 T. R. 638 ; Palmer *v.* Lawson 1 Sid. 333 ; Lake *v.* Raw, Carth. 8 ; Williams *v.* Fowler, Str. 410.

1 Sir Ralph Bovy's Case, 1 Vent. 217.

2 Stowell *v.* Ld. Zouch, Plow. 376.

3 Walsingham's Case, *ibid.* 564. Sir Ralph Bovy's Case, *ubi supra.*

4 St. John *v.* St. John, Hob. 78.

not been averred in the declaration that a survey was taken, and short tonnage made to appear. But the court held that, if such survey had *not* been taken, this was matter of defence, which ought to have been shown by the defendants, and refused to arrest the judgment.[1]

But where the matter is such, that *its affirmation* or denial *is essential to the apparent or prima facie* right of the party pleading, there it ought to be affirmed or denied by him in the first instance, though it may be such as would otherwise properly form the subject of objection on the other side.

Example: In an action of trespass on the case, brought by a commoner against a stranger, for putting his cattle on the common, *per quod communiam in tam amplo modo habere non potuit* (on account of which he could not have common in so full a manner), the defendant pleaded a license from the lord to put his cattle there, but did not aver that there was sufficient common left for the commoners. This was held, on demurrer, to be no good plea, for, though it may be objected that the plaintiff may reply that there was not enough common left, yet, as he had already alleged in his declaration that his enjoyment of the common was obstructed, the contrary of this ought to have been shown by the plea.[2]

EXCEPTIONS : PLEAS OF ESTOPPEL, AND OF ALIEN ENEMY.

There is an exception to the rule in question, in the case of certain pleas, which are regarded unfavorably by the courts, as having the effect of excluding the truth. Such are all pleadings in *estoppel*,[3] and the plea of *alien enemy*. It is said that these must be *certain in every particular;* which seems to amount to this, that they must meet and remove, by anticipation, every possible answer of the adversary.

Example: In a plea of alien enemy, the defendant must state not only that the plaintiff was born in a foreign country, now at enmity with the king, but that he came here without letters of

---

[1] Hotham *v.* East India Company, 1 T. R. 638.

[2] Smith *v.* Feverell, 2 Mod. 6 ; s. c.

1 Freeman, 190; Greenhow *v.* Ilsley, Willes, 619.

[3] Co. Litt. 352 b, 303 a; Dovaston *v.* Payne, 2 H. Bl. 530.

safe conduct from the king;[1] whereas, according to the general rule in question, such safe conduct, if granted, should be averred by the plaintiff in reply, and need not, in the first instance, be denied by the defendant.

(4) *It is not necessary to allege circumstances necessarily implied.*[2]

Examples: (1) In an action of debt on a bond, conditioned to stand to and perform the award of W. R., the defendant pleaded that W. R. made no award. The plaintiff replied that, after the making of the bond, and before the time for making the award, the defendant, by his certain writing, revoked the authority of the said W. R., contrary to the form and effect of the said condition. Upon demurrer, it was held that this replication was good, without averring that W. R. had notice of the revocation, because that was implied in the words "revoked the authority;" for there could be no revocation without notice to the arbitrator; so that, if W. R. had no notice, it would have been competent to the defendant to tender issue "that he did not revoke in manner and form as alleged."[3]

(2) So, if a feoffment be pleaded, it is not necessary to allege livery of seisin, for it is implied in the word "enfeoffed."[4]

(3) So, if a man plead that he is heir to A., he need not allege that A. is dead, for it is implied.[5]

(5) *It is not necessary to allege what the law will presume.*[6]

Examples: (1) In debt on a replevin bond, the plaintiffs declared that, at the city of C., and within the jurisdiction of the mayor of the city, they distrained the goods of W. H. for rent, and that W. H., at the said city, made his plaint to the mayor, etc., and prayed deliverance, etc., whereupon the mayor took from him and the defendant the bond on which the action was

---

[1] Casseres *v.* Bell, 8 T. R. 166.

[2] Vynior's Case, 8 Co. Rep. 81 b; Bac. Ab. Pleas, &c I. 7; Com. Dig. Pleader, E. 9; Co. Litt. 303 b; 2 Saund. 305 a, n. 13; Reg. Plac. 101; Sheers *v.* Brooks, 2 H. Bl. 120; Handford *v.* Palmer, 2 Brod. & Bing. 361; Marsh *r.* Bulteel, 5 Barn. & Ald. 507.

[3] Vynior's Case, *ubi supra;* Marsh *v.* Bulteel, *ubi supra*, S. P.; but judgment on the demurrer should be for the defendant, for the plaintiff did not put his claim on the revocation of the submission, but on an alleged non-performance of the award; such was the judgment in Marsh *v.* Bulteel.

[4] Co. Litt. 303 b; Doct. Pl. 48, 49; 2 Saund. *ubi supra.*

[5] 2 Saund. *ubi supra;* Com. Dig. *ubi supra;* Dal. 67.

[6] Wilson *v.* Hobday, 4 M. & S. 125; Chapman *v.* Pickersgill, 2 Wils. 147.

24

brought, conditioned that W. H. should appear before the mayor or his deputy, at the next court of record of the city, and there prosecute his suit, etc., and thereupon the mayor replevied, etc. It was held not to be necessary to allege in this declaration a custom for the mayor to grant replevin and take bond, and show that the plaint was made in court, because all these circumstances must be *presumed* against the defendant, who executed the bond and had the benefit of the replevin.[1]

(2) In an action for slander, imputing theft, the plaintiff need not aver that he is not a thief, because the law presumes his innocence till the contrary be shown.[2]

(6) *A general mode of pleading is allowed where great prolixity is thereby avoided.*[3]

It has been objected, with truth, that this rule is indefinite in its form.[4] Its extent and application, however, may be collected with some degree of precision from the examples by which it is illustrated in the books, and by considering the limitations which it necessarily receives from the rules tending to certainty, as enumerated in a former part of this work.

Examples : (1) In *assumpsit*, on a promise by the defendant to pay for all such necessaries as his friend should be provided with by the plaintiff, the plaintiff alleged that he provided necessaries amounting to such a sum. It was moved, in arrest of judgment, that the declaration was not good, because he had not shown what necessaries in particular he had provided. But Coke, C. J., said, " this is good, as is here pleaded, for avoiding such multiplicities of reckonings ; " and Doddridge, J., " this general allegation, that he had provided him with all necessaries, is good, without showing in particular what they were." And the court gave judgment unanimously for the plaintiff.[5]

(2) In *assumpsit* for labor and medicines, for curing the defendant of a distemper, the defendant pleaded infancy. The

---

[1] Wilson *v.* Hobday, 4 M. & S. 125.

[2] Chapman *v.* Pickersgill, 2 Wils. 147.

[8] Co. Litt. 303 b ; 2 Saund. 116 b, 411, n. 4; Bac. Ab. Pleas, &c. I. 3 ; Jermy *v.* Jenny, 1 Ld. Raym. 8 ; Aglionby *v.* Towerson, *ibid.* 400 ; Parkes *v.* Middleton, Lutw. 421 ; Keating *v.* Irish, *ibid.* 590 ; Cornwallis *v.* Savery, 2 Burr. 772 ; Mints *v.* Bethil, Cro. Eliz. 749 ; Braban *v.* Bacon, *ibid.* 916 ; Church *v.* Brownwick, 1 Sid. 334 ; Cryps *v.* Baynton, 3 Bulst. 31 ; Banks *v.* Pratt, Sty. 428 ; Huggins *v.* Wiseman, Carth. 110 ; Groenvelt *v.* Burnell, *ibid.* 491 ; J'Anson *v.* Stuart, 1 T. R. 753 ; Shum *v.* Farrington, 1 Bos. & Pull. 640 ; Barton *v.* Webb, 8 T. R. 459 ; Hill *v.* Montagu, 2 M. & S. 378.

[4] 1 Arch. 211.

[5] Cryps *v.* Baynton, 3 Bulst. 31.

plaintiff replied that the action was brought for necessaries generally. On demurrer to the replication, it was objected, that the plaintiff had not assigned, in certain, how or in what manner the medicines were necessary; but it was adjudged that the replication, in this general form, was good; and the plaintiff had judgment.[1]

(3) In debt on a bond, conditioned that the defendant should pay, from time to time, the moiety of all such money as he should receive, and give account of it, he pleaded, generally, that he had paid the moiety of all such money, etc. *Et per curiam* (and by the court), "This plea of payment is good, without showing the particular sums, and that in order to avoid stuffing the rolls with multiplicity of matter." Also, they agreed that, if the condition had been to pay the moiety of such money as he should receive, without saying *from time to time*, the payment should have been pleaded specially.[2]

(4) In an action on a bond, conditioned that W. W., who was appointed agent of a regiment, should pay all such sum and sums of money as he should receive from the paymaster general for the use of the regiment, and faithfully account to and indemnify the plaintiff, the defendant pleaded a general performance, and that the plaintiff was not damnified. The plaintiff replied, that W. W. received from the paymaster general, for the use of the said regiment, several sums of money, amounting in the whole to £1,400, for and on account of the said regiment and of the commissioned and non-commissioned officers and soldiers of the same, according to their respective proportions, and that he had not paid a great part thereof among the colonel, officers, and soldiers, etc., according to the several proportions of their pay. Upon demurrer, the court said, that "there was no need to spin out the proceedings to a great prolixity, by entering into the detail, and stating the various deductions out of the whole pay, upon various accounts, and in different proportions."[3]

(5) In debt on bond, conditioned that R. S. should render to the plaintiff a just account, and make payment and delivery of all moneys, bills, etc., which he should receive as his agent, the defendant pleaded performance. The plaintiff replied, that R. S. received, as such agent, divers sums of money, amounting to £2,000, belonging to the plaintiff's business, and had not rendered a just account, nor made payment and delivery of the said

---

[1] Huggins *v.* Wiseman, Carth. 110.
[2] Church *v.* Brownwick, 1 Sid. 334;
and see Mints *v.* Bethil, Cro. Eliz. 749.

[3] Cornwallis *v.* Savery, 2 Burr. 772.

sum, or any part thereof. The defendant demurred specially, assigning for cause, that it did not appear by the replication from whom, or in what manner, or in what proportions, the said sums of money, amounting to £2,000, had been received. But the court held the replication "agreeable to the rules of law and precedents." [1]

(7) *A general mode of pleading is often sufficient, where the allegation on the other side must reduce the matter to certainty.* [2]

This rule comes into most frequent illustration in pleading *performance,* in *actions of debt on bond.* It has been seen that the general rule as to certainty requires that the time, place, and manner of such performance should be specially shown. Nevertheless, by virtue of the rule now under consideration, it may be sometimes alleged in general terms only ; and the requisite certainty of issue is in such cases secured by throwing on the plaintiff the necessity of showing a special breach in his replication. This course, for example, is allowed in cases where a more special form of pleading would lead to inconvenient prolixity.

Example : In debt on bond, conditioned that the defendant should at all times, upon request, deliver to the plaintiff all the fat and tallow of all beasts which he, his servants, or assigns, should kill or dress before such a day, the defendant pleaded that, upon every request made unto him, he delivered unto the plaintiff all the fat and tallow of all beasts which were killed by him, or any of his servants or assigns, before the said day. On demurrer, it was objected, "that the plea was not good in such generality; but he ought to have said that he had delivered so much fat or tallow, which was all, etc. ; or that he had killed so many beasts, whereof he had delivered all the fat." But the court held "that the plea was good ; for where the matters to be pleaded tend to infiniteness and multiplicity, whereby the rolls shall be encumbered with the length thereof, the law allows of a general pleading in the affirmative. And it hath been resolved, by all the justices of England, that in debt, upon an obligation to perform the covenant in an indenture, it sufficeth to allege performance generally. So, where one is obliged to deliver all

---

[1] Shum *v.* Farrington, 1 Bos. & Pull. 640 ; and see a similar decision, Burton *v.* Webb, 8 T. R. 459.

[2] Co. Litt. 303 b ; Mints *v.* Bethil, Cro. Eliz. 749 ; 1 Saund. 117, n. 1 ; 2 Saund. 410, n. 3 ; Church *v.* Brownwick, 1 Sid. 334.

his evidences, or to assure all his lands, it sufficeth to allege that he hath delivered all, etc., or assured all his lands, and it ought to come on the other side to show the contrary in some particular."[1]

Another illustration is afforded by the plea of *non damnificatus*, on an action of debt on an indemnity bond, or bond conditioned " *to keep the plaintiff harmless and indemnified*," etc. This is in the nature of a plea of performance, being used where the defendant means to allege that the plaintiff has been kept harmless and indemnified, according to the tenor of the condition; and it is pleaded in general terms, without showing the particular manner of the indemnification.

Example : If an action of debt be brought on a bond, conditioned that the defendant " do, from time to time, acquit, discharge, and save harmless the churchwardens of the parish of P., and their successors, etc., from all manner of costs and charges, by reason of the birth and maintenance of a certain child; " if the defendant means to rely on the performance of the condition, he may plead in this general form : " *That the churchwardens of the said parish, or their successors, etc., from the time of making the said writing obligatory, were not in any manner damnified by reason of the birth or maintenance of the said child ;* "[2] and it will then be for the plaintiff to show in the replication how the churchwardens were damnified.

But with respect to the plea of *non damnificatus*, the following distinctions have been taken : First, if, instead of pleading in that form, the defendant alleges affirmatively that he " *has saved harmless*," etc., the plea will in this case be bad, unless he proceeds to show specifically *how* he saved harmless.[3] Again, it is held that if the condition does not use the words " indemnify," or " save harmless," or some equivalent term, but stipulates for the performance of some *specific act*, intended to be by way of indemnity, such as the payment of a sum of money by the defendant to a third person, in exon-

[1] Mints *v.* Bethil. Cro. Eliz. 749 ; and see Church *v.* Brownwick, 1 Sid. 334.

[2] Richard *v.* Hodges, 2 Saund. 84 ; Hayes *v.* Bryant, 1 H. Bl. 253 ; Com. Dig. Pleader, E. 25, 2 W. 33 ; Manser's Case, 2 Co. Rep. 4 a ; 7 Went. Index, 615 ; 5 Went. 531.

[3] 1 Saund. 117, n. 1 ; White *v.* Cleaver, Str. 681 ; Hillier *v.* Plympton, *ibid.* 422.

eration of the plaintiff's liability to pay the same sum, the plea of *non damnificatus* will be improper : and the defendant should plead performance specifically, as, " *that he paid the said sum*," etc.[1] It is also laid down that, if the condition of the bond be to " discharge " or " acquit " the plaintiff from a particular thing, the plea of *non damnificatus* will not apply, but the defendant must plead performance specially, " *that he discharged and acquitted*," etc., and must also show the manner of such acquittal and discharge.[2] But, on the other hand, if a bond be conditioned to " discharge and acquit the plaintiff *from any damage* " by reason of a certain thing, *non damnificatus* may then be pleaded, because that is, in truth, the same thing with a condition to " indemnify and save harmless," etc.[3]

The rule under consideration is also exemplified in the case where the condition of a bond is for performance of covenants, or other matters, *contained in an indenture, or other instrument collateral to the bond, and not set forth in the condition.* In this case, also, the law often allows (upon the same principle as in the last) a general plea of performance, without setting forth the manner.[4]

Examples: (1) In an action of debt on bond, where the condition is, that T. J., deputy postmaster of a certain stage, " shall and will, truly, faithfully, and diligently, do, execute, and perform all and every the duties belonging to the said office of deputy postmaster of the said stage, and shall faithfully, justly, and exactly observe, perform, fulfill, and keep all and every the instructions, etc., from his majesty's postmaster general," and such instructions are in an affirmative and absolute form, as follows : " You shall cause all letters and packets to be speedily and without delay, carefully and faithfully, delivered, that shall from time to time be sent unto your said stage, to be dispersed there, or in the towns and parts adjacent, that all persons receiving such letters may have time to send their respective answers," etc., it is sufficient for the defendant to plead (after setting forth the instructions)

[1] Holmes v. Rhodes, 1 Bos & Pull. 638.

[2] 1 Saund. 117, n. 1 ; Bret v. Audar, 1 Leon. 71 ; White v. Cleaver, Str. 681 ; Leneret v. Rivet, Cro. Jac. 503 ; Harris v. Pett, 5 Mod. 243 ; s. c. Carth. 375.

[3] 1 Saund. *ubi supra.*

[4] Mints v. Bethil, Cro. Eliz. 749 ; Bac. Ab. Pleas, &c. I. 3 ; 2 Saund. 410, n. 3 ; 1 Saund. *ubi supra ;* Com. Dig. Pleader, 2, V. 13 ; Earl of Kerry v. Baxter, 4 East, 340.

"*that the said T. J., from the time of the making the said writing obligatory, hitherto hath well, truly, faithfully, and diligently done, executed, and performed all and every the duties belonging to the said office of deputy postmaster of the said stage, and faithfully, justly, and exactly observed, performed, fulfilled, and kept all and every the instructions, etc., according to the true intent and meaning of the said instructions,*" without showing the manner of performance, as that he did cause certain letters or packets to be delivered, etc., being all that were sent.[1]

(2) If a bond be conditioned for fulfilling all and singular the covenants, articles, clauses, provisos, conditions, and agreements, comprised in a certain indenture, on the part and behalf of the defendant, which indenture contains covenants of an affirmative and absolute kind only, it is sufficient to plead (after setting forth the indenture) that the defendant always hitherto hath well and truly fulfilled all and singular the covenants, articles, clauses, provisos, conditions, and agreements comprised in the said indenture, on the part and behalf of the said defendant.[2]

But the adoption of a mode of pleading so general as in these examples will be improper, where the covenants, or other matters mentioned in the collateral instrument, are either in the *negative* or the *disjunctive* form;[3] and, with respect to such matters, the allegation of performance should be more specially made, so as to apply exactly to the tenor of the collateral instrument.

Example: In the example above given, of a bond conditioned for the performance of the duties of a deputy postmaster, and for observing the instructions of the postmaster general, if, besides those in the *positive* form, some of these instructions were in the *negative*, as, for example, " you shall not receive any letters or packets directed to any seaman, or unto any private soldier, etc., unless you be first paid for the same, and do charge the same to your account as paid," it would be improper to plead merely that T. J. faithfully performed the duties belonging to the office, etc., and all and every the instructions, etc. Such plea will apply sufficiently to the positive, but not to the negative part of the instructions.[4] The form, therefore, should be as follows: " *That*

[1] 2 Saund. 403 b, 410, n. 3.

[2] Gainsford v. Griffith, 1 Saund 55, 117, n. 1; Earl of Kerry v. Baxter, 4 East 340.

[3] Earl of Kerry v. Baxter, ubi supra.

supra; Oglethorp v. Hyde, Cro. Eliz. 233; Lord Arlington v. Merricke, 2 Saund. 410, and n. 3, *ibid.*

[4] Lord Arlington v. Merricke, *ubi supra.*

the said T. J., from the time of making the said writing obligatory, hitherto hath well, truly, faithfully, and diligently executed and performed all and every the duties belonging to the said office of deputy postmaster of the said stage, and faithfully, justly, and exactly observed, performed, fulfilled, and kept all and every the instructions, etc., according to the true intent and meaning of the said instructions. And the said defendant further says, that the said T. J., from the time aforesaid, did not receive any letters or packets directed to any seaman, or private soldier, etc., unless he, the said T. J., was first paid for the same, and did so charge himself, in his account, with the same as paid," etc.[1]

And the case is the same where the matters mentioned in the collateral instrument are in the *disjunctive or alternative* form; as, where the defendant engages to do either one thing or another. Here, also, a general allegation of performance is insufficient; and he should show which of the alternative acts was performed.[2]

The reasons why the general allegation of performance does not properly apply to negative or disjunctive matters are, that, in the first case, the plea would be indirect or *argumentative* in its form; in the second, *equivocal;* and would, in either case, therefore, be objectionable, by reason of certain rules of pleading, which we shall have occasion to consider in the next section.

It has been stated in a former part of this work that where a party founds his answer upon any matter not set forth by his adversary, but contained in a deed, of which the latter makes *profert*, he must demand *oyer* of such deed, and set it forth. In pleading performance, therefore, of the condition of a bond, where (as is generally the case) the plaintiff has stated in his declaration nothing but the bond itself, without the condition, it is necessary for the defendant to demand *oyer* of the condition, and set it forth.[3] And *in pleading performance of matters contained in a collateral instrument, it is necessary not only to do this, but also to make profert, and set forth the whole substance of the collateral instrument,*[4] for otherwise it will not appear that that instrument did not stipulate for the

[1] 2 Saund. 410, and n. 3 *ibid.*   [3] 2 Saund. 410, n. 2.
[2] Oglethorp *v.* Hyde, Cro. Eliz 233.   [4] *Ibid.*

performance of negative or disjunctive matters,[1] and, in that case, the general plea of performance of the matters therein contained would (as above shown) be improper.

(8) *No greater particularity is required than the nature of the thing pleaded will conveniently admit.*[2]

Thus, though generally, in an action for injury to goods, the *quantity* of the goods must be stated, yet, if they can not, under the circumstances of the case, be conveniently ascertained by number, weight, or measure, such certainty will not be required.

Examples : (1) In trespass for breaking the plaintiff's close, with beasts, and eating his peas, a declaration, not showing the quantity of peas, has been held sufficient; "because nobody can measure the peas that beasts can eat." [3]

(2) In an action on the case for setting a house on fire, *per quod* the plaintiff, amongst divers other goods, *ornatus pro equis amisit* (provisions for his horses lost), after verdict for the plaintiff, it was objected, that this was uncertain ; but the objection was disallowed by the court. And, in this case, Windham, J., said, that if he had mentioned only *diversa bona* (sundry goods), yet it had been well enough, as a man can not be supposed to know the certainty of his goods when his house is burnt; and added, that, to avoid prolixity, the law will sometimes allow such a declaration.[4]

(3) In an action of debt brought on the statute 23 Hen. VI. c. 15, against the sheriff of Anglesea, for not returning the plaintiff to be a knight of the shire in Parliament, the declaration alleged that the plaintiff " was chosen and nominated a knight of the same county, etc., by the greater number of men then resident within the said county of Anglesea, present, etc., each of whom could dispend 40s. of freehold by the year," etc. On demurrer, it was objected that the plaintiff " does not show the certainty of the number ; as to say, that he was chosen by 200, which was the greater number; and thereupon, a certain issue might arise, whether he was elected by so many, or not." But it was held that the declaration was " good enough, without showing

---

1 See Earl of Kerry *v.* Baxter, 4 East, 340.

2 Bac. Ab. Pleas, &c (B. 5) 5, and 409, 5th ed. ; Buckley *v* Rice Thomas, Plow. 118; Wimbish *v.* Tailbois, *ibid.* 54 ;

Partridge *v.* Strange, *ibid.* 85 ; Hartley *v.* Herring, 8 T. R. 130.

3 Bac. Ab. *ubi supra.*

4 Bac. Ab. Pleas, &c. 409, 5th ed.

the number of electors ; for the election might be made by voices, or by hands, or such other way, wherein it is easy to tell who has the majority, and yet very difficult to know the certain number of them." And it was laid down that, to put the plaintiff "to declare a certainty, where he can not, by any possibility, be presumed to know or remember the certainty, is not reasonable nor requisite in our law." [1]

(4) In an action for false imprisonment, where the plaintiff declared that the defendant imprisoned him until he made a certain bond, by duress, to the defendant, "and others unknown," the declaration was adjudged to be good, without showing the names of the others; "because it might be that he could not know their names ; in which case, the law will not force him to show that which he can not." [2]

(9) *Less particularity is required, when the facts lie more in the knowledge of the opposite party, than of the party pleading.* [3]

This rule is exemplified in the case of alleging title in an adversary, where (as formerly explained) a more general statement is allowed, than when title is set up in the party himself.

Examples: (1) In an action of covenant, the plaintiff declared that the defendant, by indenture, demised to him certain premises, with a covenant that he, the defendant, had full power and lawful authority to demise the same, according to the form and effect of the said indenture ; and then the plaintiff assigned a breach, that the defendant had not full power and lawful authority to demise the said premises, according to the form and effect of the said indenture. After verdict for the plaintiff, it was assigned for error, that he had not in his declaration shown, " what person had right, title, estate, or interest, in the lands demised, by which it might appear to the court that the defendant had not full power and lawful authority to demise." But, "upon conference and debate amongst the justices, it was resolved that the assignment of the breach of covenant was good ; for he has followed the words of the covenant negatively, and it lies more properly in the knowledge of the lessor, what estate he himself

---

[1] Buckley *v.* Rice Thomas, Plow. 118.

[2] Cited *ibid.* See also Wimbish *v.* Tailbois, Plow. 54, 55; Partridge *v.* Strange, Plow. 85.

[3] Rider *v.* Smith, 3 T. R. 766; Derisley *v.* Custance, 4 T. R. 77; Attorney General *v.* Meller, Hard. 459; Denham *v.* Stephenson, 1 Salk. 355; Robert Bradshaw's Case, 9 Co. Rep. 60 b ; Gale *v.* Read, 8 East, 80; Com Dig Pleader, C. 26.

has in the land which he demises, than the lessee, who is a stranger to it." [1]

(2) Where the defendant had covenanted that he would not carry on the business of a rope-maker, or make cordage for any person, except under contracts for government, and the plaintiff, in an action of covenant, assigned for breach, that after the making of the indenture, the defendant carried on the business of a rope-maker, and made cordage for divers and very many persons, other than by virtue of any contract for government, etc.; the defendant demurred specially, on the ground that the plaintiff "had not disclosed any and what particular person or persons for whom the defendant made cordage, nor any and what particular quantities or kinds of cordage the defendant did so make for them, nor in what manner, nor by what acts, he carried on the said business of a rope-maker, as is alleged in the said breach of covenant." But the court held, "that as the facts alleged in these breaches lie more properly in the knowledge of the defendant, who must be presumed cognizant of his own dealings, than of the plaintiff, there was no occasion to state them with more particularity;" and gave judgment accordingly.[2]

(10) *Less particularity is necessary in the statement of matter of inducement, or aggravation, than in the main allegations.*[3]

This rule is exemplified in the case of the derivation of title; where, though it is a general rule *that the commencement of a particular estate must be shown*, yet an exception is allowed, if the title be alleged by way of *inducement* only.

Examples: (1) Where, in *assumpsit*, the plaintiff declared that, in consideration that, at the defendant's request, he had given and granted to him, by deed, the next avoidance of a certain church, the defendant promised to pay £100, but the declaration did not set forth any time or place at which such grant was made; upon this being objected, in arrest of judgment, after verdict, the court resolved, that "it was but an inducement to the action, and therefore needed not to be so precisely alleged;" and gave judgment for the plaintiff.[4]

---

[1] Robert Bradshaw's Case, 9 Co. Rep. 60 b.

[2] Gale *v.* Read, 8 East, 80.

[3] Co. Litt. 303 a; Bac. Ab. Pleas, &c 322, 348, 5th ed.; Com. Dig. Pleader, C. 31, C. 43, E. 10, E. 18; Doct. Pl. 283; Wetherell *v.* Clerkson, 12 Mod. 597; Chamberlain *v.* Greenfield, 3 Wils. 292; Alsope *v.* Sytwell, Yelv. 17; Riggs *v.* Bullingham, Cro. Eliz. 715; Woolaston *v.* Webb, Hob. 18; Bishop of Salisbury's Case, 10 Co. Rep. 59 b; 1 Saund. 274, n. 1.

[4] Riggs *v.* Bullingham, *ubi supra.*

(2) In trespass, the plaintiff declared that the defendant broke and entered his dwelling-house, and " wrenched and forced open, or caused to be wrenched and forced open, the closet-doors, drawers, chests, cupboards, and cabinets of the said plaintiff." Upon special demurrer, it was objected, that the number of closet-doors, drawers, chests, cupboards, and cabinets, was not specified. But it was answered, "that the breaking and entering the plaintiff's house was the principal ground and foundation of the present action; and all the rest are not foundations of the action, but matters only thrown in to aggravate the damages; and on that ground need not be particularly specified." And of that opinion was the whole court; and judgment was given for the plaintiff.[1]

(11) *With respect to acts valid at common law, but regulated, as to the mode of performance, by statute, it is sufficient to use such certainty of allegation, as was sufficient before the statute.*[2]

By the common law, a lease for any number of years might be made by parol only; but, by the statute of frauds (29 Car. II. c. 3, s. 1, 2), all leases and terms for years made by parol, and not put into writing, and signed by the lessors or their agents authorized by writing, shall have only the effect of leases at will, except leases not exceeding the term of three years from the making. Yet in a declaration of debt for rent on a demise, it is sufficient (as it was at common law) to state a demise for any number of years, without showing it to have been in writing.[3] So, in the case of a promise to answer for the debt, default, or miscarriage of another person (which was good by parol, at common law, but by the statute of frauds, section 4, is not valid unless the agreement, or some memorandum or note thereof, be in writing, and signed by the party, etc.), the declaration, on such promise, need not allege a written contract.[4]

And on this subject, the following difference is to be remarked, that " where a thing is originally made by act of Parliament, and required to be in writing, it must be

---

[1] Chamberlain v. Greenfield, 3 Wils. 292.

[2] 1 Saund. 276, n. 2; 211, n. 2; Anon. 2 Salk. 519; Birch v. Bellamy,

12 Mod. 540; Bac. Ab. Statute, L. 3; 4 Hen. VII. 8.

[3] 1 Saund. 276, n. 1.

[4] 1 Saund. 211, n. 2; Anon. 2 Salk. 519.

pleaded with all the circumstances required by the act; as in the case of a will of lands, it must be alleged to have been made in writing; but where an act makes writing necessary to a matter, where it was not so at the common law, as where a lease for a longer term than three years is required to be in writing by the statute of frauds, it is not necessary to plead the thing to be in writing, though it must be proved to be so, in evidence." [1]

Distinction : As to the rule under consideration, however, a distinction has been taken between a *declaration* and a *plea ;* and it is said, that though in the former the plaintiff need not show the thing to be in writing, in the latter the defendant must.

Example : In an action of *indebitatus assumpsit,* for necessaries provided for the defendant's wife, the defendant pleaded, that before the action was brought, the plaintiff and defendant, and one J. B., the defendant's son, entered into a certain agreement, by which the plaintiff, in discharge of the debt mentioned in the declaration, was to accept the said J. B. as her debtor for £9, to be paid when he should receive his pay as a lieutenant; and that the plaintiff accepted the said J. B. for her debtor, etc. Upon demurrer, judgment was given for the plaintiff, for two reasons: first, because it did not appear that there was any consideration for the agreement; secondly, that, admitting the agreement to be valid, yet, by the statute of frauds, it ought to be in writing, or else the plaintiff could have no remedy thereon; "and though, upon such an agreement, the plaintiff need not set forth the agreement to be in writing, yet when the defendant pleads such an agreement in bar, he must plead it so as it may appear to the court that an action will lie upon it; for he shall not take away the plaintiff's present action, and not give her another, upon the agreement pleaded." [2]

---

[1] 1 Saund. 276, d, e, n. 2.

[2] Case *v.* Barber, 1 Ld. Raym. 450. It is to be observed, that the plea was at all events a bad one with respect to the first objection. The case is, perhaps, therefore, not decisive as to the validity of the second.

CHAPTER XIII.

OF RULES WHICH TEND TO PREVENT OBSCURITY AND CONFUSION IN PLEADING.

RULE I. PLEADINGS MUST NOT BE INSENSIBLE NOR REPUGNANT.[1]

(1) If a pleading be unintelligible (or, in the language of pleading, *insensible*), by the omission of material words, etc., this vitiates the pleading.[2]

(2) If a pleading be inconsistent with itself, or *repugnant*, this is ground for demurrer.

Examples: (1) Where, in an action of trespass, the plaintiff declared for taking and carrying away certain timber, lying in a certain place, for the completion of a house then lately built, — this declaration was considered as bad for repugnancy; for the timber could not be for the building of a house already built.[3]

(2) Where the defendant pleaded a grant of a rent, out of a *term of years*, and proceeded to allege that, by virtue thereof, he was seised in his demesne, *as of freehold*, for the term of his life, the plea was held bad for repugnancy.[4]

EXCEPTION.

If the second allegation, which creates the repugnancy, is merely superfluous and redundant, so that it may be rejected from the pleading, without materially altering the general sense and effect, it shall, in that case, be rejected, at least, if laid under a *videlicet*, and shall not vitiate the pleading; for the maxim is, *utile, per inutile, non vitiatur.*[5]

---

[1] Com. Dig Pleader, C. 23 ; Wyat v. Aland, 1 Salk. 324 ; Bac. Ab. Pleas, &c. I. 4; Nevill v. Soper, 1 Salk 213 ; Butt's Case, 7 Co. Rep. a ; Hutchinson v. Jackson, 2 Lut. 1324; Vin. Ab. Abatement, D. a.

[2] Com. Dig. *ubi supra;* Wyat *v.* Aland, *ubi supra.*

[3] Nevill *v.* Soper, *ubi supra.*

[4] Butt's Case, *ubi supra.*

[5] Gilb. C. P. 131, 132 ; The King *v.* Stevens, 5 East, 255 ; Wyat *v.* Aland, *ubi supra;* 2 Saund. 291, n. 1, 306, n. 14; Co. Litt. 303 b.

RULE II.   PLEADINGS MUST NOT BE AMBIGUOUS, OR DOUBTFUL, IN MEANING ; AND WHEN TWO DIFFERENT MEANINGS PRESENT THEMSELVES, THAT CONSTRUCTION SHALL BE ADOPTED WHICH IS MOST UNFAVORABLE TO THE PARTY PLEADING.[1]

Examples : (1) If in trespass *quare clausum fregit*, the defendant pleads, that the *locus in quo* was his freehold, he must allege that it was his freehold *at the time of the trespass ;* otherwise the plea is insufficient.[2]

(2) In debt on a bond, conditioned to make assurance of land, if the defendant pleads that he executed a release, his plea is bad, if it does not express *that the release concerns the same land.*[3]

(3) In trespass *quare clausum fregit,* and for breaking down two gates and three perches of hedges, the defendant pleaded that the said close was within the parish of R., and that all the parishioners there, from time immemorial, had used to go over the said close, upon their *perambulation in rogation week ;* and because the plaintiff had wrongfully erected *two gates and three perches of hedges,* in the said way, the defendant, being one of the parishioners, broke down those gates and those three perches of hedges.   On demurrer, it was objected, that though the defendant had justified the breaking down two gates and three perches of hedges, it does not appear that they were the *same gates and hedges,* in respect of which the plaintiff complained ; it not being alleged that they were the gates and hedges " *aforesaid,*" or the gates and hedges " *in the declaration mentioned.*"   " And thereto agreed all the justices, that this fault in the bar was incurable. For Walmsley said, that he thereby doth not answer to that for which the plaintiff chargeth him."   And he observed, that the case might be, that the plaintiff had erected *four* gates and *six* perches of hedges ; and that the defendant had broken down the whole of these, having the justification mentioned in the plea, in respect of two gates and three perches only, and no defence as to the remainder ; and that the action might be brought in respect of the latter only.[4]

A pleading, however, is not objectionable, as ambiguous or obscure, if it be *certain to a common intent ;*[5] that is, if it be

---

[1] Co. Litt. 303 b ; Purcell *v.* Bradley, Yelv. 36 ; Rose *v.* Standen, 2 Mod. 295 ; Dovaston *v.* Payne, 2 H. Bl. 530 ; Thornton *v.* Adams, 5 M. & S. 38 ; Lord Huntingtower *v.* Gardiner, 1 Barn. & Cress. 297 ; Fletcher *v.* Pogson, 3 Barn. & Cress. 192.

[2] Com Dig. Pleader, E. 5.

[3] Com. Dig. *ubi supra* ; Manser's Case, 2 Co. Rep. 3.

[4] Goodday *v.* Michell, Cro. Eliz. 441.

[5] Com. Dig. Pleader, E. 7, F. 17 ; 1 Saund. 49, n 1 ; Long's Case, 5 Co. Rep. 121 a ; Doct. Pl. 58 ; Colthirst *v*

clear enough, according to reasonable intendment or construction, though not worded with absolute precision.[1]

Examples: (1) In debt on a bond, conditioned to procure A. S. to surrender a copyhold to the use of the plaintiff, — a plea that A. S. surrendered and released the copyhold to the plaintiff, in full court, and the plaintiff accepted it, without alleging that the surrender was *to the plaintiff's use,* is sufficient; for this shall be intended.[2]

(2) In debt on a bond, conditioned that the plaintiff shall enjoy certain land, etc., — a plea that after the making of the bond, until the day of exhibiting the bill, the plaintiff did enjoy, is good, though it be not said, that *always* after the making, until, etc., he enjoyed; for this shall be intended.[3]

NEGATIVE PREGNANT.

It is under this head, of *ambiguity,* that the doctrine of *negatives pregnant* appears most properly to range itself. A *negative pregnant* is such a form of negative expression as may imply, or carry within it, an affirmative. This is considered as a fault in pleading; and the reason why it is so considered, is, that the meaning of such a form of expression is ambiguous.

Examples: (1) In trespass, for entering the plaintiff's house, the defendant pleaded, that the plaintiff's daughter gave him license to do so; and that he entered by that license. The plaintiff replied, that *he did not enter by her license.* This was considered as a *negative pregnant ;* and it was held, that the plaintiff should have traversed the entry by itself, or the license by itself, and not both together.[4] It will be observed that this form of traverse may imply, or carry within it, that a license was given, though the defendant did not enter by that license. It is, therefore, in the language of pleading, said to be pregnant with that admission, viz., that a license was given.[5] At the same time, the

---

Bejushin, Plow. 26, 28, 33 ; Fulmerston *v.* Steward, *ibid.* 102 ; Cooper *v.* Monke, Willes, 52 ; The King *v.* Lyme Regis, 1 Doug. 158 ; Hamond *v.* Dod, Cro. Car. 5 ; Poynter *v.* Poynter, *ibid.* 194 ; Dovaston *v.* Payne, 2 H. Bl. 530 ; Jacobs *v.* Nelson, 3 Taunt. 423. See especially Chit. Pl. 212-218.

1 It will be observed, that the word " certain " is here used, not in the sense of *particular* or *specific,* as in former parts of this work, — but in its other meaning, of *clear* or *distinct.*

2 Hamond *v.* Dod, Cro. Car. 6.

3 Harlow *r.* Wright, *ibid.* 105.

4 Myn *r.* Cole, Cro. Jac. 87.

5 Bac. Ab. Pleas, &c. 420, 5th ed.

license is not expressly admitted; and the effect, therefore, is to leave it in doubt whether the plaintiff means to deny the license or to deny that the defendant entered by virtue of that license. It is this *ambiguity* which appears to constitute the fault.[1]

(2) In an action for negligently keeping a fire, by which the plaintiff's houses were burned, the defendant pleaded that *the plaintiff's houses were not burned by the defendant's negligence in keeping his fire;* and it was objected that the traverse was not good, for it has two intendments: one that the houses were not burned; the other that they were burned, but not by negligent keeping of the fire; and so it is a negative pregnant (28 Hen. VI. 7).

(3) In trespass, for assault and battery, the defendant justified, for that he, being master of a ship, commanded the plaintiff to do some service in the ship; which he refusing to do, the defendant moderately chastised him. The plaintiff traversed, with an *absque hoc, that the defendant moderately chastised him;* and this traverse was held to be a negative pregnant; — for, while it apparently means to put in issue only the question of excess (admitting, by implication, the chastisement), it does not necessarily and distinctly make that admission; and is, therefore, ambiguous in its form.[2]

If the plaintiff had replied *that the defendant immoderately chastised him*, the objection would have been avoided; but the proper form of traverse would have been *de injuria sua propria absque tali causa.*[3] This, by traversing the whole "cause alleged," would have distinctly put in issue all the facts in the plea; and no ambiguity or doubt, as to the extent of the denial, would have arisen.[4]

This rule, however, against a negative pregnant, appears in modern times, at least, to have received no very strict construction. For many cases have occurred in which, upon various grounds of distinction from the general rule, that form of expression has been held free from objection.[5]

---

[1] 28 Hen. VI. 7; Slade *v.* Drake, Hob. 295; Styles' Pract. Reg. tit. Negative Pregnant.

[2] Auberie *v.* James, Vent. 70; s. c. 1 Sid. 444; 2 Keb. 623.

[3] Auberie *v.* James, *ubi supra.*

[4] Since Mr. Stephen published this edition, the case of Auberie *v.* James has been over-ruled by the later case of Penn *v.* Ward, 2 Cromp. M. & R. 338. The moderation of the chastisement can not be put in issue by the traverse *de injuria;* for this purpose a new assignment of the *excess* of chastisement is required.

[5] Com. Dig. Pleader, R. 6.

25

Example : In debt on a bond, conditioned to perform the covenants in an indenture of lease, one of which covenants was
that the defendant, the lessee, would not deliver possession to
any but the lessor, or such persons as should lawfully evict him,
the defendant pleaded, that he *did not deliver the possession to
any but such as lawfully evicted him.* On demurrer to this plea,
it was objected, that the same was ill, and a *negative pregnant ;*
and that he ought to have said that such a one lawfully evicted
him, to whom he delivered the possession ; or that he did not
deliver the possession to any ; but the court held the plea, as
pursuing the words of the covenant, good — being in the negative
— and that the plaintiff ought to have replied, and assigned
a breach ; and therefore judgment was given against him.[1]

Rule III. Pleadings must not be argumentative.[2]

In other words, the pleadings must advance their positions
of fact in an absolute form, and not leave them to be collected
by inference and argument only.

Examples : (1) In an action of trover, for ten pieces of money,
the defendant pleaded that there was a wager between the plaintiff and one C., concerning the quantity of yards of velvet in a
cloak ; and the plaintiff and C. each delivered into the defendant's hand ten pieces of money, to be delivered to C. if there
were ten yards of velvet in the cloak, and if not, to the plaintiff ;
and proceeded to allege *that, upon measuring of the cloak, it was
found that there were ten yards of velvet therein ;* whereupon the
defendant delivered the pieces of money to C. Upon demurrer,
" Gawdy held the plea to be good enough ; for the measuring
thereof is the fittest way for trying it : and when it is so found
by the measuring, he had good cause to deliver them out of his
hands, to him who had won the wager. But Fenner and Popham
held that the plea was not good ; for it may be that the measuring was false ; and therefore he ought to have averred, in
fact, that there were ten yards, and that it was so found upon the
measuring thereof." [3]

(2) In an action of trespass, for taking and carrying away the
plaintiff's goods, the defendant pleaded that the plaintiff never

---

[1] Pullin *v.* Nicholas, 1 Lev. 83 ; see
Com. Dig. Pleader, R. 6; *Semb. cont.*
Lea *v.* Luthell, Cro. Jac. 559.

[2] Bac. Ab. Pleas, &c. I. 5 ; Com.
Dig. E. 3 ; Co. Litt. 303 a ; Dy. 43 a ;
Wood *v.* Butts, Cro. Eliz. 260 ; Ledesham

v. Lubram, *ibid.* 870 ; Blackmore *v.*
Tidderley, 11 Mod. 38 ; s c. 2 Salk. 423 ;
Murray *v.* East India Company, 5 Barn.
& Ald. 215.

[3] Ledesham *v.* Lubram, *ubi supra.*

had any goods. "This is an infallible *argument*, that the defendant is not guilty, and yet it is no plea." [1]

(3) In ejectment, the defendant pleaded a surrender of a copyhold, by the hand of Fosset, then steward of the manor. The
plaintiff traversed *that Fosset was steward*. All the court held
this to be no issue, and that the traverse ought to be *that he
did not surrender;* for if he were not steward, the surrender is
void.[2]

The reason of this last decision appears to be, that to
deny that Fosset was steward could be only so far material as
it tended to show that the surrender was a nullity; and that
it was, therefore, an argumentative denial of the surrender;
which, if intended to be traversed, ought to be traversed in
a direct form.

Two Affirmatives do not make a Good Issue.

It is a branch of this rule *that two affirmatives do not make
a good issue*.[3] The reason is, that the traverse by the second
affirmative is *argumentative* in its nature.

Example: If it be alleged by the defendant that a party died
seised in fee, and the plaintiff allege that he died seised in tail,
this is not a good issue,[4] because the latter allegation amounts to
a denial of a seisin in fee, but denies it by argument or inference
only.

It is this branch of the rule against *argumentativeness* that
gave rise (as in part already explained) to the form of a
special traverse. Where, for any of the reasons mentioned
in a preceding part of this work, it becomes expedient for
a party traversing to set forth new affirmative matter tending to explain or qualify his denial, he is allowed to do
so; but as this, standing alone, will render his pleading
argumentative, he is required to add to his affirmative allegation an express denial, which is held to cure or prevent the
argumentativeness.[5] Thus, in the example last given, the

[1] Doct. Pl. 41; Dy. 43 a.
[2] Wood *v.* Butts, Cro. Eliz. 260.
[3] Com. Dig. Pleader, R. 3; Co. Litt.
126 a; per Buller, J., Chandler *v.*
Roberts, Doug. 60; Doct. Pl. 43, 360;
Zouch and Bamfield's Case, 1 Leon. 77.

[4] Doct. Pl. 349; 5 Hen. VII. 11, 12.
[5] Bac. Ab. Pleas, &c. H. 3; Courtney
v. Phelps, Sid. 301; Herring *v.* Blacklow,
Cro. Eliz. 30; 10 Hen. VI. 7, Pl. 21.

plaintiff may allege, if he pleases, that the party died seised in tail; but then he must add, *absque hoc, that he died seised in fee*, and thus resort to the form of a special traverse.[1]

Exception to Rule.

The doctrine, however, that two affirmatives do not make a good issue, is not taken so strictly but that the issue will, in some cases, be good, if there is sufficient negative and affirmative in *effect*, though, in the *form of words*, there be a double affirmative.

Example: In debt on a lease for years, where the defendant pleaded that the plaintiff had nothing at the time of the lease made, and the plaintiff replied that he was seised in fee, this was held a good issue.[2]

Two Negatives do not make a Good Issue.

Another branch of the rule against argumentativeness is *that two negatives do not make a good issue.*[3]

Example: If the defendant plead that he requested the plaintiff to deliver an abstract of his title, but that the plaintiff did not, when so requested, deliver such abstract, but neglected so to do, the plaintiff can not reply that *he did not neglect and refuse to deliver* such abstract, but should allege affirmatively that *he did deliver.*[4]

Rule IV. Pleadings must not be Hypothetical, or in the Alternative.[5]

Examples: (1) In an action of debt against a jailer for the escape of a prisoner, where the defendant pleaded that *if* the said prisoner did, at any time or times after the said commitment, &c., go at large, he so escaped without the knowledge of the defendant, and against his will; and that, *if* any such escape was made, the prisoner voluntarily returned into custody before the defendant knew of the escape, &c.; the court held the plea bad: for "he can not plead hypothetically that if there has been an escape there

---

[1] Doct. Pl. 349.

[2] Co. Litt. 126 a; Reg. Plac. 297, 298; and see Tomlin *v.* Burlace, 1 Wils. 6.

[3] Com. Dig. Pleader, R. 3.

[4] Martin *v.* Smith, 6 East, 557.

[5] Griffiths *v.* Eyles, 1 Bos. & Pul. 413; Cook *v.* Cox, 3 M. & S. 114; The King *v.* Brereton, 8 Mod. 330; Witherley *v.* Sarsfield, 1 Show. 127.

has also been a return.   He must either stand upon an averment that there has been no escape, or that there have been one, two, or ten escapes, after which the prisoner returned." [1]

(2) Where it was charged that the defendant wrote and published, *or* caused to be written and published, a certain libel, this was considered as bad for uncertainty. [2]

RULE V.   PLEADINGS MUST NOT BE BY WAY OF RECITAL, BUT MUST BE POSITIVE IN THEIR FORM. [3]

Example: If a declaration in trespass, for assault and battery, make the charge in the following form of expression: "*and thereupon the said A. B., by ——, his attorney, complains, for that whereas the said C. D. heretofore, to wit, &c., made an assault,*" &c., instead of "*for that the said C. D. heretofore, to wit, &c., made an assault,*" &c. — this is bad; for nothing is positively affirmed. [4]

Where a deed or other instrument is pleaded, it is generally not proper to allege (though in the words of the instrument itself) that *it is witnessed (testatum existit)* that such a party granted, &c.; but it should be stated absolutely and directly that he granted, &c.   But, as to this point, a difference has been established between declarations and other pleadings.   In the former (for example, in a declaration of covenant) it is sufficient to set forth the instrument with a *testatum existit*, though not in the latter.   And the reason given is, that, in a declaration, such statement is merely inducement; that is, introductory to some other direct allegation.   Thus, in covenant, it is introductory to the assignment of the breach. [5]

---

[1] Griffiths *v.* Eyles, 1 Bos. & Pul. 413.

[2] The King *v.* Brereton, 8 Mod. 330.

[3] Bac. Ab. Pleas, &c. B. 4; Sherland *r.* Heaton, 2 Bulst. 214; Wettenhall *v.* Sherwin, 2 Lev. 206; Mors *v.* Thacker, *ibid.* 193; Hore *v.* Chapman, 2 Salk. 636; Dunstall *v.* Dunstall, 2 Show. 27; Gourney *v.* Fletcher, *ibid.* 295; Dobbs *v.* Edmunds, 2 Ld. Raym. 1413; Wilder *v.* Handy, Str. 1151; Marshall *v.* Riggs, *ibid.* 1162.

[4] See the authorities last cited. *It*

will be observed, however, that in trespass on the case, the "whereas" is unobjectionable, being used only as introductory to some subsequent positive allegation. See also Min. Inst. IV. 572, 1017, 1018. Professor Minor recommends the use of the following formula: "*for this, to wit.*"

[5] Bultivant *v.* Holman, Cro. Jac. 537; 1 Saund. 274, n. 1. (See the form of declaring with a *testatum existit*. 3 Went. 352, 523.)

RULE VI. THINGS ARE TO BE PLEADED ACCORDING TO THEIR
LEGAL EFFECT OR OPERATION.[1]

The meaning is, that in stating an instrument or other
matter in pleading, it should be set forth, not according to its
terms, or its *form*, but according to its *effect in law;* and the
reason seems to be, that it is under the latter aspect that it
must principally and ultimately be considered; and therefore,
to plead it in terms or form only, is an indirect and circuitous
method of allegation.

Examples: (1) If a joint tenant conveys to his companion by
the words " gives," " grants," &c., his estate in the lands holden
in jointure, this, though in its terms a *grant*, is not properly
such in operation of law, but amounts to that species of conveyance called a *release*. It should therefore be pleaded, not
that he " *granted,*" &c., but that he " *released,*" &c.[2]

(2) If a tenant for life grant his estate to him in reversion,
this is, in effect, a *surrender*, and must be pleaded as such, and
not as a *grant*.[3]

(3) Where the plea stated that A. was entitled to an equity of
redemption, and, subject thereto, that B. was seised in fee, and
that they, by lease and release, granted, &c., the premises, excepting and reserving to A. and his heirs, &c., a liberty of
hunting, &c., it was held upon general demurrer, and afterwards upon writ of error, that as A. had no legal interest in
the land there could be no *reservation* to him; that the plea,
therefore, alleging the right (though in terms of the deed) by
way of *reservation* was bad; and that if (as was contended in
argument) the deed would operate as a *grant* of the right, the
plea should have been so pleaded, and should have alleged a
grant and not a *reservation*.[4]

The rule in question is, in its terms, often confined to
deeds and *conveyances*. It extends, however, to all instruments in writing, and contracts, written or verbal; and,

---

[1] Bac. Ab. Pleas, &c. I. 7; Com.
Dig. Pleader, C. 37; 2 Saund. 97, and
97 b, n. 2; Barker *v.* Lade, 4 Mod. 150;
Howel *v.* Richards, 11 East, 633; Moore
v. Earl of Plymouth, 3 Barn. & Ald. 66;
Stroud *v.* Lady Gerard, 1 Salk. 8; 1
Saund. 235 b, n. 9.

[2] 2 Saund. 97; Barker *v.* Lade, 4
Mod. 150, 151.

[3] Barker *v.* Lade, 4 Mod. 151.

[4] Moore *v.* Earl of Plymouth, *ubi
supra.*

indeed, it may be said, generally, to all matters or transactions whatever which a party may have occasion to allege in pleading, and in which the form is distinguishable from the legal effect.[1]

EXCEPTION.

But *there is an exception in the case of a declaration for written or verbal slander*, where (as the action turns on the words themselves) *the words themselves must be set forth;* and it is not sufficient to allege that the defendant published a libel, containing false and scandalous matters, in substance as follows, &c., or used words to *the effect* following, &c.[2]

RULE VII. PLEADINGS SHOULD OBSERVE THE KNOWN AND ANCIENT FORMS OF EXPRESSION, AS CONTAINED IN APPROVED PRECEDENTS.[3]

Thus, so long ago as in the time of Bracton, in the count on a writ of right there were certain words of form, besides those contained in the writ, which were considered as essential to be inserted. It was necessary to allege "*the seisin*" of the ancestor "*in his demesne as of fee*" — and "*of right*" — "*by taking the esplees*" — "*in the time of such a king*" — and (if the seisin were alleged at a period of civil commotion) "*in time of peace.*"[4] And all this is equally necessary in framing a count on a writ of right at the present day; and no parallel or synonymous expressions will supply the omission.[5] So, too, the *general issues* are examples of forms of expression fixed by ancient usage from which it is improper

---

[1] Stroud *v.* Lady Gerard, 1 Salk 8.

[2] Wright *v.* Clements, 3 Barn. & Ald. 503; Cook *r.* Cox, 3 M. & S. 110; Newton *v.* Stubbs, 2 Show. 435. But in an action for a malicious prosecution, if the declaration states merely that the defendant, without reasonable or probable cause, indicted the plaintiff for perjury, without setting forth the indictment, this is sufficient after verdict. (Pippet *v.* Hearn, 5 Barn. & Ald. 634.) See also Blizard *v.* Kelly, 2 Barn. & Cress. 283; Davis *v.* Noake, 6 M. & S. 33.

[3] Com. Dig. Abatement, G. 7; Buckley *v.* Rice Thomas, Plow. 123; Dally *v.* King, 1 H. Bl 1; Slade *v.* Dowland, 2 Bos. & Pul 570; Dowland *v.* Slade, 5 East, 272; King *v.* Fraser, 6 East, 351; Dyster *r.* Battye, 3 Barn. & Ald. 448; per Abbott, C. J., Wright *v.* Clements, *ibid.* 507.

[4] Bract. 373 a, b.

[5] Slade *v.* Dowland, *ubi supra;* Dally *v.* King, *ubi supra;* Dowland *v.* Slade, *ubi supra.*

to depart. And another illustration of this rule occurs in the following modern case : —

Example : To an action on the case, the defendants pleaded the statute of limitations, viz., *that they were not guilty within six years, &c.* The court decided, upon special demurrer, that this form of pleading was bad, upon the ground that "from the passing of the statute to the present case the invariable form of pleading the statute to an action on the case for a wrong has been to allege *that the cause of action did not accrue within six years, &c. ;*" and that "it was important to the administration of justice that the usual and established forms of pleading should be observed."[1]

It may be remarked, however, with respect to this rule, that the allegations to which it relates are of course only those of frequent and ordinary recurrence ; and that even as to these, it is rather of uncertain application, as it must be often doubtful whether a given form of expression has been so fixed by the course of precedent as to admit of no variation.

Another rule, connected in some measure, with the last, and apparently referable to the same object, is the following :

RULE VIII. PLEADINGS SHOULD HAVE THEIR PROPER FORMAL COMMENCEMENTS AND CONCLUSIONS.[2]

This rule refers to certain *formulæ* occurring at the *commencement* of pleadings subsequent to the declaration, and to others occurring at the *conclusion.*

A formula of the latter kind, inasmuch as it prays the judgment of the court for the party pleading, is often denominated the *prayer of judgment,* and occurs (it is to be observed) *in all pleadings that do not tender issue,* but in *those only.*

FORMAL COMMENCEMENTS AND CONCLUSIONS OF DILATORY PLEAS.

A PLEA TO THE JURISDICTION has usually no *commencement* of the kind in question.[3] Its *conclusion* is as follows :

---

[1] Dyster *v.* Battye, 3 Barn. & Ald. 448.

[2] Co. Litt. 303 b ; Com. Dig. Pleader, E. 27, E. 28, E. 32, E. 33, F. 4, F. 5, G. 1 ; Com. Dig. Abatement, I. 12 ; 2

Saund. 209, n. 1 ; per Holt, C. J., Bowyer *v.* Cook, 5 Mod. 146.

[3] But sometimes it has such commencement. Chit Pl. 399.

— the said C. D. prays judgment if the court of our lord the king here will or ought to have further cognizance of the plea[1] aforesaid.

or (in some cases) thus : —

— the said C. D. prays judgment if he ought to be compelled to answer to the said plea here in court.[2]

A PLEA IN SUSPENSION seems also to be generally pleaded without a formal *commencement*.[3] Its *conclusion* (in the case of a plea of *nonage)* is thus : —

— the said C. D. prays that the parol may demur (or that the said plea may stay and be respited) until the full age of him, the said C. D., &c.[4]

A PLEA IN ABATEMENT is also usually pleaded without a formal *commencement*, within the meaning of this rule.[5] The *conclusion* is thus : —

in case of plea to the *writ* or *bill*,

— prays judgment of the said writ and declaration *(or* bill), and that the same may be quashed.[6]

in case of plea to the *person*,

— prays judgment if the said A. B. ought to be answered to his said declaration *(or* bill).[7]

---

[1] 1 Went. 49 ; Bl. Com. III. 303 * ; Powers *v.* Cook, 1 Ld. Raym. 63.

[2] 1 Went. 41, 49 ; Bac. Ab. Pleas, &c. E. 2 ; per Holt, C. J., Bowyer *v.* Cook, 5 Mod. 146 ; Powers *v.* Cook, *ubi supra.*

[3] Plasket *v.* Beeby, 4 East, 485.

[4] 1 Went. 43. As to the form, in *other* pleas in suspension, see Lib. Plac. 9, 10 ; 1 Went. 15 ; 2 Saund. 210, n. 1 ; John Trollop's Case, 8 Co. Rep. 69 ; Reg. Plac 180 ; Onslow *v.* Smith, 2 Bos. & Pul. 384.

[5] 2 Saund. 209 a, n. 1 ; 1 Arch. 305 ; Lutw. 11. But if a matter *apparent on the face of the writ* be pleaded, there should be a *commencement*. See this matter explained, Saund. and Arch. *ibid.*, to which the reader is referred generally for the learning on the subject of these *formulæ* of pleas in abatement.

[6] Powers *v.* Cook, *ubi supra ;* 2 Saund. *ubi supra ;* Com. Dig. Abatement, I. 12. Yet in some instances, it seems, it may be *si curia cognoscere velit* (if the court will take cognizance). (Chatland *v.* Thornly, 12 East, 544.) In proceedings by *bill*, it seems that it is informal to pray judgment of the *declaration*, or of the *bill and declaration*.

[7] Co. Litt. 128 a ; Com. Dig. Abatement, I. 12 ; 1 Went. 58, 62.

FORMAL COMMENCEMENTS AND CONCLUSIONS OF PLEAS IN BAR.

A PLEA IN BAR has this *commencement :* —

— says that the said A. B. ought not to have or maintain his aforesaid action against him, the said C. D., because, he says, &c.

This formula is commonly called *actio non.*

The *conclusion* is,

— prays judgment if the said A. B. ought to have or maintain his aforesaid action against him.

FORMAL COMMENCEMENTS AND CONCLUSIONS OF REPLICATIONS.

A REPLICATION TO A PLEA TO THE JURISDICTION has this *commencement :* —

— says that notwithstanding anything by the said C. D. above alleged, the court of our lord the king here ought not to be precluded from having further cognizance of the plea aforesaid, because, he says, &c.[1]

or this : —

— says that the said C. D. ought to answer to the said plea here in court, because, he says, &c.[2]

and this *conclusion :* —

— wherefore he prays judgment, and that the court here may take cognizance of the plea aforesaid, and that the said C. D. may answer over, &c.[3]

A REPLICATION TO A PLEA IN SUSPENSION (in the case of a plea of *nonage)* has this *commencement :* —

— says that notwithstanding anything by the said C. D. above alleged, the parol ought not further to demur *(or,* the said plea ought not further to stay, or be respited), because, he says, &c.[4]

And (if there be any case in which such replication does not tender issue) it should probably have this *conclusion :* —

[1] 1 Went. 60; Lib. Plac. 348.
[2] 1 Went. 39.
[3] Lib. Plac. 348; 1 Went. 39.
[4] Liber Intrat.

— wherefore he prays judgment if the parol ought further to demur *(or*, if the said plea ought further to stay, or be respited), and that the said C. D. may answer over.

A REPLICATION TO A PLEA IN ABATEMENT has this *commencement :* —

where the plea was to the *writ* or *bill,*

— says that his said writ and declaration *(or* bill), by reason of anything in the said plea alleged, ought not to be quashed; because, he says, &c.[1]

where the plea was to the *person,*

— says that notwithstanding anything in the said plea alleged, he, the said A. B., ought to be answered to his said declaration *(or* bill) ; because he says, &c.[2]

The *conclusion,* in most cases, is thus : —

where the plea was to the *writ* or *bill,*

— wherefore he prays judgment, and that the said writ and declaration *(or* bill) may be adjudged good, and that the said C. D. may answer over, &c.

where the plea was to the *person,*

— wherefore he prays judgment, and that the said C. D. may answer over, &c.[3]

A REPLICATION TO A PLEA IN BAR has this *commencement : —*

— says that by reason of anything in the said plea alleged, he ought not to be barred from having and maintaining his aforesaid action against him, the said C. D. ; because, he says, &c.

This formula is commonly called *precludi non.*

The *conclusion* is thus : —

in *debt,*

— wherefore he prays judgment, and his debt aforesaid, together

---

[1] 1 Arch. 309; Rast. Ent. 126 a; Sabine *v.* Johnstone, 1 Bos. & Pul. 60.

[2] 1 Went. 42; 1 Arch. 309.

[3] 1 Went. 43, 45, 54; 1 Arch. 309; Rast. Ent. 126 a; Bisse *v.* Harcourt, 3 Mod. 281; s. c. 1 Salk. 177; 1 Show. 155; Carth. 137. As to the cases in which the *conclusion* should be different, and should pray damages, see 2 Saund. 211, n. 3 ; Medina *v.* Stoughton, 1 Ld. Raym. 594; Co. Ent. 160 a; Lil. Ent. 123 ; Lib. Plac. 1.

with his damages by him sustained by reason of the detention thereof, to be adjudged to him.

in *covenant,*

— wherefore he prays judgment, and his damages by him sustained by reason of the said breach of covenant, to be adjudged to him.

in *trespass,*

— wherefore he prays judgment, and his damages by him sustained by reason of the committing of the said trespasses, to be adjudged to him.

in *trespass on the case, in assumpsit,*

— wherefore he prays judgment, and his damages by him sustained by reason of the not performing of the said several promises and undertakings, to be adjudged to him.

in *trespass on the case, in general,*

— wherefore he prays judgment, and his damages by him sustained by reason of the committing of the said several grievances, to be adjudged to him.

And so, in all *other actions,* the replication concludes with a prayer of judgment for damages or other appropriate redress, according to the nature of the action.

PLEADINGS SUBSEQUENT TO THE REPLICATION.

With respect to PLEADINGS SUBSEQUENT TO THE REPLICATION, it will be sufficient to observe, generally, that those on the part of the defendant follow the same form of *commencement* and *conclusion* as the plea; those on the part of the plaintiff, the same as the replication.

These forms are subject to the following variations : —

First, with respect to *pleas in abatement.* Matters of abatement, generally, only render the writ *abatable* upon plea; but there are others, such as the death of the plaintiff or defendant before verdict or judgment by default, that are said to abate it *de facto ;* that is, by their own immediate effect, and before plea; the only use of the plea, in such cases, being to give the court notice of the fact.[1] Where the writ is merely *abatable*, the forms of *conclusion* above given are to be observed; but, when abated *de facto*, the *conclusion* must pray, "*whether the court will further proceed;*" for the writ being already, and *ipso facto*, abated, it would be improper to pray "*that it may be quashed.*"[2]

Again, when a plea in bar is pleaded *puis darreign continuance*, it has, instead of the ordinary *actio non*, a *commencement* and *conclusion* of *actio non ulterius* (action not further).

So, if a plea in bar be founded on any matter arising *after the commencement of the action*, though it be not pleaded *after a previous plea*, and therefore not *puis darreign continuance*, yet it pursues, in that case also, in its *commencement* and *conclusion*, the same form of *actio non ulterius*, instead of *actio non* generally;[3] for the *actio non* is taken to refer, in point of time, to the commencement of the suit, and not to the time of plea pleaded, and would, therefore, in the case supposed, be improper.[4]

COMMENCEMENTS AND CONCLUSIONS OF PLEADINGS BY WAY OF ESTOPPEL.

All pleadings by way of *estoppel* have a *commencement* and *conclusion* peculiar to themselves.

A *plea* in estoppel has the following *commencement :* —

"*says that the said A. B. ought not to be admitted to say*" (stating the allegation to which the estoppel relates);

and the following *conclusion :* —

"*wherefore he prays judgment if the said A. B. ought to be admitted, against his own acknowledgment, by his deed aforesaid*" (or otherwise, according to the matter of the estoppel), "*to say that*" (stating the allegation to which the estoppel relates).[5]

---

1 Bac. Ab. Abatement, K., G., F.; Com. Dig. Abatement, E. 17; 2 Saund. 210, n. 1.

2 Com. Dig. Abatement, H. 33, I. 12; 2 Saund. 210, n. 1; Hallowes v. Lucy, 3 Lev. 120.

3 Le Bret v. Papillon, 4 East, 502.

4 Le Bret v. Papillon, *ubi supra;* Evans v. Prosser, 3 T. R. 186; Selw. N. P. 138.

5 1 Arch. 202; Veale v. Warner, 1 Saund 325; 3 Edw. III. 21.

A *replication*, by way of estoppel, to a plea, either in abate-ment or bar, has this *commencement :* —

" *says that the said C. D. ought not to be admitted to plead the said plea by him above pleaded ; because, he says,*" &c.[1]

Its *conclusion,* in case of a plea in *abatement,* is as follows :

" *wherefore he prays judgment if the said C. D. ought to be admitted to his said plea, contrary to his own acknowledgment, &c., and that he may answer over,*" &c.

In case of a plea in *bar :* —

wherefore he prays "*judgment if the said C. D. ought to be admitted, contrary to his own acknowledgment, &c., to plead, that* " (stating the allegation to which the estoppel relates).

Rejoinders and subsequent pleadings follow the forms of pleas and replications respectively.[2]

When Pleading is to a Part only of Adverse Matter.

If any pleading be intended to apply to part only of the matter adversely alleged, it must be qualified accordingly, in its *commencement* and *conclusion.*[3]

Variations in Replevin.

Another variation occurs in the action of *replevin.*

Avowries and cognizances, instead of being pleaded with *actio non* commence thus : an avowry, that the defendant "*well avows ;* " a cognizance, that he "*well acknowledges*" the tak-ing, &c. ; and conclude thus : that the defendant "*prays judg-ment and a return of the said goods and chattels, together with his damages, &c., according to the form of the statute in such case made and provided, to be adjudged to him,*" &c.

And the subsequent pleadings have corresponding variations.

Variations in Actions of Debt on Bond.

Lastly, when in an action of *debt on bond,* some matter is pleaded in bar, tending to show that the plaintiff *never had any right of action,* and not matter *in discharge of a right*

---

[1] Took *v.* Glascock, 1 Saund. 257.   [3] Weeks *v.* Peach, 1 Salk. 179.
[2] Veale *v.* Warner, 1 Saund. 325.

once existing (as, for example, when it is pleaded that the bond was void for some illegality), the plea in that case, instead of *actio non*, has the following *commencement*, commonly called *onerari non* :

" *says that he ought not to be charged with the said debt, by virtue of the said supposed writing obligatory, because, he says,*" &c.

And the *conclusion* is thus : " *wherefore he prays judgment if he ought to be charged with the said debt by virtue of the said supposed writing obligatory.*"[1]

EXCEPTION TO RULE.

While pleadings have thus, generally, the formal *commencements* and *conclusions*, there is an exception (as already noticed) in the case of all such pleadings as *tender issue*. These, instead of the conclusion with a *prayer of judgment*, as in the above forms, conclude (in the case of the trial by jury) *to the country ;* or (if a different mode of trial be proposed) with other appropriate *formulæ*, as already explained. Pleadings which tender issue have, however, the formal *commencements*, with the exception of the *general issues*, which have neither formal commencement nor conclusion, in the sense to which the present rule refers.

EFFECT OF ERROR IN FORMAL COMMENCEMENTS OR CONCLUSIONS OF PLEADINGS.

A defect or impropriety in the *commencement* and *conclusion* of a pleading is generally ground for demurrer.[2] But if the *commencement* pray the proper judgment, it seems to be sufficient, though judgment be prayed in an improper form in the *conclusion*.[3] And the converse case, as to a right prayer

---

[1] Com. Dig. Pleader, E. 27 ; Brown *v.* Cornish, Salk. 516 ; Bennet *v.* Filkins, 1 Saund. 14 b.; *ibid.* 290, n. 3.

[2] Nowlan *v.* Geddes, 1 East, 634 ; Wilson *v.* Kemp, 2 M. & S. 549 ; Le Bret *v.* Papillon, 4 East, 502 ; Com. Dig. Pleader, E. 27 ; Weeks *v.* Peach, 1 Salk. 179 ; Powell *v.* Fullerton, 2 Bos. & Pul. 420. But in some cases, a bad conclusion makes the plea a mere nullity, and operates as a *discontinuance.* Bisse *v.* Harcourt, 3 Mod. 281 ; s. c. 1 Salk. 177 ; 1 Show. 155 ; Carth. 137 ; Weeks *v.* Peach, *ubi supra.*

[3] Street *v.* Hopkinson, Rep. Temp Hard. 345.

in the *conclusion*, with an improper *commencement*, has been decided the same way.[1] So, if judgment be simply prayed, without specifying *what* judgment, it is said to be sufficient; and it is laid down that the court will, in that case, *ex officio*, award the proper legal consequence.[2] It seems, however, that these relaxations from the rule do not apply to pleas in *abatement;* the court requiring greater strictness in these pleas, in order to discourage their use.[3]

THE CONCLUSION MAKES THE PLEADING.

It will be observed that the *commencement* and *conclusion* of a plea are in such form as to indicate the intention with which it is pleaded, and to mark its object and tendency, as being either *to the jurisdiction, in suspension, in abatement,* or *in bar.* It is therefore held that the class and character of a plea depend upon these, its formular parts; this is ordinarily expressed by the maxim, *conclusio facit placitum* (the conclusion makes the plea).[4] Accordingly, *if it commence and conclude as in bar, but contain matter sufficient only to abate the writ, it is a bad plea in bar, and no plea in abatement.*[5] And, on the other hand, it has been held that *if a plea commence and conclude as in abatement, and show matter in bar, it is a plea in abatement and not in bar.*[6]

As the *commencement* and *conclusion* have this effect of defining the character of the *plea*, so they have the same tendency in the *replication* and *subsequent pleadings.* For example, they serve to show whether the pleading be intended as in *confession and avoidance* or *estoppel*, and whether intended to be pleaded *to the whole* or *to part.* From these considerations it is apparent that they are forms which, on

---

[1] Talbot *v.* Hopewood, Fort. 335.

[2] Le Bret *v.* Papillon, 4 East, 502; 1 Saund. 97, n. 1; Chit. Pl. 394, 395, 476, 477.

[3] The King *v.* Shakespeare, 10 East, 83; Attwood *v.* Davis, 1 Barn. & Ald. 172.

[4] Street *v.* Hopkinson, Rep. Temp. Hard. 346; Medina *v.* Stoughton, 1 Ld.

Raym. 593; Talbot *v.* Hopewood, *ubi supra.*

[5] Nowlan *v.* Geddes, 1 East, 634; Wallis *v.* Savil, 1 Lutw. 41; 2 Saund. 209 d, n. 1; per Littleton, J., 36 Hen. VI. 18; Medina *v.* Stoughton, *ubi supra.*

[6] Medina *v.* Stoughton, *ubi supra;* Godson *v.* Good, 6 Taunt. 587.

the whole, materially tend to clearness and precision in pleading; and they have, for that reason, been considered under this section.

In connection with the rule last mentioned, and to further the same objects of clearness and precision, the following rule is established : —

RULE IX. A PLEADING WHICH IS BAD IN PART IS BAD ALTOGETHER.[1]

The meaning of this rule is that, *if in any material part of a pleading*, or with reference to any of the material things which it undertakes to answer, or to either of the parties answering, *the pleading be bad*, though in other respects it be free from objection, *the whole of it is open to demurrer ;* so that, if the objection be good, the whole pleading in question is overruled, and judgment given accordingly.

Examples : (1) If in a declaration of *assumpsit* two different promises be alleged in two different counts, and the defendant plead in bar to both counts conjointly the statute of limitations, viz., that he did not promise within six years, and the plea be an insufficient answer as to one of the counts, but a good bar to the other, *the whole plea* is bad, and neither promise is sufficiently answered.[2]

(2) Where to an action of trespass for false imprisonment against two defendants, they pleaded that one of them, A., having ground to believe that his horse had been stolen by the plaintiff, gave him in charge to the other defendant, a constable, whereupon the constable and A., in his aid and by his command, laid hands on the plaintiff, &c., the plea was adjudged to be bad as to both defendants, because it showed no reasonable ground of suspicion: for A. could not justify the arrest without showing such ground ; and though the case might be different as to the constable, whose duty was to act on the charge, and not to deliberate, yet as he had not pleaded separately, but had joined in A.'s justification, the plea was bad as to him also.[3]

---

[1] Com. Dig. Pleader, E. 36, F. 25; 1 Saund. 28, n. 2; Webb v. Martin, 1 Lev. 48; Rowe v. Tutte, Willes, 14; Trueman v. Hurst, 1 T. R. 40; Webber v. Tivill, 2 Saund. 127; Duffield v. Scott, 3 T. R. 374; Hedges v. Chapman, 2 Bing. 523; Earl of St. Germains v. Willan, 2 Barn. & Cress. 216.

[2] Webb v. Martin, *ubi supra.*

[3] Hedges v. Chapman, *ubi supra.*

This rule seems to result from that which requires each pleading to have *its proper formal commencement and conclusion.* For by those forms (it will be observed) the matter which any pleading contains is offered as *an entire answer to the whole* of that which last preceded.

Example: In the first example above given, the defendant would allege, in the commencement of his plea, that the plaintiff *"ought not to have or maintain his action"* for the reason therein assigned; and, therefore, he would pray judgment, &c., as to the whole *action* in the conclusion. If, therefore, the answer be insufficient as to one count, it can not avail as to the other; because, if taken as a plea to the latter only, the *commencement* and *conclusion* would be wrong. It is to be observed that there is but one plea, and consequently but one commencement and conclusion; but if the defendant should plead the statute in bar *to the first count separately,* and then plead it to the second count with a new commencement and conclusion, *thus making two pleas instead of one,* the invalidity of one of these pleas could not vitiate the other.

RULE NOT APPLICABLE TO THE DECLARATION.

As the *declaration* contains no commencement or conclusion of the kind to which the last rule relates, so, on the other hand, the *declaration* does not fall within the rule now in question. Therefore, if a declaration be good in part, though bad as to another part relating to a distinct demand divisible from the rest, and the defendant demur to the whole, instead of confining his demurrer to the faulty part only, the court will give judgment for the plaintiff.[1] It is also to be observed that the rule *applies only to material allegations;* for where the objectionable matter is *mere surplusage,* and unnecessarily introduced (the answer being complete without it), its introduction does not vitiate the rest of the pleading.[2]

---

[1] 1 Saund. 286, n. 9; Bac. Ab. Pleas, &c. B. 6; Cutforthay *v.* Taylor, 1 Ld. Raym. 395; Judin *v.* Samuel, 1 N. R. 43; Benbridge *v.* Day, 1 Salk. 218; Pow-dick *v.* Lyon, 11 East, 565; Amory *v.* Brodrick, 5 Barn. & Ald. 712.

[2] Duffield *v.* Scott, 3 T. R. 377.

CHAPTER XIV.

OF RULES WHICH TEND TO PREVENT PROLIXITY AND DELAY IN PLEADING.

RULE I. THERE MUST BE NO DEPARTURE IN PLEADING.[1]

A DEPARTURE TAKES PLACE WHEN, IN ANY PLEADING, THE PARTY DESERTS THE GROUND THAT HE TOOK IN HIS LAST ANTECEDENT PLEADING AND RESORTS TO ANOTHER.[2]

"Each party," says Lord Coke, "must take heed of the ordering of the matter of his pleading, lest his replication *depart* from his count, or his rejoinder from his bar. A departure in pleading is said to be when the second plea containeth matter not pursuant to his former, and which *fortifieth* not the same."[3]

A departure obviously can never take place till the *replication*.

A DEPARTURE MAY BE EITHER:

(1) *In Point of Fact;*
(2) *In Point of Law.*

(1) DEPARTURE IN POINT OF FACT.

Of departure in the *replication* the following is an

Example: In *assumpsit* the plaintiffs, as executors, declared on several promises alleged to have been *made to the testator* in his lifetime. The defendant pleaded that she did not promise within six years before the obtaining of the original writ of the

---

[1] Co. Litt. 304; Richards *v.* Hodges, 2 Saund. 84; Dudlow *v.* Watchorn, 16 East, 39; Tolputt *v.* Wells, 1 M. & S. 395; Fisher *v.* Pimbley, 11 East, 188; Winstone *v.* Linn, 1 Barn. & Cress. 460. And see the numerous authorities collected in Com. Dig. Pleader, F. 7, F. 11; Bac. Ab. Pleas, &c. L.; Vin. Ab. tit. Departure; 1 Arch. 247, 253.

[2] Co. Litt. 304 a; 2 Saund. 84, n. 1.

[3] Co. Litt. *ubi supra.*

plaintiffs. The plaintiffs replied that, within six years before the obtaining of the original writ, the letters testamentary were granted to them, whereby the action accrued *to them, the said plaintiffs*, within six years. The court held this to be a departure; as in the declaration they had *laid promises to the testator*, but in the replication *alleged the right of action to accrue to themselves as executors*.[1] They ought to have laid promises to themselves, as executors, in the declaration, if they meant to put their action on this ground.

But a departure does not occur so frequently in the replication as in the *rejoinder*.

Examples : (1) In debt on a bond conditioned to perform an award, so that the same were delivered to the defendant by a certain time, the defendant pleaded that the arbitrators *did not make any award*. The plaintiff replied that the arbitrators did make an award to such an effect, and that the same was tendered by the proper time. The defendant rejoined *that the award was not so tendered*. On demurrer, it was objected that the rejoinder was a departure from the plea in bar; "for, in the plea in bar, the defendant says that the arbitrators *made no award;* and now, in his rejoinder, he has *implicitly confessed* that the arbitrators *have made an award*, but says that *it was not tendered* according to the condition; which is a plain departure: for it is one thing *not to make an award* and another thing *not to tender it when made*. And although both these things are necessary by the condition of the bond to bind the defendant to perform the award, yet the defendant ought only to rely upon one or the other by itself," &c. "But if the truth had been that although the award was made, yet it was not tendered according to the condition, the defendant should have pleaded so at first in his plea," &c. And the court gave judgment accordingly.[2]

(2) In debt on a bond conditioned to keep the plaintiffs harmless and indemnified from all suits, &c., of one Thomas Cook, the defendants pleaded *that they had kept the plaintiffs harmless*,[3] &c. The plaintiffs replied that Cook sued them, and so the defendants had not kept them harmless, &c. The defendants rejoined *that they had not any notice of the damnification*. And the court held, first, that the matter of the rejoinder was bad, as the plaintiffs were not bound to give notice; and,

---

[1] Hickman *v.* Walker, Willes, 27.

[2] Roberts *v.* Mariett, 2 Saund. 188.

[3] This plea was bad, for not showing

how they had kept harmless (1 Saund. 117, n. 1); but *the court held the fault cured by pleading over*.

secondly, that the rejoinder was a departure from the plea in bar; "for, in the bar, the defendants pleaded that they have saved harmless the plaintiffs, and, in the rejoinder, confess that they have not saved harmless, but that they had not notice of the damnification; which is a plain departure."[1]

(3) In debt on a bond conditioned to perform the covenants in an indenture of lease, one of which was that the lessee, at every felling of wood, would make a fence, the defendant pleaded *that he had not felled any wood, &c.* The plaintiff replied that he felled two acres of wood, but made no fence. The defendant rejoined *that he did make a fence.* This was adjudged a departure.[2]

These, it will be observed, are cases in which the party deserts, in point of *fact*, the ground that he had first taken.

(2) DEPARTURE IN POINT OF LAW.[3]

But it is also a departure if he puts the same facts on a new ground in point of *law;* as if he relies on *the effect of the common law* in his declaration, and *on a custom* in his replication; or on the effect of the common law in his plea, and on a *statute* in his rejoinder.

Examples: (1) Thus, where the plaintiff declared in covenant on an indenture of apprenticeship, by which the defendant was to serve him for seven years, and assigned, as breach of covenant, that the defendant departed within the seven years, and the defendant pleaded infancy, to which the plaintiff replied that, by the custom of London, infants may bind themselves apprentices, this was considered as a departure.[4]

(2) In trespass, the defendant made title to the premises, pleading a *demise for fifty years* made by the college of R. The plaintiff replied that there was another prior lease of the same premises, which had been assigned to the defendant, and which was unexpired at the time of making the said lease for fifty years; and alleged a proviso in the act of 31 Hen. VIII. c. 13, avoiding all leases by the colleges to which that act relates made under such circumstances as the lease last mentioned. The defendant, in his rejoinder, pleaded another proviso in the statute, which allowed such leases to be good *for twenty-one years*, if made to the same person, &c.; and that, by virtue thereof, the demise

---

[1] Cutler *v.* Southern, 1 Saund. 116.
[2] Dy. 253 b.
[3] For a recent case involving this

sort of departure, see Union Pacific R. R. Co. *v.* Wyler, 158 U. S. 285.
[4] Mole *v.* Wallis, 1 Lev. 81.

stated in his plea was available for twenty-one years at least. The judges held the rejoinder to be a departure from the plea; "for, *in the bar, he pleads a lease of fifty years,* and, in the rejoinder, *he concludes upon a lease for twenty-one years,*" &c. And they observed that "the defendant might have shown the statute and the whole matter at first."[1]

To show more distinctly the nature of a departure, it may be useful, on the other hand, to give some examples of cases that have been held *not* to fall within that objection.

Examples: (1) In debt on a bond conditioned to perform covenants, one of which was that the defendant should account for all sums of money that he should receive, the defendant pleaded performance. The plaintiff replied that £26 came to his hands for which he had not accounted. The defendant rejoined that he accounted *modo sequente* (in manner following), viz., that certain malefactors broke into his counting-house and stole the money, of which fact he acquainted the plaintiff. And it was argued on demurrer "that the rejoinder is a departure; for fulfilling a covenant to account can not be intended but by actual accounting; whereas the rejoinder does not show an account, but an excuse for not accounting." But the court held that showing he was robbed is giving an account, and therefore there was no departure.[2]

(2) In debt on a bond conditioned to indemnify the plaintiff from all tonnage of certain coals due to W. B., the defendant pleaded *non damnificatus;* to which the plaintiff replied that for £5 of tonnage of coals due to W. B. his barge was distrained; and the defendant rejoined that *no tonnage was due* to W. B. for the coals. To this the plaintiff demurred, "supposing the rejoinder to be a departure from the plea; for the defendant having pleaded generally that the plaintiff was not damnified, and the plaintiff having assigned a breach, the matter of the rejoinder is only by way of excuse, confessing and avoiding the breach; which ought to have been done at first, and not after a general plea of indemnity. On the other side, it was insisted that it was not necessary for the defendant to set out all his case at first, and it suffices that his bar is supported and strengthened by his rejoinder. And of this opinion was the court."[3]

[1] Fulmerston *v.* Steward, Plowd. 102; s. c. Dy. 102 b.
[2] Vere *v.* Smith, 2 Lev. 5; s. c. 1 Vent. 121.
[3] Owen *v.* Reynolds, Fort. 341; cited Bac. Ab. Pleas, &c. 452, 5th ed.

(3) In an action of trespass on the case, for illegally taking toll, the plaintiff, in his declaration, set forth a charter of 26 Hen. VI., discharging him from toll. The defendant pleaded a statute resuming the liberties granted by Hen. VI. The plaintiff replied that by the statute 4 Hen. VII. such liberties were revived. And this was held to be no departure.[1]

(4) In an action of debt on a bond conditioned for the performance of an award, the defendant pleaded that the arbitrators *did not make any award :* the plaintiff replied that they duly made their award, setting part of it forth ; and the defendant, in his rejoinder, set forth the whole award *verbatim ;* by which it appeared that the award was *bad in law,* being made as to matters not within the submission. To this rejoinder the plaintiff demurred, on the ground that it was a departure from the plea ; for by the plea it had been alleged that there was no award, which meant no award in fact ; but by the rejoinder it appeared that there had been an award in fact. The court, however, held that there was no departure ; that the plea of no award meant no legal and valid award, according to the submission ; and that consequently the rejoinder, in setting the award forth, and showing that it was not conformable to the submission, maintained the plea.[2]

IN ALL CASES WHERE THE VARIANCE BETWEEN THE FORMER AND THE LATTER PLEADING IS ON A POINT NOT MATERIAL, THERE IS NO DEPARTURE.

Example : In *assumpsit,* if the declaration, in a case where the time is not material, state a promise to have been made on a given day *ten years ago,* and the defendant plead that he did not promise within six years, the plaintiff may reply that the defendant *did promise within six years* without a departure,[3] because the time laid in the declaration was immaterial.

The rule against departure is evidently necessary to prevent the retardation of the issue. For while the parties are respectively confined to the grounds they have first taken in their declaration and plea, *the process of pleading will,* as formerly

---

[1] Wood v. Hawkshead, Yelv. 13.

[2] Fisher v. Pimbley, 11 East, 188; and see Dudlow v. Watchorn, 16 East, 29 N. B. The first of these cases seems, in effect, to have overruled some former decisions. See Morgan v. Man, 1 Sid. 180; s. c. 1 Ld. Raym. 94; Harding v. Holmes, 1 Wils. 122; Praed v. Duchess of Cumberland, 4 T. R. 585; 2 H. Bl. 280.

[3] Lee v. Rogers, 1 Lev. 110; Cole v. Hawkins, 10 Mod. 348, S. P.

demonstrated, *exhaust, after a few alternations of statement, the whole facts involved in the cause*, and thereby develop the question in dispute. But if a new ground be taken in any part of the series, a new state of facts is introduced, and the result is consequently postponed. Besides, if one departure were allowed, the parties might, on the same principle, shift their ground as often as they pleased ; and an almost indefinite length of altercation might, in some cases, be the consequence.[1]

RULE II. WHERE A PLEA AMOUNTS TO THE GENERAL ISSUE IT SHOULD BE SO PLEADED.[2]

It has been already explained, that in most actions there is an appropriate form of plea, called the *general issue*, fixed by ancient usage as the proper method of traversing the declaration, when the pleader means to deny the whole or the principal part of its allegations. The meaning of the present rule is, that *if, instead of traversing the declaration in this form, the party pleads in a more special way matter which is constructively and in effect the same as the general issue, such plea will be bad, and the general issue ought to be substituted.*

Examples : (1) To a declaration in trespass for entering the plaintiff's garden, the defendant pleaded *that the plaintiff had no such garden.* This was ruled to be " no plea, for it amounts to nothing more than *not guilty ;* for if he had no such garden, then the defendant is not guilty." So the defendant withdrew his plea, and said *not guilty.*[3]

(2) In trespass for *depasturing the plaintiff's herbage, non depascit herbas* is no plea : it should be, *not guilty.*[4]

(3) In debt for the price of a horse sold, *that the defendant did not buy* is no plea, for it amounts to *nil debet.*[5]

(4) In trespass for entering the plaintiff's house, and keeping possession thereof for a certain time, the defendant pleaded

---

[1] See 2 Saund. 84 a, n. 1.

[2] Co. Litt. 303 b ; Doct. & Stud 271, 272 ; Com. Dig. Pleader, E. 14 ; Bac. Ab. Pleas, &c. 370–376, 5th ed. ; 10 Hen. VI. 16 ; 22 Hen. VI. 37 ; Holler v. Bush, Salk. 394 ; Birch v. Wilson, 2 Mod. 277 ; Lynnet v. Wood, Cro. Car. 157 ; Warner v. Wainsford, Hob. 127 ;

Anon. 12 Mod. 537 ; Saunders's Case, *ibid.* 513 ; Hallet v. Byrt, 5 Mod. 252.

[3] 10 Hen. VI. 16.

[4] Doct. Pl. 42, cites 22 Hen. VI. 37.

[5] Vin. Ab. Certainty in Pleadings, E. 15, cites Bro. Traverse, &c. pl. 275 ; 22 Edw. IV. 29.

that J. S. was seised in fee thereof, and, being so seised, gave license to the defendant to enter into and possess the house till he should give him notice to leave it; that thereupon the defendant entered and kept the house for the time mentioned in the declaration, and had not any notice to leave it all the time. The plaintiff demurred specially, on the ground that this plea amounted to the general issue, *not guilty;* and the court gave judgment, on that ground, for the plaintiff.[1]

(5) In an action of trover for divers loads of corn, the defendant in his plea entitled himself to them as tithes severed. The plaintiff demurred specially, on the ground that the plea " amounted but to *not guilty;* " and the court gave judgment for the plaintiff.[2]

(6) In trespass for breaking and entering the plaintiff's close, if the defendant plead a demise to him by the plaintiff, by virtue whereof he, the defendant, entered and was possessed, this is bad, as amounting to the general issue, *not guilty.*[3]

(7) In debt on a bond, the defendant by his plea confessed the bond, but said that it was executed to another person, and not to the plaintiff; this was bad, as amounting to *non est factum.*[4]

These examples show that a special plea, thus improperly substituted for the general issue, may be sometimes in a *negative*, sometimes in an *affirmative* form. When in the *negative*, its *argumentativeness* will often serve as an additional test of its faulty quality. Thus, the plea in the first example, " *that the plaintiff had no such garden,*" is evidently but an argumentative allegation that the defendant did not commit, because he *could* not have committed, the trespass. This, however, does not universally hold; for, in the second and third examples, the allegations that the defendant " *did not depasture,*" and " *did not buy,*" seem to be in as direct a form of denial as that of *not guilty.* If the plea be in the *affirmative*, the following considerations will always tend to detect the improper construction. If a good plea, it must (as formerly shown) be taken either as a traverse, or as in confession and avoidance. Now, taken as a traverse, such a plea is clearly

---

[1] Saunders's Case, 12 Mod. 513.
[2] Lynnet *v.* Wood, Cro. Car. 157.
[3] Jaques's Case, Sty. 355.
[4] Gifford *v.* Perkins, 1 Sid. 450; s. c. 1 Vent. 77.

open to the objection of *argumentativeness ;* for two affirmatives make an argumentative issue.   Thus, in the fourth
example, the allegations show that the house in question was
the house of J. S.; and they therefore deny argumentatively
that it was the house of the plaintiff, as stated in the declaration.   On the other hand, if a plea of this kind be intended
by way of confession and avoidance, it is bad *for want of color*,
for it admits no apparent right in the plaintiff.   Thus, in the
same example, if it be true that J. S. was seised in fee, and
gave license to the defendant to enter, who entered accordingly, this excludes all title of possession in the plaintiff; and
without such a title he has no color to maintain an action of
trespass.[1]   In the example where the defendant pleads the
plaintiff's own demise, the same observation applies; for if
the plaintiff demised to the defendant, who entered accordingly, the plaintiff would then cease to have any title of possession; and he consequently has no color to support an
action of trespass.

Effect of giving Express Color.

The fault of *wanting color* being in this manner connected
with that of *amounting to the general issue*, it is accordingly
held that a plea will be saved from the latter fault where
express color is given.[2]   And where sufficient *implied* color is
given, a plea will never be open to this kind of objection.
It is further to be observed that, where sufficient implied
color is given, the plea will be equally clear of this objection,
even though it consist of matter which *might, by a relaxation
of practice, be given in evidence under the general issue.*   The
relaxation here referred to is that formerly noticed, by which
defendants are allowed, in certain actions, to prove, under this
issue, matters in the nature of confession and avoidance; as,
for example, in *assumpsit*, a release or payment.   In such
cases the defendant (as formerly stated), though allowed, is not

---

[1] See Holler *v.* Bush, Salk. 394.

[2] Anon. 12 Mod. 537; Saunders's
Case, *ibid.* 513; Lynnet *v.* Wood, Cro.
Car. 157; Birch *v.* Wilson, 2 Mod. 274.
Indeed, the fiction of express color was
resorted to in order that this rule might
be evaded, and that an argumentative
traverse might be pleaded as a plea by
way of confession and avoidance.

obliged to plead *non assumpsit*, but may, if he pleases, plead specially the payment or release ; and if he does, such plea is not open to the objection that it amounts to the general issue.[1]

THIS RULE NOT ABSOLUTE.

It is said that the court is not bound to allow this objection, but that *it is in its discretion to allow a special plea, amounting to the general issue*, if it involve such matter of law as might be unfit for the decision of a jury.[2] It is also said that as the court has such discretion, the proper method of taking advantage of this fault is not by *demurrer*, but by motion to the court to set aside the plea and enter the general issue instead of it.[3] It appears from the books, however, that the objection has frequently been allowed on demurrer.

As a plea amounting to the general issue is usually open also to the objection of being *argumentative*, or that of *wanting color*, we sometimes find the rule in question discussed as if it were founded entirely upon those objections. This, however, does not seem to be a sufficiently wide foundation for the rule ; for there are instances of pleas which are faulty, as amounting to the general issue, which yet do not (as already observed) seem fairly open to the objection of argumentativeness, and which, on the other hand, being of the negative kind or by way of traverse, require no color. Besides, there is express authority for holding that the true object of this rule is *to avoid prolixity*, and that it is therefore properly classed under the present section. For it is laid down that "the reason of pressing a general issue is not for insufficiency of the plea, but not to make long records when there is no cause."[4]

---

1 Holler *v.* Bush, Salk. 394 ; Hussey *v.* Jacob, Carth. 356 ; Carr *v.* Hinchliff, 4 Barn. & Cress. 547.

2 Bac. Ab. Pleas, &c. 374, 5th ed. ; Birch *v.* Wilson, 2 Mod. 274 ; Carr *v.* Hinchliff, *ubi supra.*

3 Warner *v.* Wainsford, Hob. 127 ; Ward & Blunt's Case, 1 Leon. 178.

4 Warner *v.* Wainsford, *ubi supra;* see also Com. Dig. Pleader, E. 13.

Rule III. Surplusage is to be Avoided.[1]

Surplusage is here taken in its large sense, as including *unnecessary matter* of whatever description.[2]

To combine with the Requisite Certainty and Precision the Greatest Possible Brevity is now justly considered as the Perfection of Pleading.

This principle, however, has not been kept uniformly in view at every era of the science. For although it appears to have prevailed at the earliest periods, it seems to have been nearly forgotten during a subsequent interval of our legal history;[3] and it is to the wisdom of modern judges that it owes its revival and restoration.

(1) Omission of Matter wholly Foreign.

The rule as to avoiding surplusage may be considered, first, as prescribing the omission of matter *wholly foreign.*

Example: When a plaintiff, suing a defendant upon one of the covenants in a long deed, sets out, in his declaration, not only the covenant on which he sues, but all the other covenants, though relating to matter wholly irrelevant to the cause, he violates this rule.[4]

(2) Omission of Matter not required to be stated.

The rule also prescribes the omission of matter which, though not wholly foreign, *does not require to be stated.* Any matters will fall within this description which, under the various rules enumerated in a former section as tending to limit or qualify the degree of certainty, it is unnecessary to allege; for example, matter of mere *evidence*, matter of *law*, or other *things which the court officially notices*, matter *coming more properly from the other side*, matter *necessarily implied*, etc.

---

[1] Bristow *v.* Wright, Doug. 667; 1 Saund. 233, n. 2; Yates *v.* Carlisle, 1 Bl. Rep. 270.

[2] In its more strict and confined meaning, it imports matter wholly foreign and irrelevant.

[3] See the remarks of Sir M. Hale, Hist. of Com. Law, ch. vii., viii.

[4] Dundass *v.* Lord Weymouth, Cowp. 665; Price *v.* Fletcher, *ibid.* 727; Phillips *v.* Fielding, 2 H. Bl. 131.

(3) Brevity in Manner of Statement.

The rule prescribes, generally, the cultivation of *brevity*, or avoidance of unnecessary prolixity, in the *manner of statement*. A terse style of allegation, involving a strict retrenchment of unnecessary words, is the aim of the best practitioners in pleading, and is considered as indicative of a good school.

Remedy for Violation of this Rule.

Surplusage is not a subject for *demurrer ;* the maxim being that *utile, per inutile, non vitiatur.*[1] But when any flagrant fault of this kind occurs and is brought to the notice of the court, *it is visited with the censure of the judges.*[2] They have also, in such cases, on motion, referred the pleadings to the master, that he might strike out such matter as is redundant and capable of being omitted without injury to the material averments ; and, in a clear case, *will themselves direct such matter to be struck out.* And the party offending will sometimes have to pay the costs of the application.[3]

Danger arising from Surplusage.

Though traverse can not be taken (as already shown) on an immaterial allegation, yet it often happens that when material matter is alleged, *with an unnecessary detail* of circumstances, the essential and non-essential parts of the statement are, in their nature, so connected as to be *incapable of separation ;* and the opposite party is therefore entitled to *include, under his traverse, the whole matter alleged.* The consequence evidently is, that the party who has pleaded with such unnecessary particularity has to sustain an increased burden of proof, and incurs greater danger of failure at the trial.

---

[1] Co. Litt. 303 b.

[2] Yates *v.* Carlisle, 1 Bl. Rep. 270 ; Price *v.* Fletcher, Cowp. 727.

[3] Price *v.* Fletcher, *ubi supra ;* Bristow *v.* Wright, Doug. 667 ; 1 Tidd, 667, 8th ed.; Nichol *v.* Wilton, 1 Chit. Rep. 449, 450; Carmack *v.* Gundry, 3 Barn. & Ald. 272 ; Brindley *v.* Dennett, 2 Bing. 184.

Most of the principal rules of pleading have now been classed with reference to certain common objects which each class or set of rules is conceived to contemplate, and have been explained and illustrated in their connection with these objects and with each other. But there still remain certain rules, also of a principal or primary character, which have been found not to be reducible within this principle of arrangement, being, with respect to their objects, of a miscellaneous and unconnected kind. These will form the subject of the following chapter.

CHAPTER XV.

OF CERTAIN MISCELLANEOUS RULES.

THESE rules relate either to the *declaration*, the *plea*, or *pleadings in general*, and shall be considered in the order thus indicated.

RULE I. THE DECLARATION SHOULD COMMENCE WITH A RECITAL OF THE ORIGINAL WRIT.[1]

The commencement of the declaration, in *personal* actions, generally consists of a *short recital of the original writ*. Accordingly, where the writ directs the sheriff to *summon* the defendant, as in debt and covenant, the declaration begins, " *C. D. was summoned to answer A. B. of a plea*," &c.

On the other hand, where by the writ the defendant is required to be *put by gages and safe pledges*, as in trespass and trespass on the case, the commencement is, " *C. D. was attached to answer A. B. of a plea*," &c. The declaration then proceeds further to recite the writ, by showing the nature of the particular requisition or exigency of that instrument; as, for example (in debt), " *of a plea that he render to the said A. B. the sum of —— pounds*," &c. In debt, covenant, detinue, and trespass, nearly the whole original writ is recited; but not in trespass on the case. The course was formerly the same in the latter action also; but, as this led to an inconvenient prolixity, it was by rule of court[2] provided, that in that and some other actions it shall be sufficient to mention generally the nature of the action; thus: " *a plea of trespass upon the case*," &c.; and such summary form has accordingly been since used.

[1] Com. Dig. Pleader, C. 12. [2] 1 Tidd, 435, 8th ed.; 1 Saund. 318, n. 3.

In *real* and *mixed* actions, the writ is generally not so for- mally recited. Thus, in the writ of right the count begins, " *A. B. demands against C. D., &c. ;* " and the case is the same in formedon and dower. It will be observed, however, that this commencement generally comprises a repetition of the tenor of the writ; and in some actions, as in *quare impedit,* the writ is as formally recited as in actions personal.

The recital of the writ is a form which the declaration has borrowed from the style in which it was entered on *record ;* for the declaration itself, when actually pronounced in court, usually began with the words, *Ceo vous monstre* (this shows to you), etc.

Though the writ, as recited at the commencement of the declaration, appear to be erroneous, yet that is no ground for demurrer to the declaration; for the court will not judge of any defect in the original writ without examination of the instrument itself.[1]

The rule under consideration of course does not apply where the proceeding is by *bill ;* but in that case also the declaration has its proper formal commencement.

The declaration by bill commences with the following for- mula: " *A. B. complains of C. D., &c. ;* " and in the King's Bench usually proceeds to allege that the defendant is " *in the custody of the marshal of the Marshalsea of our lord the now king, before the king himself;* " [2] *i. e.,* that he is a pris- oner of the court ; but, in case of an action against an attorney or officer of the court, it alleges the defendant to be such attor- ney or officer, without stating him to be in custody, etc.   In the Common Pleas, the capacity of the defendant, as attorney or officer, is in a similar manner alleged; and in the Ex- chequer, the declaration commences by describing the plaintiff as " *a debtor to our sovereign lord the king.*"   The meaning of these *formulæ* has been explained in the remarks upon " process."

---

[1] Com. Dig. Pleader, C. 12 ; 1 Saund.   [2] Com. Dig. Pleader, C. 8.
318, n. 3 ; Helliot *v.* Selby, Salk. 701.

Rule II. The Declaration must be conformable to the Original Writ.[1]

This is a rule of high antiquity, being laid down by Bracton,[2] who wrote when the system of pleading was in a very rude and imperfect state.

Examples: (1) In detinue, where the writ stated the value of the goods which were the subject of action to be £20, and the declaration alleged £40, the variance was, in an old case, considered as a ground for reversing the judgment upon writ of error.[8]

(2) In trespass, where the writ charged the defendant with breaking the *close* of the plaintiff, and the declaration with breaking his *closes*, the decision was the same.[4]

The rule is to be taken, however, subject to this qualification : that the declaration generally may, and does, so far vary from the writ, that (as has been seen) it states the cause of action more *specially*.[5]

Though it has been thought desirable to notice this rule, it is, at the same time, to be observed that it has lost much of its practical importance, as it can rarely now be enforced. For, if the declaration varied from the original, the only modes of objecting to the variance (unless the fault happened to appear by the recital in the commencement of the declaration) were by plea in abatement or by writ of error.[6] But by a change of practice already explained, a plea in abatement, in respect of such variance, can now no longer be pleaded ; and, by the statutes of *jeofails* and amendments, the objection can not now be taken by way of writ of error after verdict ; nor, if the variance be in a matter of *form* only, can it be taken after judgment by confession, *nil dicit,* or *non sum informatus.*[7] However, the effect of the rule is still felt in pleading ; for its long and ancient observance had fixed the frame and language of the declaration in conformity with the original

---

[1] Com. Dig. Pleader, C. 13 ; Bac. Ab. Pleas, &c., B. 4 ; Co. Litt. 303 a ; Bract. 431 a, 435 b.

[2] Bract., *ubi supra.*

[8] Young *v.* Watson, Cro. Eliz 308.

[4] Edward *v.* Watkin, *ibid.* 185.

[5] Com. Dig. Abatement, G. 8, Pleader, C. 15 ; Co. Litt. 303 b.

[6] 1 Saund. 318, n. 3.

[7] 5 Geo. I. c. 13 ; 21 Jac. I. c. 13 ; 4 Ann. c. 16. See 2 Tidd, 958, 959, 8th ed. ; 1 Saund., *ubi supra.*

27

writ in each form of action ; and, by a rule which has already
been considered, to depart from the known and established
tenor of pleadings is a fault ; consequently a declaration must
still be framed in conformity with the language of the original
writ appropriate to the form of action, as much as when a
variance from the writ actually sued out might have become
the subject of a plea in abatement.

In proceedings by *bill*, the rule in question is, of course,
inapplicable ; yet, even in these, the declaration pursues the
same forms of expression as if founded on an original writ in
the same form of action. Thus, the declaration in debt by
bill is worded exactly in the same manner as the declaration
in debt by original, the formal commencement only excepted ;
and the case is the same in all other actions.

RULE III.   THE DECLARATION SHOULD, IN CONCLUSION, LAY
   DAMAGES, AND ALLEGE PRODUCTION OF SUIT.

(1) THE DECLARATION MUST LAY DAMAGES.[1]

In *personal* and *mixed* actions [2] the declaration must allege,
in conclusion, that the injury is to the *damage* of the plaintiff,
and must specify the amount of that damage.[3] In *personal*
actions, there is the distinction formerly explained between
actions that *sound in damages* and those that do not ; but in
either of these cases it is equally the practice to lay damages.
There is, however, this difference : that in the former case
damages are the main object of the suit, and are, therefore,
always laid high enough to cover the whole demand ; but in the
latter, the liquidated debt or the chattel demanded being the
main object, damages are claimed in respect of the *detention*
only of such debt or chattel, and are, therefore, usually laid at
a small sum.

THE PLAINTIFF CAN NOT RECOVER GREATER DAMAGES THAN
HE HAS LAID IN THE CONCLUSION OF HIS DECLARATION.[4]

---

[1] The student should bear in mind
the difference between *general* and
special damages ; the latter must always
be alleged specially. Chit. Pl. 346,
347. (See also any standard treatise on
"Torts," *sub voc.* "*special damages.*")

[2] But *penal* actions are an exception.

[3] Com. Dig. Pleader, C. 84 ; Robert
Pilford's Case, 10 Co. Rep. 116 b, 117 a, b.

[4] Com. Dig. Pleader. C. 84 ; Vin.
Ab. Damages, R. ; Robert Pilford's
Case, *ubi supra*. But if an excess in

In *real* actions, no damages are to be laid; because, in these, the demand is specifically for the land withheld, and damages are in no degree the object of suit.

(2) THE DECLARATION SHOULD ALSO CONCLUDE WITH THE PRODUCTION OF SUIT.

This applies to actions of all classes — real, personal, and mixed.

In ancient times, as has been seen, the plaintiff was required to establish the truth of his declaration, *in the first instance*, and before it was called into question upon the pleading, by the simultaneous production of his *secta*, that is, a number of persons prepared to confirm his allegations.[1] The practice of thus producing a *secta* gave rise to the very ancient formula, almost invariably used at the conclusion of a declaration as entered on record : *et inde producit sectam ;* [2] and though the actual production has for many centuries fallen into disuse, the formula still remains.[3] Accordingly, all declarations, except the count on a writ of right and in dower, constantly conclude thus : " *And therefore he brings his suit, &c.*" The count on a writ of right did not, in ancient times, conclude with the ordinary production of suit, but with the following formula, peculiar to itself : " *et quod tale sit jus suum offert disrationare per corpus talis liberi hominis*" (and that his right is such he offers to dereign by the body of a certain free-man), &c.,[4] and it concludes at the present day with an abbreviated translation of the same phrase : " *And that such is his right, he*

---

the verdict be not discovered until after the jury has been discharged, reference may be had to the writ, in order to sustain the proceedings, and if the damages found by the verdict do not exceed those laid in the writ, the verdict will be good. Min. Inst. IV. 1051, 1052.

[1] See Bract. 214 b. *Et inde statim producat (i. e., after the declaration in an action of prohibition) sectam sufficientem, duos ad minus, vel tres, vel plures, si possit. (And then at once let him produce a sufficient suit, two at least, or three, or more if he can.) (Ibid.,* 410 a.) " *Producit sectam,* was proffer-

ing to the court the testimony of the witnesses or followers." (Gilb. C. P. 48.)

[2] See the entries in the *Placitorum Abbreviatio, passim, temp. Ric. I., Edw. II.*

[3] As early as 7 Edw. II. it had become a mere form ; for it is said in a case reported of that year, *cest court (i. e.,* the Common Pleas) *ne soeffre mye la sute estre examine (this court never permits the suit to be examined). (7 Edw. II. 242.)*

[4] Bract. 372, b. Glanville gives it thus : *Et hoc promptus sum probare per hunc liberum meum hominem,* &c. (Glan Lib. 2, c. 3.)

offers, &c." The count in dower is an exception to the rule in question, and concludes without any production of suit; a peculiarity which appears always to have belonged to that action.[1]

We may again notice, in this place, that subjoined to the declaration, in proceedings by *bill*, there is an addition of the names of two persons, now fictitious ones, as *pledges for the prosecution of the suit.* By the old law, it was necessary that, before the sheriff executed the original writ, the plaintiff should give him security that he would pursue his claim.[2] This regulation seems to have been extended to proceedings by bill also; but, in these proceedings, the security would appear to have been given, not to the sheriff, but to the court itself, and the time for giving it was apparently that of filing the bill. Hence the practice in question of entering *pledges* at the foot of declarations by bill. These *pledges*, however, are now, in all cases, a mere matter of form; no such security being actually given in proceedings either by bill or original.

RULE IV. PLEAS MUST BE PLEADED IN DUE ORDER.[3]

The order of pleading, as established at the present day, is as follows: —

Pleas.

1. To the jurisdiction of the court.

2. To the disability of the person: { 1. Of plaintiff.
                                       { 2. Of defendant.

3. To the count or declaration.

4. To the writ: { 1. To the form of the writ: { 1. For matter apparent on the face of it.
                 {   { 2. For matter dehors the writ.
                 { 2. To the action of the writ.

5. To the action itself in bar thereof.[4]

---

[1] Booth, and Co. Ent. tit. Dower.

[2] Hussey *v.* More, Cro. Jac. 414; s. c., 3 Bulst. 279. This practice is still indicated by the form of the original writs, which always contain the clause of *si te fecerit securum.*

[3] Co. Litt. 303 a; Longueville *v.* Thistleworth, 2 Ld. Raym. 970.

[4] Com. Dig. Abatement, C.; Chit. Pl. 379.

In this order the defendant may plead all these kinds of pleas successively. Thus, *he may first plead to the jurisdiction*, and, *upon demurrer* and judgment of *respondeat ouster* thereon, *may resort to a plea to the disability of the person;* and *so to the end of the series.*

But *he can not plead more than one plea of the same kind or degree.* Thus, he can not offer two successive pleas to the jurisdiction, or two to the disability of the person.[1]

So *he can not vary the order;* for *by a plea of any of these kinds he is taken to waive or renounce all pleas of a kind prior in the series.*

And, if issue *in fact* be taken upon any plea, though of the dilatory class only, the judgment on such issue (as elsewhere explained) either terminates or (in case of a plea of suspension) suspends the action, so that he is not at liberty, in that case, to resort to any other kind of plea.

RULE V. PLEAS MUST BE PLEADED WITH DEFENCE.[2]

The nature and meaning of *defence* have been already fully explained.

Its form varies in some degree according to the nature of the action.

In the *writ of right*, where the demandant claims on *his own* seisin, it is thus: "*And the said C. D., by E. F., his attorney, comes and defends the right of the said A. B., and his seisin, when, &c., and all, &c., and whatsoever, &c., and chiefly of the tenements aforesaid, with the appurtenances, as of fee and right, &c., and says;*" and then the matter of the plea is stated.

In a writ of right, when the demandant claims on the seisin *of his ancestor*, it is thus: "*And the said C. D., by E. F., his attorney, comes and defends the right of the said A. B., and the seisin of the said G. B. (the ancestor), when, &c., and all, &c., and whatsoever, &c., and chiefly of the tenements aforesaid, with the appurtenances, as of fee and right, &c., and says.*"[3]

[1] Com. Dig. Abatement, I. 3; Bac. Ab. Abatement, O.

[2] Co. Litt. 127 b; Tampian *v.* New-

sam, Yelv. 210; Hampson *v.* Bill, 3 Lev. 240.

[3] Booth, 94; Co. Ent. 181 b.

In *formedon* the defence is: "*And the said C. D., by E. F., his attorney, comes and defends his right, when, &c., and says.*"[1]

The action of *dower* is an exception to the rule, and in this suit defence is not made.[2]

In *quare impedit* the defence is: "*And the said C. D., by E. F., his attorney, comes and defends the wrong and injury, when, &c., and says.*"

In *trespass:* "*And the said C. D., by E. F., his attorney, comes and defends the force and injury, when, &c., and says.*"

In *other personal actions:* "*And the said C. D., by E. F., his attorney, comes and defends the wrong and injury, when, &c., and says.*"

The word "comes" expresses the *appearance* of the defendant in court. It is taken from the style of the entry of the proceedings on the record, and formed no part of the *viva voce* pleading. It is accordingly not considered as in strictness constituting a part of the plea.[3]

The word "*defends,*" as used in these *formulæ*, has not its popular sense. It imports *denial*, being derived from the law Latin *defendere*, or the law French *defendre* (both of which signify *to deny*); and the effect of the expression is that the defendant denies the right of the plaintiff, or the force or wrong charged. This denial, however, is now mere matter of form; for the defence is used, not merely when the plea is by way of denial or traverse, but when by confession and avoidance also; and, even when the plea does deny, other words are employed for that purpose, as we have seen, besides those of the formal *defence.*

The *&c.*'s supply the place of words which were formerly inserted *at length*. In a personal action, for example, the form, if fully given, would be as follows: "*And the said C. D., by E. F., his attorney, comes and defends the force*" (*or* "*wrong*") "*and injury, when and where it shall behoove*

---

[1] Booth, 148. Defendit jus *suum*, &c., is the Latin phrase; but this is ungrammatically put, as Blackstone conjectures, for *ejus*, and refers to the right of the *demandant*. (See Bl. Com. III. 297*.)

[2] Rast. Ent. 228.

[3] Stephens *v.* Arthur, Salk. 544; Chit. Pl. 367, 469.

him, and the damages, and whatsoever else he ought to defend, and says." [1]

FULL DEFENCE AND HALF DEFENCE.

At a time when this formula was of more importance than it now is, particular effects were assigned to its different clauses. It was said that, by defending *"when and where it shall behoove him,"* the defendant impliedly acknowledged the jurisdiction of the court; and, by defending the *" damages, and whatsoever else he ought to defend,"* he in effect admitted the competency of the plaintiff to sue; that by the former words, therefore, he was excluded from proceeding to plead to the jurisdiction, and by the latter from pleading to the disability of the plaintiff. Hence arose a distinction between *"full defence"* and *" half defence,"* the former being that in which all the clauses were inserted; the latter being abridged thus: *" And the said C. D., by E. F., his attorney, comes and defends the force "* (or *" wrong")* *"and injury, and says."* Half defence was used where the defendant intended to plead to the jurisdiction or in disability, and full defence in other cases. All this doctrine, however, is now, in effect, superseded by the uniform practice of making defence with an *&c.,* as in the forms first above given; it having been decided that *such method will operate either as full defence or half defence,* as the nature of the plea may require. [2]

Defence is used in almost all actions. It has been seen, however, that *dower* is an exception; and the case is the same with an *assize;* the form of commencing the plea in these actions being merely *" comes and says,"* and not *" comes and defends."* [3]

Defence is used, too, in almost every description of plea in those actions in which it obtains.

---

[1] Bac. Ab. Pleas, &c. D.

[2] Co. Litt. 127 b; Alexander *v.* Mawman, Willes, 40; Wilkes *v.* Williams, 8 T. R. 633; 2 Saund. 209 c, n. 1; Chit. Pl. 368, 369.

[3] Booth, 118. In *scire facias* also no defence is made. (Bac. Ab. Pleas, &c. D.)

RULE VI. PLEAS IN ABATEMENT MUST GIVE THE PLAINTIFF A BETTER WRIT OR BILL.[1]

The meaning of this rule is, that *in pleading a mistake* of form in abatement of the writ or bill, *the plea must*, at the same time, *correct the mistake*, so as to enable the plaintiff to avoid the same objection in framing his new writ or bill.

Example: If a misnomer in the Christian name of the defendant be pleaded in abatement, the defendant must, in such plea, show what his true Christian name is, and even what is his true surname;[2] and this though the true surname be already stated in the declaration, lest the plaintiff should a second time be defeated by error in the name.

These pleas, as tending to delay justice, are not favorably considered in law, and the rule in question was adopted in order to check their repetition.

This condition of requiring the defendant to give a better writ is often a criterion to distinguish whether a given matter should be pleaded in *abatement* or in *bar*.[3] The latter kind of plea, as impugning the right of action altogether, can, of course, give no better writ; for its effect is to deny that, under any form of writ, the plaintiff could recover in such action. If, therefore, a better writ can be given, this shows that the plea ought not to be in bar, but in abatement.

RULE VII. DILATORY PLEAS MUST BE PLEADED AT A PRELIMINARY STAGE OF THE SUIT.

Dilatory pleas are generally not allowable after *full defence;*[4] nor after a *general imparlance;*[5] nor after *oyer,*[6] or a *view;*[7] nor after *voucher;*[8] nor after a *plea in bar.*[9] And, besides these, there are other proceedings also which have the effect of excluding a subsequent dilatory plea; but, being

---

[1] Com. Dig. Abatement, I. 1; Evans v. Stevens, 4 T. R. 227; Mainwaring v. Newman, 2 Bos. & Pul. 120; Haworth v. Spraggs, 8 T. R. 515.

[2] Haworth v. Spraggs, 8 T. R. 515.

[3] 1 Saund. 284, n. 4; Evans v. Stevens, *ubi supra.*

[4] Com. Dig. Abatement, I. 16.

[5] *Ibid.*, I. 20.

[6] *Ibid.*, I. 22.

[7] *Ibid.*, I. 25.

[8] *Ibid.*, I. 28.

[9] *Ibid.*, I. 23.

of a less ordinary and general kind, it is not necessary here to notice them more distinctly.[1]

RULE VIII. ALL AFFIRMATIVE PLEADINGS WHICH DO NOT CONCLUDE TO THE COUNTRY MUST CONCLUDE WITH A VERIFICATION.[2]

Where an issue is tendered to be tried by jury, it has been shown that the pleading concludes *to the country*. In all other cases pleadings, if in the affirmative form, must conclude with a formula of another kind, called a *verification* or an *averment*.

The verification is of two kinds, (1) *common* and (2) *special*.

(1) The common verification is that which applies to ordinary cases, as in the following form: "*And this the said A. B.*" (or "*C. D.*") "*is ready to verify.*"

(2) The special verifications are used only where the matter pleaded is intended to be tried by record, or by some other method than a jury. They are in the following forms: "*And this the said A. B.*" (or "*C. D.*") "*is ready to verify by the said record,*" or, "*And this the said A. B.*" (or "*C. D.*") "*is ready to verify when, where, and in such manner as the court here shall order, direct, or appoint.*"

The origin of this rule is as follows: —

It was a doctrine of the ancient law, little, if at all, noticed by modern writers, that every pleading affirmative in its nature must be supported by an offer of some *mode of proof;* and the reference to a jury (who, as formerly explained, were in the nature of witnesses to the fact in issue) was considered as an offer of *proof* within the meaning of that doctrine. When the proof proposed was that by jury, the offer was made in the *viva voce* pleading, by the words *prest d'averrer,* or *prest, &c.,* which in the record was translated, *Et hoc paratus est verificare (and this he is prepared to prove).*[3]

---

[1] See the instances, Com. Dig. Abatement, I. 26, &c.

[2] Com. Dig. Pleader, E. 32, E. 33; Co. Litt. 303 a; Finch, Law, 359.

[3] See 10 Edw. III. 23; *ibid.*, 25, and the Year Books, *passim.*

On the other hand, where other modes of proof were intended, the record ran, *Et hoc paratus est verificare per recordum (and this he is prepared to prove by the record)*, or *Et hoc paratus est verificare quocunque modo curia consideraverit (and this he is prepared to prove in whatever manner the court shall determine)*.

But while these were the forms generally observed, there was the following exception, that on the *attainment of an issue* to be tried by jury, the record marked that result by a change of phrase, and substituted, for the verification, the conclusion *ad patriam*, to the *country*.[1]

The written pleadings (which, it will be remembered, are framed in the ancient style of the record) still retain the same *formulæ* in these different cases, and with the same distinctions as to their use. They preserve the conclusion to the country, to mark the attainment of an issue triable by jury, but in other cases conclude with a translation of the old Latin phrase, *Et hoc paratus, &c.;* and hence the rule, that an affirmative pleading that does not conclude to the country must conclude with a verification.[2]

As the ancient rule requiring an offer of proof extended only to *affirmative* pleadings (those of a *negative* kind being generally incapable of proof), so the rule in question now applies to the former only, no verification being in general *necessary* in a negative pleading,[3] but it is nevertheless the practice to conclude with a verification all negative as well as affirmative pleadings that do not conclude to the country.

RULE IX.   IN ALL PLEADINGS WHERE A DEED IS ALLEGED, UNDER WHICH THE PARTY CLAIMS OR JUSTIFIES, PROFERT OF SUCH DEED MUST BE MADE.[4]

Where any party pleads a deed, and claims or justifies under it, the mention of the instrument is accompanied

---

[1] See 10 Edw. III. 25, 26, &c.

[2] "Every plea or bar, replication, &c., *must be offered to be proved true*, by saying in the plea, *Et hoc paratus est verificare*, which we call an averment." (Finch, Law, 359.) This gives confirmation, it will be observed, to the account of the origin of this rule contained in the text.

[3] Co. Litt. 303 a; Millner *v.* Crowdall, 1 Show. 338.

[4] Com. Dig. Pleader, O. 1; Leyfield's Case, 10 Co. Rep. 92 a.

with a formula to this effect: "*One part of which said indenture*" (or other deed), "*sealed with the seal of the said ——, the said —— now brings here into court, the date whereof is the day and year aforesaid.*"

This formula is called *making profert* of the deed. Its present practical import is that the party has the instrument ready for the purpose of giving *oyer;* and at the time when the pleading was *viva voce* it implied an *actual production* of the instrument in *open court* for the same purpose.

The Rule, in General, applies to Deeds only.

No *profert*, therefore, is necessary of any written agreement or other instrument not under seal,[1] nor of any instrument which, though under seal, does not fall within the technical definition of a *deed;* as, for example, a sealed will or award.[2] This, however, is subject to exception in the case of *letters testamentary* and *letters of administration;* executors and administrators being bound, when plaintiffs,[3] to support their declaration by making *profert* of these instruments.

Limitations of Rule.

The rule applies only to cases where there is occasion to *mention the deed in pleading.* When the course of allegation is not such as to lead to any mention of the deed, a *profert* is not necessary, even though in fact it may be the foundation of the case or title pleaded.

The rule extends only to cases where the party claims under the deed, or justifies under it; and therefore, when the deed is mentioned *only as inducement* or introduction to some other matter, on which the claim or justification is founded, or alleged, not to show right or title in the party pleading, but for some collateral purpose, *no profert is necessary.*[4]

---

[1] Com. Dig. Pleader, O. 3; Aylesbury *v.* Harvey, 3 Lev. 205.

[2] Com. Dig. Pleader, *ubi supra;* 2 Saund. 62 b, n. 5.

[3] But *semb.* that they are not bound to make *profert* where they have occasion to plead the letters testamentary, &c. as *defendants.* (See Marsh *v.* Newman, Poph. 163, 164, cites 36 Hen. VI. 36.)

[4] Bellamy's Case, 6 Co. Rep. 38 a; Holland *v.* Shelley, Hob. 303; Banfill *v.* Leigh, 8 T. R. 571; Com. Dig. Pleader, O. 8, O. 16; 1 Saund. 9 a, n. 1.

The rule is confined, too, to cases where the party relies on the *direct and intrinsic operation of the deed.*[1]

Example: In pleading a conveyance under the statute of uses, it is not necessary to make *profert* of the lease and release, because it is the *statute* that gives effect to the conveyance, and the deeds do not intrinsically establish the title.

Another exception to the rule obtains where the deed is *lost or destroyed* through time or accident, or is *in the possession of the opposite party.*[2] These circumstances dispense with the necessity of a *profert,* and the formula is then as follows: " *Which said writing obligatory* " (or other deed) " *having been lost by lapse of time* " (or " *destroyed by accidental fire,*" or " *being in the possession of the said* ——"), " *the said* —— *can not produce the same to the court here.*"

REASON OF RULE.

In his text Mr. Stephen has the following speculations as to the reason of this rule: —

"The reason assigned for the rule requiring *profert* is, that the court may be enabled by inspection to judge of the sufficiency of the deed.[3] The author, however, presumes to question whether the practice of making *profert originated* in any view of this kind. It will be recollected that, by an ancient rule, all affirmative pleadings were formerly required to be supported by *an offer of some mode of proof.* As the pleader, therefore, of that time concluded in some cases by offering to prove by jury or by the record, so, in others, he maintained his pleading by producing a *deed* as proof of the case alleged. In so doing he only complied with the rule that required an offer of proof. Afterwards, the trial by jury becoming more universally prevalent, it was often applied (as at the present day) to determine questions arising as to the genuineness or validity of the deed

---

[1] Banfill *v.* Leigh, 8 T. R. 573; Read *v.* Brookman, 3 T. R. 156.

[2] Read *v.* Brookman, *ubi supra;* Carver *v.* Pinkney, 3 Lev. 82.

[3] Leyfield's Case, 10 Co. Rep. 92 b; Co. Litt. 35 b.

itself so produced; and from this time a deed seems to have been no longer considered as a method of proof, distinct and independent of that by jury. Consequently it became the course to introduce, as well in pleadings where the party relied on a deed as in other cases, the common *verification* or offer to prove by *jury;* and the true object of the *profert* was in this manner not only superseded, but forgotten, though in practice it still continued to be made."

, The foregoing observations of Mr. Stephen have been confirmed very strikingly by later writers. The subject is so interesting that the student should have fuller information here with respect to it, although it more properly belongs to the law of evidence.

Among the Anglo-Saxons "written documents were largely introduced through the influence of the Roman Church, and became the strongest and most natural means of proof. . . . Not that the appeal to the oath and the use of witnesses were laid aside; but the document was not only a more serviceable, but also as good a means of proof as these."[1] More than this: a certain mystery attached to it. "The written document, which few have the art to manufacture, is regarded with mystical awe. . . . The act of setting one's hand to it is a *stipulatio* (a formal contract); it is delivered over as a *symbol* along with *twig* and *turf* and *glove*. . . . It is broadly stated that, according to the *Lex Romana* (Roman Law), any one who contravenes or will not perform a written agreement is infamous and to be punished."[2] What more natural than that the plaintiff should, if he relied on such foundation for his claim, produce it as the unanswerable proof of the demand? As we have seen, "it was the office of the *secta* to support the plaintiff's case, in advance of any answer from the defendant. This support might be such as to preclude any denial, . . . where the defendant's own . . . document was produced. . . . Documents, tallies, the production of the mainour, the showing of the wound in mayhem, all belong under this general conception. The

---

[1] Anglo-Saxon Law, 230, 231.   [2] P. & M. Hist. II. 190.

history of our law from the beginning of it is strewn with cases of the *profert* of documents." [1]

Of trial by charters or documents, but little can be said here. "The effect and interpretation of documents were ordinarily matter for the judges; and trial by charters had, in consequence, more of the features of trials of the present day than any other form of litigation, except that by inquisition and recognition. The event was not, as it was in trial by wager of law and by party-witness, largely and often wholly in the hands of the party who had delivered the last good pleading. Nor was it necessarily left to some external test, incapable in fact of discovering to the court the truth. But as in the case of trial by inquisition, the truth was, if possible, sought by a rational and satisfactory mode of inquiry; as by a comparison of the seal [2] in question with other seals of the same party, admitted to be genuine. [3]

"Whatever a defendant pleaded in answer to the plaintiff's claim of title or right by charter, or whatever the plaintiff may have replied to a defence of right or title by charter, the charter must be produced at the trial and become the main subject of contest. The defendant or plaintiff must allege either that the charter did not cover the subject-matter of the suit, or, if it did, that it had been annulled, suspended, or defeated by some other competent charter, document, or act, or that the charter itself was incomplete or a forgery. Whichever of these positions was taken, the charter in question, with the counter-charter, if such were set up, must be produced, and the trial thus became a trial by charter. . . .

"When, however, there was no means of determining of the genuineness of the seal (for if that was genuine, the charter at the time when it was executed was valid) by inspection or comparison, then the party offering the impeached document might have recourse to the duel to establish the seal by any proper witness (champion),

---

[1] Thay. Jury, 13.

[2] By Stephen's day, "men were beginning to look for a seal as an essential part of a charter." P. & M. Hist. II. 221.

[3] Glanvill, Lib. 10, c. 12, sec. 4.

especially by one whose name had been inserted by authority in the charter in question."[1]

After the introduction of trial by jury, this question was naturally referred to that mode of trial for solution.

"*Profert* was required of a deed only, because in the case of no other species of evidence was it possible. . . . Records were writings in public custody, which the party could not bring into court, because they were confined by law to some certain place. . . . Unsealed writings were, at the time of the invention of *profert*, no evidence at all. Of oral testimony, for obvious reasons, *profert* could not be made, nor could it have been necessary or useful. . . . *Profert* was then to be made of a deed, and of nothing else, because a deed was the only description of evidence of which it was possible, or could be useful."[2]

RULE X. ALL PLEADINGS MUST BE PROPERLY ENTITLED OF THE COURT AND TERM.[3]

With respect to the title of the *court*, it generally consists of a superscription of the name of the court, thus : " *In the King's Bench*," " *In the Common Pleas*," or " *In the Exchequer*."[4] But in a *declaration by bill in the King's Bench* it consists of a superscription of *the name of the prothonotary*.

With respect to the title of the *term*, it is either *general*, thus : " *Trinity term, in the fourth year of the reign of King George the Fourth;*" or *special*, thus : " *Monday next, after fifteen days of the Holy Trinity, in the fourth year of the reign of King George the Fourth*."

Such title refers to the time when the party is supposed to deliver his oral allegation in open court; and as it was only in *term* time that the court anciently sat to hear the pleading, it is therefore always of a *term* that the pleadings are entitled, though they are often in fact filed or delivered in vacation time. The term of which any pleading is entitled is usually

---

[1] Glanvill, Lib. 10, c. 12, sec. 3, 4; Hist. Pr. 316, 317, 318.

[2] Evans, Pl 27, 28.

[3] 1 Arch. 72, 162; Topping *v* Fuge,

[1] Marsh. 341 , Chit. Pl. 376, 397, 468.

[4] Com. Dig Pleader, C. 7; Chit Pl. 376, 468.

that in which it is actually filed or delivered;[1] or, where this takes place in vacation time, the title is of the term last preceding.

The most frequent practice is to entitle *generally* (according to the first form above given). But it is to be observed that a pleading so entitled is by construction of law presumed, unless proof be given to the contrary, to have been pleaded on the *first day* of the term. And the effect of this is, that if a *general* title be used, it will sometimes occasion an apparent objection.

Example: In the case of a declaration so entitled, it may appear in evidence on the trial that the cause of action arose in the course and after the first day of the term of which the declaration is entitled, or this may appear on the face of the declaration itself; and, in either case, this objection would arise, that the plaintiff would appear to have declared before his cause of action arose; whereas the cause of action ought of course always to exist at the time the action is commenced.[2]

The means of avoiding this difficulty is to entitle *specially* (according to the second form above given) of the *particular day* in the term when the pleading was actually filed or delivered.

RULE XI. ALL PLEADINGS OUGHT TO BE TRUE.[3]

While this rule is recognized, it is at the same time to be observed, that generally there is no means of *enforcing* it as a rule of pleading, because regularly there is no way of proving the falsehood of an allegation till issue has been taken and trial had upon it.

It may also be observed, that, notwithstanding this rule, a practice has prevailed of what is called *sham pleading;* that

---

[1] But *dilatory pleas,* though pleaded in a term subsequent to that of which the declaration is entitled (as is sometimes the case), must yet always be entitled of the same term with the declaration, unless pleaded with a special or general special imparlance. See this further explained, Chit. Pl. 397, 398.

[2] But where this objection arises on the trial, it may be answered by giving evidence that the declaration was actually filed on a subsequent day in the term. (Granger v. George, 5 Barn. & Cress. 149.)

[3] Bac. Ab. Pleas, &c., G. 4; Slade v. Drake, Hob. 295; Smith v. Yeomans, 1 Saund. 316.

is, pleading, for the mere purpose of delay, a matter which the pleader knows to be false. There are certain pleas of this kind which, in consequence of their having been long and frequently used in practice, have obtained toleration from the courts, and, though discouraged, are tacitly allowed; as, for example, the common plea of *judgment recovered*, viz., that judgment has been already recovered by the plaintiff for the same cause of action. But in other cases a sham plea, when ascertained to be so, is not allowed. It is true that, as already observed, it can not generally, and in the regular course, be proved that a plea is false till the trial; but where a plea is not in the usual and tolerated form of a sham plea, and the matter pleaded is at the same time very improbable, and presumably intended as a plea of that description, the court will, *on motion*, supported by affidavit of its falsehood, allow judgment to be signed by the plaintiff as for want of plea, and make the defendant or his attorney pay the costs.[1] And the court has in all cases power to punish for sham pleading, and has often strongly censured the practice.

FICTIONS AN EXCEPTION TO RULE.

Lastly, there is an exception to the rule in question, in the case of certain *fictions* established in pleading for the convenience of justice.

Examples : The declaration in ejectment always states a fictitious demise made by the real claimant to a fictitious plaintiff; and the declaration in trover uniformly alleges, though almost always contrary to the fact, that the defendant *found* the goods in respect of which the action is brought.

---

[1] Thomas *v.* Vandermoolen, 2 Barn. & Ald. 197 ; Bartley *v.* Godslake, *ibid.* 199 ; Shadwell *v.* Berthoud, 5 Barn. & Ald. 750, 751 ; Richley *v.* Proone, 1 Barn. & Cress. 286 ; Merington *v.* Becket, 2 Barn. & Cress. 81 ; Bell *v.* Alexander, 6 M. & S. 133 ; Young *v.* Gadderer, 1 Bing. 380.

CONCLUSION.

THE concluding observations of Mr. Stephen, excellent as they are, do not add anything to the principles of special pleading. The student who desires to consider in detail the merits and the defects of this science can, however, profitably study what Mr. Stephen has said under these heads, as also the extended remarks upon the same points by Professor Minor.[1]

The present work can well end with the following words of Chief Justice, afterwards Chancellor, Kent.[2]

"I entertain a decided opinion that the established principles of pleading, which compose what is called its science, are rational, concise, luminous, and admirably adapted to the investigation of truth, and ought consequently to be very carefully touched by the hand of innovation."

[1] Min. Inst. IV. 1066–1088.
[2] Bayard v. Malcolm, 1 Johns. Rep. 471 (Kent, C. J., 1806).

APPENDIX.

———◆———

SPECIMENS OF COMMON LAW RECORDS.

I.

ACTION FOR ASSAULT AND BATTERY, BY BILL IN KING'S BENCH.

HAWE *versus* PLANNER.

Trin. 17 Car. II. Regis, Roll. 925.

Berkshire, } Be it remembered that heretofore, to wit. } to wit, in the term of St. Hilary last past, before our lord the king at Westminster, came Henry Hawe by James Rouse his attorney, and brought here into the court of our said lord the king, then there, his certain bill against John Planner, of the parish of Wokingham, in the county aforesaid, yeoman, in the custody of the marshal, &c. of a plea of trespass, and there are pledges of prosecution, to wit, John Doe and Richard Roe, which said bill follows in these words; that is to say, *Berkshire,* to wit, Henry Hawe complains of John Planner, of the parish of Wokingham in the county aforesaid, yeoman, being in the custody of the marshal of the Marshalsea of our lord the king before the king himself, for that he on the 4th day of September, in the 16th year of the reign of our lord Charles the Second, now King of England, &c. with force and arms, &c. made an assault upon him the said Henry Hawe, at Wokingham aforesaid, in the county aforesaid, and him the said Henry then and there beat, wounded, and ill treated, so that his life was greatly despaired of, and other wrongs to him then and there did, against the peace of our said lord the now king, and to the damage of him the said Henry of 100*l.* and therefore he brings suit, &c.

Plea.

And now at this day, to wit, on Friday next after the Morrow of the Holy Trinity in this same term, until which day the said John had leave to imparl to the bill aforesaid, and then to answer, &c., before our lord the king at Westminster, comes as well the said Henry by his said attorney, as the said John by William Willmer, his attorney ; and the said John Planner defends the force and injury when, &c. And as to the coming with force and arms, or whatever that is against the peace of our said lord the now king, and also as to the said wounding above supposed to be done, the said John Planner saith that he is not guilty thereof, and of this he puts himself upon the country, and the said Henry thereof likewise, &c.

As to the force and arms, &c., and the wounding, defendant pleads not guilty.

And as to the residue of the trespass and assault aforesaid above supposed to be done, the said John Planner saith that the said Henry ought not to have or maintain his said action thereof against him ; because he saith, that before the said time when the said trespass and assault is supposed to be done, and at the time when, &c., he the said John was one of the churchwardens of the parish of Wokingham aforesaid, duly elected and appointed ; and that the said Henry before the said time, when, &c., and at the same time when, &c., was an inhabitant of the said parish ; and that the said Henry so being an inhabitant of the said parish before the said time when, &c., to wit, on the 21st day of August, in the 16th year aforesaid, being Sunday, was in the church of the parish aforesaid during the time that divine service was celebrated in the said church, and that the said Henry, at the time when prayers were made in the same church by the congregation of the people there, irreverently had his head covered with his hat ; whereupon he, the said John, being such churchwarden as aforesaid, then and there admonished and requested the said Henry to uncover his head, which the said Henry refused and neglected to do ; whereupon he the said John then and there took from the head of the said Henry his said hat, and then and there delivered the same to the said

And as to the residue of the trespass, actio non ;

because defendant was one of the churchwardens of Wokingham, and plaintiff an inhabitant there ;

and the plaintiff was in church during the time of divine service with his hat on ;

whereupon defendant requested him to take his hat off his head ; which he refused ; therefore defendant took plaintiff's hat off his head and delivered it to him, which is the same assault; and traverses being guilty at any other time than the day mentioned in the plea.

Henry, as it was well lawful for him to do; which said taking of the said hat of the said Henry from his head is the same assaulting, beating, and ill treating whereof the said Henry above thereof complains against him the said John : without this, that he the said John is guilty of the said assaulting, beating or ill-treating on the said 4th of September, or at any other time than on the said 21st day of August, in the 16th year aforesaid, or otherwise, or in any other manner, as the said Henry Hawe above thereof complains against him the said John; and this he the said John is ready to verify; wherefore he prays judgment if the said Henry ought to have or maintain his said action thereof against him the said John, &c. (A general demurrer and a joinder in demurrer.)

Curia advisare vult.

But because the court of our said lord the king now here is not yet advised of giving their judgment of and upon the premises whereof the parties aforesaid have put themselves upon the judgment of the court, a day thereof is given to the said parties before our lord the king at Westminster until the   day next after   to hear their judgment of and upon the premises,

Ven. fac. tam ad triand. quam ad inquirend.

because the court of our lord the king here thereof is not yet, &c.; and as well to try the said issue above joined between the said parties to be tried by the country, as to inquire what damages the said Henry Hawe has sustained on occasion of the said trespass and assault, whereof the said parties have put themselves upon the judgment of the court, if it shall happen that the judgment should be given for the said Henry Hawe against the said John Planner, let a jury thereof come before our lord the king at Westminster on   day next   and who neither, &c. to recognize, &c. because as well, &c. the same day is given to the said parties there, &c.; at which Tuesday next after fifteen days of the Holy Trinity, before our lord the king at Westminster, come the parties aforesaid by their attornies aforesaid. And because the court of our said lord the king here is not yet advised of giving their judgment of and

upon the premises, a day thereof is further given
to the said parties before our lord the king at
Westminster until Monday next after three weeks
of St. Michael, to hear their judgment of and
upon the premises because the court of our said
lord the king now here is thereof not yet, &c.;

Adjournment to Oxford. before which day the said plaint was adjourned by
our said lord the king's writ of common adjourn-
ment before our said lord the king at Oxford, in
the county of Oxford, until Saturday in the octave
of St. Martin; at which day, before our lord the
king at Oxford, come the parties aforesaid by their
attornies aforesaid. And because the court of our
said lord the king now here is not yet advised of
giving their judgment of and upon the premises,
a further day thereof is given to the said parties,
before our lord the king at Oxford, until Saturday
on the Morrow of the Purification of the Blessed
Mary to hear their judgment of and upon the
premises, because the court of our said lord the

*Term ad-
journed to
Windsor.* king now here is thereof not yet, &c.; before
which day the said plaint was adjourned by our
said lord the king's writ of common adjournment
before our said lord the king, until the said Morrow of the Purification of the Blessed Mary, at
the castle of Windsor, in the county of Berks;
at which day before our lord the king, at the said
castle of Windsor, come the said parties by their
said attornies. And because the court of our said
lord the king now here is not yet advised of giving
their judgment of and upon the premises, a further
day thereof is given to the said parties, before our
lord the king, at the said castle of Windsor, until
Friday next, in the octave of the Purification of
the Blessed Mary, to hear their judgment of and
upon the premises, because the court of our said
lord the king here is thereof not yet, &c. Before
which day the said plaint was adjourned by our

*Adjournment
to Westminster.* said lord the king's writ of common adjournment
before our said lord the king, until the said octave
of the Purification of the Blessed Mary at Westminster, in the county of Middlesex. At which
day, before our lord the king at Westminster,

come the parties aforesaid by their attornies aforesaid. And because the court of our said lord the king here is not yet advised of giving their judgment of and upon the premises, a further day thereof is given to the said parties before our lord the king at Westminster, until Monday next after the Morrow of the Ascension of our Lord, to hear their judgment of and upon the premises, because the court of our said lord the king here is thereof not yet, &c. At which day, before our lord the king at Westminster, come the parties aforesaid by their attornies aforesaid. (Further continuances for two terms.) At which day, before our lord the king at Westminster, come the parties aforesaid by their attornies aforesaid. And thereupon the premises being seen, and by the court here fully understood, it seems to the said court that the said plea by him the said John Planner, in manner and form aforesaid above pleaded, and the matter in the same contained, are good and sufficient in law to bar the said Henry Hawe from having his said action thereof against him the

Judgment. said John Planner. Therefore it is considered that the said Henry Hawe take nothing by the bill; and that he and his pledges of prosecution, to wit, John Doe and Richard Roe, be thereof in mercy for his false claim, and that the said John Planner go thereof without day, &c.

1 Saunders' Reports, 10.

II.

ACTION FOR TRESPASS (q. c. f.) BY ORIGINAL IN KING'S BENCH.

MELLOR *versus* SPATEMAN.
Pasch. 21 Car. II. Regis, Roll. 249.

Derbyshire, } John Spateman late of Derby in the
    to wit.   } said county gent. was attached to answer Henry Mellor gent. of a plea wherefore with force and arms he broke and entered the close of the said Henry, called Littlefield, at Derby aforesaid, and his grass then and there lately growing, with feet in walking, and with his cattle eat up, trod down, and consumed, and other wrongs to him did, to the great damage, &c., and against the peace of our said lord the now king, &c. And whereupon the said Henry, by Alvered Motteram his attorney, complains that the said John, on the 20th day of October in the 20th year of the reign of our said lord Charles the Second now king of England, &c. with force and arms, &c., broke and entered the said close at Derby aforesaid in the county aforesaid, and his grass, to the value of 100 shillings, then and there lately growing, with his feet in walking, and with his cattle, to wit, horses, bulls, cows, sheep, and swine, eat up, trod down, and consumed, and other wrongs, &c., to the great damage, &c., and against the peace, &c.; wherefore he says that he is worse, and has damage to the value of 20*l.* ; and therefore he brings suit, &c.

Plea.   And the said John Spateman, by John Chambers his attorney, comes and defends the force and injury when, &c.; and as to the coming with force and arms, or whatever else is against the peace of our said lord the now king, and also the whole trespass aforesaid with the said cattle, except with two geldings and two mares, he the said John Spateman says that he is not thereof guilty, and of this he puts himself upon the country; and the said Henry thereof likewise, &c.: and as to the said trespass with two geldings and two mares, and with feet in walking, above supposed to be done, he the said John Spateman says, that he the said Henry ought not to have or maintain his said

Locus in quo part of Little-field.

action thereof against him, because he says that the said close, and also the place in which the said trespass is above supposed to be done, are, and at the said time when, &c., were, 20 acres of land with the appurtenances, in Derby aforesaid, which said 20 acres of land with the appurtenances, are, and at the said time when, &c., and also from time whereof the memory of man is not to the contrary, were parcel of a certain common field

Derby an ancient borough, and defendant a burgess of it.

called Littlefield, in Derby aforesaid. And the said John Spateman further says, that the borough of Derby in the county of Derby is an ancient borough; and that he the said John Spateman is, and at the said time when, &c. and long before was, and yet is one of the burgesses of the said borough; and that the burgesses of the said borough, from time whereof the memory of man is not to the contrary, until the 11th day of July in the 14th year of the reign of the lord Charles the

The burgesses of the said borough were immemorially a body corporate by the name of Bailiffs, &c. until 11th July, 14 Car. I.; then they were incorporated by the name of the mayor and burgesses of the borough of Derby;

First, late king of England, were a body politic and corporate by the name of the bailiffs and burgesses of the borough of Derby, and by the said name were used to plead and be impleaded. And the said John Spateman further saith, that in and upon the 11th day of July in the 14th year of the reign of the lord Charles the First, late king of England, &c., the said lord the king Charles the First by his letters patent made under his great seal of England, bearing date at Westminster the said 11th day of July in the said 14th year of his reign, constituted and created the bailiffs and burgesses of the said borough to be from thenceforth forever a corporation by the name of the mayor and burgesses of the borough of Derby aforesaid, as by the said letters patent, which he

the said John brings here into court, more fully
appears. And the said John further says, that
the bailiffs and burgesses of the said borough from
time whereof the memory of man is not to the
contrary until the said 11th day of July in the 14th
year of the reign of the said lord Charles the First,
and the mayor and burgesses of the said borough,
upon the said 11th day of July in the 14th year
aforesaid, and continually afterwards hitherto,
have had, and for the whole time aforesaid have
been accustomed to have, for themselves and every
burgess of the said borough, common of pasture in
the said field called Littlefield whereof, &c., for all
their commonable cattle; that is to say, in every
two years running together, when the said field
called Littlefield whereof, &c., was sown with any
corn, after the said corn growing in the said
field called Littlefield, whereof, &c., was reaped,
gathered, and carried away, until the said field, or
some part thereof, should be resown with any
corn; and in every third year when the said
field called Littlefield whereof, &c., lay fresh and
fallow, then during the whole year. Whereupon
the said John Spateman at the said time when,
&c., because the corn in that year growing in the
said field called Littlefield whereof, &c., was then
reaped, gathered, and from thence carried away,
and no part of the said field called Littlefield
whereof, &c., was resown with any corn, put the
said two geldings and two mares, which said two
geldings and two mares were the proper cattle of
him the said John Spateman, into the said field
called Littlefield whereof, &c., to depasture the
grass then growing in the same, to use his said
common, and the said grass then growing in the
said close in which, &c., with the said geldings
and mares, and with his feet in walking at the
said time when, &c., &c., eat up, trod down, and
consumed, as it was lawful for him to do for the
cause aforesaid; and this he is ready to verify:
wherefore he prays judgment if the said Henry
ought to have or maintain his said action thereof
against him, &c. — (To this there is a general de-

Marginal notes:

and prescribes in the said corporation for a right of common in Littlefield as one of the burgesses;

and put his cattle into the common.

Demurrer

murrer, and a joinder in demurrer, and then the.
entry proceeds.)

But because the court of our said lord the king
now here is not yet advised of giving their judgment of and upon the premises, a day thereof is
given to the said parties before our lord the king

Curia advisare at Westminster, until   day next after
vult. to hear their judgment of and upon the premises,
because the court of our said lord the king now

And as well as here is not yet, &c. And as well to try the said
to try the said issue above joined between the said parties to be
issue as to in-
quire of contin- tried by the country, as to inquire what damages
gent damages on the said Henry Mellor has sustained on occasion
the demurrer. of the said trespass, whereof the said parties have
put themselves upon the judgment of the court,
if it happen that judgment shall be thereof given
for the said Henry against the said John Spate-

Venire man, let a jury thereof come before our lord the
awarded. king at Westminster, on   day next after
and who neither, &c., to recognize, &c.; because
as well, &c.: the same day is given to the said
parties there, &c. At which day here came as
well the said Henry as the said John by their

Curia ulterius attornies aforesaid. And because the court here
advisare vult. is not yet advised of giving their judgment of
and upon the premises whereof the said parties
have above put themselves on the judgment of the
court, a day thereof is further given to the said
parties before our said lord the king, from the day
of St. Michael in three weeks wheresoever, &c.,
to hear their judgment thereof, because the court

Vic. non misit of our said lord the king here is thereof not yet,
breve. &c., and as to try the said issue above joined between the said parties to be tried by the country,

Alias venire. the sheriff hath not yet returned the writ, &c. :
therefore, as before, the sheriff is commanded that
he cause to come before our lord the king at the
said term wheresoever, &c., twelve, &c., to recog-
nise in form aforesaid; the same day is given to
the said parties there, &c. At which day here
come as well the said Henry as the said John by
their said attornies ; and thereupon the premises,
whereof the said parties have above put them-

selves on the judgment of the court, being seen, and by the court here fully understood, and mature deliberation thereof had, for that it appears to the court of our said lord the king here, that the said plea of the said John, as to the said trespass with the said two geldings and two mares, and with feet in walking, above supposed to be done by the said John in manner and form aforesaid above pleaded, are not sufficient in law to bar the said Henry from having his said action thereof against the said John, it is considered that the said Henry should recover his damages against the said John on occasion of the said trespass committed with the said two geldings and two mares, and with feet in walking, &c. And as to the trial of the said issue above joined between the said parties to be tried by the country, the sheriff has not returned his writ, &c.: and thereupon he the said Henry freely here in court acknowledges, that he will not any further prosecute against the said John for the said residue of the said trespass above supposed to be done, but altogether disavows and refuses any further to prosecute against the said John for the said residue of the said trespass; therefore let the said John be thereof quit, &c.: and the said Henry prays judgment, and his damages on occasion of the said trespass committed with the said two geldings and two mares, and with feet in walking, to be given to him against the said John. But because it is not known to the court of our said lord the king now here what damages the said Henry has sustained, as well on the occasion of the said trespass as for his costs and charges by him about his suit in that behalf expended, therefore the sheriff is commanded that, by the oath of good and lawful men of his bailiwick, he diligently inquire what damages he the said Henry has sustained as well on occasion of the said trespass with the said two geldings and two mares, and with feet in walking, as for his costs and charges by him about his suit in that behalf expended, and the inquisition which, &c., should send to our said lord the king, in the

Judgment.

Nolle prosequi as to the issue.

Writ of inquiry of damages awarded.

octave of St. Hilary wheresoever, &c., under the seal, &c., and seals, &c., together with the writ of our said lord the king to him thereof directed. The same day is given to the said Henry there, &c. At which day, before our lord the king at Westminster, comes the said Henry Mellor by his said attorney; and the sheriff, to wit, Cornelius

Inquisition returned.

Clarke esquire, returns a certain inquisition, indented, taken before him at Derby in the county of Derby, on the 28th day of January in the 21st year of the reign of our said lord the now king, by the oath of twelve good, &c., whereby it is found that the said Henry Mellor hath sustained damages on the occasion aforesaid, besides his costs and charges by him about his suit in that behalf expended, to two pence; and for those costs and

Judgment.

charges, to two pence: therefore it is considered that the said Henry do recover against the said John his said damages by the said inquisition in form aforesaid found, and also eight pounds nineteen shillings and eight pence for his said costs and charges of increase adjudged to the said Henry by the court of our said lord the king now here with his assent; which said damages in the whole amount to nine pounds: and let the said John Spateman be taken, &c.

1 Saunders' Reports, 339.

III.

WRIT OF ERROR IN KING'S BENCH TO COUNTY OF DURHAM (A COUNTY PALATINE).

PEACOCK *versus* BELL AND KENDAL.

Mich. 18 Car. II. Regis, Roll. 230.

Writ of Error. *England,* } Our lord the king has sent to his jus-
to wit. } tices itinerant, in the county of Durham
and Sadberg, and other his justices in the same
county, and to every of them, his writ close in these
words, to wit: Charles the Second, by the Grace of
God, of England, Scotland, France, and Ireland, king,
defender of the faith, &c., to our justices itinerant in
the county of Durham and Sadberg, and to our other
justices in the same county, and to every of them,
greeting; forasmuch as in the record and process,
and also in the giving of judgment of the plaint
which was before you in our court, in the said
county, by our writ between Richard Bell and
Benjamin Kendal, and John Peacock alderman, of
a certain plea of trespass upon the case, done by
the said John to the said Richard and Benjamin,
manifest error has intervened, as it is said, to the
great damage of the said John, as from his complaint we have been informed, We, being willing
that the error, if any there be, should be duly
amended, and full and speedy justice done to the
said parties in this behalf, command you, that if
judgment be thereon given, you send to us, openly
and distinctly, under your seal, the said record and
process, with all things touching the same, and this
writ, so that we may have the same from the day
of St. Martin, in fifteen days, wheresoever we
shall then be in England, that inspecting the said
record and process we cause further to be done
therein for amending the said error, what of right,
and according to the law and custom of our realm

of England, shall be meet to be done. Witness ourself at Westminster, the 24th day of August, in the 18th year of our reign.

On the 24th day of September, in the 18th year of king Charles the Second, by the court; the answer of the justices of our lord the king within written; the execution of this writ appears in a certain schedule annexed to this writ. John Tempest, John Morland. This writ is allowed by us, John Tempest, William Bellasys, John Morland.

Durham, to wit. Pleas at Durham, before W. Blakiston, esq., Samuel Davison, esq., William Bellasys senior, esq., Lewis Hall, esq., and John Morland, esq., and their fellows, justices itinerant of our lord the now king, in the county of Durham and Sadberg, of his session or court of pleas holden at Durham the 6th day of June, in the 18th year of the reign of our lord Charles the Second, by the grace of God, of England, Scotland, France, and Ireland, king, defender of the faith, &c.

Warrant of attorney by the plaintiffs.

Durham, to wit. Richard Bell and Benjamin Kendal put in their place Ralph Adamson their attorney against John Peacock, late of the city of Durham, in the said County, alderman, of a plea of trespass upon the case.

Like for the defendant.

Durham, to wit. John Peacock, late of the city of Durham, in the said county, alderman, puts in his place Christopher Bell, his attorney, against the said Richard Bell and Benjamin Kendal, of a plea of trespass upon the case.

Declaration. Recital of the writ.

Durham, to wit. John Peacock, late of the city of Durham, in the said county, alderman, was attached to answer Richard Bell and Benjamin Kendal, of a plea, wherefore, whereas the said John, on the 11th day of November, in the 17th year of the reign of our lord Charles the Second, now king of England, &c., at the city of Durham, in the said county, was indebted to the said Richard and Benjamin in 39*l*. of lawful money of England, for divers wares and merchandises by the said Richard and Benjamin before that time sold and delivered to the said John Peacock at his special instance and request; and being so indebted, he the said John, in consideration thereof, undertook, and then and there faithfully promised the said Richard and Benjamin, that he the said John Peacock would well and faithfully pay and content the said 39*l.* to the said Richard and Benjamin when he should be thereunto requested; yet the said John not regarding his said promise and undertaking in form aforesaid made, but contriving and fraudulently intending craftily and subtily to deceive and defraud them the said Richard and Benjamin of the said 39*l.* has not yet paid the said 39*l.* or any penny thereof, to the said Richard and Benjamin, or any ways contented them for the same, (although so to do the said John afterwards, to wit, on the last day of November, in the said 17th year of the reign of our lord Charles the Second, now king of England, &c., at the city of Durham, in the said county, was often requested by the said Richard and Benjamin), but to pay the same to them, or in any ways to content them for the same, has altogether refused, and still refuses, to the damage of the said Richard and Benjamin of 40*l.* &c. And whereupon the said Richard and Benjamin, by Ralph Adamson their attorney, complain, that whereas the said John, on the 11th day of November, in the 17th year of the reign of our lord Charles the Second, now king of England, &c., at the city of Durham, in the said county, was indebted to the said Richard and Benjamin in 39*l.* of lawful money of England, for divers wares and merchandises by the said Richard and Benjamin before that time sold and delivered to the said John Peacock at his special instance and request; and being so indebted, he the said John, in consideration thereof, undertook, and then and there faithfully promised the said Richard and Benjamin, that he the said John Peacock would well and faithfully pay and content the said 39*l.* to the said Richard and Benjamin when he should be thereunto requested; yet the said John, not regarding his said promise and undertaking in form aforesaid made, but contriving and fraudulently intending craftily and subtily to deceive and defraud them the said Richard and Benjamin of the said 39*l.* has not yet paid the said 39*l.* or any penny thereof, to the said Richard and Benjamin, or any ways contented them for the same, (although so to do the said John afterwards, to wit, on the last day of November, in the said 17th year of the reign of our lord Charles the Second, now king of England, &c., at the city of Durham, in the said county, was often requested by the said Richard and Benjamin), but to pay the same to them, or in any ways to content them for the same has altogether refused, and still refuses, to the damage of the said Richard and Benjamin of 40*l.* &c.; and therefore they bring suit, &c.

Imparlance.

And the said John by Christopher Bell, his attorney, comes and defends the wrong and injury when, &c. and prays leave to imparl thereto here, until the 23d day of June instant, and he has it, &c.; the same day is given to the said Richard and Benjamin here, &c. At which day here come as well the said Richard and Benjamin as the said John, by their said attornies; and thereupon the said John further prays leave to imparl thereto here, until the 14th day of July next following; and he has it, &c.; the same day is given to the said Richard and Benjamin here, &c. At which day here come as well the said Richard and Benjamin as the said John, by their said attornies; and thereupon the said John further prays leave to imparl here, until the 30th day of July instant; and he has it, &c.; the same day is given to the said Richard and Benjamin here, &c. At which day here come as well the said Richard and Benjamin as the said John, by their said attornies; and thereupon the said Richard and Benjamin pray that the said John may answer the said declaration. And the said John, as before, defends the wrong and injury when, &c. and says, that he did not undertake and promise in manner and form as the said Richard and Benjamin have above thereof complained against him; and of this he puts himself upon the country, &c. And the

Plea.

Non assumpsit.

Issue.

29

Venire.

said Richard and Benjamin likewise, &c. Therefore the sheriff is commanded that he cause to come here on Thursday the 16th day of August next coming, at eight o'clock in the forenoon of the same day, twelve, &c., by whom, &c., and who neither, &c., to recognize, &c., because as well, &c. At which day and hour here come as well the said Richard and Benjamin as the said John, by their said attornies; and the sheriff, to wit, Thomas Davison knight, now returns the said writ of our lord the king of *venire facias* to him in form aforesaid directed, together with a panel of the names of the jurors annexed to the same, in all things served and executed; and the jury impanelled thereon, being called, do not come; there-

Habeas corpora juratorum.

fore the sheriff is commanded that he have their bodies here the same Thursday the 16th day of August, instant, at two o'clock in the afternoon of the same day; the same day and hour are given to the said parties here, &c. At which day and hour come as well the said Richard and Benjamin as the said John, by their said attornies; and the sheriff, to wit, Thomas Davison knight, now returns here the said writ of *habeas corpora juratorum* to him in form aforesaid directed, together with a panel of the names of the jurors thereto annexed, in all things served and executed; and the jury impanelled therein, being called, likewise come; and being chosen, tried, and sworn to speak the truth of the premises, upon their oath say,

Verdict for the plaintiffs.

that the said John did undertake and promise in manner and form as the said Richard and Benjamin have above declared against him; and they assess the damages of the said Richard and Benjamin, on occasion of the non-performance of the said promise and undertaking, besides their costs and charges by them about their suit in that behalf expended, to 30*l*. 11*s*. 2*d*. and for those costs

Judgment for the plaintiffs.

and charges to 40*s*. Therefore it is considered that the said Richard and Benjamin recover against the said John their said damages to 32*l*. 11*s*. 2*d*. by the said jurors in form aforesaid assessed, and also 5*l*. by the court here awarded of increase to the said Richard and Benjamin at their request, for their said costs and charges, which said damages in the whole amount to 37*l.* 11*s.* 2*d.*; and the said John in mercy, &c.

Afterwards, to wit, on Wednesday next after the octave of St. Hilary then next following, before our lord the king at Westminster, comes the said John Peacock by W. Bigg, his attorney, and says, that in the said record and process, and also in giving the judgment aforesaid, there is manifest error in this, that it appears by the said record that the said judgment was given for the said Richard Bell and Benjamin Kendal against the said John Peacock; whereas judgment ought by the law of the land to have been given for the said John Peacock against the said Richard Bell and Benjamin Kendal, therefore in that there is manifest error; and the said John Peacock prays the writ of our said lord the king to warn the said Richard Bell and Benjamin Kendal to be before our lord the king to hear the record and process aforesaid, and it is granted to him, &c. Whereupon the sheriff is commanded, that by good, &c., he make known to the said Richard Bell and Benjamin Kendal that they be before our lord the king on the octave of the Purification of the Blessed Virgin Mary, wheresoever, &c., to hear the said record and process, if, &c., and further, &c., the same day is given to the said John Peacock, &c. At which day, before our lord the king at Westminster, comes the said John Peacock by his said attorney, and the sheriff has not sent the writ thereof, &c. And the said Richard Bell and Benjamin Kendal on the same day being solemnly called, likewise come by A. B. their attorney: whereupon the said John Peacock, as before, says that in the said record and process, and also in giving the said judgment, there is manifest error, alleging the said errors by him in form aforesaid alleged, and prays that the said judgment, for the said errors, and others being in the said record and process, may be revoked, annulled, and entirely held for nothing, and that he may be restored to

*Error.
General error
assigned.*

Scire facias.

*Vicecomes non
misit breve.*

all things which he has lost by occasion of the said judgment; and that the court of our said lord the king here may proceed as well to the examination of the said record and process, as of the said matter above assigned for error; and that the said Richard Bell and Benjamin Kendal may re-

Nullo est erratum. join to the said errors, &c. Whereupon the said Richard Bell and Benjamin Kendal say, that neither in the said record and process, nor in giving the said judgment, is there any error; and they pray that the court of our said lord the king here may proceed as well to the examination of the said record and process, as of the said matters above assigned for errors.

1 Saunders' Reports, 69.

INDEX.

ABATEMENT,
  of nuisances, a method of self-help, 16.
  of actions,
    by death, of a sole party, 62.
      at common law, 62, 118 n., 396.
      under the statute, 17 Car. II. c. 8. 62.
    of a tort-feasor, 114, 118 n.
  by the king's demise, 140.

ABATEMENT, PLEA IN,
  for non-joinder or misjoinder of parties, 112, 135, 136, 176, 177.
  of the writ, a dilatory plea, 175. (See *Pleas.*)
    for variance, 176, 178.
    when former action is pending, 176.
  to the person of the plaintiff, or of the defendant, 176.
  to the count or declaration, 177.
  to the original writ, 177.
  applies to proceedings by bill, 178.
  effect of allowing, 178, 217.
  verification of, 178.
  when overruled on demurrer, judgment of respondeat ouster, 235.
  mistake in name of person, when ground for, 340.
  commencement and conclusion of, 396, 400.
  must give a better writ or bill, 424.

ABSQUE HOC, 255, 256, 260, 263, 266, 388.

ACCORD,
  a method of self-help, 17.

ACCOUNT,
  a formed action ex contractu, 48, 60.

ACT OF PARLIAMENT,
  illegality arising from, matter for special plea, 245.

ACTIONS. (See *Mixed Actions; Personal Actions; Real Actions.*)
  origin and history of, 24, 38.
  forms of, 38–108.
  formerly rigid, and forms prevailed over rights, 22–24, 38.
  division of, into real personal, and mixed actions, 40–48.
      local and transitory actions, 329–334.

ACTIONS — *continued.*
  Personal actions divided :
    (1) formed actions ex contractu,
      debt, 48–55. (See *Debt.*)
      detinue, 48, 55–57. (See *Detinue.*)
      covenant, 48, 57–60. (See *Covenant.*)
      account, 48, 60.
      scire facias, 48, 60–63. (See *Scire facias.*)
    (2) formed actions ex delicto,
      trespass, 63–73, 100, 101. (See *Trespass.*)
      replevin, 63, 73–77. (See *Replevin.*)
    the formed actions inadequate, 77, 83.
    upon the case, 77–82. (See *Case, Action upon the*)
    new forms of,
      assumpsit, 79, 82–89. (See *Assumpsit.*)
      trover, 79, 90–93. (See *Trover.*)
  Mixed actions divided:
      waste, 45.
      quare impedit, 45.
    ejectment, 93–99.
      for mesne profits, 100.
    consequences of mistake in form of action, 101.
    extraordinary forms of, 102–108.
    joinder, of forms of actions, 109, 110.
      of rights of action, 110, 111.
    election of, 111–115. (See *Election.*)
    parties to, 116–136. (See *Parties.*)
    the original writ, 137–148.
    proceedings in, 148–225. (See *Issue : Judgment ; Pleading ; Process.*)
    pleas in suspension of, 175, 176, 217.
ADJECTIVE LAW,
  formerly controlled the substantive, 24, 38.
ADMINISTRATOR. (See *Executor.*)
AGENT. (See *Principal and Agent.*)
ALIEN ENEMY,
  plea of, to be certain in every particular, 368.
ALLEGATION. (See *Pleading.*)
AMBIGUITY,
  in pleading, not allowed, 383–386. (See *Pleading.*)
AMENDMENT,
  of action to another of same class, 101.
  of pleadings, 189, 190, 239.
    leave for, 190.
  statutes of, and jeofails. (See *Jeofails.*)
AMERCEMENTS,
  recoverable in debt, 50, 52.
  judgment in misericordia, 219, 220.

ANIMALS,
>   when trespass lies for taking or injuring, 70, 72.
>   injuries by, remedy in case, 79, 80.

ANNUITY,
>   a formed action ex contractu, 48 n.

ANSWER, 169.

APPEALS, 103, 172.
>   to King's Bench, 35.
>   to Exchequer Chamber, 36.
>   to House of Lords, 36.
>   as private prosecutions, 66.
>   de pace et plagis, 66, 67.

APPEARANCE,
>   of defendant, 158, 159, 422.

ARBITRATION,
>   the source of civil jurisdiction, 13.
>   a method of self-help, 18.
>   award does not convey realty, 18.
>   debt lay upon an award, 52.
>   also assumpsit for other performance than payment of money, 87.

ARGUMENTATIVENESS,
>   in pleading, not allowed, 260, 386–388. (See *Pleading.*)

ARREST OF JUDGMENT. (See *Judgment.*)

ARSON, 65, 66.

ASSAULT AND BATTERY,
>   action of trespass for, 67, 70, 435.
>   form of original writ in, 144.
>   declaration in, 166, 167.

ASSIZE,
>   of mort d'ancestor, 43, 172 n.
>   of novel disseisin, 14, 42-45, 199.
>   grand, 199.
>   petty, 171, 172, 199, 200.
>   giving color in, 277.
>   defence not made to, 423.

ASSUMPSIT,
>   an action of tort, developing into one of contract, 82, 86.
>   special, 83, 87, 88.
>   general, 85, 87, 88.
>   quantum meruit, 85, 89.
>   declaration in, 86, 89.
>   damages in, 84, 86.
>   joinder of counts in, 110.
>   election between, and trespass. or case, 112, 113, 115
>   general issue in, 247, 248

ATTACHMENT, 149, 158.
  of privilege, 155, 168.
ATTORNEY, 22.
  if negligent, liable in case, 80.
AUDITA QUERELA, 102 n.
AULA REGIS, 28–33, 137.
AUTHORITY,
  how far the pleadings must show, 355–358.
  averments of, to be strictly proved, 358.
AVERMENT. (See *Declaration; Issue; Pleading.*)
AVOWRY, 76.
  of liberum tenementum, 351.
  the statute, 11 Geo. II., c. 19, § 22, 355.
  commencement and conclusion of, 398.

AWARD. (See *Arbitration.*)
  alleging breach of, 288.

BAIL, 156.
BAILMENTS,
  remedies respecting,
    in detinue, 56.
    in trespass, 70, 71.
    in trover, 92.
  election of actions respecting, 112, 115.
BANKRUPT,
  as party plaintiff, 122, 132.
        defendant, 128, 134.
BANKRUPTCY, PLEA OF, 113.
BARRISTER,
  to sign pleadings, 164.
BATTLE,
  offer of, 170.
  trial by, 195, 196.
BILL OF EXCEPTIONS, 206.
BILL OF MIDDLESEX, 153, 167.
BLOOD-FEUD, 64, 65.
BOND. (See *Debt; Deed.*)
  with condition, 303 n.
BOT, 65, 66.
BURDEN OF PROOF,
  usually rests upon party maintaining the affirmative, 204, 258.

CAPIAS AD RESPONDENDUM, 149, 158.

CAPIAS IN WITHERNAM, 74, 106.

CAPIAS UTLAGATUM, 151.

CASE AGREED, 209.

CASE, TRESPASS UPON THE, 77–93.
    when it lies, 79–82.
    declaration in, 82.
    trover, 90–93.
    election between, and assumpit, 112, 113, 115.
            and trespass, 114.

CASSETER BREVE, 217, 219.

CERTAINTY IN THE ISSUE,
    reasons for, 229 and n. 2, 372.
    required as to place, 323–334. (See *Venue*.)
        as to time, 334–336. (See *Time*.)

CERTIORARI,
    an extraordinary remedy, 107.

CHANCERY. (See *Equity*)
    original writs issued from, 39, 139–144, 148.
        in replevin, 74.
        in case, 77, 81.
        procedendo, 103.
        prohibition from, 103.
        mainprize from, 105.

CHATTELS,
    recoverable in detinue, 56, 57.
    real, 93.

CHILD,
    injury to, remedy in trespass, 70.
    seduction of female, 70, 80.
    liberty of, restored by habeas corpus, 107.

CIRCUITS, 30, 32, 33.

CLERGY,
    jurisdiction over of Anglo-Saxon courts, 26–28.

COGNIZANCES, 76.
    the statute of 11 Geo. II. c. 19, § 22, 355.
    commencement and conclusion of, 398.

COLOR,
    in pleading, 273–279. (See *Confession and Avoidance, Pleas in*.)

COMMENCEMENT,
    of pleadings, 392–400. (See *Pleading*.)

COMMON BAR, 285, 350.

COMMON COUNTS. (See *Counts*)
    included what, and how supported, 88, 89.
    joinder of, 316, 317.

COMMON PLEAS, COURT OF, 31, 35.
  jurisdiction, 35.
  prohibition from, 103.
COMMON TRAVERSE. (See *Traverse.*)
  a tender of issue, 240, 241.
COMPOSITION,
  in lieu of vengeance, 64.
COMPURGATION, 193.
CONCLUSION,
  of pleadings, 392–401. (See *Pleading.*)
CONFESSION AND AVOIDANCE, PLEAS IN,
  defined and explained, 178–181.
  motion for judgment non obstante veredicto, effect upon, 212, 213.
  in assumpsit, 248.
  inducement cannot be answered by, 266.
  division of, with respect to their subject-matter, into
      pleas in justification or excuse, 272.
      pleas in discharge, 272, 273.
  conclude with a verification and prayer for judgment, 273.
  must give color by admitting an apparent right and setting up new
      matter to defeat it, 273.
      implied color, 274.
      express color, 274–279, 410.
CONFESSION, JUDGMENT BY, 218, 219, 221.
CONSIDERATION,
  for contracts, 47, 50, 83.
  originally a mere promise was not a, 50.
  detriment as a, 82, 84.
  to be pleaded in assumpsit, 89.
CONSTITUTION,
  of the United States, Art. I., § 9, par. 2, 107.
CONSTRUCTION,
  of pleadings. (See *Issue; Pleading.*)
CONSULTATION, WRIT OF, 104.
CONTEMPT,
  by violating a procedendo, 103.
      or a prohibition, 104.
CONTINUANCES, 163.
  puis darreign continuance, 182, 397.
  imparlances, 187, 188, 449.
CONTRACT,
  law of, not early developed, 46, 47.
      under Roman law, 46, 47, 429.
  consideration, 47, 50, 82, 83. (See *Consideration.*)
  the actions of debt, detinue, and covenant preceded the idea of, 48.

CONTRACT — *continued.*
  formed actions upon, included
      debt, 48–55.
      detinue, 48, 55–57.
      covenant, 48.
      account, 48.
      scire facias, 48.
  debt lay, upon sealed, 51.
      when upon unsealed, 52.
  waiver of, by suing in tort, 112, 114.
  suits upon, parties plaintiff, 117–123.
                      defendant, 124–130.

CONTRA PACEM,
  when material words, in trespass, 68, 73.
  not used in case, 82.

CONVERSION. (See *Trover.*)

CORPORATION,
  mandamus against, 103.
  as party plaintiff, 120, 121.
          defendant, 126, 133.

COSTS,
  a part of the judgment, 219.

COUNT,
  the plaintiff's statement in real actions, 164.

COUNTS,
  several,
      when they may be joined without duplicity, 313–317.
      the object of using, 315, 316.
      common money counts, 89, 316, 317.

COUNTERPLEAS, 188.

" COUNTRY,"
  when and how pleadings conclude to it, 196, 289, 290, 292, 399, 425, 426.

COUNTY COURT, 25, 27, 33.

COURTS,
  defined, 20.
  of record, 21.
  not of record, 21.
  in general, 21.
  ancient prominence of procedure, 22.
  the Anglo-Saxon, 24–28.
  Court Baron, 26.
  of the Hundred, 26.
  county, 25, 27.
  lathe court, 27.
  court leet, 27.
  Anglo-Norman, 28.

COURTS — *continued.*
    the Aula Regis, or Curia Regis, 28–33, 36, 137.
    Court of Exchequer, 29, 32, 35, 153–155.
    Justices in Eyre, 30.
    Court of Common Pleas, 31, 32, 35.
        of King's Bench, 31, 32, 34, 67, 102, 152, 153.
        of Exchequer Chamber, 36.
        of House of Lords, 36.
    inferior, controlled by mandamus, procedendo, prohibition, and certiorari, 102, 103, 107.
    Germanic, 64, 192.
    Supreme Court of Judicature, 22, 156, 166, 167.

COVENANT, ACTION OF,
    a formed action upon contract, 48, 57–60.
    supported only by a deed, 58.
    damages recoverable in, 58–60.
    declaration in, 59, 60, 204.
    general issue in, 114 and n., 242 and n. 2.
    election between, and debt, 114.

COVENANTS,
    real, 123 n., 184.
    implied, 129.
    of warranty, 184.
    when debt lies upon, in cases of lease and devise, 52, 53, 59, 93.

COVERTURE. (See *Husband and Wife.*)
    pleading specially, 250 n.

CRIMINAL LAW,
    private prosecution, 13.
    origin and aim of, 65, 66.
    relation to trespass, 66, 67.
    exceptio de odio et atia, 200.

CUMULATIVE TRAVERSES,
    do not make a pleading double, 310–313.

CURIA REGIS, THE, 28–33, 36, 137.

DAMAGES,
    in debt, 55.
    in covenant, 58–60, 93.
    in account, 60.
    origin of in bot, 65, 66.
    in trespass, 66–68, 444.
    exemplary, 68.
    in replevin, 75, 76.
    in case, 79.
    in assumpsit, 84, 86, 89.
    in trover, 90–93.

DAMAGES— *continued.*
 in ejectment, 95, 100.
 effect upon, of election of actions, 114, 115.
 award of, by jury, 203, 216, 217.
 excessive, new trial, 212.
 general and special, 418 n.
DAMNUM ABSQUE INJURIA, 12.
DAY IN BANC, 146, 209.
DEATH. (See *Survival of Actions.*)
DEBT, ACTION OF,
 originated in procedure, 24.
 the earliest formed action upon contract, 48.
 began as a real action, 49.
 first lay for money loaned, then extended. 50.
 on records, 51, 55, 61.
 on statutes, 51.
 on sealed contracts, 51, 205.
 on unsealed contracts, when, 52.
 upon ouster of a lessee in part, 52.
 upon a devisor's convenant, 52.
 for arrears of rent, 52, 53.
 when it did not lie, 52–55.
 differs from detinue, 55.
 dependent upon the omission of a duty, 50, 55.
 deficiencies in, remedied by assumpsit, 83, 87.
 information for, 105.
 general issue in, 114.
 election between, and covenant, 114.
 judgment on default in, 115.
 original writ of, 144.
 declaration in, 165, 227, 338.
 demurrer in, form, 174, 227.
 on bond, commencement and conclusion of pleading, 398, 399.
DECEIT,
 remedy for, in case, 80.
  in assumpsit, 86, 87.
DECLARATION, 164–167, 181. (See *Pleading.*)
 in detinue, 57.
 in covenant, 59, 204.
 in trespass, 73, 161, 166, 285.
  for mesne profits, 100.
 in replevin, 74, 76.
 in case, 82.
 in assumpsit, 86, 89.
 in trover, 93.
 in ejectment, 97, 98, 100.
 in debt, 165, 227, 338.
 production of suit, 168, 418.

DECLARATION — *continued.*
    new assignment as a new, 287.
    duplicity in the, 303, 305.
    is not within the rule that a pleading bad in part is bad alto-
      gether, 402.

DEED,
    in England, the original form of contract, 47.
    in support of the action of covenant, 58.
    remedy on, when in debt, 51.
                     in assumpsit, 87.
    suit upon, party plaintiff, 117, 118.
                 defendant, 124.
    profert and oyer of, 185–187.
    estoppel by, 271.
    when to be alleged in pleading, 349, 350.

DEFAULT,
    judgment by, 115, 152, 218, 219, 221.

DEFENCE, THE, 169–171. (See *Issue ; Pleading*)

DE HOMINE REPLEGIANDO,
    writ of, 74, 106.

DE INJURIA, (*de son tort demesne*).
    the traverse, 251–254. (See *Replication ; Traverse.*)

DEMAND,
    in detinue, 57.
    in trover, 92.
    in ejectment, 99.
    of view, 183.
    of oyer, 185–187.
    of jury trial, 200.

DEMESNE,
    as of fee, pleading, 345, 400.

DEMURRER,
    office of, 101, 174.
    for non-joinder or misjoinder of parties, lies when, 135, 136.
    joinder in, 180, 227, 228, 293.
    when profert omitted, 186.
    to evidence, 206–208.
    in place of adding the similiter, 293.
    none upon a demurrer, 294.
    joinder of, with another pleading, 317 n., 319, 322.
    (1) nature and properties of,
        general, for insufficiency in substance, 232–234.
        special, for insufficiency in form, 232–234.
        effect of demurrer,
            admits facts sufficiently pleaded, 234.
            court considers the whole record on, 234–236.
                exceptions, 235, 236.

DEMURRER — *continued.*
  (2) effect of pleading over without, 236–239, 322.
    insufficiency in adverse pleading, when available without, 236.
    defective pleading, when aided by, 236, 237.
            when by verdict, 237.
            when cured by the statutes of amendments
              and jeofails, 211, 214, 224, 238, 239.
  (3) election to demur or plead,
    a question of expediency in matters of form, 239.
    also in matters of substance as to manner of statement, 239, 240

DEMURRER-BOOK, 189.

DE ODIO ET ATIA WRIT, 106, 172, 200.

DEPARTURE,
    in pleading, 403–408. (See *Pleading.*)

DETINUE, ACTION OF,
    a formed action upon contract, 48.
    an offspring of the action of debt, 49, 55.
    how different from debt, 55, 56.
    could be joined therewith, 56.

DILAPIDATION, 134 n.

DILATORY PLEAS. (See *Pleas.*)
    judgment upon, 217.

DISCONTINUANCE. (See *Issue*)
    of action, 163, 280.
    what pleading is a, 293 n., 294 n.
    how cured after verdict or certain judgments, 280 n.

DISTRESS,
    originally required judicial sanction, 16.
    a method of self-help, 16, 73.
    property exempt from, 16.
    remedies against, when illegal, 17, 71.
    when remediable in replevin, 73, 76.

DISTRINGAS, 149, 202, 209.

DOMESDAY BOOK, 198.

DOUBLE PLEAS. (See *Duplicity.*)

DOWER, ACTION OF,
    defence not made in, 422, 423.

DUPLICITY,
    the rule against, — that pleadings must not be double, — applies both
      to the declaration and to subsequent pleadings, 303–305.
    it is applied only to enforce a single issue upon a single subject of
      claim or defence, 305, 306.
    it does not compel each of several defendants to make the same
      answer, 307.
    a pleading is double that contains several answers, whatever be the
      class or quality of the answer, 307.

DUPLICITY — *continued.*

a pleading may be made double by matter ill-pleaded, 307, 308.

but not by immaterial matter, 308, 309.

or by matter pleaded only as an inducement to another allegation, 309, 310.

or by multifarious matters which together constitute but one connected proposition or entire point, 310.

    this applies to cumulative traverses, including the replication de injuria absque tali causa and the general issue in some cases, 310–313.

or by a protestation, 313.

the rule against, qualified by

    the use of several counts, 313–317.

    the use of several pleas, 313, 317–321.

DURESS,

deed made under, voidable, 245.

may be pleaded specially, 250 n.

ECCLESIASTICAL COURTS,

jurisdiction of, 34.

early enforced nude pacts, 47, 48.

controlled by prohibition, 104.

EJECTIONE FIRMÆ, 94, 95.

EJECTMENT, ACTION OF,

not a mixed action, 45.

history of, 82, 93–99.

quare ejecit infra terminum, 94.

ejectione firmæ, 94–96.

damages in, 95, 100.

judgment in, 95, 97, 99, 100.

under statutes, 99.

election between, and trespass, 112.

parties in, 134.

ELECTION,

of remedies, considerations governing,

    (1) the nature of the plaintiff's right, as depending upon possession or title, 111, 112.

    (2) the effect of non-joinder of parties, in contract and in tort, 112, 113.

    (3) joinder of several demands, 113.

    (4) depriving the defendant of defences by the form of action, 113, 114.

    (5) choice between local and transitory actions, 114.

    (6) death of defendant, effect on tort and contract, 114.

    (7) infants and lunatics liable in tort but not in contract, 114.

    (8) damages in different actions, 114, 115.

    (9) choosing tort where stringent process exists for it against defendant, 115.

ELECTION — *continued.*
> (10) when immediate execution issues on the judgment, 115.
> between ejectment and trespass, 112.
> to demur or plead, 239, 240.

ENTRY UPON LANDS,
> a method of self-help, 15.

ENTRY, WRITS OF, 44, 45.

EQUITY,
> growth of, 34, 78, 81, 86, 171.
> jurisdiction of, 81.
> in the exchequer, 34, 36.
> possession restored in, to lessees, 95.
> pleading in, 226.

ERROR, WRIT OF, 103, 108, 206, 446.
> coram nobis or vobis, 222–224.
> questions of substance open upon, 101, 135, 136, 223, 224, 236, 240.

ESPLEES, 165, 400.

ESSOIN DAY, 146.

ESTOPPEL,
> by matter of record, 271.
> by deed, 271, 272.
> by matter in pais, 271.
> pleadings in, 283, 292.
> title need not be shown where opposite party estopped from denying, 354.
> plea of, to be certain in every particular, 368.
> commencement and conclusion of pleadings by, 397, 398, 400.

EVIDENCE,
> effect and admissibility of, decided by the judge, 203, 205.
> weight of, by jury, 203.
> demurrer to, 206–208.
> verdict against, new trial, 210.
> certainty in, under issue, 229 n.
> examination of the plaintiff's suit, 169, 170.
> need not be pleaded, 362.

EXCEPTIO, 171–173, 199, 200.

EXCEPTIONS, BILL OF, 206.

EXCHEQUER, COURT OF, 29, 35.
> jurisdiction, 35, 153–155, 168.
> equity jurisdiction, 34, 36.
> prohibition from, 103.
> informations from, 105.
> quo minus in, 155, 168.

EXCHEQUER CHAMBER, COURT OF, 36.

EXECUTION, 221.
> against the person first used in the action of account, 60.

EXECUTION. — *continued.*
    in ejectment, 98, 99.
    immediate, as affecting election of actions, 115.
EXECUTOR,
    retainer by, 18.
    joinder of claims by and against, 111.
    as party plaintiff, 122, 123, 132.
           defendant, 129, 134.
EXEMPLARY DAMAGES, 68.
EXIGENT, 150.
EXTRAORDINARY REMEDIES,
    mandamus, 102, 103.
    procedendo, 103.
    prohibition, 103, 104.
    quo warranto, 104, 105.
    informations, 105.
    habeas corpus, 105–107.
    certiorari, 107.
    writs of error, 108.

FEE. (See *Title.*)
FELONY,
    appeals of, 66.
FEOFFMENT,
    meaning of, 348 n., 369.
    includes what, 279.
    how to be pleaded, 349.
FEUD, 64.
FICTIONS OF LAW,
    an exception to the rule that pleadings must be true, 433.
    in ejectment, 95, 99.
    morality of, 98 and n. 3.
FINE,
    covenant first used to convey land by way of, 58.
FINES,
    in trespass, 65, 67.
    in quo warranto, 105.
FIXTURES,
    replevin does not lie for, 75.
    nor trover, 91.
FORCIBLE ENTRY AND DETAINER,
    punished by criminal proceedings, 45.
FORFEITURES,
    recoverable in debt, 50.
    of recognizances, scire facias lay for execution, 63.
    informations for, 105.

FORM OF PLEADING. (See *Issue ; Pleading.*)

FRANCHISE,
 repealable by scire facias, 62.
 quo warranto respecting, 104.

FRANK-PLEDGE, 26.

FRAUD,
 remedy for, in case, 80.

FRAUDS, STATUTE OF,
 may be pleaded specially, 250 n.
 effect of, on pleading, 349, 350, 380.

FREEHOLD,
 none less than life estate, 40, 93.
 real actions lay for only, 40, 71, 72.
 trover does not lie for injuries to, 91.
 replevin does not lie for injury to things affixed to, 75.
 rent of, how recovered formerly, 53.
 general freehold title, how alleged and sustained, 350, 351.

GAGE,
 a pledge of faith, 47, 48.

GENERAL DEMURRER,
 lies for insufficiency in substance, 232–234.

GENERAL ISSUE, THE,
 when pleadable, 114.
 in different actions, 241–251. (See *Traverse.*)
 as a cumulative traverse, 312.
 fixed forms of, 391.
 a plea amounting to the, to be so pleaded, 408–411. (See *Pleading.*)

GOODS SOLD,
 a common count, 89, 338.

GRAND ASSIZE, 33, 199.

HABEAS CORPORA JURATORUM, 202, 209, 450.

HABEAS CORPUS,
 an extraordinary remedy, 105–107.

HEALTH,
 remedy for injuries to, in case, 68, 77, 80.

HERIOT, 17.

HILARY RULES (1834), 251 n.

HOUSE OF LORDS, 36.

HUNDRED, THE, 25.
 jurors from, 327.

HUNDRED COURT, THE, 26, 27.

HUNDRED GEMOTE, 26.

HUSBAND AND WIFE. (See *Wife.*)
    as parties plaintiff, 121, 131, 134.
              defendant, 127, 128.
    plea of coverture and of non-coverture, 178, 250 n.

IMMATERIAL ISSUE. (See *Issue.*)

IMMATERIAL TRAVERSE. (See *Traverse.*)

IMPARLANCE,
    defined, 187, 188.
    general and special, 187.
    a dilatory plea not usually allowable after a general, 424.
    illustrated, 449.

INCORPOREAL HEREDITAMENTS,
    injuries to, remediable in case, not trespass, 62, 81.
    not recoverable in ejectment, 99.
    alleging title of possession in, 341, 342.

INDEBITATUS ASSUMPSIT, 85, 338.

INDUCEMENT, THE, 263–266. (See *Traverse.*)
    title as matter of, 341 n.

INFANT,
    election of remedies against, 114.
    as party defendant in contract, 127.
                   in tort, 134.
    plea of non-age, 176, 193, 250 n.
    deed of, voidable, 245.

INFORMATION,
    an extraordinary remedy, 105.

INQUEST, 33, 199, 200.

INQUIRY, WRIT OF, 216, 217.

INQUISITION, 197, 198, 216, 217.

INTERDICT UNDE VI, 42.

INTERLOCUTIO, 187. (See *Imparlance.*)

INTRUSION,
    information for, 105.

ISSUE, 179–181, 189.
    joinder in (*similiter*), 180, 228, 292–294.
    entering, 190.
    trial of, in law, 191, 215–218.
           in fact, 191–193, 203, 210–215.
    to be single, material, and certain, 226, 229, 230.
    to specify particulars, including place and time, 230.

ISSUE — *continued.*
Rules tending simply to production of :
    RULE I. After declaration, at each stage, parties must, with certain exceptions, demur, or plead by way of traverse, or of confession and avoidance, 231.
      1. Of demurrers. (See *Demurrer.*)
        nature and properties of, 232–236.
        effect of pleading over without, 236–239.
        determining election to demur or plead, 239, 240.
      2. Of pleadings :
        (A) Of the nature and properties of traverses, 240–272. (See *Traverse.*)
          the common traverse, 240, 241.
          the general issues, 241–251, 391.
          the traverse de injuria, 251–254.
          the special traverse, 255–266.
          in general, 266–272.
        (B) Pleadings in confession and avoidance. (See *Confession and Avoidance, Pleas in.*)
          division of, 272, 273.
          conclusion of, 273.
          to give color, 273–279.
        (C) The nature and properties of pleadings in general :
          (1) Every pleading must be an answer to the whole of what is adversely alleged; discontinuance, 279–281.
          (2) It confesses such traversable matters alleged on the other side as it does not traverse ; protestation, 281, 282.
    Exceptions to Rule I. : —
      (1) Where a dilatory plea is interposed, 283.
      (2) Pleadings in estoppel, 283, 292.
      (3) Where a new assignment is necessary; new assignment extra viam, 283–289.
    RULE II. Upon a traverse, issue must be tendered, 289–292.
      Exception : When new matter is introduced, the pleading concludes with a verification, 290–292.
    RULE III. Issue, when well tendered, must be accepted, 292–294.
      the similiter, 292–294.
      joinder in demurrer, 180, 293, 294.
Rules tending to secure the materiality of the :
    RULE. All pleadings must contain matter pertinent and material, 295–302.
      as applied to traverses :
        (1) Traverse must not be taken on an immaterial point, which includes matter prematurely alleged, matter of aggravation, and of inducement, 295, 296.
        but traverse may be taken on any of several material allegations, 297.

ISSUE — *continued.*

(2) A traverse must not be either too large or too narrow,
297–302.

it is too large if taken on an immaterial allegation,
or on more of a material allegation than is material, 297–299.

or if taken in the conjunctive, instead of
the disjunctive, 299.

it is not too large when taken on a material allegation of title or estate, to the extent alleged, though
unnecessarily alleged to that extent, 299.

it is too narrow if it does not fully answer the whole
of the allegation which it proposes to answer, 300–
302.

this includes a traverse to part only of an indivisible and entire allegation, 301, 302.

Rules tending to produce singleness or unity in :

RULE I.   Pleadings must not be double, 303.   (See *Duplicity.*)
this rule, how applied, 303–313.

qualified by

the use of several counts, 313–317.

the use of several pleas, 313, 317–321.

RULE II.   It is not allowable both to plead and to demur to the
same matter, 322.

effect of this rule, 322.

not changed by the statute 4 Anne, c. 16, § 4, 322.

Rules tending to produce certainty or particularity in the:

RULE I.   The pleadings must have certainty of place; venue,
323–334.   (See *Venue.*)

RULE II.   The pleadings must have certainty of time, 334–336.
(See *Time.*)

RULE III.   The pleadings must specify quality, quantity, and
value, 336–339.

Exceptions, 338, 339.

RULE IV.   The pleadings must specify the names of persons,
339, 340.   (See *Name.*)

RULE V.   The pleadings must show title, 341–355.   (See *Title.*)

Exceptions : (1) when the opposite party is estopped from
denying title, 354, 355.

(2) avowries and cognizances, 355.

RULE VI.   The pleadings must show authority, 355–358.
averments of authority to be strictly proved, 358.

RULE VII.   In general, whatever is alleged in pleading, must
be alleged with certainty, 358–381.

Exceptions, 359–362.

subordinate rules : —

(1) Mere matter of evidence not to be pleaded, 362–364.

(2) Matter of which the court takes notice ex officio
need not be stated, 364–366.

ISSUE — *continued.*

    (3) Or matter coming more properly from the other side, 366–368.

        but pleas of estoppel, and of alien enemy, must be certain in every particular, 368.

    (4) Circumstances necessarily implied need not be alleged, 369.

    (5) So of what the law will presume, 369.

    (6) A general mode of pleading is allowed to avoid great prolixity, 370–372.

    (7) Such mode is often sufficient where the opposing allegation must reduce the matter to certainty, 372–377.

    (8) No greater particularity required than the nature of the thing pleaded will conveniently admit, 377, 378.

    (9) Less particularity required when the facts lie more in the opposite party's knowledge, 378, 379.

    (10) And in the statement of matter of inducement or aggravation, 379, 380.

    (11) Such certainty only is required, as to acts valid at common law, but regulated as to performance by statute, as sufficed before the statute, 380, 381.

    (For further rules, see *Pleading.*)

ISSUE ROLL, 220.

JEOFAILS, STATUTES OF,

    an aid to defective pleading, when, 238–240, 280 n., 334 n., 336, 337 n., 417.

JOINDER,

    of detinue with debt, 56, 109.

    of different forms of actions, 109.

    of different rights of action, 110, 113, 313.

    of issue (similiter), 180, 228.

    in demurrer, 180, 293.

JUDGMENT, 160, 215. 228. (See *Verdict.*)

    debt lay upon, 50, 51.

    in trover, 93.

    in ejectment, 95, 100.

    motion in arrest of, 101, 135, 136, 211, 214, 224, 236, 238, 239.

    when a bar, 101.

    relief from, by audita querela, 102 n.

        for delay, by procedendo. 103.

    effect upon, of misjoinder of counts, 111.

    upon voucher to warranty. 184.

    signing for want of plea, 187 n.

    medial, 192.

JUDGMENT — *continued.*
    non obstante veredicto, 212–214, 236.
    for the plaintiff, 216, 217.
        respondeat ouster, 216, 218.
        quod recuperet, interlocutory and final, 216–219.
    for the defendant, 217.
        quod breve casseter, 217, 219.
        nil capiat per breve, 217.
    by default, confession, &c., 115, 152, 218–221.
    how pronounced, 220.
    entering, 220, 221.
    given upon the whole record, 235, 236.
        exceptions, 235, 236.
    upon demurrer, not now generally final, 239 n.
    prayer for, when pleadings conclude with, 392–400.
JUDICIAL CIRCUITS, 30, 32, 33.
JURISDICTION,
    trespass lay for acts beyond court's, 69.
    lack of, prohibition for, 103, 104.
        habeas corpus, 106.
    of King's Bench and Exchequer, extended by Bill of Middlesex,
        latitat, and quo minus, 153.
    pleas to the, 175, 420, 421.
JURY,
    trial by, 173, 197–212. (See *Damages; Hundred; Verdict.*)
        conduct of, 203, 204.
    view by, 183.
    as witnesses, 229, 323.
JUSTICES IN EYRE, 30, 33.

KING'S BENCH, COURT OF, 31, 32, 152.
    jurisdiction, 34, 67, 153, 167.
    a court of appeal, 35.
    mandamus from, 102.
    prohibition from, 103.
    bill of Middlesex and latitat in, 153, 167.

LA PEINE FORTE ET DURE, 199, 201.
LATHE COURT, 27.
LATITAT, 150, 153, 167.
LEASES,
    when debt lies upon, 52, 53.
    remedy upon, in covenant, 59, 93.
        in ejectment, 93–99
    technical words in, 129 n.

LEAVE OF COURT,
    to amend pleadings, 190.
    to plead several pleas, 318, 321.
LETTERS-PATENT,
    repealable by scire facias, 62.
LIBEL,
    remediable in case, 80.
    truth of charge to be pleaded specially, 249 n.
    words of, to be set forth, 391.
LIBERUM TENEMENTUM,
    plea or avowry of, 350, 351.
LIFE ESTATE,
    the lowest freehold, 40, 93.
LIMITATIONS, STATUTE OF,
    applies to amendments, 101.
        in cases of fraud, 113, 203.
    provable under what pleas, 246 n., 248 n.
LOCAL AND TRANSITORY ACTIONS, 329-334.
LUNATIC,
    election of remedies against, 114.
    deed of, void, 245.
    lunacy pleaded specially, 250 n.

MAINPRIZE, WRIT OF, 105.
MALFEASANCE,
    injuries by, remediable in case, 79.
        in assumpsit, 83.
MANDAMUS,
    an extraordinary remedy, 102, 103.
MANOR COURT, 26, 30.
MASTER AND SERVANT,
    when trespass does not lie for servant's act, 69.
    when it lies for injury to servant, 70.
MATERIALITY OF ISSUE, 295-302. (See *Issue.*)
MATTER IN PAIS,
    estoppel by, 271.
MAYHEM, 66.
MEDIAL JUDGMENT, 192.
MESNE PROFITS, 100.
MISCHIEVOUS ANIMALS. (See *Animals.*)
MISFEASANCE,
    injuries by, remediable in case, 79.
        in assumpsit, 83.

MISJOINDER. (See *Parties*.)

MISNOMER,
    remedy for, 178, 181, 340.

MISTAKE,
    of form, plea in abatement must correct, 424.

MIXED ACTIONS, 40, 45.
    quare impedit, 45.
    waste, 45.
    no view in, 183.
    no voucher to warranty in, 184.
    oyer in, 185.
    judgment in, 218, 219.

MONEY COUNTS,
    included in the common counts, 89.
    joinder of, 316, 317.

MONEY DUE ON ACCOUNT STATED, 316.

MONEY HAD AND RECEIVED,
    a common count, 86, 89, 316.

MONEY LENT,
    a common count, 89, 316.

MONEY PAID,
    a common count, 89, 316.

MOTION IN ARREST OF JUDGMENT,
    when effective, 101, 135, 136, 211, 214, 224, 236, 238, 239, 417.

MULTIPLICITY OF ACTIONS,
    joinder of counts in one action to prevent, 109–111, 113.

NAME,
    of person, to be specified in pleadings, 339, 340.
    this applies to names of a party and of a person not a party, 339, 310.
    consequences of mistake in specifying, 178, 181, 340.

NEGATIVE PREGNANT,
    what amounts to, in a traverse, 384–386.

NEGLIGENCE,
    remediable in case, 80.
            in trover, 92.
    election between action for, and on an implied promise, 112, 115.

NEGOTIABLE INSTRUMENTS,
    when debt lies upon, 53, 54.

NEW ASSIGNMENT, 283–289. (See *Issue.*)
    extra viam, 285–289.

NEW TRIAL,
    grounds and motion for, 206, 210, 211, 222.
    granting motion for, discretionary, 211.

NIL CAPIAT,
  judgment of, 219.
NIL DEBET,
  the general issue in debt on simple contract, 241, 242 n., 245, 24⁷,
    312. (See *Traverse.*)
NIL DICIT,
  judgment by, 218, 238, 417.
NISI FECERIS, 139.
NISI PRIUS, 201, 202.
NOLLE PROSEQUI, 219, 444.
NON ASSUMPSIT,
  plea of, 243, 247–250. (See *Traverse.*)
NON CEPIT,
  the general issue in replevin, 243, 251. (See *Traverse.*)
NON DAMNIFICATUS,
  plea of, 360, 373, 374.
NON DETINET,
  the general issue in detinue, 242, 246. (See *Traverse.*)
NON EST FACTUM. (See *Traverse.*)
  the general issue in debt on specialties, 241, 244, 245, 270, 271.
                      in covenant, 242, 244, 245.
NONFEASANCE,
  trespass does not lie for, 68.
  injuries by, remediable in case, 79.
                      in assumpsit, 83.
NON OBSTANTE VEREDICTO,
  judgment of, 212–214, 236.
NON PROS.,
  judgment by, 219, 232.
NONSUIT,
  for non-joinder of parties, 112, 135, 136.
  judgment of, 335.
NON SUM INFORMATUS,
  judgment by, 218, 238, 417.
NORMANS,
  inquisition of the, 197, 198.
NOT GUILTY,
  the general issue in trespass and case, 242. 243, 246, 247, 249, 250,
    312. (See *Traverse.*)
NOTICE,
  judicial, of what matters taken, 364–366.
  of set-off, 248 n.
NOVEL DISSEISIN,
  assize of, 14, 42–45, 199. (See *Assize.*)

NUISANCE,
   remedy in case for a, 77, 78.
NUL TIEL RECORD,
   issue of, 196.

OATH,
   assertory, 193.
   trial by, 193, 194.
OFFER OF PROOF, 170.
OFFICE,
   patent for, repealed by scire facias, 62.
ORDEAL, TRIAL BY, 194, 195.
ORIGINAL WRIT, THE,
   history and nature of, 137–148.
OUSTER,
   partial, of lessee, when debt lies against him, 52.
   remedy for, in ejectment, 94, 96–99.
   by quo warranto, 104.
OUTLAWRY,
   as punishment and as process, 66, 67, 151.
OYER. (See *Profert.*)
   pleas in abatement based on, of the original writ, **177.**
   demand of, when profert is made, 185, 376.
   form of, 227.
   demandable, in all actions, 185.
      not now of records or original writs; and of deeds, &c.,
      only when profert is necessarily made, 186, 427.
      only at the term at which profert is made, 186.
   when deed is set forth in the plea, effect, 186, 187.
   not granted, but demurrer proper, when profert is improperly omit-
      ted, 186.
   demand of, and copy set forth in plea, effect, 187.
   counterpleas to, 188, 189.
   demurrer instead of counterplea, 188.

PAPER–BOOK, 189, 292.
PAROL, THE, 160. (See *Pleading.*)
PAROL DEMURRER, 176.
PARTICULAR ESTATES, 346–348, 352. (See *Title.*)
PARTICULARITY,
   in issue, 323–334. (See *Issue.*)

PARTIES TO ACTIONS,
> scire facias to change or add, 61, 62.
> non-joinder or misjoinder of, effect, 112, 135, 136.
> Dicey's rules as to, 116-136.
>> for actions of contract, 116-130.
>>> of tort, 130-134.
> consequences of non-joinder and of misjoinder of, 135, 136.

PARTNERS,
> as parties plaintiff, 119, 120, 131.
>> defendant, 126, 133.

PAYMENT OF MONEY INTO COURT,
> plea of, 288, n. 1.

PEACE,
> local, 64.
> the king's, 64, 67, 68, 139.

PENALTIES,
> recoverable in debt, 50.

PERFORMANCE,
> how pleaded, 360, 375, 376.

PERSONAL ACTIONS, 40, 46-48. (See *Actions*.)
> no view in, 183.
> no voucher to warranty in, 184.
> oyer in, 185.
> judgment in, 218.
> defence in, 422.

PERSONAL PROPERTY,
> injuries respecting, remedy in replevin, 63, 73-77.
>> in trespass, 70, 71, 92.
>> in case, 79, 80.
>> in trover, 91, 92.
> includes chattels real, 93.

PETTY ASSIZES, 171, 172, 199, 200.

PLACE, 323-334. (See *Venue*)
> when to be proved as laid, 353.

PLEADING. (See *Declaration; Demurrer; Issue; Pleas.*)
> special, 1-10, 171-173, 199, 200, 251 n.
> originally oral, 159, 163, 229.
> to be signed by a barrister, 164.
> by bill, 153, 167, 168.
> after view, 183.
> after voucher to warranty, 184.
> profert and oyer, 177, 185-187.
> imparlances, 187, 188.
> amendment of, 189, 190.
> repleader, 212-215. (See *Repleader.*)

PLEADING — *continued*.

    Rules tending to prevent obscurity or confusion in:

        RULE I. Pleadings must not be insensible or repugnant, 382.

           Exception, 382.

        RULE II. Pleadings must not be ambiguous, or doubtful ; and of different meanings the one most unfavorable to the pleader is adopted, 383–386.

           negative pregnant, 384–386.

        RULE III. Pleadings must not be argumentative, 386–388.

           two affirmatives do not make a good issue, 387, 388.

               Exception, 388.

           two negatives do not make a good issue, 388.

        RULE IV. Pleadings must not be hypothetical, or in the alternative, 388, 389.

        RULE V. Pleadings must not be by way of recital, but must be positive in their form, 389.

        RULE VI. Things are to be pleaded according to their legal effect or operation, 390, 391.

           Exception, 391.

        RULE VII. Pleadings should observe the known and ancient forms of expression, as contained in approved precedents, 391, 392.

        RULE VIII. Pleadings should have their proper formal commencements and conclusions, 392–401.

           of dilatory pleas, 392, 393.

           of pleas in bar, 394.

           of replications, 394–396, 398.

           of pleadings subsequent to the replication, 396, 397.

           of pleadings by way of estoppel, 397, 398.

           pleadings to part only of adverse matter, 398.

           in replevin; avowries and cognizances, 398.

           in debt on bond, 398, 399.

           in pleadings which tender issue, 399.

           effect of error in, 399, 400.

        RULE IX. A pleading bad in part is bad altogether, 401, 402.

           not applicable to the declaration, 402.

    Rules tending to prevent prolixity and delay in :

        RULE I. There must be no departure in pleading, 403–408.

           (1) in point of fact, 403–405.

           (2) in point of law, 405–407.

           none where the variance is on an immaterial point, 407, 408.

        RULE II. A plea amounting to the general issue should be so pleaded, 408–411.

           effect of giving color, 410.

           Rule II. not absolute, 411.

        RULE III. Surplusage is to be avoided, 412–414. (See *Surplusage*.)

    Certain miscellaneous rules discussed, viz.: —

        RULE I. The declaration should commence with a recital of the writ, 415, 416.

PLEADING — *continued.*

    Rule II. The declaration must be conformable to the original writ, 417, 418.

    Rule III. The declaration should conclude (1) by laying damages ; (2) and allege production of suit, 418-420.

    Rule IV. Pleas must be pleaded in due order, 420, 421.

    Rule V. Pleas must be pleaded with defence, 421-423.

        full defence and half defence, 423.

    Rule VI. Pleas in abatement must give the plaintiff a better writ or bill, 424.

    Rule VII. Dilatory pleas must be pleaded at a preliminary stage of the suit, 424.

    Rule VIII. All affirmative pleadings which do not conclude to the country must conclude with a verification, 425, 426.

    Rule IX. Profert must always be made of a deed alleged under which a party claims or justifies, 426-431.

        this rule, in general, applies only to deeds, 427.

            its limitations, 427, 428.

            its reason, 428-431.

    Rule X. All pleadings must be properly entitled of the court and term, 431, 432.

    Rule XI. All pleadings ought to be true, 432, 433.

        fictions as an exception, 433.

        (For further rules, see *Issue.*)

PLEAS,

    determined the right to join counts, 110.

    effect upon, of election of actions, 113.

    general issue, 114.

    dilatory, 175-178, 217, 283, 321, 392, 393, 424, 432 n.

    peremptory, 175, 178, 217.

    puis darreign continuance, 182.

    special, 251.

    in confession and avoidance, 272-279. (See *Confession and Avoidance, Pleas in.*)

    of tender and payment into court, 288, n. 1.

    duplicity in, 304, 306, 308 n.

    different, to different parts of the declaration, 317 n.

    several,

        use of, 317-321.

        effect of the statute of 4 Anne, c. 16, 212, 313, 318-322.

    laying venue in, 325.

    of liberum tenementum, 351.

    order of, &c., 420-424. (See *Pleading.*)

PLEDGE,

    detinue for, 57.

PLEDGES,

    formerly required of plaintiff at institution of suit, 145.

PLEDGES — *continued.*
in replevin, 74.
when sheriff took insufficient, scire facias lay against, 63.

POSSESSION,
what sufficient to support trespass, as to personalty, 70, 71.
as to real property, 71, 72.
immediate right to, necessary in detinue, 57.
in replevin, 76.
in trover, 91.
in ejectment, 99.
restored under leases, in equity and in ejectment, 96–100.
title of, how laid, 341–344, 350.
alleging, as against a wrongdoer, 342.

POSTEA,
the formal entry of the verdict, 205.

PRÆCIPE, 138, 139, 145, 147, 315.

PRAYER OF JUDGMENT,
in pleadings, 392–400.

PRESCRIPTION,
rights by, how pleaded, 344 n.

PREST, &c., 425.

PRESUMED FACTS,
need not be alleged, 369.

PRINCIPAL AND AGENT,
as parties plaintiff, 118, 119, 131.
defendant, 125, 133.

PRIVITY OF ESTATE,
where it exists, debt lies for rent, 52, 53.

PROCEDENDO, WRIT OF,
an extraordinary r. medy, 103.

PROCEDURE,
ancient prominence of, 22, 38.
the Judicature Acts and Rules, 22.
formerly related chiefly to realty, 46.

PROCESS,
outlawry as. 66.
remedy in trespass, abuse of, 69.
in case, 80.
original and judicial, 147, 148.
summons, attachment, distringas, and capias ad respondendum,
148–150.
latitat et discurrit, exigent, proclamation, and capias utlagatum,
150, 151.

PROCLAMATION, WRIT OF, 150.

PRODUCTION OF SUIT, 168, 169, 419.

PROFERT. (See *Oyer; Pleading.*)
    nature and form of, 185, 227, 427–431.
    made in open court, effect, 185.
    oyer demandable only when it is made, 186.
                  not at a term subsequent to, 186.
    improper omission of, only ground for demurrer, 186, 187.
    when necessary, 427, 428, 431.

PROHIBITION,
    an extraordinary remedy, 103, 104.

PROLIXITY,
    in pleading, discountenanced, 370, 403–408. (See *Pleading.*)

PROMISE,
    as a consideration, 82.
    originally not a consideration, 50.
    implied, 85, 88.
    election between implied, and breach of duty, 112, 115.

PROTESTATION,
    use of, 281, 282.
    does not make a pleading double, 313.

PUIS DARREIGN CONTINUANCE,
    plea of, 182.
    commencement and conclusion of, 397.

PUNITIVE DAMAGES, 68.

QUALITY,
    when and how to be specified in pleadings, 336–339.

QUANTITY,
    when and how to be specified in pleadings, 336–339.
    when to be proved as laid, 353.

QUANTUM MERUIT,
    a common count, 85, 89.
    whether debt properly lay upon a, 84 n.

QUANTUM VALEBANT,
    a common count, 89.

QUARE CLAUSUM FREGIT, 67, 71, 72.

QUARE EJECIT, 94, 95.

QUARE IMPEDIT,
    a mixed action, 45.
    defence in, 422.

QUASI-CONTRACTS,
    remedy upon, 85.

QUE ESTATE, 344 n., 352.

QUOD CASSETER BREVE,
    judgment of, 217, 219.

QUOD RECUPERET,
> judgment of, 216, 218, 219.

QUO MINUS, 155, 168.

QUO WARRANTO,
> an extraordinary remedy, 104, 105.

REAL ACTIONS, 40-45.
> development of, 42.
> lay only for freehold estates, 40.
> dealt originally with the title, and not with mere seisin, 40
> Writs of Right, 41, 421.
> Writs in the Nature of Writs of Right, 41.
> development of, 42-45.
> novel disseisin, 42.
> assize of mort d'ancestor, 43.
> to recover arrears of freehold rents, 53.
> scire facias lay in, when, 61.
> view in, 183.
> voucher to warranty in, 184.
> oyer in, 185.
> judgment in, 218.

REAL PROPERTY. (See *Real Actions.*)
> does not pass by an award, 18.
> remitter applies only to, 19.
> consequential injuries to, remedy in case, 79.
> detinue does not lie for, 56.
> injuries to, remediable in trespass, 67, 71, 72.
> in case, 79, 81.

REBUTTER,
> defined, 181.

RECAPTION,
> a method of self-help, 15.

RECOGNITION,
> the jurors' answer, 198.

RECORD,
> debt lay upon, 51, 55, 61.
> scire facias upon, 61.
> transcript of, by certiorari, 107.
> of courts, a perpetual memorial, 162.
> no oyer now demandable of a, 185, 186, 431.
> entering the issue on, 190.
> trial by the, 196.
> estoppel by matter of, 271.

REJOINDER,
> defined, 181.
> form of, 228.

REJOINDER — *continued.*
>joinder of parties in, 307 and n.
>commencement and conclusion of, 396, 398, 400.

RELEASE,
>pleading a, 250 n., 349.
>plea of, is a plea in discharge, 272.

REMEDIES,
>exist for all rights violated, 11.
>extraordinary, 102–108.

REMITTER,
>a method of self-help, 19.

RENT,
>when debt lay for, 52, 53.
>election to sue for, in debt or covenant, 59.

REPLEADER, 212–215.
>before and after the statute 4 Anne, c. 16, 212, 213.
>motion for a, 213, 215.
>granted only for a formal defect in the pleadings, 214, 215.

REPLEVIN, ACTION OF,
>a formed action in tort, 63, 73–77.
>forms of, 74, 106.
>effect of the Statute of Marlebridge (52 H. III.), 75.
>damages in, 75, 76.
>declaration in, 74, 76, 343.
>pleas in, 76.
>when it lies, 75, 76.
>election between, and trespass, 115.
>commencement and conclusion in pleadings in, 398.

REPLICATION,
>defined, 180, 181.
>exception met by, 173.
>on a counterplea to oyer, 189.
>form of, 227, 228.
>new assignment is in the nature of a, 286.
>the traverse de injuria, 252–254.
>duplicity in the, 305, 306.
>de injuria absque tali causa, as a cumulative traverse, does not make a pleading double, 311.
>de injuria sua propria absque residuo causæ, 254.
>statute 4 Anne, c. 16, § 4, did not extend to, 320.
>laying venue in, 325.
>formal commencement and conclusion of, 394–396, 398, 400.
>departure in the, 403, 405.

REPRISAL,
>a method of self-help, 15.

REPUGNANCY,
    in pleadings, ground for demurrer, 282, 382.

REPUTATION,
    remedy for injury to, in case, 68, 77, 80.

RESPONDEAT OUSTER,
    judgment of, 216, 218, 235.

RETAINER,
    a method of self-help, 18.

RETRAXIT,
    judgment of, 219.

REVERSION,
    assignee's remedy against lessee, 59.
    injury to, remediable in case, 79, 81.

RIGHT, WRIT OF, 41, 42, 421.

RIGHTS,
    developed by actions, 3.
    anciently subordinate to procedure, 23.

ROMAN LAW,
    influence of, 13, 28, 38, 42, 46, 78, 171–173, 226.
    contracts and writings under, 46, 47, 429.
    exceptio, 171–173.
    aimed at restitution or compensation, 65.
    pleading in, 226.

SALE,
    remedy upon, in debt, 50, 52, 86.
        in assumpsit, 86, 89.

SCIRE FACIAS, 48, 60–63.
    a judicial, not an original writ, 60.
    upon records, 61.
    in real actions, 61.
    in personal actions, 61.
    to change or add parties, 61, 62.
    upon exceptions, 62.
    as an original action, 62, 63.

SECTA. (See *Suit.*)

SEDUCTION,
    remedy for, in trespass, 70.
        in case, 80.

SEISIN,
    how pleaded, 345.
    not protected by real actions, 41.
    assize of novel disseisin, 42, 43.
        of mort d'ancestor, 43.

SELF-DEFENCE. (See *Self-help.*)

SELF-HELP, 12-19.
 (1) By the act of parties : —
  by self-defence, 15.
  by recaption of persons or of goods, 15.
  by entry upon lands, 15.
  by abatement of nuisances, 16.
  by distress, 16.
 (2) By the joint act of all parties : —
  by accord, 17.
  by arbitration, 18.
 (3) By sole operation of law : —
  by retainer, 18.
  by remitter, 19.
 history of, 12-14, 63.
 repressed under Anglo-Saxon courts, 25.

SERVANTS,
 injuries to, remedy in trespass, 70.
      in case, 80.

SET-OFF,
 election of actions as affected by, 113.
 not usually evidence under plea of nil debet or non-assumpsit, 246 n.,
 248 n.

SEVERAL COUNTS. (See *Counts.*)
 when properly joined in one action, 113, 313-317.

SEVERAL ISSUES, 307, 314, 319.

SEVERAL PLEAS. (See *Pleas.*)
 when allowed, 212, 313, 317-322.

SEVERANCE IN PLEADING, 307.

SHAM PLEADING, 432, 433.

SHERIFF,
 a judicial officer under Anglo-Saxon procedure, 25, 27.
 scire facias against, 63.
 remedies against, in trespass, 69, 71.
      in case, 80.
 view under the, 183.

SHIREEVE'S TURN, 27.

SIMILITER. (See *Issue.*)
 is a joinder in issue, 180.
 illustration of, 228.
 origin of, and when used, 292-294.
 special, 292.

SINGLE BOND,
 debt lay upon, 51.

SINGLENESS,
 of issue, 303-322. (See *Issue.*)

SLANDER. (See *Libel.*)
    remediable in case, 80.

SON ASSAULT DEMESNE,
    plea of, 272.

SPECIAL CASE, 209.

SPECIAL DEMURRER,
    lies for insufficiency in form, 232–234.

SPECIAL ISSUES, 251.

SPECIAL PLEADING,
    statements in the Introduction as to, 1–10.
    origin of, 171–173.
    meaning of, 251 n.
    development of, 199, 200.

SPECIAL TRAVERSE, 255–266. (See *Traverse.*)

SPECIALTY,
    debt lies upon, 51, 55.
    when assumpsit lies upon, 87.

STATUTE,
    debt lies upon a, 51.
    plea of, as to usury or gaming, 245 and note.
    a public, not to be pleaded, 365.

STATUTE OF FRAUDS. (See *Frauds, Statute of.*)

STATUTE OF LIMITATIONS. (See *Limitations, Statute of.*)

STATUTES CITED,
    Constitution of Clarendon, 48, 199.
    Magna Carta, 31, 39, 143, 152, 200.
    Provisions of Oxford, 142.
    St. of Marlebridge (52 Henry III.), 74.
    Westminster 1. c. 17, 73.
            " 1 (13 Edw. I.), c. 24, 40, 77, 81, 82, **142.**
            " 2 (" "), c. 30, 33.
            " 2 (" "), c. 31, 206.
            " 2 (" "), St. 1, c. 45, 61.
    5 Rich. II., St. 1, 45.
    32 Henry VIII. c. 1, 349.
    32 " " c 28, § 1, 350.
    32 " " c. 34, 59.
    34 " " c. 5, 349.
    27 Elizabeth, c. 5, 9, 233.
    27 " c. 6, 326 n., 327 n.
    16 Charles I. c. 10, 107.
    16 & 17 Charles II. c. 8, 327, 331, 333.
    29 Charles II. c. 3, §§ 1, 2, 4, 349, 380.
    31 Charles II. c. 2, 107.
    4 Anne, c. 16, 233.
            " " § 4, 212, 313, 316–322.

STATUTES CITED — *continued.*
    4 Anne, c. 16, § 6, 328.
      "   " § 11, 178.
    8 Anne, c. 14, 53.
    9 Anne, c. 20, 104.
    11 George II. c. 19, § 22, 355.
    5 George III. c. 17, 53.
    59 George III. c. 46, 196.
    6 George IV. c. 50, § 13, 328 n.
    9 George IV. c. 14, § 5, 127 n.
    3 & 4 William IV. c. 42, 134.
    43 & 44 Vict. c. 42 (Employer's Liability Act), 12.
    Common Law Procedure Act, 2.
    Supreme Court of Judicature Acts, The, 22, 156, 166, 167.

SUBSTANTIVE LAW,
    formerly subordinate to procedure, 24.

SUIT,
    defined, 20.

SUIT (SECTA),
    production of, 168.
    examination of, 169.

SUMMONS, 148, 156–158.
    ad warrantizandum, 184.

SUPREME COURT OF JUDICATURE ACTS,
    change of courts by the, 22.
    process under the, 156.
    forms of actions under the, 166, 167.

SURGEONS,
    negligent, liable in case, 80.

SURPLUSAGE,
    is to be avoided, 412–414.
    this rule requires
        (1) the omission of matter wholly foreign, 412.
        (2)   or not required to be stated, 412.
        (3) brevity in manner of statement, 413.
    remedy when the rule is violated, 413.
    danger arising from, 413.

SUR-REBUTTER,
    replies to rebutter, 181.

SUR-REJOINDER,
    replies to rejoinder, 181.

SURRENDER,
    how pleaded, 349.

SURVIVAL OF ACTIONS, 114, 118, 120, 122, 123, 125, 126, 129, 131, 132, 133, 134.

TENANTS IN COMMON,
>   when trespass lies between, 71, 72.
>   when trover, 92.

TENDER,
>   not evidence under nil debet or non-assumpsit, 246 n., 248 n.
>   plea of, 288, n. 1.

TERMS OF COURT, 145, 146.
>   no oyer at term subsequent to profert, 186.
>   pleadings to be entitled of the court and term, 431, 432.

TESTATUM CAPIAS, 153.

THWERTUTNAY, 173.

TIME,
>   pleadings must have certainty of, 334–336.
>   averments of, when material, 335.
>>   when not, 335, 336, 353.

TITLE. (See *Possession*.)
>   the pleadings must show title, 341–355.
>   I. When a party alleges title in himself, or in another whose authority
>   he pleads : —
>>   (A) it is often sufficient to allege a title by possession, 341, 342.
>>>   as against a wrong-doer it is sufficient to allege possession,
>>>   342–344.
>>   (B) cases in which a superior title must be shown, 344.
>>   (C) where title by possession is inapplicable or insufficient, the
>>>   title should, generally, be stated in its full and precise
>>>   extent, 345–351.
>>>   as to the allegation of the title itself, 345.
>>>   as to the derivation of the title, 345–351.
>>>>   (1) generally it is sufficient to state a seisin in fee simple
>>>>   per se, 345.
>>>>   (2) when necessary to show the derivation of the fee, 346.
>>>>   (3) the commencement of particular estates must gen-
>>>>   erally be shown, 346–348.
>>>>   (4) claims by inheritance, how shown, 348.
>>>>   (5) the nature of claims by conveyance or alienation
>>>>   must, generally, be shown, 348.
>>>>   (6) the nature of the conveyance or alienation should
>>>>   be stated according to its legal effect, 348, 349.
>>>>   (7) deeds or writings, when required to be alleged in
>>>>   pleading, 349, 350.
>>>>>   allegation of general freehold title, when
>>>>>   sufficient; plea or avowry of liberum tene-
>>>>>   mentum, 350, 351.
>   II. When a party alleges title in his adversary:
>>   It is not necessary to allege title more precisely than to show a
>>   liability in the party charged or to defeat his present claim,
>>   351–355.

TITLE — *continued.*
> when sufficient to allege a title of possession, 351, 352.
> when superior title must be shown, 352, 353.
> averments of title must be strictly proved, 353.

cases of estoppel, and avowries and cognizances are exceptions to the general rule requiring title to be shown, 354, 355.

TITLE OF COURT AND TERM,
> all pleadings required to be properly entitled of the court and term, 431, 432.

TORT,
> formed actions in (trespass and replevin), 63–77.
> assumpsit as an action of, 82, 86.
> election between, and contract, 112, 114.
> of infant, lunatic, or wife, 114.
> parties plaintiff in, 130–132.
>> defendant in, 132–134.

TRANSITORY AND LOCAL ACTIONS, 329–334.

TRAVERSE. (See *Issue: Pleading.*)
> the common traverse, a tender of issue, 178–181, 240, 241.
> the general issues : —
>> in debt, non est factum on specialties, 241, 244, 245.
>>> nil debet on simple contract, 241, 245, 246.
>> in covenant, non est factum, 242, 244, 245.
>> in detinue, non detinet, 242, 246.
>> in trespass, not guilty, 242, 246, 247.
>> in case, in assumpsit, the plea of non-assumpsit on both implied and express promises, and including matters in confession and avoidance, 243, 247–250.
>>> in general, not guilty, 243, 249, 250.
>> in replevin, non cepit, 243, 251.
> the traverse de injuria : —
>> always tenders issue, 251.
>> occurs only in replications in certain actions, 252–254.
>> the replication de injuria sua propria absque residuo causæ, 254.
> the special traverse : —
>> includes the inducement, which affirmatively details inconsistent circumstances, the absque hoc, which denies a fact of the preceding pleading, and a verification and prayer for judgment, 255, 259–261, 290.
>> employed, when a general denial is opposed to a rule of law, 255, 256.
>>> to show that in the particular case certain averments of fact are material and should be truly pleaded, 256–258.
>>> to separate questions of law from those of fact, 258.
>>> to secure to the pleader the opening and concluding of the cause, 258, 259.

TRAVERSE — *continued.*

answer to, 259.

when applicable, formerly and now, 261–263.

the inducement,

must itself amount to a sufficient answer in substance to the last pleading, 263.

must not consist of a direct denial, 263, 264.

must not be in the nature of a confession and avoidance, 264.

cannot be traversed, *i. e.* "there must be no traverse upon a traverse," except when the first is bad, 264, 265.

cannot be answered by a confession and avoidance, 266.

traverses in general,

must deny " modo et forma," 266, 267.

must not be taken on matter of law, 268, 269.

or upon matter not alleged, except when necessarily implied, 269, 270.

a party to a deed, who traverses it, must plead "non est factum;" the doctrine of estoppel, 270–272.

must be pertinent and material, 295–302. (See *Issue.*)

must not be too large or too narrow, 297–302. (See *Issue.*)

cumulative, does not make a pleading double, 310–313. (See *Issue.*)

TRESPASS,

action of, lies when, 17, 68–73, 101.

a formed action in tort, 63–73.

origin of, 66, 67.

de bonis asportatis, 67, 70, 71.

quare clausum fregit, 67, 71, 153, 440.

for assault and battery, 67, 70, 435.

vi et armis, 68, 82, 161.

ab initio, 69, 71, 72.

ejectione firmæ, 94.

for mesne profits, 100.

joinder of counts in, 110

election between, and ejectment, 112.

and case, 114.

and assumpsit, 112, 115.

and replevin, 115.

original writ of, 144.

bill of Middlesex, latitat, and quo minus, 153.

declaration in, 73, 161, 166, 285 n.

defence in, 422.

TRESPASS UPON THE CASE. (See *Case, Trespass upon the.*)

TRIAL. (See *Judgment; Verdict.*)

of issues in law, 191.

in fact, 191–193.

by witnesses, 193.

by oath, 193, 194.

TRIAL — *continued.*
    by ordeal, 194.
    by battle, 195.
    by the record, 196.
    by jury, 194, 197–212.
    at nisi prius, 201, 202.
    at bar, 202, 203.
    verdict, 203–212.
    burden of proof, 204.
    variance, 204.

TRITHING, 27.

TROVER, ACTION OF,
    an action of tort, 79, 90–93.
    when it lies, 91.
    joinder of counts in, 110.
    election between, and assumpsit, 112, 113.

TRUSTEE,
    as party plaintiff, 121, 122, 132.
              defendant, 128, 134.

UNITY OF ISSUE, 303–322. (See *Issue.*)

USE AND OCCUPATION, 52, 87, 89.
    trespasser cannot be sued for, 115.

USURY,
    plea of, 245 and note, 250 n.

VALUE,
    when and how to be specified in pleadings, 336–339.
    when to be proved as laid, 353.

VARIANCE,
    defined, 204.
    not vital as to formal or immaterial matters, 205, 267.
    between writ and declaration, not ground for demurrer, 416.
    how taken advantage of, 244 n., 417, 418.
    in assumpsit, what material, 87.
    when local facts are not truly laid, 331.
    mistake in name of a person in the pleadings, when a, 340.
    title to be strictly proved as laid, 353.

VENIRE FACIAS, 201, 202, 323.
    de novo, 215.

VENUE,
    meaning of, 323, 324.
    present law of, 324, 325.
    of the traversable allegations, 325.
    ancient use of the, 326.

VENUE — *continued.*

changes in practice as to, 327.

    in law of venue, 327, 328.

modern rule as to, 328.

to be truly laid,

    in local actions, 329, 330.

    not in transitory actions, 329, 330.

    as to facts arising out of the realm, 330.

change of, by defendant in a transitory action, 330.

of local facts, to be truly laid, 331.

transitory facts are laid with the venue of the action, 331, 332.

effect of allegations under a videlicet, 332.

local matters occurring out of the realm, how to be alleged, 332, 333

place alleged as description, and not as venue, to be truly stated, 333.

defects in laying, how objected to, 333, 334.

VERDICT,

special, 207–209.

general, subject to a special case, 208, 209.

principles for the jury to consider, 203, 204.

form of, 203, 205, 228, 450.

entry of (the postea), 205.

effect of, how avoided, 210–215.

limited to amount alleged, 339, 418.

avoiding, by motions : —

    for a new trial, 210, 211.

    in arrest of judgment, 211, 212.

    for judgment non obstante veredicto, 212–214.

    for a repleader, 213–215.

    for a venire facias de novo, 215.

    aider by, of defective pleading, 237, 238.

VERIFICATION. (See *Issue ; Pleading.*)

origin and use of, 260–262.

general and special, 425.

used, when new matter introduced, 260, 290.

    in affirmative pleadings not concluding to the country, 425.

    in negative pleadings, when, 426.

of dilatory pleas required, 178.

VIDELICET,

effect of allegations under a, as to the venue of the action, 332.

laying time under a, 334, 353.

"VI ET ARMIS,"

to be inserted in trespass, 68, 73.

not inserted in case, 82.

VIEW,

demand of, 183.

no dilatory plea after a, 424.

VOUCHER TO WARRANTY, 184.

no dilatory plea after, 424.

WAGER OF LAW, 50, 77, 194, 201
    none in the Exchequer, 53.
    a defence in debt and detinue, 56, 90.
    escaped by assumpsit and trover, 87.

WAPENTAKE, 26.

WARRANTY,
    voucher to, 184.

WASTE,
    a mixed action, 45.
    remediable in case, 81, 258.
    dilapidation, 134 n.

WAY, RIGHT OF,
    remedy for injuries to, 68, 81, 431, 432.

WIFE,
    injury to, remedy in trespass, 70.
                  in case, 80.
    liberty of, restored by habeas corpus, 107.
    torts of, 114.
    as party in contract, plaintiff, 121.
                       defendant, 127, 128.

WITE, 65.

WITENAGEMOTE, THE, 27, 28, 137.

WITHERNAM, WRIT OF, 74, 106.

WITNESSES,
    trial by, 193.
    as jurors, 229, 323.

WRITS,
    the English system, 38, 108.
    extension of jurisdiction by, 35, 36, 38, 137–147.
    issued from the Chancery, 39, 74, 77, 78, 81, 139–144.
    of Right, 41, 421.
    in the Nature of Writs of Right, 42.
    new forms in real actions, 42–45.
    of entry, 44, 45.
    in debt, 49.
    of covenant, 57.
    in scire facias, 60, 62.
    of trespass, 66.
    of replevin, 73.
    de homine replegiando, 74, 106.
    capias in withernam, 74, 106.
    in case, 77–82.
    in assumpsit, 82.
    in trover, 90.
    quare ejecit infra terminum, 94.

WRITS — *continued.*
ejectione firmæ, 94.
of error. (See *Error, Writ of.)*
of mandamus, 102, 103.
of procedendo, 103.
of prohibition, 103.
of consultation, 104.
of quo warranto, 104.
of habeas corpus, 105–107.
of mainprize, 105.
de odio et atia, 106.
of certiorari, 107
the original writ, 137–148.
oyer of, 186.
of præcipe, 138, 139, 147.
register of, 143.
testing and return, 145.
of judicial writs, 148.
of attachment, distringas, and capias ad respondendum, 149, 150.
of latitat et discurrit, exigent, of proclamation, and capias utlagatum, 150, 151.
bill of Middlesex, latitat, and quo minus, 153, 167.
summons, 148, 156–158.
indorsements on, 157.
pleas in abatement of, 175–178.
for view, 183.
summons ad warrantizandum, 184.
of venire facias, 201, 202, 323.
de novo, 215.
of habeas corpora juratorum, 202.
of inquiry, 216, 217.
of execution, 221.